VERSIONS OF HISTORY FROM ANTIQUITY TO THE ENLIGHTENMENT

EDITED BY DONALD R. KELLEY

¶ Versions of History

from Antiquity to the Enlightenment

YALE UNIVERSITY PRESS NEW HAVEN & LONDON

Published with assistance from the foundation established in memory of
Amasa Stone Mather of the Class of 1907, Yale College.

Set in Garamond No. 3 type by G & S Typesetters. Printed in the United
States of America by Vail-Ballou Press, Binghamton, New York.

Library of Congress Cataloging-in-Publication Data

Versions of history from antiquity to the Enlightenment / edited by
    Donald R. Kelley.
        p.   cm.
    Includes bibliographical references and index.
    ISBN 0-300-04775-4. — ISBN 0-300-04776-2 (pbk.)
    1. History—Philosophy.   I. Kelley, Donald R.
  D16.8.V46   1991
  901—dc20   90-26606
                                                    CIP

The paper in this book meets the guidelines for permanence and dura-
bility of the Committee on Production Guidelines for Book Longevity of
the Council on Library Resources.

10 9 8 7 6 5 4 3 2 1

For my son John
who grew up with all this

To be ignorant of history is to remain always a child.

Cicero, 46 B.C.

Philip Melanchthon, 1558

Bolingbroke, 1735

℈ Contents

❡ Preface

The idea of this project was conceived many years ago, back in the 1960s, on the premise—which I had not yet learned to call hermeneutical—that critical investigation of the past required an understanding of the tradition of interpretation separating us from and yet connecting us to the object of our investigations. The form first taken by this historiographical enterprise was an optimistic plan to replace the classic work of Eduard Fueter, *Geschichte der neueren Historiographie* (1911), translated into French and Italian but never English, and perhaps James Westfall Thompson's massive *History of Historical Writing* (1942). Even in the technologically antediluvian 1960s it became clear that a prerequisite for such an undertaking would include an extensive survey and classification of sources as well as bibliographical preparation which only cooperative (and nowadays computer-assisted) research could accomplish. It soon became clear, too, that such a project should expand its horizons beyond the "normal science" of narrative and analytical history and take into account adjacent areas of inquiry and interpretation and, further, make use of insights and ideas beyond the standard historiographical canon, especially in fields of philosophy, social science, and literary criticism.

This plan remained a "Madonna of the Future"; and indeed nothing like it has ever been realized or even attempted by anyone, as far as I know, although the field of historiography has expanded vastly in the past twenty years. What remains here—the dim reflection of an old dream, a fragment of a projected monument—is a gathering of materials illustrating the tradition, or rather traditions, of Western historical inquiry, and reconstructing, from a small selection of accessible texts, a putative canon of writings on the nature, aims, and methods of "history," more or less as it has been understood, practiced, and theorized about since Herodotus.

In this long, if intermittent, effort I have accumulated many debts, and I cannot begin to count the conversations and correspondence I have had with students and colleagues over more than twenty years at the State University of New York at Binghamton, Harvard, and Rochester. I should at least recall the formative exchanges in the earliest days with Myron Gilmore, Hans Baron, Samuel Kinser, George Huppert, Joseph Levine, Fritz Stern, and the late Felix Gilbert and Eric Cochrane. Several generations of students, both in historiography courses and as research assistants, have also contributed to the project, and I am grateful for the recent services and counsel of the late John D'Amico, Tina Isaacs, and John Ehman, without whose labors this book would still be gestating (if not "history" in a pejorative sense).

As so often before, the essential inspiration has come from Bonnie Smith, who brings her own enlightening, enhancing, and sobering perspective to history and historiography, and who does even more to brighten present and future.

1
❡ Introduction: Looking Backward

"How curious, after all, is the way in which we moderns think about our world!"[1] The opening sentence of E. A. Burtt's famous book applies not only to scientific thought but also to modern historical consciousness. What possible motives could we have for prying into a departed and usually disillusioning past? Vanity or nostalgia, perhaps, but these sentiments hardly operate outside our circle of memories, whereas one of the goals—indeed, one of the defining characteristics— of Western culture is "to discover, 'awaken,' and repossess the most exotic and peripheral societies," as Mircea Eliade put it; it is "no less than to revive the entire past of humanity."[2] A curious goal, to rummage among the relics of aliens, to honor the ancestors of other peoples.

There has been talk of a "Copernican revolution" in historical studies, referring loosely to the romantic period. But in fact, history, unlike science and notwithstanding the views of certain philosophers and social scientists, does not seek a single, ever more perfect model of the world and then proceed to discard old visions: if the work of Archimedes has lost all but an antiquarian interest for scientists, that of Thucydides has fulfilled his wish that it should be "a possession for all times" (reading no. 4). And although admirers of the nineteenth-century historical school might believe that there was no history worthy of the name before B. G. Niebuhr and Leopold von Ranke, more people probably continue

1. E. A. Burtt, *Metaphysical Foundations of Modern Science* (New York, 1926), 1.
2. *Myth and Reality* (New York, 1963), 113.

to read Livy and Francesco Guicciardini, whose works Niebuhr and Ranke set out to supersede, than these founders of "scientific history."[3] As Lord Acton said, there were "heroes born before Agamemnon."[4] Unlike revolutions, history does not devour its children, though it may well be subject to distortions and even to a kind of amnesia.

Without denying technical progress, the proliferation of auxiliary sciences, and the increase in sheer information, one may wonder whether many of the most essential features of historical understanding have been present in some form from the beginning. From at least the time of Herodotus, people have been interested in the customs and behavior of ancients as well as moderns, of barbarians as well as brothers. By the fifth century B.C., Herodotus and probably others were recognizing the disparity and divergences of particular societies (no. 3). They were realizing that the past was indeed a "foreign country" and that people really did things differently there.[5] This recognition of pastness, this consciousness of and curiosity about remote and alien experience, marks the beginnings of the critical study of "history."

Undoubtedly much of the wonderment about the past has stemmed from religious concerns. Questions about beginnings—the problem, the myth, of ultimate origins, which has plagued historians through the ages—may well be the taproot of historical inquiry. Like philosophy, history seems to represent a triumph of *logos* over *mythos:* historical perspective, the expansion of one's consciousness beyond personal recollection, is likewise an elevation of intellect—the temporal parallel to the formulation of general ideas. As science begins with the question "what are things made of?" so history begins with the question "what really happened?"

What gives further coherence to the tradition of historical inquiry is that history, being open to the direct pressure of human experience and possessing only tenuous links with any form of systematic thought, has never lost its connection to myth. "More than anywhere else," Eliade remarks, "[mythical thought] survives in historiography."[6] (David Fischer's study of historians' fallacies makes this embarrassingly obvious.)[7] But there is a positive side to this link as well. The mythological

3. Fritz Stern, ed., *The Varieties of History* (New York, 1956), 54, 46.

4. "German Schools of History," in *Historical Essays and Studies,* ed. J. N. Figgis and R. V. Lawrence (London, 1907), 344.

5. David Lowenthal, *The Past Is a Foreign Country* (Cambridge, 1985).

6. *Myth and Reality,* 113.

7. *Historians' Fallacies: Toward a Logic of Historical Thought* (New York, 1970).

strain in history, whether disguised as theory, models, or imaginative conjecture, has served both as a shield against the excesses of historical Pyrrhonism and as an aid to interpretation where evidence is lacking. Consider the thesis about the mythical or poetic origin of history, which can itself be traced back from Giambattista Vico and Niebuhr through Renaissance humanism to classical antiquity: when pushed to excess it may illustrate the "genetic fallacy," but it has also illuminated some of the dark corners of ancient and medieval history. The study of history, like the human condition it affects to portray, cannot entirely disengage itself from the irrational and the subconscious; as a form of human memory, it cannot entirely escape its own primitive heritage.

Identifying the object of study, pastness, does not define but does open up the field which we, after Herodotus, call "history"—though the fortunes of this multifaceted and multidimensional term range far beyond the subject of history as we think of it today (nos. 1, 9, 15, and others). Over its twenty-four-century life, this word, in Greek, Latin, and vernacular, has been construed in a variety of ways: as the past itself, whether human, natural, or both; as a particular form of literary expression, such as rhetoric, biography, or prose in general; as the body of knowledge accumulated by historians over the centuries; as a particular method of inquiry; as the process of change in a general sense; as a particular interpretation of this process, whether evolutionary, revolutionary, or degenerative, cyclical or random; as the break with nature caused by the "awakening of consciousness" (Jacob Burckhardt); and even as a philosophy of "life as a whole" (Benedetto Croce).[8] In this way, too (adapting Carl Becker's phrase), "Everyman [is] His Own Historian."

The debate continues, and although most historians agree with Herodotus's view of history as investigation of the past rather than Cicero's "light of truth" (no. 15)—"not 'the light and the truth,'" as Johann Gustav Droysen put it, "but the search therefor"[9]—there is still no generally accepted definition. What is important to realize, and difficult to grasp, is that history actually requires this fundamental indefinability. History must take into account a whole trajectory or life process in some sense. "In the beginning was the word" may hold for theologians but certainly not for historians; for them the logos comes only at the end of the inquiry and creative process.

---

8. Burckhardt, *Force and Freedom,* ed. J. H. Nichols (New York, 1955), 102; Croce, *History as the Story of Liberty,* trans. S. Sprigge (New York, 1941), 65.

9. Stern, *Varieties,* 144.

The inference is that a historical view ought to be, as far as possible, critical rather than hagiographical, and here, too, we should study the foreign as well as the familiar. Once again, there is an illuminating analogy with the history of science, which has itself been undergoing a kind of "historiographical revolution."[10] Historians of science have turned increasingly from the kind of ancestor worship that consists in sorting out supposedly scientific truth from error and then compiling a chronicle of these triumphs on the basis of an a priori pattern of continuous progress through the gradual accumulation of discrete discoveries. This is Butterfield's "Whig fallacy" with a vengeance—or Fischer's "Baconian fallacy," or the fallacy of biographers of famous men (de viris illustribus, no. 63), saints (vitae sanctorum), and martyrs (no. 81), who all tell their stories in a teleological fashion.[11] It seems even less useful for an understanding of history, whose career has been still more checkered, whose aims have been more vacillating, and whose values have been more disputed.

In many ways, then, the history of history does not exhibit a pattern of growing enlightenment and utility, whether because historians are by nature backward looking or because they are concerned with more fundamental aspects of the human condition. In fact it might be more fairly represented as a series of unending debates on topics of enduring, or at least recurrent, interest. "We go on generation after generation," Frederick Teggart once observed, "echoing confusedly the views which have been accumulated by our predecessors in the course of centuries."[12] My purpose with this collection is to give a hearing to some of the earlier, sometimes less confused, statements about the nature and function of history.

Most historians have shared at least one assumption about the character of history: what Friedrich Meinecke called the principle of individuality, taking Goethe's *Individuum est ineffabile* as his motto.[13] The

10. Traceable to Thomas Kuhn, *The Structure of Scientific Revolutions* (Chicago, 1962), a book which has spawned a vast literature.

11. Herbert Butterfield, *The Whig Interpretation of History* (Cambridge, 1931); Fischer, *Historians' Fallacies*.

12. "A Problem in the History of Ideas," *Journal of the History of Ideas*, 1 (1940): 503.

13. Meinecke, *Historism: The Rise of a New Historical Outlook*, trans. J. E. Anderson (London, 1972), vi; cf. Stern, *Varieties*, 267ff.

method of history, as Ranke put it, must be pursued through the perception of the particular;[14] history is distinguished from poetry, according
to Aristotle (no. 9), because its statements are of the nature not of universals but of singulars. In the theoretical statements not only of the
nineteenth century but also of the Renaissance, especially in the "methods" of François Baudouin and Jean Bodin (no. 91), this point was made
precisely for the purpose of distinguishing epistemologically between
natural and historical sciences.[15]

A consensus has emerged that history ought to concern itself with
human affairs. *Natural history* is an exception to this, and so is *history* in
the Baconian sense of empirical data (no. 94), which is how some political and social scientists understand the term today. However, with the
decline of the medieval chronicle, in which natural and human disasters
were recorded indiscriminately, and with the growing assumption that a
grasp of divinity was beyond the ordinary historian, the focus of narrative history shifted increasingly to humanity. Even before modern science set nature apart from and scientifically above mankind, naturalists
and humanists alike commonly distinguished between two cultures,
or at least two conceptual realms. As Galileo and his colleagues gave
mathematical definition to natural philosophy, so Vico conceptualized,
through philology, the sphere of human history, which was the main
thrust of his "new science" (no. 109). This historical distinction between nature and culture was formulated more systematically, or at least
more familiarly, in the writings of Wilhelm Windelband and Heinrich
Rickert.[16]

Further, there has been some agreement that history's province was,
or ought to be, that of literal (though perhaps not unadorned) truth.
Such was the force of Quintilian's often quoted threefold distinction
between history, poetry, and argument (no. 16). Such was the force of
Cicero's "first law" of history, repeated ad nauseam by later authors

14. Stern, *Varieties*, 58.

15. D. R. Kelley, *Foundations of Modern Historical Scholarship* (New York,
1970), and "The Theory of History," in *The Cambridge History of Renaissance
Philosophy*, ed. C. B. Schmitt and Q. Skinner (Cambridge, 1988), 746–761;
Julian Franklin, *Jean Bodin and the Sixteenth-Century Revolution in the Methodology
of Law and History* (New York, 1963).

16. Windelband, "Geschichte und Naturwissenschaft" (1894), in his
Präludien (Tübingen, 1911), 2:136–160, and Rickert, *Kulturwissenschaft und
Naturwissenschaft* (Freiburg, 1899).

(no. 15). Such was also one of the basic points of both the "arts of history" of the Renaissance and the "arts of poetry" on which the *artes historicae* were modeled (nos. 88–93).[17] And such has been the common claim of most historians, including a number of liars, fools, and hired propagandists, ever since.

This principle has at least two corollaries. One is to rely on eyewitness testimony, if not firsthand experience, as was the boast of Thucydides and the argument used by many authors of handbooks of historical method since the sixteenth century, most notably Bodin (no. 91) and Baudouin, who favored using primary sources (*primi autores*) over secondary traditions. The other corollary is to avoid personal bias, to write "without passion or prejudice" (*sine ira et studio*), as Tacitus preached (though by no means practiced; no. 20); to "leave aside the praise and blame of men and to represent their actions faithfully," as La Popelinière put it (though he, too, fell short of this ideal).[18] Many historians have echoed the old injunction of Lucian, that "historians must describe the event as it really happened" (no. 11).[19] Leopold von Ranke's injunction to describe the past "as it really was" (*wie es eigentlich gewesen*) is the most famous expression of the ancient ideal of objectivity, whose more recent fortunes have been examined by Peter Novick.[20]

Related to these commonplaces is the age-old debate as to whether history is a science ("no more, no less," declared J. B. Bury in a much-cited manifesto) or an art ("Clio, a Muse," was George Macaulay Trevelyan's rejoinder).[21] In the Renaissance, the controversy was between Italianate "arts of history" and French "methods" of a historical "science." More recently, the polarity of art and science has been between historians devoted to the access to hard reality promised by the social sciences and those committed to the idea that the practice of history is essentially the construction of plot and narrative. In all cases, the rationale is much the same.

Both the "new social historians" and the historiographical textualists, trying in their own way to rethink history, claim novel approaches. Yet the terms of the debate were posed by the ancients, specifically in discus-

---

17. G. Cotroneo, *I Trattatisti dell' "Ars Historica"* (Naples, 1971).
18. Kelley, *Foundations,* 139.
19. Stern, *Varieties,* 57.
20. *That Noble Dream* (Princeton, 1989).
21. Stern, *Varieties,* 209, 227.

sions about the relative merits of utility (*utilitas*) and pleasure (*voluptas*) in historical narrative and, more conspicuously, in disputes between those who linked history with political science and factors of geography and environment (Polybius, no. 5; Strabo, no. 6), and those who linked it with rhetoric (Cicero, no. 15). Here, as elsewhere, the archetypes are Herodotus, the crowd-pleasing teller of tales, and Thucydides, with his analytical and unromantic narrative. This debate, too, was resurrected during the Renaissance: on one side were the Italian "arts of history" of the sixteenth century, emphasizing the rhetorical heritage of history and the problems of literary form; on the other, the French "methods of history," reverting to the Polybian view of a political and "pragmatic" history (*historia pragmatike*). By virtue of this methodizing of history and its political relevance, history was formally promoted from art to science, and, by Polybius's translator Isaac Casaubon, to the level of philosophy.[22]

Another theme that has occupied historians over the ages is the identification of history with philosophy. Underlying this is a long tradition of viewing history as the true source of wisdom and self-knowledge. This is perhaps most conspicuous in the sixteenth-century handbooks of historical method, although this attitude was implicit in the whole humanist movement. To Andrea Alciato, for example, history was the "most certain philosophy" (*certissima philosophia*).[23] Once more, however, the ultimate source is classical, the most famous expression being the phrase of Dionysius of Halicarnassus revived by Lord Bolingbroke, that history is "philosophy teaching by example" (nos. 8, 105).

Another familiar topic of debate has been the relative merits of recent and more remote history. Which is the most instructive, ancient or contemporary studies? Since Herodotus, the study of antiquities and archaeology has fascinated scholars. One classic argument in favor of ancient over modern history is the preface of Dionysius of Halicarnassus (no. 8), which suggests that the seeds of Rome's political greatness were present from the beginning. "Why follow the windings of the rivers?" as Hugh of St. Victor later said. "Lay hold of the source and you shall have all."[24] This was also the assumption of Vico's "new science" (no. 109), perhaps the most philosophical expression of this genetic approach,

---

22. *Polybii . . . historiarum qui supersunt* (Paris, 1609), prefatory letter to Henry IV.

23. Kelley, *Foundations*, 95.

24. *Didascalicon* 3 : xi.

which has served advocates of ancient or premodern history down to the present day.

In opposition to proponents of ancient history are the presentists; Herodotus's rival Thucydides is the prototype for this group. Like many later critics, Thucydides eschewed earlier history—events beyond living memory—as being fabulous and inaccessible. The most common feature of this school of historical thought, represented also by Polybius and Guicciardini (nos. 5, 74), is the assumption that history must be immediately applicable—relevant or (in the phrase of Polybius) "pragmatic history." This utilitarian and presentist attitude has often carried with it a deliberate myopia associated with some particular contemporary crisis or shaping event which determines the historian's perspective. For Thucydides, the Peloponnesian War was "the greatest event yet known in history"; for Machiavelli and Guicciardini, the "calamity" (*la Calamità*) was the French invasion of Italy in 1494.[25]

Another feature of this pragmatic history is the tendency to select particular factors, to identify particular causal sequences, and often to affix guilt to particular individuals. In contrast to the Herodotean view that history should be a "picture of the whole past," which was the editorial aim of the *English Historical Review,*[26] this attitude is expressed by J. R. Seeley's famous dictum that "history is past politics and politics is present history." Like Seeley, Polybius believed that history was "the truest education and training for public life" (no. 5), and his "pragmatic history" is not descriptive but prescriptive, oriented less toward self-knowledge than toward policy making. Such was the direction, too, of Machiavelli's "untrodden path," of Guicciardini's political reflections, and of Bodin's naturalistic view of history (nos. 73, 74, 91).

If pragmatic history has been constricting in terms of chronology and subject matter, it has also had the effect of broadening the geographic horizons of historical study. One consequence of the historicist myth and the genetic fallacy has been to encourage a parochially national view. This Livian model, as we might call it (nos. 12, 64)—illustrated also by Josephus (no. 32) and implicit, perhaps, in the approach of Herodotus, despite his omnivorous curiosity—has been preserved from antiquity right down to such contemporary works as those of Henri Pirenne on the

25. Felix Gilbert, *Machiavelli and Guicciardini* (Princeton, 1965); cf. Burckhardt, *Force and Freedom,* 256, as well as Randolph Starn, "Historians and 'Crisis,'" *Past & Present,* no. 52 (1971): 3–22.

26. Stern, *Varieties,* 174.

Belgians, Daniel Boorstin on the Americans, Winston Churchill on the English, and innumerable collaborative series on national history. From antiquity, there have been protests against such ethnocentrism. The classic defense of world ("catholic") history is that of Polybius, who inveighed against specialists and national historians and portrayed history as "a body whose members may not be severed" (no. 5). A second tradition of universal history was established by Eusebius and the Christian world chroniclers and given new life by Protestants in the sixteenth century (nos. 31, 37, 96, 98). This is a style preserved in the metahistorical and cryptotheological observations of such scholars as Oswald Spengler, Eric Voegelin, Arnold Toynbee, and even Hans Blumenberg.

The universality both of Polybian and of Eusebian history is more apparent than real, however. *Romanitas* and *Christianitas* were both identified with mankind as a whole, but in fact there was very little room for "barbarians" in this concentration on what, with similar parochialism, we call Western civilization. Already in the Renaissance objections were made to such an ethnocentric attitude. What was implicit in the intercultural view of Pico della Mirandola, who aspired to review the cultural traditions of all peoples, became explicit in the historical method of Bodin, who rejected as impermissibly narrow the theory of four dominating "world monarchies" and the concomitant imperialist idea of a "translation of empire" from Rome to the Germans (no. 91).

Geographic breadth and explanatory rigor have not justified pragmatic history in the eyes of many critics, especially those in the antiquarian and rhetorical traditions, whose attitudes toward humanity required a broader view, according to which history was enlisted in the service of the liberal arts and the Renaissance ideal of encyclopedic learning (nos. 67, 68, 69). That nothing human was alien to history was at least implicit in Herodotus and authors of his persuasion, though the application of this idea was most conspicuous in the works of such philologists as Aulus Gellius (no. 17) and, in modern times, Lorenzo Valla (no. 65), who had a direct and significant impact on historical scholarship.[27]

The encyclopedic ideal has been preserved, especially in the form of various "new" histories, from the sixteenth century to the present, but the impulse of pragmatic history has always been prominent, though not necessarily in political form. The history of economic, diplomatic,

27. Kelley, *Foundations,* chap. 1; see also Peter Burke, *The Renaissance Sense of the Past* (New York, 1969).

military, or scientific activities, as well as women's history may give a utilitarian focus and a "Whiggish" form to narrative and analytical history. For the most part, these specialized branches of study are the product of the last half-century or so. As a separate discipline, economic history, for example, is post-Marxian. Particular economic insights (emphasis on money, power, material motivation, the economic basis of leisure and hence of culture, and similar observations) may be traced back to antiquity, and in particular to Thucydides (no. 4), but these elements were generally subordinate to political or psychological interpretations.

There are several exceptions to the modernity of historical specialties. One is ecclesiastical history, and specifically what may be called the Eusebian tradition, especially as revived during the Reformation. As Johann Sleidan argued in his pioneering history (no. 79), his age could not be understood in purely political terms; for a full picture it was necessary to attend to spiritual as well as material affairs, and especially to the spread of the Word. For later Lutheran historians such as Flacius Illyricus, this enjoinder became even more urgent because of the need to justify and to publicize Protestantism (but as Eusebius defended early Christianity) as traditional and nonrevolutionary. What this branch of historiography signified, perhaps inadvertently, was a special religious interpretation which has informed historical narrative down to Ranke.[28]

Equally ancient was the genre that has become the history of law. This dates back at least to the second century B.C., when the Roman jurist Pomponius composed his account of "the origins of law" (no. 14). Out of this conventional topic of conventional jurisprudence and legal education has emerged, by way of Renaissance commentaries on Pomponius (as preserved in Justinian's *Digest*), the subject of legal history. In the sixteenth century, discussions of the sources of law not only spread into other legal traditions, especially feudal, but as a result of the humanist movement also converged with historiography proper. These works reveal as well some of the remote beginnings of modern institutional and social history.[29]

28. A. G. Dickens and John Tonkin, *The Reformation in Historical Thought* (Cambridge, Mass., 1985), complements Wallace K. Ferguson, *The Renaissance in Historical Thought* (Boston, 1948).

29. Kelley, "The Rise of Legal History in the Renaissance," *History and Theory* 9 (1970): 174–194; repr. in Kelley, *History, Law and the Human Sciences* (London, 1984). Same pagination.

The Renaissance also produced pioneering efforts in the history of art, literature, language, philosophy, and other aspects of what became cultural history—for example, in Christophe Milieu's little-known method of history, published in 1551, which sets down a program for a history not only of literature but also of thought or "wisdom" more generally. This encyclopedic tradition opened up historical studies to social, intellectual, and cultural interests in the early modern period.[30] This is evident in a variety of innovating works by sixteenth-century French historians such as Etienne Pasquier, Louis Le Roy, La Popelinière (especially the "New History" appended to his *History of Histories*, 1599), and Pierre Droit de Gaillard (no. 92). These works anticipate the so-called synthetic history of Henri Berr and some of his *Annaliste* disciples and—in spirit as well as in word—the "new history" of James Harvey Robinson and perhaps also such Enlightenment historians as Voltaire.[31] Nor have we seen the end of "new histories," as evidenced by the "new cultural history" and the "new historicism" of the 1980s.

Other common patterns since the time of Aristotle have to do with attempts at large-scale interpretation. Frequently, efforts have been made to apply organic models or metaphors to the process of historical change.[32] There are hints of such life analogies in Herodotus and Thucydides, but especially since Polybius the natural cycle of coming to be and passing away has been a significant part of historians' vocabulary (no. 5). In the Renaissance, Machiavelli, Le Roy, and others preserved the Polybian metaphor of corruption and generation in terms of Aristotle's three species of constitutions, and it has never ceased to fascinate political writers (nos. 73, 71). Directly associated with this pattern was the notion of generational conflict—in one form, the old topos of the battles between "ancients" and "moderns" (see no. 20)—as the particular source of short-term historical change; this, too, has been preserved in modern conceptions of historical change.

Other efforts have been made to form broad interpretations beyond the national level (the Livian success-tragedy model); of these perhaps the most enduring has been the idea of a "translation of empire" (*translatio imperii*)—with attendant notions of "translations" of learning, of fortune, and even of wisdom (*translatio studii, translatio fortunae, trans-*

---

30. Kelley, *Foundations,* 303.
31. Stern, *Varieties,* 35.
32. See J. Schlobach, *Zyklentheorie und Epochenmetaphorik* (Munich, 1980).

latio sapientiae; nos. 59, 60).[33] A major premise here is that knowledge and power—Minerva and Mars—are constant companions, illustrated most conspicuously in the coincidence of Roman cultural and political achievement. The corollary is that, because of the instability of human nature, such ascents of fortune can be only temporary. Thus, whether through natural cycles or the will of God, this political and cultural preeminence passes from one people to another—classically from the Medes to the Persians to the Greeks to the Romans and thence to the Germans, as modern political beneficiaries of Rome; this idea of four world monarchies was rejected by Bodin and other French historians as contradicting their own claims to a share of the ancient inheritance (no. 91).

The theme of universal empire has never been forsaken; one can see an unending series of attempts to appropriate the idea illustrated in the archetypal creation of Charlemagne (see no. 60)—in the imperial constructs and claims of the Spain of Philip II, the France of Louis XIV and Napoleon, the Third Reich of Hitler, and betimes in the aspirations of Soviet and American expansionists in the twentieth century. Parallel to this is the series of republican myths, rooted in the achievement and especially the rhetoric of fifth-century Athens, first-century Rome, Renaissance Florence and Venice, and perhaps Reformation Strasbourg and Geneva, not to mention the Netherlands and England. Although the principal vehicle of these republican impulses has been associated with the "Machiavellian moment," there is obviously a broader set of traditions on which Western historical thought has been able to draw.[34] "Westward the Course of Empire" was continued in the New World, too: Frederick Jackson Turner's frontier thesis is another variation on the old theme of the westward translation of empire—and of culture.[35]

Through the ages, history has sometimes shown a less attractive face: if Herodotus was the father of *historia,* he was also "the father of lies."[36] Although history was, for some enthusiasts, the "fountain of learning," it was, for others, the "fountain of errors": such were the contradictory views offered by two sixteenth-century French authors, Pierre Droit

33. W. Goez, *Translatio Imperii* (Tübingen, 1958).
34. J. G. A. Pocock, *The Machiavellian Moment* (Princeton, N.J., 1976).
35. Stern, *Varieties,* 198.
36. Juan Luis Vives, *De Disciplinis,* Bk. 12, cited by Arnaldo Momigliano, *Studies in Historiography* (London, 1966), 139.

de Gaillard and Charles de la Ruelle. From the beginning, critics have complained about the tendency of historians toward bias, flattery, and other intellectual vices. Some, notably Henry Cornelius Agrippa (no. 70), have suggested that it is impossible for history to achieve its ideal of truthfulness. These doubters have used terms ranging from the most crude (Voltaire's "lies agreed upon," Henry Ford's "bunk") to the most sophisticated (historical "Pyrrhonism," as it was referred to from the sixteenth century, though its source is ancient).

Time-honored, too, is the habit of mutual carping, whether in the form of attacking a rival interpreter or of reviewing all the literature on a subject. To compare H. R. Richardson and G. O. Sayles's assault on Bishop Stubbs with Poggio Bracciolini's attack on Lorenzo Valla, or William of Newburgh's on Geoffrey of Monmouth, or Josephus's on Apion, or Plutarch's on Herodotus, suggests that the style of such criticism has not changed fundamentally over the centuries (nos. 50, 32, 10). Much the same might be said for the chronic, even obsessive practice of revisionism, often introduced by the wholesale rejection of earlier interpretations. Consider the remarks of Polybius on the distortions of nationally oriented historians, or the critiques by Leonardo Bruni of the theory of the Trojan origins of Florence, by Valla of the Donation of Constantine, and by Bodin of the idea of four world monarchies (nos. 64, 65, 91). These are only a few examples of the historiographical version of the old quarrel between ancients and moderns.

The subject of historical criticism may be the most important—it is certainly the most difficult to assess—of all the themes in Western historical thought. Historical criticism begins with the simple expression of doubt—Herodotus's recognition, for example, of the "logos that is not"—but the motives for such skepticism stem as often from ideology as from disinterested rationality. Probably the major vehicle of criticism is classical philology, which focuses on problems of language, style, and anachronism and on the effort to understand the ideas, customs, and institutions underlying ancient texts. Philological criticism was revived in the Renaissance by Petrarch, Lorenzo Valla, Angelo Poliziano, Joseph Justus Scaliger, and a legion of vernacularist disciples; it was systematized by Mabillon and other seventeenth-century scholars (nos. 63, 65, 95).[37]

37. Kelley, "Humanism and History," in *Renaissance Humanism*, ed. A. Rabil (Philadelphia, 1988), 3:236–270.

The critical practice and theory of Renaissance humanism was by no means exclusively scientific. As elsewhere, rhetorical motives often outweighed philosophical ones; and what has been called "the topos of critical rejection" (*anasceua*) was often the basis for attacking received wisdom, such as the theory of the Trojan origins of various European cities and states.[38] In many respects, the vaunted historical sense of such scholars as Scaliger derived as much from the desire to imitate the ancients as it did from pure curiosity. Yet an increasing number of ancient legends and errors (such as the presumed Egyptian origins of the Hermetic books and the Roman origins of feudalism) were discredited once and for all in the Renaissance. In short, philology did in effect become a science in the sixteenth and seventeenth centuries and finally the basis for the "new science" of Vico, which was the first effort to give definition to "the history of human ideas" (no. 109).

Central to Western historical thought has always been the problem of language, whether in terms of translation and making sense of an alien past or in terms of accurate description and utilization of historical sources for a suitable narrative or analytical reconstruction of social action and cultural creation. Many times and in many contexts historical scholars attempted to carry out a kind of linguistic turn against transcendent impulses. In many cases, of course, the philosophy of history proved too tempting, as did the pull toward literary concerns; not infrequently the result was rejection of conventional historical form altogether.[39]

These observations have no doubt tended to overemphasize the continuities of historical thought and writing, yet many of these themes have been carried on, often inadvertently, by nineteenth- and twentieth-century historians. The chronic and unseemly claims of historians to an unending series of new histories suggest that not only social scientists but even historians, who presumably should know better, are victims of that scholarly amnesia detected by Pitirim Sorokin, which leads them to pose as "new Columbuses" and to assume, in his words, that "nothing

38. Frank Borchardt, *German Antiquity in Renaissance Myth* (Baltimore, 1971), 55.

39. Compare the literary discussion of the art of history in the Renaissance with the recent rhetorical approaches to historiography, most notably in Hayden White, *Metahistory: The Historical Imagination in Nineteenth-Century Europe* (Baltimore, 1973).

important has been discovered in their fields during all the preceding centuries . . . and that the real scientific era in these disciplines began only in the last two or three decades with the publications of their own researches and those of members of their own clique."[40] This in itself suggests that there is (in Thomas Kuhn's phrase) a "role for history" not only in science but in history itself.[41]

It seems worthwhile to preserve some appreciation of the larger heritage of the art and science of history, which spans over two-and-a-half millennia and most of the literate culture of the world, as well as Western civilization. Modern scholars have perhaps fewer causes for satisfaction than they pretend to believe. Presentism, parochialism, neglect of gender questions, self-serving or utilitarian attempts to explain, to surrender to ideological assumptions which represent a contemporary counterpart of myth—these and other limitations are shared by ancients and moderns alike, and it is surely useful to be aware of these occupational hazards. Similarly, the concern for the critical examination and interpretation (and, if necessary, restoration) of original texts is an old scholarly tradition which has changed more in technical than in conceptual terms. Most important, the original impulse of *historia*—human curiosity joined betimes with a desire for self-knowledge—serves in the most fundamental way to link the encyclopedic learning of the ancients, medievals, and early moderns with the much better equipped and organized, if less abundantly endowed, moderns and postmoderns. Perhaps the old Ciceronian saying (no. 15), repeated by Melanchthon and many other modern scholars, still represents the final justification for the attempt to gain wisdom by looking backward: "Without history what can we be but forever children?"

The following selections, some well known but many unfamiliar or inaccessible, have been gathered to illustrate the Western canon of historical thought from the Greeks to Edward Gibbon. Passages have been taken especially from prefaces to historical works, essays in encyclopedias, letters, occasional poems, and treatises on the reading, writing, validation, celebration, and application of history. Most texts are from standard translated editions (listed in the bibliography); a few (e.g., Leland) have been slightly modernized; others (Isidore of Seville, Cam-

40. *Fads and Foibles in Modern Sociology* (Chicago, 1956), 3–4.
41. Kuhn, *The Structure of Scientific Revolutions*, pp. 1–9.

panella, Gaillard, Muret, Menestrier, Voltaire, and others) are my own translations.

The purpose of this collection is not to supply examples of narrative history in the fashion of Peter Gay's *Historians at Work* but rather, like Fritz Stern's *Varieties of History,* which begins where this volume leaves off, to document some of the central and recurring issues of the practice and theory of history: methodological, epistemological, literary, hermeneutical, and ideological. The arrangement is mainly chronological, but there is a topical focus and coherence which may be suggested by referring to a few of these major themes. Of course, some pieces reflect several themes, but I have organized them according to their primary thrust.

The word and the concept *history* can be traced in a series of contexts, including Homer, Herodotus, Aristotle, Cicero and the Roman rhetoricians, Augustine and other Christian fathers, Isidore, Petrarch, Valla, various Renaissance "arts" and "methods" of history, and the encyclopedic works of the Enlightenment.

Theoretical discussions of the art and method of history—questions of truth, sources, verification, criticism, utility, style, and so on—are undertaken most directly by Lucian, Cicero, Quintilian, Pliny, Cassiodorus, Isidore, Bruni, Vergerio, Vives, Sleidan, Muret, Campanella, Heinsius, Bodin, Gaillard, Blundeville, Bacon, and Bolingbroke.

Political and pragmatic history and the presentist analysis of causes are pursued by Thucydides, Polybius, Tacitus, Commynes, Machiavelli, Guicciardini, Sleidan, Hobbes, de Thou, and Pufendorf. By contrast, a longer perspective and broader cultural interests characterize the work of Herodotus, Diodorus of Sicily, Dionysius of Halicarnassus, Otto of Freising, such Renaissance historians as Bodin, Le Roy, Gaillard, and Sleidan, and philosophical historians of the Enlightenment such as Vico, Herder, Robertson, Voltaire, and Condorcet.

Universal history is the genre developed especially by Diodorus, Polybius, Eusebius, Orosius, Bede and other medieval chroniclers, Otto, Bodin, Raleigh, Ussher, Bossuet, Vico, and Herder. National or civic history is represented especially by Livy, Villani, Bruni, Machiavelli, Guicciardini, Commynes, Bebel, Leland, Camden, Hotman, and some historians of the Enlightenment; the religious counterpart, confessional history, is illustrated variously by the early Christian fathers—Justin, Clement, Tertullian, and Eusebius—and such Protestant historians as Bucer, Calvin, Sleidan, and Foxe.

The history of historiography and criticism of earlier historians are continuous themes from Diodorus of Sicily, Lucian, Plutarch, Cicero, Josephus, and Cassiodorus to Vives, Sleidan, and Bodin. Philology and antiquarian research is the primary aim of Aulus Gellius, Petrarch, Bruni, Valla, Mabillon, and authors of relevant articles in eighteenth-century encyclopedias; the historical problems of translation are taken up by Origen, Jerome, Hugh of St. Victor, Bruni, and Luther.

The structure, patterns, direction, and philosophy of history (cycles, degeneration, and various kinds of progress) are treated by Hesiod, Polybius, Daniel and his commentators, Prudentius, Augustine, Chrétien de Troyes, Otto of Freising, Alexander of Roes, Joachim of Flora, Machiavelli, Louis Le Roy, Bucer, Calvin, Leibniz, Vico, Herder, d'Alembert, and Condorcet.

Particular aspects of historical experience are separated and treated variously: geography by Polybius, Strabo, Diodorus of Sicily, Bodin, Robertson, and others; law and institutions by Gaius, Pomponius, Justinian, Bodin, Pufendorf, and Vico; and psychological factors by Tacitus, Procopius, Comnena, Commynes, Machiavelli, Guicciardini, and other writers of historical biography and political history.

2
℣ Greece

The term and to some extent the concept of *history* begins with the Greeks. First as a method of inquiry and then as a kind of prose narrative concerned with such inquiry, history appeared in the fifth century B.C. and produced a variety of literary offspring devoted to the investigation, description, and analysis of the remote as well as the recent past. Born of human curiosity and nourished by the epic tradition, it matured into a form of knowledge which, despite links with Ionian science and the humanistic thrust of the Socratic revolution, was distinct from philosophy and so (according to the Aristotelian formula) from poetry.

Herodotus and Thucydides illustrated the two principal types of historical writing. The first of these was concerned with remote antiquity and all aspects of human culture, and the second with recent political and military affairs—the first with a wide range of anthropological investigation, and the second with analysis and determination of causes of change. In reality, these pioneering Greek historians were not pure types, and their work represented some of both tendencies. Yet the thrust of their interests was clear, and the divergence became increasingly obvious in the writings of their successors, epigones, and critics.

What these two historiographical traditions had in common was a fascination with humanity as reflected not in biological or psychological nature but in the processes of political, social, and cultural change—though such change was explained by analogy with natural physical change, especially with the introduction of medical and philosophical terminology. This was especially the case with Polybius: he interpreted history organistically and Roman history in particular as a universal process (*historia katholike*) which in political terms followed a fundamentally cyclical pattern (the famous constitutional cycle, *anacyclosis,* a formula revived in the Renaissance). The ties between history and geography (which implied medico-astrological formulations) could only reinforce this sort of scientific approach to historiography.

Because of such naturalistic and cyclical inclinations, the Greek sense of history has often been denied, especially in comparison with the providential and linear Judaeo-Christian view. This judgment has an ancient precedent, most notably in the criticism launched by Josephus against Greek historiography as false, foreshortened, and unprofitable, especially in comparison with such Near Eastern traditions as the Egyptians and the Jews; Greek historians did indeed try to link themselves to these older cultures.

The universal history that flourished after Polybius was marked by antiquarian interests as well as rhetorical motives. In his *Library of History,* Diodorus of Sicily accepted Polybius's notion of the organic unity of history; he expanded his horizons to include cultural affairs and the oriental, and especially the Egyptian, background to the story of the rise of Rome in the Mediterranean. In his *Ancient History (Archaiologia),* Dionysius of Halicarnassus praised Herodotus over Thucydides (as he praised Greece over Rome) because antiquity presented more elevated themes than contemporary history; yet he was closer to Thucydides in maintaining that history was "philosophy teaching by example."

Born of a curiosity linked both to Homeric myth and to Ionian science, the study of history was shaped and distorted by a variety of political and rhetorical forces and ended up, for the Greeks, as a literary genre. In a sense, Lucian's second-century A.D. *How to Write History,* a self-conscious critique of this genre, marked the culmination of history as developed by the epigones of Herodotus and Thucydides, but it also marked an extraordinary shift of emphasis from substance to style. The concern of Lucian, though Thucydides was his model, was literary impact rather than human wisdom, and he was interested in preaching rather than practicing the virtues of historical knowledge. This, too, has been a familiar pattern in historiographical styles over the centuries.

❡ MYTHISTORY

> 1. The *Iliad* of HOMER (ninth century B.C.) contains the first usage of the word *histor* (the etymological ancestor of *historian*),

Homer, *The Iliad.* Trans. Andrew Lang, Walter Leaf, and Ernest Myers. London: Macmillan, 1919. P. 381.

meaning one who sees or knows, hence a kind of judge or referee. The passage concerns the Olympian god Hephaestus, inventor of fire and promoter of civilization, and in particular one of the cities he fashioned on his cosmic shield. The histor's business, already linked to the law, was to choose between contending parties; he received payment for such work.

Also he fashioned therein two fair cities of mortal men. In the one there were espousals and marriage feasts, and beneath the blaze of torches they were leading the brides from their chambers through the city, and loud arose the bridal song. And young men were whirling in the dance, and among them flutes and viols sounded high; and the women standing each at her door were marvelling. But the folk were gathered in the assembly place; for there a strife was arisen, two men striving about the blood-price of a man slain; the one claimed to pay full atonement, expounding to the people, but the other denied him and would take naught; and both were fain to receive arbitrament at the hand of a daysman [*histor*]. And the folk were cheering both, as they took part on either side. And heralds kept order among the folk, while the elders on polished stones were sitting in the sacred circle, and holding in their hands staves from the loud-voiced heralds. Then before the people they rose up and gave judgment each in turn. And in the midst lay two talents of gold, to be given unto him who should plead among them most righteously [should utter among them the most righteous doom].

> 2. HESIOD (eighth century B.C.), is the author of *Works and Days,* a bleak poem about the hard life in Boeotia. His pessimism, like that of Petrarch over two thousand years later (and expressed in strikingly similar terms), itself implies a historical sense, however unconscious. This well-known fragment illustrates one man's groping for perspective, mythological as it is, three centuries before Herodotus.

And now with art and skill I'll summarize
Another tale, which you should take to heart,
Of how both gods and men began the same.
The gods, who live on Mount Olympus, first
Fashioned a golden race of mortal men;

Hesiod, *Works and Days*. In Hesiod, *Theogony, Works and Days, Theognis, Elegies*. Trans. Dorothea Wender. New York: Penguin, 1973. Pp. 62–65.

These lived in the reign of Kronos, king of heaven,
And like the gods they lived with happy hearts
Untouched by work or sorrow. Vile old age
Never appeared, but always lively limbed,
Far from all ills, they feasted happily.
Death came to them as sleep, and all good things
Were theirs; ungrudgingly, the fertile land
Gave up her fruits unasked. Happy to be
At peace, they lived with every want supplied,
[Rich in their flocks, dear to the blessed gods.]

And then this race was hidden in the ground.
But still they live as spirits of the earth,
Holy and good, guardians who keep off harm,
Givers of wealth: this kingly right is theirs.
The gods, who live on Mount Olympus, next
Fashioned a lesser, silver race of men:
Unlike the gold in stature or in mind.
A child was raised at home a hundred years
And played, huge baby, by his mother's side.
When they were grown and reached their prime, they lived
Brief, anguished lives, from foolishness, for they
Could not control themselves, but recklessly
Injured each other and forsook the gods;
They did not sacrifice, as all tribes must, but left
The holy altars bare. And, angry, Zeus
The son of Kronos, hid this race away,
For they dishonoured the Olympian gods.

The earth then hid this second race, and they
Are called the spirits of the underworld,
Inferior to the gold, but honoured, too.
And Zeus the father made a race of bronze,
Sprung from the ash tree, worse than the silver race,
But strange and full of power. And they loved
The groans and violence of war; they ate
No bread; their hearts were flinty-hard; they were
Terrible men; their strength was great, their arms
And shoulders and their limbs invincible.
Their weapons were of bronze, their houses bronze;
Their tools were bronze: black iron was not known.
They died by their own hands, and nameless, went

To Hades' chilly house. Although they were
Great soldiers, they were captured by black Death,
And left the shining brightness of the sun.

But when this race was covered by the earth,
The son of Kronos made another, fourth,
Upon the fruitful land, more just and good,
A godlike race of heroes, who are called
The demi-gods—the race before our own.
Foul wars and dreadful battles ruined some;
Some sought the flocks of Oedipus, and died
In Cadmus' land, at seven-gated Thebes;
And some, who crossed the open sea in ships,
For fair-haired Helen's sake, were killed at Troy.
These men were covered up in death, but Zeus
The son of Kronos gave the others life
And homes apart from mortals, at Earth's edge.
And there they live a carefree life, beside
The whirling Ocean, on the Blessed Isles.
Three times a year the blooming, fertile earth
Bears honeyed fruits for them, the happy ones.
[And Kronos is their king, far from the gods,
For Zeus released him from his bonds, and these,
The race of heroes, well deserve their fame.

Far-seeing Zeus then made another race,
The fifth, who live now on the fertile earth.]
I wish I were not of this race, that I
Had died before, or had not yet been born.
This is the race of iron. Now, by day,
Men work and grieve unceasingly; by night,
They waste away and die. The gods will give
Harsh burdens, but will mingle in some good;
Zeus will destroy this race of mortal men,
When babies shall be born with greying hair.
Father will have no common bond with son,
Neither will guest with host, nor friend with friend;
The brother-love of past days will be gone.
Men will dishonour parents, who grow old
Too quickly, and will blame and criticize
With cruel words. Wretched and godless, they
Refusing to repay their bringing up,
Will cheat their aged parents of their due.

Men will destroy the towns of other men.
The just, the good, the man who keeps his word
Will be despised, but men will praise the bad
And insolent. Might will be Right, and shame
Will cease to be. Men will do injury
To better men by speaking crooked words
And adding lying oaths; and everywhere
Harsh-voiced and sullen-faced and loving harm,
Envy will walk along with wretched men.
Last, to Olympus from the broad-pathed Earth,
Hiding their loveliness in robes of white,
To join the gods, abandoning mankind,
Will go the spirits Righteousness and Shame.
And only grievous troubles will be left
For men, and no defence against our wrongs.

3. HERODOTUS (ca. 495–425 B.C.) was apparently a straight-forward man, but there is something of a mystery about his work. What led him to travel in the Near East? On what business and on what income? Above all, why did he set down the results of his research (*historia*) for posterity? Granted, he was a man of irre-pressible curiosity and a born storyteller, but who did he think would take the trouble to read his book? The answer to the last question must be that in his day there was already an attentive public ready to listen to stories about the barbarians as well as about their own past. Public life implies public memory, and it was this field that Herodotus began to explore.

The subject of his book is the confrontation of East and West, of barbarism and civilization; the book ends with the salvation of this civilization through the heroic efforts of the Athenians. But if it is a paean to the Greek love of liberty, it is not limited to this theme. Equally important are the digressions and anecdotes (*logoi*) on such topics as the origins, mythologies, religious practices, and customs of peoples outside the circle of the Hellenic world. Necessarily, Herodotus's methods were crude—a blend of sightseeing and oral tradition—but he was by no means uncritical. He distinguished, for example, between truth and myth, between eyewitness and hearsay evidence, and between cause (*aitia*) and pretext (*prophasis*).

Herodotus, *Histories,* trans. George Rawlinson as *The Persian Wars.* New York: Modern Library, 1947. Pp. 3–6, 229–230, 497–498, 655–656, and 714.

He was the originator, too, of some of the vocabulary and concepts of historical explanation: fate and fortune, change and growth, national character and laws, among others. Many of his notions and habits are still with us today in some form.

Before Herodotus there were storytellers (*logographoi*), philosophers curious about the nature of things, and poets curious about the origins of peoples. His contribution was to combine curiosity about the past with rational inquiry, mythology with science. There may have been mute, inglorious historians before Herodotus, but there is still no reason to disagree with Cicero, who called him "the father of history."

These are the researches [histories] of Herodotus of Halicarnassus, which he publishes, in the hope of thereby preserving from decay the remembrance of what men have done, and or preventing the great and wonderful actions of the Greeks and the Barbarians from losing their due meed of glory; and withal to put on record what were their grounds of feud.

According to the Persians best informed in history, the Phoenicians began the quarrel. This people, who had formerly dwelt on the shores of the Red Sea, having migrated to the Mediterranean and settled in the parts which they now inhabit, began at once, they say, to adventure on long voyages, freighting their vessels with the waves of Egypt and Assyria. They landed at many places on the coast, and among the rest at Argos, which was then pre-eminent above all the states included now under the common name of Hellas. Here they exposed their merchandise, and traded with the natives for five or six days; at the end of which time, when almost everything was sold, there came down to the beach a number of women, and among them the daughter of the king, who was, they say, agreeing in this with the Greeks, Io, the child of Inachus. The women were standing by the stern of the ship intent upon their purchases, when the Phoenicians, with a general shout, rushed upon them. The greater part made their escape, but some were seized and carried off. Io herself was among the captives. The Phoenicians put the women on board their vessel, and set sail for Egypt. Thus did Io pass into Egypt, according to the Persian story, which differs widely from the Phoenician: and thus commenced, according to their authors, the series of outrages.

At a later period, certain Greeks, with whose name they are unacquainted, but who would probably be Cretans, made a landing at Tyre, on the Phoenician coast, and bore off the king's daughter, Europe. In this they only retaliated; but afterwards manned a ship of war, and sailed to Aea, a city of Colchis, on the river Phasis; from whence, after despatching the rest of the business on which they had come, they carried off Medea, the daughter of the king of the land. The monarch sent a herald into Greece to demand reparation of the wrong, and the restitution of his child; but the Greeks made answer, that having received no reparation of the wrong done them in the seizure of Io the Argive, they should give none in this instance.

In the next generation afterwards, according to the same authorities, Alexander the son of Priam, bearing these events in mind, resolved to procure himself a wife out of Greece by violence, fully persuaded, that as the Greeks had not given satisfaction for their outrages, so neither would he be forced to make any for his. Accordingly he made prize of Helen; upon which the Greeks decided that, before resorting to other measures, they would send envoys to reclaim the princess and require reparation of the wrong. Their demands were met by a reference to the violence which had been offered to Medea, and they were asked with what face they could now require satisfaction, when they had formerly rejected all demands for either reparation or restitution addressed to them.

Hitherto the injuries on either side had been mere acts of common violence; but in what followed the Persians consider that the Greeks were greatly to blame, since before any attack had been made on Europe, they led an army into Asia. Now as for the carrying off of women, it is the deed, they say, of a rogue; but to make a stir about such as are carried off, argues a man a fool. Men of sense care nothing for such women, since it is plain that without their own consent they would never be forced away. The Asiatics, when the Greeks ran off with their women, never troubled themselves about the matter; but the Greeks, for the sake of a single Lacedaemonian girl, collected a vast armament, invaded Asia, and destroyed the kingdom of Priam. Henceforth they ever looked upon the Greeks as their open enemies. For Asia, with all the various tribes of barbarians that inhabit it, is regarded by the Persians as their own; but Europe and the Greek race they look on as distinct and separate.

Such is the account which the Persians give of these matters. They trace to the attack upon Troy their ancient enmity towards the Greeks. The Phoenicians, however, as regards Io, vary from the Persian statements. They deny that they used any violence to remove her into Egypt; she herself, they say, having formed an intimacy with the captain, while his vessel lay at Argos, and suspecting herself to be with child, of her own free will accompanied the Phoenicians on their leaving the shore, to escape the shame of detection and the reproaches of her parents. Which of these two accounts is true I shall not trouble to decide. I shall proceed at once to point out the person who first within my knowledge commenced aggressions on the Greeks, after which I shall go forward with my history, describing equally the greater and the lesser cities. For the cities which were formerly great, have most of them become insignificant; and such as are at present powerful, were weak in the olden time. I shall therefore discourse equally of both, convinced that human happiness never continues long in one stay. . . .

Thus it appears certain to me, by a great variety of proofs, that Cambyses was raving mad; he would not else have set himself to make a mock of holy rites and long-established usages. For if one were to offer men to choose out of all the customs in the world such as seemed to them the best, they would examine the whole number and end by preferring their own; so convinced are they that their own usages far surpass those of all others. Unless, therefore, a man was mad, it is not likely that he would make sport of such matters. That people have this feeling about their laws may be seen by very many proofs: among others, by the following. Darius, after he had got the kingdom, called into his presence certain Greeks who were at hand, and asked what he should pay them to eat the bodies of their fathers when they died. To which they answered, that there was no sum that would tempt them to do such a thing. He then sent for certain Indians, of the race called Callatians, men who eat their fathers, and asked them, while the Greeks stood by, and knew by the help of an interpreter all that was said, what he should give them to burn the bodies of their fathers at their decease. The Indians exclaimed aloud, and bade him forbear such language. Such is men's custom; and Pindar was right, in my judgment, when he said, "Law is king over all." . . .

[Xerxes, speaking to an assembly of the noblest Persians] . . . My intent is to throw a bridge over the Hellespont and march an army through Europe against Greece, that thereby I may obtain vengeance from the Athenians for the wrongs committed by them against the Persians and against my father. Your own eyes saw the preparations of Darius against these men; but death came upon him, and balked his hopes of revenge. In his behalf, therefore, and in behalf of all the Persians, I undertake the war, and pledge myself not to rest till I have taken and burned Athens, which has dared, unprovoked, to injure me and my father. Long since they came to Asia with Aristagoras of Miletus, who was one of our slaves, and entering Sardis, burnt its temples and its sacred groves; again, more lately, when we made a landing upon their coast under Datis and Artaphernes, how roughly they handled us you do not need to be told. For these reasons, therefore, I am bent upon this war; and I see likewise therewith united no few advantages. Once let us subdue this people, and those neighbours of theirs who hold the land of Pelops the Phrygian, and we shall extend the Persian territory as far as God's heaven reaches. The sun will then shine on no land beyond our borders; for I will pass through Europe from one end to the other, and with your aid make all the lands which it contains one country. For thus, if what I hear be true, affairs stand: The nations whereof I have spoken, once swept away, there is no city, no country left in all the world, which will venture so much as to withstand us in arms. By this course then we shall bring all mankind under our yoke, alike those who are guilty and those who are innocent of doing us wrong. For yourselves, if you wish to please me, do as follows: When I announce the time for the army to meet together, hasten to the muster with a good will, every one of you; and know that to the man who brings with him the most gallant array I will give the gifts which our people consider the most honourable. This then is what you have to do. But to show that I am not self-willed in this matter I lay the business before you, and give you full leave to speak your minds upon it openly. . . .

After [the envoys of the Medes had spoken] the Athenians returned this answer to Alexander, "We know, as well as you do, that the power of the Mede is many times greater than our own: we did not need to have that cast in our teeth. Nevertheless we cling so to freedom that we shall offer what resistance we may. Seek not to persuade us into making terms with the barbarian—say what you will, you will never gain our assent. Return rather at once, and tell Mardonius that our answer to him is this, 'So long as the sun keeps his present course, we will never join alliance with Xerxes. Nay, we shall oppose him unceasingly, trusting in the aid of those gods and heroes whom he has lightly esteemed, whose houses and whose images he has burnt with fire.' And come not again to us with words like these; nor, thinking to do us a service, persuade us to unholy actions. You are the guest and friend of our nation—we would not that you should receive hurt at our hands."

Such was the answer which the Athenians gave to Alexander. To the Spartan envoys they said, "It was natural no doubt that the Lacedaemonians should be afraid we might make terms with the barbarian; but nevertheless it was a base fear in men who knew so well of what temper and spirit we are. Not all the gold that the whole earth contains—not the fairest and most fertile of all lands—would bribe us to take part with the Medes and help them to enslave our countrymen. Even could we have brought ourselves to such a thing, there are many very powerful motives which would now make it impossible. The first and chief of these is the burning and destruction of our temples and the images of our gods, which forces us to make no terms with their destroyer, but rather to pursue him with our resentment to the uttermost. Again, there is our common brotherhood with the Greeks: our common language, the altars and the sacrifices of which we all partake, the common character which we bear—did the Athenians betray all these, of a truth it would not be well. Know then now, if you have not known it before, that while one Athenian remains alive, we will never join alliance with Xerxes. . . ."

It was the grandfather of this Artayctes, one Artembares by name, who suggested to the Persians a proposal, which they readily embraced, and thus urged upon Cyrus, "Since Zeus," they said, "has overthrown Astyages, and given the rule to the Persians, and to you chiefly, O Cyrus, come now, let us quit this land wherein we dwell—for it is a scant land and a rugged—and let us choose ourselves some other better country. Many such lie around us, some nearer, some further off: if we take one of these, men will admire us far more than they do now. Who that had the power would not so act? And when shall we have a fairer time than now, when we are lords of so many nations, and rule all Asia?" Then Cyrus, who did not greatly esteem the counsel, told them they might do so, if they liked—but he warned them not to expect in that case to continue rulers, but to prepare for being ruled by others—soft countries gave birth to soft men—there was no region which produced very delightful fruits, and at the same time men of a warlike spirit. So the Persians departed with altered minds, confessing that Cyrus was wiser than they; and chose rather to dwell in a churlish land, and exercise lordship, than to cultivate plains, and be the slaves of others.

❡ PRAGMATIC HISTORY

4. THUCYDIDES (471?–400? B.C.) built upon the work of Herodotus, but he deliberately took issue with his standards and per-

Thucydides, *The Peloponnesian War.* In *The Complete Writings of Thucydides: The Peloponnesian War,* trans. R. Crawley. New York: Modern Library, 1934. 1:3–5, 6, 7–8, 9, 10–11, and 12–15.

spective. Not for Thucydides the inquiry into foreign behavior, the investigation of ancient fables, or the self-indulgence of romantic storytelling. His field of inquiry was past politics, but not of the distant past. Specifically, his subject was the war in which he himself had taken part—and which happened also to be "the greatest event in history." He investigated the causes of the conflict between Athens and Sparta and thereby revealed certain general behavior patterns. In doing so, he not only shed light upon the future but also created a work that he hoped would be "a possession for all times."

Compared to Herodotus, Thucydides shows a much sharper focus, narrower horizons, and a more critical attitude toward truth. Despite some poetic influence, especially from Attic drama, his work belongs, retrospectively, in the category of history as science. This is evident from the sophistication with which he analyzes power, economic as well as political, and from the way he distinguishes between immediate and underlying causes. It is also evident from his assumptions about the immutability of human nature and from certain overtones derived from medical thought, such as his diagnosis of the cause (*prophasis*) of the decline of Athens. Like many of his successors, Thucydides was more prescriptive than descriptive; hence the attraction of his work to readers who demand relevance and some immediately intelligible reasons for historical change and who prefer a man of action.

Thucydides, an Athenian, wrote the history of the war between the Peloponnesians and the Athenians, beginning at the moment that it broke out, and believing that it would be a great war, and more worthy of relation than any that had preceded it. This belief was not without its grounds. The preparations of both the combatants were in every department in the last state of perfection; and he could see the rest of the Hellenic race taking sides in the quarrel; those who delayed doing so at once having it in contemplation. Indeed this was the greatest movement yet known in history, not only of the Hellenes, but of a large part of the barbarian world—I had almost said of mankind. For though the events of remote antiquity, and even those that more immediately precede the war, could not from lapse of time be clearly ascertained, yet the evidence which an inquiry carried as far back as practicable leads me to trust, all point to the conclusion that there was nothing on a great scale, either in war or in other matters.

For instance, it is evident that the country now called Hellas had in ancient times no settled population; on the contrary, migrations were of frequent occurrence, the several tribes readily abandoning their homes under the pressure of superior numbers. Without commerce, without freedom of communication either by land or sea, cultivating no more of their territory than the exigencies of life required, destitute of capital, never planting their land (for they could not tell when an invader might not come and take it all away, and when he did come they had no walls to stop him), thinking that the necessities of daily sustenance could be supplied at one place as well as another, they cared little for shifting their habitation, and consequently neither built large cities nor attained to any other form of greatness. The richest soils were always most subject to this change of masters; such as the district now called Thessaly, Boeotia, most of the Peloponnese, Arcadia excepted, and the most fertile parts of the rest of Hellas. The goodness of the land favoured the aggrandizement of particular individuals, and thus created faction which proved a fertile source of ruin. It also invited invasion. Accordingly Attica, from the poverty of its soil enjoying from a very remote period freedom from faction, never changed its inhabitants. And here is no inconsiderable exemplification of my assertion, that the migrations were the cause of there being no correspondent growth in other parts. The most powerful victims of war or faction from the rest of Hellas took refuge with the Athenians as a safe retreat; and at an early period, becoming naturalized, swelled the already large population of the city to such a height that Attica became at last too small to hold them, and they had to send out colonies to Ionia.

There is also another circumstance that contributes not a little to my conviction of the weakness of ancient times. Before the Trojan war there is no indication of any common action in Hellas, nor indeed of the universal prevalence of the name; on the contrary, before the time of Hellen, son of Deucalion, no such appellation existed, but the country went by the names of the different tribes, in particular of the Pelasgian. It was not till Hellen and his sons grew strong in Phthiotis, and were invited as allies into the other cities, that one by one they gradually acquired from the connection the name of Hellenes; though a long time elapsed before that name could fasten itself upon all. The best proof of this is furnished by Homer. Born long after the Trojan war, he nowhere calls all of them by that name, nor indeed any of them except the followers of Achilles from Phthiotis, who were the original Hellenes: in his poems they are called Danaans, Argives, and Achaeans. He does not even use the term barbarian, probably because the Hellenes had not yet

been marked off from the rest of the world by one distinctive appellation. It appears therefore that the several Hellenic communities, comprising not only those who first acquired the name, city by city, as they
came to understand each other, but also those who assumed it afterwards
as the name of the whole people, were before the Trojan war prevented
by their want of strength and the absence of mutual intercourse from
displaying any collective action.

Indeed, they could not unite for this expedition till they had gained
increased familiarity with the sea. . . .

With respect to their towns, later on, at an era of increased facilities of
navigation and a greater supply of capital, we find the shores becoming
the site of walled towns, and the isthmuses being occupied for the purposes of commerce, and defence against a neighbour. . . .

The coast populations now began to apply themselves more closely to
the acquisition of wealth, and their life became more settled; some even
began to build themselves walls on the strength of their newly acquired
riches. For the love of gain would reconcile the weaker to the dominion
of the stronger, and the possession of capital enabled the more powerful
to reduce the smaller towns to subjection. And it was at a somewhat later
stage of this development that they went on the expedition against Troy.

What enabled Agamemnon to raise the armament was more, in my
opinion, his superiority in strength, than the oaths of Tyndareus, which
bound the Suitors to follow him. . . . The strength of his navy is shown
by the fact that his own was the largest contingent, and that of the
Arcadians was furnished by him; this at least is what Homer says, if his
testimony is deemed sufficient. Besides, in his account of the transmission of the sceptre, he calls him

"Of many an isle, and of all Argos king."

Now Agamemnon's was a continental power; and he could not have been
master of any except the adjacent islands (and these would not be many),
but through the possession of a fleet.

And from this expedition we may infer the character of earlier enterprises. . . . We may safely conclude that the armament in question surpassed all before it, as it fell short of modern efforts; if we can here also
accept the testimony of Homer's poems, in which, without allowing for
the exaggeration which a poet would feel himself licensed to employ, we
can see that it was far from equalling ours. . . . If [the Hellenes] had
brought plenty of supplies with them, and had persevered in the war
without scattering for piracy and agriculture, they would have easily

defeated the Trojans in the field; since they could hold their own against them with the division on service. In short, if they had stuck to the siege, the capture of Troy would have cost them less time and less trouble. But as want of money proved the weakness of earlier expeditions, so from the same cause even the one in question, more famous than its predecessors, may be pronounced on the evidence of what it effected to have been inferior to its renown and to the current opinion about it formed under the tuition of the poets.

Even after the Trojan War Hellas was still engaged in removing and settling, and thus could not attain to the quiet which must precede growth. The late return of the Hellenes from Ilium caused many revolutions, and factions ensued almost everywhere; and it was the citizens thus driven into exile who founded the cities. . . .

But as the power of Hellas grew, and the acquisition of wealth became more an object, the revenues of the states increasing, tyrannies were by their means established almost everywhere,—the old form of government being hereditary monarchy with definite prerogatives,—and Hellas began to fit out fleets and apply herself more closely to the sea. It is said that the Corinthians were the first to approach the modern style of naval architecture, and that Corinth was the first place in Hellas where galleys were built. . . . Subsequently the Ionians attained to great naval strength in the reign of Cyrus, the first king of the Persians, and of his son Cambyses, and while they were at war with the former commanded for a while the Ionian sea. . . .

All the [Greek navies'] insignificance did not prevent their being an element of the greatest power to those who cultivated them, alike in revenue and in dominion. They were the means by which the islands were reached and reduced, those of the smallest area falling the easiest prey. Wars by land there were none, none at least by which power was acquired; we have the usual border contests, but of distant expeditions with conquest for object we hear nothing among the Hellenes. There was no union of subject cities round a great state, no spontaneous combination of equals for confederate expeditions; what fighting there was consisted merely of local warfare between rival neighbours. . . . Thus for a long time everywhere in Hellas do we find causes which make the states alike incapable of combination for great and national ends, or of any vigorous action of their own.

But at last a time came when the tyrants of Athens and the far older tyrannies of the rest of Hellas were, with the exception of those in Sicily, once and for all put down by Lacadaemon; for this city, though after the settlement of the Dorians, its present inhabitants, it suffered from factions for an unparalleled length of time, still at a very early period obtained good laws, and enjoyed a freedom from tyrants which was unbroken; it has possessed the same form of government for more than four hundred years, reckoning to the end of the late war, and has thus been in a position to arrange the affairs of the other states. Not many years after the deposition of the tyrants, the battle of Marathon was fought between the Medes and the Athenians. Ten years afterwards the barbarians returned with the armada for the subjugation of Hellas. In the face of this great danger the command of the confederate Hellenes was assumed by the Lacedaemonians in virtue of their superior power; and the Athenians having made up their minds to abandon their city, broke up their homes, threw themselves into their ships, and became a naval people. This coalition, after repulsing the barbarian, soon afterwards split into two sections, which included the Hellenes who had revolted from the king, as well as those who had aided him in the war. At the head of the one stood Athens, at the head of the other Lacedaemon, one the first naval, the other the first military power in Hellas. For a short time the league held together, till the Lacedaemonians and Athenians quarrelled, and made war upon each other with their allies, a duel into which all the Hellenes sooner or later were drawn, though some might at first remain neutral. So that the whole period from the Median war to this, with some peaceful intervals, was spent by each power in war, either with its rival, or with its own revolted allies, and consequently afforded them constant practice in military matters, and that experience which is learnt in the school of danger. . . .

Having how given the result of my inquiries into early times, I grant that there will be a difficulty in believing every particular detail. The way that most men deal with traditions, even traditions of their own country, is to receive them all alike as they are delivered, without applying any critical test whatever. The general Athenian public fancy that Hipparchus was tyrant when he fell by the hands of Harmodius and Aristogiton; not knowing that Hippias, the eldest of the sons of Pisistratus, was really supreme, and that Hipparchus and Thessalus were his brothers; and that Harmodius and Aristogiton suspecting, on the very day, nay at the very moment fixed for the deed, that information had been conveyed to Hippias by their accomplices, concluded that he had been warned, and did not attack him, yet, not liking to be apprehended and risk their lives for nothing, fell upon Hipparchus near the temple of the daughters of Leos, and slew him as he was arranging the Panathenaic procession.

There are many other unfounded ideas current among the rest of the Hellenes, even on matters of contemporary history which have not been obscured by time. For instance, there is the notion that the Lacedaemonian kings have two votes each, the fact being that they have only one; and that there is a company of Pitane, there being simply no such thing. So little pains do the vulgar take in the investigation of truth, accepting readily the first story that comes to hand. On the whole, however, the conclusions I have drawn from the proofs quoted may, I believe, safely be relied on. Assuredly they will not be disturbed either by the lays of a poet displaying the exaggeration of his craft, or by the compositions of the chroniclers that are attractive at truth's expense; the subjects they treat of being out of the reach of evidence, and time having robbed most of them of historical value by enthroning them in the region of legend. Turning from these, we can rest satisfied with having arrived at conclusions as exact as can be expected in matters of such antiquity. To come to this war; despite the known disposition of the actors in a struggle to overrate its importance, and when it is over to return to their admiration of earlier events, yet an examination of the facts will show that it was much greater than the wars which preceded it.

With reference to the speeches in this history, some were delivered before the war began, others while it was going on; some I heard myself, others I got from various quarters; it was in all cases difficult to carry them word for word in one's memory, so my habit has been to make the speakers say what was in my opinion demanded of them by the various occasions, of course adhering as closely as possible to the general sense of what they really said. And with reference to the narrative of events, far from permitting myself to derive it from the first source that came to hand, I did not even trust myself, partly on what others saw for me, the accuracy of the report being always tried by the most severe and detailed tests possible. My conclusions have cost me some labour from the want of coincidence between accounts of the same occurrences by different eye-witnesses, arising sometimes from imperfect memory, sometimes from undue partiality for one side or the other. The absence of romance in my history will, I fear, detract somewhat from its interest; but if it be judged useful by those inquirers who desire an exact knowledge of the past as an aid to the interpretation of the future, which in the course of human things must resemble if it does not reflect it, I shall be content. In fine, I have written my work, not as an essay which is to win the applause of the moment, but as a possession for all time.

The Median war, the greatest achievement of past times, yet found a speedy decision in two actions by sea and two by land. The Peloponnesian war was prolonged to an immense length, and long as it was it was short without parallel for the misfortunes that it brought upon Hellas. Never had so many cities been taken and laid desolate, here by the barbarians, here by the parties contending (the old inhabitants being sometimes removed to make room for others); never was there so much banishing and blood-shedding, now on the field of battle, now in the strife of action. Old stories of occurrences handed down by tradition, but scantily confirmed by experience, suddenly ceased to be incredible; there were earthquakes of unparalleled extent and violence; eclipses of the sun occurred with a frequency unrecorded in previous history; there were great droughts in sundry places and consequent famines, and that most calamitous and awfully fatal visitation, the plague. All this came upon them with the late war, which was begun by the Athenians and Peloponnesians by the dissolution of the thirty years' truce made after the conquest of Euboea. To the question why they broke the treaty, I answer by placing, first an account of their grounds of complaint and points of difference, that no one may ever have to ask the immediate cause which plunged the Hellenes into a war of such magnitude. The real cause I consider to be the one which was formally most kept out of sight. The growth of the power of Athens, and the alarm which this inspired in Lacedaemon, made war inevitable. Still it is well to give the grounds alleged by either side, which led to the dissolution of the treaty and the breaking out of the war.

5. POLYBIUS (ca. 198–117 B.C.) was born into a Greek family of some political eminence and served on various diplomatic missions. He spent most of his life as an intermediary between the Greeks and Romans, as emissary, hostage, friend of leading repub-

Polybius, *The Histories of Polybius,* trans. W. R. Paton. Loeb Classical Library. 1:3–13, 2:71–73 and 139–143; 3:271–273, 277–279, and 283–289; 5:27–31; 6:397–399. Reprinted by permission of the publishers and the Loeb Classical Library from Polybius, Volumes 1, 2, 3, 5, and 6, trans. W. R. Paton, Cambridge, Mass.: Harvard University Press, 1922, 1923, 1926, 1927.

licans (including Scipio Africanus), and finally as historian. During his sixteen years of captivity, he adopted their culture; his greatest work was a celebration of Roman expansion during the third and second centuries. In an intellectual sense, then, if not diplomatically, he succeeded in forging links between Greece and Rome: he introduced both Thucydidean history and the Hellenic ideal of world civilization, the *oicumene,* to the Latins. *Romanitas* became the equivalent of civilization and, for Polybius, the purpose (*telos*) of history. Polybius went one step beyond Herodotus: he not only investigated the barbarians, he actually joined them.

Pragmatic history, universal history (*historia pragmatike, historia katholike*)—these were the slogans of Polybius's historical writing. He combined didactic and scientific aims more inflated than those of Thucydides with horizons wider than those of Herodotus. To these he added some of the generalizing habits of Greek political philosophy, apparent especially in his famous law of constitutional change (*anacyclosis*), a cyclical adaptation of the Aristotelian threefold division of governmental species; in his elaborate theory of historical causation and motivation; and above all in his conviction that history itself had a fundamental, organic kind of unity—ideas which would all be taken up again in the Renaissance. He also insisted upon the value of what were later called the auxiliary sciences of history, particularly geography and chronology. Possessing its own method and categories, history was indeed philosophical in Polybius's view.

Even more than Thucydides, then, Polybius was the archetype of the scientific historian. On the whole, however, his reach exceeded his grasp, and his historical accounts have always been less interesting than his remarks on historical method. Yet his theories and ideals of historical writing have made him perhaps the most influential of all ancient historians.

Had previous chroniclers neglected to speak in praise of History in general, it might perhaps have been necessary for me to recommend everyone to choose for study and welcome such treatises as the present, since men have no more ready corrective of conduct than knowledge of the past. But all historians, one may say without exception, and in no half-hearted manner, but making this the beginning and end of their labour, have impressed on us that the soundest education and training for a life of active politics is the study of History, and that the surest and indeed the only method of learning how to bear bravely the vicissitudes of fortune, is to recall the calamities of others. Evidently therefore no one, and least of all myself, would think it his duty at this day to repeat what has been so well and so often said. For the very element of unexpectedness in the events I have chosen as my theme will be sufficient to challenge and incite everyone, young and old alike, to peruse my systematic history. For who is so worthless or indolent as not to wish to know by what means and under what system of polity the Romans in less than fifty-three years have succeeded in subjecting nearly the whole inhabited world to their sole government—a thing unique in history? Or who again is there so passionately devoted to other spectacles or studies as to regard anything as of greater moment than the acquisition of this knowledge?

How striking and grand is the spectacle presented by the period with which I purpose to deal, will be most clearly apparent if we set beside and compare with the Roman dominion the most famous empires of the past, those which have formed the chief theme of historians. Those worthy of being thus set beside it and compared are these. The Persians for a certain period possessed a great rule and dominion, but so often as they ventured to overstep the boundaries of Asia they imperilled not only the security of this empire, but their own existence. The Lacedaemonians, after having for many years disputed the hegemony of Greece, at length attained it but to hold it uncontested for scarce twelve years. The Macedonian rule in Europe extended but from the Adriatic region to the Danube, which would appear a quite insignificant portion of the continent. Subsequently, by overthrowing the Persian empire they became supreme in Asia also. But though their empire was now regarded as the greatest geographically and politically that had ever existed, they left the larger part of the inhabited world as yet outside it. For they never even made a single attempt to dispute possession of Sicily, Sardinia, or Libya, and the most warlike nations of Western Europe were, to speak the simple truth, unknown to them. But the Romans have subjected to their rule not portions, but nearly the whole of the world [and possess an empire which is not only immeasurably greater than any which preceded it, but need not fear rivalry in the future]. In the course of this work it will become more clearly intelligible [by what steps this power was acquired], and it will also be seen how many and how great advantages accrue to the student from the systematic treatment of history.

The date from which I propose to begin my history is the 140th Olympiad [220–216 B.C.], and the events are the following: (1) in Greece the so-called Social War, the first waged against the Aetolians by the Achaeans in league with and under the leadership of Philip of Macedon, the son of Demetrius and father of Perseus, (2) in Asia the war for Coele-Syria between Antiochus and Ptolemy Philopator, (3) in Italy, Libya, and the adjacent regions, the war between Rome and Carthage, usually known as the Hannibalic War. These events immediately succeed those related at the end of the work of Aratus of Sicyon. Previously the doings of the world had been, so to say, dispersed, as they were held together by no unity of initiative, results, or locality; but ever since this date history has been an organic whole, and the affairs of Italy and Libya have been interlinked with those of Greece and Asia, all leading up to one end. And this is my reason for beginning their systematic history from that date. For it was owing to their defeat of the Carthaginians in the Hannibalic War that the Romans, feeling that the chief and most essential step in their scheme of universal aggression had now been taken, were first emboldened to reach out their hands to grasp the rest and to cross with an army to Greece and the continent of Asia.

Now were we Greeks well acquainted with the two states which disputed the empire of the world, it would not perhaps have been necessary for me to deal at all with their previous history, or to narrate what purpose guided them, and on what sources of strength they relied, in entering upon such a vast undertaking. But as neither the former power nor the earlier history of Rome and Carthage is familiar to most of us Greeks, I thought it necessary to prefix this Book and the next to the actual history, in order that no one after becoming engrossed in the narrative proper may find himself at a loss, and ask by what counsel and trusting to what power and resources the Romans embarked on that enterprise which has made them lords over land and sea in our part of the world; but that from these Books and the preliminary sketch in them, it may be clear to readers that they had quite adequate grounds for conceiving the ambition of a world-empire and adequate means for achieving their purpose.

For what gives my work is peculiar quality, and what is most remarkable in the present age, is this. Fortune has guided almost all the affairs of the world in one direction and has forced them to incline towards one and the same end; a historian should likewise bring before his readers under one synoptical view the operations by which she has accomplished her general purpose. Indeed it was this chiefly that invited and encouraged me to undertake my task; and secondarily the fact that none of my contemporaries have undertaken to write a general history, in which case

I should have been much less eager to take this in hand. As it is, I observe that while several modern writers deal with particular wars and certain matters connected with them, no one, as far as I am aware, has even attempted to inquire critically when and whence the general and comprehensive scheme of events originated and how it led up to the end. I therefore thought it quite necessary not to leave unnoticed or allow to pass into oblivion this the finest and most beneficent of the performances of Fortune. For though she is ever producing something new and ever playing a part in the lives of men, she has not in a single instance ever accomplished such a work, ever achieved such a triumph, as in our own times. We can no more hope to perceive this from histories dealing with particular events than to get at once a notion of the form of the whole world, its disposition and order, by visiting, each in turn, the most famous cities, or indeed by looking at separate plans of each: a result by no means likely. He indeed who believes that by studying isolated histories he can acquire a fairly just view of history as a whole, is, at it seems to me, much in the case of one, who, after having looked at the dissevered limbs of an animal once alive and beautiful, fancies he has been as good as an eyewitness of the creature itself in all its action and grace. For could anyone put the creature together on the spot, restoring its form and the comeliness of life, and then show it to the same man, I think he would quickly avow that he was formerly very far away from the truth and more like one in a dream. For we can get some idea of a whole from a part, but never knowledge of the whole and conviction of its truth. It is only indeed by study of the interconnexion of all the particulars, their resemblances and differences, that we are enabled at least to make a general survey, and thus derive both benefit and pleasure from history.

I shall adopt as the starting-point of this Book the first occasion on which the Romans crossed the sea from Italy. . . .

It might be said by some of these who look on such things without discernment, that these are matters which it was not necessary for me to treat in such detail. My answer is, that if there were any man who considered that he had sufficient force in himself to face any circumstances, I should say perhaps that knowledge of the past was good for him, but not necessary; but if there is no one in this world at least who would venture to speak so of himself either as regards his private fortunes or those of his country—since, even if all is well with him now no man of sense could from his present circumstances have any reasonable confidence that he will be prosperous in the future—I affirm for this reason that such knowledge is not only good but in the highest degree necessary. For how can anyone when wronged himself or when his country is wronged find helpmates and allies; how can he, when desirous of acquiring some possession or initiating some project, stir to action those whose co-operation he wishes; how, finally, if he is content with present conditions, can he rightly stimulate others to establish his own convictions and maintain things as they are, if he knows nothing at all of the past history of those he would influence? For all men are given to adapt themselves to the present and assume a character suited to the times, so that from their words and actions it is difficult to judge of the principles of each, and in many cases the truth is quite overcast. But men's past actions, bringing to bear the test of actual fact, indicate truly the principles and opinions of each, and show us where we may look for gratitude, kindness, and help, and where for the reverse. It is by this means that we shall often and in many circumstances find those who will compassionate our distresses, who will share our anger or join us in being avenged on our enemies, all which is most helpful to life both in public and in private. Therefore both writers and readers of history should not pay so much attention to the actual narrative of events, as to what preceded, what accompanies, and what follows each. For if we take from history the discussion of why, how, and wherefore each thing was done, and whether the result was what we should have reasonably expected, what is left is a clever essay but not a lesson, and while pleasing for the moment of no possible benefit for the future. . . .

That no part of history requires more circumspection and more correction by the light of truth than this is evident from many considerations and chiefly from the following. While nearly all authors or at least the greater number have attempted to describe the peculiarities and the situation of the countries at the extremities of the known world, most of them are mistaken on many points. We must therefore by no means pass over the subject, but we must say a word to them, and that not casually and by scattered allusions, but giving due attention to it, and in what we say we must not find fault with or rebuke them, but rather be grateful to them and correct them when wrong, knowing as we do that they too, had they the privilege of living at the present day, would correct and modify many of their own statements. In old times, indeed, we find very few Greeks who attempted to inquire into the outlying parts of the world, owing to the practical impossibility of doing so; for the sea had so many perils that it is difficult to enumerate them, and the land ever so many more. Again, even if anyone by his own choice or by the force of circumstances reached the extremity of the world, that did not mean that he was able to accomplish his purpose. For it was a difficult matter to see many things at all closely with one's own eyes, owing to some of the countries being utterly barbarous and others quite desolate, and it was still more difficult to get information about the things one did see, owing to the difference of the language. Then, even if anyone did see for himself and observe the facts, it was even still more difficult for him to be moderate in his statements, to scorn all talk of marvels and monsters and, preferring truth for its own sake, to tell us nothing beyond it.

As, therefore, it was almost impossible in old times to give a true account of the regions I speak of, we should not find fault with the writers for their omissions or mistakes, but should praise and admire them, considering the times they lived in, for having ascertained something on the subject and advanced our knowledge. But in our own times since, owing to Alexander's empire in Asia and that of the Romans in other parts of the world, nearly all regions have become approachable by sea or land; since our men of action in Greece are relieved from the ambitions of a military or political career and have therefore ample means for inquiry and study, we ought to be able to arrive at a better knowledge and something more like the truth about lands which were formerly little known. This is what I myself will attempt to do when I find a suitable place in this work for introducing the subject, and I shall then ask those who are curious about such things to give their undivided attention to me, in view of the fact that I underwent the perils of journeys through Africa, Spain, and Gaul, and of voyages on the seas that lie on the farther side of these countries, mostly for this very purpose of correcting the errors of former writers and making those parts of the world also known to the Greeks. . . .

What chiefly attracts and chiefly benefits students of history is just this—the study of causes and the consequent power of choosing what is best in each case. Now the chief cause of success or the reverse in all matters is the form of a state's constitution; for springing from this, as from a fountain-head, all designs and plans of action not only originate, but reach their consummation.

In the case of those Greek states which have often risen to greatness and have often experienced a complete change of fortune, it is an easy matter both to describe their past and to pronounce as to their future.

For there is no difficulty in reporting the known facts, and it is not hard to foretell the future by inference from the past. But about the Roman state it is neither at all easy to explain the present situation owing to the complicated character of the constitution, nor to foretell the future owing to our ignorance of the peculiar features of public and private life at Rome in the past. Particular attention and study are therefore required if one wishes to attain a clear general view of the distinctive qualities of their constitution. . . .

Perhaps this theory of the natural transformations into each other of the different forms of government is more elaborately set forth by Plato and certain other philosophers; but as the arguments are subtle and are stated at great length, they are beyond the reach of all but a few. I therefore will attempt to give a short summary of the theory, as far as I consider it to apply to the actual history of facts and to appeal to the common intelligence of mankind. For if there appear to be certain omissions in my general exposition of it, the detailed discussion which follows will afford the reader ample compensation for any difficulties now left unsolved.

What then are the beginnings I speak of and what is the first origin of political societies? When owing to floods, famines, failure of crops or other such causes there occurs such a destruction of the human race as tradition tells us has more than once happened, and as we must believe will often happen again, all arts and crafts perishing at the same time, then in the course of time, when springing from the survivors as from seeds men have again increased in numbers and just like other animals form herds—it being a matter of course that they too should herd together with those of their kind owing to their natural weakness—it is a necessary consequence that the man who excels in bodily strength and in courage will lead and rule over the rest. We observe and should regard as a most genuine work of nature this very phenomenon in the case of the other animals which act purely by instinct and among whom the strongest are always indisputably the masters—I speak of bulls, boars, cocks, and the like. It is probable then that at the beginning men lived thus, herding together like animals and following the lead of the strongest and bravest, the ruler's strength being here the sole limit to his power and the name we should give his rule being monarchy.

But when in time feelings of sociability and companionship begin to grow in such gatherings of men, then kingship has struck root; and the notions of goodness, justice, and their opposites begin to arise in men. . . .

For the people maintain the supreme power not only in the hands of these men themselves, but in those of their descendants, from the conviction that those born from and reared by such men will also have principles like to theirs. And if they ever are displeased with the descendants, they now choose their kings and rulers no longer for their bodily strength and brute courage, but for the excellency of their judgement and reasoning powers, as they have gained experience from actual facts of the difference between the one class of qualities and the others. . . . But when they received the office by hereditary succession and found their safety now provided for, and more than sufficient provision of food, they gave way to their appetites owing to this superabundance, and came to think that the rulers must be distinguished from their subjects by a peculiar dress, that there should be a peculiar luxury and variety in the dressing and serving of their viands, and that they should meet with no denial in the pursuit of their amours, however lawless. These habits having given rise in the one case to envy and offence and in the other to an outburst of hatred and passionate resentment, the kingship changed into a tyranny; the first steps towards its overthrow were taken by the subjects, and conspiracies began to be formed. These conspiracies were not the work of the worst men, but of the noblest, most high-spirited, and most courageous, because such men are least able to brook the insolence of princes.

The people now having got leaders, would combine with them against the ruling powers for the reasons I stated above; kingship and monarchy would be utterly abolished, and in their place aristocracy would begin to grow. . . . But here again when children inherited this position of authority from their fathers, having no experience of misfortune and none at all of civil equality and liberty of speech, and having been brought up from the cradle amid the evidences of the power and high position of their fathers, they abandoned themselves some to greed of gain and unscrupulous moneymaking, others to indulgence in wine and the convivial excess which accompanies it, and others again to the violation of women and the rape of boys; and thus converting the aristocracy into an oligarchy aroused in the people feelings similar to those of which I just spoke, and in consequence met with the same disastrous end as the tyrant.

For whenever anyone who has noticed the jealousy and hatred with which they are regarded by the citizens, has the courage to speak or act against the chiefs of the state he has the whole mass of the people ready to back him. Next, when they have either killed or banished the oligarchs, they no longer venture to set a king over them, as they still remember with terror the injustice they suffered from the former ones, nor can they entrust the government with confidence to a select few, with the evidence before them of their recent error in doing so. Thus the only hope still surviving unimpaired is in themselves, and to this they resort, making the state a democracy instead of an oligarchy and assuming the responsibility for the conduct of affairs. Then as long as some of those survive who experienced the evils of oligarchical dominion, they are well pleased with the present form of government, and set a high value on equality and freedom of speech. But when a new generation arises and the democracy falls into the hands of the grandchildren of its founders, they have become so accustomed to freedom and equality that they no longer value them, and begin to aim at pre-eminence; and it is chiefly those of ample fortune who fall into this error. So when they begin to lust for power and cannot attain it through themselves or their own good qualities, they ruin their estates, tempting and corrupting the people in every possible way. And hence when by their foolish thirst for reputation they have created among the masses an appetite for gifts and the habit of receiving them, democracy in its turn is abolished and changes into a rule of force and violence. For the people, having grown accustomed to feed at the expense of others and to depend for their livelihood on the property of others, as soon as they find a leader who is enterprising but is excluded from the honours of office by his penury, institute the rule of violence; and now uniting their forces massacre, banish, and plunder, until they degenerate again into perfect savages and find once more a master and monarch.

Such is the cycle of political revolution, the course appointed by nature in which constitutions change, disappear, and finally return to the point from which they started. Anyone who clearly perceives this may indeed in speaking of the future of any state be wrong in his estimate of the time the process will take, but if his judgement is not tainted by animosity or jealousy, he will very seldom be mistaken as to the stage of growth or decline it has reached, and as to the form into which it will change. And especially in the case of the Roman state will this method enable us to arrive at a knowledge of its formation, growth, and greatest perfection, and likewise of the change for the worse which is sure to follow some day. For, as I said, this state, more than any other, has been formed and has grown naturally, and will undergo a natural decline and change to its contrary. The reader will be able to judge of the truth of this from the subsequent parts of this work. . . .

Since some authors of special histories have dealt with this period comprising the attempt on Messene and the sea battles I have described, I should like to offer a brief criticism of them. I shall not criticize the whole class, but those only whom I regard as worthy of mention and detailed examination. These are Zeno and Antithenes of Rhodes, whom for several reasons I consider worthy of notice. For not only were they contemporary with the events they described, but they also took part in politics, and generally speaking they did not compose their works for the sake of gain but to win fame and do their duty as statesmen. . . . Now I would admit that authors should have a partiality for their own country but they should not make statements about it that are contrary to facts. Surely the mistakes of which we writers are guilty and which it is difficult for us, being but human, to avoid are quite sufficient; but if we make deliberate misstatements in the interest of our country or of friends or for favour, what difference is there between us and those who gain their living by their pens? For just as the latter, weighing everything by the standard of profit, make their works unreliable, so politicians, biased by their dislikes and affections, often achieve the same result. Therefore I would add that readers should carefully look out for this fault and authors themselves be on their guard against it. . . .

It should not surprise anyone if abandoning here the style proper to historical narrative I express myself in a more declamatory and ambitious manner. Some, however, may reproach me for writing with undue animosity, it being rather my first duty to throw a veil over the offences of the Greeks. Now neither do I think that a man who is timid and afraid of speaking his mind should be regarded by those qualified to judge as a sincere friend, nor that a man should be regarded as a good citizen who leaves the path of truth because he is afraid of giving temporary offence to certain persons; and in a writer of political history we should absolutely refuse to tolerate the least preference for anything but the truth. For inasmuch as a literary record of facts will reach more ears and last longer than occasional utterances, a writer should attach the highest value to truth and his readers should approve his principle in this respect. In times of danger it is true those who are Greek should help the

Greeks in every way, by active support, by cloaking faults and by trying to appease the anger of the ruling power, as I myself actually did at the time of the occurrences; but the literary record of the events meant for posterity should be kept free from any taint of falsehood, so that instead of the ears of readers being agreeably tickled for the present, their minds may be reformed in order to avoid their falling more than once into the same errors. Enough on this subject.

> 6. STRABO (ca. 63 B.C.–A.D. 21), though best known as "the geographer," was also affiliated with the Herodotean tradition. Like Herodotus, he traveled widely and had an insatiable curiosity about the life and customs of barbarian peoples. As a student of Aristotle, he also had philosophic interests, was called "philos" by Plutarch, and wrote a continuation (no longer extant) of Polybius. He combined the encyclopedic scope of Herodotus with the critical spirit of Polybius, at least in theory, and he tried to sort out the historical and mythical elements in the writings of his predecessors.

A peculiar thing has happened in the case of the account we have of the Amazons; for our accounts of other peoples keep a distinction between the mythical and the historical elements; for the things that are ancient and false and monstrous are called myths, but history wishes for the truth, whether ancient or recent, and contains no monstrous element, or else only rarely. But as regards the Amazons, the same stories are told now as in early times, though they are marvellous and beyond belief. For instance, who could believe that an army of women, or a city, or a tribe, could ever be organised without men, and not only be organised, but even make inroads upon the territory of other people, and not only overpower the peoples near them to the extent of advancing as far as what is now Ionia, but even send an expedition across the sea as far as Attica? For this is the same as saying that the men of those times were women and that the women were men. Nevertheless, even at the present time these very stories are told about the Amazons, and they intensify the peculiarity abovementioned and our belief in the ancient accounts rather than those of the present time. . . .

Strabo, *Geograpy,* trans. Horace Leonard Jones. Loeb Classical Library. 4:39; 5:235–237 and 239–241. Reprinted by permission of the publishers and the Loeb Classical Library from Strabo, Volumes 4 and 5, trans. Horace Leonard Jones, Cambridge, Mass.: Harvard University Press, 1927, 1928.

The stories that have been spread far and wide with a view to glorifying Alexander are not accepted by all; and their fabricators were men who cared for flattery rather than truth. For instance: they transferred the Caucasus into the region of the Indian mountains and of the eastern sea which lies near those mountains from the mountains which lie above Colchis and the Euxine; for these are the mountains which the Greeks named Caucasus, which is more than thirty thousand stadia distant from India; and here it was that they laid the scene of the story of Prometheus and of his being put in bonds; for these were the farthermost mountains towards the east that were known to writers of that time. And the expedition of Dionysus and Heracles to the country of the Indians looks like a mythical story of later date, because Heracles is said to have released Prometheus one thousand years later. And although it was a more glorious thing for Alexander to subdue Asia as far as the Indian mountains than merely to the recess of the Euxine and to the Caucasus, yet the glory of the mountain, and its name, and the belief that Jason and his followers had accomplished the longest of all expeditions, reaching as far as the neighbourhood of the Caucasus, and the tradition that Prometheus was bound at the ends of the earth on the Caucasus, led writers to suppose that they would be doing the king a favour if they transferred the name Caucasus to India. . . .

But Hecataeus of Miletus says that the Epeians are a different people from the Eleians; that, at any rate, the Epeians joined Heracles in his expedition against Augeas and helped him to destroy both Augeas and Elis. And he says, further, that Dyme is an Epeian and an Achaean city. However, the early historians say many things that are not true, because they were accustomed to falsehoods on account of the use of myths in their writings; and on this account, too, they do not agree with one another concerning the same things.

❡ ANTIQUITIES

7. DIODORUS OF SICILY (ca. 90–20 B.C.), like Polybius and Strabo, provides a link between the Greek and Roman worlds and

Diodorus of Sicily, *Library of History,* trans. C. H. Oldfather. Loeb Classical Library. 1:5–25 and 29–35. Reprinted by permission of the publishers and the Loeb Classical Library from Diodorus of Sicily, Volume 1, trans. C. H. Oldfather, Cambridge, Mass.: Harvard University Press, 1933.

also between the Alexandrian and Augustan periods. After learning Latin, he traveled widely in Europe and Asia before devoting more than thirty years to his great *Library of History*. Like Polybius, he had a grand vision of universal history (*koina historia*) in terms of geography. His model, however, was Herodotus, "a curious inquirer if ever a man was," rather than Thucydides and Xenophon, who might have been more accurate but whose scope was so limited that they neglected to consider Egypt.

Diodorus's book spans the time from creation to 59 B.C. and the world from Spain to India. Burdened with ancient lore and anecdotes in the style of the old *logographoi,* it nevertheless follows a strictly annalistic plan and tends to rely upon one author at a time (one of its major values is in preserving passages of certain lost works). It is, in short, both a mine and a mess. Yet it does express Diodorus's view of history: history is intended not for pleasure but for utility (in a famous rhetorical formula); it is not an art form but a body of knowledge that made the Greeks superior to the barbarians and that presumably could do the same for other men.

It is fitting that all men should ever accord great gratitude to those writers who have composed universal histories, since they have aspired to help by their individual labours human society as a whole; for by offering a schooling, which entails no danger, in what is advantageous they provide their readers, through such a presentation of events, with a most excellent kind of experience. For although the learning which is acquired by experience in each separate case, with all the attendant toils and dangers, does indeed enable a man to discern in each instance where utility lies . . . , yet the understanding of the failures and successes of other men, which is acquired by the study of history, affords a schooling that is free from actual experience of ills. Furthermore, it has been the aspiration of these writers to marshal all men, who, although united one to another by their kinship, are yet separated by space and time, into one and the same orderly body. And such historians have therein shown themselves to be, as it were, ministers of Divine Providence. For just as Providence, having brought the orderly arrangement of the visible stars and the natures of men together into one common relationship, continually directs their courses through all eternity, apportioning to each that which falls to it by the direction of fate, so likewise the historians, in recording the common affairs of the inhabited world as though they were those of a single state, have made of their treatises a single reckoning of past events and a common clearinghouse of knowledge concerning them. For it is an excellent thing to be able to use the ignorant mistakes of others as warning examples for the correction of error, and, when we confront the varied vicissitudes of life, instead of having to investigate what is being done now, to be able to imitate the successes which have been achieved in the past. Certainly all men prefer in their counsels the oldest men to those who are younger, because of the experience which has accrued to the former through the lapse of time; but it is a fact that such experience is in so far surpassed by the understanding which is gained from history, as history excels, we know, in the multitude of facts at its disposal. For this reason one may hold that the acquisition of a knowledge of history is of the greatest utility for every conceivable circumstance of life. For it endows the young with the wisdom of the aged, while for the old it multiplies the experience which they already possess; citizens in private station it qualifies for leadership, and the leaders it incites, through the immortality of the glory which it confers, to undertake the noblest deeds; soldiers, again, it makes more ready to face dangers in defence of their country because of the public encomiums which they will receive after death, and wicked men it turns aside from their impulse towards evil through the everlasting opprobrium to which it will condemn them.

In general, then, it is because of that commemoration of goodly deeds which history accords men that some of them have been induced to become founders of cities, that others have been led to introduce laws which encompass man's social life with security, and that many have aspired to discover new sciences and arts in order to benefit the race of men. And since complete happiness can be attained only through the combination of all these activities, the foremost meed of praise must be awarded to that which more than any other thing is the cause of them, that is, to history. For we must look upon it as constituting the guardian of the high achievements of illustrious men, the witness which testifies to the evil deeds of the wicked, and the benefactor of the entire human race. For if it be true that the myths which are related about Hades, in spite of the fact that their subject-matter is fictitious, contribute greatly to fostering piety and justice among men, how much more must we assume that history, the prophetess of truth, she who is, as it were, the mother-city of philosophy as a whole, is still more potent to equip men's characters for noble living! For all men, by reason of the frailty of our nature, live but an infinitesimal portion of eternity and are dead throughout all subsequent time; and while in the case of those who in their lifetime have done nothing worthy of note, everything which has pertained to them in life also perishes when their bodies die, yet in the case of those who by their virtue have achieved fame, their deeds are remembered for evermore, since they are heralded abroad by history's voice most divine. . . .

History also contributes to the power of speech, and a nobler thing than that may not easily be found. For it is this that makes the Greeks superior to the barbarians, and the educated to the uneducated, and, furthermore, it is by means of speech alone that one man is able to gain ascendancy over the many; and, in general, the impression made by every measure that is proposed corresponds to the power of the speaker who presents it, and we describe great and good men as "worthy of speech," as though therein they had won the highest prize of excellence. And when speech is resolved into its several kinds, we find that, whereas poetry is more pleasing than profitable, and codes of law punish but do not instruct, and similarly, all the other kinds either contribute nothing to happiness or else contain a harmful element mingled with the beneficial, while some of them actually pervert the truth, history alone, since in it word and fact are in perfect agreement, embraces in its narration all the other qualities as well that are useful; for it is ever to be seen urging men to justice, denouncing those who are evil, lauding the good, laying up, in a word, for its readers a mighty store of experience.

Consequently we, observing that writers of history are accorded a merited approbation, were led to feel a like enthusiasm for the subject . . . ; [and] we resolved to write a history after a plan which might yield to its readers the greatest benefit and at the same time incommode them the least. For if a man should begin with the most ancient times and record to the best of his ability the affairs of the entire world down to his own day, so far as they have been handed down to memory, as though they were the affairs of some single city, he would obviously have to undertake an immense labour, yet he would have composed a treatise of the utmost value to those who are studiously inclined. For from such a treatise every man will be able readily to take what is of use for his special purpose, drawing as it were from a great fountain. . . .

And so we, appreciating that an undertaking of this nature, while most useful, would yet require much labour and time, have been engaged upon it for thirty years, and with much hardship and many dangers we have visited a large portion of both Asia and Europe that we might see with our own eyes all the most important regions and as many others as possible; for many errors have been committed through ignorance of the sites, not only by the common run of historians, but even by some of the highest reputation. As for the resources which have availed us in this undertaking, they have been, first and foremost, that enthusiasm for the work which enables every man to bring to completion the task which seems impossible, and, in the second place, the abundant supply which Rome affords of the materials pertaining to the proposed study. For the supremacy of this city, a supremacy so powerful that it extends to the bounds of the inhabited world, has provided us in the course of our long residence there with copious resources in the most accessible form. For since the city of our origin was Agyrium in Sicily, and by reason of our contact with the Romans in that island we had gained a wide acquaintance with their language, we have acquired an accurate knowledge of all the events connected with this empire from the records which have been carefully preserved among them over a long period of time. Now we have begun our history with the legends of both Greeks and barbarians, after having first investigated to the best of our ability the accounts which each people records of its earliest times. . . .

As for the periods included in this work, we do not attempt to fix with any strictness the limits of those before the Trojan War, because no trustworthy chronological table covering them has come into our hands: but from the Trojan War we follow Apollodorus of Athens in setting the interval from then to the Return of the Heracleidae as eighty years, from then to the First Olympiad three hundred and twenty-eight years, reckoning the dates by the reigns of the kings of Lacedaemon, and from the First Olympiad to the beginning of the Celtic War, which we have made the end of our history, seven hundred and thirty years; so that our whole treatise of forty Books embraces eleven hundred and thirty-eight years, exclusive of the periods which embrace the events before the Trojan War.

We have given at the outset this precise outline, since we desire to inform our readers about the project as a whole, and at the same time to deter those who are accustomed to make their books by compilation, from mutilating works of which they are not the authors. And throughout our entire history it is to be hoped that what we have done well may not be the object of envy, and that the matters wherein our knowledge is defective may receive correction at the hands of more able historians. . . .

Now as regards the first origin of mankind two opinions have arisen

among the best authorities both on nature and on history. One group
which takes the position that the universe did not come into being and
will not decay, has declared that the race of men also has existed from
eternity, there having never been a time when men were first begotten;
the other group, however, which holds that the universe came into being
and will decay, has declared that, like it, men had their first origin at a
definite time. . . .

Concerning the first generation of the universe this is the account
which we have received. But the first men to be born, they say, led an
undisciplined and bestial life, setting out one by one to secure their
sustenance and taking for their food both the tenderest herbs and the
fruits of wild trees. Then, since they were attacked by the wild beasts,
they came to each other's aid, being instructed by expediency, and when
gathered together in this way by reason of their fear, they gradually came
to recognize their mutual characteristics. And though the sounds which
they made were at first unintelligible and indistinct, yet gradually they
came to give articulation to their speech, and by agreeing with one
another upon symbols for each thing which presented itself to them,
made known among themselves the significance which was to be attached to each term. But since groups of this kind arose over every part of
the inhabited world, not all men had the same language, inasmuch as
every group organized the elements of its speech by mere chance. This is
the explanation of the present existence of every conceivable kind of
language, and, furthermore, out of these first groups to be formed came
all the original nations of the world.

Now the first men, since none of the things useful for life had yet been
discovered, led a wretched existence, having no clothing to cover them,
knowing not the use of the dwelling and fire, and also being totally
ignorant of cultivated food. For since they also even neglected the har-
vesting of the wild food, they laid by no store of its fruits against their
needs; consequently large numbers of them perished in the winters because of the cold and the lack of food. Little by little, however, experience taught them both to take to the caves in winter and to store fruits as
could be preserved. And when they had become acquainted with fire and
other useful things, the arts also and whatever else is capable of further-
ing man's social life were gradually discovered. Indeed, speaking generally, in all things it was necessity itself that became man's teacher, supplying in appropriate fashion instruction in every matter to a creature

which was well endowed by nature and had, as its assistants for every purpose, hands and speech and sagacity of mind. . . .

Now as to who were the first kings we are in no position to speak on our own authority, nor do we give assent to those historians who profess to know; for it is impossible that the discovery of writing was of so early a date as to have been contemporary with the first kings. But if a man should concede even this last point, it still seems evident that writers of history are as a class a quite recent appearance in the life of mankind. Again, with respect to the antiquity of the human race, not only do Greeks put forth their claims but many of the barbarians as well, all holding that it is they who are autochthonous and the first of all men to discover the things which are of use in life, and that it was the events in their own history which were the earliest to have been held worthy of record. So far as we are concerned, however, we shall not make the attempt to determine with precision the antiquity of each nation or what is the race whose nations are prior in point of time to the rest and by how many years, but we shall record summarily, keeping due proportion in our account, what each nation has to say concerning its antiquity and the early events in its history. The first peoples which we shall discuss will be the barbarians, not that we consider them to be earlier than the Greeks, as Ephorus has said, but because we wish to set forth most of the facts about them at the outset, in order that we may not, by beginning with the various accounts given by the Greeks, have to interpolate in the different narrations of their early history any event connected with another people. And since Egypt is the country where mythology places the origin of the gods, where the earliest observations of the stars are said to have been made, and where, furthermore, many noteworthy deeds of great men are recorded, we shall begin our history with the events connected with Egypt.

8. DIONYSIUS OF HALICARNASSUS (latter part of the first century B.C.) was another link between the Hellenistic and Roman worlds and another encyclopedic historian whose reach exceeded

Dionysius of Halicarnassus, *Roman Antiquities,* trans. Earnest Cary. Loeb Classical Library. 1 : 3–9, 15, 17–23, and 25–29. Reprinted by permission of the publishers and the Loeb Classical Library from Dionysius of Halicarnassus, Volume 1, trans. Earnest Cary, Cambridge, Mass.: Harvard University Press, 1937.

his grasp, a seemingly universal fate among those who preferred antiquities to contemporary history. Although he had a good knowledge of chronology and made use of nonliterary sources such as inscriptions and although he attached much importance to literary form, his book was neither critical nor well fashioned. Like Polybius, he emphasized geographic scope and the need to reveal the sequence of cause and effect; but he expressly subordinated pragmatic history to antiquarian research, for which he presented the classic justification—that the earliest period of national history was not humble and unworthy but on the contrary contained the seeds of later greatness. Such was the eclectic and genetic basis of his *Roman Antiquities*.

The controlling factor in Dionysius's view of history was rhetoric, which is not surprising, as he taught oratory at Rome and wrote several works on the subject. Because of its rhetorical qualities, the work of Herodotus (also a native of Halicarnassus) seemed to Dionysius superior to that of Thucydides. It was also preferable in terms of subject matter (more universal and varied), form (topical rather than chronological), and attitude (not bitter and fault-finding but balanced and fair). Dionysius's conviction that utility was as significant as the aesthetic and formal aspects of history was expressed most famously in his rhetorical formula that history is "philosophy teaching by example" (*De arte rhetorica*, XI, 2).

Although it is much against my will to indulge in the explanatory statements usually given in the prefaces to histories, yet I am obliged to prefix to this work some remarks concerning myself. In doing this it is neither my intention to dwell too long on my own praise, which I know would be distasteful to the reader, nor have I the purpose of censuring other historians, as Anaximenes and Theopompus did in the prefaces to their histories, but I shall only show the reasons that induced me to undertake this work and give an accounting of the sources from which I gained the knowledge of the things I am going to relate. For I am convinced that all who propose to leave such monuments of their minds to posterity as time shall not involve in one common ruin with their bodies, and particularly those who write histories, in which we have the right to assume that Truth, the source of both prudence and wisdom, is enshrined, ought, first of all, to make choice of noble and lofty subjects and such as will be of great utility to their readers, and then, with great care and pains, to provide themselves with the proper equipment for the treatment of their subject. For those who base historical works upon deeds inglorious or evil or unworthy of serious study, either because they crave to come to the knowledge of men and to get a name of some sort or other, or because they desire to display the wealth of their rhetoric, are neither admired by posterity for their fame nor praised for their eloquence; rather, they leave this opinion in the minds of all who take up their histories, that they themselves admired lives which were of a piece with the writings they published, since it is a just and a general opinion that a man's works are the images of his mind. Those, on the other hand, who, while making choice of the best subjects, are careless and indolent in compiling their narratives out of such reports as chance to come to their ears gain no praise by reason of that choice; for we do not deem it fitting that the histories of renowned cities and of men who have held supreme power should be written in an offhand or negligent manner. As I believe these considerations to be necessary and of the first importance to historians and as I have taken great care to observe them both, I have felt unwilling either to omit mention of them or to give it any other place than in the preface to my work.

That I have indeed made choice of a subject noble, lofty and useful to many will not, I think, require any lengthy argument, at least for those who are not utterly unacquainted with universal history. For if anyone turns his attention to the successive supremacies both of cities and of nations, as accounts of them have been handed down from times past, and then, surveying them severally and comparing them together, wishes to determine which of them obtained the widest dominion and both in peace and war performed the most brilliant achievements, he will find that the supremacy of the Romans has far surpassed all those that are recorded from earlier times, not only in the extent of its dominion and in the splendour of its achievements—which no account has as yet worthily celebrated—but also in the length of time during which it has endured down to our day. For the empire of the Assyrians, ancient as it was and running back to legendary times, held sway over only a small part of Asia. That of the Medes, after overthrowing the Assyrian empire and obtaining a still wider dominion, did not hold it long, but was overthrown in the fourth generation. The Persians, who conquered the Medes, did, indeed, finally become masters of almost all Asia; but when they attacked the nations of Europe also, they did not reduce many of them to submission, and they continued in power not much above two hundred years. The Macedonian domination, which overthrew the might of the Persians, did, in the extent of its sway, exceed all its predecessors, yet even it did not flourish long, but after Alexander's death began to decline; for it was immediately partitioned among many commanders from the time of the Didochi, and although after their time it was able to go on to the second or third generation, yet it was weakened by its own dissensions and at the last destroyed by the Romans. But even the Macedonian power did not subjugate every country and every sea; for it neither conquered Libya, with the exception of the small portion bordering on Egypt, nor subdued all Europe, but in the North advanced only as far as Thrace and in the West down to the Adriatic Sea.

Thus we see that the most famous of the earlier supremacies of which history has given us any account, after attaining to so great vigour and might, were overthrown. As for the Greek powers, it is not fitting to compare them to those just mentioned, since they gained neither magnitude of empire nor duration of eminence equal to theirs. . . .

For to this day almost all the Greeks are ignorant of the early history of Rome and the great majority of them have been imposed upon by sundry false opinions grounded upon stories which chance has brought to their ears and led to believe that, having come upon various vagabonds without house or home and barbarians, and even those not free men, as her founders, she in the course of time arrived at world domination, and this not through reverence for the gods and justice and every other virtue, but through some chance and the injustice of Fortune, which inconsiderately showers her greatest favours upon the most undeserving. . . .

In order, therefore, to remove these erroneous impressions, as I have called them, from the minds of the many and to substitute true ones in their room, I shall in this Book show how the founders of the city were, at what periods the various groups came together, and through what turns of fortune they left their native countries. By this means I engage to prove that they were Greeks and came together from nations not the smallest nor the least considerable. And beginning with the next Book I shall tell of the deeds they performed immediately after their founding of the city and of the customs and institutions by virtue of which their descendants advanced to so great dominion; and, so far as I am able, I shall omit nothing worthy of being recorded in history, to the end that I may instill in the minds of those who shall then be informed of the truth the fitting conception of this city,—unless they have already assumed an utterly violent and hostile attitude toward it,—and also that they may neither feel indignation at their present subjection, which is grounded on reason (for by an universal law of Nature, which time cannot destroy, it is ordained that superiors shall ever govern their inferiors), nor rail at Fortune for having wantonly bestowed upon an undeserving city a supremacy so great and already of so long continuance, particularly when they shall have learned from my history that Rome from the very beginning, immediately after its founding, produced infinite examples of virtue in men whose superiors, whether for piety or for justice or for lifelong self-control or for warlike valour, no city, either Greek or barbarian, has ever produced. . . .

The first historian, so far as I am aware, to touch upon the early period of the Romans was Hieronymus of Cardia, in his work on the Epigoni. After him Timaeus of Sicily related the beginnings of their history in his general history and treated in a separate work the wars with Pyrrhus of Epirus. Besides these, Antigonus, Polybius, Silenus and innumerable other authors devoted themselves to the same themes, though in different ways, each of them recording some few things compiled without accurate investigation on his own part but from reports which chance had brought to his ears. Like to these in all respects are the histories of those Romans, also, who related in Greek the early achievements of the city; the oldest of these writers are Quintus Fabius and Lucius Cincius, who both flourished during the Punic wars. Each of these men related the events at which he himself had been present with great exactness, as being well acquainted with them, but touched only in a summary way upon the early events that followed the founding of the city. For these reasons, therefore, I have determined not to pass over a noble period of history which the older writers left untouched, a period, moreover, the accurate portrayal of which will lead to the following most excellent and just results: In the first place, the brave men who have fulfilled their destiny will gain immortal glory and be extolled by posterity, which things render human nature like unto the divine and prevent men's deeds from perishing together with their bodies. And again, both the present and future descendants of those godlike men will choose, not the pleasantest and easiest of lives, but rather the noblest and most ambitious, when they consider that all who are sprung from an illustrious origin ought to set a high value on themselves and indulge in no pursuit unworthy of their ancestors. And I, who have not turned aside to this work for the sake of flattery, but out of a regard for truth and justice, which ought to be the aim of every history, shall have an opportunity, in the first place, of expressing my attitude of goodwill toward all good men and toward all who take pleasure in the contemplation of great and noble deeds; and, in the second place, of making the most grateful return that I may to the city in remembrance of the education and other blessings I have enjoyed during my residence in it. . . .

I begin my history, then, with the most ancient legends, which the historians before me have omitted as a subject difficult to be cleared up without diligent study; and I bring the narrative down to the beginning of the First Punic War, which fell in the third year of the one hundred and twenty-eighth Olympiad. I relate all the foreign wars that the city waged during that period and all the internal seditions with which she was agitated, showing from what causes they sprang and by what methods and by what arguments they were brought to an end. I give an account also of all the forms of government Rome used, both during the monarchy and after its overthrow, and show what was the character of each. I describe the best customs and the most remarkable laws; and, in short, I show the whole life of the ancient Romans. As to the form I give this work, it does not resemble that which the authors who make wars alone their subject have given to their histories, nor that which others who treat of the several forms of government by themselves have adopted, nor is it like the annalistic accounts which the authors of the *Atthides* have published (for these are monotonous and soon grow tedious to the reader), but it is a combination of every kind, forensic, speculative and narrative, to the intent that it may afford satisfaction both to those who occupy themselves with political debates and to those who are devoted to philosophical speculations, as well as to any who may desire mere undisturbed entertainment in their reading of history. Such things, therefore, will be the subjects of my history and such will be its form. I, the author, am Dionysius of Halicarnassus, the son of Alexander. And at this point I begin.

❡ The object of the present treatise is not to make an onslaught on the plan and ability of Thucydides, nor to make an enumeration of his

Dionysius of Halicarnassus, *On Thucydides*. In *Dionysius of Halicarnassus: On Thucydides,* trans. W. Kendrick Pritchett. Berkeley: University of California Press, 1975. Pp. 2–3, 4, 5, 7–8, and 44. Permission granted by the Regents of the University of California and the University of California Press.

faults, nor to disparage his merits, nor to engage in any other undertaking of the sort, in which I would pay no attention to the author's felicities and merits and would dwell only on his less happy utterances. The present work is an evaluation of the style of his discourse; it embraces all the qualities that he possesses either in common with others or distinct from them. Hence, it was inevitable for me to mention also faults that were found side by side with the virtues. Human nature is never so well endowed as to be unerring in either word or action, and that nature is best which meets with the greatest success and the least failure. Let everyone therefore examine from this point of view what I am about to say, and let him not question the purpose of this work instead of examining the peculiar products of the genius of the man. But I am not the first to attempt such a thing as this. There have been many men, both ancients and contemporaries, who have chosen to cite two of them, Aristotle and Plato. Aristotle is persuaded that not everything that his teacher Plato has said is of the highest excellence; so, for example, what he has to say about ideas, and the good, and the state. Then, too, Plato himself desires to show that Parmenides and Protagoras and Zeno, and not a few of the other natural scientists, have been guilty of mistakes. Yet no one censures him for this in view of the fact that the aim of natural science is the knowledge of the truth, and it is this too that reveals the true end of life. So when no one finds fault with the honest intentions of those men who differ in matters of dogma, if they do not speak well of all the views of their elders, surely no one will censure those who have chosen to reveal the peculiarities of genius, if they do not testify to the possession of all virtues by their predecessors, even those they do not possess.

There is still another point that seems to require explanation. The charge is an odious one and one that gives much pleasure to the rabble, and yet it will be easy to show that it is not sound. It does not follow that if we are inferior in ability to Thucydides and other men, we therefore forfeit the right to form an estimate of them. For men who do not possess the same skill as Apelles, Zeuxis, Protogenes, and other famous artists, are not thereby prevented from judging the art of these men, nor are men of inferior skill debarred from judging the works of Phidias, Polyclitus and Myron. I forbear to state that the layman is often a better judge of many works than the artist himself,—I mean all such works as appeal to irrational impression and emotion . . . ; and these are the criteria that every form of art has in view, and upon them it is based. But enough of this lest my whole treatise seem to be nothing more than an introduction. . . .

Thucydides . . . was unwilling either to confine his history to a single region, as did Hellanicus, or to elaborate into a single work the achievements of Greeks and barbarians in every land, as did Herodotus; but scorning the former as trifling and petty and of little value to the readers, and rejecting the latter as too comprehensive to fall within the purview of the human mind, if one would be very exact, he selected a single war, the war that was waged between the Athenians and Peloponnesians, and gave his attention to writing about this. Since he was physically robust and sound of mind, living through the duration of the war, he put together his narrative not from chance rumors but on the basis of personal experience, in cases where he was present himself, and on information from the most knowledgeable people, where he was in the dark as a result of his exile. In this way, then, he differed from the historians before him, and I say this since he chose a subject which neither consists entirely of one member nor is divided into many irreconcilable parts. Moreover, he did not insert anything of the mythical into his history, and he refused to divert his history to practice deception and magic upon the masses, as all the historians before him had done, telling of Lamias issuing from the earth in woods and glens, and of amphibious nymphs arising from Tartarus and swimming through the seas, partly shaped like beasts, and having intercourse with human beings; telling also about demi-gods, the offspring of mortals and gods, and many other stories that seem incredible and very foolish to our times. . . .

Philosophers and rhetoricians, if not all of them, yet most of them, bear witness to Thucydides that he has been most careful of the truth, the high-priestess of which we desire history to be. He adds nothing to the facts that should not be added, and takes nothing therefrom, nor does he take advantage of his position as a writer, but he adheres to his purpose without wavering, leaving no room for criticism, and abstaining from envy and flattery of every kind, particularly in his appreciation of men of merit. For in the first book, when he makes mention of Themistocles, he unstintingly mentions all of his good qualities, and in the second book in the discussion of the statesmanship of Pericles, he pronounces a eulogy such as was worthy of a man whose reputation has penetrated everywhere. Likewise, when he was compelled to speak about Demosthenes the general, Nicias the son of Niceratus, Alcibiades the son of Clinias, and other generals and speakers, he has spoken so as to give each man his due. To cite examples is unnecessary to readers of his history. This then is what may be said about the historian's success in connection with the treatment of his subject-matter—points that are good and worthy of imitation.

The defects of Thucydidean workmanship and the features that are criticized by some persons relate to the more technical side of his subject matter, what is called the economy of the discourse, something that is desirable in all kinds of writing, whether one chooses philosophical or oratorical subjects. The matter in question has to do with the division, order, and development. . . .

He ought . . . , when he began his search for the causes (aitiai) of the war, first to give an account of the real cause and the one he believed to be so. For the very nature of things (physis) would require the earlier to take precedence over the later and truth over falsehood, and the introduction (eisbole) of his narrative would have been far more effective, if such had been the method of arrangement (oikonomia). For none of those who would like to defend him could offer as an excuse that the events were small and insignificant, or a matter of common treatment and worn out by his predecessors, so that it was better for him not to start with them.

To sum up then, it is unreasonable to say that both kinds are equally deserving of emulation, the parts of his writings that are not clearly expressed by the historian and those that along with the other virtues have the added quality of clearness. One must admit that the more perfect portions are superior to the less perfect ones, and the passages that are characterized by lucidity are superior to those that are obscure. Why then do some of us praise the entire style of Thucydides and insist on saying that to the people of his own time what Thucydides wrote was familiar and intelligible but that the author took no account of us who were to follow after, whilst others banish from courts and public meetings all the language (lexis) of Thucydides as useless, instead of admitting that with but few exceptions the narrative portion is admirable and adapted to every purpose, whereas the speeches are not in their entirety suitable for imitation, but only those parts which are easily understood by all but whose composition does not lie within the range of everybody?

I might have written you more pleasant things about Thucydides, my dearest Quintus Aelius Tubero, but nothing that would be more true.

❡ METHOD

9. ARISTOTLE (384–322 B.C.) put in his *Poetics* what was to become the classic statement of the essential difference between history, poetry, and, if only implicitly, philosophy. Though somewhat invidiously intended by Aristotle, this characterization was later used to underline the value and sometimes the superiority of the study of history.

From what we have said it will be seen that the poet's function is to describe, not the thing that happened, but a kind of thing that might happen, i.e. what is possible as being probable or necessary. The distinction between historian and poet is not in the one writing prose and the other verse—you might put the work of Herodotus into verse, and it would still be a species of history; it consists really in this, that the one describes the thing that has been, and the other a kind of thing that might be. Hence poetry is something more philosophic and of graver import than history, since its statements are of the nature rather of universals, whereas those of history are singulars.

10. PLUTARCH (A.D. 45/50–120/27), a product of both Greek and Roman culture and best known as the author of paired (Greek and Roman) biographies, though by no means above reproach himself, took partisan and small-minded aim at Herodotus (as Renaissance skeptics later also did) as representing the failings of historiography, especially the ways of creating prejudice and neglecting to do justice to worthy subjects.

Many people, my dear Alexander, have been deceived by the style of Herodotus, which is apparently so simple and effortless, slipping easily from one subject to another; but more people still have suffered a similar delusion with regard to his moral character. Not only is it the height of injustice (as Plato puts it) "to seem just when one is not so," but it is an act of supreme malice to put on a false show of good humour and frankness which baffles detection. And this is exactly what Herodotus does,

Aristotle, *Poetics,* 1451a36–1451b8. My translation.

Plutarch, *On the Malice of Herodotus,* trans. Lionel Pearson and F. H. Sandbach. Loeb Classical Library. 11:9, 11–13, 15, 17, 19, and 21. Reprinted by permission of the publishers and the Loeb Classical Library from Plutarch, Volume 11, trans. Lionel Pearson and F. H. Sandbach, Cambridge, Mass.: Harvard University Press, 1965.

flattering some people in the basest possible manner, while he slanders and maligns others. Hitherto no one has dared to expose him as a liar. Since his principal victims are the Boeotians and the Corinthians, though he spares no one, I think it is proper that I should now stand up for the cause of my ancestors and the cause of truth and show how dishonest this part of his work is. . . .

I think . . . that I had better make some kind of outline, and list, in general terms, the indications by which we can determine whether a narrative is written with malice or with honesty and good will; then the individual passages examined can be classified under the different headings, if they fit the pattern.

First, then, the man who in his narrative of events uses the severest words and phrases when gentler terms will serve; if, for example, when he might have called Nicias "too much addicted to pious practices," he called him "a fanatical bigot"; or if he spoke of Cleon's "rashness and insanity" instead of his "unwise speech"—such a writer is clearly lacking in good will; he is apparently deriving pleasure out of another man's misfortune by making a clever story out of it.

Secondly, when something is discreditable to a character, but not relevant to the issue, and the historian grasps at it and thrusts it into his account where there is no place for it, drawing out his story and making a detour so as to include someone's ill-success or foolish unworthy act, there is no doubt that he delights in speaking ill of people. Thus Thucydides, even in writing about Cleon, never gave any specific account of his misdeeds, numerous though they were, and he was content with a single adjective to deal with Hyberbolus, the demagogue, calling him "a bad character" and letting him go with that. . . .

My fourth sign of ill will in history-writing is a preference for the less creditable version, when two or more accounts of the same incident are current. Sophists are permitted, on occasion, to adopt the worse cause and make the best of it; but this is for practice or display; they are not really inducing any firm belief in their cause and they may even admit that they are trying to startle people by a defence of the incredible. The historian, on the other hand, if he is to be fair, declares as true what he knows to be the case and, when the facts are not clear, says that the more creditable appears to be the true account rather than the less creditable. . . .

Furthermore, with respect to the way in which a deed is accomplished, a historian's narrative is open to the charge of malice if it asserts that the success was won not by valour but by money (as some say of Philip), or easily and without any trouble (as they say of Alexander), or not by intelligence but by good luck (as the enemies of Timothes claimed, when they painted pictures showing the cities entering of their own accord into a kind of lobster-trap while Timothes slept). It is evident that writers detract from the greatness and virtue of deeds when they deny that they were done in a noble spirit or by hard work or by valour or by a man's own effort. . . .

One might enumerate more characteristics of this kind; but these are enough to convey an idea of the man's purpose and method.

> 11. LUCIAN of Samosata (ca. A.D. 125–200) wrote the only surviving ancient treatise on historiography, remarking that "everyone wants to be a Thucydides, a Herodotus, or a Xenophon." With humor and literary exaggeration, and drawing extensively on Thucydides, Lucian took up problems of selecting and organizing material, combining rhetorical qualities with accuracy and truthfulness, and the importance of political understanding.

No, ever since the present situation arose—the war against the barbarians, the disaster in Armenia and the run of victories—every single person is writing history; nay more, they are all Thucydideses, Herodotuses and Xenophons to us, and very true, it seems, is the saying that "War is the father of all things" since at one stroke it has begotten so many historians. . . .

So in my own case, Philo, to avoid being the only mute in such a polyphonic time, pushed about open-mouthed without a word like an extra in a comedy, I thought it a good idea to roll a history or even merely chronicle the events—I'm not so bold as that: don't be afraid that I should go that far. . . .

. . . In fact, I shall offer a little advice and these few precepts to historians, so that I may share in the erection of their building, if not the inscription on it, by putting at any rate my finger-tip on the mortar. . . .

. . . History is not one of those things that can be put in hand without effort and can be put together lazily, but is something which needs,

Lucian, *How to Write History,* trans. K. Kilburn. Loeb Classical Library. 6:5–13, 49–65, and 71. Reprinted by permission of the publishers and the Loeb Classical Library from Lucian, Volume 6, trans. K. Kilburn, Cambridge, Mass.: Harvard University Press, 1959.

if anything does in literature, a great deal of thought if it is to be what Thucydides calls "a possession for evermore." Now I know that I shall not convert very many: some indeed will think me a great nuisance, particularly anyone whose history is already finished and has already been displayed in public. And if in addition he was applauded by his audience it would be madness to expect his sort to remodel or rewrite any part of what has once been ratified and lodged, as it were, in the royal palace. . . .

To begin with, let us look at this for a serious fault: most of them neglect to record the events and spend their time lauding rulers and generals, extolling their own to the skies and slandering the enemy's beyond all reserve; they do not realise that the dividing line and frontier between history and panegyric is not a narrow isthmus but rather a mighty wall; as musicians say, they are two diapasons apart, since the encomiast's sole concern is to praise and please in any way he can the one he praises, and if he can achieve his aim by lying, little will he care; but history cannot admit a lie, even a tiny one, any more than the windpipe, as sons of doctors say, can tolerate anything entering it in swallowing.

Again, such writers seem unaware that history has aims and rules different from poetry and poems. In the case of the latter, liberty is absolute and there is one law—the will of the poet. . . .

I maintain then that the best writer of history comes ready equipped with these two supreme qualities: political understanding and power of expression; the former is an unteachable gift of nature, while power of expression may come through a deal of practice, continual toil, and imitation of the ancients. These then need no guiding rules and I have no need to advise on them; my book does not promise to make people understanding and quick who are not so by nature. . . .

So give us now a student of this kind—not without ability to understand and express himself, keen-sighted, one who could handle affairs if they were turned over to him, a man with the mind of a soldier combined with that of a good citizen, and a knowledge of generalship; yes, and one who has at some time been in a camp and has seen soldiers exercising or drilling and knows of arms and engines; again, let him know what "in column," what "in line" mean, how the companies of infantry, how the cavalry, are maneuvered, the origin and meaning of "lead out" and "lead around," in short not a stay-at-home or one who must rely on what people tell him. . . .

This, as I have said, is the one thing peculiar to history, and only to Truth must sacrifice be made. When a man is going to write history, everything else he must ignore. In short, the one standard, the one yardstick is to keep in view not your present audience but those who will meet your work hereafter. Whoever serves the present will rightly be counted a flatterer—a person on whom history long ago right from the beginning has turned its back, as much as has physical culture on the art of make-up. . . . Homer indeed in general tended towards the mythical in his account of Achilles, yet some nowadays are inclined to believe him; they cite as important evidence of his truthfulness the single fact that he did not write about him during his lifetime: they cannot find any motive for lying.

That then, is the sort of man the historian should be: fearless, incorruptible, free, a friend of free expression and the truth, intent, as the comic poet says, on calling a fig a fig and a trough a trough, giving nothing to hatred or to friendship, sparing no one, showing neither pity nor shame nor obsequiousness, an impartial judge, well disposed to all men up to the point of not giving one side more than its due, in his books a stranger and a man without a country, independent, subject to no sovereign, not reckoning what this or that man will think, but stating the facts.

Thucydides laid down this law very well: he distinguished virtue and vice in historical writing, when he saw Herodotus greatly admired to the point where his books were named after the Muses. For Thucydides says that he is writing a possession for evermore rather than a prize-essay for the occasion, that he does not welcome fiction but is leaving to posterity the true account of what happened. He brings in, too, the question of usefulness and what is, surely, the purpose of sound history: that if ever again men find themselves in a like situation they may be able, he says, from a consideration of the records of the past to handle rightly what now confronts them. . . .

Let his mind have a touch and share of poetry, since that too is lofty and sublime, especially when he has to do with battle arrays, with land and sea fights; for then he will have need of a wind of poetry to fill his sails and help carry his ship along, high on the crest of the waves. Let his diction nevertheless keep its feet on the ground, rising with the beauty and greatness of his subjects and as far as possible resembling them, but without becoming more unfamiliar or carried away than the occasion warrants. For then its greatest risk is that of going mad and being swept

down into poetry's wild enthusiasm, so that at such times above all he
must obey the curb and show prudence, in the knowledge that a stal-
lion's pride in literature as in life is no trifling ailment. It is better, then,
that when his mind is on horseback his exposition should go on foot,
running alongside and holding the saddle-cloth, so as not to be left
behind.

Again, in putting words together one should cultivate a well-
tempered moderation, without excessive separation or detachment—for
that is harsh—and not, as most people, almost link them by means of
rhythm; the latter deserves our censure, the former is unpleasant to the
audience.

As to the facts themselves, he should not assemble them at random,
but only after much laborious and painstaking investigation. He should
for preference be an eyewitness, but, if not, listen to those who tell a
more impartial story, those whom one would suppose least likely to
subtract from the facts or add to them out of favour or malice. When this
happens let him show shrewdness and skill in putting together the more
credible story. When he has collected all or most of the facts let him first
make them into a series of notes, a body of material as yet with no beauty
or continuity. Then, after arranging them into order, let him give it
beauty and enhance it with the charms of expression, figure, and
rhythm. . . .

Above all, let him bring a mind like a mirror, clear, gleaming-bright,
accurately centered, displaying the shape of things just as he receives
them, free from distortion, false colouring, and misrepresentation. His
concern is different from that of the orators—what historians have to
relate is fact and will speak for itself, for it has already happened: what is
required is arrangement and exposition. So they must look not for what
to say but how to say it. In brief, we must consider that the writer of
history should be like Phidias or Praxiteles or Alcamenes or one of the
other sculptors—they certainly never manufactured their own gold or
silver or ivory or their other material; no, their material was before
them, put into their hands by Eleans or Athenians or Argives, and they
confined themselves to fashioning it, sawing the ivory, polishing, glu-
ing, aligning it, setting it off with the gold, and their art lay in handling
their material properly.

The task of the historian is similar: to give a fine arrangement of
events and illuminate them as vividly as possible. And when a man who
has heard him thinks thereafter that he is actually seeing what is being

described and then praises him—then it is that the work of our Phidias of history is perfect and has received its proper praise. . . .

Again, if a myth comes along you must tell it but not believe it entirely; no, make it known for your audience to make of it what they will—you run no risk and lean to neither side.

In general please remember this—I shall repeat it time and again—: do not write with your eye just on the present, to win praise and honour from your contemporaries; aim at eternity and prefer to write for posterity: present your bill for your book to them, so that it may be said of you: "He was a free man, full of frankness, with no adulation or servility anywhere, but everywhere truthfulness." That, if a man were sensible, he would value above all present hopes, ephemeral as they are.

3

℘ Rome

In Rome, history became identified in particular with national tradition and in general with the rhetorical genre devoted to true accounts of past deeds which had been set down in writing for the needs and desires of the present. As with the Greeks, the term *history* referred either to the past (*res gestae*) or to descriptions thereof (*rei gestae narratio*), but the emphasis was more often on its literary form than on its "real" content. By origin, Roman history was tied more to pontifical and consular records than to poetry, and it preserved its original prosaic and public character.

Though not often noticed, the importance of Roman law for the development of historical study and interpretation was considerable, due in part to the classical revival of the early modern period. Roman jurists not only insisted on investigating legal sources but took an antiquarian interest in the development of legal history and their profession.

With the Romans, as with the Greeks, history took an antiquarian as well as a contemporary form. As a genre, it ranged from the fragmented erudition of Varro and Aulus Gellius (who was also interested in civil law), or the rhetorical excesses of Cicero and Quintilian, to the practical and forceful narrative of Caesar, Sallust, and Tacitus. All these features met in the work of Livy, who was in a sense both the Herodotus and the Thucydides of Roman history, venturing in a classic fashion into the mythical origins of Rome but also (in writings no longer extant) carrying the account of national tradition down to the crisis of the republic and the coming of the empire. A greater historian on every count, even Tacitus was little more than a continuator of the Livian project, though to be sure an extraordinarily astute and elegant one.

The Roman theory of history was extracted (and in some respects almost indistinguishable) from rhetoric, especially by Cicero, with some help from Quintilian and Pliny. Their commonplaces about the utility and elegance of history have resounded over the centuries, especially in the wake of Renaissance humanism. Cicero tried to see historiography itself in historical terms and lamented the shallowness of Roman historical writing, especially concerning antiquity. Neither this challenge nor the theoretical discussion of the art of history was taken seriously until early modern times, when authors first showed their historical awareness through intense efforts at imitation of the ancients.

❡ FROM THE FOUNDING

12. LIVY (Titus Livius, ca. 59 B.C.–A.D. 17) wrote, "from the founding of the city" (*ab urbe condita*), of the rise, decline, and, in his own day, degeneration of Rome. Following an annalistic arrangement and relying mainly on literary sources, Livy viewed the past in psychological and moralistic terms, although he provided an unusual amount of economic, social, and especially religious information. After recounting various fables, including the famous foundation myth of Romulus and Remus, Livy tried to trace the trajectory of Roman fortunes from the republican age of civic virtue, aristocratic piety, military strength, and senatorial order to the social and political corruption of the imperial age. Declaring his purpose to be commemoration of the past as well as profit for the present, he nonetheless claimed to avoid partisanship. Although only thirty-five books have survived (1–10 and 21–45 from the first third of the *Decades*), Livy's work takes its place among historical works as the archetypal national history.

Whether I am likely to accomplish anything worthy of the labour, if I record the achievements of the Roman people from the foundation of the city I do not really know, nor if I knew would I dare to avouch it; perceiving as I do that the theme is not only old but hackneyed, through the constant succession of new historians, who believe either that in their facts they can produce more authentic information, or that in their

Livy, *Ab Urbe Condita,* trans. B. O. Foster. Loeb Classical Library. 1:3–9. Reprinted by permission of the publishers and the Loeb Classical Library from Livy, Volume 1, trans. B. O. Foster, Cambridge, Mass.: Harvard University Press, 1919.

style they will prove better than the rude attempts of the ancients. Yet, however this shall be, it will be a satisfaction to have done myself as much as lies in me to commemorate the deeds of the foremost people of the world; and if in so vast a company of writers my own reputation should be obscure, my consolation would be the fame and greatness of these whose renown will throw mine into the shade. Moreover, my subject involves infinite labour, seeing that it must be traced back above seven hundred years, and that proceeding from slender beginnings it has so increased as now to be burdened by its own magnitude; and at the same time I doubt not that to most readers the earliest origins and the period immediately succeeding them will give little pleasure, for they will be in haste to reach these modern times, in which the might of a people which has long been very powerful is working its own undoing. I myself, on the contrary, shall seek in this an additional reward for my toil, that I may avert my gaze from the troubles which our age has been witnessing for so many years, so long at least as I am absorbed in the recollection of the brave days of old, free from every care which, even if it could not divert the historian's mind from the truth, might nevertheless cause it anxiety.

Such traditions as belong to the time before the city was founded, or rather was presently to be founded, and are rather adorned with poetic legends than based upon trustworthy historical proofs, I purpose neither to affirm nor to refute. It is the privilege of antiquity to mingle divine things with human, and so to add dignity to the beginnings of cities; and if any people ought to be allowed to consecrate their origins and refer them to a divine source, so great is the military glory of the Roman People that when they profess that their Father and the Father of the Founder was none other than Mars, the nations of the earth may well submit to this also with as good a grace as they submit to Rome's dominion. But to such legends as these, however they shall be regarded and judged, I shall, for my own part, attach no great importance. Here are the questions to which I would have every reader give his close attention—what life and morals were like; through what men and by what policies, in peace and in war, empire was established and enlarged; then let him note how, with the gradual relaxation of discipline, morals first gave way, as it were, then sank lower and lower, and finally began the downward plunge which has brought us to the present time, when we can endure neither our vices nor their cure.

What chiefly makes the study of history wholesome and profitable is this, that you behold the lessons of every kind of experience set forth as on a conspicuous monument; from these you may choose for yourself and for your own state what to imitate, from these mark for avoidance what is shameful in the conception and shameful in the result. For the rest, either love of the task I have set myself deceives me, or no state was ever greater, none more righteous or richer in good examples, none ever was where avarice and luxury came into the social order so late, or where humble means and thrift were so highly esteemed and so long held in honour. For true it is that the less men's wealth was, the less was their greed. Of late, riches have brought in avarice, and excessive pleasures the longing to carry wantonness and licence to the point of ruin for oneself and of universal destruction.

But complaints are sure to be disagreeable, even when they shall perhaps be necessary; let the beginning, at all events, of so great an enterprise have none. With good omens rather would we begin, and, if historians had the same custom which poets have, with prayers and entreaties to the gods and goddesses, that they might grant us to bring to a successful issue the great task we have undertaken.

> 13. GAIUS (d. A.D. 178?) was the author of a seminal *Institutes of Civil Law* (rediscovered in the nineteenth century) and wrote as well on legal antiquities; in this authoritative fragment from his work on the *Twelve Tables,* he explains the legal grounds for a historical method.

Since I am aiming to give an interpretation of the ancient laws, I have concluded that I must trace the law of the Roman people from the very beginnings of their city. This is not because I like making excessively wordy commentaries, but because I can see that in every subject a perfect job is one whose parts hang together properly. And to be sure that most important part of anything is its beginning. Moreover, if it is regarded as a sin (so to speak) for people arguing cases in court to launch straight into an exposition of the case to the judge without having made any prefatory remarks, will it not be all the more unfitting for people who promise an interpretation of a subject to deal straight off with that subject matter, leaving out its beginnings, failing to trace its origin, not even, as I might say, giving their hands a preliminary wash? In fact, if I

Gaius, *Twelve Tables.* In *The Digest of Justinian,* ed. Theodor Mommsen with Paul Krueger and trans. Alan Watson. Philadelphia: University of Pennsylvania Press, 1985. 1:3.

mistake not, such introductions both lead us more willingly into our reading of the proposed subject matter, and, when we have got to the point, give us a far clearer grasp of it.

> 14. POMPONIUS (second century A.D.), a Roman jurist, wrote a handbook, the *Enchiridion*, prefaced by a sketch of legal history. Because of its position in the first title of Justinian's *Digest*, "On the Origin of Law," this sketch (or rather the corrupt, postclassical text in which it was preserved) had a significant impact on later scholarship and became a point of departure for modern legal and institutional history.

Accordingly, it seems that we must account for the origin and development of law itself. The fact is that at the outset of our *civitas*, the citizen body decided to conduct its affairs without fixed statute law or determinate legal rights; everything was governed by the kings under their own hand. When the *civitas* subsequently grew to a reasonable size, then Romulus himself, according to the tradition, divided the citizen body into thirty parts, and called them *curiae* on the ground that he improved his curatorship of the commonwealth through the advice of these parts. And accordingly, he himself enacted for the people a number of statutes passed by advice of the *curiae {leges curiatae}*; his successor kings legislated likewise. All these statutes have survived written down in the book by Sextus Papirius, who was a contemporary of Superbus, son of Demeratus the Corinthian, and was one of the leading men of his time. That book, as we said, is called *The Papirian Civil Law*, not because Papirius put a word of his own in it, but because he compiled in unitary form laws passed piecemeal. Then, when the kings were thrown out under a Tribunician enactment, these statutes all fell too, and for a second time, the Roman people set about working with vague ideas of right and with customs of a sort rather than with legislation, and they put up with that for nearly twenty years. After that, to put an end to this state of affairs, it was decided that there be appointed, on the authority of the people, a commission of ten men by whom were to be studied the laws of the Greek city states and by whom their own city was to be endowed with laws. They wrote out the laws in full on ivory tablets and put the tablets together in front of the *rostra*, to make the laws all the

Pomponius, *Manual*. In *The Digest of Justinian*, ed. Theodor Mommsen with Paul Krueger and trans. Alan Watson. Philadelphia: University of Pennsylvania Press, 1985. 1:3–5.

more open to inspection. They were given during that year sovereign right in the *civitas,* to enable them to correct the laws, if there should be a need for that, and to interpret them without liability to any appeal such as lay from the rest of the magistracy. They themselves discovered a deficiency in that first batch of laws, and accordingly, they added two tablets to the original set. It was from this addition that the laws of the *Twelve Tables* got their name. Some writers have reported that the man behind the enactment of these laws by the Ten Men was one Hermodorus from Ephesus, who was then in exile in Italy. After the enactment of these laws, there arose a necessity for forensic debate, as it is the normal and natural outcome that problems of interpretation should make it desirable to have guidance from learned persons. Forensic debate, and jurisprudence which without formal writing emerges as expounded by learned men, has no special name of its own like the other subdivisions of law designated by name (there being proper names given to these other subdivisions); it is called by the common name "civil law." Then about the same time actions-at-law whereby people could litigate among themselves were composed out of these statutes [the law of the *Twelve Tables*]. To prevent the citizenry from initiating litigation any old how, the lawmakers' will was that the actions-at-law be in fixed and solemn terms. This branch of law has the name *legis actiones,* that is, statutory actions-at-law. And so these three branches of law came into being at almost the same time: once the statute law of the *Twelve Tables* was passed, the *jus civile* started to emerge from them, and *legis actiones* were put together from the same source. In relation to all these statutes, however, knowledge of their authoritative interpretation and conduct of the actions at law belonged to the College of Priests, one of whom was appointed each year to preside over the private citizens. The people followed this practice for nearly a hundred years. . . . Then, since in the *civitas* there was the statute law of the *Twelve Tables* and on top of that the *jus civile* and on top of that the statutory *legis actiones,* it came to pass that the *plebs* fell at odds with the members of the senatorial class and seceded and set up laws for itself, which laws are called plebiscites. Soon after the *plebs* had been wheedled back, because these plebiscites were giving rise to many disputes, the decision was made in the *lex Hortensia* that they were to be deemed to have the force of statutes. And so it came about that although there was a difference as to the method of passing plebiscites and *leges* (statutes), they had the same legal force. Next, because it grew hard for the *plebs* to assemble, and to be sure much harder for the entire citizenry to assemble, being now such a vast crowd of men, the very necessity of the case imposed upon the senate trusteeship of the commonwealth. And thus did the senate come to exercise authority, and whatever it resolved upon was respected, and such a law was called a *senatus consultum* (senate resolution). At the same time, the magistrates also were settling matters of legal right, and in order to let the citizens know and allow for the jurisdiction which each magistrate would be exercising over any given matter, they took to publishing edicts. These edicts, in the case of the praetors, constituted the *jus honorarium* (honorary law); "honorary" is the term used, because the law in question had come from the high honor of praetorian office. Most recently, just as there was seen to have been a transition toward fewer ways of establishing law, a transition effected by stages under dictation of circumstances, it has come about that affairs of state have had to be entrusted to one man (for the senate had been unable latterly to govern all the provinces honestly). An emperor, therefore, having been appointed, to him was given the right that what he had decided be deemed law. Thus, in our state the constitutional course is determined by law, that is, by statute law; or there is our own *jus civile,* which is grounded without formal writing in nothing more than interpretation by learned jurists; or there are statutory actions-at-law, which govern forms of process; or there is plebiscite law, which is settled without the advice and consent of the senate; or there is a magisterial edict, whence honorary law derives; or there is a *senatus consultum,* which is brought in without statutory authority solely on the decision of the senate; or there is an imperial enactment (*constitutio*), the principle being that what the emperor himself has decided is to be observed as having statutory force.

◊ HISTORY AND RHETORIC

15. Marcus Tullius CICERO (106–43 B.C.) combined the roles of author and public figure to an extraordinary degree and was the most popular and influential of all Roman writers down to the twentieth century. He epitomized the theory and practice of rhetoric, and it is in this connection that he contributed to the classical notion of history. The Roman orator stood as the model of the historian, just as rhetoric possessed the major qualities of historical

Cicero, *Laws,* trans. Clinton Walker Keyes. Loeb Classical Library. 16:301–307. Reprinted by permission of the publishers and the Loeb Classical Library from Cicero, Volume 16, trans. Clinton Walker Keyes, Cambridge, Mass.: Harvard University Press, 1928.

narrative: truth, elegance, persuasiveness, and a concern for public benefit. In a variety of works, Cicero commented on the origin, nature, and goals of the study of history; his pronouncements became the *loci classici* of the idea of history down to the present.

Q[uintus]. As I understand it, then, my dear brother, you believe that different principles are to be followed in history and in poetry.

M[arcus Tullius]. Certainly, Quintus; for in history the standard by which everything is judged is the truth, while in poetry it is generally the pleasure one gives; however, in the works of Herodotus, the Father of History, and those of Theopompus, one finds innumerable fabulous tales. . . .

A[tticus]. There has long been a desire, or rather a demand, that you should write a history. For people think that, if you entered that field, we might rival Greece in this branch of literature also. And to give you my own opinion, it seems to me that you owe this duty not merely to the desires of those who take pleasure in literature, but also to your country, in order that the land which you have saved you may also glorify. For our national literature is deficient in history, as I realize myself and as I frequently hear you say. But you can certainly fill this gap satisfactorily, since, as you at least have always believed, this branch of literature is closer than any other to oratory. Therefore take up the task, we beg of you, and find the time for a duty which has hitherto been either overlooked or neglected by our countrymen. For after the annals of the chief pontiffs, which are records of the driest possible character, when we come to Fabius, or to Cato (whose name is always on your lips), or to Piso, Fannius, or Vennonius, although one of these may display more vigour than another, yet what could be more lifeless than the whole group? . . . Therefore this task is yours; its accomplishment is expected of you, that is, if Quintus agrees with me.

Q. Indeed I agree perfectly, and Marcus and I have frequently discussed the matter. But there is one small point on which we disagree.

A. What is that?

Q. The question of the period at which he should begin his history. I think it should be the earliest, for the records of that age have been written in such a style that they are never read at all. But he prefers to write of his own lifetime, in order to include those events in which he himself has taken part.

A. Indeed I agree rather with him. For most important events have taken place within the memory of our generation; besides, he will be able to glorify the deeds of his dear friend Gnaeus Pompeius, and to include a description of the illustrious and memorable year of his own consulship. I should rather have him write of these events than "of Romulus and Remus," as the saying is.

M. Certainly I realize that the accomplishment of this task has long been demanded of me, Atticus. And I should not refuse to undertake it, if I were granted any unoccupied or leisure time. But so great a task cannot be undertaken when one's time is filled or his attention distracted; one must be free from both work and worry.

❡ Nor, while he [the orator] is acquainted with the divine order of nature, would I have him ignorant of human affairs. He should understand the civil law, which is needed daily in practice in the courts of law. What is more disgraceful than to attempt to plead in legal and civil disputes when ignorant of statutes and the civil law? He should also be acquainted with the history of the events of past ages, particularly, of course, of our state, but also of imperial nations and famous kings; here our task has been lightened by the labour of our friend Atticus, who has comprised in one book the record of seven hundred years, keeping the chronology definite and omitting no important event. To be ignorant of what occurred before you were born is to remain always a child. For what is the worth of human life, unless it is woven into the life of our ancestors by the records of history? Moreover, the mention of antiquity and the citation of examples give the speech authority and credibility as well as affording the highest pleasure to the audience.

❡ It is the part of the orator, when advising on affairs of supreme importance, to unfold his opinion as a man having authority: his duty too it is to arouse a listless nation, and to curb its unbridled impetuosity. By one and the same power of eloquence the deceitful among mankind are brought to destruction, and the righteous to deliverance. Who more

Cicero, *Orator,* trans. H. M. Hubbell. Loeb Classical Library. 5 : 395. Reprinted by permission of the publishers and the Loeb Classical Library, from Cicero, Volume 5, trans. H. M. Hubbell, Cambridge, Mass.: Harvard University Press, 1939.

Cicero, *De Oratore,* trans. E. W. Sutton and H. Rackham. Loeb Classical Library. 3 : 223–225, 239, and 243–245. Reprinted by permission of the publishers and the Loeb Classical Library from Cicero, Volume 3, trans. E. W. Sutton and H. Rackham, Cambridge, Mass.: Harvard University Press, 1942.

passionately than the orator can encourage to virtuous conduct, or more zealously than he reclaim from vicious courses? Who can more austerely censure the wicked, or more gracefully praise men of worth? Whose invective can more forcibly subdue the power of lawless desire? Whose comfortable words can soothe grief more tenderly?

And as History, which bears witness to the passing of the ages, sheds light upon reality, gives life to recollection and guidance to human existence, and brings tidings of ancient days, whose voice, but the orator's, can entrust her to immortality? For if there be any other art, which pretends to skill in the coinage and choice of language, or if it be claimed for anyone but the orator that he gives shape and variety to a speech, and marks it out with highlights of thought and phrase, or if any method be taught, except by this single art, for producing proofs or reflections, or even in the distribution and arrangement of subject-matter, then let us admit that the skill professed by this art of ours either belongs really to some other art, or is shared in common with some other. Whereas, if all reasoning and all teaching really belong to this one art alone, then even though professors of other arts have expressed themselves with success, it does not therefore follow that such instruction is not the monopoly of this single art; but . . . just as the orator is best qualified to discuss the subjects pertaining to the other arts, assuming always that he has acquainted himself with them, so the masters of the other arts expound their own topics with the better grace, if they have learned something from the art with which we are dealing. . . .

No wonder {returned Antonius} if this subject has never yet been brilliantly treated in our language. For not one of our own folk seeks after eloquence, save with an eye to its display at the Bar and in public speaking, whereas in Greece the most eloquent were strangers to forensic advocacy and applied themselves chiefly to reputable studies in general, and particularly to writing history. Indeed even of renowned Herodotus, who first imparted distinction to such work, we have heard that he was in no way concerned with lawsuits, and yet his eloquence is of such quality as to afford intense pleasure, to myself at any rate, so far as I can comprehend what is written in Greek. After his day Thucydides, in my judgement, easily surpassed all others in dexterity of composition: so abounding is he in fullness of material that in the number of his ideas he well-nigh equals the number of his words, and furthermore he is so exact and clear in expression that you cannot tell whether it be the narrative that gains illumination from the style, or the diction from the thought. Yet even of him, though a man of public affairs, we are not told that he was numbered among forensic speakers; and it is related that when writing the volumes in question, he was far away from civic life, having in fact been driven into exile, as generally happened at Athens to anyone of excellence. . . .

Do you see how great a responsibility the orator has in historical writing? I rather think that for fluency and diversity of diction it comes first. Yet nowhere do I find this art supplied with any independent directions from the rhetoricians; indeed its rules lie open to the view. For who does not know history's first law to be that an author must not dare to tell anything but the truth? And its second that he must make bold to tell the whole truth? That there must be no suggestion of partiality anywhere in his writings? Nor of malice? This groundwork of course is familiar to every one; the completed structure, however, rests upon the story and the diction. The nature of the subject needs chronological arrangement and geographical representation: and since, in reading of important affairs worth recording, the plans of campaign, the executive actions and the results are successively looked for, it calls also, as regards such plans, for some intimation of what the writer approves, and, in the narrative of achievement, not only for a statement of what was done or said, but also of the manner of doing or saying it; and, in the estimate of consequences, for an exposition of all contributory causes, whether originating in accicent, discretion or foolhardiness; and, as for the individual actors, besides an account of their exploits, it demands particulars of the lives and characters of such as are outstanding in renown and dignity. Then again the kind of language and type of style to be followed are the easy and the flowing, which run their course with unvarying current and a certain placidity, avoiding alike the rough speech we use in Court and the advocate's stinging epigrams. Upon all these numerous and important points, do you observe that any directions are to be found in the rhetoricians' systems?

> 16. QUINTILIAN (Marcus Fabius Quintilianus, A.D. 35/40–ca. 96) was a rhetorician and literary critic who, like Cicero, emphasized the ties between oratory and history; his *Institutes of Oratory* contain a number of classic and familiar characterizations of the value and purpose of the reading and writing of history.

Quintilian, *Institutes of Oratory,* trans. H. E. Butler. Loeb Classical Library. 4:19–21 and 407–409. Reprinted by permission of the publishers and the Loeb Classical Library, from Quintilian, Volume 4, trans. H. E. Butler, Cambridge, Mass.: Harvard University Press, 1922.

History, also, may provide the orator with a nutriment which we may compare to some rich and pleasant juice. But when we read it, we must remember that many of the excellences of the historian require to be shunned by the orator. For history has a certain affinity to poetry and may be regarded as a kind of prose poem, while it is written for the purpose of narrative, not of proof, and designed from beginning to end not for immediate effect or the instant necessities of forensic strife, but to record events for the benefit of posterity and to win glory for its author. . . .

Above all, our orator should be equipped with a rich store of examples both old and new: and he ought not merely to know those which are recorded in history or transmitted by oral tradition or occur from day to day, but should not neglect even those fictitious examples invented by the great poets. For while the former have the authority of evidence or even of legal decisions, the latter also either have the warrant of antiquity or are regarded as having been invented by great men to serve as lessons to the world. He should therefore be acquainted with as many examples as possible. It is this which gives old age so much authority, since the old are believed to have a larger store of knowledge and experience, as Homer so frequently bears witness. But we must not wait till the evening of our days, since study has this advantage that, as far as knowledge of facts is concerned, it is capable of giving the impression that we have lived in ages long gone by.

> 17. AULUS GELLIUS (ca. 169–123 B.C.) studied rhetoric, law, and philosophy and is known chiefly for his learned miscellany called *Attic Nights,* named perhaps from his stay in Athens. Included among the wide range of topics are literature, philosophy, and religion, as well as essays in historical criticism, bibliophilia, chronology, antiquities, anachronisms, and legal and philological questions. Though his work has the appearance of unfocused pedantry, it displays a great sensitivity to the texture of history and to heuristic questions.

As to the age of Homer and of Hesiod opinions differ. Some, among whom are Philichorus and Xenophanes, have written that Homer was

Aulus Gellius, *Attic Nights,* trans. John C. Rolfe. Loeb Classical Library. 1:275, 357–359, and 433–437; 2:139, 315, and 343–345; 3:113, 167–169, 273, 275, and 279. Reprinted by permission of the publishers and the Loeb Classical Library from Aulus Gellius, Volumes 1, 2, and 3, trans. John C. Rolfe, Cambridge, Mass.: Harvard University Press, 1927.

older than Hesiod; others that he was younger, among them Lucius
Accius the poet and Euphorus the historian. But Marcus Varro, in the
first book of his *Portraits,* says that it is not at all certain which of the two
was born first, but that there is no doubt that they lived partly in the
same period of time, and that this is proved by the inscription engraved
upon a tripod which Hesiod is said to have set up on Mount Helicon.
Accius, on the contrary, in the first book of his *Didascalica,* makes use of
very weak arguments in his attempt to show that Hesiod was the elder:
"Because Homer," he writes, "when he says at the beginning of his poem
that Achilles was the son of Peleus, does not inform us who Peleus was;
and this he unquestionably would have done, if he did not know that the
information had already been given by Hesiod. Again, in the case of
Cyclops," says Accius, "he would not have failed to note such a striking
characteristic and to make particular mention of the fact that he was one-
eyed, were it not that this was equally well known from the poems of his
predecessor Hesiod. . . ."

The elegance of Sallust's style and his passion for coining and introducing new words was met with exceeding great hostility, and many
men of no mean ability tried to criticize and decry much in his writings.
Many of the attacks on him were ignorant or malicious. Yet there are
some things that may be regarded as deserving of censure, as for example
the following passage in the *History of Catiline,* which has the appearance
of being written somewhat carelessly. Sallust's words are these: "And for
myself, although I am well aware that by no means equal repute attends
the narrator and the doer of deeds, yet I regard the writing of history as
one of the hardest of tasks; first because the style and diction must be
equal to the deeds recorded; and in the second place, because such criticisms as you make of others' shortcomings are thought by most men to
be due to malice and envy. . . ." The critics say: "He declared that he
would give the reasons why it appears to be 'hard' 'to write history'; and
then, after mentioning the first reason, he does not give a second, but
gives utterance to complaints. . . ."

But Sallust does not use *arduus* merely in the sense of "hard," but as
the equivalent of the Greek word *chalepos,* that is, both difficult and also
troublesome, disagreeable and intractable. And the meaning of these
words is not inconsistent with that of the passage which was just quoted
from Sallust.

Some think that history differs from annals in this particular, that
while each is a narrative of events, yet history is properly an account of
events in which the narrator took part; and that this is the opinion of

some men is stated by Verrius Flaccus in the fourth book of his treatise *On the Meaning of Words*. He adds that he for his part has doubts about the matter, but he thinks that the view may have some appearance of reason, since *historia* in Greek means a knowledge of current events. But we often hear it said that annals are exactly the same as histories, but that histories are not exactly the same as annals; just as a man is necessarily an animal, but an animal is not necessarily a man.

Thus they say that history is the setting forth of events or their description, or whatever term may be used; but that annals set down the events of many years successively, with observance of the chronological order. When, however, events are recorded, not year by year, but day by day, such a history is called in Greek *ephemeris,* or "a diary," a term of which the Latin interpretation is found in the first book of Sempronius Asellio. I have quoted a passage of some length from that book, in order at the same time to show what his opinion is of the difference between history and chronicle.

"But between those," he says, "who have desired to leave us annals, and those who have tried to write the history of the Roman people, there was this essential difference. The books of annals merely made known what happened and in what year it happened, which is like writing a diary, which the Greeks call *ephemeris.* For my part, I realize that it is not enough to make known what has been done, but that one should also show with what purpose and for what reason things were done." A little later in the same book Asellio writes: "For annals cannot in any way make men more eager to defend their country, or more reluctant to do wrong. Furthermore, to write over and over again in whose consulship a war was begun and ended, and who in consequence entered the city in a triumph, and in that book not to state what happened in the course of the war, what decrees the senate made during that time, or what law or bill was passed, and with what motives these things were done—that is to tell stories to children, not to write history. . . ."

The tyrant Pisistratus is said to have been the first to establish at Athens a public library of books relating to the liberal arts. Then the Athenians themselves added to this collection with considerable diligence and care; but later Xerxes, when he got possession of Athens and burned the entire city except the citadel, removed them off to Persia. Finally, a long time afterwards, king Selucus, who was surnamed Nicanor, had all those books taken back to Athens.

At a later time an enormous quantity of books, nearly seven hundred thousand volumes, was either acquired or written in Egypt under the

kings known as Ptolemies; but these were all burned during the sack of
the city in our first war with Alexandria, not intentionally or by anyone's
order, but accidentally by the auxiliary soldiers. . . .

To use words that are too antiquated and worn out, or those which are
unusual and of a harsh and unpleasant novelty, seems to be equally
faulty. But for my own part I think it more offensive and censurable to
use words that are new, unknown and unheard of, than those that are
trite and mean. Furthermore, I maintain that those words also seem new
which are out of use and obsolete, even though they are of ancient date.
In fact, it is a common fault of lately acquired learning, or *opsimathia* as
the Greeks call it, to make a great point anywhere and everywhere, and
in connection with any subject whatever, to talk about what you have
never learned and of which you were long ignorant, when at last you have
begun to know something about it. . . .

Draco the Athenian was considered a good man and of great wisdom,
and he was skilled in law, human and divine. This Draco was the first of
all to make laws for the use of Athenians. In those laws he decreed and
enacted that one guilty of any theft whatsoever should be punished with
death, and added many other statutes that were excessively severe.

Therefore his laws, since they seemed very much too harsh, were abolished, not by order and decree, but by the tacit, unwritten consent of the
Athenians. After that, they made use of other, milder laws, compiled by
Solon. This Solon was one of the famous seven wise men. He thought
proper by his law to punish thieves, not with death, as Draco had formerly done, but by a fine of twice the value of the stolen goods.

But our decemvirs, who after the expulsion of the kings compiled laws
on *Twelve Tables* for the use of the Romans, did not show equal severity in
punishing thieves of any kind, nor yet too lax leniency. For they permitted a thief who was caught in the act to be put to death, only if it was
night when he committed the theft, or if in the daytime he defended
himself with a weapon when taken. But other thieves taken in the act, if
they were freemen, the decemvirs ordered to be scourged and handed
over to the one from whom the theft had been made, provided they had
committed the theft in daylight and had not defended themselves with a
weapon. Slaves taken in the act were to be scourged and hurled from the
rock, but they decided that boys under aged should be flogged at the
discretion of the praetor and the damage which they had done made
good. Those thefts also which were detected by the girdle and mask,
they punished as if the culprit had been caught in the act. . . .

Hellanicus, Herodotus, and Thucydides, writers of history, enjoyed great glory at almost the same time, and did not differ very greatly in age. For Hellanicus seems to have been sixty-five years old at the beginning of the Peloponnesian war, Herodotus fifty-three, Thucydides forty. This is stated in the eleventh book of Pamphila. . . .

One day there was a cessation of business in the Forum at Rome, and as the holiday was being joyfully celebrated, it chanced that one of the books of the *Annals* of Ennius was read in an assembly of very many persons. In this book the following lines occurred:

> With shield and savage sword in Proletarius armed
> At public cost; they guard our walls, our mart and town.

Then the question was raised there, what *proletarius* meant. And seeing in that company a man who was skilled in the civil law, a friend of mine, I asked him to explain the word to us; and when he rejoined that he was an expert in civil law and not in grammatical matters, I said: "You in particular ought to explain this, since, as you declare, you are skilled in civil law. For Quintus Ennius took this word from your *Twelve Tables,* in which, if I remember aright, we have the following, 'For a freeholder let the protector be a freeholder. For a proletariate citizen let whoso will be protector.' We therefore ask you to consider that not one of the books of Quintus Ennius' *Annals,* but the *Twelve Tables* are being read, and interpret the meaning of 'proletariate citizen' in that law." "It is true," said he, "that if I had learned the law of the Fauns and Aborigines, I ought to explain and interpret this. But since *proletarii, adsidui, sanates, vades, subvades,* 'twenty-five asses,' 'retaliation,' and trials for theft 'by plate and girdle' have disappeared, and since all the ancient lore of the *Twelve Tables,* except for legal questions before the court of the centumviri, was put to sleep by the Aebutian law, I ought only to exhibit interest in, and knowledge of, the law and statutes and legal terms which we now actually use."

Just then, by some chance, we caught sight of Julius Paulus passing by, the most learned poet within my recollection. We greeted him, and when he was asked to enlighten us as to the meaning and derivation of that word, he said: "Those of the Roman commons who were humblest and of smallest means, and who reported no more than fifteen hundred asses at the census, were called *proletarii,* but those who were rated as having no property at all, or next to none, were termed *capite censi,* or 'counted by head.' . . ."

I wished to have a kind of survey of ancient times and also of the famous men who were born in those days, lest I might in conversation chance to make some careless remark about the date and life of celebrated men, as that ignorant sophist did who lately, in a public lecture, said that Carneades the philosopher was presented with a sum of money by King Alexander, son of Philip, and that Panatius the Stoic was intimate with the elder Africanus. In order, I say, to guard against such errors in dates and periods of time, I made notes from the books known as *Chronicles* of the times when those Greeks and Romans flourished who were famous and conspicuous either for talent or for political power, between the founding of Rome and the second Punic war. . . .

I shall begin, then, with the illustrious Solon; for, as regards Homer and Hesiod, it is agreed by almost all writers, either that they lived at approximately the same period, or that Homer was somewhat the earlier; yet that both lived before the founding of Rome, when the Silvii were ruling in Alba, more than a hundred and sixty years after the Trojan war, as Cassius has written about Homer and Hesiod in the first book of his *Annals,* but about a hundred and sixty years before the founding of Rome, as Cornelius Nepos says of Homer in the first book of his *Chronicles.*

Well then, we are told that Solon, one of the famous sages, drew up laws for the Athenians when Tarquinius Priscus was king at Rome, in the thirty-third year of his reign. Afterwards, when Servius Tullius was king, Pisistratus was tyrant at Athens, Solon having previously gone into voluntary exile, since he had not been believed when he predicted that tyranny. . . .

At about that time Empedocles of Agrigentum was eminent in the domain of natural philosophy. But at Rome at that epoch it is stated that a board of ten was appointed to codify laws, and that at first they compiled ten tables, to which afterwards two more were added.

Then the great Peloponnesian war began in Greece, which Thucydides has handed down to memory, about three hundred and twenty-three years after the founding of Rome. At that time Olus Postumius Tubertus was dictator at Rome, and executed his own son, because he had fought against the enemy contrary to his father's order. The people of Fidenae and the Aequinians were then at war with the Roman people. During that period Sophocles, and later Euripides, were famous and renowned as tragic poets, Hippocrates as a physician, and as a philosopher, Democritus; Socrates the Athenian was younger than these, but was in part their contemporary.

18. PLINY THE YOUNGER (Gaius Plinius Caelius Secundus, A.D. 61/62–113), nephew and namesake of the encyclopedist, student of Quintilian, and colleague of Tacitus, had a distinguished legal career and continued the great tradition of Roman oratory. His letters treat a wide range of subjects, including his private and public life, literary interests, the rise of Christianity, and the nature of history.

[To Titinius Capito]

Your suggestion that I should write history has often been made, for a good many people have given me the same advice. I like the idea: not that I feel at all sure of being successful—it would be rash in an amateur—but because the saving of those who deserve immortality from sinking into oblivion, and spreading the fame of others along with one's own, seem to me a particularly splendid achievement. Nothing attracts me so much as that love and longing for a lasting name, man's worthiest aspiration, especially in one who is aware that there is nothing in him to blame and so has no fear if he is to be remembered by posterity. So day and night I wonder if "I too may rise from earth"; that would answer my prayer, for "to hover in triumph on the lips of man" is too much to hope. "Yet O if I could—" but I must rest content with what history alone seems able to guarantee. Oratory and poetry win small favour unless they reach the highest standard of eloquence, but history cannot fail to give pleasure however it is presented. Humanity is naturally inquisitive, and so factual information, plain and unadorned, has its attraction for anyone who can enjoy small talk and anecdote.

In my case family precedent is an additional incentive to work of this kind. My uncle, who was also my father by adoption, was a historian of scrupulous accuracy, and I find in the philosophers that it is an excellent thing to follow in the footsteps of one's forbears, provided that they trod an honest path. Why then do I delay? I have acted in certain important and complicated cases, and I intend to revise my speeches (without building too many hopes on them) so that all the work I put into them will not perish with me for want of this last attention. For if one looks to posterity, anything left unfinished might as well not have been begun.

Pliny the Younger, *Letters,* trans. Betty Radice. Loeb Classical Library. 1: 357–363 and 559–563. Reprinted by permission of the publishers and the Loeb Classical Library from Pliny the Younger, Volume 1, trans. Betty Radice, Cambridge, Mass.: Harvard University Press, 1969.

You will tell me that I can rewrite my speeches and write history at the same time. I wish I could, but both are such great undertakings that it will be more than enough to carry out one. I was eighteen when I began my career at the bar, and it is only now, and still only dimly, that I begin to realize the true qualities of the orator. What would happen if I shouldered a new burden in addition to the old? It is true that oratory and history have much in common, but they differ in many of the points where they seem alike. Both employ narrative, but with a difference: oratory deals largely with the humble and trivial incidents of everyday life, history is concerned with profound truths and the glory of great deeds. The bare bones of narrative and a nervous energy often distinguish the one, a fullness and a certain freedom of style the other. Oratory succeeds by its vigour and severity of attack, history by the ease and grace with which it develops its theme. Finally, they differ in vocabulary, rhythm and period-structure, for, as Thucydides says, there is all the difference between a "lasting possession" and a "prize essay": the former is history, the latter oratory. For these reasons I am not inclined to blend and mix two dissimilar subjects which are fundamentally opposed in the very quality to which each owes its prominence, lest I am swept away in the resultant confusion and treat one in the manner proper to the other. And so, to keep to my own language, for the time being I apply for an adjournment.

You however, can be considering now what period of history I am to treat. Is it to be ancient history which has had its historians? The material is there, but it will be a great labour to assemble it. Or shall it be recent times which no one has handled? I shall receive small thanks and give serious offence for beside the fact that there is much more to censure than to praise in the serious vices of the present day, such praise as one gives, however generous, is considered grudging, and however restrained one's blame it is said to be excessive. But I have enough courage of my convictions not to be deterred by such considerations. All I ask of you is to prepare the way for what you want me to do and to choose me a subject; or another good reason for delay and hesitation may arise when I am ready to start at last.

[To Cornelius Tacitus]

I believe that your histories will be immortal; a prophecy which will surely prove correct. That is why (I frankly admit) I am anxious to appear in them. We are usually careful to see that none but the best artists shall portray our features, so why should we not want our deeds to be blessed by a writer like yourself to celebrate them? So here is an account of an incident which can hardly have escaped your watchful eye, since it appeared in the official records; but I am sending it so that you may be the more assured of my pleasure if this action of mine, which gained interest from the risks attending it, shall be distinguished by the testimony of your genius.

The Senate had instructed me to act with Herennius Senecio as counsel for the province of Baetica against Baebius Massa, and after Massa's conviction had passed the resolution that his property should be kept in official custody. Senecio then discovered that the consuls would be willing to hear Massa's claims for restitution, so sought me out and proposed that we should continue to act in unity as we had done in carrying out the prosecution entrusted to us: we should approach the consuls and ask them not to allow the dispersal of the property which they were responsible for holding in custody. I pointed out that we had acted as counsel by appointment of the Senate, and asked him to consider whether perhaps we had come to the end of our role now that the case was over. "You can set what limit you like to your own responsibilities," he said, "For you have no connexion with the province except the recent one of the services you have rendered, but I was born in Baetica and served as quaestor there." "If your mind is made up," I said, "I will act with you, so that if any ill-will results, you will not have to face it alone."

We went to the consuls. Senecio said what was necessary and I added a few words. We had scarcely finished speaking when Massa complained that Senecio had displayed the animosity of a personal enemy rather than a professional counsel's honour, and demanded leave to prosecute him for failing in his duty. Amidst the general consternation I began to speak: "Most noble consuls, I am afraid that by not including me in his accusation Massa's very silence has charged me with collusion with himself." These words were acclaimed at once and subsequently much talked about; indeed, the deified Emperor Nerva (who never failed to notice anything done for the good of the State even before he became Emperor) sent me a most impressive letter in which he congratulated not only me but our generation for being blessed with an example so much (he said) in the best tradition.

Whatever the merit of this incident, you can make it better known and increase its fame and importance, but I am not asking you to go beyond what is due to the facts. History should always confine itself to the truth, which in its turn is enough for honest deeds.

℘ POLITICAL HISTORY

19. SALLUST (Gaius Sallustius Crispus, 86–ca. 34 B.C.) retired from politics to take up the preferable vocation of historian. In his historical works—especially on the conspiracy of Catiline and the Jugurthine War—he chronicled, illustrated, and deplored the decline of the Roman republic, which in his view had begun after, and in part because of, the destruction of Carthage.

It becomes all men, who desire to excel other animals, to strive, to the utmost of their power, not to pass through life in obscurity, like the beasts of the field, which nature has formed grovelling and subservient to appetite.

All our power is situate in the mind and in the body. Of the mind we rather employ the government; of the body, the service. The one is common to us with the gods; the other with the brutes. It appears to me, therefore, more reasonable to pursue glory by means of the intellect than of bodily strength, and, since the life which we enjoy is short, to make the remembrance of us as lasting as possible. For the glory of wealth and beauty is fleeting and perishable; that of intellectual power is illustrious and immortal.

Yet it was long a subject of dispute among mankind, whether military efforts were more advanced by strength of body, or by force of intellect. For, in affairs of war, it is necessary to plan before beginning to act, and, after planning, to act with promptitude and vigour. Thus, each being insufficient of itself, the one requires the assistance of the other.

In early times, accordingly, kings (for that was the first title of sovereignty in the world) applied themselves in different ways; some exercised the mind, others the body. At that period, however, the life of man was passed without covetousness; every one was satisfied with his own. But after Cyrus in Asia, and the Lacedaemonians and Athenians in Greece, began to subjugate cities and nations, to deem the lust of dominion a reason for war, and to imagine the greatest glory to be in the most extensive empire, it was then at length discovered, by proof and experience, that mental power has the greatest effect in military operation. And, indeed, if the intellectual ability of kings and magistrates were exerted to the same degree in peace as in war, human affairs would not see governments shifted from hand to hand, and things universally

Sallust, *The Conspiracy of Catiline.* In *Sallust, Florus, and Velleius Paterculus,* trans. John Selby Watson. London: Henry G. Bohn, 1852. Pp. 2–10.

changed and confused. For dominion is easily secured by those qualities by which it was at first obtained. But when sloth has introduced itself in the place of industry, and covetousness and pride in that of moderation and equity, the fortune of a state is altered together with its morals; and thus authority is always transferred from the less to the more deserving.

Even in agriculture, in navigation, and in architecture, whatever man performs owes the dominion of intellect. Yet many human beings, resigned to sensuality and indolence, uninstructed and unimproved, have passed through life like travellers in a strange country; to whom, certainly, contrary to the intention of nature, the body was a gratification, and the mind a burden. Of these I hold the life and death in equal estimation; for silence is maintained concerning both. But he only, indeed, seems to me to live, and to enjoy life, who, intent upon some employment, seeks reputation from some ennobling enterprise, or honourable pursuit.

But in the great abundance of occupations, nature points out different paths to different individuals. To act well for the Commonwealth is noble, and even to speak well for it is not without merit. Both in peace and in war it is possible to obtain celebrity; many who have acted, and many who have recorded the actions of others, receive their tribute of praise. And to me, assuredly, though by no means equal glory attends the narrator and the performer of illustrious deeds, it yet seems in the highest degree difficult to write the history of great transactions; first because deeds must be adequately represented by words; and next, because most readers consider that whatever errors you mention with censure, are mentioned through malevolence and envy; while, when you speak of the great virtue and glory of eminent men, every one hears with acquiescence only that which he himself thinks easy to be performed; all beyond his own conception he regards as fictitious and incredible.

I myself, however, when a young man, was at first led by inclination, like most others, to engage in political affairs; but in that pursuit many circumstances were unfavourable to me; for, instead of modesty, temperance, and integrity, there prevailed shamelessness, corruption, and rapacity. And although my mind, inexperienced in dishonest practices, detested these vices, yet, in the midst of so great corruption, my tender age was ensnared and infected by ambition; and, though I shrunk from the vicious principles of those around me, yet the same eagerness for honours, the same abloquy and jealousy, which disquieted others, disquieted myself.

When, therefore, my mind had rest from its numerous troubles and trials, and I had determined to pass the remainder of my days unconnected with public life, it was not my intention to waste my valuable leisure in indolence and inactivity, or, engaging in servile occupations, to spend my time in agriculture or hunting; but, returning to those studies from which, at their commencement, a corrupt ambition had allured me, I determined to write, in detached portions, the transactions of the Roman people, as any occurrence should seem worthy of mention; an undertaking to which I was the rather inclined, as my mind was uninfluenced by hope, fear, or political partisanship. I shall accordingly give a brief account, with as much truth as I can, of the Conspiracy of Catiline; for I think it an enterprise eminently deserving of record, from the unusual nature both of its guilt and of its perils. But before I enter upon my narrative, I must give a short description of the character of the man.

> 20. Cornelius TACITUS (A.D. 56–120), "greatest of the Roman historians," as Ronald Syme calls him, wrote on rhetoric (*Dialogue on Oratory*) before composing narrative surveys of imperial history—the *Annals,* which began with Augustus (A.D. 14), and the *Histories,* with Nero (A.D. 68)—and his seminal *Germany.* In these elegant narratives, Tacitus includes reflections on history, his passion for the Roman past and its senatorial traditions, his ironic and often critical view of the character and characters of the contemporary age (especially in contrast with the idealized republican past and the barbarian tribes). In various ways he reveals a sharp sense of time and temporal change. Like Livy, Tacitus became a historical and literary model in the Renaissance.

Assuredly, said Aper, I will not allow our age to be condemned, unheard and undefended, by this conspiracy of yours. First, however, I will ask you whom you call ancients, or what period of orators you limit by your definition? When I hear of ancients, I understand men of the past, born ages ago; I have in my eye Ulysses and Nestor, whose time is about thirteen hundred years before our day. But you bring forward Demosthenes and Hyperides who flourished, as we know, in the period of Philip and Alexander, a period, however, which they both outlived.

Tacitus, *Dialogue.* In *The Complete Works of Tacitus,* trans. Alfred John Church and William Jackson Brodribb. New York: Modern Library, 1942. P. 747.

Hence we see that not much more than four hundred years has intervened between our own era and that of Demosthenes. If you measure this space of time by the fraility of human life, it perhaps seems long; if by the course of the ages and by the thought of this boundless universe, it is extremely short and is very near us. For indeed, if, as Cicero says in his *Hortensius,* the great and the true year is that in which the position of the heavens and of the stars at any particular moment recurs, and if that year embraces twelve thousand nine hundred and ninety-four of what we call years, then your Demosthenes, whom you represent as so old and ancient, began his existence not only in the same year, but almost in the same month as ourselves.

But I pass to the Latin orators. Among them, it is not, I imagine, Menenius Agrippa, who may seem ancient, whom you usually prefer to the speakers of our day, but Cicero, Caelius, Calvus, Brutus, Asinius, Messala. Why you assign them to antiquity rather than to our own times, I do not see.

¶ Rome at the beginning was ruled by kings. Freedom and the consulship were established by Lucius Brutus. Dictatorships were held for a temporary crisis. The power of the decemvirs did not last beyond two years, nor was the consular jurisdiction of the military tribunes of long duration. The despotisms of Cinna and Sulla were brief; the rule of Pompeius and of Crassus soon yielded before Caesar; the arms of Lepidus and Antonius before Augustus; who, when the world was wearied by civil strife, subjected it to empire under the title of "Prince." But the successes and reverses of the old Roman people have been recorded by famous historians; and fine intellects were not wanting to describe the times of Augustus, till growing sycophancy scared them away. The histories of Tiberius, Caius, Claudius, and Nero, while they were in power, were falsified through terror, and after their death were written under the irritation of a recent hatred. Hence my purpose is to relate a few facts about Augustus—more particularly his last acts, then the reign of Tiberius, and all which follows, without either bitterness or partiality, from any motives to which I am far removed.

When after the destruction of Brutus and Cassius there was no longer

Tacitus, *Annals.* In *The Complete Works of Tacitus,* trans. Alfred John Church and William Jackson Brodribb. New York: Modern Library, 1942. Pp. 3–4, 5, 116–117, 131, and 162–163.

any army of the Commonwealth, when Pompeius was crushed in Sicily, and when, with Lepidus pushed aside and Antonius slain, even the Julian faction had only Caesar left to lead it, then, dropping the title of triumvir, and giving out that he was a consul, and was satisfied with a tribune's authority for the protection of the people, Augustus won over the soldiers with gifts, the populace with cheap corn, and all men with the sweets of repose, and so grew greater by degrees, while he concentrated in himself the functions of the Senate, the magistrates, and the laws. He was wholly unopposed, for the boldest spirits had fallen in battle, or in the proscription, while the remaining nobles, the readier they were to be slaves, were raised the higher by wealth and promotion, so that, aggrandised by revolution, they preferred the safety of the present to the dangerous past. Nor did the provinces dislike that condition of affairs, for they distrusted the government of the Senate and the people, because of the rivalries between the leading men and the rapacity of the officials, while the protection of the laws was unavailing, as they were continually deranged by violence, intrigue, and finally by corruption. . . . Thus the State had been revolutionised, and there was not a vestige left of the old sound morality.

Mankind in the earliest age lived for a time without a single vicious impulse, without shame or guilt, and, consequently, without punishment and restraints. Rewards were not needed when everything right was pursued on its own merits; and as men desired nothing against morality, they were debarred from nothing by fear. When, however, they began to throw off equality, and ambition and violence usurped the place of self-control and modesty, despotisms grew up and became perpetual among many nations. Some from the beginning, or when tired of kings, preferred codes of laws. These were at first simple, while men's minds were unsophisticated. The most famous of them were those of the Cretans, framed by Minos; those of the Spartans, by Lycurgus, and, subsequently, those which Solon drew up for the Athenians on a more elaborate and extensive scale. Romulus governed us as he pleased; then Numa united our people by religious ties and a constitution of divine origin, to which some additions were made by Tullus and Ancus. But Servius Tullius was our chief legislator, to whose laws even kings were to be subject.

After Tarquin's expulsion, the people, to check cabals among the Senators, devised many safeguards for freedom and for the establishment of unity. Decemvirs were appointed; everything specially admirable

elsewhere was adopted, and the Twelve Tables drawn up, the last specimen of equitable legislation. For subsequent enactments, though occasionally directed against evildoers for some crime, were oftener carried
by violence amid class dissensions, with a view to obtain honours not as
yet conceded, or to banish distinguished citizens, or for other base ends.
Hence the Gracchi and Saturnini, those popular agitators, and Drusus
too, as flagrant a corrupter in the Senate's name; hence, the bribing of
our allies by alluring promises and the cheating of them by tribunes
vetoes. Even the Italian and then the Civil wars did not pass without the
enactment of many conflicting laws, till Lucius Sulla, the Dictator, by
the repeal or alteration of past lesiglation and by many additions, gave us
a brief lull in this process, to be instantly followed by the seditious
proposals of Lepidus, and soon afterwards by the tribunes recovering
their license to excite the people just as they chose. And now bills were
passed, not only for national objects but for individual cases, and laws
were most numerous when the commonwealth was most corrupt. . . .

Why then in old times was economy in the ascendant? Because every
one practised self-control; because we were all members of one city. Nor
even afterwards had we the same temptations, while our dominion was
confined to Italy. Victories over the foreigner taught us how to waste the
substance of others; victories over ourselves, how to squander our own.
What a paltry matter is this of which the aediles are reminding us! What
a mere trifle if you look at everything else! No one represents to the
Senate that Italy requires supplies from abroad, and that the very existence of the people of Rome is daily at the mercy of uncertain waves and
storms. And unless masters, slaves, and estates have the resources of the
provinces as their mainstay, our shrubberies, forsooth, and our country
houses will have to support us. . . .

All nations and cities are ruled by the people, the nobility, or by one
man. A constitution, formed by selection out of these elements, it is easy
to commend but not to produce; or, if it is produced, it cannot be
lasting. Formerly, when the people had power or when the patricians
were in the ascendant, the popular temper and the methods of controlling it, had to be studied, and those who knew most accurately the spirit
of the Senate and aristocracy had the credit of understanding the age and
of being wise men. So now, after a revolution, when Rome is nothing
but the realm of a single despot, there must be good in carefully noting
and recording this period, for it is but few who have the foresight to
distinguish right from wrong or what is sound from what is hurtful,

while most men learn wisdom from the fortunes of others. Still, though this is instructive, it gives very little pleasure. Descriptions of countries, the various incidents of battles, glorious deaths of great generals enchain and refresh a reader's mind. I have to present in succession the merciless biddings of a tyrant, incessant prosecutions, faithless friendships, the ruin of innocence, the same causes issuing in the same results, and I am everywhere confronted by a wearisome monotony in my subject matter. Then again, an ancient historian has but few disparagers, and no one cares whether you praise more heartily the armies of Carthage or Rome. But of many who endured punishment or disgrace under Tiberius, the descendants yet survive; or even though the families themselves may be now extinct, you will find those who, from a resemblance of character, imagine that the evil deeds of others are a reproach to themselves. Again, even honour and virtue make enemies, condemning, as they do, their opposites by too close a contrast. But I return to my work.

¶ The Germans themselves I should regard as aboriginal, and not mixed at all with other races through immigration or intercourse. For, in former times, it was not by land but on shipboard that those who sought to emigrate would arrive; and the boundless and, so to speak, hostile ocean beyond us, is seldom entered by a sail from our world. And, beside the perils of rough and unknown seas, who would leave Asia, or Africa, or Italy for Germany, with its wild country, its inclement skies, its sullen manners and aspect, unless indeed it were his home? In their ancient songs, their only way of remembering or recording the past, they celebrate an earth-born god, Tuisco, and his son Mannus, as the origin of their race, as their founders. To Mannus they assign three sons, from whose names, they say, the coast tribes are called Ingaevones; those of the interior, Herminones; all the rest, Istaevones. Some, with the freedom of the conjecture permitted by antiquity, assert that the god had several descendants, and the nation several appellations, as Marsi, Gambrivii, Suevi, Vandilii, and that these are genuine old names. The name Germany, on the other hand, they say, is modern and newly introduced, from the fact that the tribes which first crossed the Rhine and drove out the Gauls, and are now called Tungrians, were then called Germans.

Tacitus, *Germany and Its Tribes*. In *The Complete Works of Tacitus*, trans. Alfred John Church and William Jackson Brodribb. New York: Modern Library, 1942. Pp. 709–710, 712–713, 714–715, 716–717, 718, 720, and 721.

Thus what was the name of a tribe, and not of a race, gradually prevailed, till all called themselves by this self-invented name of Germans, which the conquerors had first employed to inspire terror. . . .

For my own part, I agree with those who think that the tribes of Germany are free from all taint of intermarriages with foreign nations, and that they appear as a distant, unmixed race, like none but themselves. Hence, too, the same physical peculiarities throughout so vast a population. All have fierce blue eyes, red hair, huge frames, fit only for a sudden exertion. They are less able to bear laborious work. Heat and thirst they cannot in the least endure; to cold and hunger their climate and their soil inure them. . . .

They choose their kings by birth, their generals for merit. These kings have not unlimited or arbitrary power, and the generals do more by example than by authority. If they are energetic, if they are conspicuous, if they fight in the front, they lead because they are admired. But to reprimand, to imprison, even to flog, is permitted to the priests alone, and that not as a punishment, or at the general's bidding, but, as it were, by the mandate of the god whom they believe to inspire the warrior. They also carry with them into battle certain figures and images taken from their sacred groves. And what most stimulates their courage is, that their squadrons or battalions, instead of being formed by chance or by a fortuitous gathering, are composed of families and clans. Close by them, too, are those dearest to them, so that they hear the shrieks of women, the cries of infants. *They* are to every man the most sacred witnesses of his bravery—*they* are his most generous applauders. The soldier brings his wounds to mother and wife, who shrink not from counting or even demanding them and who administer both food and encouragement to the combatants.

Tradition says that armies already wavering and giving way have been rallied by women who, with earnest entreaties and bosoms laid bare, have vividly represented the horrors of captivity, which the Germans fear with such extreme dread on behalf of their women, that the strongest tie by which a state can be bound is the being required to give, among the number of hostages, maidens of noble birth. They even believe that the sex has a certain sanctity and prescience, and they do not despise their counsels, or make light of their answers. In Vespasian's days we saw Veleda, long regarded by many as a divinity. In former times, too, they venerated Aurinia, and many other women, but not with servile flatteries, or with sham deification. . . .

About minor matters the chiefs deliberate, about the most important the whole tribe. Yet even when the final decision rests with the people, the affair is always thoroughly discussed by the chiefs. They assemble, except in the case of a sudden emergency, on certain fixed days, either at new or at full moon; for this they consider the most auspicious season for the transaction of business. Instead of reckoning by days as we do, they reckon by nights, and in this manner fix both their ordinary and their legal appointments. Night they regard as bringing on day. Their freedom has this disadvantage, that they do not meet simultaneously or as they are bidden, but two or three days are wasted in the delays of assembling. When the multitude think proper, they sit down armed. Silence is proclaimed by the priests, who have on these occasions the right of keeping order. Then the king or the chief, according to age, birth, distinction in war, or eloquence, is heard, more because he has influence to persuade than because he has power to command. If his sentiments displease them, they reject them with murmurs; if they are satisfied, they brandish their spears. The most complimentary form of assent is to express approbation with their weapons.

In their councils an accusation may be preferred or a capital crime prosecuted. Penalties are distinguished according to the offence. Traitors and deserters are hanged on trees; the coward, the unwarlike, the man stained with abominable vices, is plunged into the mire of the morass, with a hurdle put over him. This distinction in punishment means that crime, they think, ought, in being punished, to be exposed, while infamy ought to be buried out of sight. Lighter offences, too, have penalties proportioned to them; he who is convicted, is fined in a certain number of horses or of cattle. Half of the fine is paid to the king or to the state, half to the person whose wrongs are avenged and to his relatives. In these same councils they also elect the chief magistrates, who administer law in the cantons and the towns. Each of those has a hundred associates chosen from the people, who support him with their advice and influence. . . .

It is well known that the nations of Germany have no cities, and they they do not even tolerate closely contiguous dwellings. They live scattered and apart, just as a spring, a meadow, or a wood has attracted them. Their villages they do not arrange in our fashion, with the buildings connected and joined together, but every person surrounds his dwelling with an open space, either as a precaution against the disasters of fire, or because they do not know how to build. No use is made by them of stone or tile; they employ timber for all purposes, rude masses without ornament or attractiveness. Some parts of their buildings they stain more carefully with a clay so clear and bright that it resembles painting, or a coloured design. They are wont also to dig out subterranean caves, and pile on them great heaps of dung, as a shelter from winter and as a receptacle for the year's produce, for by such places they mitigate the rigour of the cold. And should an enemy approach, he lays waste the open country, while what is hidden and buried is either not known to exist, or else escapes him from the very fact that it has to be searched for. . . .

Thus with their virtue protected they live uncorrupted by the allurements of public shows or the stimulant of feastings. Clandestine correspondence is equally unknown to men and women. Very rare for so numerous a population is adultery, the punishment for which is prompt, and in the husband's power. Having cut off the hair of the adulteress and stripped her naked, he expels her from the house in the presence of her kinsfolk, and then flogs her through the whole village. The loss of chastity meets with no indulgence; neither beauty, youth, nor wealth will procure the culprit a husband. No one in Germany laughs at vice, nor do they call it the fashion to corrupt and to be corrupted. Still better is the condition of those states in which only maidens are given in marriage, and where the hopes and expectations of a bride are then finally terminated. They receive one husband, as having one body and one life, that they may have no thoughts beyond, nor further-reaching desires, that they may love not so much the husband as the married state. To limit the number of their children or to destroy any of their subsequent offspring is accounted infamous, and good habits are here more effectual than good laws elsewhere. . . .

A race without either natural or acquired cunning, they disclose their hidden thoughts in the freedom of the festivity. Thus the sentiments of all having been discovered and laid bare, the discussion is renewed on the following day, and from each occasion its own peculiar advantage is derived. They deliberate when they have no power to dissemble; they resolve when error is impossible. . . .

In quenching their thirst they are not equally moderate. If you indulge their love of drinking by supplying them with as much as they desire, they will be overcome by their own vices as easily as by the arms of an enemy. . . .

Of lending money on interest and increasing it by compound interest they know nothing,—a more effectual safeguard than if it were prohibited.

❡ I begin my work with the time when Servius Galba was consul for the second time with Titus Vinius for his colleague. Of the former period, the 820 years dating from the founding of the city, many authors have treated; and while they had to record the transaction of the Roman people, they wrote with equal eloquence and freedom. After the conflict at Actium, and when it became essential to peace, that all power should be centered on one man, these great intellects passed away. Then too the truthfulness of history was impaired in many ways; at first, through men's ignorance of public affairs, which were now wholly strange to them, then, through their passion for flattery, or, on the other hand, their hatred of their masters. And so between the enmity of the one and the servility of the other, neither had any regard for posterity. But while we instinctively shrink from a writer's adulation, we lend a ready ear to detraction and spite, because flattery involves the shameful imputation of servility, whereas malignity wears the false appearance of honesty. I myself knew nothing of Galba, of Otho, or of Vitellius, either from benefits or from injuries. I would not deny that my elevation was begun by Vespasian, augmented by Titus, and still further advanced by Domitian; but those who profess inviolable truthfulness must speak of all without partiality and without hatred. I have reserved as an employment for my old age, should my life be long enough, a subject at once more fruitful and less anxious in the reign of the Divine Nerva and the empire of Trajan, enjoying the rare happiness of times, when we may think what we please, and express what we think.

I am entering on the history of a period rich in disasters, frightful in its wars, torn by civil strife, and even in peace full of horrors. Four emperors perished by the sword. There were three civil wars; there were more with foreign enemies; there were often wars that had both characters at once. There was success in the East, and disaster in the West. There were disturbances in Illyricum; Gaul wavered in its allegiance; Britain was thoroughly subdued and immediately abandoned; the tribes on the Suevi and the Sarmatae rose in concert against us; the Dacians had

Tacitus, *History.* In *The Complete Works of Tacitus,* trans. Alfred John Church and William Jackson Brodribb. New York: Modern Library, 1942. Pp. 419–421 and 659.

the glory of inflicting as well as suffering defeat; the armies of Parthia were all but set in motion by the cheat of a counterfeit Nero. Now too Italy was prostrated by disasters either entirely novel, or that recurred only after a long succession of ages; cities in Campania's richest plains were swallowed up and overwhelmed; Rome was wasted by conflagrations, its oldest temples consumed, and the Capitol itself fired by the hands of citizens. Sacred rites were profaned; there was profligacy in the highest ranks; the sea was crowded with exiles, and its rocks polluted with bloody deeds. In the capital there were yet worse horrors. Nobility, wealth, the refusal or the acceptance of office, were grounds for accusation, and virtue ensured destruction. The rewards of the informers were not less odious than their crimes; for while some seized on consulships and priestly offices, as their share of the spoil, others on procuratorships, and posts of more confidential authority, they robbed and ruined in every direction amid universal hatred and terror. Slaves were bribed to turn against their masters, and freedmen to betray their patrons; and those who had not an enemy were destroyed by friends.

Yet the age was not so barren in noble qualities, as not also to exhibit examples of virtue. Mothers accompanied the flight of their sons; wives followed their husbands into exile; there were brave kinsmen and faithful sons in law; there were slaves whose fidelity defied even torture; there were illustrious men driven to the last necessity, and enduring it with fortitude; there were closing scenes that equalled the famous deaths of antiquity. Besides the manifold vicissitudes of human affairs, there were prodigies in heaven and earth, the warning voices of the thunder, and other intimations of the future, auspicious or gloomy, doubtful or not to be mistaken. Never surely did more terrible calamities of the Roman People, or evidence more conclusive, prove that the Gods take no thought for our happiness, but only for our punishment.

I think it proper, however, before I commence my purposed work, to pass under review the condition of the capital, the temper of the armies, the attitude of the provinces, and the elements of weakness and strength which existed throughout the whole empire, that so we may become acquainted, not only with the vicissitudes and the issues of events, which are often matters of chance, but also with their relations and their causes. . . .

Moyses, wishing to secure for the future his authority over the nation, gave them a novel form of worship, opposed to all that is practised by other men. Things sacred with us, with them have no sanctity, while they allow what with us is forbidden. In their holy place they have consecrated an image of the animal by whose guidance they found deliverance from their long and thirsty wanderings. They slay the ram, seemingly in derision of Hammon, and they sacrifice the ox, because the Egyptians worship it as Apis. They abstain from swine's flesh, in consideration of what they suffered when they were infected by the leprosy to which this animal is liable. By their frequent fasts they still bear witness to the long hunger of former days. . . .

This worship, however introduced, is upheld by its antiquity; all their other customs, which are at once perverse and disgusting, owe their strength to their very badness. The most degraded out of other races, scorning their national beliefs, brought to them their contributions and presents. This augmented the wealth of the Jews, as also did the fact, that among themselves they are inflexibly honest and ever ready to shew compassion, though they regard the rest of mankind with all the hatred of enemies. They sit apart at meals, they sleep apart, and though, as a nation, they are singularly prone to lust, they abstain from intercourse with foreign women; among themselves nothing is unlawful.

> 21. AMMIANUS MARCELLINUS (ca. 330–400), continuing the work of Tacitus and ending the line of classical Roman historians, described Roman affairs down to the death of Valens in 378, celebrated the old institutions of empire and senate, and noted the appearance of Christianity in the Germanic nations. In the course of his narrative, he also sought lessons for the "quieter times" in which he wrote.

Now I think that some foreigners who will perhaps read this work (if I shall be so fortunate) may wonder why it is that when the narrative turns to the description of what goes on at Rome, I tell of nothing save dissensions, taverns, and other similar vulgarities. Accordingly, I shall briefly touch upon the reasons, intending nowhere to depart intentionally from the truth.

At the time when Rome first began to rise into a position of worldwide splendour, destined to live so long as men shall exist, in order that

Ammianus Marcellinus, *History,* trans. John C. Rolfe. Loeb Classical Library. 1 : 37–39, 45, 47, 49, and 53; 3 : 381–387. Reprinted by permission of the publishers and the Loeb Classical Library from Ammianus Marcellinus, Volumes 1 and 3, trans. John C. Rolfe, Cambridge, Mass.: Harvard University Press, Volume 1, 1935, revised 1950; Volume 3, 1939.

she might grow to a towering stature, Virtue and Fortune, ordinarily at variance, formed a pact of eternal peace; for if either one of them had failed her, Rome had not come to complete supremacy. Her people, from the very cradle to the end of their childhood, a period of about three hundred years, carried on wars about her walls. Then, entering upon adult life, after many toilsome wars, they crossed the Alps and the sea. Raised to manly vigour, from every region which the vast globe includes, they brought back laurels and triumphs. And now, declining into old age, and often owing victory to its name alone, it has come to a quieter period of life. Thus the venerable city, after humbling the proud necks of savage nations, and making laws, the everlasting foundations and moorings of liberty, like a thrifty parent, wise and wealthy, has entrusted the management of her inheritance to the Caesars, as to her children. And although for some time the tribes have been inactive and the centuries at peace, and there are no contests for votes but the tranquillity of Numa's time has returned, yet throughout all regions and parts of the earth she is looked up to as mistress and queen; everywhere the white hair of the senators and their authority is respected and honoured.

But this magnificence and splendour of the assemblies is marred by the rude worthlessness of a few, who do not consider where they were born, but, as if licence were granted to vice, descend to sin and wantonness. For as the lyric poet Simonides tells us, one who is going to live happy and in accord with perfect reason ought above all else to have a glorious fatherland. Some of these men eagerly strive for statues, thinking that by them they can be made immortal, as if they would gain a greater reward from senseless brazen images than from the consciousness of honourable and virtuous conduct. . . .

I pass over the gluttonous banquets and the various allurements of pleasures, lest I should go too far, and I shall pass to the fact that certain persons hasten without fear of danger through the broad streets of the city and over the upturned stones of the pavements as if they were driving post-horses with hoofs of fire (as the saying is), dragging after them armies of slaves like bands of brigands and not leaving even Sannio at home, as the comic writer says. And many matrons, imitating them, rush about through all quarters of the city with covered heads and in closed litters. . . .

In consequence of this state of things, the few houses that were formerly famed for devotion to serious pursuits now teem with the sports of sluggish indolence, re-echoing to the sound of singing and the tinkling of flutes and lyres. In short, in place of the philosopher the singer is called in, and in place of the orator the teacher of stagecraft, and while the libraries are shut up forever like tombs, water-organs are manufactured and lyres as large as carriages, and flutes and huge instruments for gesticulating actors. . . .

There is no doubt that when once upon a time Rome was the abode of all the virtues, many of the nobles detained here foreigners of free birth by many kindly attentions, as the Lotus-eaters of Homer did by the sweetness of their fruits. But now the vain arrogance of some men regard everything born outside the pomerium [the space on each side of the walls] of our city as worthless, except the childless and unwedded. . . .

And it is most remarkable to see an innumerable crowd of plebians, their minds filled with a kind of eagerness, hanging on the outcome of the chariot races. These and similar things prevent anything memorable or serious from being done in Rome. Accordingly, I must return to my subject. . . .

However, the seed and origin of all the ruin and various disasters that the wrath of Mars aroused, putting in turmoil all places with unwonted fires, we have found to be this. The people of the Huns, but little known from ancient records, dwelling beyond the Maeotic Sea near the ice-bound ocean, exceed every degree of savagery. Since there the cheeks of the children are deeply furrowed with the steel from their very birth, in order that the growth of hair when it appears at the proper time, may be checked by the wrinkled scars, they grow old without beards and without any beauty, like eunuchs. They all have compact, strong limbs and thick necks, and are so monstrously ugly and misshapen, that one might take them for two-legged beasts or for the stumps, rough-hewn into images, that are used in putting sides to bridges. But although they have the form of men, however ugly, they are so hardy in their mode of life that they have no need of fire nor of savory food, but eat the roots of wild plants and the half-raw flesh of any kind of animal whatever, which they put between their thighs and the backs of their horses, and thus warm it a little. They are never protected by any buildings, but they avoid these like tombs, which are set apart from everyday use. For not even a hut thatched with reed can be found among them. But roaming at large amid the mountains and woods, they learn from the cradle to endure cold, hunger, and thirst. When away from their homes they never enter a house unless compelled by extreme necessity; for they think they are not safe when staying under a roof. They dress in linen cloth or in the skins of field-mice sewn together, and they wear the same clothing indoors and out. But when they have once put their necks into a faded tunic, it is not taken off or changed until by long wear and tear it has been reduced to rags and fallen from them bit by bit. They cover their heads with round caps and protect their hairy legs with goatskins; their shoes are formed upon no lasts, and so prevent their walking with free step. For this reason they are not at all adapted to battles on foot, but they are almost glued to their horses, which are hardy, it is true, but ugly, and sometimes they sit them woman-fashion and thus perform their ordinary tasks. From their horses by night or day every one of that nation buys and sells, eats and drinks, and bowed over the narrow neck of the animal relaxes into a sleep so deep as to be accompanied by many dreams. And when deliberation is called for about weighty matters, they all consult as a common body in that fashion. They are subject to no royal restraint, but they are content with the disorderly government of their important men, and led by them they force their way through every obstacle. They also sometimes fight when provoked, and they enter the battle drawn up in wedge-shaped masses, while their medley of voices makes a savage noise. And as they are lightly equipped for swift motion, and unexpected in action, they purposely divide suddenly into scattered bands and attack, rushing about in disorder here and there, dealing terrific slaughter; and because of their extraordinary rapidity of movement they are never seen to attack a rampart or pillage an enemy's camp. And on this account you would not hesitate to call them the most terrible of all warriors, because they fight from a distance with missiles having sharp bone, instead of their usual points, joined to the shafts with wonderful skill; then they gallop over the intervening spaces and fight hand to hand with swords, regardless of their own lives; and while the enemy are guarding against wounds from the sabre-thrusts, they throw strips of cloth plaited into nooses over their opponents and so entangle them that they fetter their limbs and take from them the power of riding or walking. No one in their country ever plows a field or touches a plowhandle. They are all without fixed abode, without hearth, or law, or settled mode of life, and keep roaming from place to place, like fugitives, accompanied by the wagons in which they live; in wagons their wives weave for them their hideous garments, in wagons they cohabit with their husbands, bear children, and rear them to the age of puberty. None of their offspring, when asked, can tell you where he comes from, since he was conceived in one place, born far from there, and brought up still farther away. In truces they are faithless and unreliable, strongly inclined to sway to the motion of every breeze of new hope that presents itself, and sacrificing every feeling to the mad impulse of the moment. Like unreasoning beasts, they are utterly ignorant of the difference between right and wrong; they are deceitful and ambiguous in speech, never bound by any reverence for religion or for superstition. They burn with an infinite thirst for gold, and they are so fickle and prone to anger, that they often quarrel with their allies without provocation, more than once on the same day, and make friends with them again without a mediator.

This race of untamed men, without encumbrances, aflame with an inhuman desire for plundering others' property, made their violent way amid the rapine and slaughter of the neighbouring peoples as far as the Halani, once known as the Massagetae.

❡ BYZANTINE EXTENSIONS

> 22. JUSTINIAN (483–565), Byzantine emperor from 527 to 565, carried out a massive project of codifying Roman law; in his prefatory constitutions to the great anthology of classical jurisprudence called the *Digest,* or *Pandects* (533), he expressed the historical significance of his undertaking and of his imperial authority.

[Deo auctore]

Governing under the authority of God our empire which was delivered to us by the Heavenly Majesty, we both conduct wars successfully and render peace honorable, and we uphold the condition of the state. We so lift our minds toward the help of the omnipotent God that we do not place our trust in weapons or our soldiers or our military leaders or our own talents, but we rest all our hopes in the providence of the Supreme Trinity alone, from whence the elements of the whole world proceeded and their disposition throughout the universe was derived. Whereas, then, nothing in any sphere is found so worthy of study as the authority of law, which sets in good order affairs both divine and human and casts out all injustice, yet we have found the whole extent of our laws which has come down from the foundation of the city of Rome and the days of

Justinian, *Digest.* In *The Digest of Justinian,* ed. Theodor Mommsen with Paul Krueger and trans. Alan Watson. Philadelphia: University of Pennsylvania Press, 1985. 1:xlvi, xlviii, lv, and lxii–lxiii.

Romulus to be so confused that it extends to an inordinate length and is beyond the comprehension of any human nature. It has been our primary endeavor to make a beginning with the most revered emperors of earlier times, to free their *constitutiones* (enactments) from faults and set them out in a clear fashion, so that they might be collected together in one *Codex,* and that they might afford to all mankind the ready protection of their own integrity, purged of all unnecessary repetition and most harmful disagreement. This work has been accomplished and collected in a single volume under our own glorious name. In our haste to extricate ourselves from minor and more trivial affairs and attain to a completely full revision of the lay, and to collect and amend the whole set of Roman ordinances and present the diverse books of so many authors in a single volume (a thing which no one has dared to expect or to desire), the task appeared to us most difficult, indeed impossible. Nevertheless, with our hands stretched up to heaven, and imploring eternal aid, we stored up this task too in our mind, relying upon God, who in the magnitude of his goodness is able to sanction and to consummate achievements that are utterly beyond hope. . . . Again, if any laws included in the old books have by now fallen into disuse, we by no means allow you to set them down, since we wish only those rules to remain valid which have either had effect in the regular course of the judicature or which the long-established custom of this generous city has sanctioned, in accordance with the text by Salvius Julian, pointing out that all *civitates* (states) ought to follow the custom of Rome, the very head of the world, and not Rome that of other *civitates* (states). And by Rome we must understand not only the old city but also our royal one, which, with the favor of God, was founded with the best auguries.

[Tanta]

So great is the providence of the Divine Humanity toward us that it ever deigns to sustain us with acts of eternal generosity. For after the Parthian wars were stilled in everlasting peace, after the Vandal nation was done away with and Carthage—nay rather, the whole of Libya—was once more received into the Roman empire, the Divine Humanity contrived that the ancient laws, already encumbered with old age, should through our vigilant care achieve a new elegance and a moderate compass, a result which no one before our reign ever hoped for or deemed to be at all possible by human ingenuity. Indeed, when Roman jurisprudence had lasted for nearly fourteen hundred years from the foundation of the city to the period of our own rule, wavering this way and that in strife within itself and spreading the same inconsistency into the imperial *constitutiones,* it was a marvelous feat to reduce it to a single harmonious whole, so that nothing should be found in it which was contradictory or identical or repetitious, and that two different laws on a particular matter should nowhere appear. Now for the Heavenly Providence this was certainly appropriate, but for human weakness in no way possible. We, therefore, in our accustomed manner, have resorted to the aid of the Immortal One and, invoking the Supreme Deity, have desired that God should become the author and patron of the whole work. . . . Now there is one thing which we decided from the outset, when with divine approval we commissioned the execution of this work, and it seems opportune to us to ordain it now also: that no one, of those who are skilled in the law at the present day or shall be hereafter, may dare to append any commentary to these laws, save only insofar as he may wish to translate them into the Greek language in the same order and sequence as those in which the Roman words are written (*kata poda,* as the Greeks call it); and if perhaps he prefers to make notes on difficulties in certain passages, he may also compose what are caller *paratitla*. But we do not permit them to put forward other interpretations—or rather, perversions—of the laws, for fear lest their verbosity may cause such confusion in our legislation as to bring some discredit upon it. This happened also in the case of the commentators on the Perpetual Edict, who, although the compass of that work was moderate, extended it this way and that to diverse conclusions and drew it out to an inordinate length, in such a way as to bring almost the whole Roman legal system into confusion. If we have not put up with them, how far can vain disputes be allowed in the future?

> 23. PROCOPIUS (ca. 490–575) was Emperor Justinian's court historian. Trained in law and experienced in government, he was secretary for a time to Belisarius and traveled widely. As a historian, he followed both Herodotus (in his geographic digressions) and Thucydides (in style). Procopius expressed his formal ideas of

Procopius, *History of the Wars,* trans. B. H. Dewing. Loeb Classical Library. 1 : 3–5. Reprinted by permission of the publishers and the Loeb Classical Library from Procopius, Volume 1, trans. B. H. Dewing, Cambridge, Mass.: Harvard University Press, 1914.

history in his *History of the Wars.* He recorded more amusing and scandalous private observations and opinions of Emperor Justinian and Empress Theodora in his *Secret History,* a classic of muckraking history.

Procopius of Caesarea has written the history of the wars which Justinian, Emperor of the Romans, waged against the barbarians of the East and of the West, relating separately the events of each one, to the end that the long course of time may not overwhelm deeds of singular importance through lack of a record, and thus abandon them to oblivion and utterly obliterate them. The memory of these events he deemed would be a great thing and most helpful to men of the present time, and to future generations as well, in case time should ever again place men under a similar stress. For men who purpose to enter upon a war or are preparing themselves for any kind of struggle may derive some benefit from a narrative of a similar situation in history, inasmuch as this discloses the final result attained by men of an earlier day in a struggle of the same sort, and foreshadows, at least for those who are most prudent in planning, what outcome present events will probably have. Furthermore he had assurance that he was especially competent to write the history of these events, if for no other reason, because it fell to his lot, when appointed adviser to the general Belisarius, to be an eye-witness of practically all the events to be described. It was his conviction that while cleverness is appropriate to rhetoric, and inventiveness to poetry, truth alone is appropriate to history. In accordance with this principle he has not concealed the failures of even his most intimate acquaintances, but has written down with complete accuracy everything which befell those concerned, whether it happened to be done well or ill by them.

It will be evident that no more important or mightier deeds are to be found in history than those which have been enacted in these wars,— provided one wishes to base his judgment on the truth. For in them more remarkable feats have been performed than in any other wars with which we are acquainted; unless, indeed, any reader of this narrative should give the place of honour to antiquity, and consider contemporary achievements unworthy to be counted remarkable.

¶ Foreword: The Purpose of this Book. In recording everything that the Roman people has experienced in successive wars up to the time of writ-

Procopius, *The Secret History.* Trans. G. A. Williamson. Penguin Classics. Baltimore: Penguin, 1966. Pp. 37–39, 94, 111, and 192–194.

ing I have followed this plan—that of arranging all the events described as far as possible in accordance with the actual times and places. But from now on I shall no longer keep to that method: in this volume I shall set down every single thing that has happened anywhere in the Roman Empire. The reason is simple. As long as those responsible for what happened were still alive, it was out of the question to tell the story in the way that it deserved. For it was impossible to avoid detection by swarms of spies, or if caught to escape death in its most agonizing form. Indeed, even in the company of my nearest relations I felt far from safe. Then again, in the case of many events which in my earlier volumes I did venture to relate I dared not reveal the reasons for what happened. So in this part of my work I feel it my duty to reveal both the events hitherto passed over in silence and the reasons for the events already described.

But as I embark on a new understanding of a difficult and extraordinarily baffling character, concerned as it is with Justinian and Theodora and the lives they lived, my teeth chatter and I find myself recoiling as far as possible from the task; for I envisage the probability that what I am now about to write will appear incredible and unconvincing to future generations. And again, when in the long course of time the story seems to belong to a rather distant past, I am afraid that I shall be regarded as a mere teller of fairy tales or listed among the tragic poets. One thing, however, gives me confidence to shoulder my heavy task without flinching: my account has no lack of witnesses to vouch for its truth. For my own contemporaries are witnesses fully acquainted with the incidents described, and will pass on to future ages an incontrovertible conviction that these have been faithfully recorded.

And yet there was something else which, when I was all agog to get to work on this volume, again and again held me back for weeks on end. For I inclined to the view that the happiness of our grandchildren would be endangered by my revelations, since it is the deeds of blackest dye that stand in greatest need of being concealed from future generations, rather than they should come to the ears of monarchs as an example to be imitated. For most men in positions of power invariably, through sheer ignorance, slip readily into imitation of their predecessors' vices, and it is to the misdeeds of earlier rulers that they invariably find it easier and less troublesome to turn. But later on I was encouraged to write the story of these events by this reflexion—it will surely be evident to future monarchs that the penalty of their misdeeds is almost certain to overtake them, just as it fell upon the persons described in this book. Then again, their own conduct and character will in turn be recorded for all time; and that will perhaps make them less ready to transgress. For how could the licentious like of Semiramis or the dementia of Sardanaplaus and Nero have been known to anyone in later days, if contemporary historians had not left these things on record? Apart from this, those who in the future, if so it happens, are similarly ill used by the ruling powers will not find this record altogether useless; for it is always comforting for those in distress to know that they are the only ones on whom these blows have fallen.

That is my justification for first recounting the contemptible conduct of Belisarius, and then revealing the equally contemptible conduct of Justinian and Theodora. . . .

Justinian's Misgovernment. When Justinian ascended the throne it took him a very little while to bring everything into confusion. Things hitherto forbidden by law were one by one brought into public life, while established customs were swept away wholesale, as if he had been invested with the forms of majesty on condition that he would change all things to new forms. Long established offices were abolished, and new ones set up to run the nation's business; the laws of the land and the organization of the army were treated in the same way, not because justice required it or the general interest urged him to it, but merely that everything might have a new look and might be associated with his name. If there was anything which he was not in a position to transform then and there, even so he would at least attach his own name to it.

Of the forcible seizure of property and the murder of his subjects he could never have enough: when he had looted innumerable houses of wealthy people he was constantly on the look-out for others, immediately squandering on one foreign tribe or another, or on crazy building schemes, all that he had amassed by his earlier looting. And when he had without any excuse got rid of thousands and thousands of people, or so it would seem, he promptly devised schemes for doing the same to others more numerous still. . . .

Frequently matters agreed between Senate and Emperor ended by being settled quite differently. The Senate sat merely as a picturesque survival, without any power either to register a decision or to do any good, assembling for the sake of appearance and in fulfillment of an old law, since no member of that assembly was ever permitted to utter one word. The Emperor and his consort for the most part made a show of taking sides in the questions at issue, but victory went to the side upon which they had already agreed. If a man had broken the law and felt that victory was not securely his, he had only to fling more gold to this Emperor in order to obtain the passage of a law going clean contrary to all existing statutes. Then if somebody else should call for the first law, which had now been repealed, His Majesty was perfectly prepared to re-enact it and substitute it for the new one. There was nothing that re-mained permanently in force, but the scales of justice wandered at ran-dom all over the place, whichever way the greater mass of gold weighing them down succeeded in pulling them. The home of justice was the market-hall, though it had once been the Palace, and there sale-rooms flaunted themselves in which not only the administration of justice by the making of laws too was sold to the highest bidder. . . .

The Arrogance of the Imperial Pair. Among the innovations which Justi-nian and Theodora made in the conduct of official business are the following.

In previous reigns, when the Senate came into the Emperor's presence it was customary to pay homage in this way. A man of patrician rank used to salute him on the right breast: the Emperor responded by kissing him on the head, and then dismissed him. Everyone else bent his right knee to the Emperor and then retired. To the Empress, however, homage was never paid. But when they came into the presence of Justin-ian and Theodora all of them, including those who held patrician rank, had to fall on the floor flat on their faces, stretch out their hands and feet as far as they could, touch with their lips one foot of each of Their Majesties, and then stand up again. For Theodora too insisted on this tribute being paid to her, and even claimed the privilege of receiving the ambassadors of Persia and other foreign countries and of bestowing gifts of money on them, as if she were mistress of the Roman Empire—a thing unprecedented in the whole course of history.

Again, in the past persons engaged in conversation with the Emperor called him "Emperor" and his wife "Empress," and addressed each of their ministers by the title appropriate to the rank he held at the mo-ment; but if anyone were to join in conversation with either of these two and refer to the "Emperor" or "Empress" and not call them "Master" and "Mistress," or attempted to speak of any of the ministers as anything but "slaves," he was regarded as ignorant and impertinent; and as if he had committed a shocking offence and had deliberately insulted the last per-son who should have been so treated, he was sent packing.

[W]hile in earlier reigns few visited the Palace, and they on rare occa-sions, from the day that these two ascended the throne officials and people of every sort spent their days in the Palace with hardly a break. The reason was that in the old days the officials were allowed to do what was just and proper in accordance with their individual judgements; this meant that while carrying out their official duties they stayed in their own offices, while the Emperor's subjects, neither seeing nor hearing of any resort to force, naturally troubled him very rarely. These two, however, all the time taking everything into their own hands to the detriment of their subjects, compelled everyone to be in constant attendance exactly like slaves. Almost any day one could see all the law-courts pretty well deserted, and at the Emperor's Court an insolent crowd, elbowing and shoving, and all the time displaying the most abject servility. Those who were supposed to be close friends of Their Majesties stood there right through the whole day and invariably for a considerable part of the night, getting no sleep or food at the normal times, till they were worn out completely: this was all that their supposed good fortune brought them.

When, however, they were released from all their misery, the poor wretches engaged in bitter quarrels as to where the wealth of the Romans had gone to. Some insisted that foreigners had got it all; others declared that the Emperor kept it locked up in a number of small chambers.

One of these days Justinian, if he is a man, will depart this life: if he is Lord of the Demons, he will lay his life aside.

Then all who chance to be still living will know the truth.

> 24. THEOPHYLACT SIMOCATTA (d. after 640), a native of Egypt, wrote a *History* of the Emperor Maurice (582–602), which describes the Byzantine wars in the Balkans and with Persia in the east and affairs in Constantinople as well as the character and religious life of the emperor. In the precious and allusive dialogue prefacing this work, he suggests the services which history can perform for Queen Philosophy.

Philosophy [speaks]. What is this, daughter? Come now, resolve this dilemma for me, since I am eager to learn, with the clarity that like a thread traverses a labyrinth which is not mythical. For I find the preliminaries of the investigation difficult to approach and hard to pursue.

History [answers]. O Philosophy, queen of all—if indeed it is proper

Theophylact Simocatta, *History.* In *The History of Theophylact Simocatta,* trans. Michael Whitby and Mark Whitby. Oxford: Clarendon Press, 1986. Pp. 3–5.

to learn from me and for you to be taught—I will answer to the best of my understanding, for "may I keep nothing fair unknown": this is my opinion as well as the Cyrenian's.

Philosophy. Gladly would I ask, daughter, by what means and how it was that only the other day you returned to life. But the great seductiveness of disbelief checks us from speech again and, as if with a bridle, restrains us to silence, lest perchance an apparition of wonders should be beguiling us. For, my child, you were long dead, ever since the steel-encircled Calydonian tyrant entered the royal court, a barbarian mongrel of the Cyclopean breed, the Centaur, who most brutally ravaged the chaste purple, for whom monarchy was a feat of wine-swilling. I will keep silent about the rest, out of respect for my own decorum and for the dignity of the audience. I too, my daughter, was ostracized then from the royal colonnade, and could not enter Attica at the time when that Thracian Anytus destroyed Socrates my king. But subsequently the Heraclidae saved and restored the state, exorcized the pollution from the palaces, and indeed settled in the royal precincts. I celebrate the royal courts and compose these antique Attic hymns. For me indeed this is the source of prosperity; but as for you, my daughter, who was your saviour and how were you saved?

History. My queen, do you not know the great high priest and prelate of the universal inhabited world?

Philosophy. Certainly I do, my daughter; this man is my oldest friend and most familiar treasure.

History. Assuredly, my queen, you have at hand the godsend you were seeking. That man brought me to life, raising me up, as it were, from a tomb of neglect, as though he were resurrecting an Alcestis with the strength of an evil-averting Heracles. He generously adopted me, clad me in gleaming raiment, and adorned me with a gold necklace. This chignon of mine—look, a golden grasshopper is sitting upon it—was glorified and made resplendent in the present congregation by this holy man, who provided an advantageously sited rostrum and unthreatened freedom of speech.

Philosophy. My daughter, I admire the hierophant for his magnanimity, and for the great ascent of good deeds he has mounted; he sits on the lofty summit of divine wisdom and makes his abode on the peak of the virtues. He clings to terrestrial excellence, and the all-perfect words are life to him, for he does not wish even the earthly order to remain disordered. May I thus profit my devotees. Either he lives as an incorporeal philosopher on earth, or he is the incarnation of contemplation dwelling as a man among men.

History. My queen, excellently indeed have you woven the garland of praises. But, if you agree, sit awhile by this plane here; for the tree is wide-spreading, and the height and shade of the chaste willow are most attractive.

Philosophy. Lead on then, my child, and insert a proem like a starting-line to your account for your attentive audience. I will fix my mind on you, just like an Ithacan, with unstopped ears, and I will listen to Sirens' tales.

History. Accordingly, I will obey your command, my queen, and will stir the lyre of history. May you be for me a most musical plectrum, for you are an Ocean of knowledge and a Tethys of words, and in you is every grace, like an island in the garland of a boundless sea.

> 25. ANNA COMNENA (1083–1148?) continued the work of her husband Nicephorus Bryennius on the life of her father, the emperor Alexius (1081–1118), in her ornate epic, *The Alexiad.* On the basis of oral as well as documentary sources, she surveys the First Crusade (to which she was an eyewitness), the Byzantine triumph, and the Comnenian revival of her father's reign. Her highly stylized and personal view of history is suggested in the preface to this work.

The stream of Time, irresistible, ever moving, carries off and bears away all things that come to birth and plunges them into utter darkness, both deeds of no account and deeds which are mighty and worthy of commemoration; as the playwright says, it "brings to light that which was unseen and shrouds from us that which was manifest." Nevertheless, the science of History is a great bulwark against this stream of Time; in a way it checks this irresistible flood, it holds in a tight grasp whatever it can seize floating on the surface and will not allow it to slip away into the depths of Oblivion.

I, Anne, daughter of the Emperor Alexius and the Empress Irene, born and bred in the Purple, not without some acquaintance with literature—having devoted the most earnest study to the Greek language, in fact, and being not unpractised in Rhetoric and having read thoroughly

Anna Comnena, *The Alexiad.* In *The Alexiad of Anna Comnena,* trans. E. R. A. Sewter. New York: Penguin, 1969. Pp. 17–20.

the treatises of Aristotle and the dialogues of Plato, and having fortified my mind with the Quadrivium of sciences (these things must be divulged, and it is not self-advertisement to recall what Nature and my own zeal for knowledge have given me, nor what God has apportioned to me from above and what has been contributed by Opportunity); I, having realized the effects wrought by Time, desire now by means of my writings to give an account of my father's deeds, which do not deserve to be consigned to Forgetfulness nor to be swept away on the flood of time into an ocean of Non-Remembrance; I wish to recall everything, the achievements before his elevation to the throne and his actions in the service of others before his coronation.

I approach the task with no intention of flaunting my skill as a writer; my concern is rather that a career so brilliant should not go unrecorded in the future, since even the greatest exploits, unless by some chance their memory is preserved and guarded in history, vanish in silent darkness. My father's actions themselves prove his ability as a ruler and show, too, that he was prepared to submit to authority, within just limits.

Now that I have decided to write the story of his life, I am fearful of an underlying suspicion: someone might conclude that in composing the history of my father I am glorifying myself; the history, wherever I express admiration for any act of his, may seem wholly false and mere panegyric. One the other hand, if he himself should ever lead me, under the compulsion of events, to criticize some action taken by him, not because of what he decided but because of the circumstances, here again I fear the cavillers: in their all-embracing jealousy and refusal to accept what is right, because they are malicious and full of envy, they may cast in my teeth the story of Noah's son Ham and, as Homer says, "blame the guiltless."

Whenever one assumes the role of historian, friendship and enmities have to be forgotten; often one has to bestow on adversaries the highest commendation (where their deeds merit it); often, too, one's nearest relatives, if their pursuits are in error and suggest the desirability of reproach, have to be censured. The historian, therefore, must shirk neither remonstrance with his friends, nor praise of his enemies. For my part, I hope to satisfy both parties, both those who are offended by us and those who accept us, by appealing to the evidence of the actual events and of eye-witnesses. The fathers and grandfathers of some men living today saw these things.

The main reason why I have to write the account of my father's deeds is this: I was the lawful wife of Caesar Nicephorus, who was descended from the Bryennii, an extremely handsome man, very intelligent, and in the precise use of words far superior to his contemporaries. To see and hear him was indeed an extraordinary experience. For the moment, however, let us concentrate on what happened afterwards, lest the story should digress. My husband, the most outstanding man of the time, went on campaign with my brother, the Emperor John, when he (John) led an army against other barbarians and also when he set out against the Syrians and again reduced the city of Antioch. Even in the midst of these wearing exertions the Caesar could not neglect his writing and, among other compositions worthy of honourable mention, he chose in particular to write the history of the Emperor Alexius, my father (on the orders of the empress), and to record the events of his reign in several books, when a brief lull in the warfare gave him the chance to turn his attention to historical and literary research. He did indeed begin the history—and in this, too, he yielded to the wishes of our empress—with references to the period before Alexius, starting with the Roman emperor Diogenes and carrying it down to the times of his original subject. In Diogenes' reign my father was only a youth; he had done nothing worthy of note, unless childhood doings are also to be made the object of encomium.

The Caesar's plan was such as I have described; his writings make that clear. However, he was disappointed in his hopes and the history was not completed. After carrying on the account to the times of the Emperor Nicephorus Botaniates he stopped writing because circumstances prevented any further progress, to the detriment of the history itself and the sorrow of its readers. That is why I have chosen to record the full story of my father's deeds myself, so that future generations may not be deprived of knowledge about them.

4

¶ The Judeo-Christian Tradition

The biblical view of history and the tradition established by later commentators contrasted in many ways with classical theory and practice. Surveying Jewish antiquity, Josephus was openly scornful of Greek credulity and apparent lack of historical sense, and Christian authors continued this criticism. Yet in constructing a Judeo-Christian tradition, historians and scholars of late antiquity had to come to terms with classical culture and conceptualization as well as the oriental background of Greco-Roman tradition. Indeed, the attempts at reconciliation between paganism and Christianity created the framework of historical thought and writing from the late imperial period to early modern times.

This reconciliation took place on two primary fronts. One centered on the problem of interpretation, beginning with the original historical sense (*sensus historicus*)—which signified literal meaning and in effect historical accuracy—and going on to various figurative constructions later codified in the patristic three- or fourfold theory of interpretation. From the time of Saint Paul, there was a tension between interpretation according to the deadening letter and that according to the life-giving spirit, but both modes contributed to historical thought and to the tradition of hermeneutics. On the one hand, allegorical (or moral, or tropological) interpretation made it possible to accommodate pagan or Jewish experience by regarding it as prefiguring or preparing the way for the Christian Word; on the other hand, the quest for the true meaning of historical experience continued to be basic to more speculative interpretation.

The second point of confrontation between Christianity and classical culture concerned the problem of chronology, which again linked ancient and modern scholarship. Here the central problem was synchronizing Old Testament genealogies and kings with classical reckoning of historical periods, though of course the major premise hinged on the dating of creation. This universal-chronicle tradition took recognizable shape in the work of Eusebius and was continued by Saint Jerome and a long series of extraordinarily repetitive Christian chroniclers down to the Renaissance.

Constructing the Christian perspective on history was the work above all both of Eusebius, who established the basic chronology and argued for the implicit or spiritual antiquity of Christian tradition, and of Saint Augustine, who created a providential view of history out of scriptural material and Christian Neoplatonism, and whose disciple Orosius wrote a history based on Augustinian principles and periodization. As the Augustinian perspective had a divine beginning, so, too, it had a final goal in divine judgment; most historians assumed this view of human origins and destiny. Later medieval chroniclers worked largely within the framework and premises of these patristic founders of Christian historiography, and modern historians struggled with these powerful ideas, which in human terms provided the most basic justification of ecclesiastical tradition, its historical mission, and its prophetic vision.

❡ HISTORICAL MISSION

26. DANIEL (whoever he was, the name referring to the hero of the lion's den) described the most celebrated of all apocalyptic visions, both his own and the dream of Nebuchadnezzar. It formed the basis of the famous four monarchies theory, which for Daniel probably meant the Babylonians, Medes, Persians, and Macedonians, but which interpreters took to indicate the Medes, Persians, Greeks, and Romans.

Thou, O king, sawest, and behold a great image. This great image, whose brightness *was* excellent, stood before thee; and the form thereof *was* terrible.

This image's head *was* of fine gold, his breast and his arms of silver, his belly and his thighs of brass,

Daniel 2:31–40 and 7:1–7, 12–19, 23–28 (King James Version).

His legs of iron, his feet part of iron and part of clay.

Thou sawest till that a stone was cut out without hands, which smote the image upon his feet *that were* of iron and clay, and brake them to pieces.

Then was the iron, the clay, the brass, the silver, and the gold, broken to pieces together, and became like the chaff of the summer threshing floors; and the wind carried them away, that no place was found for them; and the stone that smote the image became a great mountain, and filled the whole earth.

This *is* the dream; and we will tell the interpretation thereof before the king.

Thou, O king, *art* a king of kings; for the God of heaven hath given thee a kingdom, power, and strength, and glory.

And wheresoever the children of men dwell, the beasts of the field and the fowls of the heaven hath he given into thine hand, and hath made thee ruler over them all. Thou *art* this head of gold.

And after thee shall rise another kingdom inferior to thee, and another third kingdom of brass, which shall bear rule over all the earth.

And the fourth kingdom shall be strong as iron: forasmuch as iron breaketh in pieces and subdueth all these, shall it break in pieces and bruise. . . .

In the first year of Belshazzar king of Babylon Daniel had a dream and visions of his head upon his bed: then he wrote the dream, *and* told the sum of the matters.

Daniel spake and said, I saw in my vision by night, and, behold, the four winds of the heaven strove upon the great sea.

And four great beasts came up from the sea, diverse one from another.

The first *was* like a lion, and had eagle's wings: I beheld till the wings thereof were plucked, and it was lifted up from the earth, and made stand upon the feet as a man, and a man's heart was given to it.

And behold another beast, a second, like to a bear, and it raised up itself on one side, and *it had* three ribs in the mouth of it between the teeth of it: and they said thus unto it, Arise, devour much flesh.

After this I beheld, and lo another, like a leopard, which had upon the back of it four wings of a fowl; the beast had also four heads; and dominion was given to it.

After this I saw in the night visions, and behold a fourth beast, dreadful and terrible, and strong exceedingly; and it had great iron teeth: it devoured and brake in pieces, and stamped the residue with the feet of it:

and it *was* diverse from all the beasts that *were* before it; and it had ten horns. . . .

As concerning the rest of the beasts, they had their dominion taken away: yet their lives were prolonged for a season and time.

I saw in the night visions, and, behold, *one* like the Son of man came with the clouds of heaven, and came to the Ancient of days, and they brought him near before him.

And there was given him dominion, and glory, and a kingdom, that all people, nations, and languages, should serve him: his dominion *is* an everlasting dominion, which shall not pass away, and his kingdom *that* which shall not be destroyed.

I Daniel was grieved in my spirit in the midst of *my* body, and the visions of my head troubled me.

I came near unto one of them that stood by, and asked him the truth of all this. So he told me, and made me know the interpretation of the things.

These great beasts, which are four, *are* four kings, *which* shall arise out of the earth.

But the saints of the most High shall take the kingdom, and possess the kingdom for ever, even for ever and ever.

Then I would know the truth of the fourth beast, which was diverse from all the others, exceeding dreadful, whose teeth *were of* iron, and his nails *of* brass; *which* devoured, brake in pieces, and stamped the residue with his feet. . . .

Thus he said, the fourth beast shall be a fourth kingdom upon earth, which shall be diverse from all kingdoms, and shall devour the whole earth, and shall tread it down, and break it in pieces.

And the ten horns out of this kingdom *are* ten kings *that* shall arise; and another shall rise after them; and he shall be diverse from the first, and he shall subdue three kings.

And he shall speak *great* words against the most High, and shall wear out the saints of the most High, and think to change times and laws: and they shall be given into his hand until a time and times and the dividing of time.

But the judgment shall sit, and they shall take away his dominion, to consume and to destroy *it* unto the end.

And the kingdom and dominion, and the greatness of the kingdom under the whole heaven, shall be given to the people of the saints of the

most High, whose kingdom *is* an everlasting kingdom, and all dominions shall serve and obey him.

Hitherto *is* the end of the matter. As for me Daniel, my cogitations
much troubled me, and my countenance changed in me: but I kept the
matter in my heart.

> 27. The apostle PAUL (d. ca. 67), on his second missionary jour-
> ney, according to this conventional account, preached to the Athe-
> nians about the "unknown" universal god honored in one of their
> monuments, urging the ecumenical character and provenance of
> Christianity, a message which was to become the central theme of
> the Christian view of history.

Therefore disputed he in the synagogue with the Jews, and with the
devout persons, and in the market daily with them that met with him.

Then certain philosophers of the Epicureans and of the Stoicks, encountered him. And some said, What will this babbler say? other some,
He seemeth to be a setter forth of strange gods: because he preached unto
them Jesus, and the resurrection.

And they took him, and brought him unto Areopagus, saying, May
we know what this new doctrine, whereof thou speakest, *is?*

For thou bringest certain strange things to our ears: we would know
therefore what these things mean.

(For all the Athenians and strangers which were there spent their time
in nothing else, but either to tell, or to hear some new thing.)

Then Paul stood in the midst of Mars' hill, and said, *Ye* men of
Athens, I perceive that in all things ye are too superstitious.

For as I passed by, and beheld your devotions, I found an altar with
this inscription, TO THE UNKNOWN GOD. Whom therefore ye ignorantly worship, him declare I unto you.

God that made the world and all things therein, seeing that he is Lord
of heaven and earth, dwelleth not in temples made with hands;

Neither is he worshipped with men's hands, as though he needed any
thing, seeing he giveth to all life, and breath, and all things;

And hath made of one blood all nations of men for to dwell on all the
face of the earth, and hath determined the times before appointed, and
the bounds of their habitation;

Paul, *Acts of the Apostles* 17 : 17 – 28 (King James Version).

That they should seek the Lord, if haply they might feel after him, and find him, though he be not far from every one of us;

For in him we live, and move, and have our being; as certain also of your own poets have said, For we are also his offspring.

> 28. JUSTIN MARTYR (ca. 100–165) received his appellation from Tertullian; he was a Greek who became dissatisfied with Platonism and other ancient schools of philosophy and turned to Christianity and its prophets. Justin Martyr undertook an extensive critique of pagan mythology and customs, contrasting these with Christian tradition; in his *Oratio ad Graecos,* he urged his view of the antiquity and continuity of the Judeo-Christian tradition on the pagan society from which he had emerged.

The antiquity of Moses proved by Greek writers. I will begin, then, with our first prophet and lawgiver, Moses; first explaining the times in which he lived, on authorities which among you are worthy of all credit. For I do not propose to prove these things only from our own divine histories, which as yet you are unwilling to credit on account of the inveterate error of your forefathers, but also from your own histories, and such, too, as have no reference to our worship, that you may know that, of all your teachers, whether sages, poets, historians, philosophers, or lawgivers, by far the oldest, as the Greek histories show us, was Moses, who was our first religious teacher. . . . Josephus certainly, desiring to signify even by the title of his work the antiquity and age of the history, wrote thus at the commencement of the history: "The Jewish antiquities of Flavius Josephus,"—signifying the oldness of the history by the word "antiquities." And your most renowned historian Diodorus, who employed thirty whole years in epitomizing the libraries, and who, as he himself wrote, travelled over both Asia and Europe for the sake of great accuracy, and thus became an eye-witness of very many things, wrote forty entire books of his own history. And he in the first book, having said that he had learned from the Egyptian priests that Moses was an ancient lawgiver, and even the first, wrote of him in these very words: "For subsequent to the ancient manner of living in Egypt which gods and heroes are fabled to have regulated, they say that Moses first per-

Justin Martyr, *Hortatory Address to the Greeks.* In *The Writings of Justin Martyr and Athenagoras,* trans. Marcus Dods, George Reith, and B. P. Pratten. Edinburgh: T. and T. Clark, 1867. Pp. 295–296 and 297–299.

suaded the people to use written laws, and to live by them; and he is recorded to have been a man both great of soul and of great faculty in social matters." Then, having proceeded a little further, and wishing to mention the ancient lawgivers, he mentions Moses first. For he spoke in these words: "Among the Jews they say that Moses ascribed his laws to that God who is called Jehovah, whether because they judged it a marvellous and quite divine conception which promised to benefit a multitude of men, or because they were of opinion that the people would be the more obedient when they contemplated the majesty and power of those who were said to have invented the laws. . . ."

Training and inspiration of Moses. These things, ye men of Greece, have been recorded in writing concerning the antiquity of Moses by those who were not of our religion; and they said that they learned all these things from the Egyptian priests, among whom Moses was not only born, but also was thought worthy of partaking of all the education of the Egyptians, on account of his being adopted by the king's daughter as her son; and for the same reason was thought worthy of great attention, as the wisest of the historians relate, who have chosen to record his life and actions, and the rank of his descent,—I speak of Philo and Josephus. For these, in their narration of the history of the Jews, say that Moses was sprung from the race of the Chaldaeans, and that he was born in Egypt when his forefathers had migrated on account of famine from Phoenicia to that country; and him God chose to honour on account of his exceeding virtue, and judged him worthy to become the leader and lawgiver of his own race, when He thought it right that the people of the Hebrews should return out of Egypt into their own land. To him first did God communicate that divine and prophetic gift which in those days descended upon the holy men, and him also did He first furnish that he might be our teacher in religion, and then after him the rest of the prophets, who both obtained the same gift as he, and taught us the same doctrines concerning the same subjects. These we assert to have been our teachers, who taught us nothing from their own human conception, but from the gift vouchsafed to them by God from above.

Heathen oracles testify of Moses. But as you do not see the necessity of giving up the ancient error of your forefathers in obedience to these teachers [of ours], what teachers of your own do you maintain to have lived worthy of credit in the matter of religion? For, as I have frequently said, it is impossible that those who have not themselves learned these so great and divine things from such persons as are acquainted with them, should either themselves know them, or be able rightly to teach others. . . .

Antiquity of Moses proved. And I think it necessary also to consider the times in which your philosophers lived, that you may see that the time which produced them for you is very recent, and also short. For thus you will be able easily to recognise also the antiquity of Moses. But lest, by a complete survey of the periods, and by the use of a greater number of proofs, I should seem to be prolix, I think it may be sufficiently demonstrated from the following. For Socrates was the teacher of Plato, and Plato of Aristotle. Now these men flourished in the time of Philip and Alexander of Macedon, in which time also the Athenian orators flourished, as the Philippics of Demosthenes plainly show us. And those who have narrated the deeds of Alexander sufficiently prove that during his reign Aristotle associated with him. From all manner of proofs, then, it is easy to see that the history of Moses is by far more ancient than all profane histories. And, besides, it is fit that you recognise this fact also, that nothing has been accurately recorded by Greeks before the era of the Olympiads, and that there is no ancient work which makes known any action of the Greeks or Barbarians. But before that period existed only the history of the prophet Moses, which he wrote in the Hebrew character by divine inspiration. For the Greek character was not yet in use, as the teachers of language themselves prove, telling us that Cadmus first brought the letters from Phoenicia, and communicated them to the Greeks. And your first of philosophers, Plato, testifies that they were a recent discovery.

> 29. CLEMENT OF ALEXANDRIA (Titus Flavius Clemens, ca. 150–215), an Athenian of pagan parentage, may have been a priest and was probably the first Christian scholar. He devoted himself to celebrating the new Logos and demonstrating the superiority of Christian belief to the folly of pagan mysteries and traditions as the choice of life over death and progress over corruption.

But, you say, it is not reasonable to overthrow a way of life handed down to us from our forefathers. Why then do we not continue to use our

Clement of Alexandria. *Exhortation to the Greeks,* trans. G. W. Butterworth. Loeb Classical Library. P. 197. Reprinted by permission of the publishers and the Loeb Classical Library from Clement of Alexandria, trans. G. W. Butterworth, Cambridge, Mass.: Harvard University Press, 1919.

first food, milk, to which, as you will admit, our nurses accustomed us from birth? Why do we increase or diminish our family property, and not keep it for ever at the same value as when we received it? Why do we no longer sputter into our parents' bosoms, nor still behave in other respects as we did when infants in our mothers' arms, making ourselves objects of laughter? Did we not rather correct ourselves, even if we did not happen to have good attendants for this purpose? Again, in voyages by sea, deviations from the usual course may bring loss and danger, but yet they are attended by a certain charm. So, in life itself, shall we not abandon the old way, which is wicked, full of passion, and without God? And shall we not, even at the risk of displeasing our fathers, bend our course towards the truth and seek after Him who is our real Father, thrusting away custom as some deadly drug? This is assuredly the noblest of all the tasks we have in hand, namely, to prove to you that it was from madness and from this thrice miserable custom that hatred of godliness sprang. For such a boon, the greatest that God has ever bestowed upon the race of men, could never have been hated or rejected, had you not been clean carried away by custom, and so had stopped your ears against us.

> 30. TERTULLIAN (Quintus Septimius Florens Tertullianus, 160?–230?), of pagan Roman background and legal education, became a Christian, placed his extraordinary literary skills in the service of his new faith, and defended it against the stock charges of immorality and disloyalty. He criticized the pagan conception of history and in its place substituted a vision of a distinguished Christian past and a still more marvelous future, concerning which he celebrated the blood of Christian martyrs as the "seed of the church."

Great antiquity provides authority for literature. Moses was the first of the Prophets; he wove from the past the account of the foundation of the world and the formation of the human race and afterwards the mighty deluge which took vengeance upon the godlessness of that age; he prophesied events right up to his own day. Then by means of condi-

Tertullian, *Apology.* In *Tertullian: Apologetical Works, and Minucius Felix: Octavius,* trans. Rudolph Arbesmann, Sister Emily Joseph Daley, and Edwin A. Quain. Fathers of the Church. Washington, D.C.: Catholic University of America Press, 1962. Pp. 56–59. Reprinted by permission of The Catholic University of America Press.

tions of his own time, he showed forth an image of times to come; according to him, too, the order of events, arranged from the beginning, supplied the reckoning of the age of the world: Moses is found to be alive about 300 years before Danaus, your most ancient of men, came over to Argos. He is 1,000 years earlier than the Trojan War and, therefore, the time of Saturn himself. For, according to the history of Thallus, where it is related that Belus, King of the Assyrians, and Saturn, King of the Titans, fought with Jupiter, it is shown that Belus antedated the fall of Troy by 332 years. It was by this same Moses, too, that their own true law was given to the Jews by God. Next, other Prophets, too, have set forth many facts more ancient than your literature; even the last of the Prophets was either a little earlier or, at any rate, a contemporary of your wise men and lawmakers.

Hence, it can be perceived that your laws as well as your learning were conceived from the law of God and divine teaching. What is first must of necessity be the seed. Thence you derive certain terms in common with us or very similar to ours: the love of wisdom is called "philosophy" from *sophia;* the striving after prophecy has derived the poetic term, "vaticination," from *prophetia.* Whatever glory men found, they have corrupted it to make it their own. Fruit has been known to deteriorate from its seed. Still, in many ways I would maintain a very firm position about the antiquity of the Sacred Books, were there not at hand a consideration of greater weight in proving their trustworthiness which results from the power of their truth rather than from the evidence of their antiquity. For, what will more powerfully defend their testimony than their daily fulfillment throughout the whole world, when the rise and fall of kingdoms, the fate of cities, the ruin of nations, the conditions of the times, correspond in all respects just as they were announced thousands of years ago? By this, too, our hope—which you deride—is animated, and our trust—which you call presumption—is strengthened. For, a review of the past is likely to incline one to trust in the future: the same voices foretold both alike; the same books noted both. In them, time—which to us seems to be split in two—is one. Thus, all that remains unproved has already been proved, as far as we are concerned, because it was foretold together with that which has been proved and with the things which at that time were yet to be. You have, I know, a Sibyl, inasmuch as this name for a true prophetess of the true God has been everywhere appropriated for all who appeared to have the gift of prophecy; and just as your Sibyls have been deceitful regarding the truth in the matter of their name, so also have your gods.

So, all the subject matter; all the material, origins, arrangements, sources of any of your ancient writings; even most of your races and cities, illustrious for their history and hoary, as far as records go; the very character of the letters whereby the events are indicated and preserved; and—I think we are still indulging in understatement—those very gods of yours, I say, and those temples, oracles, and sanctuaries—all are antedated by centuries by the writings of a single Prophet, in which it appears that there has been collected the store of knowledge of the entire Jewish religion and, from thence, of our own religion, too. You may have heard, in the meanwhile, of Moses; he would be of the same age as the Argive Inachus; by nearly 400 years—actually, it was seven years less—he antedated Danaus, whom you consider the most ancient of your race; he lived about 1,000 years before the death of Priam; I might even say that he was about 1,500 years earlier than Homer, too, and I have reliable authorities to follow. As for the rest of the Prophets, too, although they lived after Moses, are not their very latest representatives older than the earliest of your philosophers, lawgivers, and historians?

The task would not be so difficult as it would be endless for us to explain by what means these points could be proved; the enumeration would not offer much trouble, but, in the present circumstances, it would take a long time. Many records, together with much mathematical calculation on the fingers, would have to be used. The archives of the most ancient of all peoples, the Egyptians, Chaldeans, and Phoenicians, would have to be laid open. We would need to have recourse to the fellow citizens of those through whom this information has come to us, men like Manetho of Egypt, Berosus of Chaldea, and Hieromus of Phoenicia, King of Tyre; their followers, too—Ptolemy of Mendes, Menander of Ephesus, Demetrius of Phalerum, King Juba, Apion, Thallus, Josephus the Jew, the native defender of Jewish antiquities, and any other who either substantiates or refutes them.

The Greeks' census lists, too, would have to be consulted to see what was done and when, that the time sequence might be made clear and the order of the records clarified; one would have to go through the foreign histories and literatures of the world. Yet, we have already introduced, as it were, a part of the proof when we have mentioned the names of some through whom all can be proved. It is much better to postpone the proof, lest, in our haste, we either accomplish too little or digress too far from the point in accomplishing it.

> 31. EUSEBIUS of Caesarea (260?–340?), ecclesiastical politician and bishop, was the authoritative historian of the Christian church. Besides theological works and imperial panegyrics, Eusebius produced his authoritative *Chronicles* and his *Ecclesiastical History*. The first surveyed in a comparative way the history of ancient nations as well as Christianity, and the second told the epic story of Christian expansion from the incarnation of Christ and organization under Augustus through expansion and various dissensions down to the legalization of Christianity by Constantine in 315. This work established the major themes of Christian historiography down to modern times.

I have purposed to record in writing the successions of the sacred apostles, covering the period stretching from our Saviour to ourselves; the number and character of the transactions recorded in the history of the Church; the number of these who were distinguished in her government and leadership in the provinces of greatest fame; the number of those who in each generation were the ambassadors of the word of God either by speech or pen; the names, the number and the age of those who, driven by the desire of innovation to an extremity of error, have heralded themselves as the introducers of Knowledge, falsely so-called, ravaging the flock of Christ unsparingly, like grim wolves. To this I will add the fate which has beset the whole nation of the Jews from the moment of their plot against our Saviour; moreover, the number and nature and time of the wars waged by the heathen against the divine word and the character of those who, for its sake, passed from time to time through the contest of blood and torture; furthermore the martyrdoms of our own time, and the gracious and favouring help of our Saviour in them all. My starting-point is therefore no other than the first dispensation of God touching our Saviour and Lord Jesus the Christ. Even at that point the project at once demands the lenience of the kindly, for confessedly it is beyond our power to fulfill the promise, complete

Eusebius, *The Ecclesiastical History,* trans. Kirsopp Lake. Loeb Classical Library. 1:7–11, 13–15, 21–25, and 29. Reprinted by permission of the publishers and the Loeb Classical Library from Eusebius, *Ecclesiastical History,* Volume 1, trans. Kirsopp Lake, Cambridge, Mass.: Harvard University Press, 1926.

and perfect, since we are the first to enter on the undertaking, as travellers on some desolate and untrodden way. We pray God to give us his guidance, and that we may have the help of the power of the Lord, for nowhere can we find even the bare footsteps of men who have preceded us in the same path, unless it be those slight indications by which in divers ways they have left to us partial accounts of the times through which they have passed, raising their voices as a man holds up a torch from afar, calling to us from on high as from a distant watch-tower, and telling us how we must walk, and how to guide the course of our work without error or danger. We have therefore collected from their scattered memoirs all that we think will be useful for the present subject, and have brought together the utterances of the ancient writers themselves that are appropriate to it, culling, as it were, the flowers of intellectual fields. We shall endeavour to give them unity by historical treatment, rejoicing to rescue the successions, if not of all, at least of the most distinguished of the apostles of our Saviour throughout those churches of which the fame is still remembered. To work at this subject I consider especially necessary, because I am not aware that any Christian writer has until now paid attention to this kind of writing; and I hope that its high value will be evident to those who are convinced of the importance of a knowledge of the history. I have already summarized the material in the chronological tables which I have drawn up, but nevertheless in the present work I have undertaken to give the narrative in full detail.

I will begin with what, apprehended in relation to Christ, is beyond man in its height and greatness,—the dispensation of God, and the ascription of divinity. For he who plans to hand on in writing the history of Christian origins is forced to begin from the first dispensation concerning the Christ himself, which is more divine than it seems to most, seeing that from him we claim to derive our very name. . . .

"In the beginning was the Logos and the Logos was with God and the Logos was God, all things were through him, and without him was no single thing." This, indeed, is also the teaching of the great Moses, as the most ancient of all prophets, when by divine inspiration he described the coming into being, and the ordering of the universe, that the creator and fabricator of all things gave up to the Christ himself, and to no other than his divine and first-born Logos, the making of subordinate things and communed with him concerning the creation of man. . . .

It must now be demonstrated why this announcement was not formerly made, long ago, to all men and all nations, as it is now. The life of men in the past was not capable of receiving the complete wisdom and virtue of the teaching of Christ. For at the beginning, after the first life in blessedness, the first man, despising the command of God, fell at once to this mortal and perishable life, and exchanged the former divine delights for this earth with its curse; and after him those who filled all our world were manifestly much worse, with the exception of one or two, and chose some brutal habit of life, unworthy of the name. They gave no thought to city or state, to art or knowledge, they had not even the name of laws and decrees or virtue and philosophy, but they lived as nomads in the wilderness like savage and unbridled beings; they destroyed by their excess of self-chosen wickedness the natural reasonings, and the germs of thought and gentleness in the human soul; they gave themselves up completely to all iniquity so that at one time they corrupted one another, at another they murdered one another, at another they were cannibals; they ventured on conflicts with God and on the battles of the giants famous among all men; they thought to wall up the earth to heaven, and in the madness of a perverted mind prepared for war against the supreme God himself. While they were leading this life, God, the guardian of all, pursued them with floods and conflagrations, as though they had been a wild forest scattered throughout the whole earth; he cut them off with perpetual famines and plagues, by wars and by thunderbolts from on high, as if he were restraining by bitter chastisement some terrible and grievous disease of their souls. Then, indeed, when the great flood of evil had come nigh overwhelming all men, like a terrible intoxication overshadowing and darkening the souls of almost all, the first-begotten and first-created Wisdom of God, the pre-existent Logos himself, in his exceeding kindness appeared to his subjects, at one time by a vision of angels, at another personally to one or two of the God-fearing men of old, as a saving power of God, yet in no other form than human, for they could not receive him otherwise.

But when the seeds of true religion had been strewn by them among a multitude of men, and a whole nation, sprung from the Hebrews, existed on earth, cleaving to true religion, he handed on to them, through the prophet Moses, images and symbols of a certain mysterious sabbath and of circumcision and instruction in other spiritual principles, but not unveiled initiation itself, for many of them had still been brought up in the old practices. Their Law became famous and spread among all men like a fragrant breeze. Beginning with them the minds of most of the heathen were softened by the lawgivers and philosophers who arose everywhere. Savage and unbridled brutality was changed to

mildness, so that deep peace, friendship, and mutual intercourse obtained. Then, at last, when all men, even the heathen throughout the
world, were now fitted for the benefits prepared for them beforehand, for
the reception of knowledge of the Father, then again that same divine
and heavenly Logos of God, the teacher of virtues, the minister of the
Father in all good things, appeared at the beginning of the Roman Empire through man. . . .

It is now time to demonstrate that the very names "Jesus," and especially "Christ," were held in honour by the ancient God-loving prophets
themselves. Moses was himself the first to recognize how peculiarly august and glorious is the name of Christ, when he delivered the tradition
of the types and symbols of heavenly things, and the mysterious images,
in accordance with the oracle which said to him, "See thou shalt make all
things according to the type which was shown thee in the mount"; for in
describing the High Priest of God as a man of supreme power, he calls
him Christ, and, as a mark of honour and glory, surrounds with the
name of Christ this rank of the High Priesthood, which with him surpassed all pre-eminence among men. Thus then he knew the divine
character of "Christ."

❡ HUMAN HISTORY

32. FLAVIUS JOSEPHUS (37–102), a Hellenized Jew who became a naturalized Roman, turned to writing after a military and
political career. Though possessing some claim to be the national
historian of the Jews, Josephus came under attack by the Jews for
conversion to the Roman side during the "great rebellion." His
major work, the *Jewish Antiquities*, was modeled on what Dionysius
of Halicarnassus had called "archaeology" (*archaiologia*), and it
served as an intercultural link, this one between Rome and the
East, celebrating in particular the lawgiver Moses and the universal value of Hebrew culture. Though partisan and apologetic,
Josephus was often critical and made pioneering use of archival
sources. The controversial aspect of his writings appears in his justification against critics, represented by the long-dead anti-Semite
Apion, which was not only an attack on Greek historians for their

Flavius Josephus, *Jewish Antiquities,* trans. H. St. J. Thackery. Loeb Classi-
cal Library. 4 : 3 – 13. Reprinted by permission of the publishers and the Loeb
Classical Library from Flavius Josephus, Volume 4, trans. H. St. J. Thackery,
Cambridge, Mass.: Harvard University Press, 1930.

ignorance, credulity, superficiality, and myopia (a theme picked up again in the Renaissance) but also an essay on historical method.

Those who essay to write histories are actuated, I observe, not by one and the same aim, but by many widely different motives. Some, eager to display their literary skill and to win the fame therefrom expected, rush into this department of letters; others, to gratify the persons to whom the record happens to relate, have undertaken the requisite labour even though beyond their power; others again have been constrained by the mere stress of events in which they themselves took part to set these out in a comprehensive narrative; while many have been induced by prevailing ignorance of important affairs of general utility to publish a history of them for the public benefit. Of the aforesaid motives the two last apply to myself. For, having known by experience the war which we Jews waged against the Romans, the incidents in its course and its issue, I was constrained to narrate it in detail in order to refute those who in their writings were doing outrage to the truth.

And now I have undertaken this present work in the belief that the whole Greek-speaking world will find it worthy of attention; for it will embrace our entire ancient history and political constitution, translated from the Hebrew records. I had indeed ere now, when writing the history of the war, already contemplated describing the origin of the Jews, the fortunes that befell them, the great lawgiver under whom they were trained in piety and the exercise of the other virtues, and all those wars waged by them through long ages before this last in which they were involuntarily engaged against the Romans. However, since the compass of such a theme was excessive, I made the *War* into a separate volume, with its own beginning and end, thus duly proportioning my work. Nevertheless, as time went on, as is wont to happen to those who design to attack large tasks, there was hesitation and delay on my part in rendering so vast a subject into a foreign and unfamiliar tongue. However, there were certain persons curious about the history who urged me to pursue it, and above all Epaphroditus, a man devoted to every form of learning . . . , and ashamed of myself that I should be thought to prefer sloth to the effort of this noblest of enterprises, I was encouraged to greater ardour. Besides these motives, there were two further considerations to which I had given serious thought, namely, whether our ancestors, on the one hand, were willing to communicate such information, and whether any of the Greeks, on the other, had been curious to learn our history.

I found then that the second of the Ptolemies, that king who was so deeply interested in learning and such a collector of books, was particularly anxious to have our Law and the political constitution based thereon translated into Greek; while, on the other side, Eleazar, who yielded in virtue to none of our high priests, did not scruple to grant the monarch the enjoyment of a benefit, which he would certainly have refused had it not been our traditional custom to make nothing of what is good into a secret. Accordingly, I thought that it became me also both to imitate the high priest's magnanimity and to assume that there are still to-day many lovers of learning like the king. For even he failed to obtain all our records: it was only the portion containing the Law which was delivered to him by those who were sent to Alexandria to interpret it. The things narrated in the sacred Scriptures are, however, innumerable, seeing that they embrace the history of five thousand years and recount all sorts of surprising reverses, many fortunes of war, heroic exploits of generals, and political revolutions. But, speaking generally, the main lesson to be learned from this history by any who care to peruse it is that men who conform to the will of God, and do not venture to transgress laws that have been excellently laid down, prosper in all things beyond belief, and for their reward are offered by God felicity; whereas, in proportion as they depart from the strict observance of these laws, things (else) practicable become impracticable, and whatever imaginary good thing they strive to do ends in irretrievable disasters. At the outset, then, I entreat those who will read these volumes to fix their thoughts on God, and to test whether our lawgiver has had a worthy conception of His nature and has always assigned to Him such actions as befit His power, keeping his words concerning Him pure of that unseemly mythology current among others; albeit that, in dealing with ages so long and so remote, he would have had ample licence to invent fictions. For he was born two thousand years ago, to which ancient date the poets never ventured to refer even the birth of their gods, much less the actions or the laws of mortals. The precise details of our Scripture records will then be set forth, each in its place, as my narrative proceeds, that being the procedure that I have promised to follow throughout this work, neither adding nor omitting anything.

But, since well-nigh everything herein related is dependent on the wisdom of our lawgiver Moses, I must first speak briefly of him, lest any of my readers should ask how it is that so much of my work, which professes to treat of laws and historical facts, is devoted to natural philosophy. Be it known, then, that that sage deemed it above all necessary, for one who would order his own life aright and also legislate for others, first to study the nature of God, and then, having contemplated his works with the eye of reason, to imitate so far as possible that best of all models and endeavour to follow it. For neither could the lawgiver himself, without this vision, ever attain to a right mind, nor would anything that he should write in regard to virtue avail with his readers, unless before all else they were taught that God, as the universal Father and Lord who beholds all things, grants to such as follow Him a life of bliss, but involves in dire calamities those who step outside the path of virtue. Such, then, being the lesson which Moses desired to instill into his fellow-citizens, he did not, when framing his laws, begin with contracts and the mutual rights of man, as others have done; no, he led their thoughts up to God and the construction of the world; he convinced them that of all God's works upon earth we men are the fairest; and when once he had won their obedience to the dictates of piety, he had no further difficulty in persuading them of all the rest. Other legislators, in fact, following fables, have in their writings imputed to the gods the disgraceful errors of man and thus furnished the wicked with a powerful excuse; our legislator, on the contrary, having shown that God possesses the very perfection of virtue, thought that men should strive to participate in it, and inexorably punished those who did not hold with or believe in these doctrines. I therefore entreat my readers to examine my work from this point of view. For, studying it in this spirit, nothing will appear to them unreasonable, nothing incongruous with the majesty of God and His love for man; everything, indeed, is here set forth in keeping with the nature of the universe; some things the lawgiver shrewdly veils in enigmas, others he sets forth in solemn allegory; but wherever straightforward speech was expedient, there he makes his meaning absolutely plain.

❡ In my history of our *Antiquities,* most excellent Epaphroditus, I have, I think, made sufficiently clear to any who may peruse that work the

Flavius Josephus, *The Life Against Apion,* trans. H. St. J. Thackery. Loeb Classical Library. 1 : 163–167, 169, 171, 173, and 185. Reprinted by permission of the publishers and the Loeb Classical Library from Flavius Josephus, Volume 1, trans. H. St. J. Thackery, Cambridge, Mass.: Harvard University Press, 1926.

extreme antiquity of our Jewish race, the purity of the original stock, and the manner in which it established itself in the country which we occupy to-day. That history embraces a period of five thousand years, and was written by me in Greek on the basis of our sacred books. Since, however, I observe that a considerable number of persons, influenced by the malicious calumnies of certain individuals, discredit the statements in my history concerning our antiquity, and adduce as proof of the comparative modernity of our race the fact that it has not been thought worthy of mention by the best known Greek historians, I consider it my duty to devote a brief treatise to all these points; in order at once to convict our detractors of malignity and deliberate falsehood, to correct the ignorance of others, and to instruct all who desire to know the truth concerning the antiquity of our race. As witnesses to my statements I propose to call the writers who, in the estimation of the Greeks, are the most trustworthy authorities on antiquity as a whole. The authors of scurrilous and mendacious statements about us will be shown to be confuted by themselves. I shall further endeavor to set out the various reasons which explain why our nation is mentioned by a few only of the Greek historians; at the same time I shall bring those authors who have not neglected our history to the notice of any who either are, or feign to be, ignorant of them.

My first thought is one of intense astonishment at the current opinion that, in the study of primeval history, the Greeks alone deserve serious attention, that the truth should be sought from them, and that neither we nor any others in the world are to be trusted. In my view the very reverse of this is the case, if, that is to say, we are not to take idle prejudices as our guide, but to extract the truth from the facts themselves. For in the Greek world everything will be found to be modern, and dating, so to speak, from yesterday or the day before: I refer to the foundation of their cities, the invention of the arts, and the compilation of a code of laws; but the most recent, or nearly the most recent, of all their attainments is care in historical composition. On the contrary, as is admitted even by themselves, the Egyptians, the Chaldaeans, and the Phoenicians—for the moment I omit to add our nation to the list—posses a very ancient and permanent record of the past. For all these nations inhabit countries which are least exposed to the ravages of the atmosphere, and they have been very careful to let none of the events in their history be forgotten, but always to have them enshrined in official records written by their greatest sages. The land of Greece, on the contrary, has experienced countless catastrophes, which have obliterated the memory of the past; and as one civilization succeeded another the men of each epoch believed that the world began with them. . . .

Surely, then, it is absurd that the Greeks should be so conceited as to think themselves the sole possessors of a knowledge of antiquity and the only accurate reporters of its history. Anyone can easily discover from the historians themselves that their writings have no basis of sure knowledge, but merely present the facts as conjectured by individual authors. More often than not they confute each other in their works, not hesitating to give the most contradictory accounts of the same events. . . .

The main responsibility for the errors of later historians who aspired to write on antiquity and for the licence granted to their mendacity rests with the original neglect of the Greeks to keep official records of current events. . . .

But a second reason must be added. Those who rushed into writing were concerned not so much to discover the truth, notwithstanding the profession which always comes readily to their pen, as to display their literary ability; and their choice of a subject was determined by the prospect which it offered them of outshining their rivals. Some turned to mythology, others sought popularity by ecomiums upon cities or monarchs; others, again, set out to criticize the facts or the historians as the road to a reputation. In short, their invariable method is the very reverse of historical. For the proof of historical veracity is universal agreement in the description, oral or written, of the same events. On the contrary, each of these writers, in giving his divergent account of the same incidents, hoped thereby to be thought the most veracious of all. While, then, for eloquence and literary ability we must yield the palm to the Greek historians, we have no reason to do so for veracity in the history of antiquity, least of all where the particular history of each separate foreign nation is concerned. . . .

Nevertheless, certain despicable persons have essayed to malign my history, taking it for a prize composition such as is set to boys at school. What an extraordinary accusation and calumny! Surely they ought to recognize that it is the duty of one who promises to present his readers with actual facts first to obtain an exact knowledge of them himself, either through having been in close touch with the events, or by inquiry from those who knew them. That duty I consider myself to have amply fulfilled in both my works.

33. Flavius Magnus Aurelius CASSIODORUS (ca. 490–575) was a Roman statesman who founded the monastery of Vivarius and in 540 retired there to devote himself to religion and scholarship. Besides work on the history of the church, on the Goths (preserved only in Jordanes), and on a world chronicle, Cassiodorus wrote a pedagogical treatise, *Divine and Human Letters,* which contains a seminal discussion of the tradition of Christian historiography.

On Christian Historians. In addition to the various writers of treatises, Christian studies also possess narrators of history, who, calm in their ecclesiastical gravity, recount the shifting movements of events and the unstable history of kingdoms with eloquent but very cautious splendor. Because they narrate ecclesiastical matters and describe changes which occur at various times, they must always of necessity instruct the minds of readers in heavenly affairs, since they strive to assign nothing to chance, nothing to the weak power of gods, as pagans have done, but to assign all things truly to the will of the Creator. Such is Josephus, almost a second Livy, who is very diffuse in his *Jewish Antiquities,* a prolix work which, in a letter to Lucinus Betticus, Father Jerome says he himself could not translate because of its great size. We, however, have had it laboriously translated into Latin in twenty-two books by our friends, since it is exceedingly subtle and extensive. Josephus has also written with remarkable grace seven other books entitled *The Jewish Captivity,* the translation of which is ascribed by some to Jerome, by others to Ambrose, and by still others to Rufinus; and since the translation is ascribed to men of this sort, its extraordinary merits are explicitly shown. The next work to be read is the history written by Eusebius in Greek in ten books, but translated and completed in eleven books by Rufinus, who has added subsequent events. Among the Greek writers Socrates, Sozomenus, and Theodoretus have written on events subsequent to Eusebius' history; with God's help we have had the work of these men translated and placed in a single codex in twelve books by the very fluent Epiphanius, lest eloquent Greece boast that it has something essential which it judges you do not possess. Orosius, who compares

Cassiodorus, *Divine and Human Letters,* trans. Leslie Webber Jones as *An Introduction to Divine and Human Readings.* Records of Civilization. New York: Columbia University Press, 1946. Pp. 115–117. Reprinted by permission of Columbia University Press.

Christian times with pagan, is also at hand, if you desire to read him. Marcellinus too has traversed his journey's path in laudable fashion, completing four books on the nature of events and the location of places with most decorous propriety; I have likewise left his work for you.

Eusebius has written chronicles, which are the mere shadows of history and very brief reminders of the times, in Greek; and Jerome has translated this work into Latin and extended it to his own time in excellent manner. Eusebius has been followed in turn by the aforesaid Marcellinus the Illyrian, who is said to have acted first as secretary of the patrician Justinian, but who later, with the Lord's help, upon the improvement of his employer's civil status, faithfully guided his work from the time of the emperor Theodosius to the beginning of the triumphant rule of the emperor Justinian, in order that he who had first been grateful in the service of his employer might later appear to be most devoted during his imperial rule. St. Prosper has also written chronicles which extend from Adam to the time of Genseric and the plundering of the City. Perhaps you will find other later writers, inasmuch as there is no dearth of chroniclers despite the continual succession of one age after another. But when, O diligent reader, you are filled with these works and your mind gleams with divine light, read St. Jerome's book *On Famous Men*, a work whose brief discussion has honored the various Fathers and their work; then read a second book, by Gennadius of Marseilles, who has very faithfully treated and carefully examined the writers on divine law. I have left you these two books joined in a single volume, lest delay in learning the matter be caused by the need of using various codices.

> 34. Aurelius PRUDENTIUS Clemens (348–after 405), who was trained in rhetoric and the law and who served under Theodosius I, was the greatest of early Christian poets. Prudentius glorified the Christian faith and, in *Contra Symmachum*, represented it as the wave of the future in contrast to retrograde and exhausted pagan culture—an early manifestation, it has been suggested, of the idea of progress.

Prudentius, *A Reply to the Address of Symmachus*, trans. H. J. Thomson. Loeb Classical Library. 1 : 379–381; 2 : 45 and 53–57. Reprinted by permission of the publishers and the Loeb Classical Library from Prudentius, Volumes 1 and 2, trans. H. J. Thomson, Cambridge, Mass.: Harvard University Press, 1949, 1953.

But her many gods have led Rome from success to success, and she worships them for their good service in that they have given her great victories. Come then, warrior city, say what power it was that subdued Europe and Africa to thee; tell us the names of the gods. Jupiter by his good favour gave thee to rule over Crete, Pallas over Argos, the Cynthian over Delphi. Isis gave up the people of the Nile, she of Cythera the Rhodians, the huntress maid resigned Ephesus to thee, and Mars the Hebrus. Bromius abandoned Thebes, Juno herself granted that the Africans should serve a race of Phrygian descent, and that city, which to make mistress of subject nations, "did but the fates allow, was even then the goddess's cherished aim," she bade live under the dominion of the sons of Romulus. Was it by the treachery of their own native gods that all these cities fell? Do their altars lie in ruins through their own betrayal? . . .

But I see the instances of ancient valour which move you. You say the world was conquered on land and sea, you recount every success and victory, and recall a thousand triumphal processions one after another, with their loads of spoil passing through the midst of Rome. Shall I tell you, Roman, what cause it was that so exalted your labours, what it was that nursed your glory to such a height of fame that it has put rein and bridle on the world? God, wishing to bring into partnership peoples of different speech and realms of discordant manners, determined that all the civilised world should be harnessed to one ruling power and bear gently bonds in harmony under the yoke, so that love of their religion should hold men's hearts in union; for no bond is made that is worthy of Christ unless unity of spirit leagues together the nations it associates. Only concord knows God; it alone worships the beneficent Father aright in peace. The untroubled harmony of human union wins his favour for the world; by division it drives Him away, with cruel warfare it makes Him wroth; it satisfies Him with the offering of peace and holds Him fast with quietness and brotherly love. In all lands bounded by the western ocean and lightened by Aurora at her rosy dawning, the raging war-goddess was throwing all humanity into confusion and arming savage hands to wound each other. To curb this frenzy God taught the nations everywhere to bow their heads under the same laws and become Romans—all whom Rhine and Danube flood, or Tagus with its golden stream, or great Ebro, those through whose land glides the horned river of the western world, those who are nurtured by Ganges or washed by the warm Nile's seven mouths. A common law made them equals and bound them by a single name, bringing the conquered into bonds of brotherhood. We live in countries the most diverse like fellow-citizens of the same blood dwelling within the single ramparts of their native city, and all united in an ancestral home. Regions far apart, shores separated by the sea, now meet together in appearing before one common court of law, in the way of trade in the products of their crafts they gather to one thronged market, in the way of wedlock they unite in legal marriage with a spouse of another country; for a single progeny is produced from the mixed blood of two different races. Such is the result of the great successes and triumphs of the Roman power. For the time of Christ's coming, be assured, was the way prepared which the general good will of peace among us had just built under the rule of Rome. For what room could there have been for God in a savage world and in human hearts at variance, each according to its different interest maintaining its own claims, as once things were? Where sentiments are thus disordered in man's breast, agreement upset, and faction in the soul, neither pure wisdom visits nor God enters. But if a supremacy in the soul, having gained authority to rule, checks the impulses of refractory appetite and rebellious flesh and controls all its passions under a single order, the constitution of life becomes stable and a settled way of thought draws in God in the heart and subjects itself to one Lord. . . .

Look at the crime-stained offerings to frightful Dis, to whom is sacrificed the gladiator laid low on the ill-starred arena, a victim offered to Phlegethon in misconceived expiation for Rome. For what means that senseless show with its exhibition of sinful skill, the killing of young men, the pleasure fed on blood, the deathly dust that ever enshrouds the spectators, the grim sight of the parade in the amphitheatre? Why, Charon by the murder of these poor wretches receives offerings that pay for his services as guide, and is propitiated by a crime in the name of religion. Such are the delights of the Jupiter of the dead, such the acts in which the ruler of dark Avernus finds content and refreshment. Is it not shameful that a strong imperial nation thinks it needful to offer such sacrifices for its country's welfare, and seeks the help of religion from the vaults of hell?

35. ISIDORE OF SEVILLE (ca. 570–636), the last of Western church fathers, is best known as the author of the standard medi-

Isidore of Seville, *Etymologies*. Cited (Latin) in *Isidori Hispalensis Episcopi, Etymologiarum sive originvm libri XX,* ed. W. M. Lindsay. Oxford: Clarendon Press, 1962. Vol. 1, bk. 1, chaps. 41–44. My translation.

eval encyclopedia, the *Etymologies,* in which the origins and nature
of disciplines are authoritatively, though sometimes imaginatively,
described. His definition of history, reflecting classical convention,
was accepted and repeated for centuries.

Grammas: On history. History is the narration of deeds [*res gestae*] by
which things done in the past are known. In Greek *history* is derived
from *see* [*videre*] or *know* [*cognoscere*]. According to the ancients, only
those wrote history who participated in it, and they wrote only what
they had seen. We apprehend by sight better than we learn by hearsay.
For things which are seen may be described without deception. This task
belongs to grammar, because whatever is worthy of memory must be
written down. But the monuments of history are said to be what carry
the memory of deeds. *Succession* [*series*] comes by derivation from *sertis,* a
wreath of flowers bound together successively.

On the first authors of histories. For us Moses first wrote history from
the beginning of the world. For the pagans, Dares Phrygius first wrote
the history of the Greeks and Trojans, which they had written on paper
of palm. But after Dares, Herodotus first established history in Greece.
After him, [?] illuminated those times in which Ezra wrote the law.

On the use of history. The histories of nations do not deprive readers of
useful things. For many wise men included in their histories past deeds
of men for the instruction of the present, so that through history the
reckoning of past ages and years is understood, and by the succession of
consuls and kings many necessary things are made known.

On the types of history. The field of history has three parts. For
ephemeres is the name for day-to-day activities. We call this a diary. For
what the Latins call diurnal, the Greeks call ephemeral. We call *calendars*
what are divided into months. Annals are things according to years.
Whatever memorable things, civil and military, on land and sea, are
noted in yearly commentaries, are called *annals* from yearly activities.
But history concerns many years and times, for which annual commentaries are carefully entered in books. But there is one difference between
history and annals, in that history concerns those times which we see,
while annals concern those years of which our age is ignorant. Whence
Sallust belongs to history, Livy, Eusebius, and Jerome to annals and to
history. There is also a difference between history, argument, and fable.
For history concerns real deeds; arguments those things which were not
done but which are possible; fables those things which neither were done
nor are possible because they are unnatural.

❡ CITY OF GOD

> 36. AUGUSTINE of Hippo (354–430), greatest of Latin church
> fathers, combined the major themes of the Christian vision: its
> ancient tradition, its terrible struggles, and predestined future in a
> classic and extraordinarily influential philosophy, or rather a theol-
> ogy, of history. *The City of God against the Pagans* was inspired by
> the need to defend Christianity from the charge that it was respon-
> sible for the decline of Rome, and in particular the sack of Rome by
> Alaric in 410. In this book, Augustine represents humanity as
> being on a pilgrimage between the two cities, secular and divine, as
> collectively living through six ages of man (corresponding to the
> six days of creation), and as passing through divinely programmed
> careers of the four world monarchies of Daniel on its way to
> judgment.

The true education of the human race, at least as far as God's people
were concerned, was like that of an individual. It advanced by steps in
time, as the individual does when a new stage of life is reached. Thus it
mounted from the level of temporal things to a level where it could grasp
the eternal, and from visible things to a grasp of invisibles. Note, however, that even at the stage when visible rewards from God were promised, the command was given that the one God must be worshipped.
The human heart was not permitted to yield homage to any but the soul's
true creator and lord, even to secure the worldly advantages of a fleeting
life. Assuredly if anyone denies that all things that either angels or other
men can bestow upon men are controlled by the mighty hand of the
Almighty and of none other, he is raving mad. Providence is without
doubt a subject that the Platonist Plotinus discusses. He demonstrates
that providence reaches down from the most high God, to whom belong
intellectual and inexpressible beauty, all the way to things here on earth
and proves it by the beauty that is seen in tiny flowers and in leaves. All
these, he maintains, inasmuch as they are so lowly and fade so fleetingly,
could not possibly have such perfectly designed harmony in their pro-

Augustine, *The City of God against the Pagans,* Loeb Classical Library.
3:313–315, 411–415, 417, and 419–421; 4:395–399; 5:383–385. Reprinted by permission of the publishers and the Loeb Classical Library from
Augustine, Volume 3, trans. David S. Wiesen, Volume 4, trans. Philip Levine,
and Volume 5, trans. Eva Matthews Sanford and William McAllen Green,
Cambridge, Mass.: Harvard University Press, 1965, 1966, 1968.

portions, should they not derive from a region where intellectual and immutable beauty continues to exist while at the same time it dwells in all things. . . .

I distinguish two branches of mankind: one made up of those who live according to man, the other of those who live according to God. I speak of these branches also allegorically as two cities, that is, two societies of human beings, of which one is predestined to reign eternally with God and the other to undergo eternal punishment with the devil. But this is their final state, which is to be treated later. At this juncture, inasmuch as I have said enough about origins, that of the angels, whose number we do not know, and that of the first two human beings, I should, I think, undertake to trace the careers of the two cities from the moment when the two human beings first produced offspring up to the time when procreation will come to an end. For the history of the aforesaid two cities that are my subject extends through this entire period or era, during which those who die make room for the new-born who take their place.

Cain then was the first-born of those two parents of the human race, one who belonged to the city of men; Abel was born later and belonged to the City of God. Now we know by experience that where the individual is concerned, as the Apostle has remarked, "it is not the spiritual which is first but the animal and then the spiritual"—hence everyone, arising as he does from a condemned stock, is first inevitably evil and carnal through Adam; but if he starts to progress through rebirth in Christ, he will later be good and spiritual. The same thing is true of the entire human race. For at the very start, when the two cities began their history through birth and death, the first to be born was the citizen of this world, and only after him came the alien in this world who is a member of the City of God, one predestined by grace and chosen by grace, one by grace an alien below and by grace a citizen above. . . .

There was indeed a kind of shadow and prophetic likeness of this City of God that served rather as a sign pointing to it than as a representation of its reality on earth when the time for its manifestation was due. The image too was called a holy city, a name which it earned by serving as a symbol, not showing directly the reality which is still to come. It is of this image in its serving role and of the free city that it foreshadows that the Apostle speaks when he says to the Galatians: "Tell me, you who desire to be under the law, have you not heard the law? For it is written that Abraham had two sons, one by a slave and one by a free woman. But the son of the slave was born according to the flesh, the son of the free woman through promise. Now this is an allegory. These women are two covenants. One is from Mount Sinai, bearing children for slavery; this is Hagar. Now Sinai is a mountain in Arabia and corresponds to the present Jerusalem, for she is in slavery with her children. But the Jerusalem above is free, and she is our mother. For it is written: 'Rejoice, O barren one that dost not bear; break forth and shout, thou who are not in travail; for the desolate hath more children than she who hath a husband.' Now we, brethren, like Isaac, are children of promise. . . ."

We find then in the earthly city two aspects: in one it manifests its own presence and in the other it serves by its presence to point to the heavenly city. Moreover, citizens of the earthly city are brought forth by a natural being that is corrupted by sin, whereas the citizens of the heavenly city are brought forth by a grace that frees nature from sin. Hence the former are called "vessels of wrath," the latter "vessels of mercy." This distinction was symbolized also in the two sons of Abraham; for one, Ishmael, the son of the slave called Hagar, was born according to the flesh, the other, Isaac, the son of the free woman Sarah, was born according to the promise. Both sons, to be sure, sprang from the seed of Abraham, but the one was produced by ordinary practice showing nature's way, the other came as a gift of the promise pointing to grace. In one case man's wont is presented, in the other God's beneficence is commended. . . .

Daniel prophesies about this last judgment in such a way as to foretell also the prior coming of Antichrist, and to continue his narrative to the everlasting reign of the saints. For when he had seen in his prophetic vision four beasts, signifying four kingdoms, and the fourth of them overcome by a certain king who is recognized as Antichrist, and thereafter the everlasting reign of the Son of man, who is understood to be Christ, he says: "The spirit of me, Daniel, was terrified in my abode, and the visions of my head disturbed me. And I drew near," he says, "to one of those who stood by, and asked of him the truth about all these things, and he told me the truth."

Then he tells what he heard from him of whom he asked about all these things, just as if it were the latter explaining them to him, as follows: "These four great beasts are four kingdoms, which shall arise upon the earth, and shall be swept away, and the saints of the Most High shall receive the kingdom and possess it for ever, even for ever and ever.

And I asked with care," he says, "about the fourth beast, which was different from every other beast, and far more terrible; his teeth were of iron, and his nails of bronze, and he devoured and ground to bits all the rest, and trod them under foot. And I asked about his ten horns, that were upon his head, and about that other horn, which rose up and struck down three of the former; in this horn there were eyes and a mouth that spoke mighty things, and its visage was larger than the rest. I looked, and this horn made war on the saints, and prevailed over them, until the ancient days came and gave the kingdom to the saints of the Most High; and the time came, and the saints took possession of the kingdom."

This, then, is what Daniel says he asked; and then he continues, telling what he heard. "And he said" (that is, he from whom Daniel had asked replied, saying): "The fourth beast is the fourth kingdom which shall be upon the earth, and which shall prevail over all kingdoms; and it shall devour the whole earth and tread it under foot and destroy it. And its horns are ten kings who shall arise; and after them shall arise another who shall surpass in wickedness all who were before him. And he shall humble three kings, and shall utter words against the Most High, and shall wear down the saints of the Most High, and shall think to change times and laws; and power shall be given into his hand for a time and times and half a time. And the judgement shall sit, and they shall take away his dominion to be destroyed and finally brought to naught; and the kingdom and the power and the might of the kings under the whole heaven shall be given to the saints of the Most High. And his kingdom shall be an everlasting kingdom, and all dominions shall serve and obey him. So far," says Daniel, "his speech continued. As for me, Daniel, my thoughts disturbed me much, and my countenance was changed; but I kept these words in my heart."

Now some have interpreted those four kingdoms as meaning those of the Assyrians, the Persians, the Macedonians and the Romans. Those who wish to know how fitting this interpretation is may read the book of the presbyter Jerome on Daniel, which is written with abundant learning and care. But even he who reads these words only half awake cannot doubt that the kingdom of Antichrist must be suffered in all its cruelty against the church, albeit for only a brief space of time, before the saints shall receive, through the last judgement of God, their everlasting reign. From the enumeration of days in a later passage it is clear that "a time and times and half a time" means a year and two years and half a year, or three years and a half, although sometimes in Scripture this idea is expressed in months. For, though "times" in Latin seems to be an inexact expression, the word so rendered is dual in number. The dual is not found in Latin, but it is said to exist in Hebrew, as it does in Greek. Hence "times" here has the meaning "two times." I admit that I am afraid that we may be mistaken about the ten kings whom Antichrist is to find, it seems, as if they were so many living men, and hence he may come unexpectedly, since there are not so many kings alive in the Roman world. For what if that number ten indicates the whole number of kings after whom he is to come, just as the idea of totality is often expressed by a thousand, or a hundred, or seven, or by sundry other numbers which I need not now specify? . . .

The very number of ages also, like the number of days in Creation, if reckoned according to the divisions of time which seem to be indicated in the Scriptures, throws more light on that sabbath rest, for it comes out as the seventh age. The first age, corresponding to the first day, is from Adam to the flood, the second, from then on till Abraham. These are equal, not in years, but in the number of generations, for each age is found to have ten. From this point, as the evangelist Matthew marks off the periods, three ages follow, reaching to the coming of Christ, each of which is completed in fourteen generations: one from Abraham to David, the second from then till the deportation to Babylon, the third from then until the birth of Christ in the flesh. Thus there are five ages in all. The sixth is now in progress, and is not to be measured by any fixed number of generations, for the Scripture says: "It is not for you to know the times which the Father has fixed by his own power." After this age God will rest, as on the seventh day, when he will cause the seventh day, that is, us, to rest in God himself. To discuss each of these separate ages studiously at this time is too long a task. But this seventh will be our sabbath, and its end will not be an evening, but the Lord's Day, an eighth eternal day, sanctified by the resurrection of Christ, which prefigures the eternal rest of both spirit and body. There we shall be still and see, shall see and love, shall love and praise. Behold what shall be in the end without end! For what else is our end, except to reach the kingdom which has no end?

In my judgement I have, with the help of the Lord, discharged my debt of completing this huge work. May those who think it too little or too much, forgive me; and may those who think it just enough rejoice and give thanks, not to me, but with me, to God. Amen. Amen.

¶ Therefore, whatever that science called history teaches us about the order of past events is a very important help to us. Through it we are aided in understanding the Sacred Books, even though we learn it outside the Church through our study as children. We often seek information on many points by using the Olympiads and the names of the consuls. An ignorance of the consulship in which the Lord was born and of that in which He suffered has caused some to make the mistake of believing that He suffered His Passion when He was forty-six years old. This is because the Jews maintained that the temple, which was a figure of His Body, was in the process of being built for that number of years. We know from the authority of the Gospel that He was baptized when He was about thirty years old. It is possible for us to compute how many years He lived after that from the sequence of His actions. Yet, in order that no shadow of doubt may come from any other source, we determine it more plainly and more accurately by comparing the history of the pagan nations with the Gospel. It will then be obvious that there was some reason for the statement that the temple was in building for forty-six years; since that number cannot be related to the Lord's age, it may be concerned with a more hidden teaching about the human body. For, with this body the only Son of God, through whom all things were made, did not disdain to clothe Himself for our sake.

In connection with the usefulness of history, to pass over the Greeks, what a troublesome controversy our Ambrose has settled for the readers and devoted followers of Plato! They slanderously dared to say that all the maxims of the Lord Jesus Christ, which they are forced to respect and acclaim, were learned by Him from the works of Plato, since it cannot be denied that Plato lived a long time before the human coming of the Lord. When that renowned bishop learned from his study of pagan history that, in the time of Jeremias, Plato had traveled to Egypt while the prophet was there, did he not prove that it was more probable that Plato

Augustine, *Christian Instruction* (Fathers of the Church, Vol. 2; Writings of Saint Augustine, Vol. 4). Trans. John J. Gavigan. Second edition. Washington, D.C.: Catholic University of America Press, 1950. Pp. 98–100. Reprinted by permission of The Catholic University of America Press.

had been initiated into our literature through Jeremias? As a result, he was capable of teaching and writing those things which are justly held in esteem. Not even Pythagoras himself, from whose disciples these men claim that Plato learned theology, lived before the time of the literature of the Hebrew nation. It was in this people that the worship of one God originated, and from it the Lord came "according to the flesh." So, through a study of dates, it is much more credible that those men obtained from our literature anything they said that was noble and truthful, rather than that the Lord Jesus Christ learned from the works of Plato, which it is the utmost madness to suppose.

Further, when the past arrangements of men are recounted in historical narration, we must not consider history itself among those human institutions. For things which have now passed away and cannot be revoked must be considered to be in the order of time, whose Creator and Administrator is God. It is one thing to relate what has been done, but another to teach what should be done. History reports honestly and profitably what has been accomplished. On the other hand, books of the soothsayers and all similar writings endeavor to teach what should be done or heeded, with the presumption of an instructor and not with the reliability of a guide.

> 37. PAULUS OROSIUS (fl. early fifth century) wrote his *Seven Books of History against the Pagans* in 417–418 for Augustine; it supplemented, reinforced and explicated historiographically the grand design of God as presented in *The City of God against the Pagans.*

I have obeyed your bidding, most blessed Father Augustine, and would that I have done so with as much competence as with pleasure. However, I am not completely convinced as to the result, whether I have done well or otherwise. . . . Since my humble self owes what I have done to your fatherly bidding and it is entirely your own, what has come from you returns to you; this work I have rendered my own, by this alone on my part, that I did it gladly.

You bade me speak out in opposition to the empty perversity of those

Paulus Orosius, *The Seven Books of History against the Pagans* (Fathers of the Church). Trans. Roy J. Deferrari. Washington, D.C.: Catholic University of America Press, 1964. 50:3, 4, 5–7, 44–45, 63, 285–287, and 363–364. Reprinted by permission of The Catholic University of America Press.

who, aliens to the City of God, are called "pagans" (*pagani*) from the crossroads and villages of country places or "heathen" (*gentiles*) because of their knowledge of earthly things. Although they do not inquire into the future, and either forget or do not know the past, yet defame present times as most unusually beset, as it were, by evils because there is belief in Christ and worship of God, and increasingly less worship of idols— accordingly you bade me set forth from all the records available of histories and annals whatever instances I have found recorded from the past of the burdens of war or ravages of disease or sorrows of famine or horrors of earthquakes or of unusual floods or dreadful outbreaks of fire or cruel strokes of lightning and storms of hail or even the miseries caused by parricides and shameful deeds, and unfold them systematically and briefly in the context of this book. . . .

Since nearly all men interested in writing, among the Greeks as among the Latins, who have perpetuated in words the accomplishments of kings and peoples for a lasting record, have made the beginning of their writing with Ninus, the son of Belus, king of the Assyrians, because they wish it to be believed in their blind opinion that the origin of the world and the creation of mankind were without beginning; yet they explain that kingdoms and wars began with him as if, indeed, the human race up to that time lived in the manner of beasts, and then for the first time, as if shaken and aroused, awoke to a new wisdom. I have decided to trace the beginning of man's wretchedness from the beginning of man's sin, touching on only a few examples and these briefly. Now from Adam, the first man, to the King Ninus, so-called the "Great," when Abraham was born, 3,184 years passed, which either have been omitted or unknown by all historians. But from Ninus or Abraham to Caesar Augustus, that is, to the birth of Christ, which was in the forty-second year of the Caesar's rule, when the Gates of Janus were closed, for peace had been made with the Parthians and wars had ceased in the whole world, 2,015 years have passed, in which between the performers and the writers the fruit of labors and occupations of all were wasted. Therefore, the subject itself demands that I touch upon briefly a few accounts from these books which, when speaking of the origin of the world, have lent credence to past events by the prediction of the future and the proof of subsequent happenings, not that we may seem to press their authority upon anyone, but because it is worthwhile to recall the general opinion which is common to all of us. Since, in the first place, if the world and man are directed by a divine providence, which as it is good, so also it is just, but man, who by his changeable nature and freedom of choice is both weak and stubborn, just as he should be guided with devotion when in need of help, so he must be reproved with justice for the immoderate use of his freedom. Everyone, whoever sees the human race through himself and in himself, perceives that from the beginning of man this world has been controlled by alternating periods of good and evil, then we are taught that sin and the punishment of sin began with the very first man. Furthermore, those who begin with the middle period, although they never recall early times, have described nothing but wars and calamities. What else should these wars be called but evils befalling on one side or the other? Moreover, such evils which existed then, just as they do now to a certain extent, are undoubtedly either manifest sins or the hidden punishments of sins. What, then, prevents our unfolding the beginning of this story, the main body of which others have described, and demonstrating, by a very brief account, that earlier ages which were much more numerous endured similar miseries?

Therefore, I intend to speak of the period from the founding of the world to the founding of the City; then up to the principle of Caesar and the birth of Christ, from which time the control of the world has remained under the power of the City, down even to our own time. Insofar as I shall be able to recall them, I think it necessary to disclose the conflicts of the human race and the world, as it were, through its various parts, burning with evils, set afire with the torch of greed, viewing them as from a watchtower, so that first I shall describe the world itself which the human race inhabits, as it was divided by our ancestors into three parts and then established by regions and provinces, in order that when the locale of wars and the ravages of diseases are described, all interested may more easily obtain knowledge, not only of the events of their time, but also of their location.

Our ancestors fixed a threefold decision [sic] of the whole world surrounded by a periphery of ocean, and its three parts they called Asia, Europe, and Africa, although some have thought that there should be two, that is, Asia and then Africa to be joined with Europe. . . .

Now I think that there is no one among men from whom it is possible to conceal that God made man in this world. Therefore also, when man sins the world is censured and, because of our failure to check the intemperance, this earth on which we live is punished by the disappearance of other living creatures and by the failure of our crops. So if we are the creation of God, we are properly also the object of his attention; for who loves us more than He who made us? Moreover, who regulates more orderly than He who both has made and loves us? Indeed, who can order and regulate our deeds more wisely and more firmly than He who both foresaw what had to be done and brought to accomplishment what He had foreseen? Therefore, that all power and all ordering are from God, both those who have not read feel, and those who have read recognize. But if powers are from God, how much the more are the kingdoms, from which the remaining powers precede; but if the kingdoms are hostile to one another, how much better it is if some one be the greatest to which all the power of the other kingdoms is subject, such as the Babylonian kingdom was in the beginning and, then, the Macedonian, afterward also, the African and, finally, the Roman which remains up to this day, and by the same ineffable plan at the four cardinal points of the world, four chief kingdoms preeminent in distinct stages, namely: the Babylonian kingdom in the East, the Carthaginian in the South, the Macedonian in the North, and the Roman in the West. Between the first and last of these, that is, between the Babylonian and the Roman, as it were, between an aged father and a little son, the intervening and brief kingdoms of Africa and Macedonia came as protectors and guardians, accepted by the power of time, not by the law of inheritance. Whether this is so, I shall try to explain as clearly as possible. . . .

In the two hundred and ninety-ninth year since the founding of the City, while the legates who had been sent to the Athenians to copy the laws of Solon were being awaited, famine and pestilence checked the Roman arms.

Moreover, in the three hundredth year, that is, in the ninety-fifth Olympiad, the *potestas* of the consuls, being given over to the decemvirate to establish the laws of Attica, brought great destruction upon the Republic. For the first of the decemvirs, although the rest retired, Appius Claudius alone continued the *imperium* for himself, and immediately there followed a conspiracy of the others, so that, ignoring the custom whereby the honor of the *imperium* rested with one but the *potestas* was common to all, all threw everything into confusion according to their own passions. Thus, among other things which they all insolently presumed, they suddenly, one by one, marched forth with the twelve fasces and with other honors of authority. When this new evil rule had begun, and the sense of duty on the part of the consuls had been cast aside, a line of tyrants sprang up; after adding two tables of laws to the ten previous ones, acting always in a most insolent and scornful manner, on the day when it was customary to lay aside their official powers, they proceeded with the same signs of authority. . . .

Although I think that I have already shown sufficiently that the peace of the Roman Empire was foreordained for His coming, nevertheless, I shall try to supplement that with a few more arguments.

At the Beginning of the second book when I touched lightly upon the time of the founding of Rome, I consistently described many points of similarity between Babylon, a city of the Assyrians, at the time the first in the world, and Rome, which today equally dominates the world. I pointed out that the former was the first and the latter the last empire; that the former gradually declined and the latter slowly gained strength; the the former lost its last king at the same time that the latter had its first; then, that the former was attacked and captured by Cyrus and, as it were, fell in death at the time when the latter, rising confidently after expelling the kings, began to enjoy the freedom of its own plans; and especially that when Rome was claiming her independence, then, too, the Jewish people, who were slaves under the kings at Babylon, regaining their freedom, returned to holy Jerusalem and, just as had been foretold by the prophets, rebuilt the temple of the Lord. Furthermore, I had said that between the Babylonian Empire which had arisen in the East, and the Roman Empire which arose in the West and was nourished by the heritage of the East, there intervened the Macedonian and African Empires, that is, that in the North and the South in brief intervals they played the roles of protector and guardian. I realize that no one has ever doubted that the Babylonian and Roman Empires are rightly called that of the East and that of the West. That the Macedonian Empire was in the North, not only its very geographical location, but also the altars of Alexander the Great which stand to this day at the foot of the Riphaean Mountains, teach us. Moreover, that Carthage surpassed all Africa and extended the boundaries of its empire, not only into Sicily, Sardinia, and other adjacent islands, but also into Spain, both the records of history and remains of cities show us. It has also been said that the two cities had stood for very much the same number of years, when Babylon was laid waste by the Medes and Rome was attacked by the Goths.

But now to these remarks I add the following, to make it clearer that God is the one ruler of all ages, kingdoms, and places. The Carthaginian

Empire, from its founding until its overthrow, lasted a little more than seven hundred years, likewise, the Macedonian Empire, from Caranus to Perses, a little less than seven hundred; yet both were terminated by the number seven, by which all things are decided. Rome herself also, although she was continued to the coming of our Lord Jesus Christ with her Empire intact, nevertheless, she, too, had difficulty on meeting this number. For in the seven hundredth year of its foundation, a fire of uncertain origin destroyed fourteen of its districts, and, as Livy says, never was the City damaged by a greater conflagration, so much so that some years later Caesar Augustus contributed a large sum of money from the public treasury for the restoration of the buildings which had then been burned. I would be able also to show that twice this same number of years remained for Babylon, which, after more than fourteen hundred years, was finally captured by King Cyrus, did not a consideration of present circumstances forbid. . . .

. . . We now learn daily, by frequent and trustworthy messages, that in the Spains wars are being carried on among the barbarian tribes and that slaughter is taking place on both sides; and they say, especially, that Wallia, the king of the Goths, is intent on concluding a peace. As a result of this, I would, in any way whatever, permit Christian times to be blamed freely, if, from the founding of the world to the present, any equally fortunate period can be pointed out. We have made manifest, I think, and are showing almost no more by words than by my finger the countless wars which have been stilled, the many usurpers who have been destroyed, and the very savage peoples who have been checked, confined, incorporated, and annihilated with a minimum loss of blood, no struggle, and almost without any slaughter. It is left now for our detractors to repent of their deeds and to blush at the truth, and to believe, fear, love, and follow the only true God who is all powerful, all of whose deeds they have learned to be good, even those which they think are evil.

I have set forth, with Christ's help, according to your bidding, most blessed Augustine, the desires and punishments of sinful men, the struggles of the world and the judgments of God, from the beginning of the world down to the present day, that is, during five thousand six hundred and eighteen years, as briefly and as simply as I could, but separating Christian times, because of the greater presence of Christ's grace, from the former confusion of unbelief. So now I enjoy the certain and only reward of my obedience, which I ought to have desired; but as for the quality of my books, you who bade me write them shall see; if you publish them, they shall be approved by you; if you destroy them, they shall be condemned by you.

> 38. THEODORET of Cyrus (d. ca. 466), bishop and theological controversialist, wrote an *Ecclesiastical History* to continue Eusebius's work down to 428 and to defend the church against new heresies.

Design of the History. When artists paint on panels and on walls the events of ancient history, they alike delight the eye, and keep bright for many a year the memory of the past. Historians substitute books for panels, bright description for pigment, and thus render the memory of past events both stronger and more permanent, for the painter's art is ruined by time. For this reason I too shall attempt to record in writing events in ecclesiastical history hitherto omitted, deeming it indeed not right to look on without an effort while oblivion robs noble deeds and useful stories of their due fame. For this cause too I have been frequently urged by friends to undertake this work. But when I compare my own powers with the magnitude of the undertaking, I shrink from attempting it. Trusting, however, in the bounty of the Giver of all good, I enter upon a task beyond my own strength.

Eusebius of Palestine has written a history of the Church from the time of the holy Apostles to the reign of Constantine, the prince beloved of God. I shall begin my history from the period at which his terminates.

Origin of the Arian Heresy. After the overthrow of the wicked and impious tyrants, Maxentius, Maximinus, and Licinius, the surge which those destroyers, like hurricanes, had roused was hushed to sleep; the whirlwinds were checked, and the Church henceforward began to enjoy a settled calm. This was established for her by Constantine, a prince deserving of all praise, whose calling, like that of the divine Apostle, was not of men, nor by man, but from heaven. He enacted laws prohibiting sacrifices to idols, and commanding churches to be erected. He appointed Christians to be governors of the provinces, ordering honour to be shown to the priests, and threatening with death those who dared to insult them. By some the churches which had been destroyed were rebuilt; others erected new ones still more spacious and magnificent.

Theodoret, *Ecclesiastical History*. In *A Select Library of Nicene and Post-Nicene Fathers of the Christian Church,* ed. and trans. Philip Schaff and Henry Wace. Second series. Grand Rapids, Mich.: Wm. B. Eerdmans, 1961. 3:33.

Hence, for us, all was joy and gladness, while our enemies were overwhelmed with gloom and despair. The temples of the idols were closed;
but frequent assemblies were held, and festivals celebrated, in the
churches. But the devil, full of all envy and wickedness, the destroyer of
mankind, unable to bear the sight of the Church sailing on with favourable winds, stirred up plans of evil counsel, eager to sink the vessel
steered by the Creator and Lord of the Universe.

> 39. The BOOK OF THE POPES (*Liber Pontificalis*) is a collection of
> papal biographies from Peter down to the ninth century (later con-
> tinuations carry the work to 1431) and has historical value from the
> late fifth century.

Preface. Jerome to the most blessed pope Damascus: We humbly beseech thy glorious holiness, . . . we bend in supplication and entreat
that thou deign to impart to us in order the record of the deeds done in
thy see from the principate of blessed Peter, the apostle, even to thine
own day; that thus we may humbly ascertain which of the bishops of the
aforesaid see attained the crown of martyrdom and which are judged to
have transgressed the canons of the apostles. Pray for us, most blessed
pope. Given April 27. Received at Rome.

Damascus, bishop of the city of Rome, to Jerome. The church rejoices
already, drinking with satisfaction at thy fountain, and the thirst grows
ever keener among its priests to hear of the past, in order that what is
right may be recognized and what is wrong rejected. So all the record
which the zeal of our see has been able to discover we send with gladness
to thee, beloved. Pray for us unto the holy resurrection, brother and
fellow priest. Farewell in Christ, our God and Lord. Given May 23.
Received September 26. Sent from Rome to Jerusalem.

I. Peter

Blessed Peter, the Antiochene, son of John, of the province of Galilee and the town of Beth-saida, brother of Andrew and chief of the apostles,

Blessed Peter, the apostle, and chief of the apostles, the Anti-ochene, son of John, of the prov-ince of Galilee and the town of Bethsaida, brother of Andrew,

Book of the Popes. Trans. Louise Ropes Loomis. New York: Columbia University Press, 1916. 1:3–6. Reprinted by permission of Columbia University
Press. The two columns represent the two earliest recensions from the early and
late seventh century.

first occupied the seat of the bishop in Anthiocia for 7 years. This Peter entered the city of Rome when Nero was Caesar and there occupied the seat of the bishop for 25 years,

1 month and 8 days.   2 months and 3 days.

He was bishop in the time of Tiberius Caesar and of Gaius and of Tiberius Claudius and of Nero.

He wrote two epistles which are called catholic, and the gospel of Mark, for Mark was his disciple and son by baptism; afterwards the whole source of the four gospels, which were confirmed by inquiring of him, that is Peter, and obtaining his testimony; although one gospel is couched in Greek, another in Hebrew, another in Latin, yet by his testimony were they all confirmed. . . .

He consecrated blessed Clement as bishop and committed to him the government of the see and all the church, saying: "As unto me was delivered by my Lord Jesus Christ the power to govern and to bind and loose, so also I commit it unto thee, that thou mayest ordain stewards over divers matters who will carry onward the work of the church and mayest thyself not become engrossed with the cares of the world but mayest strive to give thyself solely to prayer and preaching to the people."

After he had thus disposed affairs he received the crown of martyrdom with Paul in the year 38 after the Lord's passion.

He was buried also on the Via Aurelia, in the shrine of Apollo, near the place where he was crucified, near the palace of Nero, in the Vatican, near the triumphal district, on June 29.

He held three ordinations, 7 deacons, 10 priests, 3 bishops, in the month of December.

He held ordinations in the month of December, 3 bishops, 10 priests, 7 deacons.

℘ SPIRIT AND LETTER

40. ORIGEN (ca. 195–253/254), perhaps the greatest scholar and theologian of Christian antiquity, devoted many of his works to the allegorical interpretation of scriptures and especially to the rec-

Origen, *Song of Songs*. In Origen, *Song of Songs, Commentary and Homilies*, trans. R. P. Lawton. London: Longmans, Green, 1957. Pp. 218 and 221.

onciliation of and correspondences between the Old and New Testaments. In particular, he expounded the influential theory of textual exegesis as a search for three levels of meaning, from literal and historical to figurative and mystical.

Paul the apostle teaches us that the invisible things of God are understood by means of things that are visible, and that the things that are not seen are beheld through their relationship and likeness to things seen [Rom 1 : 20; 2 Cor 4 : 18]. He thus shows that this visible world teaches us about that which is invisible, and that this earthly scene contains certain patterns of things heavenly. Thus it is to be possible for us to mount up from the things we see on earth the things that belong to heaven. . . . And as to what he says about *the beginning and the end and the middle of the times*, he is speaking of the visible world, a beginning which Moses put at not quite six thousand years ago; the middle is a term relative to the total count of the time; and the end is that for which we hope, when *heaven and earth shall pass away* [Mt 24 : 17; Mk 13 : 21]. . . . Moreover, he relates *the alterations of courses and the changes of seasons and the revolutions of the year* of the things that are to be seen to the unseen changes and alterations of incorporeal things. And *the revolutions of the temporal years* of our present estate he relates to those most ancient and eternal years after the manner of him who said: "I had in my mind the eternal years" [Cf. Ps 77 : 5].

¶ Paul says somewhere in writing to the Corinthians: "For we know that our fathers were all under the cloud, and all were baptized into Moses in the cloud and in the sea, and all ate the same supernatural food and all drank the same supernatural drink. For they drank from the supernatural Rock which followed them, and the Rock was Christ" (1 Cor 10 : 1−4). You can see how different Paul's tradition is from the historical reading: what the Jews think is a crossing of the sea, Paul calls baptism; where they see a cloud, Paul puts the Holy Spirit; and it is in this way that he wants us to understand what the Lord commanded in the gospels when he said: "Whoever is not born again of water and the

Origen, *On Interpreting the Scripture.* In *Origen, Spirit and Fire: A Thematic Anthology of His Writings,* ed. and trans. Hans Urs von Balthasar. Washington, D.C.: Catholic University of America Press, 1984. Pp. 100−104 and 148−149. Reprinted by permission of The Catholic University of America Press.

Holy Spirit cannot enter into the kingdom of heaven" (cf. Jn 3 : 5). And the manna too, which the Jews think of as food for the stomach and satisfaction for hunger, Paul calls "spiritual food" (1 Cor 10 : 3). And not just Paul, but the Lord too, says in the same gospel: "Your fathers ate the manna in the wilderness, and they died. Whoever eats of the bread which I give him will not die for ever" (cf. Jn 6 : 49, 50). And right after that: "I am the bread which came down from heaven" (Jn 6 : 51). Hence Paul speaks quite openly about "the rock which followed them": "And the Rock was Christ" (1 Cor 10 : 4). How then are we to act, who have received such principles of interpretation from Paul, the teacher of the church? Does it not seem right that such a method coming to us from the tradition should serve as a model in all other instances: Or shall we, as some would like, abandon what so great and holy an apostle has given us and turn back to "Jewish myths" (Ti 1 : 14)? I at least, if I am interpreting this differently than Paul, think that in this I am extending my hands to the enemies of Christ, and that this is what the prophet says: "Woe to him who gives his neighbor to drink from the turmoil of confusion" (Hb 2 : 15).

With this we learn something of general import: if a sign signifies something, then each of the signs in scripture (whether in a historical or law text) is a sign indicative of something to be fulfilled later. Thus "the sign of Jonah" coming forth after three days from "the belly of the whale" was a sign of the resurrection of our Savior rising from the dead after "three days and three nights" (Mt 12 : 39–40). And what is called circumcision is a "sign" (Rom 4 : 11) of what Paul explained in the words: "We are the circumcision" (Phil 3 : 3). You too now should search out every sign in the old scriptures as a type of something in the new, and what is called sign in the new covenant as indicative of something either in the age to come or in the generations after that in which the sign took place.

Something is called a sign when, through something that is visible something else is meant. So for example . . . the sign of Jonah, and what is meant is Christ. . . .

Since this is so, we now have to sketch out what seems to us to be the marks of the proper understanding of the scripture. First, it must be shown that the purpose of the Spirit, which by God's providence through the WORD who "was in the beginning with God" (Jn 1 : 2) illuminating the ministers of truth, the prophets and the apostles, was first of all to teach us something about the hidden mysteries regarding

the fate of human beings. . . . A second purpose, because of those unable to bear the burden of investigating matters so important, was to
conceal the doctrine concerning the things just mentioned in the revealed accounts which contained information about the physical work of
creation, the creation of human beings and their growth through generation from the first pair to a great multitude. The Spirit also did this in
other histories recounting both the deeds of the just and—since they
were human—their occasional sins, and the wickedness, licentiousness
and greed of the lawless and impious. And most remarkable, in the
accounts about wars, the conquered and the conquerors, some mysteries
are revealed to those able to examine them closely. And even more remarkably, the laws of truth are predicted through the written laws; and
all this is written down in an order and with a power truly befitting the
wisdom of God. For it was intended that the covering over of the spiritual things—that is, the bodily part of the scriptures—should not be
without profit in many things and that it should be able, as far as possible, to bring improvements to the multitude. . . .

There are some things which are in no way to be observed according to
the letter of the law, and there are some things which allegory should not
change at all but are to be observed in every way just as the scripture has
them; [finally, there are also] some things which can also stand according
to the letter, but in which it is also necessary for allegory to be sought.

We have often pointed out that there is a threefold mode of understanding in the holy scripture: a historical, a moral and a mystical. We
understand from this that there is in scripture a body, a soul and a spirit.

The first glimpse of the letter is bitter enough: it prescribes the circumcision of the flesh; it gives the laws of sacrifice and all the rest that is
designated by the letter that kills (cf. 2 Cor 3 : 6). Cast all this aside like
the bitter rind of a nut. You then, secondly, come to the protective
covering of the shell in which the moral doctrine or counsel of conti-
nence is designated. These are of course necessary to protect what is
contained inside, but they too are doubtless to be smashed and broken
through. We would say, for example, that abstinence from food and
chastisement of the body is necessary as long as we are in this body,
corruptible as it is and susceptible to passion. But when it is broken and
dissolved and, in the time of its resurrection, gone over from corruption
into incorruption and from animal to spiritual, then it will be domi-
nated no longer by the labor of affliction or the punishment of abstinence, but rather by its own quality and not by any bodily corruption.

This is why abstinence seems necessary now and afterwards will have no point. Thirdly you will find hidden and concealed in these the sense of the mysteries of the wisdom and knowledge of God (cf. Col 2 : 3) in which the souls of the saints are nourished and fed not only in the present life but also in the future. This then is that priestly fruit about which the promise is given to those "who hunger and thirst for righteousness, for they shall be satisfied" (Mt 5 : 6). In this way, therefore, the gradation of this threefold mystery runs through all the scripture.

The Church in the Old Covenant, 368. You are not to think that it is only since the coming of Christ in the flesh that it has been called bride or church, but from the beginning of the human race and the very foundation of the world, or rather, to follow Paul's lead in seeking the origin of the mystery even earlier, even "before the foundation of the world." For his words are: "Even as he chose us in him before the foundation of the world, that we should be holy and blameless before him. He destined us in love to be his sons" (Eph 1 : 4–5). In the Psalms too it is written: "Remember your congregation which you have gathered from the beginning" (Ps 74 : 2). For the first foundations of the congregation of the church were laid right "from the beginning," which is why the Apostle says that the church "is built" not only "on the foundation of the apostles," but also on that of "the prophets" (Eph 2 : 20). But among the prophets is also counted Adam who prophesied a great mystery in Christ and in the church. This is found in the words: "Therefore a man leaves his father and his mother and cleaves to his wife, and they become one flesh" (Gn 2 : 24).

❡ Let no one, however, entertain the suspicion that we do not believe any history in Scripture to be real, because we suspect certain events related in it not to have taken place; or that no precepts of the law are to be taken literally, because we consider certain of them, in which either the nature or possibility of the case so requires, incapable of being observed; or that we do not believe those predictions which were written of the Saviour to have been fulfilled in a manner palpable to the senses; or that His commandments are not to be literally obeyed. We have therefore to state in answer, since we are manifestly so of opinion, that the truth of the history may and ought to be preserved in the majority of instances. For who can deny that Abraham was buried in the double cave

Origen, *De Principiis.* In *The Writings of Origen,* trans. Frederick Crombie. Edinburgh: T. and T. Clark, 1869. 1 : 323 and 325.

at Hebron, as well as Isaac and Jacob, and each of their wives? Or who doubts that Shechem was given as a portion to Joseph? or that Jerusalem is the metropolis of Judea, on which the temple of God was built by Solomon?—and countless other statements. . . . And yet I have no doubt that an attentive reader will, in numerous instances, hesitate whether this or that history can be considered to be literally true or not; or whether this or that precept ought to be observed according to the letter or no. And therefore great pains and labour are to be employed, until every reader reverentially understand that he is dealing with divine and not human words inserted in the sacred books.

> 41. JEROME (ca. 347–420), Augustine's friend and colleague, was one of the greatest biblical and classical scholars; his letters vividly depict the troubles of the collapsing Western empire. In connection with his controversial translation of the Bible (eventually the authoritative Vulgate), Jerome discussed problems of interpretation and the relation between figurative and historical meaning.

For I myself not only admit but freely proclaim that in translating from the Greek (except in the case of the holy scriptures where even the order of the words is a mystery) I render sense for sense and not word for word. For this course I have the authority of Tully who has so translated the Protagoras of Plato, the Oeconomicus of Xenophon, and the two beautiful orations which Aeschines and Demosthenes delivered one against the other. What omissions, additions, and alterations he has made substituting the idioms of his own for those of another tongue, this is not the time to say. I am satisfied to quote the authority of the translator who has spoken as follows in a prologue prefixed to the orations. "I have thought it right to embrace a labour which though not necessary for myself will prove useful to those who study. I have translated the noblest speeches of the two most eloquent of the Attic orators, the speeches which Aeschines and Demosthenes delivered one against the other; but I have rendered them not as a translator but as an orator, keeping the sense but altering the form by adapting both the metaphors and the words to suit our own idiom. I have not deemed it necessary to render word for word but I have reproduced the general style and empha-

Jerome, *Letters*. In *A Select Library of Nicene and Post-Nicene Fathers of the Christian Church*, ed. and trans. Philip Schaff and Henry Wace. Second series. Grand Rapids, Mich.: Wm. B. Eerdmans, 1961. 6:113–114 and 130.

sis. I have not supposed myself bound to pay the words out one by one to the reader but only to give him an equivalent in value." Again at the close of his task he says, "I shall be well satisfied if my rendering is found, as I trust it will be, true to this standard. In making it I have utilized all the excellences of the originals, I mean the sentiments, the forms of expression and the arrangement of the topics, while I have followed the actual wording only so far as I could do so without offending our notions of taste. If all that I have written is not to be found in the Greek, I have at any rate striven to make it correspond with it." Horace too, an acute and learned writer, in his Art of Poetry gives the same advice to the skilled translator:—

> And care not thou with over anxious thought
> To render word for word.

. . . I shudder when I think of the catastrophes of our time. For twenty years and more the blood of Romans has been shed daily between Constantinople and the Julian Alps. Scythia, Thrace, Macedonia, Dardania, Dacia, Thessaly, Achaia, Epirus, Dalmatia, the Pannonias—each and all of these have been sacked and pillaged and plundered by Goths and Sarmatians, Quades and Alans, Huns and Vandals and Marchmen. How many of God's matrons and virgins, virtuous and noble ladies, have been made the sport of these brutes! Bishops have been made captive, priests and those in minor orders have been put to death. Churches have been overthrown, horses have been stalled by the altars of Christ, the relics of martyrs have been dug up.

> Mourning and fear abound on every side
> And death appears in countless shapes and forms.

The Roman world is falling: yet we hold up our heads instead of bowing them. What courage, think you, have the Corinthians now, or the Athenians or the Lacedaemonians or the Arcadians, or any of the Greeks over whom the barbarians bear sway?

❡ The truth is that I have partly discharged the office of a translator and partly that of a writer. I have with the utmost fidelity rendered the Greek

Jerome, *Preface to the Chronicle of Eusebius.* In *A Select Library of Nicene and Post-Nicene Fathers of the Christian Church,* ed. and trans. Philip Schaff and Henry Wace. Second series. Grand Rapids, Mich.: Wm. B. Eerdmans, 1961. 6:484.

portion, and at the same time have added certain things which appeared to me to have been allowed to slip, particularly in the Roman history, which Eusebius, the author of this book, as it seems to me, only glanced at; not so much because of ignorance, for he was a learned man, as because, writing in Greek, he thought them of slight importance to his countrymen. So again from Ninus and Abraham, right up to the captivity of Troy, the translation is from the Greek only. From Troy to the twentieth year of Constantine there is much, at one time separately added, at another intermingled, which I have gleaned with great diligence from Tranquillus and other famous historians. Moreover, the portion from the aforesaid year of Constantine to the sixth consulship of the Emperor Valens and the second of Valentinianus is entirely my own. Content to end here, I have reserved the remaining period, that of Gratianus and Theodosius, for a wider historical survey; not that I am afraid to discuss the living freely and truthfully, for the fear of God banishes the fear of man; but because while our country is still exposed to the fury of the barbarians everything is in confusion.

> 42. HUGH OF ST. VICTOR (d. 1142) was a teacher of arts and theology, biblical exegete, and the author of the *Didascalicon,* a guidebook for students which treats the correct method of textual interpretation and the origin and value of disciplines, including history, the foundation of sacred as well as secular learning.

Concerning the Origin of Logic. Such was the origin of all the arts; scanning them all, we find this true. Before there was grammar, men both wrote and spoke; before there was dialectic, they distinguished the true from the false by reasoning; before there was rhetoric, they discoursed upon civil laws; before there was arithmetic there was knowledge of counting; before there was an art of music, they sang; before there was geometry, they measured fields; before there was astronomy, they marked off periods of time from the course of the stars. But then came the arts, which, though they took their rise in usage, nonetheless excel it.

This would be the place to set forth who were the inventors of the separate arts, when these persons flourished and where, and how the

Hugh of St. Victor, *Didascalicon.* In *The Didascalicon of Hugh of St. Victor: A Medieval Guide to the Arts,* trans. Jerome Taylor. New York: Columbia University Press, 1961. Pp. 59–60, 91–92, 120–121, 135–136, and 138–139. Reprinted by permission of Columbia University Press.

various disciplines made a start in their hands: first, however, I wish to distinguish the individual arts from one another by dividing philosophy into its parts, so to say. I should therefore briefly recapitulate the things I have said thus far, so that the transition to what follows may more easily be made. . . .

Concerning Order in Expounding a Text. . . . Order in the disciplines is arranged to follow nature. In books it is arranged according to the person of the author or the nature of the subject matter. In narration it follows an arrangement which is of two kinds—either natural, as when deeds are recounted in the order of their occurrence, or artificial, as when a subsequent event is related first and a prior event is told after it. In the exposition of a text, the order followed is adapted to inquiry.

Exposition includes three things: the letter, the sense, and the inner meaning. The letter is the fit arrangement of words, which we also call construction; the sense is a certain ready and obvious meaning which the letter presents on the surface; the inner meaning is the deeper understanding which can be found only through interpretation and commentary. Among these, the order of inquiry is first the letter, then the sense, and finally the inner meaning. And when this is done, the exposition is complete. . . .

Concerning the Threefold Understanding. First of all, it ought to be known that Sacred Scripture has three ways of conveying meaning—namely, history, allegory, and tropology. To be sure, all things in the divine utterance must not be wrenched to an interpretation such that each of them is held to contain history, allegory, and tropology all at once. Even if a triple meaning can appropriately be assigned in many passages, nevertheless it is either difficult or impossible to see it everywhere. . . . Thus is it that, in a wonderful manner, all of Sacred Scripture is so suitably adjusted and arranged in all parts through the Wisdom of God that whatever is contained in it either resounds with the sweetness of spiritual understanding in the manner of strings; or, containing utterances of mysteries set here and there in the course of a historical narrative or in the substance of a literal context, and, as it were, connecting these up into one object, it binds them together all at once. . . .

Concerning the Order Which Exists in the Disciplines. First of all, the student of Sacred Scripture ought to look among history, allegory, and tropology for that order sought in the disciplines—that is, he should ask which of these three precedes the others in the order of study.

In this question it is not without value to call to mind what we see happen in the construction of buildings, where first the foundation is laid, then the structure is raised upon it, and finally, when the work is all finished, the house is decorated by the laying on of color.

Concerning History. So too, in fact, must it be in your instruction. First you learn history and diligently commit to memory the truth of the deeds that have been performed, reviewing from beginning to end what has been done, when it has been done, where it has been done, and by whom it has been done. For these are the four things which are especially to be sought for in history—the person, the business done, the time, and the place. Nor do I think that you will be able to become perfectly sensitive to allegory unless you have first been grounded in history. Do not look down upon these least things. The man who looks down on such smallest things slips little by little. If, in the beginning, you had looked down on learning the alphabet, now you would not even find your names listed with those of the grammar students. . . .

But just as you see that every building lacking a foundation cannot stand firm, so also is it in learning. The foundation and principle of sacred learning, however, is history, from which, like honey from the honeycomb, the truth of allegory is extracted. As you are about to build, therefore, "Lay first the foundation of history; next, by pursuing the 'typical' meaning, build up a structure in your mind to be a fortress of faith. Last of all, however, through the loveliness of morality, paint the structure over as with the most beautiful colors."

You have in history the means through which to admire God's deeds, in allegory the means through which to believe his mysteries, in morality the means through which to imitate his perfection. Read, therefore, and learn that "in the beginning God created heaven and earth." Read that in the beginning he planted "a paradise of pleasure wherein he placed man whom he had formed." Him sinning God expelled and thrust out into the trials of this life. Read how the entire offspring of the human race descended from one man; how, subsequently, flood destroyed sinners; how, in the midst of the waters, the divine mercy preserved the man Noah with his sons; next, how Abraham received the mark of faith, but afterwards Israel went down into Egypt; how God thereafter led the sons of Israel out of Egypt by the hand of Moses and Aaron, brought them through the Red Sea and through the desert, gave them the Law, and settled them in the land of promise; how often he delivered them as sinners into the hands of their enemies and afterwards freed them again when they were penitent; how first through judges, then through kings, he rules his people: "He took his servant David from following the ewes great with young." Solomon he enlightened with wisdom. For the weeping Ezechiel he added on fifteen years. Thereafter he sent the straying people captive into Babylon by the hand of Nabuchodonosor. After seventy years he brought them back, through Cyrus. At last, however, when that time was already declining, he sent his Son into our flesh, and he, having sent his apostles into all the world, promised eternal life to those who were repentant. He foretold that he would come at the end of the ages to judge us, to make a return to each man according to his deeds—namely, eternal fire for sinners, but for the just, eternal life and the kingdom of which there shall be no end. See how, from the time when the world began until the end of the ages, the mercies of God do not slacken.

5
❡ The Middle Ages

The "barbarian" historians of early medieval Europe worked within the general Christian framework of universal history beginning with creation and with some vague recollection of classical historiography; but their theme was the story, sometimes legendary, of particular national traditions: Gothic, Frankish, Lombard, Anglo-Saxon, and others. The cultural activities accompanying the Carolingian renovation of empire to some extent renewed ties with classical culture, but monasteries formed the center of historical writing for much of the later medieval period, most notably in England and France.

The "renaissance of the twelfth century," as C. H. Haskins described it, included a revival of historical scholarship and writing as well as of Greek science and Roman law. A sense of history was apparent not only in the renewed interest in classical antiquity and in the narrative form of history but also in the approach (historical in the sense of literal and nonfigurative) to biblical and legal texts and in criticism of forgeries and legends. The Eusebian and Augustinian scheme of universal history was preserved and elaborated in different ways by such authors as Otto of Freising, Vincent of Beauvais, and Joachim of Flora.

In the later Middle Ages, the vernacular began to rival and eventually to replace Latin as the medium of narrative history. French, English, and Italian chronicles, local, urban, national, and ecclesiastical, recorded and investigated social, cultural, and political affairs and became vehicles of propaganda and controversy. Yet the old Ciceronian conception of history, especially regarding its truthfulness and utility, continued to be invoked; to that extent, European historiography represents a continuation of the enterprise begun by Herodotus and Thucydides.

❧ BARBARIAN HISTORY

43. JORDANES (d. 554?) based his *Gothic History* (ca. 550) on the lost work of Cassiodorus. Though somewhat crude and credulous, this book is the first account of Germanic migrations, drawn presumably (in Livian fashion) from legends and oral tradition. Its discussion of *Getica* sets a style for barbarian history.

Though it had been my wish to glide in my little boat by the edge of the peaceful shore and, as a certain writer says, to catch little fishes from the pools of the ancients, you, brother Castalius, bid me set my sails toward the deep. You urge me to leave the little work I have in hand, that is, the abbreviation of the Chronicles, and to condense in my own style in this small book the twelve volumes of Senator on the origin and deeds of the Getae from olden time to the present day, descending through the generations of the kings. Truly a hard command, and imposed by one who seems unwilling to realize the burden of the task. Nor do you note this, that my utterance is too slight to fill so magnificent a trumpet of speech as his. But worse than every other burden is the fact that I have no access to his books that I may follow his thought. Still— and let me lie not—I have in times past read the books a second time by his steward's loan for a three days' reading. The words I recall not, but the sense and the deeds related I think I retain entire. To this I have added fitting matters from some Greek and Latin histories. I have also put in an introduction and a conclusion, and have inserted many things of my own authorship. Wherefore reproach me not, but receive and read with gladness what you have asked me to write. If aught be insufficiently spoken and you remember it, do you as a neighbor to our race add to it, praying for me, dearest brother. The Lord be with you. Amen. . . .

Now from this island of Scandza, as from a hive of races or a womb of nations, the Goths are said to have come forth long ago under their king, Berig by name. As soon as they disembarked from their ships and set foot on the land, they straightaway gave their name to the place. And even to-day it is said to be called Gothiscandza. Soon they moved from here to the abodes of the Ulmerugi, who then dwelt on the shores of Ocean, where they pitched camp, joined battle with them and drove

Jordanes, *The Origin and Deeds of the Goths*. In *The Gothic History of Jordanes*, trans. Charles Christopher Mierow. Princeton, N.J.: Princeton University Press, 1915. Pp. 51, 57–58, and 142.

them from their homes. Then they subdued their neighbors, the Vandals, and thus added to their victories. But when the number of the people increased greatly and Filimer, son of Gadaric, reigned as king—about the fifth since Berig—he decided that the army of the Goths with their families should move from that region. In search of suitable homes and pleasant places they came to the land of Scythia, called *Oium* in that tongue. Here they were delighted with the great richness of the country, and it is said that when half the army had been brought over, the bridge whereby they had crossed the river fell in utter ruin, nor could anyone thereafter pass to or fro. For the place is said to be surrounded by quaking bogs and an encircling abyss, so that by this double obstacle nature has made it inaccessible. And even to-day one may hear in that neighborhood the lowing of cattle and may find traces of men, if we are to believe the stories of travellers, although we must grant that they hear these things from afar.

This part of the Goths, which is said to have crossed the river and entered with Filimer into the country of Oium, came into possession of the desired land, and there they soon came upon the race of the Spali, joined battle with them and won the victory. Thence the victors hastened to the farthest part of Scythia, which is near the sea of Pontus; for so the story is generally told in their early songs, in almost historic fashion. Ablabius also, a famous chronicler of the Gothic race, confirms this in his most trustworthy account. Some of the ancient writers also agree with the tale. Among these we may mention Josephus, a most reliable relator of annals, who everywhere follows the rule of truth and unravels from the beginning the origin of things;—but why he has omitted the beginnings of the race of the Goths, of which I have spoken, I do not know. He barely mentions Magog of that stock, and says they were Scythians by race and were called so by name.

Before we enter on our history, we must describe the boundaries of this land, as it lies. . . .

And now we have recited the origin of the Goths, the noble line of the Amali and the deeds of brave men. This glorious race yielded to a more glorious prince and surrendered to a more valiant leader, whose fame shall be silenced by no ages or cycles of years; for the victorious and triumphant Emperor Justinian and his consul Belisarius shall be named and known as Vandalicus, Africanus and Geticus.

Thou who readest this, know that I have followed the writings of my ancestors, and have culled a few flowers from their broad meadows to weave a chaplet for him who cares to know these things. Let no one believe that to the advantage of the race of which I have spoken—though indeed I trace my own descent from it—I have added aught besides what I have read or learned by iniquity. Even thus I have not included all that is written or told about them, nor spoken so much to their praise as to the glory of him who conquered them.

> 44. GREGORY OF TOURS (Georgius Florentinus Gregorius, 538–594) was bishop of that city after 573 and had some education in the liberal arts, though more in Scripture. He was the author of devotional works and, from 574 on, of the *History of the Franks*. After a conventional survey of universal history, he devoted his book to the Christian phase of Frankish history down to his own day. For Gregory, the Christian Creed was the centerpiece and starting point of his history, as Providence was its foundation; yet his attention was monopolized by the details of violence, warfare, and the sin of misery, which formed the substance of human history.

Here Begins Gregory's First Preface. With liberal culture on the wane, or rather perishing in the Gallic cities, there were many deeds being done both good and evil: the heathen were raging fiercely; kings were growing more cruel; the church, attacked by heretics, was defended by Catholics; while the Christian faith was in general devoutly cherished, among some it was growing cold; the churches also were enriched by the faithful or plundered by traitors—and no grammarian skilled in the dialectic art could be found to describe these matters either in prose or verse; and many were lamenting and saying: "Woe to our day, since the pursuit of letters has perished from among us and no one can be found among the people who can set forth the deeds of the present on the written page." Hearing continually these complaints and others like them I [have undertaken] to commemorate the past, in order that it may come to the knowledge of the future; and although my speech is rude, I have been unable to be silent as to the struggles between the wicked and the upright; and I have been especially encouraged because, to my surprise, it has often been said by men of our day, that few understand the learned words of the rhetorician but many the rude language of the common people. I have decided also that for the reckoning of the years

Gregory of Tours, *History of the Franks*. Trans. Ernest Brehaut. New York: W. W. Norton, 1969. Pp. 1, 5, and 6–7.

the first book shall begin with the very beginning of the world, and I have given its chapters below. . . .

In Christ's Name. Here Begins the First Book of the Histories. As I am about to describe the struggles of kings with the heathen enemy, of martyrs with pagans, of churches with heretics, I desire first of all to declare my faith so that my reader may have no doubt that I am Catholic. I have also decided, on account of those who are losing hope of the approaching end of the world, to collect the total of past years from chronicles and histories and set forth clearly how many years there are from the begining of the world. But I first beg pardon of my readers if either in letter or in syllable I transgress the rules of the grammatic art in which I have not been fully instructed, since I have been eager only for this, to hold fast, without any subterfuge or irresolution of heart, to that which we are bidden in the church to believe, because I know that he who is liable to punishment for his sin can obtain pardon from God by untainted faith.

I believe, then, in God the Father omnipotent. I believe in Jesus Christ his only Son, our Lord God, born of the Father, not created. [I believe] that he has always been with the Father, not only since time began but before all time. For the Father could not have been so named unless he had a son; and there could be no son without a father. But as for those who say: "There was a time when he was not," I reject them with curses, and call men to witness that they are separated from the church. I believe that the word of the Father by which all things were made was Christ. I believe that this word was made flesh and by its suffering the world was redeemed, and I believe that humanity, not deity, was subject to the suffering. . . .

I believe that the soul is immortal but that nevertheless it has no part in deity. And I faithfully believe all things that were established at Nicaea by the three hundred and eighteen bishops. But as to the end of the world I hold beliefs which I learned from our forefathers, that Antichrist will come first. . . .

As to the reckoning of this world, the chronicles of Eusebius, bishop of Caesarea, and of Jerome the priest, speak clearly, and they reveal the plan of the whole succession of years. Orosius too, searching into these matters very carefully, collects the whole number of years from the beginning of the world down to his own time. Victor also examined into this connection with the time of the Easter festival. And so we follow the works of the writers mentioned above and desire to reckon the complete series of years from the creation of the first man down to our own time, if the Lord shall deign to lend his aid. And this we shall more easily accomplish if we begin with Adam himself.

> 45. THE CHRONICLE OF FREDEGAR (7th century) was a compilation of universal history from creation, using Eusebius as well as Gregory and Isidore of Seville. It continued Gregory's story of the Franks and included the first mention of the theory of their Trojan origins.

Unless the Almighty helps me, I cannot tell how I can express in one word the labour on which I am embarking and how, in striving to succeed, my long struggle devours days already too short. "Translator" in our own vernacular gives the wrong sense, for if I feel bound to change somewhat the order of words, I should appear not to abide by a translator's duty. I have most carefully read the chronicles of St. Jerome, of Hydatius, of a certain wise man, of Isidore and of Gregory, from the beginning of the world to the decline of Guntramm's reign; and I have reproduced successively in this little book, in suitable language and without many omissions, what these learned men have recounted at length in their five chronicles.

Further, I have judged it necessary to be more thorough in my striving for accuracy, and so I have noted in the above-mentioned chronicles, as it were a source of material for a future work, all the reigns of the kings and their chronology. I have brought together and put into order in these pages, as exactly as I can, this chronology and the doings of many peoples and have inserted them in the chronicles (a Greek word meaning in Latin the record of the years) compiled by these wise men, chronicles that copiously gush like a spring most pure. I could have wished that I had the same command of language, or at least approached it; but it is harder to draw from a spring that flows intermittently. And now the world grows old, which is why the fine point of wisdom is lost to us. Nobody now is equal to the orators of past times, or could even pretend to equality. Thus I am compelled, so far as my rusticity and ignorance permit, to hand on as briefly as possible whatever I have learned from the books of which I have spoken; and if any reader doubts me, he has only to

The Chronicle of Fredegar. In *The Fourth Book of the Chronicle of Fredegar with Its Continuations,* trans. J. M. Wallace–Hadrill. London: Thomas Nelson and Sons, 1960. Pp. 1–3.

turn to the same author to find that I have said nothing but the truth. At
the end of Gregory's work I have not fallen silent but have continued on
my own account with facts and deeds of later times, finding them wherever they were recorded, and relating of the deeds of kings and the wars
of peoples all that I have read or heard or seen that I could vouch for. Here
I have tried to put in all I could discover from that point at which
Gregory stopped writing, that is, from the death of King Chilperic.

ℭ CHRONICLES

46. BEDE (673–735), the father of English history, was a learned
Northumbrian monk who wrote many works, including a pioneering treatise on chronology, in which he established the convention
of dating "from the Lord's incarnation" ("A.D."). He also continued Isidore of Seville's chronicle, making use of the Augustinian
scheme of six ages. Most influential was his *Ecclesiastical History,*
the greatest of barbarian histories, covering secular as well as
church history from 597 to 731. Modeled on Eusebius's history,
Bede's book began with an account of England's geography and first
inhabitants and carried the story from Caesar's landing (55 B.C.)
through the conversion of the Anglo-Saxons and spread of the faith
down to his own day. His efforts to collect sources, continental as
well as English, and his view of the utility of history are expressed
in his preface.

To the Most Glorious King Ceowulf. Bede the Priest and Servant of Christ.

Some while ago, at Your Majesty's request, I gladly sent you the history of the Church in England which I had recently completed, in order
that you might read it and give it your approval. I now send it once again
to be transcribed, so that Your Majesty may consider it at greater leisure.
I warmly welcome the diligent zeal and sincerity with which you study
the words of Holy Scripture, and your eager desire to know something
of the doings and sayings of great men of the past, and of our own nation
in particular. For if history records good things of good men, the

Bede, *A History of the English Church and People.* Trans. Leo Sherley-Price.
Penguin Classics. Baltimore: Penguin, 1955. Pp. 33–39.

thoughtful hearer is encouraged to imitate what is good: or if it records evil of wicked men, the good, religious listener or reader is encouraged to avoid all that is sinful and perverse, and to follow what he knows to be good and pleasing to God. Your Majesty is well aware of this; and since you feel so deeply responsible for the general good of those over whom divine Providence has set you, you wish that this history may be better known both to yourself and to your people.

But in order to avoid any doubts as to the accuracy of what I have written in the minds of yourself or of any who may listen to or read this history, allow me briefly to state the authorities upon whom I chiefly depend.

My principal authority and adviser in this work has been the most reverend Abbot Albinus, an eminent scholar educated in the church of Canterbury by Archbishop Theodore and Abbot Hadrian, both of them respected and learned men. He carefully transmitted to me verbally or in writing through Nothelm, a priest of the church of London, anything he considered worthy of mention that had been done by disciples of the blessed Pope Gregory in the province of Canterbury or the surrounding regions. Such facts he ascertained either from records or from long established traditions. Nothelm himself later visited Rome, and obtained permission from the present Pope Gregory (II) to examine the archives of the holy Roman Church. He found there letters of Pope Gregory (I) and other Popes, and when he returned, the reverend father Albinus advised him to bring them to me for inclusion in this history. So from the period at which this volume begins until the time when the English nation received the Faith of Christ, I have drawn extensively on earlier writers. But from that time until the present, I owe much of my information about what was done in the See of Canterbury by the disciples of Pope Gregory and their successors, and under what kings events occurred, to the remarkable industry of Abbot Albinus made known to me through Nothelm. They also provided some of my information about the bishops and kings under whom the provinces of the East and West Saxons, the East Angles, and the Northumbrians received the grace of the Gospel. Indeed, it was due to the persuasion of Albinus that I was encouraged to begin this work. Also the most reverend Bishop Daniel of the West Saxons sent to me in writing certain facts about the history of the Church in his province, in the adjoining province of the South Saxons, and in the Island of Vectis. I am indebted to the brethren of Lastingham monastery for their careful account of the conversion of the province of Mercia to

Christ by the holy priests Cedd and Ceadda, their founders; of how the province of the East Saxons rejected and recovered the Faith; and of how their holy fathers lived and died. In addition, I have traced the progress of the Church in the province of the East Angles, partly from old traditions, and partly from the account given by the most reverend Abbot Esi. The growth of the Christian Faith and succession of bishops in the province of Lindsey I have learned either from the letters of the most reverend Bishop Cynebert, or by word of mouth from other reliable persons. But with regard to events in the various districts of the province of Northumbria, from the time that it received the Faith of Christ up to the present day, I am not dependent on any one author, but on countless faithful witnesses who either know or remember the facts, apart from what I know myself. In this connexion, it should be noted that whatever I have written concerning our most holy father and Bishop Cuthbert, whether in this book or in my separate account of his life and doings, I have in part taken and accurately copied from a Life already compiled by the brethren of the Church of Lindisfarne; and I have carefully added to this whatever I could learn from the reliable accounts of those who knew him. Should the reader discover any inaccuracies in what I have written, I humbly beg that he will not impute them to me, because, as the laws of history require, I have laboured honestly to transmit whatever I could ascertain from common report for the instruction of posterity.

I earnestly request all who may hear or read this history of our nation to ask God's mercy on my many failings of mind and body. And in return for the diligent toil that I have bestowed on the recording of memorable events in the various provinces and places of greater note, I beg that their inhabitants may grant me the favour of frequent mention in their devout prayers. . . .

Britain, formerly known as Albion, is an island in the ocean, facing between north and west, and lying at a considerable distance from the coasts of Germany, Gaul, and Spain, which together form the greater part of Europe. It extends 800 miles northwards, and is 200 in breadth, except where a number of promontories stretch further, the coastline round which extends to 3675 miles. To the south lies Belgic Gaul, from the nearest shore of which travellers can see the city known as Rutubi Portus, which the English have corrupted to Reptacestir. The distance from these across the sea to Gessoriacum, the nearest coast of the Morini, is fifty miles, or, as some write it, 450 furlongs. On the opposite side of Britain, which lies open to the boundless ocean, lie the isles of the Orcades. Britain is rich in grain and timber; it has good pasturage for cattle and draught animals, and vines are cultivated in various localities. There are many land and sea birds of various species, and it is well known for its plentiful springs and rivers abounding in fish. There are salmon and eel fisheries, while seals, dolphins, and sometimes whales are caught. There are also many varieties of shell-fish, such as mussels, in which are often found excellent pearls of several colours, red, purple, violet, and green, but mainly white. Cockles are abundant, and a beautiful scarlet dye is extracted from them which remains unfaded by sunshine or rain; indeed, the older the cloth, the more beautiful its colour. The country has both salt and hot springs, and the waters flowing from them provide hot baths, in which the people bathe separately according to age and sex. As Saint Basil says: "Water receives its heat when it flows across certain metals, and becomes hot, and even scalding." The land has rich veins of many metals, including copper, iron, lead, and silver. There is also much black jet of fine quality, which sparkles in firelight: when burned, it drives away snakes, and, like amber, when it is warmed by friction, it clings to whatever is applied to it. In old times, the country had twenty-eight noble cities, and innumerable castles, all of which were guarded by walls, towers, and barred gates.

Since Britain lies far north toward the pole, the nights are short in summer, and at midnight it is hard to tell whether the evening twilight still lingers or whether dawn is approaching; for in these northern latitudes the sun does not remain long below the horizon at night. Consequently both summer days and winter nights are long, and when the sun withdraws southwards, the winter nights last eighteen hours. In Armenia, Macedonia, and Italy, and other countries of that latitude, the longest day lasts only fifteen hours and the shortest nine.

At the present time there are in Britain, in harmony with the five books of the divine law, five languages and four nations—English, British, Scots, and Picts. Each of these have their own language, but all are united in their study of God's truth by the fifth—Latin—which has become a common medium through the study of the scriptures. The original inhabitants of the islands were the Britons, from whom it takes its name, and who, according to tradition, crossed into Britain from Armorica, and occupied the southern parts. When they had spread northwards and possessed the greater part of the island, it is said that some Picts from Scythia put to sea in a few longships, and were driven by storms around the coasts of Britain, arriving at length on the north coast of Ireland. Here they found the nation of the Scots, from whom they asked permission to settle, but their request was refused. Ireland is the largest island after Britain, and lies to the west. It is shorter than Britain to the north, but extends far beyond it to the south towards the northern coasts of Spain, although a wide sea separates them. These Pictish seafarers, as I have said, asked for a grant of land to make a settlement. The Scots replied that there was not room for them both, but said: "We can give you good advice. There is another island not far to the east, which we often see in the distance on clear days. Go and settle there if you wish; should you meet resistance, we will come to your help." So the Picts crossed into Britain, and began to settle in the north of the island, since the Britons were in possession of the south. Having no women with them, these Picts asked wives of the Scots, who consented on condition that, when any dispute arose, they should choose a king from the female royal line rather than the male. This custom continues among the Picts to this day. As time went on, Britain received a third nation, that of the Scots, who migrated from Ireland under their chieftain Reuda, and by a combination of force and treaty, obtained from the Picts the settlements that they still hold. From the name of this chieftain, they are still known as Dalreudians, for in their tongue *dal* means a division.

> 47. EADMER (ca. 1060–1128), who was born before the Norman Conquest and who served in the household of Archbishop Lanfranc of Canterbury, took as his theme the life of Lanfranc's successor Anselm, both in a biography and in his *History of the Recent Events in England*.

What an inestimable benefit have they conferred on posterity who with an eye to the good of future generations have committed to writing a record of the events of their own times. This is the conclusion which seems to be borne in upon me when I note how men of the present day under stress or difficulties of one kind or another search laboriously into the doings of their predecessors, anxious to find there a source of comfort and strength and yet, because of the scarcity of written documents which has resulted in the events being all too quickly buried in oblivion, they cannot for all their pains succeed in doing so as they would wish. I cannot doubt that those who have composed such records, provided they have laboured with a good motive, will receive from God a good reward.

Eadmer, *History of the Recent Events in England*. Trans. Geoffrey Bosanquet. London: Cresset, 1964. Pp. 1–2.

Accordingly, having this consideration in mind I have determined, while aiming at brevity, to set down in writing the things which I have seen with my own eyes and myself heard. This I do both to comply with the wishes of my friends who strongly urge me to do so and at the same time to render some slight service to the researches of those who come after me if they should chance to find themselves involved in any crisis in which the events which I record can in any respect afford a helpful precedent. I may add that the main purpose of this work is first to describe how Anselm, Abbot of the Monastery of Bec, was made Archbishop of Canterbury, and then to shew how it came about that, a disagreement having arisen between him and the Kings of England, he was so often and for so long absent in exile from the country and what has been the outcome of the question in dispute between them.

Now it would seem that the question which gave rise to this dispute is a matter entirely new to this century of ours and, at any rate from the time that the Normans began to rule here, to say nothing of the time before that, no such question had ever been heard by people in England. From the time that William, Duke of Normandy, conquered England and subdued it no one was ever made a bishop or abbot there without first being made the King's man and receiving from the King investiture by the presentation of the pastoral staff. To this rule there were only two exceptions, namely Ernest and Gundulf, who successively presided over the Church of Rochester. They, as was customary in the case of that diocese, were invested by Lanfranc, Archbishop of Canterbury. Now Anselm wished to put an end to this practice of investiture by the King, as being contrary to God and to the canons of the Church, and thereby to prune away the mischiefs resulting from it. It was on this account that he incurred the enmity of the Kings of England and was forced to quit the country; not that there were not also other reasons for his departure as the course of events will shew.

My story will also include a number of other occurrences which took place in England before, during and after the matters already mentioned, occurrences of which we do not think it right that those who come after us should be deprived of all knowledge, so far as it is within our power to prevent it. But in the preface this brief reference to all these matters is enough.

We come then to the plan of our narrative. We should, we think, begin by going a little further back and tracing in brief outline what was, so to speak, the actual planting of the seed from which grew the developments which we are to record. This should be our starting point.

> 48. WILLIAM OF MALMESBURY (ca. 1095–1143), a monk and librarian who was born of a French knight and an English mother, was probably the best of the many English historians after Bede. His *Chronicle of the Kings of England* and *Modern History* (*Historia novella*) tried to tell the story of England, from Caesar to Henry II, with "Roman art": with some attempt at causal sequence and critical use of his predecessors.

The history of the English, from their arrival in Britain to his own times, has been written by Bede, a man of singular learning and modesty, in a clear and captivating style. After him you will not, in my opinion, easily find any person who has attempted to compose in Latin the history of this people. Let others declare whether their researches in this respect have been, or are likely to be, more fortunate; my own labour, though diligent in the extreme, has, down to this period, been without its reward. There, are, indeed, some notices of antiquity, written in the vernacular tongue after the manner of a chronicle, and arranged according to the years of our Lord. By means of these alone, the times succeeding this man have been rescued from oblivion: for of Elward, a noble and illustrious man, who attempted to arrange these chronicles in Latin, and whose intention I could applaud if his language did not disgust me, it is better to be silent. Nor has it escaped my knowledge, that there is also a work of my Lord Eadmer, written with a chastened elegance of style, in which, beginning from King Edgar, he has but hastily glanced at the times down to William the First: and thence, taking a freer range, gives a narrative, copious, and of great utility to the studious, until the death of Archbishop Ralph. Thus from the time of Bede there is a period two hundred and twenty-three years left unnoticed in his history; so that the regular series of time, unsupported by a connected relation, halts in the middle. This circumstance has induced me, as well out of love to my country, as respect for the authority of those who have enjoined me the undertaking, to fill up the chasm, and to season the crude materials with Roman art. And that the

William of Malmesbury, *Chronicle of the Kings of England from the Earliest Period to the Reign of King Stephen.* Ed. and trans. J. A. Giles. London: George Bell and Sons, 1904. Pp. 3–5.

work may proceed with greater regularity, I shall cull somewhat from Bede, whom I must quote, glancing at a few facts, but omitting more.

The First Book, therefore, contains a succinct account of the English, from the time of their descent on Britain, till that of King Egbert, who, after the different Princes had fallen by various ways, gained the monarchy of almost the whole island.

But as among the English arose four powerful kingdoms, that is to say, of Kent, of the West Saxons, of the Northumbrians, and of the Mercians, of which I purpose severally to treat if I have leisure, I shall begin with that which attained the earliest to maturity, and was also the first to decay. This I shall do more clearly, if I place the kingdoms of the East Angles, and of the East Saxons, after the others, as little meriting either my labours, or the regard of posterity.

The Second Book will contain the chronological series of the Kings to the coming of the Normans.

The three following Books will be employed upon the history of three successive kings, with the addition of whatever, in their times, happened elsewhere, which, from its celebrity, may demand a more particular notice. This, then, is what I purpose, if the Divine favour shall smile on my undertaking, and carry me safely by those rocks of rugged diction, on which Elward, in his search after sounding and farfetched phrases, so unhappily suffered shipwreck. "Should any one, however," to use the poet's expression, "peruse this work with sensible delight," I deem it necessary to acquaint him, that I vouch nothing for the truth of long past transactions, but the consonance of the time; the veracity of the relation must rest with its authors. Whatever I have recorded of later times, I have either myself seen, or heard from credible authority. However, in either part, I pay but little respect to the judgment of my contemporaries: trusting that I shall gain with posterity, when love and hatred shall be no more, if not a reputation for eloquence, at least credit for diligence. . . .

In the year of the incarnation of our Lord 449, Angles and Saxons first came into Britain; and although the cause of their arrival is universally known, it may not be improper here to subjoin it: and, that the design of my work may be the more manifest, to begin even from an earlier period. That Britain, compelled by Julius Caesar to submit to the Roman power, was held in high estimation by that people, may be collected from their history, and be seen also in the ruins of their ancient buildings. Even their emperors, sovereigns of almost all the world, eagerly embraced opportunities of sailing hither, and of spending their days here. Finally, Severus and Constantius, two of their greatest princes, died upon the island, and were there interred with the utmost pomp.

> 49. HENRY OF HUNTINGDON (1109–1155), who gained the rank of archdeacon, began his history sometime before 1133 and carried the story up to 1129. Drawing on the Anglo-Saxon chronicle, Bede, and others, Henry included poems and ballads as well as a narrative of English affairs—among them the formation of baronial parties—and such continental events as the Crusade.

To Alexander Bishop of Lincoln.

As the pursuit of learning in all its branches affords, according to my way of thinking, the sweetest earthly mitigation of trouble and consolation in grief, so I consider that precedence must be assigned to History, as both the most delightful of studies and the one which is invested with the noblest and brightest prerogatives. Indeed, there is nothing in this world more excellent than accurately to investigate and trace out the course of worldly affairs. For where is exhibited in a more lively manner the grandeur of heroic men, the wisdom of the prudent, the uprightness of the just, and the moderation of the temperate, than in the series of actions which history records? We find Horace suggesting this, when speaking in praise of Homer's story, he says:—

> His works the beautiful and base contain,—
> Of vice and virtue more instructive rules
> Than all the sober sages of the schools.

Crantor, indeed, and Chrysippus composed laboured treatises on moral philosophy, while Homer unfolds, as it were in a play, the character of Agamemnon for magnanimity, of Nestor for prudence, of Menelaus for uprightness, and on the other hand portrays the vastness of Ajax, the feebleness of Priam, the wrath of Achilles, and the fraud of Paris; setting forth in his narrative what is virtuous and what is profitable, better than is done in the disquisitions of philosophers.

But why should I dwell on profane literature? See how sacred history

Henry of Huntingdon, *History of the English*. In *The Chronicle of Henry of Huntingdon,* trans. Thomas Forester. London: Henry G. Bohn, 1853. Pp. xxv–xxviii.

teaches morals; while it attributes faithfulness to Abraham, fortitude to Moses, forbearance to Jacob, wisdom to Joseph; and while, on the contrary, it sets forth the injustice of Ahab, the weakness of Oziah, the recklessness of Manasseh, the folly of Roboam. O God of mercy, what an effulgence was shed on humility, when holy Moses, after joining with his brother in an offering of sweet-smelling incense to God, his protector and avenger, threw himself into the midst of a terrible danger, and when he shed tears for Miriam, who spoke scornfully of him, and was ever interceding for those who were malignant against him! How brightly shone the light of humanity when David, assailed and grievously tried by the curses, the insults, and the foul reproaches of Shimei, would not allow him to be injured, though he himself was armed, and surrounded by his followers in arms, while Shimei was alone and defenceless; and afterwards, when David was triumphantly restored to his throne, he would not suffer punishment to be inflicted on his reviler. So, also, in the annals of all people, which indeed display the providence of God, clemency, munificence, honesty, circumspection, and the like, with their opposites, not only provoke believers to what is good, and deter them from evil, but even attract wordly men to goodness, and arm them against wickedness.

History brings the past to the view, as if it were present, and enables us to judge of the future by picturing to ourselves the past. Besides, the knowledge of former events has this further pre-eminence, that it forms a main distinction between brutes and rational creatures. For brutes, whether they be men or beasts, neither know, nor wish to know, whence they come, nor their own origin, nor the annals and revolutions of the country they inhabit. Of the two, I consider men in this brutal state to be the worst, because what is natural in the case of beasts, is the lot of men from their own want of sense; and what beasts could not acquire if they would, such men will not though they could. But enough of these, whose life and death are alike consigned to everlasting oblivion.

With such reflections, and in obedience to your commands, most excellent prelate, I have undertaken to arrange in order the antiquities and history of this kingdom and nation, of which you are the most distinguished ornament. At your suggestion, also, I have followed, as far as possible, the Ecclesiastical History of the venerable Bede, making extracts, also, from other authors, with compilations from the chronicles preserved in antient libraries. Thus, I have brought down the course of past events to times within our own knowledge and observation. The attentive reader will learn in this work both what he ought to imitate, and what he ought to eschew; and if he becomes the better for this imitation and this avoidance, that is the fruit of my labours which I most desire; and, in truth, the direct path of history frequently leads to moral improvement. But, as we undertake nothing without imploring divine assistance, let us commence by invoking God's holy name.

> 50. WILLIAM OF NEWBURGH (1135/36–1198) wrote a *History of English Affairs* which concentrated on the period 1066–1198 and which commented on social as well as ecclesiastical and political matters. In the spirit of twelfth-century dialectic and science, William rejected the Arthurian legends which, though not found in Bede, had been endorsed by Geoffrey of Monmouth's popular *History of the Kings of Britain* (ca. 1136).

The history of our English nation has been written by the venerable Beda, a priest and monk, who, the more readily to gain the object he had in view, commenced his narrative at a very remote period, though he only glanced, with cautious brevity, at the more prominent actions of the Britons, who are known to have been the aborigines of our island. The Britons, however, had before him a historian of their own, from whose work Beda has inserted an extract; this fact I observed some years since, when I accidentally discovered a copy of the work of Gildas. His history, however, is rarely to be found, for few persons care either to transcribe or possess it—his style being so coarse and unpolished: his impartiality, however, is strong in developing truth, for he never spares even his own countrymen; he touches lightly upon their good qualities, and laments their numerous bad ones: there can be no suspicion that the truth is disguised, when a Briton, speaking of Britons, declares, that they were neither courageous in war, nor faithful in peace.

For the purpose of washing out those stains from the character of the Britons, a writer in our times has started up and invented the most ridiculous fictions concerning them, and with unblushing effrontery, extols them far above the Macedonians and Romans. He is called Geoffrey, surnamed Arthur, from having given, in a Latin version, the fabulous exploits of Arthur (drawn from the traditional fictions of the Britons, with additions of his own), and endeavored to dignify them

William of Newburgh, *History of English Affairs*. In *The Church Historians of England,* trans. Joseph Stevenson. London: Seeleys, 1856. Vol. 4, pt. 2, pp. 398–402.

with the name of authentic history; moreover, he has unscrupulously promulgated the mendacious predictions of one Merlin, as if they were genuine prophecies, corroborated by indubitable truth, to which also he has himself considerably added during the process of translating them into Latin. He further declared, that this Merlin was the issue of a demon and woman, and, as participating in his father's nature, attributes to him the most exact and extensive knowledge of futurity; whereas, we are rightly taught, by reason and the holy scriptures, that devils, being excluded from the light of God, can never by mediation arrive at the cognizance of future events; though by means of some types, more evident to them than to us, they may predict events to come rather by conjecture than by certain knowledge. Moreover, even in their conjectures, subtle though they be, they often deceive themselves as well as others: nevertheless, they impose on the ignorant by their feigned divinations, and arrogate to themselves a prescience which, in truth, they do not possess. The fallacies of Merlin's prophecies are indeed evident in circumstances which are known to have transpired in the kingdom of England after the death of Geoffrey himself, who translated these follies from the British language; to which, as is truly believed, he added much from his own invention. Besides, he so accommodated his prophetic fancies (as he easily might do) to circumstances occurring previous to, or during, his own times, that they might obtain a suitable interpretation. Moreover, no one but a person ignorant of ancient history, when he meets with that book which he calls the History of the Britons, can for a moment doubt how impertinently and impudently he falsifies in every respect. For he only who has not learnt the truth of history indiscreetly believes the absurdity of fable. I omit this man's inventions concerning the exploits of the Britons previous to the government of Julius Caesar, as well as the fictions of others which he has recorded, as if they were authentic. I make no mention of his fulsome praise of the Britons, in defiance of the truth of history, from the time of Julius Caesar, when they came under the dominion of the Romans, to that of Honorius, when the Romans voluntarily retired from Britain, on account of the more urgent necessities of their own state. . . .

Now, since it is evident that these facts [up to Bede's time] are established with historical authenticity by the venerable Beda, it appears that whatever Geoffrey has written, subsequent to Vortigen, either of Arthur, or his successors, or predecessors, is a fiction, invented either by himself or by others, and promulgated either through an unchecked propensity to falsehood, or a desire to please the Britons, of whom vast numbers are said to be so stupid as to assert that Arthur is yet to come, and who cannot bear to hear of his death. . . . Moreover, he depicts Arthur himself as great and powerful beyond all men, and as celebrated in his exploits as he chose to feign him. First, he makes him triumph, at pleasure, over Angles, Picts, and Scots; then, he subdues Ireland, the Orkneys, Gothland, Norway, Denmark, partly by war, partly by the single terror of his name. To these he adds Iceland, which, by some, is called the remotest Thule. . . .

Next this fabler, to carry his Arthur to the highest summit, makes him declare war against the Romans, having, however, first vanquished a giant of surprising magnitude in single combat, though since the times of David we never read of giants. Then, with a wider licence of fabrication, he brings all the kings of the world in league with the Romans against him; that is to say, the kings of Greece, Africa, Spain, Parthia, Media, Iturea, Libya, Egypt, Babylon, Bithynia, Phrygia, Syria, Boethia, and Crete, and he relates that all of them were conquered by him in a single battle; whereas, even Alexander the Great, renowned throughout all ages, was engaged for twelve years in vanquishing only a few of the potentates of these mighty kingdoms. Indeed, he makes the little finger of his Arthur more powerful than the loins of Alexander the Great; more especially when, previous to the victory over so many kings, he introduces him relating to his comrades the subjugation of thirty kingdoms by his and their united efforts; whereas, in fact, this romancer will not find in the world so many kingdoms, in addition to those mentioned, which he had not yet subdued. Does he dream of another world possessing countless kingdoms, in which the circumstances he has related took place? Certainly, in our own orb no such events have happened. For how would the elder historians, who were ever anxious to omit nothing remarkable, and even recorded trivial circumstances, pass by unnoticed so incomparable a man, and such surpassing deeds? How could they, I repeat, by their silence, suppress Arthur, the British monarch (superior to Alexander the Great), and his deeds, or Merlin, the British prophet (the rival of Isaiah), and his prophecies? For what less in the knowledge of future events does he attribute to this Merlin than we do to Isaiah, except, indeed, that he durst not prefix to his productions, "Thus saith the Lord;" and was ashamed to say, "Thus saith the Devil," though this had been best suited to a prophet the offspring of a demon.

Since, therefore, the ancient historians make not the slightest mention of these matters, it is plain that whatever this man published of Arthur and of Merlin are mendacious fictions, invented to gratify the curiosity of the undiscerning. . . .

Therefore, let Beda, of whose wisdom and integrity none can doubt, possess our unbounded confidence, and let this fabler, with his fictions, be instantly rejected by all.

There were not wanting, indeed, some writers after Beda, but none at all to be compared with him, who detailed from his days the series of times and events of our island until our own recollection; men deserving of praise for their zealous and faithful labours, though their narrative be homely. In our times, indeed, events so great and memorable have occurred, that, if they be not transmitted to lasting memory by written documents, the negligence of the modern must be deservedly blamed. Perhaps a work of this kind is already begun, or even finished, by one or more persons, but nevertheless, some venerable characters, to whom I owe obedience, have deigned to enjoin such a labour, even to so insignificant a person as myself, in order that I, who am unable to make my offerings with the rich, may yet be permitted, with the poor widow, to cast somewhat of my poverty into the treasury of the Lord; and, since we are aware that the series of English history has been brought down by some to the decease of king Henry the first, beginning at the arrival of the Normans in England, I shall succinctly describe the intermediate time, that, by the permission of God, I may give a more copious narrative from Stephen, Henry's successor, in whose first year I, William, the least of the servants of Christ, was born unto death in the first Adam, and born again unto life in the Second.

> 51. ROGER OF WENDOVER (d. 1236) gathered the "flowers of history" in a world chronicle that begins with creation and focuses on English history from 447. It draws on continental sources as well as Bede, William of Malmesbury, and Henry of Huntingdon, among others, though from 1201 Wendover's account of the reigns of John and Henry III, which makes use of royal and papal charters, is original.

We have thought good briefly to note the chief events of past times, and to give the lineage of our Saviour from the beginning, with the

Roger of Wendover, *Flowers of History*. In *Roger of Wendover's Flowers of History*, trans. J. A. Giles. London: Henry G. Bohn, 1849. 1:1–3.

successions of certain kingdoms of the world and of their rulers, for the instruction of posterity, and to aid the diligence of the studious hearer. But, first we will address a word to certain dull cavillers, who ask what need there is of recording men's lives and deaths, or the various chances which befall them; or of committing to writing the different prodigies of heaven, earth, and the elements? Now, we would have such persons know that the lives of good men in times past are set forth for the imitation of succeeding times; and that the examples of evil men, when such occur, are not to be followed, but to be shunned. Moreover, the prodigies and portentous occurrences of past days, whether in the way of pestilence, or in other chastisements of God's wrath, are not without admonition to the faithful. Therefore is the memory of them committed to writing, that if ever the like shall again occur, men may presently betake themselves to repentance, and by this remedy appease the divine vengeance. For this cause, therefore, among many others, Moses, the law-giver, sets forth in the sacred history, the innocence of Abel, the envy of Cain, the sincerity of Job, the dissimulation of Esau, the malice of eleven of the sons of Israel, the goodness of Joseph the twelfth, the punishment of the five cities in their destruction by fire and brimstone, to the end that we may imitate the good, and carefully turn from the ways of the wicked; and this not only does Moses, but also all the writers of the sacred page, who, by commending virtue, and holding up vice to detestation, invite us to the love and fear of God. They are, therefore, not to be heeded, who say that books of chronicles, especially those by catholic authors, are unworthy of regard; for through them, whatever is necessary for human wisdom and salvation, the studious inquirer may be able to acquire by his memory, apprehend by his learning, and set forth by his eloquence.

The following work, then, is divided into two books, the first of which treats briefly of the Old Testament of the law of God, through five ages of the world, unto the coming of the Saviour, as the same are marked by Moses the law-giver, with the successions of the kings of the Gentiles and of their kingdoms, without which the law of God could not conveniently be set forth. For Luke, the evangelist, in writing the Gospel of Christ, made mention of Tiberius Caesar, and the kings of the Jewish nation, whose days and years were well known to all, to the end that the advent of the Saviour among men, and His works, which were of lowly origin, might come to the knowledge of all, by means of that which had more of splendour and notoriety; and this indeed was the way of almost all the writers of the sacred page, for the reasons above mentioned. The second book of this work treats of the New Testament, commencing with the incarnation of Christ and his nativity, and notices every year, without omitting one, down to our times, on whom the ends of the world are come, which we will treat of more at large in its proper place. Nevertheless, for the sake of fastidious readers, who are easily wearied, we think it good to aim at brevity in this our history, to the end that while they experience delight in a short and pleasing narration, we may kindle in their minds a love of reading that which does not weary, and, from listless hearers and fastidious readers, convert them into diligent students. Finally, that which follows has been taken from the books of catholic writers worthy of credit, just as flowers of various colours are gathered from various fields, to the end that the very variety, noted in the diversity of the colours, may be grateful to the various minds of the readers, and by presenting some which each may relish, may suffice for the profit and entertainment of all. . . .

The second book of this work, commencing with the time of grace, treats of the nativity of our Saviour, and of his works in the flesh, of the calling of the apostles, and of the saints of God now glorified in heaven, arranged according to the years of incarnation, without omitting one, down to our times, on whom the ends of the world are come; in the course of which it treats of all the Roman pontiffs and emperors. It treats, moreover, of archbishops, bishops, and other dignities of the church, of kings, and princes, and other great men, who in their times lived in different regions, and of their acts, whether good or evil. It treats, moreover, of the various chances that have befallen mankind, the prodigious and portentous manifestations of God's wrath, to the end that, being admonished by past evils, men may betake themselves to humiliation and repentance, taking an example for imitation from the good, and shunning the ways of the perverse.

> 52. ORDERICUS VITALIS (1075–1142), a scholarly monk and book hunter, wrote a history of the monastery of Saint Evroul which expanded into a larger, secular history of Normandy. Ordericus's view of history's lessons and its providential framework was conventional enough, but his *Ecclesiastical History* is valuable for its scope and detail.

Ordericus Vitalis, *Ecclesiastical History.* In *The Ecclesiastical History of Orderic Vitalis,* ed. and trans. Marjorie Chibnall. Oxford: Clarendon Press, 1980. 1:131–133.

Our predecessors in their wisdom have studied all the ages of the erring world from the earliest times, have recorded the good and evil fortunes of mortal men as a warning to others, and, in their constant eagerness to profit future generations, have added their own writings to those of the past. This we see achieved by Moses and Daniel and other writers of the Hagiographa; this we find in Dares Phrygius and Pompeius Trogus and other historians of the gentiles, this too we perceive in Eusebius and the *De Ormesta mundi* of Orosius and Bede the Englishman and Paul of Monte Cassino and other ecclesiastical writers. I study their narratives with delight, I praise and admire the elegance and value of their treatises, I exhort the learned men of our own time to imitate their remarkable erudition. Because it is not my lot to direct others in what they should do, I can at least endeavour to shun vain idleness, and bestir myself to undertake something which may give pleasure to my ordinary fellow-students.

In the narrative of the restauration of the abbey of Saint-Evroul, which at the command of Abbot Roger I undertook to write plainly to the best of my ability, I have occasion to touch truthfully on some matters concerning the good or evil leaders of this wretched age. Now, equipped with no literary skill to support me and endowed with neither knowledge nor eloquence, but inspired by the best intentions, I set about composing an account of the events which we witness and endure. It is fitting that, since new events take place every day in this world, they should be systematically committed to writing to the glory of God, so that—just as past deeds have been handed down by our forebears—present happenings should be recorded now and passed on by the men of today to future generations. My purpose is to speak truthfully about ecclesiastical affairs as a simple son of the Church; eagerly striving to follow the early Fathers according to the small measure of my ability, I have set out to investigate and record the fortunes of the Christian people in this present time, and therefore I have ventured to call this work the *Ecclesiastical History*. For although I cannot explore Macedonian or Greek or Roman affairs and many other matters worthy of the telling, because as a cloister monk by my own free choice I am compelled to unremitting observance of my monastic duty, nevertheless I can strive with the help of God and for the consideration of posterity to explain truthfully and straightforwardly the things which I have seen in our own times, or know to have occurred in nearby provinces. I firmly believe, following the prognostications of earlier writers, that in time someone will come with greater understanding than myself, and greater capacity for interpreting the various events taking place on earth, who will perhaps derive something from my writings and those of others like me, and will graciously insert this in his chronicle or history for the information of future generations. I hold this opinion all the more confidently because I began this work at the clear command of the venerable old abbot, Roger, and am now offering it to you, Father Warin, his legitimate successor according to the custom of the Church, so that you may delete what is superfluous, correct its infelicities, and set the seal of your wisdom and authority on the emended version. First of all I will tell of the Beginning that has no beginning, by whose aid I aspire to come to the End that has no ending, where I may sing devout praises with those above for ever and ever, to him who is alpha and omega.

> 53. JOHN OF SALISBURY (d. 1180), ecclesiastical statesman, diplomat, famed medieval humanist, and political theorist, composed his ecclesiastical history in the mode of Eusebius; his narrative, written in exile from notes taken during residency in Rome, was critical, opinionated, and centered on events in Rome, though it attended also to the empire and Norman Sicily.

Jerome, the renowned father of the church, a man of wide learning, had so high an opinion of the Book of Chronicles as to assert that anyone who claimed to know holy scripture without it would make himself a laughingstock. The reason he gave was that it touched on events omitted from other books which were the key to many problems in the gospels. For it is, as it were, a comprehensive epilogue to the Old Testament in which, with the books of Esdras and Maccabees, we may read the mighty works of divine mercy manifested to us in our fathers; up to the time when, in a moment of universal silence, the needs of humanity and the purpose of the divine will required that the consubstantial and coeternal Son of God should enter the womb of an immaculate Virgin, that the Word might be made flesh and dwell among us. At this point the holy evangelists take up the story, teaching what God as man performed in man for man; and, flying on swift wings to the four corners of the earth, spread the word which saves the souls of the faithful and unites the church without spot or stain to Christ.

Luke, Paul's disciple, who described the acts of the apostles, covered

John of Salisbury, *Pontifical History*. In *John of Salisbury's Memoires of the Papal Court*, trans. Marjorie Chibnall. London: Thomas Nelson and Sons, 1956. Pp. 1–4.

the infancy of the newly-born church; and Eusebius of Caesarea, who succeeded him as an interpreter of scripture, told the story of the church in its youth, and finally, in describing the torments and triumphs of illustrious Christians, showed it as it came to manhood. Then Cassiodorus, who was converted from a Gentile to a Christian, from a senator to a monk, from an orator to a doctor of the church, lauded the palms that the Christian host had seen and received from the fathers; and, following in the path of other chroniclers, left as successors men distinguished in this art. Orosius, Isidore and Bede, and others whom it would be tedious to enumerate practised it; our own age too is not without numerous scholars who have undertaken to enrich their contemporaries with work of this kind. Amongst them one of the latest is Master Hugh, canon of St. Victor of Paris, who related the order of events from the beginning of the world up to the time of Pope Innocent II and Louis, most Christian king of the Franks, and included all the vicissitudes of kingdoms in the concise narrative. After him, Sigebert, monk of Gembloux, wove the pattern of his narrative from the first year of Valetinian and Gratian to the council of Rheims, celebrated in the year of our lord 1148, in the time of Louis king of the Franks, when Conrad was reigning in Germany. From that time, however, there is not a single chronicle that I can discover; though I have found in church archives notes of memorable events which could be of help to any future writers who may appear. Sigebert, however, did not even describe everything that took place in the time of Pope Innocent; he was silent on several important points, either because they had escaped his notice, or for some other reason. For although he was anxious to handle great events in many kingdoms, he gave more space and care to those which concerned his Germans. Out of zeal for them, probably, he inserted some things in his chronicle which seem contrary to the privileges of the Roman church and the traditions of the holy fathers. And so, my dearest friend and master, I gladly obey your command; and will undertake, by the grace of God, as you bid, to give a short account of events touching papal history, omitting all else. My aim, like that of other chroniclers before me, shall be to profit my contemporaries and future generations. For all these chroniclers have had a single purpose: to relate noteworthy matters, so that the invisibile things of God may be clearly seen by the things that are done, and men may by examples of reward or punishment be made more zealous in the fear of God and pursuit of justice. Yes indeed, anyone ignorant of these things, who claims knowledge of holy writ or worldly wisdom, may be said to make himself a laughingstock. For, as the pagan says, "The lives of others are our teachers"; and whoever knows nothing of the past hastens blindly into the future. Besides, the records of the chronicles are valuable for establishing or abolishing customs, for strengthening or destroying privileges; and nothing, after knowledge of the grace and law of God, teaches the living more surely and soundly than knowledge of the deeds of the departed.

In what I am going to relate I shall, by the help of God, write nothing but what I myself have seen and heard and know to be true, or have on good authority from the testimony or writings of reliable men. So may the beginning of my discourse be that Son of the immaculate Virgin who "in the beginning was the Word"; and may He guide the work I have undertaken for our salvation and the welfare of His church, for He is the guide of all who walk rightly and the end of all that we do.

> 54. FULCHER OF CHARTRES (ca. 1059–1127), who had some classical learning, wrote a chronicle of the First Crusade, based in part on eyewitness testimony and expressing marvel at the grandeur of his theme and the actions of his protagonists.

Prologue.

Here Beginneth Master Fulcher's Prologue *To The Work Which Follows.*   It is a joy to the living and even profitable to the dead when the deeds of brave men, especially those fighting for God, are read from written records, or retained in the recesses of the memory, are solemnly recited among the faithful. For those still living in this world, on hearing of the pious purposes of their predecessors, and how the latter following the precepts of the Gospels spurned the finest things of this world and abandoned parents, wives, and their possessions however great, are themselves inspired to follow God and embrace Him with enthusiasm [Matth. 12:29; Marc. 10:29; Luc. 18:29; Matth. 16:24; Marc. 8:34; Luc. 9:23]. It is very beneficial for those who have died in the Lord when the faithful who are still alive, hearing of the good and pious deeds of

Fulcher of Chartres, *Chronicle of the First Crusade.* In Fulcher of Chartres, *A History of the Expedition to Jerusalem, 1095–1127.* Trans. Frances Rita Ryan. Knoxville, Tenn.: University of Tennessee Press, 1969. Pp. 57–59.

their forebears, bless the souls of the departed and in love bestow alms with prayers in their behalf whether they, the living, knew the departed or not.

2. For this reason, moved by the repeated requests of some of my comrades, I have related in a careful and orderly fashion the illustrious deeds of the Franks when by God's most express mandate they made a pilgrimage in arms to Jerusalem in honor of the Savior. I have recounted in a style homely but truthful what I deemed worthy of remembrance as far as I was able or just as I saw things with my own eyes on the journey itself.

3. Although I dare not compare the above-mentioned labor of the Franks with the great achievements of the Israelites or Maccabees or of many other privileged people whom God has honored by frequent and wonderful miracles, still I consider the deeds of the Franks scarcely inferior since God's miracles often occurred among them. These I have taken care to commemorate in writing. In what way do the Franks differ from the Israelites or Maccabees? Indeed we have seen these Franks in the same regions, often right with us, or we have heard about them in places distant from us, suffering dismemberment, crucifixion, flaying, death by arrows or by being rent apart, or other kinds of martyrdom, all for the love of Christ. They could not be overcome by threats or temptations, nay rather if the butcher's sword had been at hand many of us would not have refused martyrdom for the love of Christ.

4. Oh how many thousands of martyrs died a blessed death on this expedition! But who is so hard of heart that he can hear of these deeds of God without being moved by the deepest piety to break forth in His praise? Who will not marvel how we, a few people in the midst of the lands of our enemies, were able not only to resist but even to survive? Who has ever heard of the like? On one side of us were Egypt and Ethiopia; on another, Arabia, Chaldea and Syria, Assyria and Media, Parthia and Mesopotamia, Persia and Scythia. Here a great sea separated us from Christendom and by the will of God enclosed us in the hands of butchers. But His mighty arm mercifully protected us. "Blessed indeed is the nation whose God is the Lord" [Psalm. 32 : 12].

5. The history which follows will tell both how this work was begun and how, in order to carry out the journey, all the people of the West freely devoted to it their hearts and hands.

Here Endeth the *Prologue*.

55. The *GRANDES CHRONIQUES DE FRANCE,* assembled by
the monks of Saint-Denis between 1274 and 1461 and translated
from Latin sources, was the first vernacular history of the French
monarchy. It divided the monarchy into the three main dynasties,
which were celebrated for their defense of learning as well as political and military success, and were (as in Fredegar) traced back to
Trojan origins.

From the one who begins this work, to all those who will read it,
greetings in the name of Our Lord. Because many people doubt the
genealogy of the kings of France and the source and line from which they
are descended, he has undertaken this work at the command of one
whom he neither could nor ought to refuse. But because his learning and
the limitation of his ability are unequal to the task of such an elevated
history, he begs at the beginning that the reader will suffer patiently and
without complaint all that he finds to blame. . . .

Everyone should know that he will treat matters more briefly than he
should, for long and confused discourse are hardly pleasant to those who
must listen, but brief and pertinent words do please listeners. This history will be told according to the rule of the Chronicles of the Abbey of
Saint-Denis in France, where the history of the deeds of all the kings
have been written. For there one may read the original of this history. . . . And everyone should understand that this work is useful to
teach the deeds of the kings to honorable people and to show everyone
where the leading figures of the world come from. It is an example of
leading a good life, even to kings and princes who have lands to govern;
for an eminent master [Vincent of Beauvais] has called history "the mirror of life." Here everyone can find good and bad, beauty and ugliness,
reason and folly, and carry on successfully by the examples of history;
and if all the things he reads in this history are not profitable, most of
them at least will be of assistance. They should know that he has nothing
of his own to add and that everything comes from the ancient authors
who have treated and compiled the histories of the deeds of the kings;
and what he says is on their behalf and his words are their words. . . .
And because there have been three dynasties of kings of France since it

*Les Grandes Chroniques de France, selon que elles sont conservées en l'église de Saint-
Denis en France.* Ed. M. Paulin. Paris: Techener, 1836. Prologue. My translation.

began, this book will be divided into three major books. In the first we shall speak of the Merovingian genealogy, in the second that of Pepin, and in the third the dynasty of Hugh Capet. And each book will be divided into several parts, according to the lives and deeds of various kings, and organized by chapters to show more the material clearly and without confusion. The Beginning of this history begins with the great line of Trojans, from which it has descended by long succession.

It is certain, then, that the kings of France, through which the kingdom has achieved glory and renown, have descended from the noble line of Troy. They were glorious in victory, noble in renown, devout in the service of the Christian faith; and indeed this nation is strong and proud and cruel to its enemies, as the name ("Frank") signifies, while it is merciful and generous to its subjects and to those it vanquishes in battle. For they do not fight, as formerly, to increase their kingdom and dominion, but to acquire the glory of victory. And it is not without reason named above other nations, for it has not long suffered the servitude of idolatry nor evil, since it has heard the preaching of the truth, and it obeys its Creator when it hears his messages, it offers and sacrifices to God the first fruits and beginnings of its reign; and it has received the Christian faith in such love and devotion that since the time it has obeyed its Creator, it has desired the propagation of the faith more than the increase of its landed possessions.

And by his grace our Lord has given it a prerogative over all lands and all nations. . . . If any other nation brings violence or grief to the holy Church, the complaint comes to France, and in France is the succor and refuge; from France comes the sword and weapons by which it is avenged; and France, as a loyal daughter, answers all its mother's needs; it is always there to give aid and assistance. If therefore faith is more fervently and strictly kept, it is not without good reasons. The first is that my lord Saint Denis, glorious martyr and apostle of France, by whose ministry it was first converted, sustains and guarantees it as his own possession, given to him to introduce the faith. The second reason is that the source of learning [*clerg*], by which the holy Church is sustained and illuminated, flourishes in Paris. And as others have said, learning has always been in accord, so that one cannot be without the other: they have always been together and, thank God, they will not be separated. In three places they have lived at different times: for in the city of Athens philosophy formerly resided, and in Greece the flower of chivalry. From

Greece they then came to Rome, and from Rome they have come to France. By God's grace let them long remain here, to praise the glory of the name of Him, who lives and reigns through all the ages. Amen.

> 56. CHRETIEN DE TROYES (1135–1185) wrote various romances, including *Cligés,* which is about a Byzantine prince, which ranges from King Arthur's court to Constantinople, and which (like the *Grandes Chroniques*) alludes here to the translation of studies (*translatio studii*), a central theme of Western cultural history adapted from the biblical idea of a translation of empire and the four world monarchies.

> In books the ancient tales are told—
> The works of men, the deeds of old.
> The Greeks, so says our book, were first
> In chivalry; they were most versed
> In laws and things divine. And next
> Passed chivalry to Rome, our text
> Declares. At last to France, we pray,
> These arts have come to us to stay.

> 57. GIOVANNI VILLANI (ca. 1280–1348), a prosperous younger contemporary of Dante, wrote a rich and diversely illustrated chronicle of Florence from the time of Noah, repeating the legends of Trojan origins, foundation by Caesar, and destruction by "Totila" and describing the political ups and downs, party conflicts, economic triumphs, cultural achievements, and natural disasters of this Guelf republic down to the Black Death of 1348.

And I, finding myself on that blessed pilgrimage; the holy city of Rome, beholding the great and ancient things therein, and reading the stories and the great doings of the Romans, written by Virgil, and by Sallust, and by Lucan, and Titus Livius, and Valerius, and Paulus Orosius, and other masters of history, which wrote alike of small things as of great, of the deeds and actions of the Romans, and also of foreign nations throughout the world, myself to preserve memorials and give examples to those which should come after took up their style and de-

Chrétien de Troyes, *Cligés.* Ed. A. Hilka. Halle: M. Niemeyer, 1971. 2:27–39. My translation.

Giovanni Villani, *Chronicle.* In *Villani's Chronicle,* trans. Rose E. Selfe and ed. Philip H. Wicksteed. London: Archibald Constable, 1906. P. 321.

sign, although as a disciple I was not worthy of such a work. But considering that our city of Florence, the daughter and creature of Rome, was rising, and had great things before her, whilst Rome was declining, it seemed to me fitting to collect in this volume and new chronicle all the deeds and beginnings of the city of Florence, in so far as it has been possible for me to find and gather them together, and to follow the doings of the Florentines in detail, and the other notable things of the universe in brief, as long as it shall be God's pleasure; in hope of which, rather than in my own poor learning, I undertook, by his grace, the said enterprise; and thus in the year 1300, having returned from Rome, I began to compile this book, in reverence to God and the blessed John, and in commendation of our city of Florence.

> 58. DINO COMPAGNI (ca. 1260–1324) wrote his chronicle around 1310, though it was not published until the eighteenth century. It is not only a celebration of Florentine achievement but also a perceptive and connected history of the conflict between the Whites (Dino's as well as Dante's party) and the Blacks.

The subject of the work and the author's motive in writing it.

The remembrance of the ancient histories has long stirred my mind to write of the events, fraught with danger and ill-fitted to bring prosperity, which the noble city, the daughter of Rome, has for many years undergone, and especially at the time of the Jubilee of the year 1300. However, for many years I excused myself from writing on the ground of my own incompetence, and in the belief that another would write: but at last, the perils having so multiplied, and the outlook having become so significant that silence might no longer be kept concerning them, I determined to write for the advantage of those who shall inherit the prosperous years, to the end that they may acknowledge that their benefits are from God, who rules and governs throughout all ages. . . .

When I began, I purposed writing the truth concerning those things of which I was certain, through having seen and heard them, because they were things noteworthy, which in their beginnings no one saw so

Dino Compagni, *Chronicle.* In *The Chronicle of Dino Compagni,* trans. Else C. M. Benecke and A. G. Ferrers Howell. London: J. M. Dent, 1906. Pp. 1–5.

clearly as I; and those things I did not clearly see, I purposed writing according to hearsay. But since many, because of their corrupt will, err in their speech, and corrupt the truth, I purposed to write according to the most authentic report. And in order that strangers may be the better able to understand the things that happened, I will describe the fashion of the noble city which is in the province of Tuscany and under the protection of the sign of Mars. It is enriched by a copious imperial river of sweet water, which divides it almost in half. The climate is equable, and the city is sheltered from hurtful winds; its territory is scanty in extent, but abounds in good produce. The citizens are valiant in arms, proud, and quarrelsome. The city is enriched by unlawful gains, and, on account of its power, is distrusted and feared, rather than loved, by the neighbouring towns. . . .

The said city of Florence is very well populated, and the good air promotes generation. The citizens are very courteous, and the women very handsome and well attired. The large houses are very beautiful, and better supplied with comforts and conveniences than those in the other cities of Italy. On this account many people come from distant lands to visit the city, not from necessity, but by reason of her flourishing industries, and for the sake of her beauty and adornment. . . .

Let her citizens, then, weep for themselves and their children, since by their arrogance, wickedness, and struggles for office they have undone so noble a city, have outraged the laws, and in a short time have bartered away the privileges which their forefathers won by much labour through long years; and let them await the justice of God, which by many tokens is threatening to bring evil upon them, as upon guilty persons who were free to avoid the possibility of its overwhelming them.

After much hurt had been received in ancient times through the quarrels of the citizens, there arose in the said city one quarrel which caused such division among them that the two parties gave, one to the other, two new hostile names of Guelfs and Ghibellines.

¶ UNIVERSAL HISTORY

59. OTTO OF FREISING (d. 1158), a German noble who studied arts and theology at Paris, joined the Cistercian order, later became

Otto of Freising, *The Deeds of Frederick Barbarossa*. Records of Civilization. Trans. Charles Christopher Mierow. New York: W. W. Norton, 1966. Pp. 24–25, 28, 144–145, and 146–148.

a bishop, and wrote a eulogistic history of the emperor Frederick Barbarossa, whom he regarded as a descendant of the ancient Caesars. Otto's major work was *The Two Cities,* which in effect brought Orosius up to date and, with a global perspective, elaborated on the Augustinian philosophy of history. In this book, Otto included the six ages of man, the four world monarchies, and the translation of empire—and along with it the translation of studies—to the Hohenstaufen state of his day, with historical, philosophical, and prophetic comments on the cultural movement from East to West and the rise and fall of states within God's larger plan for humanity.

This, I think, has been the purpose of all who have written history before us: to extol the famous deeds of valiant men in order to incite the hearts of mankind to virtue, but to veil in silence the dark doings of the base or, if they are drawn into the light, by the telling to place them on record to terrify the minds of those same mortals.

Hence I judge those who write at this time to be in a certain measure happy. For, after the turbulence of the past, not only has an unprecedented brightness of peace dawned again, but the authority of the Roman empire prevails so greatly by reason of the virtues of our most victorious prince that the people living under his jurisdiction rest in humble quiet, and whatever barbarian or Greek dwells outside his bounds is overawed by the weight of his authority and trembles. . . .

And thus let the proposed history take its beginning, in the name of God. . . .

But the citizens of Rome, learning of the prince's arrival, decided to sound out his inclinations in advance by an embassy. Therefore they appointed scholarly and learned men as their representatives to meet him between Sutri and Rome, having first received a safe conduct for their protection. And thus being presented before the consistory of His Royal Excellency, the men began to speak as follows:

"We the ambassadors of the City—no insignificant part of the City— O Excellent King, have been sent to Your Excellency by the senate and people of Rome. Hear with calm mind and gracious ears what is brought to your attention by the City that is the kindly mistress of the world— the City of which, by God's aid, you shall soon be prince, emperor, and lord. If you have come—nay, because, as I [the People] believe, you have come—in peace, I rejoice. You seek authority over the world; I arise willingly to give you the crown. I meet you with rejoicing. For why should not a prince come peacefully to visit his people? Why should he not treat with notable munificence the people who have awaited his coming with great and protracted expectation, in order to shake off the unseemly yoke of the clergy? I pray for the return of the former times. I ask for the return of the privileges of the renowned City. May the City under this prince take the helm of the world once more. May the insolence of the world be checked under this emperor and be subjected to the sole rule of the City! May such a ruler be adorned with the fame as well as with the name of Augustus! . . ."

Hereupon the king, inflamed with righteous anger by the tenor of a speech as insolent as it was unusual, interrupted the flow of words of those ambassadors concerning the jurisdiction of their republic and of the empire, as they were about to spin out their oration in the Italian fashion by lengthy and circuitous periods. Preserving his royal dignity with modest bearing and charm of expression, he replied without preparation but not unprepared.

"We have heard much heretofore concerning the wisdom and the valor of the Romans, yet more concerning their wisdom. Wherefore we cannot wonder enough at finding your words insipid with swollen pride rather than seasoned with the salt of wisdom. You set forth the ancient renown of your city. You extol to the very stars the ancient status of your sacred republic. Granted, granted! To use the words of your own writer, 'There was, *there was once* virtue in this republic.' 'Once' I say. And O that we might truthfully and freely say 'now'! Your Rome—any, ours also—has experienced the vicissitudes of time. She could not be the only one to escape a fate ordained by the Author of all things for all that dwell beneath the orb of the moon. What shall I say? It is clear how first the strength of your nobility was transferred from this city of ours to the royal city of the East, and how for the course of many years the thirsty Greekling sucked the breasts of your delight. Then came the Frank, truly noble, in deed as in name, and forcibly possessed himself of whatever freedom was still left to you. Do you wish to know the ancient glory of your Rome? The worth of the senatorial dignity? The impregnable disposition of the camp? The virtue and the discipline of the equestrian order, its unmarred and unconquerable boldness when advancing to a conflict? Behold our state. All these things are to be found with us. All these have descended to us, together with the empire. Not in utter nakedness did the empire come to us. It came clad in its virtue. It brought its adornments with it. With us are your consuls. With us is your senate. With us is your soldiery. These very leaders of the Franks must rule you by their counsel, these very knights of the Franks must

avert harm from you with the sword. You boastfully declare that by you I
have been summoned, that by you I have been made first a citizen and
then the prince, that from you I have received what was yours. How
lacking in reason, how void of truth this novel utterance, may be left to
your own judgment and to the decision of men of wisdom! Let us ponder
over the exploits of modern emperors, to see whether it was not our
divine princes Charles and Otto who, by their valor and not by anyone's
bounty, wrested the City along with Italy from the Greeks and the Lombards and added it to the realms of the Franks. Desiderius and Berengar
teach you this, your tyrants, of whom you boasted, on whom you relied
as your princes. We have learned from reliable accounts that they were
not only subjugated and taken captive by our Franks, but grew old and
ended their lives in their servitude. Their ashes, buried among us, constitute the clearest evidence of this fact. But, you say: 'You came on my
invitation,' I admit it; I was invited. Give me the reason why I was
invited! You were being assailed by enemies and could not be freed by
your own hand or by the effeminate Greeks. The power of the Franks was
invoked by invitation. I would call it entreaty rather than invitation. In
your misery you besought the happy, in your frailty the valiant, in your
weakness the strong, in your anxiety the carefree. Invited after that
fashion—if it may be called an invitation—I have come. I have made
your prince my vassal and from that time until the present have transferred you to my jurisdiction. I am the lawful possessor. Let him who
can, snatch the club from Hercules."

¶ For His Majesty Frederick, victorious, renowned and triumphant,
emperor of the Romans, august forever, Otto, by the grace of God
[bishop] of the church of Freising, prays for a continuance of the good
fortune that now is his, in Him that "giveth salvation unto kings."
    Your Imperial Majesty requested of my humble self that the book
which several years ago by reason of the beclouded condition of the times
I wrote on the vicissitudes of history be now transmitted to your Serene
Highness. I have therefore obeyed your command willingly and gladly,

Otto of Freising, *The Two Cities*. In *The Two Cities: A Chronicle of Universal
History to the Year 1146 A.D.*, trans. Charles Mierow and ed. Austin Evans and
Charles Knapp. New York: Columbia University Press, 1928. Pp. 87–91,
93–97, 167, 220–221, 318–319, 322–323, 453, and 454. Reprinted by
permission of Columbia University Press.

so much the more devotedly as I regard it as thoroughly in accord with your royal preeminence that you desire to know what was done in olden times by kings and emperors, and to know this not only for the better protection of the state by arms, but also for its better molding by laws and statutes. Even so great a king of the Persians, Ahasuerus or Artaxerxes, although he had not attained to the knowledge of the true light through the worship of the one God, yet, realizing by reason of the nobility of his soul that this was of profit to royal grandeur, commanded that the yearbooks which had been written during his own reign or under his predecessors be examined, and so he gained glory thereby, his purpose being that the innocent should not be punished as if he were guilty and that the guilty should not escape punishment as though he were blameless.

Furthermore, while no earthly personage is found who is not subject to the laws of the universe and kept under constraint by such subjection, kings alone, as being set above the laws and reserved to be weighed in the divine balances only, are not held in restraint by the laws of this world. . . . But you, most glorious Prince, are indeed The Peace Maker, and are rightly so called, since you have changed the night of mist and rain into the delightful splendor of morning calm by preserving for each man what is his, and have restored lovable peace to the world. Therefore, since God—who was also the beginning [of all this achievement]— bestowed upon you the power to persevere therein by grace of divine mercy, you will not fall into the condemnation of this bitter sentence.

The knowledge of history, therefore, will be proper and advantageous to Your Excellency, for thereby, considering the deeds of brave men and the strength and power of God, who changeth monarchs and giveth thrones to whomsoever He will, and suffereth changes to come to pass, you shall live ever in His fear, and, advancing in propsperity, shall reign through many circling years. Accordingly, let Your Nobility know that I wrote this history in bitterness of spirit, led thereto by the turbulence of that unsettled time which preceded your reign, and therefore I did not merely give events in their chronological order, but rather wove together, in the manner of a tragedy, their sadder aspects, and so ended with a picture of unhappiness each and every division of the books even down to the seventh and the eighth. In the latter books the rest of souls and the double garment of the resurrection are shadowed forth.

And so, if it shall please Your Majesty to commend to writing to be remembered by posterity the glorious sequence of your exploits, then, if you will arrange the main topics with the aid of the secretaries of Your Highness and transmit them to me, I shall not be slow to prosecute this joyous task with joyful mind, if I have God's grace and if life attend me, expecting nothing as a reward save that Your Imperial Clemency shall be graciously minded to aid in its times of need the church which I serve. . . .

Regarding the expedition which you have planned against the arrogance of the Milanese, I have heard of it with gladness for the honor of the empire and the exaltation of your own person, and have dutifully undertaken the task you have enjoined upon me regarding this matter, a task imposed on my lowly self. I have sent as bearers of these presents the venerable Abbot Raboto of St. Stephen's and our chaplain, Rahewin, who took down this history from my lips, that they may by your grace make suitable response on our behalf concerning this matter.

To the friend of his heart, Rainald, the noble Chancellor of the greatest prince among princes of the earth, Otto, by the grace of God bishop of the church of Freising, sends greeting and pledge of respectful allegiance.

"Since I believe," as Boethius says, "that the greatest solace in life is to be found in handling and thoroughly learning all the teachings of philosophy," I devote myself to your noble character the more intimately and the more gladly because I know that you have labored zealously hitherto in the pursuit of this very study and that you are preeminently proficient in it. Therefore I write with the more assurance to Your Industrious Highness, not as to a novice but as to a philosopher, regarding the book which I am sending to His Majesty the Emperor, praying that in regard to certain matters therein set down I may find you not an unfavorable but kindly interpreter. For you know that all teaching consists of two things: avoidance and selection. To begin therefore with that which comes first for those who are approaching philosophy, namely grammar, this study itself is the one which, in accordance with the training it gives, teaches us to select those things which are in harmony with our purpose and to avoid such matters as are a hindrance to our purpose. . . . Logic also, the application of which has principally in view the teaching of syllogisms, by clarifying and training the judgment clears away and avoids the admixture of propositions useless for the formation of syllogisms, but selects the useful and arranges them properly. . . . The geometrician also, by employing the *reductio ad absurdum* in the case of part of an incorrect diagram, shows that such a figure is to be avoided, and proves by cogent reasoning that his own demonstration must be accepted. So also the art of the historians has certain things to clear away and to avoid and others to select and arrange properly; for it avoids lies and selects the truth. Therefore let not Your Discreet Highness be offended or (as I have said before) interpret the matter in an unfavorable light in the hearing of the emperor, if it shall appear that in our history certain matters have been spoken in criticism of his predecessors or ancestors, that the truth may be held in esteem, inasmuch as it is better to fall into the hands of men than to abandon the function of a historian by covering up a loathsome sight by colors that conceal the truth.

Next, I shall briefly explain the order in which this history proceeds, that, when this is known, the nature of the work may be the more readily apparent. That there were from the beginning of the world four principal kingdoms which stood out above all the rest, and that they are to endure unto the world's end, succeeding one another in accordance with the law of the universe, can be gathered in various ways, in particular from the vision of Daniel. I have therefore set down the rulers of these kingdoms, listed in chronological sequence: first the Assyrians, next (omitting the Chaldeans, whom the writers of history do not deign to include among the others) the Medes and the Persians, finally the Greeks and the Romans, and I have recorded their names down to the present emperor, speaking of the other kingdoms only incidentally, to make manifest the fluctuations of events. I have also discoursed concerning the various orders of holy men, and have given a list of the kings who reigned in Laurentum, Latium, and Alba Longa before the founding of the City and after the City was founded, and finally a catalogue of emperors and of the popes of Rome to the time of the present incumbents. And so in the eighth book I have brought my work to a conclusion by speaking of the resurrection of the dead and of the end of The Two Cities. Moreover, I have shown how kingdom was supplanted by kingdom up to the time of the empire of the Romans, believing that the fulfillment of what is said of that empire—that it must be utterly destroyed by a stone cut out from a mountain—must be awaited until the end of the ages, as Methodius states. Farewell.

In pondering long and often in my heart upon the changes and vicissitudes of temporal affairs and their varied and irregular issues, even as I hold that a wise man ought by no means to cleave to the things of time, so I find that it is by the faculty of reason alone that one must escape and find release from them. For it is the part of a wise man not to be whirled about after the manner of a revolving wheel, but through the stability of his powers to be firmly fashioned as a thing foursquare. Accordingly, since things are changeable and can never be at rest, what man in his right mind will deny that the wise man ought, as I have said, to depart from them to that city which stays at rest and abides to all eternity? This is the City of God, the heavenly Jerusalem, for which the children of God sigh while they are set in this land of sojourn, oppressed by the turmoil of the things of time as if they were oppressed by the Babylonian captivity. For, inasmuch as there are two cities—the one of time, the other of eternity; the one of the earth, earthly, the other of heaven, heavenly; the one of the devil, the other of Christ—ecclesiastical writers have declared that the former is Babylon, the latter Jerusalem.

But, whereas many of the Gentiles have written much regarding one of these cities, to hand down to posterity the great exploits of men of old (the many evidences of their merits, as they fancied), they have yet left to us the task of setting forth what, in the judgment of our writers, is rather the tale of human miseries. There are extant in this field the famous works of Pompeius Trogus, Justin, Cornelius [i.e., Tacitus], Varro, Eusebius, Jerome, Orosius, Jordanes, and a great many others of our number, as well as of their array, whom it would take too long to enumerate; in those writings the discerning reader will be able to find not so much histories as pitiful tragedies made up of mortal woes. We believe that this has come to pass by what is surely a wise and proper dispensation of the Creator, in order that, whereas men in their folly desire to cleave to earthly and transitory things, they may be frightened away from them by their own vicissitudes, if by nothing else, so as to be directed by the wretchedness of this fleeting life from the creature to a knowledge of the Creator. But we, set down as it were at the end of time, do not so much read of the miseries of ourselves in consequence of the experiences of our own time. For, to pass over other things, the empire of the Romans, which in Daniel is compared to iron on account of its sole lordship—monarchy, the Greeks call it—over the whole world, a world subdued by war, has in consequence of so many fluctuations and changes, particularly in our day, become, instead of the noblest and the foremost, almost the last. So that, in the words of the poet, scarcely

"a shadow of its mighty name remains."

For being transferred from the City to the Greeks, from the Greeks to the Franks, from the Franks to the Lombards, from the Lombards again to the German Franks, that empire not only became decrepit and senile through lapse of time, but also, like a once smooth pebble that has been rolled this way and that by the waters, contracted many a stain and developed many a defect. The world's misery is exhibited, therefore, even in the case of the chief power in the world, and Rome's fall foreshadows the dissolution of the whole structure.

But what wonder if human power is changeable, seeing that even mortal wisdom is prone to slip? We read that in Egypt there was so great wisdom that, as Plato states, the Egyptians called the philosophers of the Greeks childish and immature. Moses also, the giver of the law, "with whom Jehovah spake as a man speaketh unto his friend," and whom He filled with wisdom divine, was not ashamed to be instructed in all the wisdom of Egypt. Did not that great patriarch, appointed by God the father of nations, Abraham, a man trained in the learning of the Chaldeans and endowed with wisdom, did he not, when called by God, desert his former manner of life [i.e., go to Egypt] and yet not lay aside his wisdom? And yet Babylon the great, not only renowned for wisdom, but also "the glory of kingdoms, the beauty of the Chaldeans' pride," has become, in the words of the prophecy of Isaiah, without hope of restoration, a shrine of owls, a house of serpents and of ostriches, the lurking-place of creeping things. Egypt too is said to be in large measure uninhabitable and impassable. The careful student of history will find that learning was transferred from Egypt to the Greeks, then to the Romans, and finally to the Gauls and the Spaniards. And so it is to be observed that all human power or learning had its origin in the East, but is coming to an end in the West, that thereby the transitoriness and decay of all things human may be displayed. This, by God's grace, we shall show more fully in what follows. . . .

In this work I follow most of all those illustrious lights of the Church, Augustine and Orosius, and have planned to draw from their fountains what is pertinent to my theme and my purpose. The one of these has discoursed most keenly and eloquently on the origin and the progress of the glorious City of God and its ordained limits, setting forth how it has ever spread among the citizens of the world, and showing which of its citizens or princes stood forth preeminent in the various epochs of the princes or citizens of the world. The other, in answer to those who, uttering vain babblings, preferred the former times to Christian times, has composed a very valuable history of the fluctuations and wretched issues of human greatness, the wars and the hazards of wars, and the shifting of thrones, from the foundation of the world down to his own time. Following in their steps I have undertaken to speak of the Two Cities in such a way that we shall not lose the thread of history, that the devout reader may observe what is to be avoided in mundane affairs by reason of the countless miseries wrought by their unstable character, and that the studious and painstaking investigator may find a record of past happenings free from all obscurity. . . .

As we are about to speak, then, concerning the sorrow-burdened insecurity of the one city and the blessed permanence of the other, let us call upon God, who endures with patience the turbulence and confusion of this world, and by the vision of himself augments and glorifies the joyous peace of the other city, to the end that by His aid we may be able to say the things which are pleasing to Him.

The first book extends to Arbaces and the transfer of the Babylonian sovereignty to the Medes, and the beginning of the Roman power.

The second extends to the civil war of the Romans, fought with Julius and Pompey as leaders, to the death of Caesar, and to our Lord's nativity.

The third extends to Constantine and the times of the Christian Empire, and the transfer of sovereignty to the Greeks.

The fourth extends to Odovacar and the invasion of the kingdom by the Rugians.

The fifth extends to Charles and the transfer of sovereignty to the Franks, and the division of the kingdom and the empire under his descendants.

The sixth extends to Henry the Fourth and the schism between the kingly power and the priestly power; it includes the anathema pronounced against the emperor, the expulsion of Pope Gregory VII from the City, and his death at Salerno.

The seventh extends to the uprising of the Roman people and the ninth year of King Conrad.

The eighth is concerned with Antichrist and the resurrection of the dead and the end of the Two Cities. . . .

Since, as I have said, Daniel wrote a prophetic account of the changes of kingdoms, it seems worthwhile to comment a little on this account. While he was interpreting the dream of the king of the Babylonians he said, "You yourself, O King, are the head of gold that you saw. After you shall arise another kingdom inferior to yours, after that yet another, after that a fourth which, because it shall be very strong, is compared to iron that breaks in pieces all things." See how the prophet in citing four kingdoms named the first, because of its magnificence from gold; the fourth he called iron on account of its power and the subjection to it of the world by war. Two intermediate kingdoms intervened. The first and the fourth, which I mentioned above, are the mighty kingdoms of the Babylonians and the Romans, one of which fell in the East, the other, as I have often remarked already, arose in the West. The empires of the Persians and the Greeks existed in the interval between them. Some, however, including the kingdom of the Persians as well as that of the Medes and the Chaldeans with the Babylonians, have put the African kingdom in the second place among the four chief empires of the world. Thus they locate the four kingdoms of the world according to the four points of the compass: the Babylonian in the East, the African in the South, the Macedonian in the North, and the Roman in the West. . . .

Now at this point I think I ought to answer the question that I put off above, why the Lord of the universe wished the whole world to be subject to the dominion of one city, the whole world to be moulded by the laws of one city. In the first place He wished it, as I have said, that the minds of men might be more ready to understand, more capable of understanding great matters. Secondly, He wished it that unity of faith might be recommended to them after they had been united in this way, in order that all men, being constrained by their fear of a single city to revere one man, might learn also that they ought to hold to one faith, and through that faith might learn that God must be revered and adored not merely as a celestial being but as the Creator of all. Hence upon His coming a census of the whole world was ordered, doubtless that men might learn that One was to come who would enroll all who came to Him as citizens in the Eternal City. Hence at His birth throughout the entire circuit of the universe the world, exhausted by calamities and wearied by its own dissensions, willed to be at peace and to serve the emperor of the Romans rather than to rebel, that understanding might be vouchsafed of the fact that He had come in the flesh who said in mercy to those weighed down and wearied by the weight of earthly burdens, "Come unto me, all ye that labor and are heavy laden, and I will give you rest." For this reason peace, at that time a new thing, was granted to the world in order that the servants of the new king might be able to journey more freely over the whole world and implant health-bringing precepts about right living. It is not therefore to accidental causes, nor to the worship of false gods, but to the true God who forms the light and creates the darkness that, in my judgment, we must ascribe the fact that the commonwealth of the Romans expanded from a poor and lowly estate to such heights and to a great sovereignty under the primacy of one man. . . .

At this point I think I must tell, as I promised above, how the Franks, of whom I have made mention, came into the Gauls and by what means they severed themselves from the control of the Romans and began to be independent. They started, as I have said, from Troy. When they had established for themselves a home in Scythia they were called Sicambri. When the world had been made into a Roman province, and they too along with everyone else had been made subject to Rome, in the course of time they were called Franks by Valentinian for the reason which we have given above, and for ten years were left free to govern themselves. Upon the completion of this period, when the Romans demanded the customary tribute, the Franks,—made imperious by liberty, as regularly happened—refused to give tribute. . . . From this time on they also began to have laws that were drawn up by Wisogastaldus and Salagastus. They say that the law which even today is called Salic, after his name, was framed by this Salagastus. This law the noblest of the Franks, who are called Salian, still use. Upon the death of Pharamond his son Clodion, who wore his hair long, succeeded him; from him the kings of the Franks were called "the longhaired." During these days, as I said above, when Francia was, so to speak, in the process of being sown, Rome began gradually to decline. By this time the peoples that before had inhabited provinces of the Romans—not kingdoms—were learning to chose kings; now they were learning to break loose from the power of the Romans and to stand in the authority set up by their own discretion. . . .

As I said above, all human power or wisdom, originating in the East, began to reach its limits in the West. Regarding human power—how it passed from the Babylonians to the Medes and the Persians and from them to the Macedonians, and after that to the Romans and then again to the Greeks under the Roman name—I think enough has been said. How it was transferred from the Greeks to the Franks, who dwell in the West, remains to be told in the present book. That wisdom was found first in the East (that is, in Babylonia) and was carried thence into Egypt, because Abraham went down to Egypt in a time of famine, Josephus makes clear in the first book of his *Antiquities,* speaking as follows concerning Abraham: "He bestowed on them a knowledge of arithmetic and himself delivered over to them also all the lore of astronomy. For before Abraham the Egyptians were absolutely ignorant of these things." That wisdom passed from Egypt to the Greeks in the time of the philosophers the same author indicates in these words: "For these are known to have been implanted by the Chaldeans in Egypt, whence also they are said to have made their way to the Greeks." Thus far Josephus. From the Greeks it appears to have been carried to the Romans, under the Scipios, Cato and Tullius, and especially in the times of the Caesars, when a group of poets sang songs of many kinds, and afterwards to the extreme West—that is, to the Gauls and the Spains—very recently, in the days of those illustrious scholars Berengar, Manegold and Anselm. Men divinely inspired were able to foresee and as it were to have a vision of these things. But we are in a position not merely to believe but also actually to see the things which were predicted, since we behold the world (which, they predicted, was to be despised for its changeableness) already failing and, so to speak, drawing the last breath of extremest old age. . . .

This work of ours, which we have entitled *The Two Cities,* is, plainly, divided into three parts. For, whereas the City of Christ, or the Kingdom of Christ with reference to its present or its future status, is called the Church, it exists in one form so long as it is seen to hold the good and the bad in one embrace; it will exist in another at that time when it shall cherish only the good in the glory of the heavenly embrace; it existed in yet another while it lived subject to princes of the heathen before "the fullness of the Gentiles" was come. . . .

The evil city likewise, we find, has three states or stages. Of these the first was before the time of grace, the second was and is during the time of grace, the third will be after this present life. The first is wretched, the second more wretched, the third most wretched. On the other hand the first condition of that other company (the people of the City of Christ) is abject, the second prosperous, the third blessed; or (to put it in other words) the first is lowly, the second intermediate, the third perfect. Enough has been said in the preceding books with regard to the twofold status of each part. The one was at first lowly while it was in obscurity. Afterwards, when not only inward blessings but outward prosperity as well had been bestowed upon it, it was not to be sure abject as before, nor was it as yet gloriously perfect and blessed as it is to be hereafter; it was rather in a middle or intermediate condition. The other, in part through the effects of infinite changes, in part through its ignorance of true religion, was at first wretched, later, after the revelation of light, so much the more wretched as it was the more inexcusable after the truth had been made manifest. It remains now to tell in this eighth book about the third state, namely, how the one City is to attain to the highest blessedness, the other to fail and to descend to the utmost misery, when the most righteous Judge shall, at the last judgment, examine and shall decide the case of each city.

> 60. ALEXANDER OF ROES (fl. late thirteenth century), a defender of the Holy Roman Empire of the German Nation and the thesis of a translation of empire from antiquity (his *Translatio Imperii* dates ca. 1281), conceived of European civilization as a cultural trinity, passed on from antiquity, with leadership provided by Italy and the Papacy in theology, by France in learning, and by Germany in politics.

Thus, it should be known that the holy Charlemagne, emperor by consent and order of the Roman pontiff, instituted and determined by divine inspiration that the empire of the Romans should always rest on canonical election by the princes of the Germans. It did not seem right to him that the sanctuary of God, that is, the kingdom of the Church, should be possessed by hereditary right, considering that he himself issued directly from the Greeks, Romans, and Germans, and that first his father Pepin and then Charles himself had, through the Franks (i.e., Germans), liberated the city of Rome and the Church of God from the infestation of the Lombards. These princes are the Archbishop of Trier (who is archchancellor of France), the Archbishop of Cologne (archchancellor of Italy), the Archbishop of Mainz (archchancellor of Germany [i.e., all of Alemania]), and the Count Palatine of Trier, once mayor of the palace, to which office Charlemagne's ancestors traced their origins.

Moreover, since Charles himself was king of the Franks (i.e., the Germans) and since that kingship had devolved upon him by inheritance, it would have been impious and indecent of him to deprive his heirs entirely of the royal dignity. Therefore, he ordered (and [his son] Louis confirmed) that the French [*Francigenae*] should have a hereditary king along with a certain portion of the kingdom of the Franks, who would recognize no superior in temporals and who, as the descendant of emperors, would owe no homage or other service. To this king, his heir,

Alexander of Roes, *Translatio Imperii*, in *Alexander von Roes Schriften*, ed. H. Grundmann and H. Heimpel. Stuttgart, 1958. Pp. 124–28. My translation.

he gave the teaching [*studium,* the term for "university"] of philosophy and liberal arts, which he transplanted from the city of Rome to Paris. And it should be noted, as required by due and necessary order, that as the Romans, who were senior, were given the priesthood [*Sacerdotium*], so the Germans [*Germani vel Franci*], who were junior, were given the empire [*Imperium*], and the French [*Francigene vel Galli*], who were more acute, were given the teaching [*Studium*] of sciences.

Thus as the constancy of the Romans firmly maintains the Catholic faith, so the magnanimity of the Germans should imperiously order it to be held, and the subtlety and eloquence of the French should, with the firmest reasoning, prove and demonstrate that it should be so held. By these three, namely, *Sacerdotium, Imperium, Studium,* as by the virtues, namely, the vital, natural, and spiritual, the Holy Catholic Church is spiritually vitalized, augmented, and ruled. By these three, as by foundation, walls, and roof, the Church is materially made perfect. And it should be noted that if one foundation and one roof suffices but not one wall, this is because one seat is enough for the priesthood (namely, Rome) and for the studium (namely, Paris), but the empire has been granted by the Holy Spirit four principal locations, namely, Aquitaine, Arles, Milan, and the city of Rome. Therefore, let those whose business it is see to it that this house remains whole and intact, lest (may it not happen) Antichrist or his precursors enter not through the gate but through the broken walls, and kill the flock and its shepherd.

> 61. JOACHIM OF FLORA (ca. 1135–1202) was a visionary and allegorical interpreter of Scriptures who modified the Augustinian and Orosian world scheme by positing not two but three ages, corresponding to the Trinity. The third period, that of the spirit, was the prelude to the Antichrist and disaster. This periodization, with accompanying apocalyptic interpretations, had an extraordinary influence on Western philosophy of history for centuries.

When we wish to expound something figuratively in the Scriptures, it should first appear to us as if there were a procession of the Holy Spirit from the Father, according to which the first period of history would be considered as that of the Father, the second that of the Spirit, then, as if

Joachim of Flora, *Super quatuor Evangelia.* In George Boas, *Essays on Primitivism and Related Ideas in the Middle Ages.* Trans. George Boas. New York: Octagon, 1948. Pp. 209 and 210–211.

there were a procession of the Holy Spirit from the Son, according to
which the second period must be considered to be that of the Son, the
third that of the Holy Spirit. . . .

Now there was one period in which men lived according to the flesh,
that is, up to the time of Christ. It was initiated by Adam. There was a
second period in which men lived between the flesh and the spirit, which
was initiated by Elisha, the prophet, or by Uzziah, king of Judah. There
is a third, in which men live according to the spirit, which will last until
the end of the world. It was initiated in the days of the blessed Benedict.
And so the fructification of the peculiarities of the first period, or to
speak more truly, of the first condition, lasted from Abraham up to
Zacharias, the father of John the Baptist. Its initiation dates from
Adam. The fructification of the third age dates from that generation
which was the twenty-second after Saint Benedict. . . .

Because in the first age the order of the laity stood out, in the second
the order of the clerics, in the third, the beginnings of which are making
themselves felt, nay, even some outstanding mysteries, the order of
monks ought to appear. Particularly, however, since the advent of Eli,
who was the first in Israel to show that spiritual life of which we are
speaking, can that order, which is partly of the flesh and partly of the
spirit, say not undeservedly of that which is wholly spiritual, "He who
cometh after me was made before me, and I baptize you in water, but he
shall baptize you with the Holy Ghost and with fire. . . ."

There must be distinguished three periods, as if by stretches of three
days, in the generations of the Church. The first ran from Zacharias, the
father of John, who had the covenant of Abraham, up to the blessed Pope
Sylvester, fourteen generations; [the second], from the blessed Pope Sylvester to Pope Zachary, fourteen generations; and [the third] from him
to the present, fourteen generations. . . .

According now to the spiritual interpretation, we may assign the Four
Gospels themselves to four periods. For in the Gospel of Matthew, which
begins with Abraham, we take up the whole divine account of the Old
Testament, which announced that the Saviour of the world would be
born of the seed of David and Abraham, according to the flesh. In the
Gospel of Luke, which concerns the boyhood and education of Christ up
to His twelfth year, we find the doctrine of Mother Church which, beginning with John the Baptist, as if by intervals of time, comes step by
step down to these our times, according to that verse of Daniel, "Many
shall run to and fro, and knowledge shall be increased." In the Gospel of

Mark, in which Christ's manhood, that is, the time of His preaching, is related, His spiritual doctrine, of which the Apostle says, "We speak wisdom among them that are perfect." That is, the spiritual doctrine beginning at the time in which Elias will come and continuing until the end of terrestrial history. In the Gospel of John we find that ineffable wisdom which will exist in the future.

> 62. CHRISTINE DE PIZAN (ca. 1363–1431), a noblewoman with classical as well as biblical learning, moved from writing poetry to history; in her *Book of the City of Ladies* she argued, in opposition to persistent masculine prejudice and error, for the virtues of women and their moral and historical significance.

I could hardly find a book on morals where, even before I had read in it its entirety, I did not find several chapters or certain sections attacking women, no matter who the author was. This reason alone, in short, made me conclude that, although my intellect did not perceive my own great faults and, likewise, those of other women because of its simpleness and ignorance, it was however truly fitting that such was the case. And so I relied more on the judgment of others than on what I myself felt and knew. I was so transfixed in this line of thinking for such a long time that it seemed as if I were in a stupor. Like a gushing fountain, a series of authorities, whom I recalled one after another, came to mind, along with their opinions on this topic. And I finally decided that God formed a vile creature when He made woman, and I wondered how such a worthy artisan could have deigned to make such an abominable work which, from what they say, is the vessel as well as the refuge and abode of every evil and vice. . . .

So occupied with these painful thoughts, my head bowed in shame, my eyes filled with tears, leaning on the pommel of my chair's armrest, I suddenly saw a ray of light fall on my lap, as though it were the sun. I shuddered then, as if wakened from sleep, for I was sitting in a shadow where the sun could not have shone at that hour. And as I lifted my head to see where this light was coming from, I saw three crowned ladies standing before me, and the splendor of their bright faces shone on me and throughout the entire room. . . .

Then she who was the first of the three smiled and began to speak,

Christine de Pizan, *The Book of the City of Ladies*. Trans. Earl Jeffrey Richards. New York: Persea, 1982. Pp. 4–5, 6, 11, 32, 59, 77–78, 151, and 256.

"Dear daughter, do not be afraid, for we have not come here to harm or trouble you but to console you, for we have taken pity on your distress, and we have come to bring you out of the ignorance which so blinds your own intellect that you shun what you know for a certainty and believe what you do not know or see or recognize except by virtue of many strange opinions. . . .

"Thus, fair daughter, the prerogative among women has been bestowed on you to establish and build the City of Ladies. For the foundation and completion of this City you will draw fresh waters from us as from clear fountains, and we will bring you sufficient building stone, stronger and more durable than any marble with cement could be. Thus your City will be extremely beautiful, without equal, and of perpetual duration in the world. . . .

". . . If anyone maintained that women do not possess enough understanding to learn the laws, the opposite is obvious from the proof afforded by experience, which is manifest and has been manifested in many women—just as I will soon tell—who have been very great philosophers and have mastered fields far more complicated, subtle, and lofty than written laws and man-made institutions. Moreover, in case anyone says that women do not have a natural sense for politics and government, I will give you examples of several great women rulers who have lived in past times. And so that you will better know my truth, I will remind you of some women of your own time who remained widows and whose skill governing—both past and present—in all their affairs following the deaths of their husbands provides obvious demonstration that a woman with a mind is fit for all tasks. . . .

"I could tell you a great deal about ladies who governed wisely in ancient times, just as what I will presently tell you will deal with this question. In France there was once a queen, Fredegund, who was the wife of King Chilperic. Although she was cruel, contrary to the natural disposition of women, nevertheless, following her husband's death, with great skill this lady governed the kingdom of France which found itself at this time in very great unrest and danger, and she was left with nothing besides Chilperic's heir, a small son name Clotair. There was great division among the barons regarding the government, and already a great civil war had broken out in the kingdom. Having assembled the barons in council, she addressed them, all the while holding her child in her arms: 'My lords, here is your king. Do not forget the loyalty which has always been present among the French, and do not scorn him because he is a child, for with God's help he will grow up, and when he comes of age he will recognize his good friends and reward them according to their deserts, unless you desire to disinherit him wrongfully and sinfully. As for me, I assure you that I will reward those who act well and loyally with such generosity that no other reward could be better.' Thus did this queen satisfy the barons, and through her wise government, she delivered her son from the hands of his enemies. . . .

"As for this queen of France, Fredegund, of whom I spoke to you before, the boldness of her deeds in battle was equally great, for, as I have already mentioned, when she was widowed by King Chilperic her husband, with Clotair her son at her breast and the kingdom beset by war, she told the barons, 'My lords, do not be afraid of all the enemies who have come upon us, for I have thought up a ruse by which we will conquer, provided you believe me. I will abandon all feminine fear and arm my heart with a man's boldness in order to increase your courage and that of the soldiers in the army, out of pity for your young prince. I will walk ahead of everyone, holding him in my arms, and you will follow me. You will do exactly as I have ordered our high constable to do. . . .'"

[I answered] "My lady, I greatly admire what I have heard you say, that so much good has come into the world by virtue of the understanding of women. These men usually say that women's knowledge is worthless. In fact when someone says something foolish, the widely voiced insult is that this is women's knowledge. In brief, the typical opinions and comments of men claim that women have been and are useful in the world only for bearing children and sewing."

She answered, "Now you can recognize the massive ingratitude of the men who say such things; they are like people who live off the goods of others without knowing their source and without thanking anyone. You can also clearly see how God, who does nothing without a reason, wished to show men that He does not despise the feminine sex nor their own, because it so pleased Him to place such great understanding in women's brains that they are intelligent enough not only to learn and retain the sciences but also to discover new sciences themselves, indeed sciences of such great utility and profit for the world that nothing has been more necessary. . . . And let no one say that I am telling you these things just to be pleasant: they are Boccaccio's own words, and his credibility is well-known and evident. . . .

"As for the great benefits brought about by women regarding spiritual matters, just as I told you before, was it not Clotilda, daughter of the king of Burgundy and wife of the strong Clovis, king of France, who first brought and spread the faith of Jesus Christ to the kings and princes of France? What greater good could have been accomplished than what she did? For after she had been enlightened by the Faith, like the good Christian and holy lady she was, she did not cease to prod and beg her lord to receive the holy Faith and be baptized. . . ."

In brief, all women—whether noble, bourgeois, or lower-class—be well-informed in all things and cautious in defending your honor and chastity against your enemies! My ladies, see how these men accuse you of so many vices in everything. Make liars of them all by showing forth your virtue, and prove their attacks false by acting well, so that you can say with the Psalmist, "the vices of the evil will fall on their heads."

6
ℐ The Renaissance

The Renaissance conception of history was based on that of classical antiquity, but to the loci classici were added new emotions, values, attitudes, and judgments. For humanists, the art of history was central to the so-called *studia humanitatis* which defined their program, and it had close ties with the other humanities, especially grammar (historical sense being equivalent to grammatical or literal sense, in contrast to figurative interpretation), rhetoric (history, too, being devoted to concrete, causal, and didactic narrative), and moral philosophy (humanists recalling the aphorism of Dionysius of Halicarnassus designating history as "philosophy teaching by example"). The distinguishing feature of history, in contrast to the other human arts (and especially poetry) was its dedication to "truth," the old Ciceronian formulas insisting on this point.

In literary terms, too, Renaissance historiography followed ancient models, especially the national history of Livy and the more popular Roman authors but increasingly the scientific history of Thucydides and Polybius as well. The dual tradition of Thucydidean (political, presentist, and critical) and Herodotean historiography (cultural, antiquarian, and betimes credulous) was revived and persisted in the Renaissance theory and practice of history.

The humanist view of history was the product of a cultural shock: the confrontation of an almost forgotten civilization which clashed in many ways with Christian tradition and yet (most notably in the writings of Petrarch) promised extraordinary rewards. Of the questions arising from this intellectual experience, the first was how to understand or interpret—how to translate—the texts and thoughts of the ancients into modern form. The new, or renewed, science of philology (especially in the work of such scholars as Bruni and Valla) suggested the way to a solution. Out of philology emerged as well the arts of historical criticism on the basis of which truth might be extricated from the myths and corrupt traditions of the past and an authentic modern history might be formed.

Modern ideas of history also had to face questions of value, and as always, opinions were divided. A few skeptics (such as Henry Cornelius Agrippa) denounced history as prideful and full of errors: Herodotus could be called the "father of lies" (Vives's phrase) as well as the "father of history." Most scholars, however, were inclined to accept the moral, pedagogical, political, and even philosophical benefits of historical studies and to look to history not only for lessons but also, increasingly, for legitimacy; imitation (*mimesis*) was a constant companion of historical curiosity. One result was that, although some legends (such as that of the Trojan origins of European nations) were exploded, other idealizations and myths—political, religious, and cultural—were created. Of these new cultural constructs, the most significant may have been the "quarrel" between the Ancients and Moderns (one of the roots of the modern idea of progress), which established the basic premise for the periodization of the historical process.

In many ways, history was accommodated to the needs and pressures of the modern world, most conspicuously in the new political history of Machiavelli and Guicciardini, who were concerned to explain the predicaments of their own times and, in Machiavelli's case, to exploit history, ancient and modern, for the purpose of finding larger patterns of change and even a kind of political science. But perhaps the most significant implication of Renaissance attitudes was the suggestion that history was not only an art but also an autonomous mode of thought which could add to the understanding of other disciplines and give form to the whole humanist encyclopedia of learning, as variously illustrated by the work of Vespasiano, Polydore Vergil, Juan Luis Vives, and Louis Le Roy. Thus history, while retaining its literary ambitions in some circles, ascended the ladder of academic learning to the level of a true science and profession.

❡ THE SENSE OF HISTORY

63. PETRARCH (Francesco Petrarca, 1304–1374) was a Florentine poet and scholar who, according to the legend disseminated by
such disciples as Boccaccio and Bruni, was "the first" (*il primo*) to
restore an understanding and appreciation of ancient culture: he
was regarded as the founding father of Renaissance humanism.
One of the main ingredients of this innovative yet backward-
looking attitude was an extraordinary sensitivity to history as well
as a sense of self in relation to the record of the past. This humanist
sense of history is displayed in ways that reflect Petrarch's feeling
that the noble classical past, that is, the Roman republican and
imperial part of Italian tradition, had indeed been lost or forgotten, but that human learning might bring it back to life and in this
way give cultural, moral, and even political renewal to what he
called "Italia mia." At first, Petrarch's emotional drive toward and
identification with antiquity was largely literary nostalgia and an
ambition to become the modern Virgil (manifested in his poem
Africa), but soon this aspiration led him to efforts of critical historical scholarship.

Petrarch's own vision of history can be seen in a number of writings, poetry as well as prose, most characteristically in his self-
conscious "letter to posterity" and his fascinating letters to classical
authors, including Homer, Livy, and Tacitus. More directly historiographical was his study of famous men of the Roman past, in
which, like Plutarch, he hoped to bring the lessons of antiquity
directly to bear upon the modern age. Petrarch's pioneering contribution to critical historical scholarship is illustrated especially in
his letter to the emperor Charles IV exposing the forged donation
(purportedly from Caesar) to the Habsburgs on grounds of anachronism and the general ignorance of history characteristic of his
still unenlightened age—to which it was Petrarch's hope to bring
knowledge, beauty, and virtue.

Living, I despise what melancholy fate
has brought us wretches in these evil years.
Long before my birth time smiled and may again,

Petrarch, sonnet from *Epistolae metricae,* 3:33. Cited (Latin) in Theodor E.
Mommsen, *Medieval and Renaissance Studies,* ed. Eugene Rice, Jr. Ithaca, N.Y.:
Cornell University Press, 1959. P. 128. My translation.

for once there was, and yet will be, more joyful days.
But in this middle age time's dregs
sweep around us, and we bend beneath a heavy
load of vice. Genius, virtue, glory now
have gone, leaving chance and sloth to rule.
Shameful vision this! We must awake or die.

❡ "To Posterity"

I possessed a well-balanced rather than a keen intellect, one prone to all kinds of good and wholesome study, but especially inclined to moral philosophy and the art of poetry. The latter, indeed, I neglected as time went on, and took delight in sacred literature. Finding in that a hidden sweetness which I had once esteemed but lightly, I came to regard the works of the poets as only amenities. Among the many subjects which interested me, I dwelt especially upon antiquity, for our own age has always repelled me, so that, had it not been for the love of those dear to me, I should have preferred to have been born in any other period than our own. In order to forget my own time, I have constantly striven to place myself in spirit in other ages, and consequently I delighted in history; not that the conflicting statements did not offend me, but when in doubt I accepted what appeared to me most probable, or yielded to the authority of the writer.

My style, as many claimed, was clear and forcible; but to me it seemed weak and obscure. In ordinary conversation with friends, or with those about me, I never gave any thought to my language, and I have always wondered that Augustus Caesar should have taken such pains in this respect. When, however, the subject itself, or the place or listener, seemed to demand it, I gave some attention to style, with what success I cannot pretend to say; let them judge in whose presence I spoke. If only I have lived well, it matters little to me how I talked. Mere elegance of language can produce at best but an empty renown.

Petrarch, *Epistolae seniles*. In James Harvey Robinson and Henry Winchester Rolfe, *Petrarch, The First Modern Scholar and Man of Letters*. New York: G. P. Putnam's Sons, 1898. Pp. 64–65.

ℌ To Marcus Tullius Cicero

Your letters I sought for long and diligently; and finally, where I least expected it, I found them. At once I read them, over and over, with the utmost eagerness. And as I read I seemed to hear your bodily voice, O Marcus Tullius, saying many things, uttering many lamentations, ranging through many phases of thought and feeling. I long had known how excellent a guide you have proved for others; at last I was to learn what sort of guidance you gave yourself.

Now it is your turn to be the listener. Hearken, wherever you are, to the words of advice, or rather of sorrow and regret, that fall, not unaccompanied by tears, from the lips of one of your successors, who loves you faithfully and cherishes your name. O spirit ever restless and perturbed! in old age—I am but using your own words—self-involved in calamities and ruin! what good could you think would come from your incessant wrangling, from all this wasteful strife and enmity? Where were the peace and quiet that befitted your years, your profession, your station in life? What Will-o'-the-wisp tempted you away, with a delusive hope of glory; involved you, in your declining years, in the wars of younger men; and, after exposing you to every form of misfortune, hurled you down to a death that it was unseemly for a philosopher to die? Alas! the wise counsel that you gave your brother, and the salutary advice of your great masters, you forgot. You were like a traveller in the night, whose torch lights up for others the path where he himself has miserably fallen.

Of Dionysius I forbear to speak; of your brother and nephew, too; of Dolabello even, if you like. At one moment you praise them all to the skies; at the next fall upon them with sudden maledictions. This, however, could perhaps be pardoned. I will pass by Julius Caesar, too, whose well-approved clemency was a harbour of refuge for the very men who were warring against him. Great Pompey, likewise, I refrain from mentioning. His affection for you was such that you could do with him what you would. But what insanity led you to hurl yourself upon Anthony? Love of the republic, you would probably say. But the republic had fallen before this into irretrievable ruin, as you had yourself admitted. Still, it is possible that a lofty sense of duty, and love of liberty, constrained you

Petrarch, *To Marcus Tullius Cicero (Fam. XXIV, 3)*. In James Harvey Robinson and Henry Winchester Rolfe, *Petrarch, The First Modern Scholar and Man of Letters*. New York: G. P. Putnam's Sons, 1898. Pp. 233–242.

to do as you did, hopeless though the effort was. That we can easily believe of so great a man. But why, then, were you so friendly with Augustus? What answer can you give to Brutus? If you accept Octavius, said he, we must conclude that you are not so anxious to be rid of all tyrants as to find a tyrant who will be well-disposed toward yourself. Now, unhappy man, you were to take the last false step, the last and most deplorable. You began to speak ill of the very friend whom you had so lauded, although he was not doing any ill to you but merely refusing to prevent others who were. I grieve, dear friend, at such fickleness. These shortcomings fill me with pity and shame. Like Brutus, I feel no confidence in the arts in which you are so proficient. What, pray, does it profit a man to teach others, and to be prating always about virtue, in high-sounding words, if he fails to give heed to his own instruction? Ah! how much better it would have been, how much more fitting for a philosopher, to have grown old peacefully in the country, meditating, as you yourself have somewhere said, upon the life that endures for ever, and not upon this poor fragment of life; to have known no fasces, yearned for no triumphs, found no Catilines to fill the soul with ambitious long-ings!—All this, however, is vain. Farewell, forever, my Cicero.

Written in the land of the living; on the right bank of the Adige, in Verona, a city of Transpadane Italy; on the 16th of June, and in the year of that God whom you never knew the 1345th. . . .

❡ To the same.

If my earlier letter gave you offence,—for, as you often have re-marked, the saying of your contemporary in the Andria is a faithful one, that compliance begets friends, truth only hatred,—you shall listen now to works that will soothe your wounded feelings and prove that the truth need not always be hateful. For, if censure that is true angers us, true praise, on the other hand, gives us delight.

You lived then, Cicero, if I may be permitted to say it, like a mere man, but spoke like an orator, wrote like a philosopher. It was your life that I criticized; not your mind, nor your tongue; for the one fills me with admiration, the other with amazement. And even in your life I

Petrarch, *To Marcus Tullius Cicero (Fam. XXIV, 4)*. In James Harvey Robin-son and Henry Winchester Rolfe, *Petrarch, The First Modern Scholar and Man of Letters*. New York: G. P. Putnam's Sons, 1898. Pp. 249–252.

feel the lack of nothing but stability, and the love of quiet that should go with your philosophic professions, and abstention from civil war, when liberty had been extinguished and the republic buried and its dirge sung.

See how different my treatment of you is from yours of Epicurus, in your works at large, and especially in the *De Finibus*. You are continually praising his life, but his talents you ridicule. I ridicule in you nothing at all. Your life does awaken my pity, as I have said; but your talents and your eloquence call for nothing but congratulation. O great father of Roman eloquence! not I alone but all who deck themselves with the flowers of Latin Speech render thanks unto you. It is from your wellsprings that we draw these streams that water our meads. You, we freely acknowledge, are the leader who marshals us; yours are the words of encouragement that sustain us; yours is the light that illumines the path before us. In a word, it is under your auspices that we have attained to such little skill in this art of writing as we may possess. . . .

You have heard what I think of your life and your genius. Are you hoping to hear of your books also; what fate has befallen them, how they are esteemed by the masses and among scholars? They still are in existence, glorious volumes, but we of to-day are too feeble a folk to read them, or even to be acquainted with their mere titles. Your fame extends far and wide; your name is mighty, and fills the ears of men; and yet those who really know you are very few, be it because the times are unfavorable, or because men's minds are slow and dull, or, as I am the more inclined to believe, because the love of money forces our thoughts in other directions. Consequently right in our own day, unless I am much mistaken, some of your books have disappeared, I fear beyond recovery. It is a great grief to me, a great disgrace to this generation, a great wrong done to posterity. The shame of failing to cultivate our own talents, thereby depriving the future of the fruits that they might have yielded, is not enough for us; we must waste and spoil, through our cruel and insufferable neglect, the fruits of your labours too, and of these of your fellows as well, for the fate that I lament in the case of your own books has befallen the words of many other illustrious men.

It is of yours alone, though, that I would speak now. Here are the names of those among them whose loss is most to be deplored; the *Republic*, the *Praise of Philosophy*, the treatises on the *Care of Property*, on the *Art of War*, on *Consolation*, on *Glory*,—although in the case of this last my feeling is rather one of hopeful uncertainty than of certain despair.

And then there are huge gaps in the volumes that have survived. It is as if indolence and oblivion had been worsted, in a great battle, but we had to mourn noble leaders slain, and others lost or maimed. This last indignity very many of your books have suffered, but more particularly the *Orator,* the *Academics,* and the *Laws.* They have come forth from the fray so mutilated and disfigured that it would have been better if they had perished outright.

Now in conclusion, you will wish me to tell you something about the condition of Rome and the Roman republic: the present appearance of the city and whole country, the degree of harmony that prevails, what classes of citizens possess political power, by whose hands and with what wisdom the reins of empire are swayed, and whether the Danube, the Ganges, the Ebro, the Nile, the Don, are our boundaries now, or in very truth the man has arisen who "bounds our empire by the ocean-stream, our fame by the stars of heaven," or "extends our rule beyond Garama and Ind," as your friend the Mantuan Virgil has said. Of these and other matters of like nature I doubt not you would very gladly hear. Your filial piety tells me so, your well-known love of country, which you cherished even to your own destruction. But indeed it were better that I refrained. Trust me, Cicero, if you were to hear of our condition to-day you would be moved to tears, in whatever circle of heaven above, or Erebus below, you may be dwelling. Farewell, forever.

Written in the world of the living, on the left bank of the Rhone, in Transalpine Gaul; in the same year, but in the month of December, the 19th day. . . .

❡ To Titus Livy

I should wish (if it were permitted from on high) either that I had been born in Thine age or thou in ours; in the latter case our age itself, and in the former I personally should have been the better for it. I should surely have been one of those pilgrims who visited thee. For the sake of seeing thee I should have gone not merely to Rome, but indeed, from either Gaul or Spain I should have found my way to thee as far as India. As it is I must fain be content with seeing thee as reflected in thy works—not

Petrarch, *To Titus Livy (Fam. XXIV, 8).* In *Petrarch's Letters to Classical Authors,* ed. and trans. M. E. Cosenza. Chicago: University of Chicago Press, 1910. Pp. 100–103.

thy whole self, alas, but that portion of thee which has not yet perished, notwithstanding the sloth of our age. We know that thou didst write one hundred and forty-two books on Roman affairs. With what fervor, with what unflagging zeal must thou have labored; and of that entire number there are now extant scarcely thirty.

Oh, what a wretched custom is this of wilfully deceiving ourselves! I have said "thirty," because it is common for all to say so. I find, however, that even from these few there is one lacking. They are twenty-nine in all, constituting three decades, the first, the third and the fourth, and the last of which has not the full number of books. It is over these small remains that I toil whenever I wish to forget these regions, these times, and these customs. Often I am filled with bitter indignation against the morals of today, when men value nothing except gold and silver, and desire nothing except sensual, physical pleasures. If these are to be considered the goal of mankind, then not only the dumb beasts of the field, but even insensible and inert matter has a richer, a higher goal than that proposed to itself by thinking man. But of this elsewhere.

It is now fitter that I should render thee thanks, for many reasons indeed, but for this in especial: that thou didst so frequently cause me to forget the present evils, and transfer me to happier times. As I read, I seem to be living in the midst of the Cornellii Scipiones Africani, of Laelius, of Fabius Maximus, Metellus, Brutus. . . . It is with these men that I live at such times and not with the thievish company of today among whom I was born under an evil star. And Oh, if it were my happy lot to possess thee entire, from what other great names would I not seek solace for my wretched existence, and forgetfulness of this wicked age! Since I cannot find all these in what I now possess of thy work, I read of them here and there in other authors, and especially in that book where thou art to be found in thy entirety, but so briefly epitomized that, although nothing is lacking as far as the number of books is concerned, everything is lacking as regards the value of the contents themselves.

Pray greet in my behalf thy predecessors Polybius and Quintus Claudius and Valerius Antias, and all those whose glory thine own greater light has dimmed; and of the later historians, give greeting to Pliny the Younger, of Verona a neighbor of thine, and also to thy former rival Crispus Sallustius. Tell them that their ceaseless nightly vigils have been of no more avail, have had no happier lot, than thine.

Farewell forever, thou matchless historian!

Written in the land of the living, in that part of Italy and in that city in which I am now living and where thou wert once born and buried, in the vestibule of the Temple of Justina Virgo, and in view of thy very tombstone; on the twenty-second of February, in the thirteen hundred and fiftieth year from the birth of Him whom thou wouldst have seen, or of whose birth thou couldst have heard, hadst thou lived a little longer.

❡ Preface to *De viris illustribus*

I should naturally call very fortunate those scholars who wrote at a time when some honor was accorded such fine endeavors. Now I judge fortunate those who are even permitted to strive for such an honor without penalty. So many enemies of excellence meet you wherever you turn that to seem to love excellence is not without danger; and whoever would turn away from the path travelled by the insane mob will be subject either to harm or to reproach. There are two roads open to men, either of greediness or pleasure, and both full of peril. And to move from these two even a little is held to be a hateful and ridiculous error, so that whoever abandons the beaten path that leads to death is seen as an utter fool or public enemy of the human race. There is another path, the most difficult but noble one, which leads to glory; it has always been travelled by a few and is now travelled by practically no one. Hence, not only Venus, but also Juno wins the palm of judgement for their endeavors; Minerva alone is neglected. What indeed can we do now, if it is dangerous to love excellence and to admire one's friends? And what use will it be to speak of these things, if the evil and cowardly despise the mention of the good and illustrious, if almost all the glory of others is subjected to their slander? Therefore, should we be silent? No, rather, it is proper to speak, for the very reason that through the remembrance of virtue we censure vice.

I have decided, therefore, to collect or rather almost to compress into one place the praise of the illustrious men who flourished with outstanding glory and whose memory—which I found spread far and wide and scattered in sundry volumes—has been handed to us through the skill of

Petrarch, *Long Preface to De viris illustribus (1351–1353)*. In Benjamin G. Kohl, "Petrarch's Prefaces to De viris illustribus." *History and Theory* 13, no. 2 (1974): 132–144. Copyright © 1974, Wesleyan University.

many learned men. I confess that I should prefer to write on things seen rather than read, contemporary rather than ancient, so that posterity would receive from me information about this age just as I have received from the ancients information about the distant past. However, being tired and desirous of rest, I thank those contemporary princes who free me from this labor, for they contribute material not for history but for satire. And though I realize that some of them have recently become famous because of military victories, these occurred because of good fortune or the inertia of the enemy, so that the success was not at all a question of military valor or true glory.

Just as it is glorious to invent new things in philosophical or poetic works, so it is forbidden to do so in history. And since it is my purpose not to compose a story but to retell history, therefore it is proper for me to follow in the footsteps of many famous authors—not, however, to transcribe their words but to describe the events themselves. It does not escape me how much work is involved in maintaining the dignity of my discourse. Since it is not permitted to me to make use of the very words of earlier historians and since it is not possible for me to surpass them in style, there is only a third course open to me. Let everyone be aware of the volume and order of the many disparate facts and if I have done my task well let him be grateful to me; if I have done it with some elegance, let him be very grateful. Also the reader should realize that as I have taken upon myself the task of collecting the facts, so I have relieved him of the burden of research. For although the things I am going to write about are found in other authors, they are not, however, found collected there in the same way. For what is lacking in one author I have supplied from another. One account I have made shorter, another clearer; there were still others whose brevity made them obscure, so I have expanded these and thus made them more lucid. I have also omitted many things which I know are found in other historians who treated of the ancients' customs and absurd religious practices (I should say superstitions); for these things would have been more tedious than useful and pleasant. I have joined together many things which were found dispersed in many histories, by one author or by several, and I have made them a whole.

In doing this I have thought that I have been able to avoid the imprudence of sterile diligence of those authors who, having collected the words of all the historians—so that they seem to have not neglected anything at all—have really contradicted one authority with another so the entire text of their history is lost in cloudy ambiguities and inexplicable conflicts. I am neither the peacemaker among conflicting historians nor the collector of every minute fact; but rather, I am the copier of those whose verisimilitude or greater authority demands that they be given greater credence. Therefore, if there are any future readers who are well-versed in history and who will have met one or another anecdote which they have not been accustomed to hear or read, I beseech and even admonish them not to pronounce judgement hastily (which is the habit of those who know only a little), but rather to reflect upon the disagreements of historians, who in many cases caused embarrassment even to Livy, who was so much closer to the events he was describing. For there are some men, especially soldiers, who, because they are very busy, select in time of leisure only one history book and, to distract themselves from their worries, take refuge in the pleasure of reading it at some time during the day or night. And thus they are so impressed by reading this one book that anything they hear which is not in it seems to them to be not just new, but even erroneous. Hence, they immediately proclaim as false anything which is told in a way that differs from how they had found it written in their own book. They consider themselves learned because they have read only one book, while if they had read many (as it is possible to do), they would have realized that they were quite ignorant. So they do not think that what is lacking in their author can be found, as it can, in others, or that what is told in the other authors in a different way can really be believed.

Now, if anyone who really wants to know all of history will say that I have left out entirely too much and have neglected the law of history which as I know was recorded by Cicero, I will defend myself by calling attention to my diligence and to the infinite quantity of events. Since it is virtually impossible to satisfy the curiosity to know everything, I have instead taken the position that I shall treat only those things which acquire splendor in the treatment. Hence, I shall observe the rule I have read in Horace's *Ars Poetica*. For who, I ask, would want to set down, in order, from the most distant past, the names of the kings of the Parthians or Macedonians, of the Goths and Huns and Vandals and other peoples which have always been obscure and that now are obliterated by time? And even if I were to try to do this, would I not seem to have forgotten my own purpose, because of the immensity of the work and the boredom for the reader, not to mention the labor and loss of time involved for me? Besides, not every rich and powerful person is similarly distinguished; these are the result of good luck, while the illustrious ones are the product of glory and virtue. In any case, I have not promised to describe lucky men, but illustrious ones. I recall an anecdote about Caesar Augustus who, when he was at Alexandria where the ashes of the kings of Egypt were preserved in precious tombs, gladly contemplated the body of Alexander of Macedon, which lay in the chamber. But when Augustus was asked if he wanted to inspect the remains of Ptolemy, he replied, "I want to see kings, not just corpses." Even though he knew that Ptolemy had been a king, the wise emperor wanted to suggest by this brief remark that there is a great difference between true kings and those who are commonly given the name of kings.

I have promised, I repeat, to describe those men whom we call illustrious and who are remembered the most by their magnificent and illustrious deeds, although in fact some of these men are relatively unknown. For if we required that each one be absolutely illustrious we would have made a very slender volume or even perhaps none at all. For who can be found who is illustrious in every way? It is a well-known fact that, as with many handsome faces, the most illustrious minds are often afflicted by nature with some grave defect. In a work of this size, I have expended long and painstaking labor in order that I might be both useful and pleasing. I have omitted many things which, as I said above, seemed to lend more to confusion than to usefulness, while I have striven at the same time for brevity and a description of the really important events. For what use is it, to give some examples, to know what slaves or dogs an illustrious man has had, what beasts of burden, what cloaks, what were the names of his servants, what was the nature of his married life, his profession, or his personal property? What use is it to know what sort of food he liked best, or what he preferred as a means of transportation, as a breastplate, as a cloak, or finally, even for sauces and vegetables?

Whoever desires to know these and similar things, let him consult other historians who propose to write a great deal, rather than just on important or glorious subjects. In my book, he will look for these things in vain, except inasmuch as they can lead to virtues or to the contraries of virtues. For, unless I am mistaken, this is the profitable goal for the historian: to point up to the readers those things that are to be followed and those to be avoided, with plenty of distinguished examples provided on either side. Whatever author would presume to wander outside this boundary, let him know that he is treading on foreign soil and wandering in foreign territory, and let him be reminded to return to the beaten path, except perhaps when he will be seeking, at a certain point, to please the readers with amusing anecdotes. For I myself cannot deny that I have often abandoned myself for long periods to such digressions, when it was pleasing for me to remember or to recall to others the manners and domestic life of illustrious men, their conversations, their pithy sayings and turns of phrases, their works, sometimes stinging, sometimes grave, which they dropped here and there and all of which seemed to me to be always diverting and sometimes even useful. And I have added reports on their bodily stature, genealogy, and manner of death when it seemed to be pleasing to know these things.

If I have succeeded in accomplishing less than I had intended, I hope that whoever reads this book will please excuse me. For while I make you judge of my success, I wish that you believe what I say concerning my intentions. And if it will seem to you, therefore, that there is too much of some material or less than you would like concerning other things, ascribe it either to a lack of genius or to a mind which has been distracted by worry, and say among yourselves: "This man would have liked to be more outstanding, more useful, more pleasing, but he was not able." If, on the other hand, the labor of my studies has perhaps at least in part quenched the thirst of your expectations, then I ask from you no other kind of reward than that I be loved by you, even though I am not known by you, even though I am shut up in my grave, even though I have turned into dust. In this same way, I have loved after a thousand years many who have helped me in my studies who were not just dead but consumed after so much time. But I realize I protest too much, and so that I do not seem to be too preoccupied with meriting your good judgement, I shall not drag on longer. Nor shall I expend on this little preface the time (and let us hope that will be granted to us) which is due only to necessities. Therefore, with him whom we call the father of the human race, I begin my very long journey.

❡ To Emperor Charles IV (1355)

On the false privilege exempting Austria from imperial jurisdiction. Lies always limp and are easily caught. It is difficult for them to escape the verdict of a keen, quick intellect. This morning I saw a manuscript

Petrarch, *Letter to Emperor Charles IV.* In Peter Burke, *The Renaissance Sense of the Past.* Trans. Peter Burke. London: Edward Arnold, 1969. Pp. 50–54.

which was full of words and empty of truth. I do not know who wrote it, but have no doubt that he was not a learned man but a schoolboy, an ignorant writer, a man with the desire to lie but without the skill to do it properly—otherwise he would not have made such stupid mistakes. Forgers usually give their falsehoods some colour of truth, so that it is possible to believe what never happened, because it is similar to things which did happen.

The author—it is utter madness—seems to have believed that with this trifle he could overthrow Roman law and the Empire too, defended as it is by arms, laws, and virtues. He might at least have produced more workmanlike lies, which did not look false even to the almost blind.

I have no doubt, Caesar, that the whole of this rascal's deceit was immediately apparent to you, and to your nobles, wise and learned men, and especially to your lynx-eyed chancellor. However, you ask me for an opinion too. I shall tell you the first impression it made on me, busy and anxious as I am. It is no small honour that Your Highness wanted me to be a party to the secret and considered me the right man to expose these deceits.

I shall not discuss the point that no one has authority over his equals, and that Julius Caesar and Nero did not make any decree which you have not the right to reverse. The rogue did not realise this when he pretended, with clumsy cunning, that they were the authors of that disgraceful privilege, as if what the best princes had decreed, and the worst confirmed, could not be revoked by anyone. I leave this question to your lawyers, or better still, to you, since, (as I learned in the law-schools when I was young), you contain all laws within yourself.

I come now to the point you are waiting for. "We," he says, "the emperor Julius Caesar, we, Caesar, worshipper of the gods, lord of the land, the imperial Augustus," etc. Who is so stupid or so ignorant that he cannot see that there are almost as many lies here as there are words? Although (as Lucan says) this dishonest plural had long been used to address great men, they did not use it themselves. So although his flattering followers had begun to speak to Caesar as if he were plural, which was never done to anyone before him (a custom which later became a general one), he himself, speaking to his troops, always referred to himself in the singular. That ox did not know this fact, or he would have bellowed more warily.

I own a number of Julius Caesar's personal letters. His speeches, many of which are to be found in the works of Lucan and other writers, and one in Sallust, were not composed by him, but by those writers themselves. But he dictated his letters in person. Here is an example.

> "Caesar to Oppius and Cornelius, greetings. I am most glad to learn from your letters that you approve completely of what was done at Confinium. I should be glad of your advice, all the more because I plan to do something that I scarcely approve of myself."

Again:

> "Caesar to Oppius and Cornelius, greetings. On the seventh day before the Ides of March I came to Brundisium and pitched camp near its walls. Pompey is at Brundisium; he sent Gn. Magius to me to discuss peace. I replied as we planned; I wanted you to know at once. When there is hope of an agreement, I will tell you immediately."

Again, writing to Cicero:

> "Although I know that you are not afraid, I do not believe that you will do anything imprudent either. But being worried by rumours, I thought I should write to you," etc.

There exists a letter of his, or rather a decree, concerning an important matter, addressed not to individual friends but to the people of Sidon, as follows:

> "G. Julius Caesar, general (*imperator*) and pontifex, and dictator for the second time, to the magistrates and people of Sidon and Cinthia, greetings. If you are well, it is good; my army and I are well. I have sent you a copy of the decree to Hircanus, son of Alexander the chief priest and ruler of the Jews, to be inserted in your public annals. I want this decree to be written on bronze in Greek and Latin. Immediately afterwards, I decreed that Hircanus and the sons of Alexander should be the rulers of the Jewish people and should always be their high-priests, according to the customs of their ancestors. I order that he and his sons should be counted among our allies and our very good friends, and that they should have all the rights of the high priest," etc.

If you want this letter, you will find it in the third book of Josephus, a most reliable author. I could give more examples: you see his style. Who does not see not only how false, but also how ridiculous it is that Julius Caesar should call himself Augustus! I thought that every schoolboy knew that that name began to be used by his successor. Read Florus, read Suetonius, read Orosius, read Eutropius, in fact read all the historians. Everyone knows, except this ass who is now braying so inappropriately.

I do not understand what follows, what invented uncle this is, something quite extraordinary, known only in these scribblings and found nowhere else; especially odd in that little or nothing is known of Caesar's father even. I would be surprised at this if I were not accustomed to believing this man's glory to be so great, his name so illustrious, that those around him paled beside him like the stars beside the sun. I do not know where this uncle sprang from, or where he was hiding for so many centuries, or for what offense he was taken to the ends of the earth. I am extremely surprised that an anonymous witness is brought into the case, and in such a great matter trust is placed in one whose name is as doubtful as his testimony. The privilege is also invalid because it lacks the name of the man to whom it was made, since privileges (as I learned when I was a boy), are of restricted application. There are many things here which weaken it, but this matter I leave to your lawyers.

Nor it is possible to argue seriously that what is called "Austria" is an eastern region. "Auster" (South) and "Priens" (East) are different. They are names for the directions of different regions, directions which vary with one's own position. From Rome, from the city from which the document claims to come, which removes this region, Austria, from imperial jurisdiction, Austria is not south, but north.

The date of the document is clearly false. It does not indicate that exact day, nor the consuls in office. Only an idiot would say "given at Rome on Friday in the first year of our reign" without adding the month and the day. What shepherd, what ploughman would write like this— let alone the man who had, besides his other great deeds, reformed the calendar! Then he says "of our reign" which is so far from the truth as to arouse indignation as well as laughter. For, as you have heard, Caesar wished to be called "general" (*imperator*), "pontifex," and "dictator"— never "king" (*rex*). We read that Rome in earliest times had seven kings. Those who wished to become kings after this were put to the sword or thrown from the rock on the Capitol hill. I admit that Caesar was suspected of wishing to be king—but only by his enemies. He was too prudent and too careful of his reputation to take a title which would have made him infamous. He would no more call himself a "king" (or allow himself to be called one) than "buffoon," "adulterer" or "pimp." In fact he was even less likely to allow it, for while the other names are shameful and filthy, that of "king" was odious, dangerous and intolerable at Rome. Here is the evidence.

When the Spanish people offered Scipio Africanus the title of "king" out of admiration for his great and glorious achievements, look at what he answered. I quote Livy's own words. "After the herald had made silence, he said that his greatest title was that of "general" (*imperator*), which his soldiers had given him. The name of "king" was a great one elsewhere, but at Rome it was not tolerated." And so Lucan said "Caesar was everything," meaning that he united in himself all the honours of Rome, where there was no royal title. Caesar could not have mentioned his "reign": had he done so he would have been execrated and rejected.

This is my answer to that ignorant and clumsy fabricator of lies concerning his stories about Julius Caesar. Much of it is also applicable to what he says about Nero, ending "given on the day of the great god Mars" [Tuesday]. Oh shameless, stupid man! How will you answer critics? What Monday and what Wednesday precede and follow this day? Who can tolerate this wild lying, this foolishness?

Caesar, you may laugh and be glad that the rebels against you are able to do you less harm than they would like; they attack your authority and claim this liberty on the basis of more lies than they realise. If they had, he would never have begun with a lie like this: "We, Nero, the friend of the gods," when we read that he despised all the gods; for Suetonius says of him in Book VI of his *Lives of the Caesars,* "He always had contempt for religion, except one, that of the goddess Syria. But he soon despised her enough to [sully her image]."

These, oh emperor, are my immediate comments without a detailed study. I omit the question of the style of both letters, which from beginning to end is both barbarous and modern. It is clear that these documents were thrown together quite recently in a childish attempt to imitate the style of the ancients. It is impossible not to see the falsehood, which is apparent in every word. The whole thing is so different from what the forger aimed at, so remote from antiquity and the style of Caesar, that a credulous old woman or a mountain peasant might perhaps be taken in, but certainly not a man of intelligence.

You have sent me a letter dictated in anger. I much approve of its style and rejoice that praise is due to you not only as a soldier and a judge, but as a writer too.

Caesar, farewell. Be mindful of me and of the empire, and lead a life such that your friends do not lie to you and your enemies fear you.

Milan, the 12th before the Kalends of April, in haste.

> 64. LEONARDO BRUNI (1370–1444) was a disciple of Petrarch who, as Florentine chancellor and publicist, expanded Petrarch's largely moral and private conception of history to a political and actively "civic" vision. Among the first Western Hellenists, Bruni translated Aristotle's works of "practical philosophy," especially the *Politics* and *Nicomachaean Ethics,* and faced the problem of rendering the terms and concepts of ancient Greek culture into modern Latin. Bruni's major concern was modern history, however, and he insisted on its value both for national tradition and for civic responsibility, shifting emphasis from the contemplative to the active life, from imperial to republican Rome, and from Roman to native Florentine origins of the city.
>
> Bruni also carried Petrarch's critical methods into the political sphere, discarding the old myth of Trojan origins and beginning to form a new myth of Florence's republican virtues (compared not only to Rome but also to ancient Athens) underlying what is conventionally called *civic humanism.* Bruni's expanded sense of history can be seen both in his panegyrical writings on Florence (composed during the crucial struggle between the republic he served and the Milanese despotism) and in his formal *History of Florence,* which became a model for later national histories composed in the humanist and Livian mode.

In my view, then, the whole essence of translation is to transfer correctly what is written in one language into another language. But no one can do this correctly who has not a wide and extensive knowledge of both languages. Nor is even that enough. There are many men who have the capacity to understand an activity, though they cannot themselves exercise it. Many persons, for instance, appreciate painting who cannot

Leonardo Bruni, *On the Correct Way to Translate.* In *The Humanism of Leonardo Bruni: Selected Texts* (Medieval and Renaissance Texts and Studies, vol. 46; Renaissance Texts, vol. 10). Trans. Gordon Griffiths, James Hankins, and David Thompson. Binghamton, N.Y.: Medieval & Renaissance Texts & Studies in conjunction with Renaissance Society of America, 1987. Pp. 218 and 219–221.

themselves paint, and many understand the art of music without themselves being able to sing.

Correct translation is therefore an extremely difficult task. One must have, first of all, a knowledge of the language to be translated, and no small or common knowledge at that, but one that is wide, idiomatic, accurate, and detailed, acquired from a long reading of the philosophers and orators and poets and all other writers. No one who has not read, comprehended, thoroughly considered and retained all these can possibly grasp the force and significance of the words, especially since Aristotle himself and Plato were, I may say, the very greatest masters of literature, and practiced a most elegant kind of writing filled with the sayings and maxims of the old poets and orators and historians, and frequently employed tropes and figures of speech that have acquired idiomatic meanings far different from their literal meanings. We in our language, for instance, employ such expressions as "I humor you," "soldiers lost in battle," "take in good part," "it would be worthwhile," "to take pains," and a thousand others like them. The rawest schoolboy knows what "pains" are, and what "to take" means, but the whole phrase means something else. To say "a hundred soldiers were lost in battle," means, literally, that "a hundred soldiers cannot be found." It is the same with the other examples: the words mean one thing, the sense is another. . . .

The Greek language covers a broad field, and there are innumerable examples in Aristotle and Plato of illustrations drawn from Homer, Hesiod, Pindar, Euripides, and other ancient poets and writers. Then, too, there is a frequent use of figures of speech, so that a man not familiar with a wide variety of every kind of author is likely to be misled and to mistake the sense of what he is to translate.

Agreed, then, that the first concern of the translator is to acquire a thorough knowledge of the language out of which he translates, and that this knowledge can only be achieved by a repeated, varied and close reading of all kinds of writers. Next he must have such a grasp of the language into which he translates, that he will have a thorough command of it, have it completely within his power, so when he must render word for word, he will not beg or borrow or leave the word in Greek out of ignorance of Latin; he will know subtly the nature and the force of words, so he will not say "middling" when he means "small," "adolescent" when he means "adolescence," "courage" when he means "strength," "war" when he means "battle," "city" when he means "city-state." He will moreover observe the distinctions between "to be fond of" and "to love," between "to choose out" and "to seek out," between "to desire" and "to wish," "to perorate" and "to persuade," "to accept" and "to grant," "to expostulate with" and "to complain of," and a thousand similar cases. He will be familiar with the idioms and figures of speech used by the best authors, and will imitate them when he translates, and he will avoid verbal and grammatical novelties, especially those that are imprecise and barbarous.

The foregoing qualities are all necessary. In addition, he must possess a sound ear so that his translation does not disturb and destroy the fullness and rhythmical qualities of the original. For since in every good writer—and most especially in Plato and Aristotle—there is both learning and literary style, he and he only will be a satisfactory translator who is able to preserve both.

In short, these are the vices of a translator: to understand badly what is to be translated, or to turn it badly; and to translate in such fashion that the beauty and precision of the original author is rendered clumsy, confused, and ugly. The man whose ignorance of learning and literature is such that he cannot avoid all those vices, is rightly criticized and condemned when he tries to translate. By mistaking one thing for another, he leads men into divers errors, and by making him seem ridiculous and absurd he threatens the majesty of his original author. . . .

For every writer has his proper style: Cicero his sonority and richness, Sallust his dry and succinct expression, Livy his rough grandeur. So the good translator in translating each will conform himself to them in such a way that he follows the style of each one. Hence, if he is translating Cicero, with a variety and richness of expression matching his, the translator must fill up the entire period with large, copious, and full phrasings, now rushing them along, now building them up. If he translates Sallust, he must needs decide in the case of nearly every word to observe propriety and great restraint, and to this end must retrench and cut down. If he translates Livy, he must imitate the latter's forms of expression. The translator should be carried away by the power of the original's style. He cannot possibly preserve the sense to advantage unless he insinuates and twists himself into the original's word order and periodic structure with verbal propriety and stylistic faithfulness. This then is the best way to translate: to preserve the style of the original as well as possible, so that polish and elegance be not lacking in the words, and the words be not lacking in meaning.

¶ It took me a long time and much inner searching before I decided to attempt a literary presentation of the deeds of the Florentine people. I wished to recount their struggles in civil and foreign wars and to tell of their great exploits in war and in peace. What appealed to me was the magnificent performance of this people, first in dealing with domestic foes, then in combatting their immediate neighbors, and finally in our own time as a great power fighting the tremendously powerful duke of Milan and the highly aggressive King Ladislas. They shook all Italy from the Alps to Apulia with the sound of Florentine arms, and even beyond Italy they caused kings and vast armies to cross the Alps from France and Germany. Add to this the conquest of Pisa. Considering the clash of character, the struggle for power, and the ultimate outcome, I think it fair to draw the parallel with Rome's defeat of Carthage. In the ultimate pacification and siege of Pisa, carried on as stubbornly by one side as by the other, deeds were done that deserve to be remembered, deeds no less impressive than those we read about and admire so much in antiquity. These actions seemed to me worthy of record and remembrance, and I thought that acquaintance with this story would serve both public and private ends. For if we think men of advanced age are wiser because they have seen more of life, how much wisdom can history give us if we read it correctly; for there the deeds and thoughts of many ages are visible and we can readily see what to imitate and what to avoid, and be inspired by the glory of great men to attempt like excellence. What held me back, however, was the labor involved in such an enterprise, and the gaps in our knowledge of certain times, and even the harsh sounding names that would hardly allow an elegant presentation, and many other problems. Having weighed all these ideas carefully and long, I came to feel mainly that any plan for writing was better than being idly silent.

In starting to write, therefore, I have been aware of my own limita-

Leonardo Bruni, *History of Florence*. In Renée Neu Watkins, *Humanism and Liberty: Writings on Freedom from Fifteenth-Century Florence*. Trans. Renée Neu Watkins. Columbia, S.C.: University of South Carolina Press, 1978. Pp. 27–29, 30–31, 33, 62–64, and 65–66.

tions and of the weight of my task. But I hope that God will favor my enterprise and will help me to fulfill my good intentions. For if my abilities are not equal to the undertaking, He will support hard work and effort. Would that the men of earlier times, whatever their wisdom and erudition, had recorded the events of their day, instead of silently letting things go by. For, unless I am mistaken, the special duty of scholars has always been to celebrate the deeds of their own time. They should have labored to rescue those deeds from oblivion and from the power of fate; they should have sought to grace those actions with immortality. Yet I suppose that each man had his reasons for remaining silent. Some shrank back from all this heavy labor; some lacked the necessary ability; some neglected history because they preferred other forms of writing. It is not hard, with some effort, to write a little book or a letter. History, however, involves at the same time a long continuous narrative, causal explanation of each particular event, and appropriately placed judgments on certain issues. The great burden of the task may overwhelm the pen—it is a dangerous thing to promise something hard to carry out. Thus, while everyone pursued his personal comfort or considered his reputation, the public good was neglected and the memory of remarkable men and heroic actions was almost wholly lost.

I have decided, therefore, to write the known history of this city, not only for my own time but for earlier ages as far as they can be studied. The story will touch on the history of all Italy, for nothing important has been done in Italy for a long time without the participation of at least some Florentines. In explaining the various embassies sent out by this city, moreover, I shall have to discuss other nations. Before I come to the times that mainly concern me, however, I shall narrate what I think is the correct tradition concerning the city's founding and its origins. The facts will contradict some commonly held beliefs, and will shed light on what is to follow.

The founders of Florence were Romans sent by Lucius Sulla to Fiesole. To veterans who had given outstanding service, particularly in the civil war against Pompey, he granted part of the land of Fiesole as well as the town itself. Such a relocation of citizens and assignment of lands was called a *colony* by the Romans, because it meant the estates cultivated [*colere*] and inhabited by the new men were given to them as homes. Why new people were sent to this area, however, must be explained.

Not many years before Sulla's dictatorship, there was a general rebellion among the peoples of Italy against the domination of the Romans. They had been allied with the Romans on many campaigns, had fought and labored by their side and shared the perils which attended their expansion, and yet, as they resentfully discovered, they had not shared in the rewards. Hence their indignation. After much conferring among themselves, they finally sent common representatives of the whole group to Rome to discuss the problem, demanding Roman citizenship and a share in the honors and offices of the empire for all Italians. The question came up during the tribunate of Marcus Crusus, and for some time the petitioners were left in suspense. Their demands were ultimately rejected, however, and then the peoples involved openly defected and declared war on their ungrateful allies. Because the war was made by former allies [*socii*] of Rome, it is known as the *Social* War. The Romans emerged victorious and severely punished the main rebellious provinces. They dealt most harshly with Picenum [the Marches] and Tuscany. The flourishing city of Asculum in Picenum was razed like an enemy town, and in Tuscany, Chiusi was likewise leveled. The people of Arezzo and Fiesole also suffered heavy blows above and beyond the war damage itself; many people's property was confiscated and many were forced to flee, so that these towns were left half-empty.

Such was the occasion, almost in fact the invitation, for Sulla's action as a dictator in granting his veterans these lands. When the veterans came to Fiesole, however, and divided the fields among themselves, many of them decided that amidst the security of the Roman empire, it was unnecessary to inhabit an inaccessible hilltop. So they came down into the valley and began to live along the banks of the Arno and Mugno. The new city located between these two rivers was at first called Fluentia. The name lasted for some time, it seems, until the city had grown and developed. Then, perhaps just through the ordinary process by which words are corrupted, or perhaps because of the flowering of the city, Fluentia became Florence.

Both Cicero and Sallust, who are great Latin writers, report the story of these colonizers. Cicero tells us, moreover, that the veterans, though excellent Roman citizens and strong men, showed no idea of moderation in spending when they found themselves suddenly and unexpectedly enriched by Sulla through civil war. They built grandly and created great households, great gatherings of people, and luxurious amenities, and soon they were buried in debt. To free them from this burden, Sulla himself would have had to return from the dead. What the father of Latin eloquence says of their buildings seems important to me, for it leads to the conclusion that the foundations of this city, from its very infancy, were magnificent. And even amidst the present splendor of Florence there still exist examples of ancient building that command our admiration. There is the aqueduct that brought water to the city from sources seven leagues away, and the great theaters placed outside the walls for popular sports and spectacles. These theaters are now located within the city limits and built over with residences. Even the temple we call the Baptistery was begun by classical builders and was consecrated by their pagan priests to Mars.

Out of nostalgia or loyalty to their old home, the colonizers seem to have consciously imitated Rome in their planning of the city and construction of buildings. . . .

Only the nearness of Rome in her grandeur limited the growth of Florence. As great trees overshadow small plants that arise in their vicinity and keep them stunted, so the weight of Rome pressed on her surroundings and let no greater city arise in Italy. Other cities that had in fact been great were pressed down by the nearby power of Rome, ceased to grow, and even became smaller. How then might the city of Florence grow? She could not augment her borders by war under the rule of the empire, nor indeed wage war at all; nor could she increase the power of her administrators, since their jurisdiction was narrowly circumscribed by jealous Roman officials. As to commerce, in case it should seem that commerce could have added to the growth of the city, in those days it could not center anywhere but at Rome. That was the place where men gathered and where there were markets. Rome had ports, islands, rights of passage everywhere, privileges, official protection. Nowhere else was there so much privilege and power. If a man of solid worth was occasionally born elsewhere within the general region, he would see the difficulties that stood in his way at home and move invariably to Rome. Thus Rome drew to herself everything wonderful that was engendered in Italy and drained all other cities. . . .

After [the Carolingian rule] the empire was far away in Germany, and few of the emperors lived in Italy permanently, though many visited as they were supposed to do and brought armies. Little by little, the Italian cities began to want liberty and to acknowledge the empire's authority nominally rather than in practice. The city of Rome and the name Rome received respect for their ancient power rather than for their present awesomeness. . . . Meanwhile those Italian cities that had survived the various floods of barbarians began to grow and flourish and to regain their original independence. . . . Florence, some say, was razed by Attila the Hun, others say by Totila, and they report that it was (after a long period) restored by Charlemagne. It seems clear to us, however, that Attila the Hun was never in Tuscany at all, and that he never crossed to this side of the river Minicius, which flows from Lake Garda to Padua. Totila, king of the Goths, did, as we have shown, fall fiercely on the Tuscan cities after Belisarius had briefly liberated them from the Goths. I am convinced, therefore, that a confusion of names has led some authors to take Totila for Attila. I think it likely that desire for vengeance burned in the heart of Totila and made him want to destroy this city to prevent any new defection, for it was here that somewhat earlier the thousands of Goths under Radagasus had been killed. Because of this painful memory angering him, he would have wished to destroy Florence, a city that stood like a monument to the defeat of his people in Etruria. If so, Florence lay in ruins for two hundred years, from Totila to Charlemagne; but it would be very surprising indeed, if while the city lay empty for so long, there were still plenty of people around it. For we cannot think that Charlemagne brought new inhabitants in from Rome, since that city had been recently involved in trouble and so much afflicted by earlier devastations as well that it needed to gain new inhabitants and could not possibly send them forth. About that time, in fact, it is recorded that, for lack of Romans to inhabit Ostia, colonists were brought there from Sardinia. I think, therefore, that Totila had indeed done great harm to Florence and killed many citizens and torn down the walls, but I don't believe that he destroyed the city altogether nor that it was entirely without inhabitants for all that time. I see still standing the rich and large temple of Mars and other buildings from before the period of Totila, and when I consider these unharmed remains I cannot believe that the whole city was destroyed nor that it was totally uninhabited for so long. More likely, I think the walls were restored by Charlemagne and he recalled the nobility, which, when the fortifications of the city were destroyed, had fortified capacious castles on their estates. I think, therefore, that the city was put back together as a city after being in a sense dismembered. Rather than refounded, in my opinion, it was essentially restored.

I have mentioned the Tuscan cities that perished. The main ones which reemerged after being long swamped by calamity were Pisa, Florence, Perugia, and Siena. The Pisans found they could dominate the sea coast with their fleet because theirs was the only Tuscan maritime center that remained after Tarquinia, Luna, and Populonium disappeared. The Florentines prospered by cultivating their land. The Perugians gained great power because of their fertile land and their strategic location. Siena stood high for the splendor of her urban amenities and her excellent old families, and she attracted the resources freed by the destruction of her near neighbors, Rusellae and Populonium. Arezzo was next door, and almost surpassed all other cities by the quality of her soil and the size of her territory, but she lay between Florence and Perugia and was held down by the power of these two sturdy neighbors. . . .

The many disputes between the popes and the emperors brought plentiful tinder to our local quarrels and fights. For the empire which began with Charlemagne and was founded mainly for the protection of the Roman church, once it was, as we have explained, transferred to Germany, fell into the hands of successors whose purpose in life seemed to be the persecution and overthrow of the popes. Where help had been looked for, there was the bitterest harm. The cause of the fighting was essentially that the church tried to hold on to certain powers of jurisdiction while the empire tried to usurp them on the basis of its ancient prerogatives. Against the emperors, the popes used decretals and powers of censure, which at that time were their only arms, and urged cities and princes to refuse obedience to the empire. Threatening heavy punishments if people obeyed the papal decrees, the emperors made themselves feared by the use of arms. The dispute remained unsettled, and people shifted from one side to the other.

Over this great issue there was so much violent dispute in Italy that finally not only cities but peoples living within the same walls were divided into parties. Two parties appeared in Tuscany: one favored the pope and was opposed to the emperors, the other was devoted to the imperial name. But the side which, as we said, opposed the emperors was essentially composed of those who were concerned about the liberty of peoples: they considered it degrading for Germans and barbarians to rule over Italians under the pretext of the Roman name. The other faction consisted of men devoted to the imperial name and forgetful of the liberty and glory of their ancestors—men who preferred to serve foreigners rather than be ruled by their own people. The struggle of these factions caused a vast amount of harm. For public affairs involved more greed and rivalry than good and honest government, and in private life there was more and more hatred and enmity. Thus the disease took hold of private and public life at the same time—first it was nourished by dispute, then it worsened and became deadly hatred, finally it burst out in arms and slaughter and the devastation of cities.

¶ I believe that from its very founding Florence conceived such a hatred for the destroyers of the Roman state and underminers of the Roman Republic that it has never forgotten to this very day. If any trace of or even the names of those corrupters of Rome have survived to the present, they are hated and scorned in Florence.

Now this interest in republicanism is not new to the Florentine people, nor did it begin (as some people think) only a short time since. Rather, this struggle against tyranny was begun a long time ago when certain evil men undertook the worst crime of all—the destruction of the liberty, honor, and dignity of the Roman people. At that time, fired by a desire for freedom, the Florentines adopted their penchant for fighting and their zeal for the republican side, and this attitude has persisted down to the present day. If at other times these political factions were called by different names, still they were not really different. From the beginning Florence has always been united in one and the same cause against the invaders of the Roman state and it has constantly persevered in this policy to the present time. By Jove, this was caused by a just hatred of tyranny more than by the well-deserved respect due to the ancient fatherland.

¶ But we must not forget that true distinction is to be gained by a wide and varied range of such studies as conduce to the profitable enjoyment of life, in which, however, we must observe due proportion in the attention and time we devote to them.

First amongst such studies I place History: a subject which must not on any account be neglected by one who aspires to true cultivation. For it is our duty to understand the origins of our own history and its development; and the achievements of Peoples and of Kings.

For the careful study of the past enlarges our foresight in contempo-

Leonardo Bruni, *Panegyric to the City of Florence*. In *The Earthly Republic: Italian Humanists on Government and Society*, ed. and trans. Benjamin G. Kohl and Ronald G. Will with Elizabeth B. Welles. Philadelphia: University of Pennsylvania Press, 1978. Pp. 151–152.

Leonardo Bruni, *Concerning the Study of Literature*. In William Harrison Woodward, *Vittorino Feltre and Other Humanist Educators: Essays and Versions*. Cambridge: Cambridge University Press, 1921. Pp. 127–128.

rary affairs and affords to citizens and to monarchs lessons of incitement or warning in the ordering of public policy. From History, also, we draw our store of examples of moral precepts.

In the monuments of ancient literature which have come down to us, History holds a position of great distinction. We specially prize such authors as Livy, Sallust and Curtius; and, perhaps even above these, Julius Caesar; the style of whose Commentaries, so elegant and so limpid, entitles them to our warm admiration. Such writers are fully within the comprehension of a studious lady. For, after all, History is an easy subject: there is nothing in its study subtle or complex. It consists in the narration of the simplest matters of fact which, once grasped, are readily retained in the memory.

The great Orators of antiquity must by all means be included. Nowhere do we find the virtues more warmly extolled, the vices so fiercely decried. From them we may learn, also, how to express consolation, encouragement, dissuasion or advice. If the principles which orators set forth are portrayed for us by philosophers, it is from the former that we learn how to employ the emotions—such as indignation, or pity—in driving home their application in individual cases. Further, from oratory we derive our store of these elegant or striking turns of expression which are used with so much effect in literary compositions. Lastly, in oratory we find that wealth of vocabulary, that clear easy-flowing style, that verve and force, which are invaluable to us both in writing and in conversation.

> 65. LORENZO VALLA (1407–1457) was the enfant terrible of Italian humanism—arch-humanist and arch-historical critic, whose career was devoted to the defense and dissemination of the liberal arts, especially rhetoric, which he regarded (on formal, literary, and moral grounds) as virtually identical with history. As a professional rhetorician, Valla celebrated the cultural tradition still reflected in Roman law and the Latin language, which he studied with lexicographical thoroughness and zeal in his *Elegances of the Latin Language* (1444). Valla also made contributions to modern historiography with his history of Ferdinand of Aragon and, more fundamentally, to historical scholarship in a variety of textual studies, including biblical and legal texts but most notably in his *Dec-*

Lorenzo Valla, *The Elegances of the Latin Language.* In *The Portable Renaissance Reader,* ed. and trans. James Bruce Ross and Mary Martin McLaughlin. New York: Viking, 1953. Pp. 131–135.

lamation on the Donation of Constantine, which applied the methods of Petrarch to this ecclesiastical forgery and cornerstone of papal supremacy and which became the locus modernus of historical criticism.

When I often consider for myself the deeds of our ancestors and the acts of other kings and peoples, ours seem to me to have excelled all others not only in empire but even in the propagation of their language. For the Persians, the Medes, the Assyrians, the Greeks, and many other peoples have seized dominion far and wide—it is certain that they have held empire[s?], even if less in extent than that of the Romans, nevertheless much more enduring in its course—but no people has spread its language so far as ours has done, who in a short space of time has made the Roman tongue, which is also called Latin from Latium where Rome is located, well-known and almost queen—even if I omit mention of that coast of Italy which was formerly called Greater Greece or Sicily which was also Greek or the entirety of Italy—almost throughout the entire West and through not a negligible part of both the North and Africa. Further, as far as the provinces are concerned, the Roman tongue was offered to mortals as a certain most excellent fruit for the sowing. Certainly this was a much more famous and splendid task than increasing the empire itself. For they who increase the extent of the empire are accustomed to be greatly honored and are called emperors; however, they who have conferred any benefices on men are celebrated not by human but rather by divine praise, especially when they further not so much the grandeur and glory of their own city but also the public utility and well-being of all men.

As our ancestors, winning high praises, surpassed other men in military affairs, so by the extension of their language they indeed surpassed themselves, as if, abandoning their dominion on earth, they had attained to the fellowship of the gods in Paradise. If Ceres, Liber, and Minerva, who are considered the discoverers of grain, wine, oil, and many others have been placed among the gods for some benefaction of this kind, is it less beneficial to have spread among the nations the Latin language, the noblest and the truly divine fruit, food not of the body but of the soul? For this language introduced those nations and all peoples to all the arts which are called liberal; it taught the best laws, prepared the way for all wisdom; and finally, made it possible for them no longer to be called barbarians.

Why would anyone who is a fair judge of things not prefer those who

were distinguished for their cultivation of the sacred mysteries of literature to those who were celebrated for waging terrible wars? For you may
most justly call those men royal, indeed divine, who not only founded
the republic and the majesty of the Roman people, insofar as this might
be done by men, but, as if they were gods, established also the welfare of
the whole world. Their achievement was the more amazing because
those who submitted to our rule knew that they had given up their own
government, and, what is more bitter, had been deprived of liberty,
though not perhaps by violence. They recognized, however, that the
Latin language had both strengthened and adorned their own, as the
later discovery of wine did not drive out the use of water, or silk expel
wool and linen, or gold the other metals, but added to these other blessings. And just as the beauty of a jewel set in a golden ring is not diminished but enhanced, so our language, in uniting with the vernacular
speech to others, conferred splendour: it did not destroy it. For not by
arms or bloodshed or wars was its domination achieved, but by benefits,
love, and concord. Of this achievement (so far as I can conjecture) the
sources have been, as I have said, first, that our ancestors perfected themselves to an incredible degree in all kinds of studies, so that no one seems
to have been pre-eminent in military affairs unless he was distinguished
also in letters, which was a not inconsiderable stimulus to the emulation
of others; then, that they wisely offered honourable rewards to the teachers of literature; finally, that they encouraged all provincials to become
accustomed to speak, both in Rome and at home, in the Roman fashion.

But since this is sufficient, I shall say no more about the comparison
between the Roman Empire and its language. The Roman dominion,
the peoples and nations long ago threw off as an unwelcome burden; the
language of Rome they have thought sweeter than any nectar, more
splendid than any silk, more precious than any gold or gems, and they
have embraced it as if it were a god sent from Paradise. Great, therefore,
is the sacramental power of the Latin language, truly great in its divinity, which has been preserved these many centuries with religious and
holy awe, by strangers, by barbarians, by enemies, so that we Romans
should not grieve but rejoice, and the whole listening earth should
glory. We have lost Rome, we have lost authority, we have lost dominion, not by our own fault but by that of the times, yet we reign still, by
this more splendid sovereignty, in a great part of the world. Ours is Italy,
ours Gaul, ours Spain, Germany, Pannonia, Dalmatia, Illyricum, and
many other lands. For wherever the Roman tongue holds sway, there is
the Roman Empire.

But now the Greeks are going around, boasting about the abundance of their languages. Impoverished as they say it is, our one language is more effective than five of their dialects, which, according to them, are so much richer than ours. The Latin language is a single tongue, like one law, for many peoples; in one Greece there is not a single language (which is a scandalous thing), but many dialects, like factions in a state. Moreover, foreigners agree with us in speaking as we do; the Greeks cannot agree among themselves, much less hope to induce others to speak their language. Among the Greeks, various authors write in Attic, Aeolic, Ionic, Doric, Koine; with us, that is among many nations, no one writes except in Latin, in the language that embraces all disciplines worthy of a free man, just as among the Greeks they are diffused in many dialects. Who does not know that when the Latin language flourishes, all studies and disciplines thrive, as they are ruined when it perishes? For who have been the most profound philosophers, the best orators, the most distinguished jurisconsults, and finally the greatest writers, but those indeed who have been most zealous in speaking well?

But when I wish to say more, sorrow hinders and torments me, and forces me to weep as I contemplate the state which eloquence had once attained and the condition into which it has now fallen. For what lover of letters and the public good can restrain his tears when he sees eloquence now in that state in which it was long ago when Rome was captured by the Gauls; everything was overturned, burned, destroyed, so that the Capitoline citadel hardly survived. Indeed, for many centuries not only has no one spoken in the Latin manner, but no one who has read Latin has understood it. Students of philosophy have not possessed, nor do they possess, the works of the ancient philosophers; nor do rhetoricians have the orators; nor lawyers the jurisconsults; nor teachers the known works of the ancients, as if after the Roman Empire had fallen, it would not be fitting to speak of [or?] in the Roman fashion, and the glory of Latinity was allowed to decay in rust and mould. I neither accept nor reject any of these, daring only to declare soberly that those arts which are most closely related to the liberal arts, the arts of painting, sculpture, modeling, and architecture, had degenerated for so long and so greatly and had almost died with letters themselves, and that in this age they have been aroused and come to life again, so greatly increased is the number of good artists and men of letters who now flourish.

But truly, as wretched as were those former times in which no learned man was found, so much the more this our age should be congratulated, in which (if we exert ourselves a little more) I am confident that the language of Rome will shortly grow stronger than the city itself, and with it all disciplines will be restored. Therefore, because of my devotion to my native Rome and because of the importance of the matter, I shall arouse and call forth all men who are lovers of eloquence, as if from a watch tower, and give them, as they say, the signal for battle.

¶ I know that for a long time now men's ears are waiting to hear the offense with which I charge the Roman pontiffs. It is, indeed, an enormous one, due either to supine ignorance, or to gross avarice which is the slave of idols, or to pride of empire of which cruelty is ever the companion. For during some centuries now, either they have not known that the Donation of Constantine is spurious and forged, or else they themselves forged it, and their successors walking in the same way of deceit as their elders have defended as true what they knew to be false, dishonoring the majesty of the pontificate, dishonoring the memory of ancient pontiffs, dishonoring the Christian religion, confounding everything with murders, disasters and crimes. They say the city of Rome is theirs, theirs the kingdom of Sicily and Naples, the whole of Italy, the Gauls, the Spains, the Germans, the Britons, indeed the whole West; for all these are contained in the instrument of the Donation itself. So all these are yours, supreme pontiff? And it is your purpose to recover them all? To despoil all kings and princes of the West of their cities or compel them to pay you a yearly tribute, is that your plan?

I, on the contrary, think it fairer to let the princes despoil you of all the empire you hold. For, as I shall show, that Donation whence the supreme pontiffs will have their right derived was unknown equally to Sylvester and to Constantine. . . .

O you scoundrel! were there in Rome churches, that is, temples, dedicated to Peter and Paul? Who had constructed them? Who would have dared to build them, when, as history tells us, the Christians had never had anything but secret and secluded meeting-places? And if there had been any temples at Rome dedicated to these apostles, they would not have called for such great lights as these to be set up in them; they were little chapels, not sanctuaries; little shrines, not temples; oratories

Lorenzo Valla, *Declamation on the Donation of Constantine.* In *The Treatise of Lorenzo Valla on the Donation of Constantine,* trans. Christopher B. Coleman. New Haven, Conn.: Yale University Press, 1922. Pp. 25–27, 97, 115, and 131–133. Reprinted by permission of Yale University Press.

in private houses, not public places of worship. So there was no need to care for the temple lights, before the temples themselves were provided. . . .

Which shall I censure the more, the stupidity of the ideas, or of the words? You have heard about the ideas; here are illustrations of his words. He says, "It seems proper for our Senate to be adorned" (as though it were not assuredly adorned), and to be adorned forsooth with "glory." And what is being done he wishes understood as already done; as, "we have proclaimed" for "we proclaim": for the speech sounds better that way. And he puts the same act in the present and in the past tense; as, "we decree," and "we have decreed." And everything is stuffed with these words, "we decree," "we decorate," "imperial," "imperial rank," "power," "glory." . . .

"If any one, moreover—which we do not believe—prove a scorner in this matter, he shall be condemned and shall be subject to eternal damnation; and shall feel the holy apostles of God, Peter and Paul, opposed to him in the present and in the future life. And he shall be burned in the lower hell and shall perish with the devil and all the impious."

This terrible threat is the usual one, not of a secular ruler, but of the early priests and flamens, and nowadays, of ecclesiastics. And so this is not the utterance of Constantine, but of some fool of a priest who, stuffed and pudgy, knew neither what to say nor how to say it, and, gorged with eating and heated with wine, belched out these wordy sentences which convey nothing to another, but turn against the author himself. First he says, "shall be subject to eternal damnation," then as though more could be added, he wishes to add something else, and to eternal penalties he joins penalties in the present life; and after he frightens us with God's condemnation, he frightens us with the hatred of Peter, as though it were something still greater. Why he should add Paul, and why Paul alone, I do not know. And with his usual drowsiness he returns again to eternal penalties, as though he had not said that before. Now if these threats and curses were Constantine's, I in turn would curse him as a tyrant and destroyer of my country, and would threaten that I, as a Roman, would take vengeance on him. But who would be afraid of the curse of an overly avaricious man, and one saying a counterfeit speech after the manner of actors, and terrifying people in the role of Constantine? This is being a hypocrite in the true sense, if we press the Greek word closely; that is, hiding your own personality under another's.

66. VESPASIANO da Bisticci (1421–1498) was a Florentine manuscript collector and book dealer who adapted to modern times the genre developed by Petrarch (and in effect also adapted the historiographical efforts of Bruni to culture and the arts) by compiling his *Vite di uomini illustri del secolo xv* (unpublished until the nineteenth century), which memorialized and celebrated the great men of the Renaissance.

I have often considered how great is the value of the light which learned writers, in times both ancient and modern, have thrown upon the actions of illustrious men; how that the fame of many worthies has come to naught because there was no one to preserve in writing the memory of their deeds, and that, if Livy and Sallust and other writers of excellence had not lived in the time of Scipio Africanus, the renown of that great man would have perished with his life. Neither would there have been any record of Metellus, or of Lycurgus, or of Cato, or of Epaminondas the Theban, or of the infinite number of men of mark who lived in Greece and Rome. But because many illustrious writers flourished amongst these people, the lives and actions of their great men have been displayed and published abroad, so that they are as real to us as if they had lived to-day, whereas they happened a thousand years and more ago. For this reason great men may well lament that, in their lifetime, there should be living no writers to record their deeds.

As to the origin of Florence, it is the opinion of Messer Lionardo and of many other learned men that the Florentines are sprung from the horse-soldiers of Sylla, but this view is difficult to justify. Pliny holds that the city must be of great antiquity, and that the Florentines were called Fluentini because their city was placed between the streams of Arno and Mugone. This is a valid testimony of its antiquity. Moreover, he cites, by way of further proof, the shape of the theatre which still exists, the Temple of Mars, now S. Giovanni, a very ancient building, and certain aqueducts which are still partially standing; but all these instances depend only on conjecture, seeing that no learned scribes have ever put the matter on record. For this reason Messer Lionardo, in writing his history of Florence, was put to much trouble through lack of documents, except for a period of some hundred and fifty years, and elsewhere he had to base his facts upon such authorities as I have named above.

Vespasiano, *Renaissance Princes, Popes, and Prelates*. Trans. William George and Emily Waters. New York: Harper Torchbooks, 1963. Pp. 13–15.

We find in Florence no writers from the foundation to the time of Dante, that is for more than a thousand years. Following Dante came Petrarch and then Boccaccio, but these tell nothing of the origin of the city because they found no records. After Dante came two other poets, Messer Coluccio and Maestro Luigi Marsigli, who was also a theologian and very learned also in astrology, geometry and arithmetic. Of the lives of these we have no detailed record, but they are mentioned occasionally by all writers. The present age has produced many distinguished men in all the faculties, as will appear to posterity if a record be kept of them, as was the practice in old times when learned writers were plentiful. In this age all the seven liberal arts have been fruitful in men of distinction, not only in Latin, but also in Hebrew and Greek; men most learned and eloquent and equal to the best of any age. In painting, sculpture and architecture we find art on its highest level, as we may see from the works which have been wrought amongst us. An immense number of these great men we cannot call by name; their fame has perished simply because no one has written of them. And this loss did not arise through lack of writers; eloquent and learned men abounded, but they were loth to undertake the burden of literature, knowing that in the end they would enjoy neither the repute nor the appreciation they deserved.

We may see how numerous men of learning were in the times of Pope Nicolas of happy memory, and of King Alfonso, because they were well rewarded and held in the highest esteem, and how many excellent works they composed or copied through the munificence of princes so liberal as the two I have named, whose fame will last for ever. Moreover, beyond the money they gave, they paid honour to men of letters and advanced them to high station. In addition to these two princes must be named a worthy successor, the Duke of Urbino, who, having followed their example in honouring and rewarding and promoting men of letters, became their protector in every respect, so that all were wont to fly to him in case of need. Thus, to help them in their labours, he paid them well for their work, so that he gained immortal fame by their writings. But when there was no longer a Duke of Urbino, and when neither the court of Rome nor any of the other courts showed any favour for letters, they perished, and men withdrew to some other calling, seeing that, as I have said, letters no longer led to profit or reward.

As it has chanced that I myself am of this same age, and that from time to time I have met many illustrious men, whom I have come to know well, I have set down a record of these in the form of a short commentary to preserve their memory, though such work is foreign to my calling. I have been moved thereto by two reasons. *First,* that their fame may not perish: *Second,* that if anyone should take the trouble to write their lives in Latin he should find before him a material from which such work could be modelled. And in order that these men of light and leading may be under a worthy chief, whom they may well follow, and because in all cases the spiritual ought to hold the first place, I will assign to Pope Nicolas the leadership of all the rest, and I will tell what I have to say concerning His Holiness with all the brevity possible, considering the praise which is his due. Had this task of mine been undertaken in ancient times, the Pope must have been portrayed as an illustrious man by anyone who might have done it. It will appear from the life of this excellent Pope how great is the power of virtue, because everyone must see that he could only have attained to his high position by virtuous dealing.

❡ THE IDEA OF HISTORY

> 67. PIER PAOLO VERGERIO (1349–1444) was a teacher of the humanities at Florence and Padua and, sometime after 1404, composed his pedagogical treatise *De Ingenuis moribus*. In characteristically humanist fashion, Vergerio, in the section recommending the studia humanitatis, gives first place to the study of history because of its elegance and utility.

I attach great weight to the duty of handing down this priceless treasure to our sons unimpaired by any carelessness on our part. How many are the gaps which the ignorance of past ages has willfully caused in the long and noble roll of writers! Books—in part or in their entirety—have been allowed to perish. What remains of others is often sorely corrupt, mutilated, or imperfect. It is hard that no slight portion of the history of Rome is only to be known through the labours of one writing in the Greek language: it is still worse that this same noble tongue, once well nigh the daily speech of our race, as familiar as the Latin language itself, is on the point of perishing even amongst its own sons and to us Italians is already utterly lost, unless we except one or two who in our time are

Pier Paolo Vergerio, *Concerning Liberal Studies.* In William Harrison Woodward, *Vittorino Feltre and Other Humanist Educators: Essays and Versions.* Cambridge: Cambridge University Press, 1921. Pp. 106–107.

tardily endeavoring to rescue something—if it be only a mere echo of it—from oblivion.

We come now to the consideration of the various subjects which may rightly be included under the name of "Liberal Studies." Amongst these I accord the first place to History on grounds both of its attractiveness and of its utility, qualities which appeal equally to the scholar and to the statesman. Next in importance ranks Moral Philosophy, which indeed is, in a peculiar sense, a "Liberal Art," in that its purpose is to teach men the secret of true freedom. History, then, gives us the concrete examples of the precepts inculcated by philosophy. The one shews what men should do, the other what men have said and done in the past, and what practical lessons we may draw therefrom for the present day. I would indicated as the third main branch of study, Eloquence, which indeed holds a place of distinction amongst the refined Arts. By philosophy we learn the essential truth of things, which by eloquence we so exhibit in orderly adornment as to bring conviction to differing minds. And history provides the light of experience—a cumulative wisdom fit to supplement the force of reason and the persuasion of eloquence. For we allow that soundness of judgment, wisdom of speech, integrity of conduct are the marks of a truly liberal temper.

> 68. POLYDORE VERGIL (ca. 1470–1555), best known as the first humanist historiographer of England, brought to his task the critical attitudes and style associated with Bruni. In 1496, Vergil published a popular Renaissance encyclopedia organized genetically according to the "first inventors of things" (*De rerum inventoribus*), in which history itself was cast in a historical, or mythical, mode.

Histories, of all other Writings, be most commendable, because it informeth all sorts of people, with notable examples of living, and doth excite Noble-men to insue such activity in enterprises, as they read to have been done by their Ancestors; and also discourageth and dehorteth wicked persons from attempting of any heinous deeds or crime, knowing, that such acts shall be registered in perpetual memory, to the praise or reproach of the doers, according to the desert of their endeavours. Pliny writeth, That Cadmus Milesius first wrote Histories among the

Polydore Vergil, *De rerum inventoribus.* In *Polydori Virgilii de Rerum Inventoribus,* trans. John Langley. New York: Burt Franklin, 1971. Pp. 29–32.

Grecians, which contained the actions of Cyrus King of Persia. Albeit, Josephus supposeth it to be made probably, that Histories were begun by the old Writers of the Hebrews; as in the time of Moses, which wrote the lives of many of the eldest Hebrews, and the creation of the World: or else to the Priests of Egypt and Babylon. For the Egyptians and Babylonians, have been of longest continuance very diligent; in setting forth things in writing; insomuch that their Priests were appointed for that purpose, of putting in writing such things as were worthy to be had in memory. As concerning the first writers of Prose, I cannot hold with Pliny, which saith, Pheresides, a Syrian, wrote first Prose, in the time of King Cyrus. For it is no doubt, but he that wrote Histories, wrote also Prose first; and Pheresides was long after Moses, which was 688 years before Joatham King of the Jews. In whose time the Olympiads began; and this Pheresides (as Eusebius writeth) was but in the first Olympiad. Of the Grecians, Xenophon, Thucydides, Herodotus, Theopompus, flourished most in writing Histories. Of the Romans; Titus Livius, and Gaius Sallustius Crispus, with divers other, were had in high estimation. Before that time they used Annals or Chronicles, which contained onely the actions and facts of every day severally. The first office of an Historiographer, is to write no lye. The second, that he shall conceal not truth for favour, displeasure or fear. The perfection of an History, restest in matter and words. The order of the matter requireth observance of times, descriptions of places, the manners and lives of men, their behaviours, purposes, occasions, deeds, sayings, casualties, atchieveings, and finishing of things. The tenour of the works asketh a brief perspicuity and sincere truth, with moderate and peaceable ornaments.

We may be sure, that by and by after men were formed, they received of God the use of speech, wherein when they perceived some words to be profitable, and some hurtfull in uttering of them; they appointed and compiled an art of speech, or communication, called Rhetorick. Which (as Diodorus saith) was invented by Mercury: but Aristotle affirmeth, that Empedocles was first author of the Oratorical Art. In Rome, this feat of eloquence was never forbidden, but in processe (as it was perceived to be profitable and honest) was had in such estimation; and so many, partly for their defence, partly for glory and ambition, employed their studies in it with such endeavour, that very many of the Commonalty were promoted into the degree of Senatours, and atchieved much worship by it; Corax and Thisias, being Sicilians, gave first precepts in writing of this Science. And their Countryman Leontinus

Gorgias succeeded them. Demosthenes was principel among the Grecians: among the Romans, Tullius Cicero had no fellow. Now as touching the effect and property of it, there be in it (as Cicero Writeth) five parts; first, to invent matter to speak; then, formally to order his devices; next, to polish it, and furnish it with elegant terms, and choyse words and to have it with a comely gesture, in such sort, that it delight: for the convenient treatableness thereof, doth teach, and plainly declare the thing, and move affections of pitty and favour, in the hearts of Judges; or if the cause permit, or time require, to excite a chearfull laughing, and abundant grave leverity. In terms of this faculty, we have this difference; we call him that defendeth matters, and pleadeth causes, an Oratour. A Rhetoritian, is he that teacheth or professeth to be a Schoolmaster in that Art. A Declamator, is he that is occupied in feigned causes, either for his own exercise, or to instruct others thereby.

> 69. JUAN LUIS VIVES (1492–1540), greatest of Spanish humanists and, like Erasmus, a cosmopolitan scholar, taught in Paris, Louvain, and England. He published an extraordinary range of scholarly, historical, philosophical, psychological, and educational works. In his encyclopedia, *De tradendis disciplinis* (1531), Vives offered in unusual detail a critical praise of history, sacred and profane, which was given an elevated place in the humanist scheme of learning.

The oldest writers of History were honoured differently by different nations. The Egyptians press on our notice their priests; the Greeks, Cadmus the son of Agenor. But it is much more certain that Abraham of Ur left behind him a history, written earlier than all those writers, and from his account Moses obtained the description of the creation of Heaven and Earth. This history was received by Abraham from the sons of Seth, who, as Josephus observes, recorded with letters on two pillars of brick and stone the beginning of the world as well as the first elements of the chief arts. Hence it appears that History took its rise at once with that of men, because it was thus expedient for the human race. It is well to learn the course of history from the beginning of the world or of a people continuously right through their course to the latest time for,

Juan Luis Vives, *On Education*. In *Vives: On Education,* trans. Foster Watson. Cambridge: Cambridge University Press, 1913. Pp. 236–240, 241–243, 244–246, and 247–249.

then, all is more rightly understood and more firmly retained than if we read it in disconnected parts, in the same way that in a description of the whole world, land and sea are placed before the eyes at a glance. For thus it is easier to see the face of the world and the arrangement of its parts one by one, and to understand how each is placed. Polybius of Megalopolis likens the history of the whole human race to a complete living being, but separate histories of races he considers are like that living being, torn to pieces, limb by limb, so that looking at its mutilated parts, no one can distinguish its form, beauty, and strength. Therefore we will so join together the limbs of history as to regard them as a connected whole, if not as a single animal, at any rate as a single building, adapted in all its parts to the whole design. Thus we should do as far as the diversity in writers will permit us, by employing the method of chronology, than which nothing is more apt and suitable in the study of history.

At first, an author should be read who weaves together history from the earliest times up to within our own memory, or approximately so, in a connected whole, so that a full historical outline is provided in the form of a summary. Such a writer is Nauclerus, or more copious, pure and laborious than he, and moreover more learned is Antonius Sabellicus. Paulus Orosius describes the course of history from the foundation of Rome to his own times, giving a suitable summary of historical events. Then the parts of history treated by whole works of authors must be summarised and be put together so as to make a connected whole, which will be a more convenient course than taking them as detached pieces. Moses treats of the Creation of the World in the book which, on this account, is entitled Genesis. On the same subject a book is published under the name of Berosus the Babylonian, but is a fabrication, wonderfully pleasing to unlearned and lazy men. In the same class of books are the *Aequivoca* of Xenophon and the fragments of Archilochus, Cato, Sempronius, and Fabius Pictor, which are gathered together in the same book by Annius of Viterbo. This material he rendered more ridiculous by his own inventions not but what there is some truth in them, for otherwise the narrative would not have such a face to it, but the body itself of the history is built up on lies, nor is it the work of the man whose name it falsely bears on the title. The Egyptian Manethon and the Persian Metasthenes are taken out of Eusebius. Next to be studied are Exodus, Numbers, Joshua, and the Judges of Israel. Philo the Alexandrine traced, in outline, history from Adam to the death of Saul. Diodorus Siculus wrote on the period between the Flood which occurred under Ogyges, a King of Boetia, to his own times, i.e. up to C. Caesar the Dictator, of whom Pliny says (I do not know on what ground) that he was the first amongst the Greeks to degenerate into trickery in historical writing, though, as a matter of fact, there is no greater inventor of tales than himself, only he has given to his work no seductive or high-sounding title but merely calls it *bibliothéke*.

Greek History up to the beginning of the Olympiads is very fabulous, nor can anyone distinguish between what is true and false. But even the history of the following ages is not free from falsities, although it contains a slightly larger amount of facts. For its study Homer supplies some help in both of his poems, although almost all of him is wrapt round with the fabulous. Dares Phyrigius and Dictys Cretensis are the inventions of those who wished to romance about that most renowned war. Dion Prusiensis prattles of the fable that Troy was, after all, not taken. Philostratus in his history corrects the great lies of Homer, by lies still more pronounced. Quintus Calaber added a completion to the Iliad of Homer. Then the student should proceed to the books of the Kings and the Paralipomena [i.e. the Chronicles], Esther, Tobias, Judith, the Apocrypha. Esdras is divided into four books, the first two of which are recognised as canonical by the Jews, but the latter two are apocryphal.

The beginnings of the history of the Romans are obscure and have reached their posterity in attenuated accounts because, as Livy says, before the city of Rome was conquered by the Gauls, there was but little experience in writing. There is a work of Josephus directed against Apion, in which he speaks of antiquity in a way that aroused the admiration of St. Jerome, who was astounded that a Jew should show such knowledge of Greek culture. Herodotus is called the Father of History, because he was the first to unite elegance and grace of style with power of narration of events. He includes very many fabulous matters, but he is excused by the title of his work. For he calls it *The Muses,* by which he indicated that some of the topics were treated somewhat freely. For this freedom is permissible to the Muses, so that the attention of readers may be enchained the more pleasantly. The severity of dry facts, which must occasionally happen in historical accounts would not secure this result. With more conscientiousness, Thucydides of Athens gives his record of the Peloponnesian War. Then follow: History of Xenophon, the Paralipomena, the Laws of Lycurgus, the *Anabasis* of the younger Cyrus. For the *paidera* of the elder Cyrus is an account of the education of that prince, not his history. . . .

The affairs of the Roman people, as Julius Florus well said, do not merely include the history of a race, but also of the whole world, and of all humanity. It will greatly lead to its due comprehension, to learn about the functions of the magistrates and priests of that city. On these points there is a little book called the *Annals* of Fenestella (this may be the name of the author or it may be the work of some unnamed author). There is also another book, that of Pomponius Laetus, taken from Fenestella. Then as to the divisions of the city, Faustus Victor has written, at brief length, but he only gives a list of bare names. Livy began the history of the deeds of the Romans from the beginning of the city. He wove together these threads up to his own times, i.e. up to the reign of Augustus, but by far the greatest part has perished. For a long time past there have been only three decades extant, out of fourteen. Lately two books have been added. And, as we are writing, five further books out of the fifth decade have been just discovered in an old library. Livy is a very painstaking author, of the highest service, as an eloquent historian, and one writing thoughtfully on affairs of state. There are some people who are not inclined to divide his work into decades, but the Prefaces to every tenth book are conclusive evidence that this division was made by the author himself. There is an *Epitome* of Livy, drawn up by Julius Florus. Florus has also composed a small work himself on Roman History. It would be impossible to imagine anything of that kind of writing more clear-sighted or more charming. Dionysius Halicarnasseus has handed down in Greek what was narrated to him by M. Varro, his master, with regard to the beginnings of the Romans and the earliest times of the city. We have to note, in the case of Polybius, as well as in that of Livy, a loss of a great portion of his writings; out of forty books of his histories merely five books remain to us. . . .

The Holy Gospel was expounded by four writers. It is the Book of Life, and the adorable history of the human race restored. The great happiness of the collection of these books belonged to the age of Augustus and Tiberius. St. Luke, who wrote the Gospel, also consigned to memory the Acts of the Apostles. Suetonius Tranquillus, the most painstaking and most uncorrupted of the Greek and Latin writers, seems to me to have written most justly on the history of the twelve Emperors. For he is silent neither as to the vices of the best princes, nor even as to the suspicion of a vice; whilst in the case of the worst Emperors, he does not omit to show any tincture of virtue. With like trustworthiness and painstaking Laertius Diogenes has composed the *Lives of the Philosophers*.

There is extant also a small work of Suetonius on the Grammarians. Cornelius Tacitus is weighty in judgments and thus directs the reader to practical wisdom. He is the more valuable because he is concerned with domestic politics rather than with warfare. There is also the book of Tacitus on the customs of the Germans. We have also the *Antiquities* of Flavius Josephus and the *War against the Jews* which the Vespasians had waged. . . .

If anyone has not yet read Paulus Orosius, then at this point he should be consulted. So, too, with Eutropius who composed an *Epitome* of Roman history from Janus up to the time of the Emperor Jovianus. Likewise let the student of history read Sextus Aurelius, who wrote a history of the Emperors from Augustus to Theodosius. Flavius Blondus (Biondo) has depicted in ten books, *Rome in its Triumphs (Roma Triumphans)*, and, in another work, *The Restoration of Italy (Italia Instaurata)*. Peter Crinitus has produced a work in five books on the Roman poets from Livius Andronicus the freed slave of Salinator, up to the time of Sidonius Apollinaris. Paul Warnefried, the Longobard also surnamed Diaconus has written on the Emperors from Valentinian to Leo. Procopius and Agathias have transmitted to posterity the deeds of Justinian. From these authors Leonardo Bruni, of Arezzo, has put together his *War against the Goths*. From these wars, up to his time, i.e. up to the Pope Pius II, Flavius Blondus has written three decades of Roman history which he has entitled: "From the Fall of the Roman Empire to the year 1440."

Church History from the time of Our Lord Jesus Christ up to the reign of Constantine has been unfolded by Eusebius in nine books, which we called the *Ecclesiastical History*. The tenth and eleventh volumes, which carry the history to the reign of Arcadius and Honorius, were added by Rufinus, the commentator on the original work. We have also read another Church History written by three writers. The book is therefore called the Threefold Work (*Tripartita*). It was brought into an abridgement by Cassiodorus, and extends from the time of the consuls and Emperors Crispus and Constantine up to the 17th year of the Emperor Theodosius Augustus. Saint Jerome has surveyed the ecclesiastical writers from Peter up to his own time, under the Emperor Theodosius. . . .

When the Roman Empire was cut up and dismembered, each separate people, relying on its own strength, carried on its own domestic and foreign affairs. Then arose separate histories of different countries.

Eginhardus the secretary of Charles the Great, committed his master's life and acts to posterity. Turpinus and lately Donatus Acciajolus (Acciolaus) (briefly yet pleasantly) have also written on Charles the Great. Gaguinus traced the history of France up to his own time, i.e. up to Louis XI, and it is said wrote it with a good deal of feeling. With more trustworthiness, Paulus Aemilius wrote an old French History, i.e. from the first Kings of the Franks, after the downfall of the Roman power, up to the time of the brothers Philip and Charles, sons of Louis. Jordan, at the suggestion of Castalius, added to posterity the history of the Goths. Roderick, Bishop of Toledo, wrote on Spanish history; Albert Cranzius (i.e., Kranzius) on Saxon history; Sabellicus on Venetian history; Maria Siculus on the history of Aragon; Hector Boethius on Scottish history; Pope Pius on Bohemian history. Beatus Rhenanus dealt with the origins, position and manners of Germany, and the customs of its inhabitants. Saxo Grammaticus wrote in a manner bordering on the fabulous with regard to the Danes, so that one might think he wished to arouse the astonishment of other races, though you will also wonder at the words and elegance of his diction, writing as he did, in that age and in such a country. Yet more fabulous are the stories, which are stated concerning the origins of Britain, tracing them from Brutus the Trojan, who never existed. . . . Peter Martyr of Milan has compiled monumental books in his records of the navigations of the ocean, and the Discovery of the New World, which took place in his time. But since then, yet vaster events have followed. These cannot but seem fabulous to our posterity, though they are absolutely true. . . .

There are many others who may help historical study, even when they are not professed historians, e.g. Cicero, Seneca, Gellius, Macrobius and, still more, Polydore Vergil in his book, *De rerum inventoribus,* and St. Augustine in his *Civitas Dei;* also Pliny and the plunderer of Pliny, Solinus. There are the geographers also, Strabo and Pius Secundus. Of the Greeks, Plato and Plutarch (i.e. in their smaller ethical works) should be mentioned. . . . Eusebius of Caesarea would be of the highest service in this respect, were it not that he has come down to posterity so faulty, through the negligence and idleness of copyists. Jerome continues the chronology of Eusebius for a further fifty years. Prosper of Aquitaine takes us another sixty years onward. Then follows the Florentine Matthew Palmerius (Palmieri) up to the year of Our Lord 1449. Then, through another thirty years, chronology is supplied by Matthias Palmerius of Pisa. In addition, some further chronological material is furnished by Sigibert, a monk of Gemblours. The work of Bede, the priest, is like that of Eusebius, but somewhat more clearly written. Herman Contractus followed him, up to the year 1066. If a man has leisure to read more on Imperial and Pontifical history, let him add the work of Archbishop Antonius of Florence. . . .

I have not mentioned those, who have written on some small race or state, such as Flanders, Liège, Utrecht. Nor have I included those writers who used the vernacular language such as the Spanish Vlaera, Froissart, Monstrelet, Philip Cominius (de Comines), of whom there are many not less worthy of being known and read than the majority of Greek and Latin histories.

But mention of the deeds achieved by those great men arouses in my soul a great grief which I frequently feel when I ponder within myself with what diligence and care the deeds of Alexander, Hannibal, Scipio, Pompey, Caesar, and other generals; of Socrates, Plato, and other philosophers, have been closely detailed and fixed on the memory for ever, so that there is no danger of their escaping recall, but the deeds of the Apostles, Martyrs, and lastly the Saints of our religion, both in the early Church, and in the later ages of the Church, are almost unknown, and involved in the greatest darkness. Yet they would be so much more fruitful both for knowledge, and for imitation, than the deeds of generals and the sayings of philosophers. For what has been written on the lives of the Saints, with few exceptions, has been polluted with many fabrications. The writer followed his own inclination, and has told us, not what the saint actually did, but what the writer would have wished him to have done, so that the writing of the *Lives of Saints* has been directed by the caprices of the writers, not by the truth of the facts. There have been those who, instead of using great scrupulousness, shaped together small falsehoods, on behalf of religion. This is dangerous, since it may take away confidence in what is true, on account of the falsity found in it; and in religion no sort of necessity can be pleaded for such a procedure. There are so many true things to produce as evidence on behalf of our religion that any falsities, like cowardly and useless soldiers, are more of a burden than a help.

The knowledge of fables must be added to that of history. But they must be of that erudite kind which is adapted to usefulness in living, that they may be applied to a practical purpose. To this class belong poetical fables, and the apologues of Aesop, and books of proverbs and maxims by which general sentiment is assimilated.

Someone may here exclaim: When is all this to be read? The answer is; when men are of ripe age, even when they are advanced in years, at such times as would otherwise be spent in play and trifling. For if anyone were to consider how much time he spends in playing, how much empty, often even, in harmful, conversation, how much in slothful ease, he would find there was plenty of time to pursue his course through all the subjects I have mentioned, and sufficient time to spare for many other things. We have an overflow of time, if we only use it wisely. It is when we dispose of it badly that it becomes so very limited. But if anyone cannot read everything for himself, let him employ a reader, after the custom of the Romans, and give heed to a clear, instructed, and fluent recital of the authors.

> 70. HENRY CORNELIUS AGRIPPA of Nettesheim (1486–1535) has gained the reputation of a modern skeptic mainly through the publication in 1520 of his *Vanity of Arts and Sciences,* an inverted encyclopedia which, largely on religious grounds, assaulted all forms of human learning as useless and immoral. High on Agrippa's list of targets was the study of human history, which he criticized as worse than useless, being full of human pride, pretentiousness, and lies.

History is a declaration of praiseworthy—or unpraiseworthy—things, which, as in a lively picture, sets before our eyes the counsels, deeds and outcomes of great events, the enterprises of princes and noblemen, with a description of times and places. And therefore, most all men call it the mistress of life, and profit by its framing. Through its many examples history both inspires excellent men, for the immortal glory of praise and renown for all worthy enterprises, and, out of fear of perpetual infamy, history keeps wicked men from misdeeds. However, the opposite has sometimes happened, and many (as Livy wrote in Manlius Capitolinus) would rather have a great, than a good fame. Although many virtuous men are unknown, evil ones will be remembered and written about because of misdeeds, as Justine recorded about Troyus, and about Pausanias the Macedonian who was famous for murdering King Phillip, and as Gelluis, Valerius and Solinus wrote about Hero-

Henry Cornelius Agrippa, *On the Vanitie and Uncertaintie of Artes and Sciences.* Ed. Catherine M. Dunn. Northridge, Calif.: California State University, 1974. Orthography modernized. Pp. 35–36, 37–39, and 40–41.

stratus, who burned the Temple of Diana at Ephesus, the most renowned building of Asia. And although laws providing extreme penalties forbade mentioning this man in word or writing, notwithstanding, he obtained the end for which he had committed such a great offense—the fame it brought him for uncountable years up to the present.

But let us return to history. This art, although it chiefly requires order, agreement and truth of all things, notwithstanding, it offers them least among all arts. Historiographers disagree mightily among themselves and write such variable and different things about one event that it is impossible that a number of them should not be liars. They disagree about the beginning of the world, the universal flood, and the building of Rome—of which beginnings they profess to write of actual events. Yet about the first of these events all men are ignorant, the other all men will not believe, and the third is uncertain among them. Since these things took place in the distant past, we can forgive them their error. But regarding later times they must be accused of lying, and so great occasions have become a multitude of discordances. Since most historians were not present when events took place or familiar with the people involved, they instead rely upon another's word and write inconsistent accounts for which vice Strabo reproved Eratostheus, Metrodorius, Septius, Posidonius, and Patrocles the Geographer. Others, when they have seen only part of an event or place, such as an army passing, or begging under pretense of prayer in making a pilgrimage, or traveling through countries, then rashly presume to write a history, such as Onosicritus and Aristobolus' histories of India. There are others who for pleasure interlace lies with truth, often omitting much of the truth, for which vice Diodorus Seculius reproves Herodotus. . . . There are also some who turn true things into fables, as Gnidius, Cresias, Hecataeus, and many other ancient historians did. There are many who impudently and shamefully profess to be historians so that they will not seem ignorant in any subject, or have paraphrased from others trifles and strange stories and have presumed to write of unknown countries that one cannot go to and have produced nothing but monstrous lies. . . .

Furthermore most of the things that Cornelius Tacitus, Marcellus, Orosius and Blondus write about Germany are far from the truth. Likewise Strabo falsely wrote that the River Ister, that is, the Danube, originates not far from the Adriatic Sea and Herodotus says that it flows from the Hesperus and springs near to the habitat of the Celts—who live the farthest away of all people of Europe—and enters into Scithia. . . .

Likewise, Conrades Celtis supposes that the people called Daci are the same as the Cimbrians, that is, that the Flemings and the Cherusci are those who we call Cerusci, and moreover he says that the Rypher Mountains are in Sarmatia, in present day Poland, and writes that the gum called amber grows out of a tree.

There are, moreover, others among historians guilty of greater lies, who when they were present at events or else had absolute knowledge of them, notwithstanding, because they were overcome with benevolence and affection, were flattered by their own renditions and preferred falsehood to the truth. Among these are some who set out to write history in order to refute or defend other men's causes and only wrote those things that served their purpose, dissembling, passing over, or dismissing the importance of the rest, thereby producing corrupt and imperfect works. Blondus reproves Orosius for this because in order not to stray from the subject upon which he set out to write, he did not mention the great ruin the Goths brought upon Italy when they ransacked Ravenna, Candanum, Aquileia, Ferrara, and in a manner all Italy.

There are, moreover, many, corrupted by fear, rancor, or hatred who write lies; others, because they desire to extol their own doings, diminish other men's prowess and write not what happened, but that which they wish had happened and which pleases them, steadfastly trusting that those whom they flattered will not fail to be defenders of their lies and act as their witnesses. This vice was notable among Greek writers, but recent historians of all nations do it too, for example, Sabellicus and Blondus writing about the Venetians, and Paulus Emilius and Ganguinus, writing on the exploits of the French. Princes accept these histories because, as Plutarch says, the majesty of history glorifies their deeds. In this way, the Greek historiographers, writing about inventors, attributed inventions to themselves that were not theirs.

And yet another most corrupt kind of flatterer tries to enlarge and extend the ancestry of his Prince and relates him to the world's most ancient kings. When they are not able to join them through a family, they resort to fables and strange beginnings and give false names of kings and places . . . there is nothing they would not lie about. . . .

There are also many who write history not so much to tell the truth but to express delight and flatter the image of a noble prince who pleases them. And if someone reproves them for lying they say they have not as

great a regard for things actually done as for posterity, and therefore they
have not written about all events exactly as they happened but how they
ought to have happened. They obstinately will not defend the truth, but
where common utility requires will either fain or provide a lie, citing
Fabius as a precedent, who said that a lie is not to be despised that avails
to the persuasion of honesty. Furthermore, alleging that they write for
posterity, they claim that it makes no great difference in what name or
what order the example of a good Prince should be published abroad—
such an example Xenophon set for Cyrus, not as it was but as it ought to
be, and wrote a resemblance and pattern of a singular good prince and
produced a proper history, but one without truth. . . .

Cicero says that in Herodotus, the father of History, in Diodorus, and
Theopompus are infinite fables stuffed full of lies, for we read in them
that the Medes drunk rivers and that men might sail over the hill Athos.

> And whatsoever lying Greece
> does dare to write in histories.

And such are the causes why in no part any credit may thoroughly be
given to histories. Although we chiefly seek truth in them it is very
difficult to attain the necessary judgment needed to discern the truth,
since historians wrote not of things that happened in public, which
declared the truth of things and stopped liars' mouths. Instead each used
his own opinion. Hereof they have gotten authority to err and lie—
whereupon among historiographers there has risen so great a discord
that, as Josephus says against Appion, they reprove one another with
their books and write very differently about the same thing.

. . . Besides this, many historiographers write many things, some of
which should be censored because it inspires men to follow evil examples. For those who with wonderful praise depict Hercules, Achilles,
Hector, Theseus, Epaminondas, Lizander, Themistocles, Xerxes,
Cyrus, Danus, Alexander, Pirrhus, Hannibal, Scipio, Pompei, Caesar,
what else have they described but great and furious thieves and famous
spoilers of the world? I confess that they were very good captains, but
doubtless very wicked men.

Yet if someone tells me that by reading history singular wisdom may
be gained, I do not deny it as long as he also grants me that out of the
same matter comes great damage. In history, as Martial said, there are
many good things, many indifferent, and many negative.

71. LOUIS LE ROY (1510–1577), disciple and biographer of the founding father of French humanism, Guillaume Budé, was a pioneering translator (into French) of Plato and Aristotle, a professor of Greek at the College of Three Languages (inspired in part by Budé), and author of what one modern scholar has called "the first history of civilization." Le Roy's *Vicissitude or Variety of Things in the Universe* (1575) gave historical form to Budé's encyclopedic program by surveying the rise, and especially the fifteenth- and sixteenth-century renaissance ("heroic age," in Budé's phrase), of the whole encyclopedia of arts and sciences, defending the superiority of the moderns over the ancients, formulating and celebrating an idea of cultural progress on the basis of various novelties, but acknowledging that within national traditions (if not on the level of universal history) the old law of generation and decay still held.

In the beginning men were quite simple and rude, differing little in any respect from wild animals. Through fields and mountains they fed upon raw flesh of beasts, or the plants with their roots, trunks, and leaves which earth produced at its pleasure through the woods, or upon the fruits of wild trees, or on venison. On the banks of seas, rivers, lakes, ponds, and marshes, [they ate] fish and birds. They dressed themselves in skins instead of robes. In order to be protected from heat and cold, and from winds, rains, and snows, they withdrew into the hollows of big trees, or under their leafy branches; into low ditches, hideous caves, or under shelters, cabins, or huts made of heavy poles, and slightly covered with branches, straw, reeds and thatch. Since they were, then, more robust, they fed themselves with stronger foods, and also they lived longer. They were almost always out of doors in constant labor, and lying down on the hard earth where sleep took them. But, becoming more feeble, and not being able to digest such viands, nor to remain uncovered, nude and bare, they were forced little by little to seek means of softening this savage and aggressive way of life that they could no longer bear. Then they learned to sow corn, which before had grown unknown among the other grasses, to trim the vines which the earth similarly produced among the other plants, to transplant and graft fruit trees, so as to give them better fruit, to care for and season the meat and

Louis Le Roy, *La Vicissitude ou variété des choses* (1575). In Werner L. Gundersheimer, *The Life and Works of Louis Le Roy*. Trans. Werner L. Gundersheimer. Geneva: Librarie Droz, 1966. Pp. 104–105.

fish, and then to build, assembling in groups in order to live in greater security and comfort. In this way they were led away from the brutal life they led to this sweetness and civility.

¶ Now just as the Tartars, Turks, Mamelukes, and Persians have by their valour drawn to the East the glory of arms, so we here in the West have in the last two hundred years recovered the excellence of good letters and brought back the study of the disciplines after they had long remained as if extinguished. The sustained industry of many learned men has led to such success that today this our age can be compared to the most learned times that ever were. For we now see the languages restored, and not only the deeds and writings of the ancients brought back to light, but also many fine things newly discovered. In this period grammar, poetry, rhetoric, and dialectic have been illumined by expositions, annotations, corrections, and innumerable translations. Never has mathematics been so well known, nor astrology, cosmography, and navigation better understood. Physics and medicine were not in a state of greater perfection among the ancient Greeks and Arabs than they are now. Arms and military instruments were never so destructive and effective, nor was there equal skill in handling them. Painting, sculpture, modelling, and architecture have been almost wholly restored. And more could not possibly have been done in eloquence and jurisprudence. Even politics, including and controlling everything, which seemed to have been left behind, has recently received much illumination. Theology, moreover, the most worthy of all, which seemed to be destroyed by the sophists, has been greatly illuminated by the knowledge of Hebrew and Greek; and the early fathers of the Church, who were languishing in the libraries, have been brought to light. Printing has greatly aided this work and has made easier its development. . . .

During the reign of Tamerlane there began the restoration of the languages and of all the discplines. The first to apply himself to this work was Francesco Petrarca, who opened up libraries which had long been closed and removed the dust and filth from the good books and ancient writers. Being a man of great understanding and excellent learning, he

Louis Le Roy, *The Excellence of This Age*. [*Vicissitude* continued] In *The Portable Renaissance Reader,* ed. and trans. James Bruce Ross and Mary Martin McLaughlin. New York: Viking, 1953. Pp. 91–92, 93, 97–98, 99, 101, 103, and 107–108.

not only embellished the Italian tongue, of which he, together with his disciple Boccaccio, is revered as an exemplar and principal author, but also laudably stimulated Latin poetry and prose. . . .

The princes who have done most to revive the arts were Pope Nicholas V and Alfonso King of Naples, who welcomed honourably and rewarded liberally those who presented to them Latin translations of Greek books. The King of France, Francis I, paid the salaries of public professors in Paris, and created a sumptuous library at Fountainebleau, full of all the good books. Without the favour and liberality of the kings of Castile and Portugal, the discovery of the new lands and the voyage to the Indies would not have come about. The Medici lords of Florence, Cosimo and Lorenzo, helped very much, receiving the learned men who came to them from all parts, supporting them honourably; and, sending scholars at their own expense to hunt throughout Greece for the good and ancient books which were being lost, they built up magnificent libraries for the common good.

Besides the restoration of ancient learning, now almost complete, the invention of many fine new things, serving not only the needs but also the pleasure and adornment of life, has been reserved to this age. Among these, printing deserves to be put first, because of its excellence, utility, and the subtlety of craftsmanship from which has come the cutting of matrices and fonts, the distribution and composing of type, the making of ink and of balls for putting it on the form, the setting of presses and the way of handling them, of dampening the paper, placing, taking out, and drying the leaves, then gathering them into volumes, going over and correcting the proof, which has already been spoken of.

Second praise must be given to the invention of the marine compass, the rose, and the steel needle which, when touched or rubbed on the lodestone, always indicates the point corresponding to the direction where the arctic pole is supposed to be.

. . . By this skill the whole ocean has been navigated, innumerable islands found, and a great part of terra firma discovered in the West and South, unknown to the ancients, and therefore called "the new world," which has been not only conquered but also converted to the Christian religion under the power of Spain. This enterprise was begun by Cristoforo Colombo the Genoese, and by Amerigo Vespucci the Florentine, a person of excellent understanding and fine judgment who deserves no less praise than the famous Hercules of Greece. . . .

I should willingly give third place to "bombard" or cannonry—

which has brought an end to all other military instruments of the past, which it surpasses in force of motion, violence, and speed—if it were not for the fact that it seems invented rather for the ruin than the utility of humankind, the enemy of generous virtue, which it attacks without distinction, breaking and destroying everything it encounters. . . .

In addition, sects have sprung up in all countries, which have greatly disturbed the public peace and chilled the mutual charity of human beings. Some more curious persons wish to attribute the cause of this to celestial movements, in view of the fact that at about the same time Luther in Saxony, Techel Cuselbas, and the Shah (Ismail) in Persia, and others elsewhere have presumed to reform the established ceremonies of the religions, and to change their accepted doctrines. . . .

But now it is time to put an end to this discourse by which we have clearly shown the vicissitude in all human affairs, arms, letters, languages, arts, states, laws, and customs, and how they do not cease to rise and fall, growing better or worse alternately.

For if the memory and knowledge of the past serve as instruction to the present and warning to the future, it is to be feared that since they have now arrived at such great excellence, the power, wisdom, disciplines, books, industry, works, and knowledge of the world may in the future decline as they have done in the past and be destroyed; that the order and perfection of today will be succeeded by confusion, refinement by crudity, learning by ignorance, elegance by barbarism. I foresee already in my mind certain peoples, strange in form, colour, and habits, pouring in upon Europe, as did formerly the Goths, Huns, Lombards, Vandals, and Saracens, who destroyed our towns, cities, castles, palaces, and churches. They will change our customs, laws, languages, and religion; they will burn our libraries, ruining everything noble they find in the countries they occupy in order to destroy their honour and virtue. I foresee wars springing up in all parts, civil and foreign; factions and heresies arising which will profane all that they touch, human and divine; famine and pestilence menacing mortals; the order of nature, the regulation of the celestial movements, and the harmony of the elements breaking down with the advent of floods on the one hand, excessive heat on the other, and violent earthquakes. And I foresee the universe approaching its end through the one or other form of dislocation, carrying with it the confusion of all things and reducing them to their former state of chaos.

Although things proceed in this way, as the physicists tell us, according to the inevitable law of the world, and have their natural causes, nevertheless their coming about depends chiefly on divine providence, which is above all nature and alone knows the times determined in advance for their decline. For this reason men of good will should not be astounded but should rather take courage, each working faithfully in the vocation to which he is called, in order to preserve as many as possible of the fine things restored or recently invented, the loss of which would be irreparable, and to transmit them to those who come after us just as we have received them from our ancestors; likewise good letters insofar as it shall please God for them to endure. We shall pray Him to preserve from indignities those who worthily profess letters in order that they may persevere in this honourable study, improving the arts and clarifying the truth to His praise, honor, and glory.

℘ POLITICAL HISTORY

72. PHILIPPE DE COMMYNES (1445–1509) served first Charles the Bold of Burgundy and then Louis XI and Charles VIII of France. At the end of his life he composed his memoirs, which described and analyzed the political and military events of French history, with particular attention to the wars of Italy beginning in 1494. Commynes was no humanist, but he believed that history had lessons to offer, and he filled his narrative with portraits; social, economic, and social observations; and especially political and psychological reflections drawn from the events he had witnessed and endured.

Your Excellence, Archbishop of Vienne, in order to comply with your request that I should commit to writing for you an account of what I have known and heard of the acts of King Louis XI (may he rest in peace), our master and benefactor, and prince most worthy of remembrance, I have kept as close to the truth as I could and as far as my memory would allow.

Of the period of his youth, I can say nothing except what I have heard him relate; but from the time when I came into his service to the hour of his death, at which I was present, I have been at his side more continu-

Philippe de Commynes, *Memoirs*. In *The Memoirs of Philippe de Commynes*, ed. Samuel Kinser and trans. Isabelle Cazeaux. Columbia, S.C.: University of South Carolina Press, 1969. 1:91–92, 121–123, 130–132, 169–170, 335–336, 353–354, 355–356, 358, 361–362, and 363–364; 2:437–438 and 567–568.

ously than anyone else, performing the duties of the position in which I
served him, which has always been at least that of chamberlain, or attending to his great affairs. In him as in all other princes whom I have
known or served, I have discerned some good and some evil, for they are
men like us. Perfection belongs to God alone. But when virtue and good
qualities exceed vices in a prince, he is worthy of great praise, since
princes are more inclined than other men to be willful in their actions,
owing to the upbringing and scarce discipline which they receive in
their youth; and when they reach manhood, most people take pains to
cater to their whims and their rank.

Since I would not wish to lie, it is possible that at some point in this
writing some detail might be found which might not entirely reflect
credit on the king; but I hope that those who read this will take into
account the above-mentioned reasons for it. And I venture to affirm in
his praise that, all things considered, I do not believe I have ever known
any prince in whom one could find fewer faults than in him. And I have
known as many princes and have been as frequently in touch with them
as any man who has lived in France in my time. I have known sovereigns
in this kingdom as well as in Brittany and in these parts of Flanders, in
Germany, England, Spain, Portugal, and Italy—temporal as well as
spiritual rulers. Several I have not seen, but I have known them by means
of communications from their embassies, or by means of letters and
instructions from them, from which one can have enough information
about their nature and character.

However, I do not intend to praise the king here to the detriment of
the honor or good reputation of others. I am merely sending you what I
could readily call to mind, hoping that you are requesting this in order
to make use of it in some writing which you intend to compose in Latin,
for you are very well versed in that language; your work will proclaim the
greatness of the prince of whom I shall speak to you and will bear witness
to your understanding of affairs. Wherever I am lacking, you may consult my lord of Bouchage and others, who will be better able to enlighten you and will couch the information in better style. But due to
the obligation of honor and because of the great intimacies and kind-
nesses which were to be uninterrupted until the death of one or the other
of us, no one should be in a position to remember him better than I am.
The losses and afflictions which have befallen me since his death also
serve to remind me of the graces which I received from him. It is not
unusual that after the decease of so great and powerful a prince great

changes should take place. Some people lose from this, and others gain. For goods and honors are not divided up according to the desire of those who request them.

In order to inform you about the period when I knew the king, that period you requested me to write about, I must begin before the time when I entered his service; and then, in orderly fashion, I shall pursue my account until the moment when I became his servant, and shall continue to his death. . . .

I speak of these [royal] offices and office-holders because they made people desire changes, and not only in our time. But during the wars which started from the time of King Charles VI [1380–1422] and lasted until the peace of Arras [1435], the English had conquered so great a part of this kingdom that the negotiations for that peace lasted a full two months. . . .

At the time of the treaty the regent of France for the English was the duke of Bedford, brother of King Henry V and husband of the sister of Duke Philip of Burgundy. He resided in Paris and the least stipend he ever received in his office was twenty thousand *ecus* per month. They lost Paris and little by little the rest of the kingdom.

Having returned to England, no one wanted to diminish his estate. There was not enough wealth in the kingdom of England to satisfy everyone. Wars broke out among them to obtain authority; they lasted for many years, and King Henry VI [1422–1461], who had been crowned king of France and England in Paris, was imprisoned in the castle of London and declared a traitor and criminal of lese majesty. He spent most of his life there and was finally put to death. The duke of York, father of the late King Edward [IV], declared himself king; a few days later he was routed in battle and slain [1460]. . . .

These wars lasted so long that all those from the houses of Warwick and Somerset were beheaded or died on the battlefield. King Edward had his brother, the duke of Clarence, drowned in a cask of malmsey because he wanted to proclaim himself king, or so it was alleged. Upon Edward's death, his second brother, the duke of Gloucester, had the two sons of Edward murdered, declared the daughters illegitimate, and had himself crowned king [Richard III (1483–1485)].

Immediately after, the count of Richmond, the present king [Henry VII (1485–1509)], who had been a prisoner in Brittany for several years, returned to England where he overthrew and killed in battle the cruel King Richard, who had his nephews killed a short time before.

And thus, as far as I can remember, at least eighty men of English royal lineage died in these civil wars of England. I knew several of them and I learned about the rest from the Englishmen who were staying with my lord of Burgundy while I was in his service.

So it is not only in Paris or in France that men fight each other for the goods and honors of this world. Princes and those who rule over large territories should take heed lest division arise in their household; for from there this fire spreads throughout the province. But I believe that nothing is effected save by divine disposition: for when princes or kingdoms have enjoyed great prosperity and wealth and disregard the source of such graces, God unexpectedly sets up an enemy or enemies against them, as you may see from the kings' names in the Bible and from the events seen several years ago in England, the house of Burgundy, and other places which you have seen and see every day. . . .

. . . I have seen many deceptions in this world, perpetrated by many servants in their relations with their masters; and the proud princes and lords who have no great desire to listen to people are deceived more often than the humble ones who listen willingly. Among all those I have ever known, the most skillful at extricating himself out of a disagreeable predicament in time of adversity was King Louis XI, our master, the most humble person in terms of speech and manner and the prince who worked more than any other to gain to his cause any man who could serve him or who could be in a position to harm him. And he was not discouraged if a man he was trying to win over at first refused to cooperate, but he continued his persuasion by promising him many things and actually giving him money and dignities which he knew the other coveted; as for those he had expelled and dispossessed in time of peace and prosperity, he repurchased their favors at a great price when he needed them, made use of them and held no grudge against them on account of things past.

He was naturally a friend of those in middle rank and an enemy of all the powerful lords who could do without him. No man ever gave ear to people to such an extent or inquired about so many matters as he did, or wished to make the acquaintance of so many persons. For indeed he knew everyone in a position of authority and of worthy character who lived in England, Spain, Portugal, Italy, in the territories of the duke of Burgundy, and in Brittany, as well as he knew his own subjects. These methods and manners which he had, of which I have spoken above, saved the crown for him, in view of the enemies he had acquired for himself at the time of his accession to the throne.

But above all his great liberality served him well. For although he was a wise leader in time of adversity, as soon as he believed himself to be secure or at least in a state of truce, he began to antagonize people by means of petty actions; this was hardly to his advantage, and it was with great difficulty that he could endure peace. He spoke slightingly of people in their presence as well as in their absence, except in the case of those he feared; and they were numerous because he was by nature rather apprehensive. When as a result of his words some harm came upon him or if he suspected that it might, he wanted to make amends and would make the following speech to the person he had offended: "I well realize that my tongue has brought me much pleasure. It is reasonable, however, that I should make reparation for my blunder." And he never said these kind words without granting the person whom he thus addressed a favor, and no small one at that.

Yet God give infinite grace to a prince when he knows the difference between good and evil, and especially when his good actions outnumber his bad ones, as was the case with the king, our above-mentioned master. In my opinion, the distress he endured in his youth when he was a fugitive from his father and escaped to Duke Philip of Burgundy, with whom he resided for six years {1456–1461}, was beneficial to him because he was forced to please those whose help he needed. Adversity taught him that, and it is no small lesson. After he had grown up and was crowned king, at the beginning of his reign he had no other thought but of revenge. The injury that resulted from this came soon, and then his repentance. He made reparations for his folly and his error by regaining those he had wronged, as you will hear shortly.

If his education had not been different from that of the lords whom I have seen brought up in this kingdom, I do not believe that he would ever have regained ground: for they are taught only to act like fools in dress and speech; of letters they have no knowledge. Not a single wise man is placed in their entourage. They have tutors to whom one speaks about matters concerning them, but not a word is said to them about it, and these tutors manage their affairs. There are some lords with income of less than thirteen silver livres who are proud to say: "Speak to my servants," and they think that by these words they imitate very important people. I have also very often seen their servants derive profit from them, making it obvious that they take them for fools. And if by chance one of them regains control and inquires about what belongs to him, it is so late that it hardly matters any more; for it should be noted that all

men who have ever been famous and have accomplished great deeds have
started very young; and that depends on one's education or the grace of
God. . . .

It is great folly for a prince to put himself in the power of another,
especially when they are at war; and it is also to their advantage if they
have studied history in their youth. They can thus realize what happens
in such assemblies and how some of the ancients committed great frauds,
impostures, and perjuries against each other, capturing and killing
those who had confidence in their word. This is not to imply that everyone acts in this manner, but a single example should be sufficient to
make many people wiser and to inspire them to guard themselves well.

It seems to me (and I speak on the basis of what I have seen in this
world, which includes eighteen years or more experience in close relationship with princes, having had intimate knowledge of the greatest
and most secret affairs which have been transacted in this kingdom of
France and in neighboring territories) that one of the surest means to
make a man wise is to have him read ancient history and learn how to
conduct and guard himself and how to manage his affairs wisely, according to histories and examples of our ancestors. For our life is so short that
it cannot give us the necessary experience in so many matters.

Besides, our life-span is diminished, and we do not live as long as men
did in former times; neither are our bodies as strong, and similarly our
faith and loyalty to one another have been weakened. I could not say by
what ties one could assure oneself with regard to the great, who are
rather inclined to do as they please without regard to any reason that can
be offered. And, worst of all, they are usually surrounded by persons who
are only interested in pleasing their masters, and they invariably praise
all their actions whether they are good or bad. And if someone is found
who wants to improve things, every one falls to quarreling.

Again I cannot help but blame lords who are ignorant. Around every
lord one is sure to find some lawyers and ecclesiastics, as is proper; and
they are indeed valuable when they are good men, but very dangerous
otherwise. At every turn they cite a law or story, and even the best story
is liable to be given a bad interpretation at their hands. But wise men
and those who have read things will never be deceived by them, nor will
anyone be so convincing that they [the wise] will accept lies. You may be
sure that God did not establish the position of king or prince to have it
filled by stupid people or by persons who pride themselves in saying: "I
am no scholar; I refer my affairs to my council and I trust them." And

without further explanation they proceed to their pleasures. If they had been better educated in their youth they would reason differently and they would want to earn the respect of others for their person and their virtues.

I do not wish to imply that all princes use the services of unworthy persons. But most of those whom I have known have been surrounded by them. I have known some wise princes who, when the necessity arose, knew how to select the advice of the best ministers and followed it without complaining.

Among all the princes whom I was privileged to know, the one who could do this best was the king, our master; and no one knew better how to honor and respect people of worth and excellence. He was rather well-read; he liked to ask questions and to learn about everything and was endowed with good natural sense, which is more important than any science that can be learned in this world. All the books that have been written would be useless if they did not serve to bring to mind past events. And one man can learn more in three months' time from reading a book than twenty men living successively could observe and understand from experience.

Thus, to conclude this digression, it seems to me that God cannot send a greater plague on my country than a prince of little understanding: for that is the source of all other misfortunes. First of all, division and war arise because he delegates his authority to others, although that is the prerogative which he should most want to reserve for himself. And from this division famine and death proceed, as well as the other afflictions which derive from war. Thus one may observe how much the subjects of a prince have reason to lament when they see his children badly educated and in the hands of men of bad temperament. . . .

Chroniclers commonly write only things which reflect credit on those whose actions they record, and they omit many things, or they do not know about them sometimes as they truly happened. But I have decided not to speak of anything which is not true and which I have not seen or heard from such great people that they are worthy of being believed, and without having any regard to praises. For it is good to think that there is no prince so wise that he does not err once in a while, and even very often, if he lives long. And so their actions would appear, if one always told the truth. The greatest senates and the greatest consuls in the world have indeed erred and still do, as it has been seen and is seen every day. . . .

All things considered, it seems to me that God has created neither man nor beast in this world without establishing some counterparts to oppose him, in order to keep him in humility and fear. And therefore Ghent is well situated where it is, for those are the territories of Christendom the most given to all the pleasures to which man is inclined and also to the greatest display and expense. The people there [in Ghent] are good Christians, and they serve and honor God well.

And this is not the only nation to whom God has given some sort of thorn. For to the kingdom of France He has opposed England; to the English He has opposed the Scotch, and to the kingdom of Spain, Portugal. I do not want to speak of Granada, for the people are enemies of the true faith; however, so far Granada has caused much trouble to the kingdom of Castile. To the princes of Italy (most of whom hold their territories without title, unless it be given to them in heaven, and about that we can only guess) who rule their subjects rather cruelly and violently in regard to taxes, God has opposed the communes of Italy, such as Venice, Florence, Genoa, and sometimes Bologna, Siena, Pisa, Lucca, and others, which often are against the lords, and the lords against them; and each keeps an eye on the other so that neither may grow. . . .

I have spoken only of Europe, for I am not well informed of the situation in the two other parts of the world, Asia and Africa; but I have heard that they have as many wars and divisions as we do, and that they are carried on even more mechanically. For I have learned that in some localities in Africa they sell their own people to Christians, and this is borne out by the Portuguese, who have had many slaves and still do.

It may seem, therefore, that these divisions are necessary in all the world and that these dissensions and oppositions, which God has given and ordered for every estate and almost for every person, as I explained above, are also necessary. And offhand, speaking as an unlearned man who wants to hold only opinions which we should, it seems to me that this is so, and principally because of the stupidity of many princes, and also because of the wickedness of others, who have enough sense and experience but wish to use it evilly.

A prince or other man of whatever estate he may be, who has power and authority over others and is well educated, learned, and experienced will either be improved as a result, or else made worse: for great knowledge makes wicked men worse and good men better. However, it is probable that knowledge does men more good than harm, if only because it makes them conscious of their bad actions and ashamed of them;

and that may be enough to prevent them from doing wrong, or at least from doing it too often. And if they are not naturally good, they will not wish to appear bad or willing to harm anyone. I have seen many such instances among great people, where they have abstained from many bad actions because of their learning, and often also because of fear of God's punishments, of which they are more aware than ignorant persons who have neither seen nor read anything.

Therefore I will say that those who are unwise for lack of having been brought up well—and perhaps also their temperament is involved here—do not understand at all the extent of power and lordship which God has given them over their subjects; for they have not seen it, nor have they heard about it from those who know it. Those who do understand these things do not generally become close to such princes; and if some of those who are close do know, they do not want to talk about it for fear of displeasing them. And if anyone wishes to make some remonstrance to them, nobody will support him; at best he will be considered mad, and perhaps his words will be taken in the worst possible sense as far as he is concerned.

Therefore one must conclude that neither our natural reason, nor our sense, nor fear of God, nor love of our neighbor will restrain us at all from doing violence to one another, or from keeping for ourselves what belongs to another, or from taking the possessions of others by all possible means. . . .

To continue with my subject, is there any king or lord in this world who has the power, outside of his own domain, to levy a single denier on his subjects without the approval and consent of those who are to pay it, unless he does it by tyranny and violence? One might object that there are certain times in which it is not possible to wait for the convocation of an assembly because it would take too long to start the war and prepare it. To this I would reply that one should not be in such a hurry and that there is always enough time for such an enterprise. And I insist that kings and princes are much stronger when they undertake some affair with the advice of their subjects; and they are more feared by their enemies. . . .

When I refer to kings or princes, I mean them and their governors; and when I say people, I mean those who have high positions and dignities under their authority. The greatest misfortunes generally proceed from the strongest, for the weak seek only to have patience.

I include women as well as men, because women are sometimes and in certain places put in a position of authority, either by their husbands' love, or for the administration of their children's affairs, or because their territories were part of their dowry. If I were to speak of the middle estates of this world and the low ones, it would take too long. It will be sufficient to speak of the high-ranking people, for it is through them that God's power and justice are made known. For if misfortunes befall a poor man or one hundred of them, no one worries about this, for it is attributed to his poverty or lack of proper care, or if he drowns or breaks his neck because no one was there to save him, people hardly talk about it. When calamity befalls a great city, however, the reaction is not the same; yet it does not arouse so much commotion as in the case of a prince.

One might ask why the power of God is more manifest against great people than against persons of low rank. It is because the humble and the poor find enough to punish them when they deserve it. Furthermore, they are frequently chastised when they have done nothing wrong, either to serve as examples for others because someone wants to get their possessions, or perhaps because of an error on the part of the judge. At other times they have deserved their punishment and justice must take its course. But as for great princes and princesses, their rich governors and provincial counselors, disorderly towns who disobey their lords and governors, who will investigate their conduct? . . .

My answer to this is that the information which will be brought against them will be the complaints and clamors of the people whom they afflict and oppress in so many ways without having any compassion or pity for them, the dolorous lamentations of the widows and orphans whose husbands and fathers they have put to death, to the detriment of their survivors, and in general the protestations of all those whom they have persecuted either in their persons or their possessions. This will be the accusation, and the great cries of the people, their complaints and their pitiful tears will bring it before Our Lord, who will be the true judge of the case, and perhaps He will not defer their punishment until the next world but will chastise them in this one.

Therefore we must assume that they will be punished because they have refused to believe and have been lacking in true faith and trust. Thus we must say that God has to show His will by means of examples and instances, so that they and everyone else may be convinced that their punishments are the result of their cruel offenses, and He must show upon them His force, His virtue and His justice. For no one else in this world has this power except Him. . . .

To continue the memoirs I have begun, I wish to tell you how it came about that King Charles VIII, who rules at present, undertook his journey to Italy, in which I took part, and left from the town of Vienne to Dauphine on the twenty-third day of August, 1495. There was much discussion about whether or not he should go, because the enterprise seemed most unreasonable to all those who were wise and experienced, and he was the only one to approve of the plan, aside from a person named Etienne de Vesc, a native of Languedoc, a man of petty lineage who had never heard or seen anything. Also involved with this affair up to that time was a man who lacked courage—a collector of taxes called the [receiver-]general Briconnet, who on account of this trip has since obtained high positions in the church, such as the cardinalate, and many benefices. The other [Etienne de Vesc] had already acquired many inheritances, and he was seneschal of Beaucaire and president des comptes in Paris, and he had served the king very well as valet de chambre during the latter's childhood; and this man attracted the said [receiver-]general to the project. And the two of them were the cause of the above-mentioned enterprise, for which few people praised them and many blamed them; for all the things necessary for such a great enterprise were lacking.

For the king was very young; he was feeble in person [but] very willful. He had few wise persons or good leaders around him. He had no ready cash; for before they left, they borrowed 100,000 francs from the bank of Sauli in Genoa at the rate of fourteen percent interest [computed] from fair to fair, and from several other sources, as I shall explain later. They had neither tents nor pavilions, and it was in winter that they began to march into Lombardy. One good thing they had, and that was a bold company full of young gentlemen, though [they were] little inclined to obedience. Therefore one must conclude that this trip, both going and returning, was led by God, because the judgment of the leaders whom I mentioned was hardly of any use to the expedition. However, they can well assert that they were the occasion of bringing great honor and great glory to their master.

Now you may realize how great are the miseries of great kings and princes who are afraid of their own children! King Louis, who was so wise and virtuous, was afraid of them (that is, of that very King Charles who reigns today); but he provided very wisely for him and he left him the crown at the age of fourteen. King Louis had frightened his father King Charles VII, and found himself in arms and in league against him with some lords and knights of the kingdom because of quarrels pertaining to the court and the government; and he told me that many times. And this happened when he was about thirteen [sixteen] years old, and it did not last. But after he became an adult he had great divisions with King Charles VII his father, and he withdrew to Dauphine and from there to Flanders, leaving the territory of Dauphine to the king his father, for they did not wage war against each other. And this matter was mentioned at the beginning of these memoirs.

No creature is exempt from suffering, and everyone eats his bread in sorrow and toil, as Our Lord promised them from the moment He created man, and He kept His word loyally to everyone; but sorrows and toil are varied, and those of the body are the least, whereas those of the mind are the greatest. Those of the wise are one sort and those of the fools of another, but the fool endures much more sorrow and suffering than the wise, although it seems otherwise to many, and he has less consolation. The poor people, who work and toil in order to feed themselves and their children and who pay taxes and other subsidies to their lords, would live in great discomfort if great princes and lords had nothing but all the pleasure in this world and they had all the worry and misery; but it happens quite differently, for if I wanted to begin to write about the suffering that I have seen high-ranking persons endure, men as well as women, during the past thirty years alone, I could make a book out of it. I do not refer to those who are of the same condition as those who are mentioned in Boccaccio's book, but I am thinking of the men and women whom one sees in perfect wealth, health, and prosperity; and those who did not frequent them as closely as I did considered them to be very happy. And I have often seen their disappointments and sorrows founded on such insignificant reasons that people who did not live close to them would hardly have wanted to believe it. Most of them are founded on suspicions and the reports [of others], which constitute a secret illness reigning in the houses of great princes, from whence comes many evils which befall their persons as well as their servants and subjects. And this shortens life so much that there is hardly a king in France since the time of Charlemagne who lived past his sixtieth year.

73. NICCOLO MACHIAVELLI (1469–1527), observer of and participant in the early phases of the Italian wars, brought the insights both of humanism and of practical experience (diplomatic, military, and administrative) to questions of political change, which the Italian calamity produced by the French invasion of 1494 had made urgently relevant. In his *Discourses on the First Ten Books of Titus Livius,* Machiavelli tried (more subtly and learnedly than he did in *The Prince*) to reflect on the process of history and to chart what he called a "new route" which would lead to a modern science of politics by drawing on the lessons of Roman experience, failures as well as successes, and by analyzing the cyclical patterns posited long before by Polybius. Machiavelli asked similar questions of the career of his own city-state, and in his *Florentine Histories*—following Bruni but shifting emphasis from external to internal and constitutional questions—he traced the social conflicts, political clashes, and decline of liberty from medieval times down to the death of Lorenzo de' Medici in 1492, which ended the golden age of Florentine republicanism.

Ever since your Holiness, while enjoying a less elevated dignity, commissioned me to write the history of the Florentine People, I have used, in order to fulfill your command, the diligence and skill which natural aptitude and experience have bestowed upon me. Having now approached in my history those times when, owing to the death of Lorenzo de' Medici, the Magnificent, the affairs of Italy so greatly changed, and having to relate those events which are in themselves of a more urgent and important character, I have to adopt a graver and more elevated style. I have, therefore, thought it proper to reduce what I have written of those previous times into a small volume, and present it to your Holiness, in order that you may taste in some degree the fruit of your sowing and of my labour.

In the first place your Holiness will see as you read that, as the Roman Empire commenced to lose its dominion in the West, Italy was desolated through many ages by a continual change of princes and governments. You will see that the Pontiffs, the Venetians, the Kingdom of Naples, and the Dukedom of Milan have taken up leading positions in the government of this country. You will see that your fatherland, owing to its factions, cast off its obedience to the empire, and persisted in its divi-

Niccolò Machiavelli, *Florentine History.* Trans. W. K. Marriott. London: J. M. Dent and Sons, 1922. Pp. xv–xvi and 1–3.

sions until it commenced to be ruled under the shadow of your house. I
was particularly charged and commanded by your Holiness to write in
such a manner of your ancestors that I could in no way be accused of
flattery, for although it may be pleasing to hear men praised with justice,
it is displeasing to see them loaded with false virtues. I greatly fear,
however, that in describing the goodness of Giovanni, the wisdom of
Cosimo, the affability of Piero, and the magnificence and foresight of
Lorenzo, I may appear to your Holiness to have transgressed your commands. For this and any similar transgressions, it is my excuse to you
and others whom I may have offended, that finding the records of these
statesmen full of praise by those writers who at various times have described them, it seemed to me that I ought to write of them as I found
them, or be charged with envy for my silence. If under their noble deeds
there lay concealed an ambition contrary to the welfare of the commonwealth, as some have said, I have not found it, and am not bound to
discuss it, for in all my history I have never sought to conceal a dishonest
action under an honest cloak, or to hide a praiseworthy deed although
inspired by a contrary motive. That I have not been prone to adulation
will be seen in every line of my history, especially in the speeches and
private discourses, whether direct or indirect, where it will be found
that the opinions and dispositions accord entirely with the characters of
the speakers. I have avoided in every place all insulting reflections, as
contributing neither to the dignity nor veracity of history. No one therefore who rightly considers my writings can charge me with adulation,
especially when it is seen that I have written so little concerning the
memory of the father of your Holiness, caused in a measure by his short
life, in which he had but few opportunities, nor have I been able to
illustrate it from his writings. Nevertheless, to have been the father of
your Holiness was a great and glorious distinction, eclipsing the deeds of
his ancestors, and ages will add to his fame far more than the malignity
of fortune did to shorten his days.

I have, however, most Holy and Blessed Father, done my best, without violating the truth, to satisfy everybody, and perhaps I have not
satisfied any one. If this be the case I shall not marvel, for I consider it
impossible for any one to write the history of his own time without
offending many. Nevertheless I shall go my way cheerfully, hoping, that
as I am honoured and sustained by the beneficence of your Holiness, so
I shall be aided and defended by the armed legions of your most sacred
judgment; and I shall continue my enterprise with the same confidence

and spirit in which I have written up to this hour, unless your Holiness should abandon me, or my life should cease.

It was in my mind when I first thought of writing the history of the Florentine people that I would commence my story with the year of the Christian religion 1434, at which time the family of the Medici, through the abilities of Cosimo and of his father Giovanni, had acquired more power than any other house in Florence. Because I thought to myself that Messer Lionardo d'Arezzo and Messer Poggio, two most excellent historians, had related in great detail all the events which had happened before that date. But after having diligently read their writings in order to see what plan and method they had adopted, that our history might profit by their example to the benefit of the readers, I found that in the descriptions of the wars waged by the Florentines against foreign princes and people they had been most exact, but upon the subject of civil discord and internal strifes and their consequences they had been entirely silent, or had written far too briefly concerning them; so that these historians have failed to convey anything either instructive or pleasing to their readers. I believe they did this, either because such incidents appeared to them so insignificant that they judged them unworthy of commemoration, or because they feared to offend the descendants of those whom in the course of their story they might have to condemn. Now—if they will allow me to say so—these two reasons are, it seems to me, quite unworthy of great men, because if anything teaches or pleases in history it is that which is described in detail, and if any reading can be profitable to citizens who may be called upon to govern republics, it is that which reveals the causes of hatreds and dissensions in a state, so that, learning wisdom from the perils of others, they may maintain themselves in unity. And if the history of any republic can exercise an influence upon us, then the example of our own will instruct us more, and to our greater advantage. For if ever the dissensions in a republic were remarkable, those of Florence have been the most remarkable, for most other republics of which we have any knowledge have been content with one division, with which, according to circumstances, they have either strengthened or ruined their state; but Florence, not content with one, has had many. In Rome, as every one knows, after the kings were driven out, there arose the strife between the patricians and plebians which lasted until Rome fell. Thus, also, it happened in Athens and in other republics which flourished in those days. But in Florence the dissensions were at first among the nobility themselves, afterwards between the nobles and the citizens, and finally between the citizens and the plebians, and many times it has happened that one of these parties, having prevailed over the other, would divide and become two parties. From these dissensions there occurred more deaths, and banishments, and general extinction of families, than ever happened in any city of which we have knowledge. And truly, according to my judgment, nothing could have so well demonstrated the vitality of our city as these dissensions, which were fierce enough to have destroyed the greatest and most powerful city. Nevertheless our republic has always seemed to thrive, the ability of its citizens, and their skill and success in aggrandising their country and themselves, being so great that those who have survived these misfortunes have been able to bring far more advantage to the republic than the untoward circumstances, which diminished their numbers, could work it evil. And doubtless had Florence been fortunate enough after she had freed herself from the empire to have adopted a form of government that would have kept her united, I know of no republic, either ancient or modern, that would have been superior to her, with such capacity and valour was she replete. After the republic had expelled the Ghibellines in such numbers that Tuscany and Lombardy were full of them, the Guelfs, with those who remained, drew from the city alone 1200 cavalry and 12,000 infantry during the war against Arezzo and a year before the battle of Campaldino. Afterwards in the war against Filippo Visconti, Duke of Milan, when, their own forces being exhausted, they were driven to rely on mercenaries, it is a matter of common knowledge that during the five years which the war lasted the Florentines raised 3,500,000 florins; and, to show the resources of the state, when that war was over they took the field against Lucca, being unable to rest satisfied with the peace. I cannot, therefore, understand by what reasoning these dissensions are deemed unworthy of commemoration. And if these noble authors were restrained by the fear of wounding the memory of those about whom they had to write, they are deceived, and show that they know little of the ambition of men and their desire to perpetuate their ancestors' names and their own. Nor has it occurred to them that many who have not had the opportunity of securing fame by praiseworthy deeds have gained it by infamous ones. Nor have they considered that actions intrinsically great, as are those of government and statecraft, however they may be handled, or to whatever end they may come, seem always to bring more honour than blame to men. These considerations have caused me to alter my plan and to commence my history with the foundation of our city. And as it is not my intention to occupy the place of other writers until 1434, I shall particularly describe those events only which occurred within the city, and of outside affairs I shall write only that which may be needful for a right understanding of these events which took place within. After the year 1434, I shall describe both in detail. Furthermore, before I shall treat of Florence, in order that this history shall be the better understood to all time, I shall describe the means by which Italy came under the sway of the rulers of those times. All these events, Italian as well as Florentine, will be contained in four books. The first will relate briefly the events which occurred in Italy from the decline of the Roman Empire until the year 1434. The second will commence with the story of the foundation of the city of Florence until the war against the pope, which arose after the expulsion of the Duke of Athens. The third will finish with the death of Ladislao, the King of Naples, in the year 1414. And with the fourth book we shall again reach 1434, from which time until the present the events which occurred both within and without the city will receive particular attention.

❡ Although the envious nature of men, so prompt to blame and so slow to praise, makes the discovery and introduction of any new principles and systems as dangerous almost as the exploration of unknown seas and continents, yet, animated by that desire which impels me to do what may prove for the common benefit of all, I have resolved to open a new route, which has not yet been followed by any one, and may prove difficult and troublesome, but may also bring me some reward in the approbation of those who will kindly appreciate my efforts.

And if my poor talents, my little experience of the present and insufficient study of the past, should make the result of my labors defective and of little utility, I shall at least have shown the way to others, who will carry out my views with greater ability, eloquence, and judgment, so that if I do not merit praise, I ought at least not to incur censure.

When we consider the general respect for antiquity, and how often—to say nothing of other examples—a great price is paid for some fragments of an antique statue, which we are anxious to possess to ornament

Niccolò Machiavelli, *Discourses on the First Ten Books of Titus Livius*. Trans. Christian E. Detmold. In *The Prince and the Discourses,* ed. Max Lerner. New York: Modern Library, 1940. Pp. 103–105, 110–117, 216, 272–275, and 530.

our houses with, or to give to artists who strive to imitate them in their own works; and when we see, on the other hand, the wonderful examples which the history of ancient kingdoms and republics presents to us, the prodigies of virtue and of wisdom displayed by the kings, captains, citizens, and legislators who have sacrificed themselves for their country,—when we see these, I say, more admired than imitated, or so much neglected that not the least trace of this ancient virtue remains, we cannot but be at the same time as much surprised as afflicted. The more so as in the differences which arise between citizens, or in the maladies to which they are subjected, we see these same people have recourse to the judgments and the remedies prescribed by the ancients. The civil laws are in fact nothing but decisions given by their jurisconsults, and which, reduced to a system, direct our modern jurists in their decisions. And what is the science of medicine, but the experience of ancient physicians, which their successors have taken for their guide? And yet to found a republic, maintain states, to govern a kingdom, organize an army, conduct a war, dispense justice, and extend empires, you will find neither prince, nor republic, nor captain, nor citizen, who has recourse to the examples of antiquity! This neglect, I am persuaded, is due less to the weakness to which the vices of our education have reduced the world, than to the evils caused by the proud indolence which prevails in most of the Christian states, and to the lack of real knowledge of history, the true sense of which is not known, or the spirit of which they do not comprehend. Thus the majority of those who read it take pleasure only in the variety of the events which history relates, without ever thinking of imitating the noble actions, deeming that not only difficult, but impossible; as though heaven, the sun, the elements, and men had changed the order of their motions and power, and were different from what they were in ancient times.

Wishing, therefore, so far as in me lies, to draw mankind from this error, I have thought it proper to write upon those books of Titus Livius that have come to us entire despite the malice of time; touching upon all those matters which, after a comparison between the ancient and modern events, may seem to me necessary to facilitate their proper understanding. In this way those who read my remarks may derive those advantages which should be the aim of all study of history; and although the undertaking is difficult, yet, aided by those who have encouraged me in this attempt, I hope to carry it sufficiently far, so that but little may remain for others to carry it to its destined end. . . .

I will leave aside what might be said of cities which from their very birth have been subject to a foreign power, and will speak only of those whose origin has been independent, and which from the first governed themselves by their own laws, whether as republics or as principalities, and whose constitution and laws have differed as their origin. Some have had at the very beginning, or soon after, a legislator, who, like Lycurgus with the Lacedaemonians, gave them by a single act all the laws they needed. Others have owed theirs to chance and to events, and have received their laws at different times, as Rome did. It is a great good fortune for a republic to have a legislator sufficiently wise to give her laws so regulated that, without the necessity of correcting them, they afford security to those who live under them. Sparta observed her laws for more than eight hundred years without altering them and without experiencing a single dangerous disturbance. Unhappy, on the contrary, is that republic which, not having at the beginning fallen into the hands of a sagacious and skilful legislator, is herself obliged to reform her laws. More unhappy still is that republic which from the first has diverged from a good constitution. And that republic is furthest from it whose vicious institutions impede her progress, and make her leave the right path that leads to a good end; for those who are in that condition can hardly ever be brought into the right road. Those republics, on the other hand, that started without having even a perfect constitution, but made a fair beginning, and are capable of improvement,—such republics, I say, may perfect themselves by the aid of events. It is very true, however, that such reforms are never effected without danger, for the majority of men never willingly adopt any new law tending to change the constitution of the state, unless the necessity of the change is clearly demonstrated; and as such a necessity cannot make itself felt without being accompanied with danger, the republic may easily be destroyed before having perfected its constitution. That of Florence is a complete proof of this: reorganized after the revolt of Arezzo, in 1502, it was overthrown after the taking of Prato, in 1512.

Having proposed to myself to treat of the kind of government established at Rome, and of the events that led to its perfection, I must at the beginning observe that some of the writers on politics distinguished three kinds of government, viz. the monarchical, the aristocratic, and the democratic; and maintain that the legislators of a people must choose from these three the one that seems to them most suitable. Other authors, wiser according to the opinion of many, count six kinds of governments, three of which are very bad, and three good in themselves, but so liable to be corrupted that they become absolutely bad. The three good

ones are those which we have just named; the three bad ones result from
the degradation of the other three, and each of them resembles its corresponding original, so that the transition from the one to the other is very
easy. Thus monarchy becomes tyranny; aristocracy degenerates into oligarchy; and the popular government lapses readily into licentiousness.
So that a legislator who gives to a state which he founds, either of these
three forms of government, constitutes it but for a brief time; for no
precautions can prevent either one of the three that are reputed good,
from degenerating into its opposite kind; so great are in these the attrac-
tions and resemblances between the good and the evil.

Chance has given birth to these different kinds of governments
amongst men; for at the beginning of the world the inhabitants were few
in number, and lived for a time dispersed, like beasts. As the human race
increased, the necessity for uniting themselves for defence made itself
felt; the better to attain this object, they chose the strongest and most
courageous from amongst themselves and placed him at their head,
promising to obey him. Thence they began to know the good and the
honest, and to distinguish them from the bad and vicious; for seeing a
man injure his benefactor aroused at once two sentiments in every heart,
hatred against the ingrate and love for the benefactor. They blamed the
first, and on the contrary honored those the more who showed themselves grateful, for each felt that he in turn might be subject to a like
wrong; and to prevent similar evils, they set to work to make laws, and
to institute punishments for those who contravened them. Such was the
origin of justice. This caused him, when they had afterwards to choose a
prince, neither to look to the strongest nor bravest, but to the wisest
and most just. But when they began to make sovereignty hereditary and
non-elective, the children quickly degenerated from their fathers; and,
so far from trying to equal their virtues, they considered that a prince
had nothing else to do than to excel all the rest in luxury, indulgence,
and every other variety of pleasure. The prince consequently soon drew
upon himself the general hatred. An object of hatred, he naturally felt
fear; fear in turn dictated to him precautions and wrongs, and thus
tyranny quickly developed itself. Such were the beginning and causes of
disorders, conspiracies, and plots against the sovereigns, set on foot, not
by the feeble and timid, but by those citizens who, surpassing the others
in grandeur of soul, in wealth, and in courage, could not submit to the
outrages and excesses of their princes.

Under such powerful leaders the masses armed themselves against the
tyrant, and, after having rid themselves of him, submitted to these

chiefs as their liberators. These abhorring the very name of prince, constituted themselves a new government; and at first, bearing in mind the
past tyranny, they governed in strict accordance with the laws which
they had established themselves; preferring public interests to their
own, and to administer and protect with greatest care both public and
private affairs. The children succeeded their fathers, and ignorant of the
changes of fortune, having never experienced its reverses, and indisposed
to remain content with this civil equality, they in turn gave themselves
up to cupidity, ambition, libertinage, and violence, and soon caused the
aristocratic government to degenerate into an oligarchic tyranny, regardless of all civil rights. They soon, however, experienced the same
fate as the first tyrant; the people, disgusted with their government,
placed themselves at the command of whoever was willing to attack
them, and this disposition soon produced an avenger, who was sufficiently well seconded to destroy them. The memory of the prince and
the wrongs committed by him being still fresh in their minds, and
having overthrown the oligarchy, the people were not willing to return
to the government of a prince. A popular government was therefore
resolved upon, and it was so organized that the authority should not
again fall into the hands of a prince or a small number of nobles. And as
all governments are at first looked up to with some degree of reverence,
the popular state also maintained itself for a time, but which was never
of long duration, and lasted generally only about as long as the generation that had established it; for it soon ran into that kind of license which
inflicts injury upon public as well as private interests. Each individual
only consulted his own passions, and a thousand acts of injustice were
daily committed, so that, constrained by necessity, or directed by the
counsels of some good man, or for the purpose of escaping from this
anarchy, they returned anew to the government of a prince, and from
this they generally lapsed again into anarchy, step by step, in the same
manner and from the same causes as we have indicated.

Such is the circle which all republics are destined to run through.
Seldom, however, do they come back to the original form of government, which results from the fact that their duration is not sufficiently
long to be able to undergo these repeated changes and preserve their
existence. But it may well happen that a republic lacking strength and
good counsel in its difficulties becomes subject after a while to some
neighboring state, that is better organized than itself; and if such is not
the case, then they will be apt to revolve indefinitely in the circle of

revolutions. I say, then, that all kinds of government are defective; those three which we have qualified as good because they are too short-lived, and the three bad ones because of their inherent viciousness. Thus sagacious legislators, knowing the vices of each of these systems of government by themselves, have chosen one that should partake of all of them, judging that to be the most stable and solid. In fact, when there is combined under the same constitution a prince, a nobility, and the power of the people, then these three powers will watch and keep each other reciprocally in check.

Amongst those justly celebrated for having established such a constitution, Lycurgus beyond doubt merits the highest praise. He organized the government of Sparta in such manner that, in giving to the king, the nobles, and the people each their portion of authority and duties, he created a government which maintained itself for over eight hundred years in the most perfect tranquillity, and reflected infinite glory upon this legislator. On the other hand, the constitution given by Solon to the Athenians, by which he established only a popular government, was of such short duration that before his death he saw the tyranny of Pisistratus arise. And although forty years afterwards the heirs of the tyrant were expelled, so that Athens recovered her liberties and restored the popular government according to the laws of Solon, yet it did not last over a hundred years; although a number of laws that had been overlooked by Solon were adopted, to maintain the government against the insolence of the nobles and the license of the populace. The fault he had committed in not tempering the power of the people and that of the prince and his nobles, made the duration of the government of Athens very short, as compared with that of Sparta.

But let us come to Rome. Although she had no legislator like Lycurgus, who constituted her government, at her very origin, in a manner to secure her liberty for a length of time, yet the disunion which existed between the Senate and the people produced such extraordinary events, that chance did for her what the laws had failed to do. Thus, if Rome did not attain the first degree of happiness, she at least had the second. Her first institutions were doubtless defective, but they were not in conflict with the principles that might bring her to perfection. For Romulus and all the other kings gave her many and good laws, well suited even to a free people; but as the object of these princes was to found a monarchy, and not a republic, Rome, upon becoming free, found herself lacking all those institutions that are most essential to liberty, and which her kings had not established. And although these kings lost their empire, for the reasons and in the manner which we have explained, yet those who expelled them appointed immediately two consuls in place of the king; and thus it was found that they had banished the title of king from Rome, but not the regal power. The government, composed of Consuls and a Senate, had but two of the three elements of which we have spoken, the monarchical and the aristocratic; the popular power was wanting. In the course of time, however, the insolence of the nobles, produced by the causes which we shall see further on, induced the people to rise against the others. The nobility, to save a portion of their power, were forced to yield a share of it to the people; but the Senate and the Consuls retained sufficient to maintain their rank in the state. It was then that the Tribunes of the people were created, which strengthened and confirmed the republic, being now composed of the three elements of which we have spoken above. Fortune favored her, so that, although the authority passed successively from the kings and nobles to the people, by the same degrees and for the same reasons that we have spoken of, yet the royal authority was never entirely abolished to bestow it upon the nobles; and these were never entirely deprived of their authority to give it to the people; but a combination was formed of the three powers, which rendered the constitution perfect, and this perfection was attained by the disunion of the Senate and the people, as we shall more fully show in the following two chapters. . . .

All those who have written upon civil institutions demonstrate (and history is full of examples to support them) that whoever desired to found a state and give it laws, must start with assuming that all men are bad and ever ready to display their vicious nature, whenever they may find occasion for it. If their evil disposition remains concealed for a time, it must be attributed to some unknown reason; and we must assume that it lacked occasion to show itself; but time, which has been said to be the father of all truth, does not fail to bring it to light. . . .

Whoever considers the past and the present will readily observe that all cities and all people are and ever have been animated by the same desires and the same passions; so that it is easy, by diligent study of the past to foresee what is likely to happen in the future in any republic, and to apply those remedies that were used by the ancients, or, not finding any that were employed by them, to devise new ones from the similarity of the events. But as such considerations are neglected or not understood by most of those who read, or, if understood by these, are unknown by those who govern, it follows that the same troubles generally recur in all republics. . . .

I repeat, then, that this practice of praising and decrying is very general, though it cannot be said that it is always erroneous; for sometimes our judgment is of necessity correct, human affairs being in a state of perpetual movement, always either ascending or declining. We see, for instance, a city or country with a government well organized by some man of superior ability; for a time it progresses and attains a great prosperity through the talents of its lawgiver. Now, if any one living at such a period should praise the past more than the time in which he lives, he would certainly be deceiving himself; and this error will be found due to the reasons above indicated. But should he live in that city or country at the period after it shall have passed the zenith of its glory and in the time of its decline, then he would not be wrong in praising the past. Reflecting now upon the course of human affairs, I think that, as a whole, the world remains very much in the same condition, and the good in it always balances the evil; but the good and the evil change from one country to another, as we learn from the history of those ancient kingdoms that differed from each other in manners, whilst the world at large remained the same. The only difference being, that all the virtues that first found a place in Assyria were thence transferred to Media, and afterwards passed to Persia, and from there they came into Italy and to Rome. And if after the fall of the Roman Empire none other sprang up that endured for any length of time, and where the aggregate virtues of the world were kept together, we nevertheless see them scattered amongst many nations, as, for instance, in the kingdom of France, the Turkish empire, or that of the Sultan of Egypt, and nowadays the people of Germany, and before them those famous Saracens, who achieved such great things and conquered so great a part of the world, after having destroyed the Roman Empire of the East. The different peoples of these several countries, then, after the fall of the Roman Empire, have possessed and possess still in great part that virtue which is so much lamented and so sincerely praised. And those who live in those countries and praise the past more than the present may deceive themselves; but whoever is born in Italy and Greece, and has not become either an Ultramontane in Italy or a Turk in Greece, has good reason to find fault with his own and to praise the olden times; for in their past there are many things worthy of the highest admiration, whilst the present has nothing that compensates for all the extreme misery, infamy, and degradation of a period where there is neither observance of religion, law, or military discipline, and which is stained by every species of the lowest brutality; and these vices are the more detestable as they exist amongst those who sit in the tribunals as judges, and hold all power in their hands, and claim to be adored.

But to return to our argument, I say that, if men's judgment is at fault upon the point whether the present age be better than the past, of which latter, owing to its antiquity, they cannot have such perfect knowledge as of their own period, the judgment of old men of what they have seen in their youth and in their old age should not be false, inasmuch as they have equally seen both the one and the other. This would be true, if men at the different periods of their lives had the same judgment and the same appetites. But as these vary (though the times do not), things cannot appear the same to men who have other tastes, other delights, and other considerations in age from what they had in youth. For as men when they age lose their strength and energy, whilst their prudence and judgment improve, so the same things that in youth appeared to them supportable and good, will of necessity, when they have grown old, seem to them insupportable and evil; and when they should blame their own judgment they find fault with the times. Moreover, as human desires are insatiable, (because their nature is to have and to do everything whilst fortune limits their possessions and capacity of enjoyment,) this gives rise to a constant discontent in the human mind and a weariness of the things they possess; and it is this which makes them decry the present, praise the past, and desire the future, and all this without any reasonable motive. I know not, then, whether I deserve to be classed with those who deceive themselves, if in these Discourses I shall laud too much the times of ancient Rome and censure those of our own day. And truly, if the virtues that ruled then and the vices that prevail now were not as clear as the sun, I should be more reticent in my expressions, lest I should fall into the very error for which I reproach others. But the matter being so manifest that everybody sees it, I shall boldly and openly say what I think of the former times and of the present, so as to excite in the minds of the young men who may read my writings the desire to avoid the evils of the latter, and to prepare themselves to imitate the virtues of the former, whenever fortune presents them the occasion. For it is the duty of an honest man to teach others that good which the malignity of the times and of fortune has prevented his doing himself; so that amongst the many capable ones who he has instructed some one perhaps, more favored by Heaven, may perform it. . . .

Wise men say, and not without reason, that whoever wishes to foresee the future must consult the past; for human events ever resemble those of preceding times. This arises from the fact that they are produced by men who have been, and ever will be, animated by the same passions, and thus they must necessarily have the same results. It is true that men are more or less virtuous in one country or another, according to the nature of the education by which their manners and habits of life have been formed. It also facilitates a judgment of the future by the past, to observe nations preserve for a long time the same character; ever exhibiting the same disposition to avarice, or bad faith, or to some other special vice or virtue. Whoever reads attentively the history of our city of Florence, and observes the events of our more immediate times, will find that the Germans and the French are full of avarice, pride, cruelty, and bad faith, from which evil qualities our city has suffered greatly at various times. As to the want of good faith, everybody knows how often the Florentines have paid money to King Charles VIII, upon his promising to restore to them the citadel of Pisa; which promises, however, he never fulfilled, thereby exhibiting his want of good faith and his greed of money. Let us come, however, to more recent events.

> 74. FRANCESCO GUICCIARDINI (1483–1540) shared many of the premises and prejudices as well as the political experiences of his older contemporary Machiavelli and, like him, made it his business to understand the sources of the Italian calamity of 1494, first in his youthful history of Florence but then more directly in his masterly *History of Italy,* which started just where Machiavelli's history ended, with the background to the French invasions of 1494. In a style more Thucydidean than Livian and with massive detail and impressive psychological insight, Guicciardini analyzed the causes of this conjuncture of events and the manifold repercussions, aiming not (like Machiavelli) at a systematic political science but, as suggested by the scattered reflections and aphorisms gathered in his *Ricordi,* at practical understanding and policy and at understanding, retrospectively, the causes of Florentine collapse.

Francesco Guicciardini, *Maxims and Reflections of a Renaissance Statesman (Ricordi).* Trans. Mario Domandi. New York: Harper Torchbooks, 1965. Pp. 59, 70, 71, and 123.

If you observe well, you will see that, from one age to another, there is a change not only in men's speech, vocabulary, dress, style of building, culture, and such things, but, what is more, even in their sense of taste. A food that was highly prized in one age will often be found far less appetizing in another. . . .

Some men write discourses on the future, basing themselves on current events. And if they are informed men, their writings will seem very plausible to the readers. Nevertheless, they are completely misleading. For since one conclusion depends upon the other, if one is wrong, all that are deduced from it will be mistaken. But every tiny, particular circumstance that changes is apt to alter a conclusion. The affairs of this world, therefore, cannot be judged from afar but must be judged and resolved day by day. . . .

To judge by example is very misleading. Unless they are similar in every respect, examples are useless, since every tiny difference in the cause may be a cause of great variations in the effects. And to discern these tiny differences takes a good and perspicacious eye. . . .

Documents are rarely falsified at the start. It is usually done later, as occasion or necessity dictates. To protect yourself, it is a good idea to have an authentic copy made immediately after the instrument or document is drawn up, and to keep it close by. . . .

Past events shed light on the future. For the world has always been the same, and everything that is and will be, once was; and the same things recur, but with different names and colors. And for that reason, not everyone recognizes them—only those who are wise, and observe and consider them diligently.

¶ I have decided to write about the events which have taken place in Italy within living memory since the time when French armies called in by our own princes began to trouble her peace with great upheavals. A very rich theme for its variety and extent, and full of appalling disasters, for Italy has suffered for many years every kind of calamity that may vex wretched mortals either through the just wrath of God or through the impious and wicked actions of their fellow men. From the understand-

Francesco Guicciardini, *History of Italy.* In *Guicciardini: History of Italy and History of Florence,* trans. Cecil Grayson and ed. John R. Hale. New York: Washington Square, 1964. Pp. 85–86, 89, and 145–146. Reprinted by permission of Pocket Books, a division of Simon and Schuster.

ing of these events, so diverse and grave, all men will be able to draw many useful lessons both for themselves and for the public good. It will appear from countless examples how unstable are human affairs—like a sea driven by the winds; how pernicious, nearly always to themselves but invariably to the common people, are the ill-judged actions of rulers when they pursue only vain error or present greed. And forgetting how often fortune changes, and converting to other peoples' harm the power vested in them for the public good, they become through lack of prudence or excess of ambition the authors of fresh upheavals.

The calamities of Italy began (and I say this so that I may make known what was her condition before, and the causes from which so many evils arose), to the greater sorrow and terror of all men, at a time when circumstances seemed universally most propitious and fortunate. It is indisputable that since the Roman Empire, weakened largely by the decay of her ancient customs, began to decline more than a thousand years ago from that greatness to which it had risen with marvelous virtue and good fortune, Italy had never known such prosperity or such a desirable condition as that which it enjoyed in all tranquility in the year of Our Lord 1490 and the years immediately before and after. For, all at peace and quietness, cultivated no less in the mountainous and sterile places than in the fertile regions and plains, knowing no other rule than that of its own people, Italy was not only rich in population, merchandise and wealth, but she was adorned to the highest degree by the magnificence of many princes, by the splendor of innumerable noble and beautiful cities, by the throne and majesty of religion; full of men most able in the administration of public affairs, and of noble minds learned in every branch of study and versed in every worthy art and skill. Nor did she lack military glory according to the standards of those times; and being so richly endowed, she deservedly enjoyed among all other nations a most brilliant reputation.

Italy was preserved in this happy state, which had been attained through a variety of causes, by a number of circumstances, but among these by common consent no little credit was due to the industry and virtue of Lorenzo de' Medici, a citizen so far above the rank of private citizen in Florence that all the affairs of the Republic were decided by his advice. Florence was at that time powerful by virtue of her geographical position, the intelligence of her people and the readiness of her wealth rather than for the extent of her dominion. . . .

Such was the state of things, such the foundation of the peace of Italy, so arranged and juxtaposed that not only was there no fear of any present disorder but it was difficult to imagine how, by what plots, incidents or forces, such tranquility might be destroyed. Then, in the month of April 1492 there occurred the death of Lorenzo de' Medici. It was bitter for him, because he was not quite forty-four years of age, and bitter for his republic, which, because of his prudence, reputation and intellect in everything honorable and excellent, flourished marvelously with riches and all those ornaments and advantages with which a long peace is usually accompanied. But it was also a most untimely death for the rest of Italy, both because of the work he constantly did for the common safety and because he was the means by which the disagreements and suspicions that frequently arose between Ferdinand and Lodovico—two princes almost equal in power and ambition—were moderated and held in check.

The death of Lorenzo was followed a few months later by that of the Pope, as day by day things moved toward the coming disaster. . . .

Now not only the preparations made by land and sea, but the heavens and mankind joined in proclaiming the future calamities of Italy. Those who profess to know the future either by science or by divine inspiration affirmed with one voice that greater and more frequent changes were at hand—events stranger and more horrible than had been seen in any part of the world for many centuries. Men were no less terrified by the widespread news that unnatural things in heaven and earth had appeared in various parts of Italy. One night in Puglia three suns stood in an overcast sky with horrible thunder and lightning. In the Arezzo district a vast number of armed men on enormous horses were seen passing through the air day after day with a hideous noise of drums and trumpets. In many places in Italy the sacred statues and images sweated visibly. Everywhere many monsters were born, both human and animal; and many other things outside the order of nature had happened in all kinds of places. All these filled the people of Italy with unspeakable fear, frightened as they were already by the rumors of the power of the French and the ferocity with which (as all the histories related) they had in the past overrun and despoiled the whole of Italy, sacked and put to fire and sword the city of Rome and conquered many provinces in Asia; indeed there was no part of the world that had not at some time felt the force of their arms. Men were only surprised that among so many portents there should not have been seen the comet which the ancients reputed a certain harbinger of the downfall of rulers and states.

The approach of realities daily increased belief in heavenly signs, predictions, prognostications and portents. For Charles, firm in his resolve,
now came to Vienne in the Dauphine. He could not be moved from his
decision to invade Italy in person either by the entreaties of all his subjects or by lack of money, which was so scarce that he was only able to
provide for his daily needs by pawning for a small sum certain jewels
loaned to him by the Duke of Savoy, the Marchioness of Monferrat and
other nobles of his court. The money he had earlier collected from the
revenues of France, and that which had been given him by Lodovico
Svorza, he had spent partly on the navy in which from the start great
hopes of victory were placed, and part he had handed out thoughtlessly
to a variety of persons before he left Lyons. As at that time princes were
not so quick to extort money from their peoples as—riding roughshod
over respect for God and men—they were later taught by avarice and
excessive greed to do, it was not easy for him to accumulate any more.
On so weak a basis was it proposed to mount so vast a war! For he was
guided more by rashness and impetuousness than by prudence and good
counsel.

❡ In the first Discourse the distinction he makes that all cities have been
built either by foreigners or by the natives of the place is right. Athens
and Venice fall into this second category, Rome too, but in a different
way, because they were built by local people needing a place of safety or
a common government. Rome, however, without any of these requirements was built rather as an Alban colony, that is, by men either Albans
or subjects under Alban rule, for love of those places where they had been
brought up or out of ambition for self-rule. Nor can Rome, because of
Aeneas, be counted with the foreign-built, because that would be seeking its origins too far back, which should not be traced to the earliest
ancestors of the builders.

As for those cities built by foreigners, it is not entirely true that
colonies sent out to relieve nations of some of the burden of population
always remain dependencies, because many nations, such as the Gauls,
Cimbrians, etc., for that reason sent out part of their peoples to make

Francesco Guicciardini, *Considerations on the "Discourses" of Machiavelli on the First Decade of T. Livy.* In *Francesco Guicciardini: Selected Writings,* ed. Cecil Grayson and trans. Margaret Grayson. London: Oxford University Press, 1965. Pp. 60–62.

new settlements which did not depend on or recognize the authority of their homeland in any way. Hence it is a truer and fuller distinction to say that those cities built by foreigners are either set up to exercise self-rule and be quite independent of their origins or are so constituted that they must accept their rule. In the second type it is true that they cannot make great strides from the beginning, but as time goes on, many events may occur to free them from their subjection, and then it may happen that their power increases remarkably. Florence was of this nature, and all the Roman colonies, for since the decline of Rome many of them have become splendid and powerful cities. Possibly if one took them individually it would be found that no fewer colonial cities had risen to notable heights than those with free beginnings. They have grown, or not, according to their site, their constitution, or the fortunes they encountered. It is true that ordinarily the latter have been slower to grow, as they began as subjects of others, but if, meanwhile, through the advantages of their site, a good constitution, or for some other reason, they have been able to expand in wealth and population, later on they have found it easy to become powerful.

The principal basis of the power and riches of cities is a large population, and it is not easy for a city in infertile country to increase its population unless, like Florence, it enjoys a productive climate or, like Venice, it enjoys the resources of the sea. Hence it is better to found the city in a fertile land for inhabitants are more readily drawn there. But if it were possible to collect a large population in a place, not of course absolutely infertile, but not very rich, there is no doubt that the need to obtain supplies would contribute more to its strength than wise laws could, for laws may be changed by men's will, while necessity is an everpresent law and stimulus. This set Rome on the right path, for, although placed in fertile country, yet having no lands of her own and surrounded by powerful states, she was forced to expand both by force of arms and through peaceful relations. This is true, not perhaps for a city wishing to live ideally, but for those wishing to rule according to the common usage of the world, as they must; otherwise, being weak, they would be crushed and oppressed by their neighbors.

75. THOMAS HOBBES (1588–1679) combined his classical training and his interest in politics for the first time in his transla-

Thomas Hobbes, *The History of the Grecian War, Written by Thucydides.* London, 1843. 1:vi–x, xiv–xv, xvi–xviii, xx–xxii, xxiv, xxv–xxvi, xxx, and xxxi–xxxii.

tion of Thucydides (1628), in which he proposed to show the value
of history and a means of understanding the causes of political
decline and in particular the dangers of democracy.

It hath been noted by divers, that Homer in poesy, Aristotle in philosophy, Demosthenes in eloquence, and others of the ancients in other
knowledge, do still maintain their primacy: none of them exceeded,
some not approached, by any in these later ages. And in the number of
these is justly ranked also our Thucydides; a workman no less perfect in
his work, than any of the former; and in whom (I believe with many
others) the faculty of writing history is at the highest. For the principal
and proper work of history being to instruct and enable men, by the
knowledge of actions past, to bear themselves prudently in the present
and providently towards the future: there is not extant any other (merely
human) that doth more naturally and fully perform it, than this of my
author. It is true, that there be many excellent and profitable histories
written since: and in some of them there be inserted very wise discourses, both of manners and policy. But being discourses inserted, and
not of the contexture of the narration, they indeed commend the knowledge of the writer, but not the history itself: the nature whereof is merely
narrative. In others, there be subtle conjectures at the secret aims and
inward cogitations of such as fall under their pen; which is also none of
the least virtues in a history, where conjecture is thoroughly grounded,
not forced to serve the purpose of the writer in adorning his style, or
manifesting his subtlety in conjecturing. But these conjectures cannot
often be certain, unless withal so evident, that the narration itself may be
sufficient to suggest the same also to the reader. But Thucydides is one,
who, though he never digress to read a lecture, moral or political, upon
his own text, nor enter into men's hearts further than the acts themselves
evidently guide him: is yet accounted the most politic historiographer
that ever writ. The reason whereof I take to be this. He filleth his narrations with that choice of matter, and ordereth them with that judgment,
and with such perspicuity and efficacy expresseth himself, that, as Plutarch saith, he maketh his auditor a spectator. For he setteth his reader in
the assemblies of the people and in the senate, at their debating; in the
streets, at their seditions; and in the field, at their battles. So that look
how much a man of understanding might have added to his experience,
if he had then lived a beholder of their proceedings, and familiar with
the men and business of the time: so much almost may he profit now, by
attentive reading of the same here written. He may from the narrations

draw out lessons to himself, and of himself be able to trace the drifts and counsels of the actors to their seat.

These virtues of my author did so take my affection, that they begat in me a desire to communicate him further: which was the first occasion that moved me to translate him. For it is an error we easily fall into, to believe that whatsoever pleaseth us, will be in like manner and degree acceptable to all: and to esteem of one another's judgment, as we agree in the liking or dislike of the same things. And in this error peradventure was I, when I thought, that as many of the more judicious as I should communicate him to, would affect him as much as I myself did. I considered also, that he was exceedingly esteemed of the Italians and French in their own tongues: notwithstanding that he be not very much beholden for it to his interpreters. Of whom (to speak no more than becomes a candidate of your good opinion in the same kind) I may say this: that whereas the author himself so carrieth with him his own light throughout, that the reader may continually see his way before him, and by that which goeth before expect what is to follow; I found it not so in them. The cause whereof, and their excuse, may be this: they followed the Latin of Laurentius Valla, which was not without some errors: and he a Greek copy not so correct as now is extant. Out of French he was done into English (for I need not dissemble to have seen him in English) in the time of King Edward the Sixth; but so, as by multiplication of error he became at length traduced, rather than translated into our language. Hereupon I resolved to take him immediately from the Greek, according to the edition of Aemilius Porta: not refusing or neglecting any version, comment, or other help I could come by. Knowing that when with diligence and leisure I should have done it, though some error might remain, yet they would be errors but of one descent; of which nevertheless I can discover none, and hope they be not many. After I had finished it, it lay long by me: and other reasons taking place, my desire to communicate it ceased.

For I saw that, for the greatest part, men came to the reading of history with an affection much like that of the people in Rome: who came to the spectacle of the gladiators with more delight to behold their blood, than their skill in fencing. For they be far more in number, that love to read of great armies, bloody battles, and many thousands slain at once, than that mind the art by which the affairs both of armies and cities be conducted to their ends. I observed likewise, that there were not many whose ears were well accustomed to the names of the places they shall meet with in this history; without the knowledge whereof it can neither patiently be read over, perfectly understood, nor easily remembered: especially being many, as here it falleth out. Because in that age almost every city both in Greece and Sicily, the two main scenes of this war, was a distinct commonwealth by itself, and a party in the quarrel. . . .

Agreeable to Thucydides' nobility, was his institution in the study of eloquence and philosophy. For in philosophy, he was the scholar (as also was Pericles and Socrates) of Anazagoras; whose opinions, being of a strain above the apprehension of the vulgar, procured him the estimation of an atheist: which name they bestowed upon all men that thought not as they did of their ridiculous religion, and in the end cost him his life. And Socrates after him for the like causes underwent the like fortune. It is not therefore much to be regarded, if this other disciple of his were by some reputed an atheist too. For though he were none, yet it is not improbable, but by the light of natural reason he might see enough in the religion of these heathen, to make him think it vain and superstitious; which was enough to make him an atheist in the opinion of the people. In some places of his history he noteth the equivocation of the oracles; and yet he confirmeth an assertion of his own, touching the time this war lasted, by the oracle's prediction. He taxeth Nicias for being too punctual in the observation of the ceremonies of their religion, when he overthrew himself and his army, and indeed the whole dominion and liberty of his country, by it. Yet he commendeth him in another place for his worshipping of the gods, and saith in that respect, he least of all men deserved to come to so great a degree of calamity as he did. So that in his writings our author appeareth to be, on the one side not superstitious, on the other side not an atheist.

In rhetoric, he was the disciple of Antiphon; one (by his description in the eighth book of this history) for power of speech almost a miracle, and feared by the people for his eloquence. Insomuch as in his latter days he lived retired, but so as he gave counsel to, and writ orations for other men that resorted to him to that purpose. It was he that contrived the deposing of the people, and the setting up of the government of THE FOUR HUNDRED. For which also he was put to death, when the people again recovered their authority, notwithstanding that he pleaded his own cause the best of any man to that day. . . .

For his opinion touching the government of the state, it is manifest that he least of all liked the democracy. And upon divers occasions he noteth the emulation and contention of the demagogues for reputation and glory of wit; with their crossing of each other's counsels, to the damage of the public; the inconsistency of resolutions, caused by the diversity of ends and power of rhetoric in the orators; and the desperate actions undertaken upon the flattering advice of such as desired to attain, or to hold what they had attained, of authority and sway amongst the common people. Nor doth it appear that he magnifieth anywhere the authority of the few: amongst whom, he saith, every one desireth to be the chief; and they that are undervalued, bear it with less patience than in a democracy; whereupon sedition followeth, and dissolution of the government. He praiseth the government of Athens, when it was mixed of the few and the many; but more he commendeth it, both when Peisistratus reigned, (saving that it was an usurped power), and when in the beginning of this war it was democratical in name, but in effect monarchical under Pericles. So that it seemeth, that as he was of regal descent, so he best approved of the regal government. . . .

How he was disposed to a work of this nature, may be understood by this: that when being a young man he heard Herodotus the historiographer reciting his history in public, (for such was the fashion both of that, and many ages after), he felt so great a sting of emulation, that it drew tears from him: insomuch as Herodotus himself took notice how violently his mind was set on letters, and told his father Olorus. When the Peloponnesian war began to break out, he conjectured truly that it would prove an argument worthy of his labour; and no sooner it began, than he began his history; pursuing the same not in that perfect manner in which we see it now, but by way of commentary or plain register of the actions and passages thereof, as from time to time they fell out and came to his knowledge. But such a commentary it was, as might perhaps deserve to be preferred before a history written by another. For it is very probable that the eighth book is left the same as it was when he first writ it: neither beautified with orations, nor so well cemented at the transitions, as the former seven books are. And though he began to write as soon as ever the war was on foot; yet began he not to perfect and polish his history, till after he was banished. . . .

Now for his writings, two things are to be considered in them: truth and elocution. For in truth consisteth the soul, and in elocution the body of history. The latter without the former, is but a picture of history; and the former without the latter, unapt to instruct. But let us see how our author hath acquitted himself in both. For the faith of this history, I shall have the less to say: in respect that no man hath ever yet called it into question. Nor indeed could any man justly doubt of the truth of that writer, in whom they had nothing at all to suspect of those things that could have caused him either voluntarily to lie, or ignorantly to deliver an untruth. He overtasked not himself by undertaking an history of things done long before his time, and of which he was not able to inform himself. He was a man that had as much means, in regard both of this dignity and wealth, to find the truth of what he relateth, as was needful for a man to have. He used as much diligence in search of the truth, (noting every thing wilst it was fresh in memory, and laying out his wealth upon intelligence), as was possible for a man to use. He affected least of any man the acclamations of popular auditories, and wrote not his history to win present applause, as was the use of that age: but for a monument to instruct the ages to come; which he professeth himself, and entitleth his book a possession for everlasting. He was far from the necessity of servile writers, either to fear or flatter. And whereas he may peradventure be thought to have been malevolent towards his country, because they deserved to have him so; yet hath he not written any thing that discovereth such passion. Nor is there any thing written of them that tendeth to their dishonour as Athenians, but only as people; and that by the necessity of the narration, not by any sought digression. So that no word of his, but their own actions do sometimes reproach them. In sum, if the truth of a history did ever appear by the manner of relating, it doth so in this history: so coherent, perspicuous and per-suasive is the whole narration, and every part thereof.

In the elocution also, two things are considerable: disposition or method, and style. Of the disposition here used by Thucydides, it will be sufficient in this place briefly to observe only this: that in his first book, first he hath, by ways of exordium, derived the state of Greece from the cradle to the vigorous statue it then was at when he began to write: and next, declared the causes, both real and pretended, of the war itself, he followeth distinctly and purely the order of time throughout; relating what came to pass from year to year, and subdividing each year into a summer and winter. The grounds and motives of every action he setteth down before the action itself, either narratively, or else con-triveth them into the form of deliberative orations in the persons of such as from time to time bare sway in the commonwealth. After the actions, when there is just occasion, he giveth his judgment of them; shewing by what means the success came either to be furthered or hindered. Digressions for instruction's cause, and other such open conveyances of precepts, (which is the philosopher's part), he never useth; as having so clearly set before men's eyes the ways and events of good and evil councils, that the narration itself doth secretly instruct the reader, and more effectually than can possibly be done by precept.

For his style, I refer it to the judgment of divers ancience and competent judges. Plutarch in his book, De gloria Atheniensium, saith of him thus: "Thucydides aimeth always at this; to make his auditor a spectator, and to cast his reader into the same passions that they were in that were beholders. . . ."

Herodotus undertook to write of those things, of which it was impossible for him to know the truth; and which delight more the ear with fabulous narrations, than satisfy the mind with truth: but Thucydides writeth one war; which, how it was carried from the beginning to the end, he was able certainly to inform himself: and by propounding in his proeme the miseries that happened in the same, he sheweth that it was a great war, and worthy to be known; and not to be concealed from posterity, for the calamities that then fell upon the Grecians; but the rather to be truly delivered unto them, for that men profit more by looking on adverse events, than on prosperity: therefore by how much men's miseries do better instruct, than their good success; by so much was Thucydides more happy in taking his argument, than Herodotus was wise in choosing his. . . .

To this [objection of Dionysius of Halicarnassus about Thucydides' neglect of an earlier event] I say, that it was the duty of him that had undertaken to write the history of the Peloponnesian war, to begin his narration no further off than at the causes of the same, whether the Grecians were then in good or in evil estate. And if the injury, upon which the war arose, proceeded from the Athenians; then the writer, though an Athenian and honoured in his country, ought to declare the same; and not to seek nor take, though at hand, any other occasion to transfer the fault. And that the acts done before the time comprehended in the war he writ of, ought to have been touched but cursorily, and no more than may serve for the enlightening of the history to follow, how noble soever those acts have been. Which when he had thus touched, without affection to either side, and not as a lover of his country but of truth; then to have proceeded to the rest with the like indifferency. And to have made an end of writing, where the war ended, which he undertook to write; not producing his history beyond that period, though that which followed were never so admirable and acceptable. All this Thucydides hath observed.

These two criminations I have therefore set down at large, translated almost verbatim, that the judgment of Dionysius Halicarnassius may the better appear concerning the main and principal virtues of a history. I think there was never written so much absurdity in so few lines. He is contrary to the opinion of all men that ever spake of this subject besides himself, and to common sense. For he makes the scope of history, not profit by writing truth, but delight of the hearer, as if it were a song. And the argument of history, he would not by any means have to contain the calamities and misery of his country; these he would have buried in silence: but only their glorious and splendid actions. Amongst the virtues of an historiographer, he reckons affection to his country; study to please the hearer; to write of more than his argument leads him to; and to conceal all actions that were not to the honour of his country. Most manifest vices. He was a rhetorician; and it seemeth he would have nothing written, but that which was most capable of rhetorical ornament. Yet Lucian, a rhetorician also, in a treatise entitled, How a history ought to be written, saith thus: "that a writer of history ought, in his writings, to be a foreigner, without country, living under his own law, subject to no king, nor caring what any man will like or dislike, but laying out the matter as it is. . . ."

Some man may peradventure desire to know, what motive Dionysius might have to extenuate the worth of him, whom he himself acknowledgeth to have been esteemed by all men for the best by far of all historians that ever wrote, and to have been taken by all the ancient orators and philosophers for the measure and rule of writing history. What motive he had to do it, I know not: but what glory he might expect by it, is easily known. For having first preferred Herodotus, his countryman, a Halicarnassian, before Thucydides, who was accounted the best; and then conceiving that his own history might perhaps be thought not inferior to that of Herodotus; by this computation he saw the honour of the best historiographer falling on himself. Wherein, in the opinion of all men, he hath misreckoned. And thus much for the objections of Denis of Halicarnasse. . . .

Lastly, hear the most true and proper commendation of him from Justus Lipsius, in his notes to his book *De Doctrina Civili* in these words: "Thucydides, who hath written not many nor very great matters, hath perhaps yet won the garland from all that have written of matters both many and great. Everywhere for elocution grave; short, and thick with sense; sound in his judgments; everywhere secretly instructing and directing a man's life and actions. In his orations and excursions, almost divine. Whom the oftener you read, the more you shall carry away; yet never be dismissed without appetite. Next to him is Polybius, &c."

And thus much concerning the life and history of Thucydides.

7
ℱ The Reformation

The Reformation, partly reinforced by the Renaissance sense of history and partly in reaction to it, powerfully shaped the European conception of history. On the one hand, evangelical reformers, following the Renaissance humanists wanted to go back to the pure sources of Christian doctrine and practice, the "primitive" and patristic periods of church history; on the other hand, they rejected the pagan implications of classicism and any notion that the "Romanists" retained ancient virtues of any sort. Like their Conciliarist predecessors (such as Henry of Langenstein), they wanted reformation in the sense of a Christian canon purged of the degenerate "human traditions" accumulated above all by the papal monarchy, its canon law, and accompanying "idolatry"; they rewrote the history of the church as a tragedy of progressive degeneration from the imitation of Christ. Martin Luther, Martin Bucer, Jean Calvin, John Foxe, and other Protestants recognized the practical, especially moral and political, virtues of human history, but their larger goal was to construct a new perspective on the European past—a perspective which stressed spiritual above institutional values and continuity and which forged links, doctrinal as well as martyrological, between sixteenth-century reform, late medieval heresy, and prophetic visions of future judgment.

The ideological conflicts accompanying the wars of religion that arose from the politicization of Protestantism gave further impetus to secular history and to the reevaluation of particular national traditions, while the study and writing of history was increasingly conscripted into political as well as confessional causes. Scholars developed national history in a Livian and Brunian mode and accommodated it to the age of religious strife. They also adapted both medieval traditions of universal history and humanist reconstructions of antiquity to the modern—and the "new"—world.

During the Reformation and its aftermath, in short, the Renaissance sense of history was wedded to the search for ideologically useful pasts. Hired historiographers—sixteenth-century equivalents of court historians—served not only cities and national states but also confessional parties. Most notable among these historiographers were Johann Sleidan, author of the first authoritative history of the Reformation, and (less officially) François Hotman, who rewrote the history of France in a Huguenot perspective. In the following century Clarendon produced a royalist version of the history of the English civil war. The study both of contemporary history (especially the compendious work of Jacques-Auguste de Thou) and of the medieval past (illustrated by the pioneering investigations of John Leland and William Camden) was reinforced by Reformation issues. In general, religious, political, and national partisanship not only distorted but in fundamental ways also intensified the humanist drive to reconstruct the political, social, and cultural past of European civilization.

❡ TRADITION RESTORED

76. HENRY OF LANGENSTEIN (d. 1397), a German master at the University of Paris, wrote his "Letter on Behalf of a Council of Peace" as a plan to end the Great Schism (1378–1417). Following the arguments of William of Ockham and Marsilius of Padua, he defended the Conciliarist idea which elevated the ecumenical council of the church above the pope (or popes, as there were two claimants at the time) and justified his arguments by invoking precedent and ecclesiastical tradition, thus illustrating the significance of history in religious and political controversy.

Henry of Langenstein, *A Letter on Behalf of a Council of Peace*. In *Advocates of Reform: From Wyclif to Erasmus* (Volume 14: The Library of Christian Classics), ed. Matthew Spinka. Pp. 106–107 and 110. First published 1953, published simultaneously in Great Britain and the United States of America by the S.C.M. Press, and The Westminster Press. Used by permission of Westminster / John Knox Press.

1. The Sins of the People are the Cause of the Schism

. . . The devil has raised himself up; virtue has been outlawed, vice has taken its place; the malice of succeeding generations has rendered the straight paths of the fathers crooked; and the decrees of the Church have been violated. It has become the custom for the Church to be built on blood relations and the sanctuary of God maintained as if it were a family possession. Hence the flock of the Lord is today deprived of its shepherd; the patrimony of the Church is consumed in vainglorious ostentation; and the temples for the worship of God lie open and in ruins. The unworthy are raised high with dignities. The ministers of the Church seek after the things of the world, despise the things of the spirit, set their minds on the laws of the world and upon the fomenting of lawsuits, and are not mighty in the Word of God to kindle men's souls.

What more? The regulations of spiritually minded men of former times, most worthy of [our] observation, are by the negligence of their successors overthrown. To them the antiquity of the fathers, out of harmony with the works of darkness, has been displeasing, while the novelty of their own inventions, vying with the law of God, has given them pleasure. . . .

4. The Solution of these Disagreements Must Be Undertaken by a General Council

. . . Now, of this schismatic iniquity, which is hindering the action of divine grace by its venomous seed, I believe an end can be made by three ways that are open to men. The first is this: that anyone who is conscious of being a party to the above-mentioned crimes take it to heart and through penance reconcile himself to God. The second: that it be arranged throughout the circle of the Universal Church to make continual supplication for divine mercy publicly in fasting, weeping, and prayer. The third: that when these preparations have been carried out for the bestowal of the grace of the Holy Spirit, a general council be called in the name of Jesus Christ to purge his Church from the iniquities and various excesses, all too common at this time, and, after these causes have been removed, to tear up from the very roots the present division in the city of God which this befouling and monstrous schism has brought forth.

Here is a way of peace, a way oft trodden by our fathers before us, a way of salvation. The record of past events, which is the teacher of modern men, ought surely to move Christian kings and princes to undertake with the greatest enthusiasm this way which is pleasing to God and demand its execution without delay. History informs us that formerly, through the devotion, patronage, and encouragement of kings, in past emergencies of the Church provincial and general synods of bishops were in the providence of God frequently called and that they faithfully submitted themselves and their lawsuits, as well as the correction and emendation of their laws, to the holy judgment of their councils. This is evident from a wide consideration of the proceedings of the councils which have been recorded.

> 77. MARTIN LUTHER (1483–1546) developed a conception of history to suit and to legitimize his critical view of the earthly life of the church. Although he took a conventional view of the human values of historical study, his concern was mainly for the spiritual tradition of Christianity culminating in his own program of reformation. From Luther's evangelical perspective, the Roman papacy followed a trajectory of decline from the purity of the primitive church to the corruption of the contemporary papal monarchy— antichrist incarnate—and the degenerate human traditions embodied in the canon law (which he ceremoniously burned as well as attacked in print). He contrasted this with his larger vision of the spiritual continuity established by the pure word of God and its witnesses. Although claiming to preserve the literal and historical sense of Scriptures, Luther also sought the life-giving spirit in his translations of the Bible.

The renowned Roman Varro says that the very best way to teach is to add an example or illustration to the word, for they help one both to understand more clearly and to remember more easily. Otherwise, if the discourse is heard without an example, no matter how suitable and excellent it may be, it does not move the heart as much, and is also not so clear and easily retained. Histories are, therefore, a very precious thing. For what the philosophers, wise men, and all men of reason can teach or devise which can be useful for an honorable life, that the histories present powerfully with examples and happenings making them visually so real, as though one were there and saw everything happen that the

Martin Luther, *Preface to Galeatius Capella's History*. In *Career of the Reformer*, ed. and trans. Lewis Spitz. Volume 34 of *Luther's Works*, ed. J. Pelikan and H. Lehmann. Philadelphia: Fortress Press, 1955–1986. Pp. 275–278.

word had previously conveyed to the ears by mere teaching. There one finds both how those who were pious and wise acted, refrained from acting, and lived, how they fared and how they were rewarded, as well as how those who were wicked and foolish and how they were repaid for it.

Upon thorough reflection one finds that almost all laws, art, good counsel, warning, threatening, terrifying, comforting, strengthening, instruction, prudence, wisdom, discretion, and all virtues well up out of the narratives and histories as from a living fountain. It all adds up to this: histories are nothing else than a demonstration, recollection, and sign of divine action and judgment, how He upholds, rules, obstructs, prospers, punishes, and honors the world, and especially men, each according to his just desert, evil or good. And although there are many who do not acknowledge God or esteem him, they must nevertheless come up against the examples and histories and be afraid lest they fare like those individuals whom the histories portray. They are more deeply moved by this than if one were simply to restrain and control them with mere words of the law or instruction. Thus we read not only in the Holy Scriptures, but also in the books of pagans how they cited as witnesses and held up the examples, words, and deeds of forebears when they wanted to carry a point with the people or when they intended to teach, admonish, warn, or deter.

The historians, therefore, are the most useful people and the best teachers, so that one can never honor, praise, and thank them enough. That may very well be a work of great lords, as the emperor, king, etc., who in their time deliberately had histories written and securely preserved in the libraries. Nor did they spare any cost necessary for supporting and educating such people as were qualified for writing histories. One can see especially in the books of Judges, Kings, and Chronicles that among the Jewish people such masters were appointed and retained. That was also the case among the kings of Persia who had such libraries in Media, as one can gather from the book of Ezra and Nehemiah [Ezra 6:2]. Nowadays the princes and lords must have their chancelleries for this purpose in which they preserve and file their affairs, both new and old. How much more should one have a history of the whole period of their rule drawn up about all or at least about the most important matters and leave it for posterity.

What should we Germans bewail more than that we do not have the history and example of our ancestors beyond a thousand years and know scarcely anything about our origin, except what we must use from histories of other nations, which perhaps must make mention of us out of necessity rather than to their honor? For since God's work goes on continuously, as Christ says, "My Father is working still, and I am working" [John 5 : 17], it cannot fail that in every age something noteworthy should have happened, that one should rightly take note of. And although not everything can be collected, at least the most important events would be concisely preserved, as some intended to do who composed songs about Dietrich von Bern and other giants and in so doing represented many very important matters concisely and plainly.

But that requires a first-rate man who has a lion's heart, unafraid to write the truth. For the greater number write in such a way that they readily pass over or put the best construction on the vices and deficiencies of their own times in the interest of their lords or friends and in turn glorify all too highly some trifling or vain virtue. On the other hand, they embellish or besmirch histories to the advantage of their fatherland and disadvantage of the foreigners, according to whether they love or hate someone. In that way histories become extremely unreliable and God's work is shamefully obscured, as the Greeks are accused of doing and as the pope's flatterers have done up to now and still do. In the end it comes down to this: that one does not know what one should believe. Thus the noble, fine, and loftiest use of histories is ruined and they become nothing but bearers of gossip. Consequently, such an important work as writing histories is open to everyone. He then writes and ignores, praises, and decries whatever he likes.

This profession should, therefore, be used by prominent people or at least by those men who are called to it. For since histories describe nothing else than God's work, that is, grace and wrath, it is only right that one should believe them, as though they were in the Bible. They should therefore indeed be written with the very greatest diligence, honesty, and truthfulness. But I am very well aware that this will not happen at present, unless that order returned which existed among the Jews. Meanwhile we must remain satisfied with our historians as they are and now and then reflect for ourselves and judge whether the writer is getting off the right track because of partiality or prejudice, whether he praises and blame too much or too little, according to how he is disposed toward people or things, even as we must tolerate it that under a lax government teamsters along the way adulterate the wine with water, so that one cannot obtain a drink of pure vintage, and we must be satisfied with receiving the better part or something out of it.

But for all that, this historian Galeatius Capella impresses me as though he wishes to represent a genuine writer of history and to set matters forth not with long-winded, unnecessary words, but briefly and thoroughly. It is for all that a subject which ought to be read and remembered. For in it one can indeed also see God's work, how marvelously he rules the children of men and how very wicked the devil is and all his, so that we learn to fear God and seek his counsel and aid in matters both large and small. To him be praise and thanks in all eternity, through our Lord Jesus Christ. Amen.

¶ Here, in Romans 3[:28], I knew very well that the word solum is not in the Greek or Latin text; the papists did not have to teach me that. It is a fact that these four letters s o l a are not there. And these blockheads stare at them like cows at a new gate. At the same time they do not see that it conveys the sense of the text; it belongs there if the translation is to be clear and vigorous. I wanted to speak German, not Latin or Greek, since it was German I had undertaken to speak in the translation. But it is the nature of our German language that in speaking of two things, one of which is affirmed and the other denied, we use the word solum (allein) along with the word nicht [not] or kein [no]. For example, we say "The farmer brings allein grain and kein money"; "No, really I have nicht money, but allein grain"; "I have allein eaten and nicht yet drunk"; "Did you allein write it, and nicht read it over?" There are innumerable cases of this kind in daily use.

In all these phrases, this is the German usage, even though it is not the Latin or Greek usage. It is the nature of the German language to add the word allein in order that the word nicht or kein may be clearer and more complete.

. . . We do not have to inquire of the literal Latin, how we are to speak German, as these asses do. Rather we must inquire about this of the mother in the home, the children on the street, the common man in the marketplace. We must be guided by their language, the way they speak, and do our translating accordingly. That way they will understand it and recognize that we are speaking German to them. . . .

Martin Luther, *On Translating: An Open Letter*. In *Word and Sacrament*, *1*, ed. and trans. E. Theodore Bachmann. Volume 35 of *Luther's Works*, ed. J. Pelikan and H. Lehmann. Philadelphia: Fortress Press, 1955–1986. Pp. 188–189 and 194–195.

Ah, translating is not every man's skill as the mad saints imagine. It requires a right, devout, honest, sincere, God-fearing, Christian, trained, informed, and experienced heart. Therefore I hold that no false Christian or factious spirit can be a decent translator. That becomes obvious in the translation of the Prophets made at Worms. It has been carefully done and approaches my German very closely. But Jews had a hand in it, and they do not show much reverence for Christ. Apart from that there is plenty of skill and craftsmanship there. So much for translating and the nature of the languages!

> 78. MARTIN BUCER (1491–1551), Luther's first major convert, was a magisterial reformer whose ecclesiastical ideas had a profound impact both on Calvin and on English Protestants. His *De regno Christi,* dedicated to the short-lived Protestant hope, King Edward VI, was a systematic expression of the evangelical view of the true church, its history, its organization in this life, and the spiritual tradition on which it claimed to be based.

The Various Periods of the Church

Here it must further be observed that this external glory and happiness are indeed due to the Church and are proper to it, but not at any particular time. For there is a time when our King, to declare his heavenly might in the infirmity of his subjects and to illustrate their faith in him, permits Satan to stir up the entire world against them, and to bring it about that they are hateful to all men for his name's sake (Matt. 10:21–22), and they are handed over to be killed with inhuman cruelty, even a brother by a brother, children by their parents, and parents by their children.

There is likewise a happy time when our King provides for his subjects a surface calm and procures the favor of men, even under the rule of tyrants, as he did in the early Church, as Luke describes in Acts, the second, fourth, and fifth chapters.

Besides this, there is a time in which our King magnificently fulfills the prophecies mentioned about the happiness and glory of the Church as he did under Constantine and the pious emperors who followed him, who adjoined and consecrated both themselves and their wealth and peoples to the Church of Christ insofar as they could.

With what ardor Blessed Constantine was aflame, Eusebius of Pamphilia, in his orations about the life of this prince, and Theodoret, in the first book of his Church History, relate. For Eusebius writes about him in his fourth oration, that he observed all Christian feasts and ceremonies with utmost reverence and was most devoted to saying his prayers; and he inflamed his armies and his court in every way to have the same sort of zeal. For he showed himself an assiduous teacher and preacher to them and always had religious services conducted in his presence even in camp. He bestowed great honors, too, on the priests of the Lord, who were really fit for their office rather than being secular and courtly; when the people of God were on the increase everywhere in the cities, he built temples for sacred assemblies; in all places he wiped out the profession and equipment of idolatry. . . .

. . . Similarly, the holy father and church histories mention very many fine things about the religion and piety of Theodosius, his zeal for the peace of the churches, as well as his kind treatment of them.

Truly in these periods the churches of Christ experienced that abundant kindness of the Lord toward themselves which the prophets had predicted.

. . . However, as even very holy men always sin and it pleases the Lord to test and try the faith of his own by various temptations, so the churches never lack his chastising and proving by heretics or false brethren or worldly men, nor will they ever, while they are here on pilgrimage and away from the Lord (cf. 2 Cor. 5 : 6).

But the most difficult time of the Church, through which it still passes in so many nations, was when it was oppressed for so many centuries in the service of Antichrists, as can be seen in so many kingdoms of Europe today. For since the Lord preserved in these churches some echo of his gospel and Holy Baptism with the invocation of his name, it cannot be doubted that he had and still has many citizens of his Kingdom among them, although these are involved in very many grave errors and labor under a weakness of faith. For the Antichrists, the pseudo-bishops and clergy, following their head, the supreme Roman Antichrist, first horribly corrupted the teaching of the gospel with numerous harmful comments about the merits of the saints and those proper to each, and about the saving power of their ceremonies, things which are obviously impious and which they also conduct impiously. Further-more, they present all this to the people of Christ in an alien tongue, and forbid the reading of the Holy Scripture. Finally, they completely over-turn the sacraments and the discipline of Christ and do everything in their power to prevent them from ever being restored. . . .

Finally, the present time of the Kingdom of Christ is as yet fluctuating and uncertain. For in some places those who exercise public power rage against no criminals more cruelly than against those who belong to the Kingdom of Christ. In other places, those who are in control make concessions to their citizens and permit them to aspire to the Kingdom of Christ. For they allow them the reading of the Holy Scriptures and the preaching of the gospel as long as they are not held responsible for this and as long as they experience no inconvenience.

During the last thirty years there have also been some, especially in Germany, who have seen to it that a right preaching of the gospel was received and who have let it be their primary concern that the religion of Christ be rightly established. On account of this they faced no small dangers. Yet there still can be found only a few who have become entirely subject to Christ's gospel and Kingdom, indeed who have allowed the Christian religion and the discipline of the churches to be restored throughout according to the laws of our King. . . .

. . . And so it has happened that in a great many places the entire doctrine of the Kingdom of Christ has been faithfully announced to the people, but I for one cannot say in what churches it has yet been firmly accepted and Christian discipline publicly constituted.

Therefore, insofar as they have refused to accept the Kingdom of Christ entire as it was offered to them, the Lord has with just judgment remitted them to the tyranny of the Roman Antichrist and the false bishops and subjected them to the trials of many other calamities.

❡ CONFESSIONAL HISTORY

79. JOHANN SLEIDAN (1506–1556) brought to the writing of Protestant history not only the values of humanist scholarship and a commitment to evangelical religion but also the political con-

Johann Sleidan, *History of the Reformation*. In *The General History of the Refor-mation of the Church, Written in Latin by John Sleidan, L.L.D., Faithfully En-glished,* trans. Edmund Bohun. London: Edw. Jones, 1689. Preface.

cerns of Machiavelli and Guicciardini. Sleidan tried to be a loyal subject of the emperor and wrote a survey of the old four monarchies theory to enhance the political claims of the Habsburgs, but his major work was commissioned by the rebellious Schmalkaldic League of Lutheran princes to chronicle their successes and to legitimize their program. Sleidan treated both sacred and profane history in a rich survey of the progress of Lutheranism from 1517 down to his own death, covering social, diplomatic, and military as well as religious affairs; his work was soon translated into many vernacular languages. More than an apologist, Sleidan prided himself on his truthfulness and objectivity and wrote a comprehensive apology in response to many critics who objected to his excessive frankness and lack of partiality.

To the most illustrious Prince Augustus, Elector and Duke of Saxony . . .

Illustrious Sir, divers authors have discovered to us the manifold and various accidents which attend human affairs and the changes in states and kingdoms, and God Himself has been pleased heretofore to instruct us with His own voice as it were to fortell us what should happen of this nature many ages before it came to pass. And as to the first four great empires of the world, He has been pleased by Daniel the prophet to inform us of their order, changes, and successions, the greatest part of whose excellent predictions are now by the event exposed and made very plain to us and afford us a knowledge which is both very sweet and full of consolation. The same holy prophet has also foretold the changes of religion and the contests concerning its doctrine, and the apostle St. Paul, who followed him, has clearly also discovered beforehand many things to that nature. And the accomplishment of these predictions has been delivered down to us and explained by various writers who have lived in the intermediate ages. But that change which has happened in our times is one of the most illustrious events which has come to pass.

The prophet has foretold that the Roman Empire should be the last, and the most powerful, and that it should be divided; and accordingly it is reduced to the lowest degree of weakness, though it was once of an immense bulk and vast extent, so that now it only subsists within the confines of Germany; and its fortunes have been very various and unsteady, partly by reason of its intestine divisions, and partly on the account of foreign combinations against it. Yet after all, God has at last given us the most potent emperor that has reigned in many ages. For in the person of this prince are united the succession of many rich and powerful kingdoms and inheritances, which by reason of their situations have afforded him the opportunity of performing great things, by sea and land, above any other of our princes. And as his power has very much exceeded all the emperors of Germany which have reigned since Charles the Great, so the things which have happened in his time, and under his government, have rendered him the most conspicuous and memorable of all our Princes.

And amongst these, the Reformation of Religion, doth justly challenge the first place which began with his reign. For this controversy had not been moved above fourteen months, when Maximillian the Emperor (his grandfather and immediate predecessor in the Empire) died. And when he was chosen by the seven electors, Luther being at the self same time provoked by his adversaries, entered the lists, and maintained a public disputation against Eck at Leipzig; by which the minds of both the contending parties were put into a great commotion. The reign therefore of this great prince is diligently to be considered, and for the better understanding of it, ought to be compared with those of former times. For God has ever used to raise up illustrious and great princes when the ecclesiastical or civil state were to be changed. Such were Cyrus, and Alexander the Macedonian, C. Julius Caesar, Constantine, Charles the Great, and the Ottos of Saxony, and now in our times at last, Charles the V.

That change I have here in this story unfolded, is such that no man who does clearly understand it, can think of it without astonishment, and the utmost degree of admiration and wonder. Its beginning was small and almost contemptible; and one man alone, a while, bore the hatred and violence of the whole world. And even he too might easily, at first, have been quieted and laid to sleep, if the condition he so offered his adversaries had been accepted by them. For he promised he would hold his peace, if they would do so too. But then they refused this and would force him to recant, and stood stiffly in this resolution that he should do it. And he on the other side as stoutly replied, that he could not retract what he had advanced, till they had shown him wherein he had erred. The debate between them improved and grew greater, and the business was brought before the Diet of Germany, by which means it dilated itself to that degree we now see it in.

But then upon what reasons it was done; what share the Popes of Rome, the universities, the kings, princes, and states of Christendom had in this affair; how Luther defended his cause before the emperor and the princes of Germany in the Diet; How many men of great learning joined themselves with him; how this business was from time to time agitated and debated in the Diets; what ways were proposed for an accommodation; how the Popes solicited the emperor and other christian princes; how they frequently promised a reformation and a general council; what persecutions and slaughters were in several places stirred up against those who embraced this doctrine; what conspiracies and leagues were set on foot to the same end, not only in Germany but in other countries, as this religion spread itself; how some forsook it, and others persevered constantly in it; what tumults, contentions, and wars were occasioned by it; these things, in my judgment are so great, and so full of variety, that I think it were a sin to suffer them to perish in silence, and not commit them to writing.

To this I may add, that I think it very reasonable to give an account what the state of the Empire has been during the reign of the prince, by the space of thirty-six years; what wars he has managed; what commotions and disturbances have happened; and what has been the fortune of the neighbor kingdoms and provinces in these times. (But then I shall show hereafter the method I have followed in this work.) For as this prince's dominions are of great extent, so he has been attacked by very potent adversaries. The things therefore that have happened during his reign, and in our memory, are strangely great. Some years since, many men of eminent learning and virtue, when these things happened to be accidentally mentioned, began to be earnest with me that I should commit to writing the affairs of our times, especially what related to religion. And this they did, not out of an opinion that I was better able to do it than another, or because there were not abler men to be found for that purpose; but because they saw me particularly fancy and love these composures; and thence they concluded that I being by nature designed to this employment, and by her powerfully excited to it, might perhaps not altogether lose or misspend my time in the attempt. On the other side, I who knew what a large sea of matter I was to enter into, and that design needed a man of greater ingenuity and eloquence than I could pretend to, and therefore I almost despaired of ever being able to accomplish it; yet being at last overcome by the authority of those who had made this motion to me, I resolved to make a trial of it. . . .

. . . The main and principal scope of my design is to set forth the affairs of religion; but then I thought it needful for order's sake to set down also the civil transactions. As to the nature of the story every man that reads it will easily see what it is.

Candor and truth are the two most becoming ornaments of an history; and in truth, I have taken the utmost care that neither of them might be wanting here. To that end I have taken up nothing upon surmise or light report, but I have studiously collected what I have here written from the public records and papers; the faith of which can justly be called in question by no man. . . .

. . . The reader will meet frequent mention of foreign affairs, especially the French and English, and to these I have pursued the same method, and I have inserted nothing but what I had good authority for. And as to the French transactions, I saw many of them in the nine years I lived in that kingdom. So that the greatest part of the persecutions and burnings, and the royal edicts against the possessors of the reformed religion, which I have mentioned; the disputation undertaken by the divines of Paris against some of their ministers; the confession of their faith which was published in print soon after, and the court factions which then were on foot, do all of them fall within that time also. As to military actions, and what passed in the wars, I have not wholly passed them over, not indeed could I, and yet I have not made them any principal part of my business, because that of religion was my main design. . . .

. . . The second ornament which I mentioned of history, is Candor or impartiality, which is ever to be observed to prevent the writers being drawn from the truth by his affections, which seems the most difficult, because it is so rarely to be found in historians. Now though perhaps I shall not be able to persuade all my readers that I have used more than ordinary diligence, as far as it was possible for me, as to this: Yet I do with repeated earnestness conjure them not to load me with unjust suspicion beforehand. This whole work, as I said above, is extracted out of the public acts, papers, or records; collected together with great diligence, and a great part of which have been already printed, partly in Latin, and partly in the vulgar tongues, viz. the German, Italian, and French. It contains many orations, petitions, and answers; very many accusations and their answers; in all these I nakedly, simply, and with good faith, recite all things as they were particularly acted. For here I do not add anything of my own, nor do I make any judgment on them; but willingly and freely leave it to my reader. I make no rhetorical flourishes, nor do I write anything out of favour or envy to any man. No, I only furnish the style, and use my own words, that the tenor of my language may be equal and always alike; and digest everything, and fix it in its proper place, as it happened to be done in order and time. . . .

. . . My mind and strength were very much supported, first, when I considered that it was for the glory of God, who was thus pleased to discover His almighty power, and admirable counsel in our times; next that the common good and advantage, which would result from it, very much wrought upon me. For even here in Germany very few clearly understand in what order everything was done; and foreign nations know nothing at all of them; but the far greatest part of men being prepossessed with prejudices, judged of the greatest part of the things quite otherwise than they ought. To all this, I may add, I have had some consideration for posterity, if yet these my writings will bear the light, and last any long time.

. . . Now though I write the history of those things which have happened during the reign of Charles V who is yet living, and at the helm of our state, and so many other great actions may perhaps follow in his times; yet because those that are past must of necessity be the first principal and greatest part of the events of it: therefore I would not delay this work any longer, wherein I have gratified many learned men, not only of Germany, but also of the other countries, who desired to see it. Without doubt there are great commotions and strange and wonderful changes coming on; and the Sacred Scriptures see clearly and plainly to foretell as much; and the present state of affairs intimate the same; so that those who are disposed to write, are not like to be destitute of matter. But in the interim, as the public good inclined me to undertake this task; so it has now at last prevailed with me to publish these thirty-five books.

Illustrious Sir,

I desire to dedicate unto your highness this my labour and work; because you are descended of that family which was first pleased to give entertainment and protection to this doctrine. Your father readily embraced it, your brother hath settled a considerable estate for the education of children in learning and piety, and your father-in-law (the king of Denmark) is a famous defender of it also; and lastly, because you too, Great Sir, pursuing with much glory their example, I cannot but be confident, this work, which I hope will be profitable to many, will be therefore acceptable to you. May God Preserve Your Highness.

Given the 23 of March 1555.

℣ Being informed that many speak very unfriendly of my history, and as I clearly see, reward my great labor very ill, I am thereby enforced to publish this *Apology* in my own defense. I have already in my preface set forth the causes that induced me to write, the methods I pursued in it, and that I designed no man's disrepute, or favor; that I was very desirous of setting down nothing but what was exactly true, and disposed beforehand, in case I were shown I had anywhere mistaken, to correct and blot out what was amiss and to caution my readers not to believe my errors. I thought this would satisfy all mankind, and the rather, because the very perusal of what I had written would clear my reputation and create a firm belief of my fidelity. But being on all hands informed, to my great dissatisfaction and sorrow, that it has happened quite otherwise, I am necessitated to add what follows to that preface.

I say then, that from the beginning of the world, it has never been the custom of men to write the *civil* and *sacred history* of their times. That this usage (as appears by their books) has most flourished in the most free and illustrious nations, especially amongst the Greeks and Romans. That the principal law and ornament of history is truth and sincerity and therefore it was that Cicero stiled it, "The witness of times, the light of truth, the life of memory, and the mistress of life." By these words the great orator hath given a noble commendation of history, and an excellent description of what ought to be aimed at in the composing of it. Now there having happened, in our times, such a change in religion, as is not to be paralleled in any age since the apostles; and there having followed it a great commotion in the civil state, as is usual. Though I was not the fittest person to undertake this work, yet at the request of many good men, I entered upon it, for the glory of God, and with great fidelity and diligence have brought it down to our own times. And I have firm hope, that all who are not highly prejudiced will confess that I have not given the reins to my passions in anything in this affair; and that I

Johann Sleidan, *Apology for His History.* In *The General History of the Reformation of the Church, Written in Latin by John Sleidan, L.L.D., Faithfully Englished,* trans. Edmund Bohun. London: Edw. Jones, 1689. No pagination.

have behaved myself, perhaps, with more moderation than any other writer.

For though I willingly profess the doctrine of the gospel, which by the mercy of God was now restored, and rejoice exceedingly that I am a member of the Reformed Church; yet I have carefully abstained from all exasperating language and simply delivered everything as it came to pass. I call God to witness, also, that I never designed to injure or hurt any man's reputation falsely; for what a madness would it have been to have delivered anything otherwise than it was, in an affair which is fresh in all men's memory? And, I hope, those who are intimately acquainted with me, have never yet discovered any such vanity in me. And yet if after all, I have by chance committed any error or mistake, I will readily confess it, whenever I shall be shown it, and also caution my reader openly, that he may not be misled by me, as I have said in my preface. As to the pains I have taken and the diligence I have used in this work, no man could possibly have done more to find out the truth, as many men can bear me witness and the very work itself will in great part show.

In this history of religion, I could not omit what concerned the civil government, because, as I have already said, they are interwoven each with the other, especially in our times, so that it was not possible to separate them. This union of the sacred and the civil state, is sufficiently discovered in the Scriptures, and is the cause that the change of religion, in any nation, is always attended presently with offenses, distractions, contentions, strifes, tumults, factions, and wars. "For this cause," Christ saith, "the Son shall be against the father, and the daughter against the mother, and that this doctrine would not bring peace, but a sword, and raise a fiery contention amongst the nearest relations." And that this has ever been the state of affairs since the beginning of the world, cannot be denied, and is also manifest from the thing itself. For in our times no sooner did this benefit, vouchsafed us by God and the doctrine of the Gospel, begin to be preached against the papal indulgences and the traditions of men, but presently all the world, but especially the clergy, became tumultuous and unquiet. This occasioned the bringing this affair before the Diet, or public convention of the state of Germany; and when thereupon some princes and free cities embraced this doctrine, this fire spread itself and the causes was exagitated with great variety, till at last it burst out into a war.

Now in the description, I have made of it, will appear what care and diligence the emperor employed to put a stop to this dissention; what the Protestants also from time to time answered, and what conditions they frequently offered. And when it came to a war, the event was various and perplexed; as for instance, the emperor (to give one example out of many) wrote to some of the princes and cities, and afterwards published in print, a declaration of his intentions and designs. This declaration was the foundation of the emperor's cause, and by the laws of history was to be represented, together with the answer of the adverse party. For, without this, what kind of history would it be thought which should only represent what one party said? . . .

I neither take form, nor add to any man's actions, more than the truth of the thing requires and allows. And in truth it is apparent this had been done by few. For the greatest part of the writers give their own judgments both of the things, and persons they mention in their histories.

To omit the more ancient historians, we know how Platina has written *The Lives of the Popes,* and Philip Commines, a knight, has in our memory published an illustrious history of his own times, and among other things which he there delivers, tells us, that after Charles the Hardy, Duke of Burgundy, was slain before Nancy in battle, Louis XII, King of France, ravished his daughter, and heir, Artois and both the Burgundies; and although Commines was a sworn subject of France, and a counsellor to that prince, yet he saith this was ill done. . . .

Commines is chiefly commended because he wrote so equally, but then he ever pursues this method, as I have said already, that he not only sets down what was done, but also gives his own judgment of it, and tells us what everyone did, well or ill; and although I would not have done this, yet it is the most usual practice of historians. But then, that what was done or said by both parties should be exactly related, is not only just and equal, and the constant usage from the most ancient times, but also absolutely necessary; for without it, it is impossible to write an history. Wherever there are factions, wars, and seditions, be sure there are complaints, accusations, and answers, and all places are filled with opposite and contradictory papers. Now he that truly relates these as they are, doth neither of the parties any injury, but follows the laws of an historian. For in these brawls and contentions, everything which the partie object against each other is not presently true and certain. Where there is contention, hatred and enmity, it is very well known and experienced how things managed for the most part on both sides. If what the Popes, and their adherents, have within thirty-six years last past belched out against the Protestants were all true, there could be found nothing more wicked and impious than they. . . .

I do not doubt but all impartial men will yield that I have in this, which I have said, clearly given the true laws of history; and I can as little think they will judge that I have broke those laws; the far greater part of my history being extracted out of pieces which were printed before. They act therefore very unfriendly, or rather injuriously with me, who traduce and defame my writings, and the more are they guilty if they understand the laws of history. But if they know them not, then I desire they would learn them from what I have written and from other historians. . . .

In truth I generally had made it my business to write in order, and as truly as I could, the story of that wonderful blessing God has been pleased to bestow upon the men of this age. And to that purpose, about sixteen years since, I collected all that I thought necessary to that work. Nor have I since made any headlong haste in the writing of it, but gone leisurely on with a steady judgment. The labour I have taken, in this great work, is know to none but God and myself. And I had respect to nothing but the glory of God in it; and laying aside the study of the civil law, which is my profession, I accordingly almost spent my whole time upon it. So that all things considered, I think, I may aver that I was drawn to it by an impulse from God, I will commend my cause to Him, seeing I have met so ill a recompence from some men, for my great labour and pains; it being His cause I defended, and I am fully assured He will look upon that work as a most pleasing and acceptable sacrifice; the conscience of which sustains and comforts me; and the more, because I see many learned men approve and applaud my work, paying me their thanks for it, and acknowedging the benefit they have reaped by it. Therefore I desire all those who are the hearty lovers of truth, that they would not believe the slanders of ill men, but kindly entertain my work, and approve my faith and diligence, without admitting any suspicion of me. Lastly, I profess that I acknowledge Charles the V now Emperor of Germany, and Ferdinand King of the Romans his brother, to be the supreme magistrates appointed by God, whom I ought in all things to obey, as Christ and His apostles have commanded, excepting only those things which are forbidden by God.

80. JEAN CALVIN (1510–1564) extended the Protestant view of history in the later (1543, 1545, 1550, 1553, 1554, etc.) editions of his systematic and (for his massive discipleship) authoritative *Institution of Christian Religion,* which drew upon the didactic value of history as well as on doctrinal argument. Like his friend and mentor Bucer as well as his predecessors Luther and Melanchthon, Calvin joined his celebration of the progress of the true church to a systematic critique of corrupt Romanist tradition, describing in detail the condition of the primitive church and later departures from this ideal, illustrated by papal claims of primacy and such human fabrications as the Donation of Constantine.

The Condition of the Ancient Church, and the Kind of Government in Use Before the Papacy

1. Fidelity of the ancient Church to the Scriptural archetype   Up to this point we have discussed the order of church government as it has been handed down to us from God's pure Word, and also those ministries established by Christ. Now to make all these matters clearer and more familiar, and also to fix them better in our minds, it will be useful to recognize in this characteristics of the ancient church the form which will represent to our eyes some image of the divine institution. For even though the bishops of those times promulgated many canons, by which they seemed to express more than was expressed in Scripture, still they conformed their establishment with such care to the unique pattern of God's Word that you may readily see that it had almost nothing in this respect alien to God's Word. But though something might be wanting in their arrangements, yet because they tried with a sincere effort to preserve God's institution and did not wander far from it, it will be most profitable here briefly to ascertain what sort of observance they had.

We have stated that Scripture sets before us three kinds of ministers. Similarly, whatever ministers the ancient church had it divided into three orders. For from the order of presbyters (1) part were chosen pastor

Jean Calvin, *Institutes of the Christian Religion.* In *Calvin: Institutes of the Christian Religion,* *1* (Volumes 20 and 21: The Library of Christian Classics), ed. John T. McNeill and trans. Ford Lewis Battles. 21 : 1068–1069, 1084, 1085, 1087, 1102, 1141, and 1224. Copyright © 1960 W. L. Jenkins. Used by permission of Westminster / John Knox Press.

and teachers; (2) the remaining part were charged with the censure and correction of morals; (3) the care of the poor and the distribution of alms were committed to the deacons. . . .

The Ancient Form of Government Was Completely Overthrown by the Tyranny of the Papacy

1. Scandalous neglect of requirements for the episcopate Now it behooves us to turn our attention to the order of church government adhered to today by the Roman see and all its satellites, and the whole picture of that hierarchy which they are always talking about; also, to compare with it our description of the first and ancient church. From such a comparison will appear the nature of that church which these men have who are raging to oppress—or rather destroy—us by its mere title.

It is best to begin with the call, that we may see who and what type are called to this ministry and in what manner. Then we shall consider how faithfully they discharge their office.

We shall give first place to bishops. Would that it were an honor to give them first place in this discussion! But the reality does not allow me to touch even lightly upon this matter, without great shame to them. . . .

The practice of having an examination of learning has, to be sure, become old-fashioned. But if learning is held in any regard, they choose a lawyer who knows how to plead in a court rather than how to preach in a church. This is certain, that for a hundred years scarcely one man in a hundred has been elected who has comprehended anything of sacred learning. . . .

2. The community deprived of the right to elect its bishop Now all the people's right in electing a bishop has been taken away. Votes, assent, subscriptions, and all their like have vanished; the whole power has been transferred to the canons alone. They confer the episcopate on whom they please; they introduce him directly before the people, but to be adored, not to be examined. . . .

3. Neglect has led to the intervention of princes But when they say that this was devised as a remedy they are lying. We read that in old times cities were often in tumult over the choice of bishops; yet no one ever dared think of taking away the right of the citizens. For they had other ways of avoiding these faults or, once they had occurred, of correcting them. The truth shall be told.

When the people began to be more negligent in holding elections, and cast that responsibility upon the presbyters as not applying to themselves, the latter abused this opportunity to usurp a tyranny for themselves which they afterward confirmed by issuing new canons.

Ordination, moreover, is nothing but pure mockery. For the kind of examination which they display there is so empty and thin that it even lacks every outward trapping.

Therefore, what the princes in some places have obtained by agreement with the Roman pontiffs—the right to nominate bishops—has caused no new loss to the church, because the election was taken away only from the canons, who had seized it without right or had actually stolen it. . . .

The Primacy of the Roman See

1. The requirement of submission to Rome   To this point we have reviewed those orders of the church which existed in the government of the ancient church but were afterward corrupted by the times, then more and more perverted, and which now keep only their name in the papal church and are actually but masks. This we have done that the godly reader might judge from comparison what sort of church the Romanists have, for the sake of which they make us guilty of schism, since we have separated from it.

But we have not discussed the capstone of the whole structure, that is, the primacy of the Roman see, from which they strive to prove that the church catholic is their exclusive possession. The reason why we have not discussed this primacy is that it originated neither in Christ's institution, nor in the practice of the ancient church, as those former offices which, as we have shown, so arose from antiquity that they utterly degenerated through corruption of the times, indeed, took on a completely new form. . . .

22. The corruption of the present-day papacy   But that I may not be compelled to pursue and examine individual points, I again appeal to those who today wish to be thought the best and most faithful patrons of the Roman see, whether they are not ashamed to defend the present state of the papacy. For it clearly is a hundred times more corrupt than it was in the times of Gregory and Bernard, though even then it greatly displeased those holy men. . . .

12. The Donation of Constantine fraudulent and absurd   As for the Donation of Constantine, those only moderately versed in the history of those times need not be taught not only how fabulous, but also how absurd, it is. But to pass over histories, Gregory himself is a fitting and complete witness of this matter. For whenever he speaks of the emperor, he calls him "most serene Lord" and himself his "unworthy servant." Likewise, in another passage: "Now let not our lord, by virtue of his earthly power, be too ready to take offense at the priests; but, with excellent consideration, for the sake of Him whose servants they are, let him so rule them that he also may give them due reverence." We see how, in common subjection, he wishes to be regarded as one of the people. For there he is pleading no other man's cause but his own. In another passage: "I trust in Almighty God that he will give long life to our pious lords and will dispose us under your hand according to his mercy." I have not quoted these statements because I intend to discuss thoroughly the question of the Donation of Constantine, but only that my readers may see in passing how childishly the Romanists lie when they try to claim earthly power for their pontiff.

The more foul, then, is the shamelessness of Augustinus Steuchus, who has dared, in this lost cause, to sell his labor and tongue to his pontiff. Valla had roundly refuted that fable—a task not difficult for a learned man with sharp wit.

> 81. JOHN FOXE (1516–1587), one of the Marian exiles with connections to the continental Protestant community, was the founder of modern English martyrology. In his famous and enormously influential *Acts and Monuments* (first edition 1557), he surveyed and celebrated the legacy and legends of the spirituality and suffering that formed the basis of the incipient English Puritan tradition, which he linked with late medieval heresies such as Lollardy. Into such religious terms Foxe, like Calvin and others but more directly and more humanly, translated conventional human-

John Foxe, *Acts and Monuments*. In *The Acts and Monuments of John Foxe: A New and Complete Edition*, ed. Stephen Reed Cattley. London: R. B. Seeley and Burnside, 1841. 1:508–509, 510, 512–515, 517, 519, 520–522, and 523.

ist views of the moral and didactic value of history while exploiting the Protestant view of history as a weapon of controversy.

To the Persecutors of God's Truth, Commonly Called Papists, Another Preface of the Author

If any other had had the doing and handling of this so tragical an history, and had seen the mad rage of this your furious cruelty, in spilling the blood of such an innumerable sort of Christ's holy saints and servants, as, in the volumes of this history, may appear by you, O ye papists (give me leave by that name to call you), I know not what he would have done therein: what vehemency of writing—what sharpness of speech and words—what roughness of style, in terming and calling you—he would have used; what exclamations he would have made against you; how little he would have spared you. So I, likewise, if I had been disposed to follow the order and example of their doing,—what I might have done herein, let your own conjectures give you to understand, but that which you have deserved. And if you think you have not deserved so to be entreated, as I have said, and worse than I have done, then see and behold, I beseech you, here in this story, the pitiful slaughter of your butchery! Behold your own handy work! consider the number, almost out of number, of so many silly and simple lambs of Christ, whose blood you have sought and sucked; whose lives you have vexed; whose bodies you have slain, racked and tormented; some also you have cast on dunghills, to be devoured of fowls and dogs; without mercy, without measure, without all sense of humanity! See, I say, and behold, here present before your eyes, the heaps of slain bodies, of so many men and women, both old, young, children, infants, new born, married, unmarried, wives, widows, maids, blind men, lame men, whole men; of all sorts, of all ages, of all degrees; lords, knights, gentlemen, lawyers, merchants, archbishops, bishops, ministers, deacons, laymen, artificers, yea, whole households and whole kindreds together; father, mother and daughter; grandmother, mother, aunt, and child, etc.; whose wounds, yet bleeding before the face of God, cry vengeance! For, whom have you spared? what country could escape your hands? See, therefore, I say, read, and behold your acts and facts; and, when you have seen, then judge what you have deserved. . . . I exhort you, that with patience you would read and peruse the history of these your own acts and doings, being no more ashamed now to read them, than you were then to do them; to the intent that, when you shall now the better revise what your doings have been, the more you may blush and detest the same. . . .

. . . Peradventure you will excuse yourselves, and say, that you did but the law; and if the law did pass upon them, you could not do with all. But here I will ask, what law do you mean? The law of God, or the law of man? If ye mean the law of God, where do you find in all the law of God, to put them to death, which, holding the articles of the creed, never blasphemed his name, but glorified it, both in life, and in their death? If you answer, by the law of man, I know the law ("ex officio" or rather ex homicidio) which you mean and follow. But who brought that law in first, in the time of king Henry IVth, but you? Who revived the same again in queen Mary's days, but you? Further, who kept them in prison before the law, till, by the law, you had made a rope to hang them withal? And think you by charging the law, to discharge yourselves? . . . And because you charge them so much with heresy, this would I know, by what learning do you define your heresy, by the scripture, or by your canon law? I know what you will answer: but whatsoever you say, your own acts and deeds will well prove the contrary. For what scripture can save him, whom your law condemneth? What heresy was there, in speaking against transubstantiation, before Innocent III did so enact it in his canon, A.D. 1215? What man was ever counted for an heretic, which, worshipping Christ in heaven, did not worship him in the priest's hands, before Honorius III, in his canon, did cause the sacrament to be elevated and adored upon the altar? "Faith only justifying," in St. Paul's time, and in the beginning church, was no heresy, before of late days the Romish canons have made it heresy! . . .

To conclude, in countries, kingdoms, cities, towns, and churches reformed, your errors and superstitious vanities be so blotted out, within the space of these forty years, in the hearts of men, that their children and youth, being so long nouseled in the sound doctrine of Christ, like as they never heard of your ridiculous trumpery, so will they never be brought to the same. And if nothing else will deface you, yet printing only will subvert your doings, do what ye can, which the Lord only hath set up for your desolation. Wherefore, forsake your cause, and your false hopes, and save yourselves. And take me not your enemy in telling you the truth, but rather your friend, in giving you good counsel—if you will follow good counsel given. Return therefore and reform yourselves; repent your murders, cease your persecutions, strive not against the Lord; but rather bewail your iniquities, which, though they be great, and greater than you are aware, yet they are not so great, but Christ is greater, if ye repent betimes. Ye see here I trust good counsel given; God grant it may as well fructify in you, as on my part it hath proceeded of an open and tender heart; wishing you well to do, as I pray God ye may, so that you and we may agree and consent together in one religion and truth, in Christ Jesus our Lord, to whom be praise for ever. Amen.

To the True and Faithful Congregation of Christ's Universal Church . . .

Upon the like trust in God's gracious goodness, if I, sinful wretch, not comparing with the building of that temple, but following the zeal of the builder, might either be so bold to ask, or so happy to speed, after my seven years' travail about this Ecclesiastical History, I would most humbly crave of Almighty God to bestow his blessing upon the same; that as the prayers of them which prayed in the outward temple were heard, so all true disposed minds which shall resort to the reading of this present history, containing the Acts of Gods holy Martyrs, and Monuments of his Church, may, by example of their life, faith, and doctrine, receive some such spiritual fruit to their souls, through the operation of his grace; that it may be to the advancement of his glory, and profit of his church, through Christ Jesus our Lord. Amen. . . .

As for me and my history, as my will was to profit all and displease none, so if skill in any part wanted to will, yet hath my purpose been simple; and certes the cause no less urgent also, which moved me to take this enterprise in hand.

For, first, to see the simple flock of Christ, especially the unlearned sort, so miserably abused, and all for ignorance of history, not knowing the course of times and true descent of the church, it pitied me that this part of diligence had so long been unsupplied in this my country church of England. Again, considering the multitude of chronicles and story-writers, both in England and out of England, of whom the most part have been either monks, or clients to the see of Rome, it grieved me to see in their Monuments the principal points which chiefly concerned the state of Christ's church, and were most necessary of all christian people to be known, either altogether pretermitted, or if any mention thereof were inserted, yet were all things drawn to the honour specially of the church of Rome, or else to the favour of their own sect of religion. Whereby the vulgar sort, hearing and reading in their writings no other church mentioned or magnified but only that church which here flourished in this world in riches and jollity, were drawn also to the same persuasion, to think no other church to have stood in all the earth but only the church of Rome. . . .

When I considered this partial dealing and corrupt handling of histories, I thought with myself nothing more lacking in the church than full and a complete story; which, being faithfully collected out of all our monastical writers and written monuments, should contain neither every vain written fable (for that would be too much), nor yet leave out any thing necessary, for that would be too little; but, with a moderate discretion, taking the best of every one, should both ease the labour of the reader from turning over such a number of writers, and also should open the plain truth of times lying long hid in obscure darkness of antiquity: whereby all studious readers, beholding as in a glass the stay, course, and alteration of religion, decay of doctrine, and the controversies of the church, might discern the better between antiquity and novelty. For if the things which be first, after the rule of Tertullian, are to be preferred before those that be later, then is the reading of histories much necessary in the church, to know what went before, and what followed after; and therefore not without cause "historia," in old authors, is called the Witness of Times, the Light of Verity, the Life of Memory, Teacher of Life, and Shewer of Antiquity, etc., without the knowledge whereof man's life is blind, and soon may fall into any kind of error; as by manifest experience we have to see in these desolate later times of the church, when the bishops of Rome, under colour of antiquity, have turned truth into heresy, and brought such new-found devices of strange doctrine and religion, as, in the former age of the church, were never heard of before, and all through ignorance of times and for lack of true history. . . .

In these miserable days, as the true visible church began now to shrink and keep in for fear, so up started a new sort of players, to furnish the stage, as school-doctors, canonists, and four orders of friars; besides other monastical sects and fraternities of infinite variety; which, ever since, have kept such a stir in the church, that none for them almost durst rout, neither Caesar, king, nor subject. What they defined, stood; what they approved, none almost could save. And thus have these, hitherto, continued, or reigned rather, in the church the space now of full four hundred years and odd. During which space the true church of Christ, although it durst not openly appear in the face of the world, was oppressed by tyranny; yet neither was it so invisible or unknown, but, by the providence of the Lord, some remnant always remained from time to time, which not only showed secret good affection to sincere doctrine, but also stood in open defence of truth against the disordered church of Rome. . . .

Wherefore, if any be so far beguiled in his opinion [as] to think the doctrine of the church of Rome, as it now standeth, to be of such antiquity, and that the same was never impugned before the time of Luther and Zuinglius now of late, let them read these histories: or if he think the said history not to be of sufficient credit to alter his persuasion, let him peruse the acts and statutes of parliaments, passed in this realm, of ancient time, and therein consider and confer the course of times; where he may find and read, in the year of our Lord 1382, of a great number (who there be called evil persons) going about from town to town in frieze gowns, preaching unto the people, etc. Which preachers, although the words of the statute do term there to be dissembling persons, preaching divers sermons containing heresies and notorious errors, to the emblemishment of christian faith, and of holy church, etc., as the words do there pretend; yet notwithstanding, every true christian reader may conceive of those preachers to teach no other doctrine, than now they hear their own preachers in pulpits preach against the bishop of Rome, and the corrupt heresies of his church. . . .

In [1570] the full seventy years of the Babylonish captivity draweth now well to an end, if we count from the first appearing of these bloody marks above-mentioned. Or if we reckon from the beginning of Luther and his persecution, then lacketh yet sixteen years. Now what the Lord will do with this wicked world, or what rest he will give to his church after these long sorrows, he is our Father in heaven, his will be done in earth as seemeth best to his divine Majesty. . . .

The Utility of This Story

. . . Now, if men commonly delight so much in other chronicles which entreat only upon matters of policy, and rejoice to behold therein the variable events of worldly affairs, the strategems of valiant captains, the roar of foughten fields, the sacking of cities, the hurlyburlies of realms and people; and if men think it such a gay thing in a commonwealth to commit to history such old antiquities of things profane, and bestow all their ornaments of wit and eloquence in garnishing the same, how much more then is it meet for Christians to conserve in remembrance the lives, acts, and doings, not of bloody warriors, but of mild and constant martyrs of Christ; which serve not so much to delight the ear, as to garnish the life, to frame it with examples of great profit, and to encourage men to all kind of christian godliness! As first, by reading thereof we may learn a lively testimony of God's might working in the life of man, contrary to the opinion of Atheists, and all the whole nest of Epicures. . . .

Over and besides this, the mild deaths of the saints do not a little avail to the stablishing of a good conscience, to learn the contempt of the world, and to come to the fear of God. Moreover, they confirm faith, increase godliness, abate pride in prosperity, and in adversity do open an hope of heavenly comfort. For what man, reading the misery of these godly persons may not therein, as in a glass, behold his own case, whether he be godly or godless? For if God give adversity unto good men, what may either the better sort promise themselves, or the evil not fear? And whereas by reading of profane stories we are made perhaps more skilful in warlike affairs; so by reading of this we are made better in our living, and besides are better prepared until like conflicts (if by God's permission they shall happen hereafter), more wise by their doctrine, and more steadfast by their example.

To be short, they declare to the world what true christian fortitude is, and what is the right way to conquer; which standeth not in the power of man, but in hope of the resurrection to come, and is now, I trust, at hand. In consideration whereof, methinks I have good cause to wish, that, like as other men, even so also kings and princes, who commonly delight in heroical stories, would diligently peruse such monuments of martyrs, and lay them always in sight, not only to read, but to follow, and would paint them upon their walls, cups, rings, and gates. . . .

Whereby it is manifest, what estimation in times past was attributed to martyrs; with what gratulation, rejoicing, mirth, and common joy, the afflictions of those godly, dying in Christ's quarrel, were sometimes received and solemnized; and that not without good reasonable cause. For the church did well consider how much she was beholden to their benefits, by whose death she understood her treasures to increase. Now then if martyrs are to be compared with martyrs, I see no cause why martyrs of our time deserve any less commendation than the others in the primitive church; which assuredly are inferior unto them in no point of praise, whether we view the number of them that suffered, or greatness of their torments, or their constancy in dying, or also consider the fruit that they brought, to the amendment of posterity, and increase of the gospel. . . .

All these premises duly of our parts considered and marked, seeing we have found so famous martyrs in this our age, let us not fail then in publishing and setting forth their doings; lest, in that point, we seem more unkind to them, than the writers of the primitive church were unto theirs. And though we repute not their ashes, chains, and swerds [swords] in the stead of relics, yet let us yield thus much unto their commemoration, to glorify the Lord in his saints, and imitate their death (as much as we may) with like constancy, or their lives at the least with like innocency. They offered their bodies willingly to the rough handling of the tormentors; and is it so great a matter then for our part to mortify our flesh, with all the members thereof? They neglected not only the riches and glory of the world for the love of Christ, but also their lives; and shall we then keep so great a stir one against another for the transitory trifles of this world? They continued in patient sufferent, when they had most wrong done unto them, and when their very hearts' blood gushed out of their bodies; and yet will not we forgive our poor brother, be the injury never so small, but are ready for every trifling offence to seek his destruction, and cut his throat? They, wishing well to all men, did of their own accord forgive their persecutors; and therefore ought we, who are now the posterity and children of martyrs, not to degenerate from their former steps, but, being admonished by their examples, if we cannot express their charity toward all men, yet at least to imitate the same to our power and strength. Let us give no cause of offence to any, and if any be given to us, let us overcome it with patience, forgiving, and not revenging, the same. And let us not only keep our hands from shedding of blood, but our tongues also from hurting the fame of others. Besides, let us not shrink, if case so require, from martyrdom, or loss of life, according to their example, and to yield up the same in the defence of the Lord's flock. Which thing if men would do, much less contention and business would be in the world than now is. And thus much touching the utility and fruit to be taken of this history.

82. Edward Hyde, first earl of CLARENDON (1608–1674), was a royalist whose history was the product of firsthand experience as

Clarendon, *History of the Rebellion*. In *Clarendon: Selections from the History of the Rebellion and the Life by Himself,* ed. G. Huehns. Oxford: Oxford University Press, 1978. Pp. 1–7.

well as reflection. Begun during the Puritan Revolution as a work
of propaganda for the cause of Charles II and for so-called mixed
monarchy, the *History of the Rebellion and the Civil War* (1671, published posthumously 1702–1704) was rewritten and transformed
into a classic narrative of the English Civil War, emphasizing social
and political rather than religious forces.

That posterity may not be deceived, by the prosperous wickedness of
these times, into an opinion, that less than a general combination, and
universal apostasy in the whole nation from their religion and allegiance, could, in so short a time, have produced such a total and prodigious alteration and confusion over the whole kingdom; and so the
memory of those few, who, out of duty and conscience, have opposed
and resisted that torrent, which hath overwhelmed them, may lose the
recompense due to their virtue; and, having undergone the injuries and
reproaches of this, may not find a vindication in a better age; it will not
be unuseful, at least to the curiosity if not the conscience of men, to
present to the world a full and clear narration of the grounds, circumstances, and artifices of this rebellion: not only from the time since the
flame hath been visible in a civil war, but, looking farther back, from
those former passages, accidents, and actions, by which the seed-plots
were made and framed, from whence these mischiefs have successively
grown to the height they are now at.

And then, though the hand and judgment of God will be very visible,
in the infatuating a people (as ripe and prepared for destruction) into all
the perverse actions of folly and madness, making the weak to contribute
to the designs of the wicked, and suffering even those, by degrees, out of
the conscience of their guilt, to grow more wicked than they intended to
be; letting the wise to be imposed upon by men of no understanding,
and possessing the innocent with laziness and sleep in the most visible
article of danger; uniting the ill, though of the most different opinions,
divided interests, and distant affections, in a firm and constant league of
mischief; and dividing those, whose opinions and interests are the same,
into faction and emulation, more pernicious to the public than the trea-
son of the others: whilst the poor people, under the pretence of zeal to
religion, law, liberty, and parliaments, (words of precious esteem in
their just signification,) are furiously hurried into actions introducing
atheism, and dissolving all the elements of Christian religion; cancelling
all obligations, and destroying all foundations of law and liberty; and
rendering, not only the privileges, but very being, of parliaments des-

perate and impossible: I say, though the immediate finger and wrath of God must be acknowledged in these perplexities and distractions; yet he who shall diligently observe the distempers and conjunctures of time, the ambition, pride, and folly of persons, and the sudden growth of wickedness, from want of care and circumspection in the first impressions, will find all this bulk of misery to have proceeded, and to have been brought upon us, from the same natural causes and means, which have usually attended kingdoms, swoln with long plenty, pride, and excess, towards some signal mortifications, and castigation of Heaven. And it may be, upon the view of the impossibility of foreseeing many things that have happened, and of the necessity of overseeing many other things, we may not yet find the cure so desperate, but that, by God's mercy, the wounds may be again bound up; though no question many must first bleed to death; and then this prospect may not make the future peace less pleasant and durable.

And I have the more willingly induced myself to this unequal task, out of the hope of contributing somewhat to that end; and though a piece of this nature (wherein the infirmities of some, and the malice of others, both things and persons, must be boldly looked upon and mentioned) is not likely to be published at least in the age in which it is writ, yet it may serve to inform myself, and some others, what we are to do, as well as to comfort us in what we have done, and then possibly it may not be very difficult to collect somewhat out of that store, more proper, and not unuseful for the public view. And as I may not be thought altogether an incompetent person for this communication, having been present as a member of parliament in those councils before and till the breaking out of the rebellion, and having since had the honour to be near two great kings in some trust, so I shall perform the same with all faithfulness and ingenuity; with an equal observation of the faults and infirmities of both sides, with their defects and oversights in pursuing their own ends; and shall no otherwise mention small and light occurrences, than as they have been introductions to matters of the greatest moment; nor speak of persons otherwise, than as the mention of their virtues or vices is essential to the work in hand: in which as I shall have the fate to be suspected rather for malice to many, than of flattery to any, so I shall, in truth, preserve myself from the least sharpness, that may proceed from private provocation, or a more public indignation, in the whole observing the rules that a man should, who deserves to be believed.

I shall not then lead any man farther back in this journey, for the discovery of the entrance into these dark ways, than the beginning of this king's reign. For I am not so sharp-sighted as those, who have discerned this rebellion contriving from (if not before) the death of queen Elizabeth, and fomented by several princes and great ministers of state in Christendom, to the time that it brake out. Neither do I look so far back as believing the design to be so long since formed; (they who have observed the several accidents, not capable of being contrived, which have contributed to the several successes, and do know the persons who have been the grand instruments toward this change, of whom there have not been any four of familiarity and trust with each other, will easily absolve them from so much industry and foresight in their mischief;) but that, by viewing the temper, disposition, and habit, of that time, of the court and of the country, we may discern the minds of men prepared, of some to do, and of others to suffer, all that hath since happened; the pride of this man, and the popularity of that; the levity of one, and the morosity of another; the excess of the court in the greatest want, and the parsimony and retention of the country in the greatest plenty; the spirit of craft and subtlety in some, and the rude and unpolished integrity of others, too much despising craft or art; like so many atoms contributing jointly to this mass of confusion now before us.

We are now entering upon a time, the representation and description whereof must be the most unpleasant and ungrateful to the reader, in respect of the subject matter of it; which must consist of no less weakness and folly on the one side, than of malice and wickedness on the other; and as unagreeable and difficult to the writer, in regard that he shall please very few who acted then upon the stage of business, but that he must give as severe characters of the persons, and severely censure the actions of many, who wished very well, and had not the least thought of disloyalty or infidelity, as well as of those, who, with the most deliberate impiety, prosecuted their design to ruin and destroy the crown; a time, in which the whole stock of affection, loyalty, and courage, which at first alone engaged men in the quarrel, seemed to be quite spent, and to be succeeded by negligence, laziness, inadvertency, and dejection of spirit, contrary to the natural temper, vivacity, and constancy of the nation; and in which they who pretended most public-heartedness, and did really wish the king all the greatness he desired to preserve for himself, did sacrifice the public peace, and the security of their master, to their own passions and appetites, to their ambition and animosities against each other, without the least design of treachery, or damage towards his majesty: a time, in which want of discretion and mere folly produced as much mischief as the most barefaced villainy could have done; and in which the king suffered as much by the irresolution and unsteadiness of his own counsels, and by the ill humour and faction of his counsellors, by their not foreseeing what was evident to most other men, and by their jealousies of what was not like to fall out; sometimes by deliberating too long without resolving, and as often resolving without any deliberation, and most of all, not executing vigorously what was well deliberated and resolved; as by the indefatigable industry, and the irresistible power and strength of his enemies.

All these things must be very particularly enlarged upon, and exposed to the naked view, in relation of what fell out in this year, 1645, in which we are engaged, except we will swerve from that precise rule of ingenuity and integrity we profess to observe; and thereby leave the reader more perplexed, to see the most prodigious causes which produced them; which would lead him into as wrong an estimate of things, and persuade him to believe, that a universal corruption of the hearts of the whole nation had brought forth those lamentable effects; which proceeded only from the folly and frowardness, from the weakness and the wilfulness, the pride and the passion of particular persons, whose memories ought to be charged with their own evil actions, rather than they should be preserved as the infamy of the age in which they lived; which did produce as many men eminent for their loyalty and incorrupted fidelity to the crown, as any that had preceded it. Nor is it possible to discourse of all these particulars, with that clearness that must subject them to common understandings, without opening a door for such reflections upon the king himself, as shall seem to call both his wisdom and his courage into question, as if he had wanted the one to apprehend and discover, and the other to prevent, the mischiefs which threatened him. All which consideration might very well discourage, and even terrify me from prosecuting this part of the work with that freedom and openness, as must call many things to memory which are forgotten, or were never understood; and rather persuade me to satisfy myself with a bare relation of what was done, and with the known event of that miserable year [1645], (which, in truth, produced all that followed in the next,) without prying too strictly into the causes of those effects, which might seem rather to be the production of Providence, and the instances of divine displeasure, than to proceed from the weakness and inadvertancy of any men, not totally abandoned by God Almighty to the most unruly lusts of their own appetite and inventions.

But I am too far embarked in this sea already, and have proceeded with too much simplicity and sincerity with reference to things and persons, and in the examinations of the grounds and oversights of counsels, to be now frighted with the prospect of those materials, which must be comprehended within the relation of this year's transactions. I know myself to be very free from any of those passions which naturally transport men with prejudice towards the persons whom they are obliged to mention, and whose actions they are at liberty to censure. There is not a man who acted the worst part, in this ensuing year, and whom I had ever the least difference, or personal unkindness, or towards whom I had not much inclination of kindness, or from whom I did not receive all invitations of farther endearments. There were many who were not free from very great faults, and oversights in the counsels of this year, with whom I had great friendship, and which I did not discontinue upon those unhappy oversights; nor did flatter them when they were past, by excusing what they had done. I knew most of the things myself which I mention, and therefore can answer for the truth of them; and other most important particulars, which were transacted in places very distant from me, were transmitted to me, by the king's immediate direction and order, even after he was in the hands and power of the enemy, out of his own memorials and journals. And as he was always severe to himself, in censuring his own oversights, so he could not but well foresee, that many of the misfortunes of this ensuing year would reflect upon some want of resolution in himself, as well as upon the gross errors and oversights, to call them no worse, of those who were trusted by him. And therefore as I first undertook this difficult work with his approbation and by his encouragement, and for his vindication, so I enter upon this part of it, principally, that the world may see (at least if there be ever a fit season for such a communication; which is not like to be in this present age) how difficult it was for a prince, so unworthily reduced to those straits his majesty was in, to find ministers and instruments equal to the great work that was to be done; and how impossible it was for him to have better success under their conduct, whom it was then very proper for him to trust with it; and then, without my being over solicitous to absolve him from those mistakes and weaknesses to which he was in truth sometimes liable, he will be found not only a prince of admirable virtue and piety, but of great parts of knowledge, wisdom, and judgment; and that the most signal parts of his misfortunes proceeded chiefly from the modesty of his nature, which kept him from trusting himself enough, and made him believe, that others discerned better, who were much inferior to him in those faculties; and so to depart often from his own reason, to follow the opinions of more unskillful men, whose affections he believed to be unquestionable to his service. And so we proceed in our relation of matter of fact.

❡ NATIONAL HISTORY

> 83. HEINRICH BEBEL (1472–1516), German humanist, friend of Erasmus and Reuchlin, poet (who received a laureate in 1501), and first professor of rhetoric at Tübingen from 1497, celebrated the cultural heritage and (following the arguments of Tacitus) superiority of Germany in this oration given for the emperor Maximilian I.

All I have to say touches on the glory of our country and on the paucity of writers who might give fitting praise to it. Let me add my voice to the laments over the destiny of our valorous forefathers, among whom we find innumerable doers of heroic deeds but not a single man who took it upon himself to record them for posterity. This fact I bemoan here in your presence, noble emperor; over this I shed my tears. For had we possessed able authors to commemorate acts of German bravery, were the achievements and virtues of our emperors Charles, Louis, Lothar, Friedrich, Otto, Henry, Konrad, Rudolf, and Albrecht fresh in the memory of our own people and the world, we would not today be disgraced by lying Greek historians who set up Theseus, Themistocles, Pericles, Militiades, Epaminondas, Pausanias, and Alcibiades as models of all virtues; nor by the mendacious Romans who eulogize their Fabians and Caesars and Scipios—men to whom our own citizens were not only equal in magnitude of achievements but whom they excelled, not least because we Germans were spurred by ideals of justice and virtue, while

Heinrich Bebel, *Oration in Praise of Germany*. In *Manifestations of Discontent in Germany on the Eve of the Reformation,* ed. and trans. Gerald Strauss. Bloomington, Ind.: Indiana University Press, 1971. Pp. 67–68, 69–70, and 71–72.

Roman conquerors were driven by nothing more than the lust for power and dominion. Our ancient German rulers faced hardship, perils, and death in order to serve God and extend the Christian faith and the sway of our religion. . . .

The books of rhetoricians, poets, historians, and philosophers are replete with the deeds of Romans and Greeks, whom they hold up as very paradigms for posterity. But who speaks of Frederick, of Charles, of Otto? No one does, and yet no finer examples could be given, and none worthier of emulation. For this neglect there is no reason except the oblivion into which the deeds of our ancestors have fallen. Whoever wishes to praise Germany as she should be praised will find that our history has no shortage of praiseworthy and virtuous deeds. Indeed he will realize that the German past can hold its own not only with attainments considered excellent in our own day but also with the greatest of the feats of antiquity. Whatever qualities the nations of the world count as their proudest, our people will be seen to possess them so that we may say with justice: Germany contains within herself all the excellent and praiseworthy things claimed by other peoples. . . .

TO COME TO THE POINT: What other nation on this earth has such well-born princes and so high-minded a nobility as ours? What people can boast braver knights and more self-sacrificing warriors? No other land is as populous and as well endowed with courage and vigor. Even the most distant peoples on the earth know this about us. . . . What other nation has extended its borders as far as we have pushed ours? Long ago, as we learn from the ancients, the limits of Germany were the Vistula and the Hungarian frontier on the east, the Rhine in the west, the Danube in the south, and the ocean in the north. Now, however, we have gone far beyond these ancient confines, not in predatory expeditions but to occupy and to hold, so that the peoples we have conquered can no longer recall the time when they belonged to another master. In the east we have vanquished the Hungarians and occupied Transylvania. . . . In the south we own the former lands of the Rhetians, Vindelicians, Bavarians, the Alpine peoples, Austria and Styria. We have advanced deep into Italy; we hold Croatia, Carniola, and Carinthia. Even Lombardy, Liguria, Tuscany, Sicily, and the Greek regions of southern Italy have fallen into our hands. . . .

And in the west how far have we Germans advanced the glory of our name! Switzerland is ours, for we have driven out the Gauls. Ours, also, the lands of [all the Gallic tribes] conquered by us. England is ours, the country that got its name from the Angles mentioned by Tacitus. . . .

Looking toward the north, finally, we see that Prussia is ours, the land whose ancient inhabitants . . . we saved from the grip of heathenism and made into civilized, Christian men. Thanks to us, Danes, Swedes, and Norwegians are Christians today, as are the peoples residing on the most distant borderlands of Germany. All this is bourne out by the most learned cosmographers and historians. . . . In sum: Few peoples in the world have not, at one time or another, felt the sharpness of German swords or have at least trembled at the terror of our name. It is true we have upon occasion been defeated by the armies of Rome, mistress of the entire earth. But we never gave the Romans an easy victory, nor did we allow them to return to their homeland without bloody losses. And often we vanquished them and subjected them to humiliating defeats. . . .

Therefore, most august emperor, my claim that our people does not lack for a past of glorious deeds. We miss only the historians who should have recorded these deeds. . . . If the older Pliny's twenty books on the Germanic-Roman wars were still extant, we would, I am sure, find in them ample material for the elaboration of our fame. But alas, they have disappeared in the destruction wrought by time. . . .

I do not wish to speak as an historian, noble emperor, and fill your ear with a long catalogue of events. Let me therefore pass from the German wars—the proper telling of which requires a stout volume rather than a brief address—to other matters. I see that many states and peoples boast of their ancient origins, but in antiquity of descent, as well as in valor, we Germans can hold our own with any nation under the sun. We may say of ourselves what the Athenians claimed for their own: our renown rests not only on what we have made of ourselves but also upon our roots and our first beginnings. We were not immigrants into our land; we are not an amalgamation of nomad groups. We are an autochthonous people, born from the soil of the land on which we now make our home. Where we live today are our ancient origins. Cornelius Tacitus, the great Roman historian, is witness to this fact. . . . Out best claim to honor and glory, however, is founded upon our superior virtue, a trait in which we excel all the other nations of mankind. What people, pray, shows greater devotion to justice? What people is more steadfast and sincere in its faith? Observe the magnificent churches, monasteries, convents and altars standing in our land; where may clearer evidence be found of a people's love and respect for divine worship and the Christian religion? Where are signs of greater devotion than the wars we have fought for the protection and propagation of our faith? Have the rulers of other countries done as much for the Roman Church and the Catholic faith, indeed for the salvation of Christendom itself? . . .

Notwithstanding this, history records not our deeds but those of other peoples. Our past is shrouded in darkness and lies hidden in obscure corners. When an occasional foreign writer does mention us, he is moved by antipathy, fear, or the need for flattery to alter historical fact or to leave out much that should be said. Do I need to cite examples of my charge? But now, at last, God has begun to look with favor upon our condition. He has given you to us, noble and august Maximilian. Under your auspices and leadership our people's magnificent exploits will shine forth in renewed brilliance, having lain neglected all these years, hidden in rust and squalor. Learning flourishes again, men's minds have become active once more, and poets respond to your magnificent encouragement, for you love men of letters and are gracious in supporting them. And not in vain, for authors and scholars return their thanks by celebrating you and your glorious accomplishments. Among the ancients those men were counted happy whom the gods had chosen either to perform great actions or to record them. Those, however, they judged happiest of all to whom it was given to do both. You, noble emperor, may therefore be called happiest, for not content with performing great deeds in the daily pursuit of affairs of state, you read history and express the desire to hear tales of memorable feats done in the past. They even say that you yourself are engaged in the writing of history and that you are planning a description of Germany to rival that of the great Julius Caesar, who won the admiration of all Rome because, while fully occupied as governor and general, he was also a devotee of arts and letters.

> 84. JOHN LELAND (1503–1552), who had studied the classics at Oxford and Paris, accepted a commission from King Henry VIII in 1533 to visit the libraries of post-Reformation England; from this extended scholarly *iter* came the seminal work in English antiquities and topography, *The Itinerary* *{The Laboriouse Journey and*

John Leland, *The Laboriouse Journey and Serche of Johan Leylande.* In *The Itinerary of John Leland, in or about the Years 1535–1543,* ed. Lucy Toulmin Smith. London: George Bell and Sons, 1907. Orthography modernized. Pp. xxxvi–xliii.

Serche of Johan Leylande}, which was to be followed and filled out by later scholars.

To my Sovereign Liege King Henry the eighth:

Whereas it pleased your highness upon very just considerations to encourage me, by the authority of your most gracious commission in the fifteenth year of your prosperous reign, to pursue and diligently to search all the libraries of monasteries and colleges of this your noble realm, to the intent that the monuments of ancient writers as well of other nations, as of this your own province might be brought out of deadly darkness to lively light, and to receive like thanks of the posterity, as they hoped for at such time as they employed their long and great studies to the public wealth; yea and furthermore that the holy Scripture of God might both be sincerely taught and learned, all manner of superstition and craftily colored doctrine of a route of the Roman bishops totally expelled out of this your most catholic realm: I think it now no less than my very duty bravely to declare to your Majesty what fruit has sprung from my laborious journey and costly enterprise, both rooted upon your infinite goodness and liberality, qualities right highly to be esteemed in all princes, and most especially in you as naturally your own well known properties.

First I have conserved many good authors, the which otherwise had been like to have perished to no small incommodity of good letters, of the which part remain in the most magnificent libraries of your royal palaces. Part also remain in my custody. Whereby I trust right shortly so as to describe your most noble realm, and to publish the Majesty and the excellent acts of your progenitors (hitherto sorely obscured both for lack of imprinting of such works as lay secretly in corners, and also because men of eloquence have not enterprised to set them forth in a flourishing style, in some times past not commonly used in England of writers, otherwise well learned, and now in such estimation that except truth be delicately clothed in purple her written verities can scant find a reader), that all the world shall evidently perceive that no particular region may justly be extolled than yours for true nobility and virtues at all points renowned. Furthermore, part of the exemplaries curiously sought by me, and fortunately found in sundry places of this your dominion, have been imprinted in Germany, and now are in the presses chiefly of Frobenius that not all only the Germans, but also the Italians themselves, that count, as the greeks did full arrogantly, all other nations to be

barbarous and unlettered saving their own, shall have a direct occasion
openly of force to say that *Britannia prima fuit parens, altrix* (addo hoc
etiam & jure quodam optimo), *conservatrix* cum virorum magnorum,
tum maxime ingeniorum [Britain was the parent and provider of great
and most able men].

And that profit has risen by the aforesaid journey in bringing full
many things to light as concerning the usurped authority of the Bishop
of Rome and his complices, to the manifest and violent derogation
of kingly dignity, I refer myself most humbly to your most prudent,
learned and high judgment to discern my diligence in the long volume
wherein I have made answer for the defense of your supreme dignity,
alone leaning to the strong pillar of holy Scripture against the whole
College of the Romanists, cloaking their crafty assertions and arguments
under the name of one poor Pighius of [Utrecht] in Germany, and standing to them as to their own ancher-hold against tempests that they know
will rise if truth may be by license let in to have a voice in the general
council.

Yet herein only I have not pitched the supreme mark of my labor
whereunto your grace most like a princely patron of all good learning did
animate me: but also considering and expending with myself how great
a number of excellently good wits and writers, learned with the best, as
the times served, have been in this your region, not only at such times as
the Roman Emperors had recourse to it, but also in those days that the
Saxons prevailed of the Britains, and the Normans of the Saxons, [I]
could not but with a fervant zeal and an honest courage commend them
to memory, else alas like to have been perpetually obscured or to have
been lightly remembered as uncertain shadows. Wherefore I, knowing
by infinite verity of books and assiduous reading of them who have been
learned, and who have written from time to time in this realm, have
digested into four books the names of them with their lives and monuments of learning, and to them added the title, *"De viris illustribus,"*
following the profitable example of Hieronyme, Gennadie, Cassiodorus,
Severiane, and Trittemie a late writer: but always so handling the matter
that I have more expatiated in this camp than they did, as in a thing that
desired to be somewhat at large, and to have ornament. The first book
beginning at the druids is deducted on [to] the time of the coming of
St. Augustine into England. The second is from the time of Augustine
on to the advent of the Normans. The third from the Normans to the end
of the most honorable reign of the mighty, famous, and prudent Prince

Henry the VII, your Father. The fourth begins with the name of your Majesty, whose glory in learning is to the world so clearly known, that though among the lives of other learned men I have accurately celebrated the names of . . . Kings and your progenitors; and also Ethelwarde, second son of Alfred the Great, [Humphrey] Duke of Glocester, and [Tiptoft] Earl of Worcester; yet conferred with [i.e., compared with] your Grace they seem as small lights (if I may freely say my judgment, your high modesty not offended) in respect of the day-star.

Now further to insinuate to your Grace of what matters the writers, whose lives I have congested into four books, have treated of, I may right boldly say, that besides the cognition of the three tongues, in the which part of them have excelled, that there is no kind of liberal science, or any feat concerning learning, in the which they have not shown certain arguments of great felicity of wit; yea and concerning the interpretation of holy Scripture, both after the ancient form, and sins in the scholastical trade, they have reigned in a certain excellency.

And as touching historical knowledge there has been to the number of a full hundred, or more, that from time to time have with great diligence, and no less faith, would to God with like eloquence, prescribed the acts of your most noble predecessors, and the fortunes of this realm, so incredibly great, that he that has not seen and thoroughly read their works can little pronounce in this part.

Wherefore after that I had perpended [i.e., pondered] the honest and profitable studies of these historiographies, I was totally inflamed with a love to see thoroughly all those parts of this your opulent and ample realm, that I had read of in the aforesaid writers: in so much that all my other occupations intermitted I have so traveled in your dominions both by the sea coasts and the middle parts, sparing neither labor nor costs, by the space of these six years past, that there is almost neither cape, nor bay, haven, creek or pier, river or confluence of rivers, breches, waschis, lakes, meres, fenny waters, mountains, valleys, moors, heaths, forests, [chases,] woods, cities, burges, castles, principal manor places, monasteries, and colleges, but [that] I have seen them and noted in so doing a whole world of things very memorable.

Thus instructed I trust shortly to see the time that like as [Charlemagne] had among his treasures three large and notable tables of silver richly enameled, one of the site and description of Constantinople, another of the site and figure of the magnificent city of Rome, and the third of the description of the world; so shall your majesty have this your world and empire of England so set forth in a quadrate table of silver, if God sends me life to accomplish my beginnings, that your grace shall have ready knowledge at the first sight of many right delectable, fruitful, and necessary pleasures, by the contemplation thereof, as often as occasion shall move you to the sight of it. And because that it may be more permanent, and further known than to have it engraved in silver or brass, I intend (by the leave of God) within the space of twelve months following, such a description to make of your realm in writing, that it shall be no mastery after[ward] for the graver or painter to make a like[ness] by a perfect example.

Yea and to wade further in this matter, whereas now almost no man can well guess at the shadow of the ancient names of havens, rivers, promontories, hills, woods, cities, towns, castles, and [the] variety of kind[r]eds of people, that Caesar, Livy, Strabo, Diodorus, Fabius Pictor, Pomponius Mela, Pliny, Cornelius Tacitus, Ptolemy, Sextus Rufus, Ammianus Marcellinus, Solinus, Antoninus, and diverse others make mention of, I trust so to open this window that the light be seen so long, that is to say, by the space of a whole thousand years, stopped up, and the old glory of your renouned Britain to reflourish through the world.

This done, I have matter at plenty already prepared to this purpose, that is to say to write a history, to the which I intend to ascribe this title, De Antiquitate Britannica, or else Civilis Historia. And this work I intend to divide into so many books as there be shires in England, and sheres and great dominions in Wales. So that I esteem that this volume will include fifty books, whereof each one severally shall contain the beginnings, increases, and memorable acts of the chief towns and castles of the province allotted to it. . . .

And to superadd a work as an ornament and a right comely garland to the enterprises aforesaid, I have selected stuff to be distributed into three books, the which I propose to entitle, De Nobilitate Britannica. Whereof the first shall declare the names of kings, queens, with their children, dukes, earls, lords, captains and rulers in this realm to the coming of the Saxons and their conquest. The second shall be of the Saxons and Danes to the victory of King William the Great. The third from the Normans to the reign of your most noble grace, descending lineally of the Britain, Saxon and Norman kings. So that all noble men shall clearly perceive their lineal parentage.

Now if it shall be the pleasure of Almighty God that I may live to perform these things that are already begun and in a great forwardness, I trust that this your realm shall be so well known, once painted with its native colors, that the renown thereof shall give place to the glory of no other region; and my great labors and costs, proceeding from the most abundant fountain of your infinite goodness toward me, your poor scholar and most humble servant, shall be evidently seen to have not all only pleased but also profited the studious, gentle, and equal readers.

This is the brief declaration of my laborious journey, taken by motion of your highness, so much studying at all hours the fruitfull preferment of good letters and ancient virtues.

Christ continue your most royal estate, and the prosperity with succession in kingly dignity of your deer and worthily beloved son Prince Edward, Granting you a number of princely sons by the most gracious, benign, and modest lady your Queen.

> 85. WILLIAM CAMDEN (1551–1623), greatest of English antiquarians and historians, not only wrote a history of the reign of Elizabeth but also followed Leland in the study of English geography and medieval sources. In order to "restore antiquity to England and England to antiquity," Camden offered in his *Britannia* (published in increasingly amplified editions from 1586 to 1607) a narrative of Roman and Anglo-Saxon England down to the Norman conquest and continued his work in a set of monographic studies of geographic, social, cultural, and institutional history.

As all the Regions with the whole worlds frame, and all therein was created by the Almightie, for his last and most perfect worke that goodly, upright, provident, subtile, wittie, and reasonable creature, which the Greekes call [*anthropos*], for his upright looke the Latines Homo, for that he was made of Molde; and we with the Germains, call Man of his principall part, the mind, being the verie image of God, and pettie world within himselfe: so he assigned in his divine providence, this so happy and worthy region to men of answerable worth, if not surpassing, yet equalling the most excellent inhabitants of the earth, both in the endowments of minde, lineaments of bodie, and their deportment both in peace and warre, as if I would enter into this discourse I could very easily shew.

But overpassing their naturall inclination by heavenly influence an-

William Camden, *The Inhabitants of Britain*. In *Remains Concerning Britain*, ed. and trans. R. D. Dunn. Toronto: University of Toronto Press, 1984. Pp. 13–14 and 15–18.

swerable to the disposition of Aries, Leo, and Sagittary, & Jupiter, with Mars Dominators for this Northwest part of the world, which maketh them impatient of servitude, lovers of liberties, martiall and couragious, I will only in particular note some what, and that summarily of the Britaines, Scottish, and English the three principall inhabitants.

The Britaines, the most ancient people of this Isle inhabited the same from sea to sea, whose valour and prowes is renowned both in Latine and Greek monuments, and may appear in these two points which I will heere onely note. First that the most puissant Roman forces, when they were at the highest, could not gaine of them, being then a halfe-naked people, in thirty whole yeares the countries from the Thames to Striviling. And when they had gained them, and brought them into forme of a province, they found them so warlike a people, that the Romanes levied as many Cohorts, companies, and ensignes of Britans from hence for the service of Armenia, Aegypt, Illyricum, their frontire Countries, as from any other of their Provinces whatsoever. As for those Britans which were farther North, and after as is most probable, called Pictes, (for that they still painted themselves when the Southerne parts were brought to Civilities,) they not onely most couragiously defended their libertie, but offended the Romans with continuall and most dangerous incursions. The other remainder of the Britans, which retyred themselves to the west parts, now called Wales, with like honour of fortitude, for many hundred years, repelled the yoake both of the English and Norman slaverie. . . .

And since they were admited to the imperiall Crowne of England, they have, to their just praise, performed all parts of dutifull loyalties and allegiance most faithfully therunto; plentifully yeelding Martiall Captaines, judicious Civillians, skilfull common Lawyers, learned Divines, complete Courtiers, and adventrous Souldiers. In which commendations their cousins the Cornishmen do participate proportionally, although they were sooner brought under the English command.

Great also is the glorie of those Britons, which in most dolefull time of the English invasion, withdrew themselves into the West parts of Gallia, then called Armorica; For they not onely seated themselves there, maugre the Romans, (then indeede low, and neare setting,) and the French: but also imposed their name to the countrey, held and defended the same against the French, untill in our grandfathers memorie, it was united to France by the sacred bonds of matrimonie.

Next after the Britans, the Scottishmen comming out of Ireland, planted themselves in this Isle on the North side of Cluid, partly by force, partly by favour of the Pictes, with whom a long time they annoyed the Southerne parts, but after many blody battels amongst themselves, the Scottishmen subdued them, and established a kingdome in those parts, which with manlike courage and warlike prowesse, they have not onely maintained at home, but also hath purchased great honour abroad. For the French cannot but acknowledge they have seldome atchieved any honourable acts without Scottish hands, who therefore are deservedly to participate the glorie with them. As also divers parts of France, Germany, and Suitzerland, cannot but confesse, that they owe to the Scottish Nation, the propagation of good letters and Christian religion amongst them.

After the Scottishmen, the Angles, Englishmen or Saxons, by Gods wonderfull providence were transplanted hither out of Germanie. A people composed of the valiant Angles, Jutes, and Saxons, then inhabiting Jutland, Holsten, and the sea coasts along to the river Rhene, who in short time subduing the Britans, and driving them into the mountanous Westerne parts, made themselves by a most compleate conquest, absolute Lords of all the better soyle thereof, as farre as Orkeney. Which cannot be doubted of, when their English tongue reacheth so farre along the East coast, unto the farthest parts of Scotland, and the people thereof are called by the Highland-men, which are the true Scots, by no other name than Saxons, by which they also call us the English.

This warlike, victorious, stiffe, stowt, and rigorous Nation, after it had as it were taken roote heere about one hundred and sixtie years, and spread his branches farre and wide, being mellowed and mollified by the mildeness of the soyle and sweete aire, was prepared in fulnes of time for the first spirituall blessing of God, I meane our regeneration in Christ, and our ingrafting into his mysticall bodie by holy baptisme. Which Beda our Ecclesiastical Historian recounteth in this manner, and I hope you will give it the reading. Gregorie the Great Bishop of Rome, on a time saw beautifull boyes to be sold in the market at Rome, & demanded from whence they were; answer was made him, out of the Isle of Britain. Then asked he againe, whither they were Christians or no? They said no. "Alas for pittie" said Gregorie, "that the foule fiend should be Lord of such faire folkes; and that they which carrie such grace in their countenance, should be voide of grace in their hearts." Then he would know of them by what name their Nation was called, and they told him "Angleshmen. And justly be they so called" (quoth he,) "for they have

Angelike faces, and seeme meete to be made coheires with the Angells in heaven."

Since which time, they made such happy progresse in the Christian profession both of faith and works, that if I should but enter into consideration thereof, I should be over-whelmed with many tides of matter. Many and admirable monuments thereof, do every where at home present themselves to your view, erected in former times, (and no small number in our age, although few men note them,) not for affectation of fame, or ostentation of wealth, but to the glorie of God, increase of faith, of learning and to maintenance of the poore. As for abroad, the world can testifie that foure Englishmen have converted to Christianitie, eight nations of Europe. Winfrid alias Boniface, the Denshire-man converted the German Saxons, Franconians, Hessians, and Thuringians. Willebrod the Northern man, the Frisians and Hollanders. Nicholas Brakspere of Middlesex, who was after called Pope Hadrian the Norwegians, and not long since, Thomas of Walden of Essex, the Lithuanians. Neither will I heere note which strangers have noted, that England hath bred more Princes renowned for sanctitie, than any Christian Nation whatsoever.

It doth also redound to the eternall honour of England, that our countrimen have twice beene schoolemaisters to France. First when they taught the Gaules the discipline of the Druides; and after, when they and the Scottishmen first taught the French the liberall Arts, and perswaded Carolus magnus to found the Universitie of Paris. They also brought into Fraunce the best lawes which the Parlament of Paris and Burdeaux have now in use. They at the lowest ebbe of learning, amazed the world with their excellent knowledge in Philosophie, and Divinitie: for that I may not particulate of "Alexander of Hales, the Irrefragable Doctor," Schoolemaster to the "Angelique" Doctor "Thomas Aquinas," one Colledge in Oxford brought forth in one age those foure lights of learning: "Scotus the Subtile, Bradwardine the Profound, Okham the Invincible, and Burley the Perspicuous," and as some say, "Baconthorpe the Resolute"; which Titles they hadde by the common consent of the judiciall and learned of that and the succeeding ages.

Yet their militarie glorie hath surpassed all, for they have terrified the whole world with their Armes in Syria, Aegypt, Cyprus, Spaine, Sicill, and India.

They have traversed with most happy victories both France and Scotland, brought away their Kings captives, conquered Ireland and the

Isle of Cyprus, which King Richard the first gave frankly to Guie of Lusignian, and lately with a maidens hand, mated the mightiest Monarch in his owne Countries. They beside many other notable discoveries, twice compassed the whole globe of the earth with admirable successe, which the Spaniards have yet but once performed. Good Lord, how spaciously might a learned pen walke in this argument!

> 86. FRANÇOIS HOTMAN (1522–1590) was a Calvinist scholar, jurist, and ideologist who composed, during the religious wars, a review of the political and institutional history of France from the perspective of the Huguenot party, which he served. His *Francogallia* (1773) traced the decline of the "ancient constitution" of the French monarchy (comparable to the thesis of his earlier work, *The State of the Primitive Church*) from Merovingian times down to the religious wars and lamented the Roman (first imperial and then "papist") "tyranny" which had come to replace Gallo-Germanic liberty and constitutional government as reflected in the French customs, the Estates General, and the popular character and "fundamental laws" of the monarchy.

There was a time when young men, anxious to learn, poured into our Francogallia from all the ends of the earth to attend the academies, coming, as it were, to sample the wares available in the arts. Now they shun them, as if they were seas infested with pirates, and curse them as though they were the lair of some barbarous Cyclops. The thought of this circumstance wounds me deeply when I consider that for nearly twelve years my miserable and unfortunate country has been scorched by the fires of civil war. My sorrow is even more bitter when I reflect that so many have stood by unconcerned, observing the flames (as Nero once watched Rome burning), and some have wickedly blown upon these fires with the bellows of their speeches and libels, while few, if any, have hastened to extinguish them. I know well enough my own slight and humble condition. Nevertheless, in a general conflagration I believe that anyone, however low his station, who can throw on a bucket of water makes a welcome contribution. In this spirit I hope that no one who loves our country will disdain the service I would render in seeking salve for its affliction.

In reflecting upon these great calamities I have, for several months

François Hotman, *Francogallia*. Trans. J. H. M. Salmon. Cambridge: Cambridge University Press, 1972. Pp. 141–145, 183, 185, 189–191, 197–199, 343–347, 349, and 523.

past (in the year 1572 and in 1573), fixed my attention on what is revealed by all the old French and German historians of our Francogallia, and from their writings I have compiled a summary of its constitution. They show that our commonwealth flourished in this form for more than a thousand years. From this review it is astonishing to find how great was the wisdom of our ancestors in constituting our commonwealth, and it does not seem possible for me to doubt in any way that the most certain remedy for our great afflictions should be sought in the constitution. For, as I gave increasing attention to the cause of these calamities, it seemed to me that, even as our own bodies decay (whether by external blows and shocks, or by the inward corruption of humours, or by old age), so, too, do commonwealths perish, some by hostile attack, some by internal dissensions, and some by senescence. Although the troubles that afflict our commonwealth are commonly thought to proceed from internal conflicts, these should be seen not as the cause but as the beginning of our troubles. That weighty writer Polybius shows in his works how important it is to distinguish between the beginning of a thing and its cause. Now I assert that the cause was the blow delivered against our constitution about one hundred years ago by one who certainly was the first to undermine the excellent institutions designed by our ancestors. Just as our bodies, when dislocated by some external blow, cannot be repaired unless each member be restored to its natural seat and place, so we may trust that our commonwealth will return to health when it is restored by some act of divine beneficence into its ancient and, so to speak, its natural state. And, because Your Highness has always proved himself to be the greatest friend of our country, I judged it to be the best thing I could do to inscribe, if not consecrate, this summary of our history to your most illustrious name, so that your patronage and authority will enable it to pass more safely into the hands of its readers. Hail and farewell, most illustrious Prince. I beseech Almighty God to suffer your illustrious house to live for ever in all blessedness and prosperity. . . .

The origin of the Franks, who, when they had occupied Gaul, changed its name to France or Francogallia

Our argument now requires us to inquire into the place of origin of the Franks, into their original settlements and the cradle of their race. It is certain that the people who bore that name occupied a large part of

Europe for many years and that they were German. Hence it is very surprising that no mention is made of them by Ptolemy, Strabo and Pliny, and especially that no reference is to be found in Cornelius Tacitus, who traced the locations and names of all the German peoples with extraordinary diligence. We offer some few examples from the many references which attest the importance of the Frankish name.

First, St. Jerome in his *Life of Hilary the Hermit* remarks: "The man whom the Emperor Constantine supported had red hair and a white skin, indicating that he was a provincial. Among the Saxons and Alemanni that people is strong rather than agreeable, and used to be called Germans by the historians, though now they are called Franks." A little further on Jerome writes: "He had known a good deal of the Frankish tongue as well as Latin." Another example is from the chronicle of Johannes Nauclerus, where he says: "Charlemagne was called king of the Franks, which is the same thing as saying he had been declared king of Germany and Gaul. It is well known that at that time the whole Transalpine Gaul and Germany, stretching from the Pyrenees as far as Pannonia, was called France [Francia]. The latter was called Germany or Eastern France, the former Gallica or Western France. All historians agree as to the truth of this statement. . . . ."

. . . Einhard in his *Life of Charlemagne* writes: "Charles had received the mighty kingdom of the Franks from his father Pepin the Great, and he so nobly extended its boundaries that he nearly doubled its size. Formerly it was not larger than that part of Gaul which lies between the Loire and the Rhine, the ocean and the Balearic Sea, and included a part of Germany between Saxony and the Danube and between the Rhine and the River Sala, which divides the Thuringians from the Sorabi. Later this area was inhabited by the so-called Eastern Franks. Beyond these the Alemanni and the Bavarians passed into the power of the Frankish kingdom. Through various memorable wars he first conquered Aquitaine, etc."

Otto of Freising writes in his chronicle concerning the kingdom of Dagobert: "The land of the Franks now extended from Spain as far as Pannonia, including two most noble duchies, Aquitaine and Bavaria." He gives much greater detail in a later passage. Godfrey of Viterbo follows him in his chronicle for the year 881. . . .

Otto of Freising writes in his fourth Chronicle: "It seems to me that the Franks who lived in Gaul adapted their language as a result of their contact with the Romans and so produced the tongue they speak today, while others who remained near the Rhine and in Germany employed Teutonic speech." In many passages this opinion has been closely followed by Godfrey of Viterbo: "The Franks seem to me," he writes, "to have learnt in those times the Roman language they still use today, and to have learnt it from those Romans who had once lived there." It is perfectly clear from these references that both the Frankish name and the breadth of their authority were widely recognised, which one might expect, since they held a large part of Europe. . . .

. . . These matters seem clearly established, and yet Gregory bishop of Tours, who wrote about the origin of the Franks eight hundred years earlier, declares at the beginning of his history that, though he had conducted detailed researches into the problem, he had found nothing at all that was certain. Gregory possessed an ancient work by one of their historians, Sulpicius Alexander, but he had nothing to say about their first place of origin nor about the origins of their kingdom. Nevertheless, we have noted that the original Franks came from that area lying between the Elbe, the Rhine and the sea, close to the country where the greater and lesser Chauci were settled, "a people," as Tacitus says, "who were the most noble among the Germans, and who maintained their greatness by following the path of justice." This was the region which bordered on the country of the Batavi, for it is generally agreed that the Frankish settlements were on the sea coast among the marshes, and that the Franks excelled in seamanship and in naval warfare. . . .

As to nearly all those others who take delight in fables and would relate the origin of the Franks to the Trojans and to a certain hypothetical Francion, son of Priam, we can only say that such an argument provides material for the work of poets, not of historians. Among them pride of place should go to Guillaume du Bellay, who, although he stood foremost in his knowledge of all the higher arts and deserved great praise for his ingenuity, yet in his book on the antiquities of Gaul and France would seem to have composed a work of fabulous deeds, after the manner of the *Amadis de Gaule,* rather than a history of Francogallia. . . .

The Public Council

We believe that they clearly show, as we said at the beginning, that our ancestors who, as Franks, were truly the guardians of liberty, did not place themselves under any tyrant or executioner who might treat his subjects as if they were cattle, but rather did they abhor all tyranny and especially the domination of any Turkish tyrant, and they held strictly to that divine precept: "LET THE WELFARE OF THE PEOPLE BE THE SUPREME LAW." Indeed our examples prove that the whole power of administering the kingdom clearly lay with the public council, which, as we said earlier, was called the placitum. Such is the term used by the anonymous chronicler of Dijon in this passage: "In the year 764 King Pepin held a great placitum among the Franks in the town of Carignan." But the origin of this word was lost, and the reason for this was that by strict Latin usage the term meant something which had been questioned and debated by many men in consultation, and a thing upon which they had finally reached agreement among themselves, whence the expression placita among philosophers, as employed by Cicero and other men of ancient times. An example is given by Gellius: "The Spartan people used to deliberate on anything that was useful and honourable and for the greatest good of the commonwealth." He goes on: "The advice they gave was accepted and approved [complacitum] by all the citizens." . . .

This being so I believe the conjecture I have already set forth in certain other books will not seem unreasonable, that is that the common phrase, "For such is our placitum," which royal clerks even today employ at the foot of laws and ordinances, was derived from the word placitum. All these ordinances used to be written in Latin (which we regard as clearly enough established from Aimon, the Capitulary of Charlemagne and other records of this kind), but later, when the royal clerks began to use the vernacular, they unwittingly, or, rather, maliciously, translated the expression as "Car tel est nostre plaisir" ["For such is our pleasure"].

There is this further evidence of the power of the people in Charlemagne's Capitulary: that, if any new clauses be added to the law, the people should be consulted about them and, when all consented to the additions, they should sign their names in confirmation of these clauses. It is manifest from these words that the people of France were formerly bound only by those laws which they had approved by their own votes in the assemblies. . . .

Lest any point by overlooked, it may be said, in conclusion, that such was the authority of this council among other peoples that even foreign princes sometimes applied for the judgment of the council on an issue in dispute between them. This is shown in the appendix to Gregory of Tours: "In the twelfth year of his reign, the district of Alsatia, where Theuderic had been brought up and which he held by command of his father, Childebert, was passed to Theudebert according to a barbarous custom. Accordingly it was agreed by the two kings to hold an assembly in the fortress by the River Sala, so that the matters might be resolved by the judgment of the Franks." . . .

The Parlements

. . . The more I track down the origin of this disease of pettifoggery, which we can very truly call the French pox, the more I am certain of the view I earlier advanced, namely that, just as the plague of superstition, and many other plagues besides, flowed out from the workshop of the Roman pontiffs, so too did the practice of the art of legal chicanery reach us from the court of Rome, because it is known to have expanded to its full extent a few years after the promulgation of the decretals. For in the decretals of Gratian there is reference to a letter from Pope Leo (whom they list in the calendar of their saints) to Louis II, who was both king of France and emperor. There it is stated that the pope submits to the edicts and ordinances of the emperors and the law established by them. The letter goes on to say that the pope begs that same emperor for his clemency and wishes the constitutions of Roman Law everywhere to be observed. Indeed, there exists a decretal of Pope Honorius III where it is clearly shown that right up to that time the popes had obeyed the provisions of Roman Law and the constitutions of the Christian emperors contained in Justinian's Code, and that these were used in disputes on oath.

Someone may ask whether we have any remedy to suggest for such ills. It is clear that the cause of all these troubles is in part impiety, and in part the incredible superstition of our people, which flowed in to us throughout those times from that same font. This shrouded the whole Christian world like a huge fog, and, when the single light of the Christian religion was extinguished as the holy scriptures were obscured and buried, all things continued to be weighed down by the thick darkness of superstition.

87. JACQUES-AUGUSTE DE THOU (1553–1617), member of a dynasty of French lawyers and educated in a humanist manner, was the greatest historian of his age. The *History of His Times*, a prod-

Jacques-Auguste de Thou, *Dedication to Henry IV*. In *The Life of Thuanus, with some Account of His Writings and a Translation of the Preface to His History*, by John Collinson. London: Longman, Hurst, Rees, and Orme, 1807. Pp. 389–395, 397–398, 405–407, 409, 421, 423–424, 430–432, 435–438, and 439.

uct of travels, correspondence, and industrious book-collecting, presented an extraordinarily comprehensive and detailed history of the European world from 1546 to 1607. The work, which Dr. Johnson once thought of translating, was placed on the Roman *Index* of forbidden books for its excessive frankness. In the preface, De Thou defends his historiographical standards, methods, and practice.

Sire, when the design of writing a history of these times first engaged my thoughts, it did not escape me that such a work, however executed, would be exposed to various censures; but I knew that ambition was not my motive, and consoled myself with the reward to be derived only from a good conscience. I hoped also that, in proportion as time gradually abated personal animosities, a love of truth might succeed, especially under the government of your Majesty; who, by the signal favor of Providence, after crushing the monstrous brood of rebellion, and extinguishing faction in its embers, have given peace to France, and at the same time united liberty and regal power, two things usually thought incompatible.

The passions of aspiring men then formed a constant source of civil war, and all hopes of peace were excluded from the public councils of the realm. Such a conjuncture I lamented for the sake of my country, but it appeared propitious to the historian, who, avoiding detraction, wished to write with freedom. On this point, however, my sentiments have altered with the times. I was induced, as I have said, to begin to write in camps, in the midst of sieges and the noise of arms, when my mind was engrossed by the variety and importance of events, and sought, in composition, a relief from public calamity. My work has been continued and completed in your Majesty's court, amongst the oppressive labours of the law, foreign journies, and other avocations; and, upon reflection, I have become apprehensive that what might have pleased, or at least have been excused in tumultuous times, may now give less satisfaction, and even offend certain morose persons. For, by the infirmity of our nature, we are more inclined to do ill, than to hear of what we have ill done.

It is the first law of history to fear to record what is false, and, in the next place, not to want courage in relating the truth. And I can affirm that I have taken sincere pains to discover, to extricate, to display the truth, when obscured or buried under party contentions, and on all occasions to deliver it with unblemished integrity to posterity. I should have been ashamed to prevaricate in a cause so honorable, and through an absurd affectation of prudence, do injustice to the singular happiness of your Majesty's times, in which every one is allowed to think what he pleases, and to speak what he thinks.

With respect to myself, I trust all who know me (and I have not lived in obscurity) know how far I am from dissimulation. Since, by your Majesty's clemency, we have been all restored to favor, I have utterly discarded all sense of any private injuries, and may, with justice, be confident that no person, however prejudiced, will accuse me of want of candor and temper, in all that relates to past transactions. I may appeal to the testimony of those very persons, whose names occur often in these books, who have always found me ready to do them all honorable service, according to the extent of the powers, entrusted to me by your Majesty.

What upright judges ought to do in determining of the fortunes and lives of men, that I have done in this work, interrogating myself at different times, whether or not any personal pique might operate to give my opinion a wrong bias. I have sometimes covered the harshness of actions with gentle expressions, continually repressed my own judgment, and abstained from digressions. Lastly I have aimed to acquire a plain and simple style, the image of a mind averse from vain and ostentatious ornament, equally free from asperity and adulation.

In return I request of my readers to lay aside private prejudices, and forbear to decide upon my history, until they have perused it with attention.

The undertaking is perhaps beyond my abilities; and my imperfections will be manifest on many occasions. But the public good, and an ardent desire to merit the good opinion of mine own age and of posterity have so far prevailed, that I had rather be thought wanting in caution, than in my affection for their service.

I am not so much in pain about my fidelity, of which I am thoroughly conscious. My industry, too, has been such, as will perhaps meet with indulgence from your Majesty, and the candid reader. But what unfortunately constitutes the greatest part of my work, will, I fear, prove offensive and unpalatable to many, who, being removed (as they think) from danger in their own persons, want both feeling and justice, in estimating the calamities of others.

I allude to the religious dissensions, which, in addition to other evils, have infested this corrupt age. This malady has for a century afflicted the Christian world, and will continue to afflict it, unless seasonable remedies, and therefore different from such as have been hitherto used, be applied by those whose province it is. Experience has taught us, that fire and sword, exile and proscription, rather irritate than heal the distemper, that has its seat in the mind. These only affect the body; but judicious and edifying doctrine, gently instilled, descends into the heart.

Other things are regulated at the discretion of the civil magistrate, and consequently of the sovereign. Religion alone is not subject to command, but is infused into well prepared minds from a pre-conceived opinion of the truth, with the concurrence of divine grace. Tortures have no influence over her: in fact, they rather tend to make men obstinate, than to subdue or persuade them. What the stoics boasted, with so much parade, of their wisdom, applies with far more justice to religion. Affliction and pain have no power over the religion man. . . .

. . . Tortures therefore by no means repress the ardor of innovators in religion: but their minds are rather hardened by them, to suffer and attempt more. From the ashes of those who perished, others arose; and as their numbers encreased, patience was converted into fury. Those who had been suppliants for mercy, began to expostulate, to make demands with importunity: those who had fled from punishment, now boldly betook themselves to arms.

France has now witnessed this visitation for forty years, and the Netherlands nearly as long. The evil is become so aggravated, that it cannot now be rooted out, as it perhaps might have been originally, by one or two public acts of punishment. It has pervaded whole countries, whole nations, and in fact the greater part of Europe: and now, not the secular arm of the magistracy, but the sword of the Lord only can avail. Mild persuasion and amicable conference may still conciliate those, whom force cannot subdue. . . .

This mild system prevailed till the time of the Vaudois. Persecution had then no effect: but the wound rankled under this improper treatment. The number of sectaries daily encreased, complete armies were raised by their party; and at length, a crusade, no less important than that which our ancestors headed against the Saracens, was decreed against them. What ensued? They were defeated, put to flight, slain, spoiled of property and honors, but they were not so convinced of their error as to be brought to a sound mind. By arms they defended themselves—by arms they were subdued, and, fleeing into Provence, and the Alps bordering upon France, found there an asylum for their lives and opinions. Part retired to Calabria, and kept themselves there even till the pontificate of Pius IV. Some passed into Germany, and others found a refuge in England. From the remnant of this sect, John Wicliff is supposed to have sprung. He taught long at Oxford; and, about three hundred years ago, after many religious contentions, died there a natural death. The secular punishment only affected his dead body; and, long after his decease, his bones were publicly burnt.

A succession of contests continued until our own age, in which, after an unhappy attempt at punishment, what began in dissension terminated in open war and revolt in Germany, England, and France. A schism being thus made and confirmed, and too long neglected by those who could and ought to have remedied it, it is uncertain whether the public tranquillity, or religion itself, has been the greater sufferer.

I do not wish to revive the old question of punishing heretics. That controversy would ill suit my time of life or condition. But I am desirous to shew that those princes have acted with prudence, and, conformably to the institutions of the ancient church, who have judged it right to appease religious contests even upon disadvantageous terms, rather than suppress them by force of arms. . . .

The progress of events brings me now to our own times: and I am preparing to handle a sore, barely to touch with, I fear, will be to my prejudice. But since I have entered on this topic, I will dismiss it in one word, and ingenuously say, (under your Majesty's reign this may be done) that war is not the legitimate mode of removing schism from the church. . . .

Your Majesty then exercised that moderation and lenity, the benefit of which you had in your own person experienced. The edicts published against the Protestants, contrary to the will of your predecessor, were revoked, and after making peace at home and abroad with great honor, you confirmed two decrees successively made in their favor by a third, which reinstated them in their estates and good name. Many were advanced to the first places of dignity: and you judged that thus concord would be more commodiously cemented, and the ferment in the minds of men subsiding, the clouds of passion and prejudice would disperse, and they would discern what is the best, that is, the most ancient religious constitution. . . .

Taught, therefore, by experience, and your Majesty's example, I have abstained from opprobrious language, and have always made honorable mention of the Protestants, especially those who excelled in learning. Neither have I concealed the faults of our own party; for I think, as the best men have thought, that the manifold heresies, which agitate the world at this day, have gathered strength, not more from the malice and intrigues of their supporters, than from our vices. . . .

The education I received from my father, (an excellent man, as is well known, and very tenacious of the old religion); the traditionary lesson, if I may so speak, delivered from my grandfather and great-grandfather, and my own disposition upon taking a part in public affairs; all have concurred to make the love of my country, next to reverence of the supreme Being, the strongest passions of my heart. I do not put in competition with it private affections, and private gratifications. I entirely adopt the sentiment of the ancients, that our country is a second God, and the laws of our country other deities. Whoever violates them, whatever color of piety he may assume, is sacrilegious, and a parricide.

These rights, these laws, are the foundation upon which France has raised herself to her present extent of dominion, and eminence of grandeur.

If there be any (and I wish there were not) who would by degrees subvert these by mines and secret engines, aware that open force would not avail, we should not be good citizens, we should be unworthy of the name of Frenchmen, if we did not make resistance unto death.

It is the voice of our ancestors, men eminent for piety, that the preservation of the laws is the heavenly pledge of public safety, the palladium of our country. While we keep it in custody, we may defy foreign machinations; but if it be lost, we are no longer secure. If through our cowardice or remissness this should ever be stolen, there is no doubt but the robber, another Ulysses skilled in Grecian wiles, will, by suborning some Sinon, introduce into France a fatal horse pregnant with foreign soldiers. Then will this most flourishing part of Europe be laid waste by a conflagration, like that which levelled Troy with the ground.

God grant us a better fate! nor have we this to fear, while your Majesty and the Dauphin are preserved to us. . . .

. . . Terrible in war, you assume the most amiable character during peace. The fine arts regard you as their patron: and those immense edifices, raised with incredible celerity, with all their costly magnificence of tapestry, painting, sculpture, in the most exquisite workmanship, are monuments of the greatness of your mind, and of your attachment to peace, which no time will deface.

What is more than all, the muses, driven from their ancient seats by the rage of war, congratulate you as their restorer. Under your auspices, the university of Paris has revived; and by the accession of Isaac Casaubon, that luminary of the age, to the custody of your Majesty's truly royal library, it has lately acquired a splendid ornament.

Thus it is plain that the uninterrupted course of so many triumphs did not serve so much as a state of progression to more ambitious projects, as it inspired you with the resolution of cultivating peace with your neighbours, and giving rest to your weary harassed people. Proceed, Sire, in this generous design; pursue the plan of confirming the peace, purchased at the expence of so many labors, by restoring vigour and authority to the laws. Assure yourself that the life and soul and judgment and understanding of the country center in the laws; and that a state without law, like a body deprived of its animating principle, is defunct and lifeless in its blood and members. Magistrates and judges are ministers and interpreters of the laws; and in fine, WE ARE ALL SERVANTS OF THE LAWS, THAT WE MAY BE FREE.

In the confidence of enjoying this freedom, I have composed my history, the first part of which I here present to the public, and dedicate it to your august name, for many just reasons, which concern both the author and the subject matter itself.

It would be ingratitude for me to forget the addition made by your Majesty to that honor, which I first received at the hands of your predecessor of blessed memory. In the course of my services in courts and in camps, I have been entrusted with many negociations of importance; and have thus obtained much of the knowledge requisite for a work of this kind. Profiting by my intercourse with several illustrious persons, who had grown old in the court, I have reduced to the scale of truth many things that have appeared in scattered publications, or on uncertain authority. Whilst I formed part of your Majesty's retinue, I exerted my diligence on this object, until the obligation of my office confined me to this slavery of the bar. . . .

. . . Another reason for inscribing this history to you is, that, as I have undertaken a work full of dangerous hazard, I stood in need of powerful patronage to screen me from the calumnious and malevolent; and also of that discerning judgment which your Majesty displays in the conduct of national affairs, to examine the truth of my relations.

8

❡ The Science
of History

In the sixteenth century, under the combined intellectual forces of the Renaissance and the Reformation, the study of history was promoted by some scholars from the level of art to that of science, which is to say from the writing of historical narrative (the principal subject of the Italianate "arts" of history) to the reading and reorganization of histories for political and philosophical purposes (the aim of the French "methods" of history). The polemical needs of Reformation controversy enlisted the services of historical study, yet without losing the legacy of classical commonplaces (history teaching by example, and so on) which had been inherited and developed by Renaissance humanists. This contrast can be seen in the conventional praises of history assembled by Tommaso Campanella, Daniel Heinsius, and the derivative work of Thomas Blundeville (though many other examples could be chosen) and the handbooks of historical method, beginning especially with the influential work of Jean Bodin.

Originally, *method* implied arrangement of historical data and categories for pedagogical purposes, but increasingly the term came to suggest techniques of historical investigation and authentication which originated in Renaissance philology and culminated in works of erudition by such writers as Jean Mabillon, whose work represented a codification of the so-called auxiliary sciences of history. One of the major disciplines serving history was the science of chronology, established in the previous century by Joseph Justus Scaliger and continued in the seventeenth century by Archbishop Ussher. On this basis, universal history was promoted from its medieval, Augustinian form (still reflected in some ways in the *Discourse* of Jacques-Bénigne Bossuet) to a comparative, comprehensive, and synchronic study of civilizations on a global scale.

For Bodin, history not only became a science but was placed "above all sciences." For Francis Bacon, on the other hand, *history* still meant either empirical data or else accounts of civil and ecclesiastical affairs; although, conceptually, it found a place in his scheme of learning and scientific method, it was identified with memory and subordinated to the higher faculty of reason. Outside the imperial terrain of natural philosophy, history continued to be regarded as both art and science (in the old-fashioned sense of organized knowledge if not of the "new science" of Bacon or Galileo), but historical method and scientific history continued to be separated from the literary tradition of historical narrative, at least until the eighteenth century.

❡ THE ART OF HISTORY

88. MARC-ANTOINE MURET (1526–1585), great classical scholar, regius professor in the College of Three Languages in Paris, and a teacher of Michel de Montaigne, delivered Latin orations on many subjects. Here he offers a standard humanist celebration of the art of history.

Cicero in his first book on Invention gives this definition of history: "History is a thing done but removed from the memory of our age." Now in this definition (though it accords with that written by Cornificius or whoever was the author of the Rhetoric to Herennius) there are almost as many faults as there are words. In the first place history is not a "thing done" but rather an exposition or narration of what has been done. For the conspiracy of Cataline and the war made by Jugurtha are not history, and it is not what these authors meant to say and does not express properly what they had in mind. This one may indeed excuse and attribute to carelessness, but one should not be negligent in a definition. As for what they added (that it is not history if not something remote from the memory), of what relevance is that? For if someone writes today about Romulus and Remus, should we admit that he writes history and

Marc-Antoine Muret, *Discours de l'histoire.* In *Discours de l'histoire extraict des memoires d'une harangue latine de Marc Ant. Muret,* trans. from the Latin by Frederic Morel. Paris: n.p., 1604. Pp. 1–2. My translation.

yet, if he puts into writing the wars between Charles V and Francis I, should we deny that he writes history because these things are not "removed from the memory of our age"? Or indeed should we say that they are not yet histories but only made such when they find somebody who remembers those things? Thus it would seem that he does not now write a history, and yet those who read his writings read a history. Even Thucydides did not write history in this sense, nor Xenophon in his book on the wars of Cyrus the younger or on the affairs of Greece, nor Sallust when he wrote about the conspiracy of Cataline or the wars of Jugurtha. One would have to say of Livy, that he wrote history when he pursued ancient things, but that in his last books, comprising what was done in his time, he ceased to write history. . . .

How should we define history? The word "history" signifies not only the description and exposition of things done but also a account of what they were. Aristotle, treating the nature and affection of animals, called his book a "history of animals," and Theophrastus called his book on plants a "history." But the books in which one investigates the causes and principles of things or in which one gives the principles of a discipline, cannot properly be called "history". . . , except where one describes and exposes something in a simple way. This is why a certain book (misattributed to Galen), in which the opinions of ancient philosophers on each subject are recited plainly without being analyzed, is justly called "philosophical history." The same description may be given to the books on the same subject which are attributed to Plutarch concerning the opinions and views of philosophers. . . . For it should be understood that what is written about a subject in general is not called history if it does not treat each thing specially and individually. This being so, we do not take for our discourse the name of history in a large and general sense. Thus reducing the force and meaning to close and narrow limits, we judge it necessary to give this definition: "History is a narration, diffuse and continuous, of things done publicly."

> 89. TOMMASO CAMPANELLA (1568–1639), a renowned Dominican scholar, was an extraordinarily eclectic and eccentric philosopher, who combined empiricism and new scientific ideas with

Tommaso Campanella, Della "philosophia rationalis." Cited (Latin) in Tutte le opere, ed. L. Firpo. Milan: Arnoldo Mondadori, 1954. Pp. 1222–1254. My translation.

neo-Platonism within a metaphysical system. In this section of his treatise on rational philosophy, he offers a philosophical formulation of historiography, its categories, and its epistemological foundations.

Historiography

Chapter 1. What historiography is and how it provides the basis of all sciences, though it forms the fifth part of Rational Philosophy. Article 1. Historiography is the art of writing history well (as the name indicates) to establish the foundation of all sciences.

Explanation. Each science has its basis in what we derive from the senses. The senses both of ourselves and of others are in a way the reporter and witness of the soul, which is the inventor, constructor, and master of the sciences. [Science] arises from the description of things, as they exist in one way or another, in order to indicate their purpose, cause, and origin, and what they are like; then to judge, define, and determine. Judgments and definitions are the principles of speculative and doctrinal science after the last stage of experience: moral judgments and precepts, the determination of practical decisions according to the cognitive understanding, appetite, and will, which are the extensions into primal nature, as we have stated in our *Physiology.* For philosophers do not understand or determine what something is if they have not first apprehended it by their senses or those of another. . . . Political scientists, economists, and moral philosophers do not arrive at a conclusion if they have not first observed through their own or another's senses.

Thus, since customs are not corporeal, the study of the moral sciences is less attractive to the young than that of physical science. The orator and judge base their questions and judgments on history, as I have shown in my *Rhetoric,* because narration is the most important part of oratory. [And so it is with medical doctors, poets, theologians, and others.]

Article 2. What history is and its main conditions. History is narrative discourse, variously formed, truthful, honest, clear, sufficient for the basis of science.

Explanation. First on "discourse" generally. "Narration" differs from a discourse which expresses desire or dislike and one which does not narrate facts but expresses sentiments and passions of the soul and does not create a basis for science except as it contains particular notions, as is stated in my *Logic*. And it is different from a dialogue or polemical discourse, which indicates and demonstrates, and from rhetoric, which persuades, praises, accuses, etc., but does not narrate as such.

[History] is said to be variously formed, as distinguished from other categories, which are formed only of a subject, predicate, and connective in order to express something, but not to narrate what is necessary to know historically, and serves rather as a principle in the explanation of a science than as its basis. It is said to be "truthful." In fact, if it is false, it is not history but either error pure and simple or a fable created to suggest something different than what is signified by the word. It is said to be "frank" because it has no other signification than what the word expresses directly, and in this differs from a parabolic expression, which indicates one thing by saying another. And it is said to be "clear," for it can be simple in a sense but enigmatic and confused if what is placed first should really come later, so that the order, style, and excessive emphasis [gravity] are causes of obscurity. . . .

Article 3. Conditions of a good historiographer. There are three requirements for a good historiographer: above all he should be well informed about the matters he narrates; then he should have a decisive mind, not giving way to timidity or inclining to mendacity; third, he should be honest and desirous of truth. In no case should direct testimony be rejected for mere opinion, as I have shown in my *Metaphysics*. So we should not reject apostolic testimony for the opinions of the Jews or the Machiavellians; nor can modern historians criticize ancient histories, except by means of something also ancient, shown in the same way through the agreement of things, places, and times. This is why we cannot accept as historians either Scaliger, for his fabulous history of the church, or Mahomet, for his history of Moses and Christ. For truth cannot contradict truth. . . . The second requirement warns the historian not to be corrupted by love of father or friend, money or flattery: it serves little to know if things are not told as they are. This is why Poggio [Bracciolini] was ridiculed by Sannazzaro for having praised his Florence:

> He was neither a bad citizen,
> Nor a good historian.

The third condition is necessary. In fact the corrupt man is pleased with his lies and has no scruples about deceiving the world. This is why Berosus would not be considered a historian except by official historiographers, but so these flatterers affirm. Once in Judaism only the prophets wrote . . . , but without divine revelation honesty without science is of little use. Giovanni Villani, certainly an honest man, wrote a kind of fable about the founding of Florence by a certain Florinus [Fiorino], though Tacitus attributed it to the Romans and Ennius to more ancient peoples. . . . Argument founded on etymology is only conjecture, not testimony, unless it can be confirmed in another way.

The disagreement of dates, places, and persons of medieval historians, or those of an earlier age, and of other essential circumstances, reveals the falsity of the historian; but the use of words, the turn of phrase, the disagreement with adversaries, the rejection of commonplaces of authority, and other accidental circumstances are not enough to discredit a historian, as I have shown in my *Topics* and *Predicaments*. This is why [Melchior] Cano has not argued successfully in rejecting Berosus, nor Torquemada in demonstrating to be false the letter of St. Clement and other older popes: even on the apostles he brings suspicions, though not criticisms.

Chapter 2. The three kinds of history.   Article 1. History has three genera: divine, which narrates the appearances of God and the things done by him among men, the creation of the world and the miracles of his saints, such as the story of Moses; the second, natural history, such as that of Pliny concerning all the things of nature and Aristotle on the animals; and the third, civil history, which narrates the deeds of men, such as Livy, Sabellico, etc.

Article 2. Sacred history is based on theology. The first part narrates the things man has learned from God, such as the discourses of the prophets, the letters of the apostles, the laws of Moses, and most of the Gospel. . . . The second part narrates the deeds of divine men, and what God himself did in human form. . . . To the third genus belongs those who write the lives of the saints and the history of the church, such as Surius, Baronius, Eusebius, etc.

Article 3. Natural history [universal and particular]. . . .

Article 4. Human history. Human history is essential for political scientists, moral philosophers, orators, poets, and those who know what, good or bad, the ancients have done in the art of governing the state, the family, children. We learn what is useful or not useful, how to derive rules from so much experience, and are able to reform science and laws and learn how one should act with particular peoples. So Homer,

Odyssey 1.3: "He who saw the customs of many men and many cities." This is why one who knows well the history of all the nations from the origin of the world to his own age has the advantage of having seen the earth from earliest times down to today. . . .

One kind of history is universal, which narrates from the origin of the world to our day the beginnings, progresses, deeds, declines, changes, and clashes of all nations, as did Sabellico, Tarcagnota, and Pineda, though the latter wrote under a false title ("ecclesiastical monarchy"). Another sort is particular history, which concerns a particular nation, as Josephus writing of Jewish history, Corio that of Milan, Villani of Florence, Sansovino that of Venice. One tells the story of the whole life of a republic or kingdom, such as Florence; another concerns only one epoch, as Thucydides describing the Peloponnesian War, and Guicciardini the events occurring in Italy as a result of the entry of King Charles VII of France, still another a single event, as Xenophon narrating the expedition of Cyrus the Younger or Sallust the wars of Jugurtha and that of Cataline, and yet another the life of a single man, as Curtius of Alexander and Tranquilla the twelve Caesars. . . .

It is essential that the historian know geography well in order to show when and how the facts he narrates occur, and to know the genealogy of the principal families and the origins of nations. He should write in a concise, clear, and unaffected style to leave as few questions as possible to posterity. He will neither praise nor blame anyone, being a reporter and not a judge, and will refer the judgment to other men of the time. . . .

Article 5. . . . One who writes the universal history of men will divide the work into five or six millenia, and each millenium into ten centuries, the centuries into decades, the decades into years. . . . He who writes particular history will divide it according to centuries, years, etc.

> 90. DANIEL HEINSIUS (1580–1685), a Dutch humanist and protégé of the great Joseph Justus Scaliger, published Latin poetry, a work on classical drama, and an edition of Aristotle's poetics. Here he celebrates in elaborate rhetoric the art of history and its human, especially political, uses.

Daniel Heinsius, *The Value of History*, trans. George W. Robinson. Pp. 7–11, 12, 14–15, 21, and 24. Reprinted by permission of the publishers from *The Value of History* by Daniel Heinsius, trans. George W. Robinson, Cambridge, Mass.: Harvard University Press, 1943.

The name of Themistocles is illustrious in the annals of the Greeks, and the shrewdest of historians bears witness to his accuracy in judgment of the present, and keenness in divining the future. At the age of a hundred and seven years, they say, seeing the imminence of death, he boldly reproached Nature, because he must depart from life when, through long experience of affairs, he had learned to live. He reckoned it harsh, forsooth, that this celestial animal, on which they have bestowed the name of man because it presents, as it were, a kind of earthly copy of divine Providence, founds and establishes cities, wages wars, regulates peace, examines and considers the diversities of events, and from them determines what may be of use to itself and others: that this being should live for one moment, but ever after abide in the darkness of death, while all its deeds end and perish with it. There was in his great and lofty spirit a glowing ardent desire for immortality. This desire took its origin and beginning, not from the perishable body, which, deprived of vital heat, returns to earth of its own accord, like the boughs and fruits of trees, but from that graft of the divine. A man worthy of that immortality to which he so strongly aspired, he saw that practical wisdom, the rule and pattern of human life, has its seat upon a lofty height; that one cannot attain to it except by certain steps; and that these steps are the deeds of men. Unless these are preserved, and set forth in clear light for all to see, necessarily men must ever live as tiros, and depart from this life in ignorance of the purposes for which they are born.

Now if some god should grant mortals this privilege, that, before they enter upon the management of affairs, the government of cities, the administration of office, they might, in order that they may not make the wonted complaint of the brevity of life, the variety of peoples and understandings, their condition and the incertitude of events, the power of fortune in human affairs, and other matters, to which men are hardly able to attain without examples, singly and once ascend a steep cliff, whence they might behold and survey the peoples of the whole earth, of all ages and generations, and their manners and character, the wars of princes, the laws of the prudent, the situation of countries and cities, all counsels, all action and their results: truly, gentlemen, they would think themselves fortunate indeed! Truly that fretful animal, whom we call man, because in life itself he ever touches only the fringes of life, would for once acquit of blame that Supreme Divinity, whose greatness he does not understand, and whose kindness he is quick to accuse.

He would be freed from the limits of time and space. Unhampered by the difficulties of travel, he would approach everything, he would be present without danger at all wars and events, he would gather into one focus the immeasurably great vastness of ages and generations. He would view in a moment an infinite multitude of matters and affairs. He would scan the affairs of the Egyptians, which are considered the most ancient, of the Persians, thought to have been richest, of the Romans, justly reckoned to have been the greatest. He would still behold Themistocles, whom we know to have been active more than two thousand years ago. The trophies of Miltiades, which did not allow Themistocles to sleep, he would see in their pristine freshness. He would attend the assemblies of the Athenians, the deliberations of the Lacedaemonians, the Roman Senate. To him nothing would be hidden by time, inaccessible through distance, closed by situation. The designs, too, and the secrets of empire, which lie concealed in the minds of kings and princes as in a hidden shrine, he would gather directly from the event, exactly like a physician who conducts a post mortem examination upon the human body. He would cast his mental eye upon the inner counsels and arts of war, which the Greeks call stratagems.

This privilege, gentlemen, not to lead you too far away, is History. History, surest pledge of the kindness of God to man, mother of truth, pattern of life, preserver of actions, and, as one among the Greeks says, metropolis of practical wisdom. History renders man contemporary with the universe. She transmits to posterity the likeness, not of the body, but of the life, the counsels, the soul, and presents it to the view of all, copied not in bronze or iron, not by the aid of picture or statue, but in monuments of letters, by the imperishable resources of facts and words. . . .

Political science belongs wholly to History. The historian seeks material only from his own field. On the other hand, political science, without History, is tortured and almost wasted away by tasteless, disgusting, and pedantic distinctions and minute divisions of philosophers. Separated also from human actions, exiled from her home, she is not read in states, where her kingdom is, but perishes where she had her birth, in the dust of the schools. . . .

They who are versed in the majestic and austere science of the law rightly exalt it, but they unjustly disparage other sciences, or consider them unworthy of a man of weight. Of them we do not ask that they appraise History in the light of the dependence upon it of Jurisprudence herself. We are not beggars, we demand only our own. But we do ask that they look to their laws to the best of their ability, leaving History to us and to princes. With pride we say it: If History have no professorship, if all universities be closed, she will always have a hospitable reception in palaces and in the innermost chambers of kings and princes. She is the inseparable companion of their minds, their counsels, and their deeds. In camps, amid trumpets and the clash of arms, as witness Scipio, where laws, as the proverb tells us, must be silent, she will find place. For I must make it clear that the exposition of History made for the benefit of kings and princes is not the same as that which we make to you. For you, we must sometimes stick closely to details, we must continually examine antiquities, we must sometimes cite parallel passages of authors. But he who would undertake before kings and princes the exposition of a great historian, such as, e.g., Polybius or Livy, would certainly resolve upon a quite different system. He would take all civil and military knowledge as his province. He would treat of the education and training of a prince, of the best order and manner of ruling, of the function and office of an ambassador. On this there was a whole section, a great part of which has survived, in the Pandects of Porphyrogenitus, which the great emperor, imitating Justinian, compiled from the historians. . . .

O divine power and dignity of letters! O preserver of men, preserver of men's deeds, preserver of chronology, preserver of all the centuries, of all years and generations the preserver, History! In thee Greece applies herself to philosophy, in thee Rome still rules, in thee likewise she waxes and flowers, begins and ends: Brutus overthrows the kingdom, Romulus founds it: Cocles plucks out the bridge, Mucius burns his hand: Cloelia swims, Lucretia is outraged. Hannibal lays waste Italy, Scipio, Carthage: Crassus is slain among the Parthians, Pompey in Egypt, Caesar in the Senate Chamber by the armed citizens, Cato gives his life for liberty. Through thee whatever has been, is, while whatever is, never ceases to be. Through thee the people has its customs, the soothsayers their sacred rites, the magistrates their badges of office. Through thee the city has its regions, aqueducts, blocks, and streets; only in thee it has its walls and boundaries. The very patron deities also, and mother Vesta, and the eternal fires, and Tarpeian Jupiter, and the Seven Hills, are never seen except in History. . . .

Let us cherish this brief time, this moment, which God hath prepared for the cultivation of this great trust, History. In her reside for us and for almost all created things glory, memory, and dignity, and finally the destined keystone of eternity itself. So in surpassing the law of our mortality under the will and favor of God immortal, we may seem to have conferred life and eternity upon all others. This must be looked for from History almost alone.

❡ THE METHOD OF HISTORY

> 91. JEAN BODIN (1530–1596) was a jurist and polyhistorical philosopher best known for his *Republic* of 1576. In his seminal treatise, the *Method for the Easy Comprehension of History,* published ten years earlier, Bodin analyzed the varieties and proper ordering (method) of history and emphasized the connections with law and geography, its "scientific" status, critical approaches to its understanding, and, traveling further down the "new route" of Machiavelli, its practical, especially political, value.

In this Method, oh most excellent President, I planned to deal with the way in which one should cull Flowers from History to gather thereof the sweetest fruits. . . .

When I came into the law courts, in order to live in the public eye, as the saying goes, and serve the people, I first proposed to myself that I should put all the time free from forensic business into legal studies and that either by writing or in whatever way I could I should make return to the state, to which, after immortal God, we owe all things. But when I observed that there are, in all, three kinds of writing: first, discovering things and collecting materials; second, arranging things in correct order and in polished form; last, in eliminating the errors in old books— it seemed to me remarkable that there were and always have been so many searchers, but rather few who have reported their findings artistically and logically. To omit the other disciplines, we have almost countless writers who by their commentaries have augmented the civil law of the Romans to such an extent that it seems to suffer from no one thing more, from no more serious malady, than its own huge size. Indeed, the more inept each one was in writing, the more did he pour forth

Jean Bodin, *Method for the Easy Comprehension of History.* Trans. Beatrice Reynolds. New York: W. W. Norton, 1945. Pp. 1–3, 4–5, 8, 9, 10–12, 13–14, 15, 17–18, 19, 21, 43, 46, 62, 66, 68–69, 153, 291, 293, 303, 319, 334–335, and 336–337.

a multitude of books; yet I see no one who has compressed into graceful form the scattered and disjointed material found. . . .

To this objective I directed all my studies—all my thoughts. At the beginning I outlined in a table a form of universal law, which I have shown to you, so that from the very sources we may trace the main types and divisions of types down to the lowest, yet in such a way that all members fit together. In this exercise, truly, I have appreciated the saying of Plato—nothing is more difficult or more nearly divine than to separate accurately. Next I have established postulates, on which the entire system rests as on the firmest foundation. Then I have added definitions. Afterward I laid down as briefly as possible precepts called "rules" according to the proposed form, as if to a norm. At one side I added, in brief notes, the interpreters of Roman law, so that from the same sources whence I have drawn, each man can take to his own satisfaction.

Then from every source I collected and added the legislation of peoples who have been famous for military and civic disciplines. In this connection, also, I made use of the standards of the jurisconsults, as well as of the historians, so that consideration is given to the decrees of the Persians, the Greeks, and the Egyptians, no less than to the Romans. From the Pandects of the Hebrews, also, chiefly from the books of the Sanhedrin, I planned to take all the best things. . . .

All this material, then, approved and confirmed by the opinions of jurisconsults and historians, makes that branch of learning more famous and more worthy of honor than if it had depended upon the will of one people, the Romans—especially when our Roman material for the most part is found to be suppositions of the later Greeks. At a time when all things suffered from the crudest barbarism, fifteen men appointed by Justinian to codify the laws so disturbed the sources of legislation that almost nothing pure is dragged forth from the filth and the mud. From this condition has originated that immense and diffuse abundance of decrees to eliminate discrepancies among the laws themselves and to put together in some way members torn from the entire body. From this we can understand that the ancient interpreters had great talent, but an almost incredible task. We obtain the same impression from their writings, which they poured out in such abundance that they seem to have spent all their days in writing and saved none for reading. . . .

Of interpreters, therefore, of whom we have a choice and whom we use for citing the laws, there are four kinds. One consists of those who

have trained their memory in the schools in perpetual discussion of enactments, yet are without exercise and forensic practice. The second
group is made up of those who by continual practice of forensic matters,
but very few precepts, have developed within themselves the wisdom for
judging. The third kind consists of those who have learned from the
latter the practice, from the former the precepts: of this type we have,
among our men, Durand, Du Faur, Guy Pape, Chasseneux, Bohier,
Baron, Connan, Tiraqueau, his colleague Brisson, and the ornament of
our college, Du Moulin. From them we have learned valuable lessons in
teaching and judging civil causes; from the others almost nothing. . . .
The last type consists of those trained not only by precepts and forensic
practice but also in the finest arts and most stable philosophy, who grasp
the nature of justice . . . laid down by eternal law . . . [and who] have
enjoyed the name "jurisconsult." . . .

But omitting those who voluntarily remove themselves from the list
of learned men, I come back to history, whence started our discourse.
From this subject then we have collected the widely scattered statutes of
ancient peoples, so that we may include them also in this work. Indeed,
in history the best part of universal law lies hidden; and what is of great
weight and importance for the best appraisal of legislation—the custom
of the peoples, and the beginnings, growth, conditions, changes, and
decline of all states—are obtained from it. The chief subject of this
Method consists of these facts, since no rewards of history are more
ample than those usually gathered about the governmental form of
states. I have written more on this topic than on the other topics, because
few have treated the problem, so vital to comprehend, and those few
only superficially. . . .

Preamble on the ease, delight, and advantage of historical reading

Although history has many eulogists, who have adorned her with
honest and fitting praises, yet among them no one has commended her
more truthfully and appropriately than the man who called her the
"master of life." This designation, which implies all the adornments of
all virtues and disciplines, means that the whole life of man ought to be
shaped according to the sacred laws of history, even as to the canon of
Polycletus. Certainly philosophy, which itself is called the "guide of

life," would remain silent among dead things, even though the extreme limits of good and evil had been set, unless all sayings, deeds, and plans are considered in relation to the account of days long past. From these not only are present-day affairs readily interpreted but also future events are inferred, and we may acquire reliable maxims for what we should seek and avoid. So it seemed to me remarkable that, among so many writers and in so learned an age, until now there has been no one who has compared famous histories of our forbears with each other and with the account of deeds done by the ancients. Yet this could be accomplished easily if all kinds of human activities were brought together and if from them a variety of examples should be arranged, appropriately and each in its place, in order that those who had devoted themselves entirely to crime might be reviled by well-earned curses, but those who were known for any virtue might be extolled according to their deserts.

This, then, is the greatest benefit of historical books, that some men, at least, can be incited to virtue and others can be frightened away from vice. . . .

But of what value is it that this branch of learning is the inventor and preserver of all the arts, and chiefly of those which depend upon action? Whatever our elders observe and acquire by long experience is committed to the treasure house of history; then men of a later age join to observations of the past reflections for the future and compare the causes of obscure things, studying the efficient causes and the ends of each as if they were placed beneath their eyes. Moreover, what can be for the greater glory of immortal God or more really advantageous than the fact that sacred history is the means of inculcating piety to God, reverence to parents, charity to individuals, and justice to all? Where, indeed, do we obtain the words of the prophets and the oracles, where the unending vitality and power of minds, unless we draw them from the fount of the Holy Scriptures?

But beyond that boundless advantage, the two things which are usually sought in every discipline, ease and pleasure, are so blended in the understanding of historical books that greater ease or equal pleasure does not seem to inhere in any other body of knowledge. The ease, indeed, is such that without help of any special skill the subject is understood by all. In other arts, because all are linked together and bound by the same chains, the one cannot be grasped without knowledge of the other. But history is placed above all branches of knowledge in the highest rank of importance and needs the assistance of no tool, not even of letters, since by hearing alone, passed on from one to another, it may be given to posterity. . . .

To ease is added the pleasure that we take in following the narrative of virtue's triumphs. This, I suppose, is so great that he who once is captivated and won over by the delights of history can never suffer himself to be torn from her sweet embrace. Moreover, if men are impelled by such eagerness for knowledge that they now take pleasure even in unreliable tales, how much greater will it be when events are recounted truthfully? Then, too, what is more delightful than to contemplate through history the deeds of our ancestors placed before our eyes as in a picture? . . .

There is more danger that while we revel in too great appreciation, we may overlook the utility (although in delight, also, there is use). . . .

Now, indeed, since history has boundless advantages, is read with great ease, and gives even greater pleasure, it has not been open to anyone's reproach. Although many have misrepresented the other arts as dangerous or useless, no one has yet been found who has marked the record of the past with any stain of infamy—unless perchance the man who accused this art of mendacity when he had declared war on all the virtues and the disciplines. But such a reproach is for fables, not for history; if the account is not true, it ought not even to be called history, as Plato thought. He says that every product of thought is either true or false: he calls the latter poetry, the former knowledge. But why argue? When so much of advantage may be extracted from the very fables of Homer, which take unto themselves the likeness of information and truth, then what sort of reward must we hope from history? Since this teaches us clearly not only the arts necessary for living but also those objectives which at all costs must be sought, what things to avoid, what is base, what is honorable, which laws are most desirable, which state is the best, and the happiest kind of life. Finally, since if we put history aside the cult of God, religion, and prophecies grow obsolete with the passing of centuries; therefore, on account of the inexpressible advantage of such knowledge, I have been led to write this book, for I noticed that while there was a great abundance and supply of historians, yet no one has explained the art and the method of the subject. Many recklessly and incoherently confuse the accounts, and none derives any lessons therefrom. Formerly men wrote books about the proper arrangement of historical treatises; how wisely, I do not discuss. They have, perhaps, a possible excuse for their project. Yet, if I may give an opinion, they seem to resemble some physicians, who are distrustful of all kinds of medicine: resolutely they once again examine their preparation and do not try to teach the strength and nature of the drugs which are proposed in such abundance or to fit them to the present illnesses. This applies also to those who write about the organization of historical material, when all books contain ample information about the past and the libraries contain the works of many historians whom they might more usefully have taken to study and imitate than to discuss oratorically the exordium, the narrative, and the ornaments of words and sentences.

Then, in order that what we are going to write about the historical method may have some outline, we shall at the beginning divide and delimit the subject, then indicate the order of reading. After this we shall arrange similar instances of human activities from history, so that this may be an aid to memory. Afterwards we shall consider the choice of individual writers. Then we shall discuss the correct evaluation of works in this field. Following this we shall speak about the governmental form of states, in which the discipline of all history is chiefly engaged. Then we shall refute those who have upheld the idea of the four monarchies and the golden age. Having explained these things, we shall try to make clear the obscure and intricate sequence of chronologies, so that one can understand whence to seek the beginning of history and from what point it ought to be traced. At length we shall refute the error of those who maintain the independent origin of races. Finally we move on to the arrangement and order of reading historians, so that it may be plainly understood what each man wrote about and in what period he lived.

Chapter 1. What History Is and of How Many Categories

Of History, that is, the true narration of things, there are three kinds: human, natural, and divine. The first concerns man; the second, nature; the third, the Father of nature. One depicts the acts of man while leading his life in the midst of society. The second reveals causes hidden in nature and explains their development from earliest beginnings. The last records the strength and power of Almighty God and of the immortal souls, set apart from all else. In accordance with these divisions arise history's three accepted manifestations—it is probable, inevitable, and holy—and the same number of virtues are associated with it, that is to say, prudence, knowledge, and faith. The first virtue distinguishes base from honorable; the second, true from false; the third, piety from impiety. The first, from the guidance of reason and the experience of practical affairs, they call the "arbiter of human life." The second, from inquiry into abstruse causes, they call the "revealer of all things." The last, due to love of the one God toward us, is known as the "destroyer of vice." From these three virtues together is created true wisdom, man's supreme and final good. Men who in life share in this good are called blessed, and since we have come into the light of day to enjoy it, we should be ungrateful if we did not embrace the heaven-offered benefit, wretched if we abandon it. Moreover, in attaining it we derive great help from history in its three phases, but more especially from the divine form, which unaided can make mankind happy, even though they have no experience of practical affairs and no knowledge of secret physical causes. Yet if the two latter are added, I believe that they will bring about a great increase in human well-being. . . .

But because human history mostly flows from the will of mankind, which ever vacillates and has no objective—nay, rather, each day new laws, new customs, new institutions, new manners confront us—so, in general, human actions are invariably involved in new errors unless they are directed by nature as leader. . . . Since for acquiring prudence nothing is more important or more essential than history, because episodes in human life sometimes recur as in a circle, repeating themselves, we judge that attention must be given to this subject, especially by those who do not lead a secluded life, but are in touch with assemblies and societies of human beings.

So of the three types of history let us for the moment abandon the divine to the theologians, the natural to the philosophers, while we concentrate long and intently upon human actions and the rules governing them. Investigation into human activity is either universal or particular: the latter includes the memorable words and deeds of a single man or, at the utmost, of a people. As the Academicians wisely did not assume any generalized concept of old women's affairs, so history should not concern itself with actions equally futile. Universal history narrates the deeds of many men or states, and in two ways: either of several peoples, for example, Persians, Greeks, Egyptians, or of all whose deeds have been handed down, or at least of the most famous. This also can be done in many ways. That is to say, when events are listed according to time—for each day, or month, or year—then the accounts are called ephemerides, or diaries, or annals. Or writers may trace from the origin of each state, or as far as memory permits, or even from the creation of the world, the beginnings, growth, established type, decline, and fall of states. This also is done in two ways: briefly or fully, and the books are accordingly called chronicles or chronologies, respectively. Other writers achieve the same end in a slightly different way. Verrius Flaccus called history a "tale spread abroad," in which the importance of affairs, persons, and places was weighed by whoever was present at these events. But Cicero gave the name "annals" to accounts reporting the deeds of each year without any ornament or troublesome inquiry into causes. History, said Cicero, is nothing but the making of annals. Diaries, or ephemerides, are the deeds of each day, as Asellio explained in the writings of Gellius. But fasti are annals in which all memorable things, the greatest magistrates, the most famous victories, defeats, triumphs, and secular games are briefly mentioned. . . .

If anyone does not wish to include mathematics with the natural sciences, then he will make four divisions of history: human, of course, uncertain and confused; natural, which is definite, but sometimes uncertain on account of contact with matter or an evil deity, and therefore inconsistent; mathematical, more certain, because it is free from the admixture of matter, for in this way the ancients made the division between the two; finally, divine, most certain and by its very nature changeless. And this is all about the delimitation of history.

Chapter 2. The Order of Reading Historical Treatises

. . . First, then, let us place before ourselves a general chart for all periods, not too detailed and therefore easy to study, in which are contained the origins of the worlds, the floods, the earliest beginnings of the states and of the religions which have been more famous, and their ends, if indeed they have come to an end. These things may be fixed in time by the creation and the founding of the City, then by the Olympiad, or even, if reason demands, by the year of Christ and the Hegira of the Arabs (which in popular chronicles is omitted). Conforming closely to this type are the works commonly called chronicles, characterized by spaces between the lines, brief indeed, but easy for beginners. Although their chronology is not exact, yet they approach fairly close to the truth of the matter. After this representation we shall use a somewhat fuller and more accurate book, which covers the origins, conditions, changes, and fall not only of illustrious peoples but also of all peoples, yet with a brevity such that one can see almost at a glance what was the established form of each state. . . .

There are, then, three kinds of historian, I think: first, those very able by nature, and even more richly endowed by training, who have advanced to the control of affairs; the second group, those who lack education, but not practice or natural gifts; the last is composed of those who, endowed to some extent by nature, lack the experience of practical affairs, yet with incredible enthusiasm and labor in collecting the materials of history have almost brought themselves level with men who have spent all their lives in public affairs. There is, however, an infinite variety of any type—the more so because each man has more or less integrity, learning, and experience. The best writers are fully equipped on all three counts, if only they could rid themselves of all emotion in writing history. It is difficult for a good man, when writing of villains, to refrain from imprecation or to avoid bestowing love and gratitude on heroes. The first attempts to embroider history occurred when it was thought fine to use an honorable lie for the praise of virtuous characters and the vituperation of evil. But if good writers fail in this type of writing, what must we judge about the evil ones? It is a matter of importance, therefore, whether the historian has written a treatise about his own concerns or those of others; whether his work deals with compatriots or foreigners; enemies or friends; military discipline or civil; finally, whether it is of his own age or of an earlier period; for his contemporaries or for posterity. . . .

Or if there is anyone who prefers to enjoy the glory of his labors in his own lifetime, let him, when he has investigated all the public and private records, recreate the deeds of a former period and from the tradition preserved by older men write history. Famous writers have done just this: Livy, Suetonius, Tacitus, Arrian, and Dionysius of Halicarnassus. We can rely more readily upon the last author than on the others, because he wrote, not of his own state, but of another and collected all the commentaries and secrets of state from the official documents. . . .

First, indeed, comes Dionysius of Halicarnassus, who, in addition to his moderate manner of speaking and his Attic purity, wrote of the antiquities of the Romans from the very foundation of the city with such diligence that he seems to excel all Greeks and Latins. The things which the Latins neglected as almost too commonplace—for example, sacrifices, games, triumphs, and magistrates' insignia, as well as the general training of the Romans in governing the state, taxes, auspices, assemblies, the difficult division of the whole population into classes and tribes, then, too, the authority of the senate, the orders of the plebs, the rule of the magistrate, and the power of the people—he alone seems to me to have reported most accurately. . . . There are those who think that Diodorus ought to be placed with the foregoing, and many place him first; yet I do not see what they admire so much in him, whether they refer to his manner of speaking, which is extremely commonplace, or to his system of histories. . . .

In this respect Cornelius Tacitus aids us greatly. For when he wrote the events of one century, from Tiberius to Nerva, he investigated most thoroughly all the most important, minor, and most trifling things. In his fourth book he promised not to tell of war, or sieges of cities, or routed armies, or struggles of the plebs and optimates. His labor would be inglorious, but yet not useless. And a little later—"We have put together despotic commands, incessant accusations, faithless friendships, the ruin of the guiltless, and developments alike in outcome." However, he carefully described all wars which occurred in those times in which he had a share or actual direction. After the victory of Actium there was no historian who treated more fully the military or legal system. He was schooled for a long time in military and civil training, and as proconsul he controlled lower Germany. In that time he described the customs, institutions, and rites of the Germans with such diligence that the Germans owe their ancient history to Tacitus alone. . . .

The works of Guicciardini are very detailed and might have been written in imitation of [G. du Bellay] if the authors had not been contemporaries. Although he always remained within the territory of Italy and cannot be compared in military renown with Du Bellay, nevertheless, in the judgment of serious people he excelled his contemporaries in writing history (and I do not know whether or not he excelled the older historians also). For where anything came under deliberation which seemed inexplicable, just there he showed the keenest sage opinions appropriately like salt. To collect a few from many: since he was most skilled in military and civil training, he implicitly accused our men of recklessness because they extended their power easily by arms, but could not retain it; they did not observe that the dominion acquired by those who do not know how to apply civil disciplines has always been not only useless but even a dangerous responsibility. Truly an unusual opinion and one worthy of a great man! Oh, that it were well known to princes! . . .

It remains for us to form an opinion about letters and disciplines also.

At one and the same time there lived a great number of learned men. Then, when the memory of letters had become almost extinct, once again others brought it back to the light of day. Plato, Aristotle, Xenocrates, Timaeus, Archytas, Isocrate, and an infinite number of orators and poets flourished at the same time. After a long interval Chrysippus, Carneades, Diogenes the Stoic, and Arcecilas appeared. Again, Varro, Cicero, Livy, and Sallust were contemporaries; then Virgil, Horace, Ovid, and Vitruvius grew famous. And not long ago, Valla, Trapezuntius, Vicino, Gaza, Bessarion, and Mirandola flourished contemporaneously. If anyone, then, having collected passages of memorable affairs, should compare with them these great trajections and ascertain the regions affected or the states changed, he will achieve fuller knowledge about the customs and the nature of peoples; then, also, he will make much more effective and reliable judgment about every kind of history. . . .

Chapter 6. The Type of Government in States

Since History for the most part deals with the state and with the changes taking place within it, to achieve an understanding of the subject we must explain briefly the origins, developed form, and ends of principalities, especially since there is nothing more fruitful and beneficial in all history. Other things, indeed, seem very valuable for a knowledge of the nature of the soul and really admirable for shaping the morals of each man, but the things gathered from the reading of historians about the beginnings of cities, their growth, matured form, decline, and fall are so very necessary, not only to individuals but to everyone, that Aristotle thought nothing was more effective in establishing and maintaining societies of men than to be informed in the science of governing a state. Yet, about this matter the opinions of great men are so varied and divergent that it is noteworthy that in so many centuries no one until now has explained what is the best kind of state.

Since Plato thought that no science of managing a state is so difficult to understand that no one could grasp it, he advocated this method of formulating laws and establishing the government on a firm foundation; if sage men, having collected all the customs and all the laws of all countries, should compare them, they might compound from them the best kind of state. Aristotle seems to have followed this plan as far as he could, yet he did not carry it out. Following Aristotle, Polybius, Dionysius of Halicarnassus, Plutarch, Dio, and Tacitus (I omit those whose writings have perished) left many excellent and important ideas about the state scattered throughout their books.

Machiavelli also wrote many things about government—the first, I think, for about 1,200 years after barbarism had overwhelmed everything. [His sayings] are on the lips of everyone, and there is no doubt but that he would have written more fully and more effectively and with a greater regard for truth, if he had combined a knowledge of the writings of ancient philosophers and historians with experience. . . .

Chapter 7. Refutation of Those Who Postulate Four Monarchies and the Golden Age

A long-established, but mistaken, idea about four empires, made famous by the prestige of great men, has sent its roots down so far that it seems difficult to eradicate. It has won over countless interpreters of the Bible; it includes among modern writers Martin Luther, Melanchthon, Sleidan, Lucidus, Funck, and Panvinio—men well read in ancient history and things divine. Sometimes, shaken by their authority, I used to think that it ought not to be doubted. I was stirred also by the prophecy of Daniel, whose reliability it is a crime to disparage, whose authority it is wicked to question. Yet afterwards I understood that the obscure and ambiguous words of Daniel could be twisted into various meanings; and in interpreting the prophecies I preferred to take that formula of the courts, "it doth not appear," than recklessly to agree with anyone because of the opinion of others which I did not understand. I thoroughly approve the reply of Calvin, not less polished than sagacious, when he was asked his opinion about the book of the Apocalypse. He candidly answered that he was totally at a loss regarding the meaning of this obscure writer, whose identity was not yet agreed upon among the erudite. Similarly, I do not see how we are to relate the wild beasts and the image discussed by Daniel to those empires which flourish everywhere now-a-days and have flourished for so many centuries. . . .

The way in which the Germans define a monarchy is absurd, that is, according to the interpretation of Philip Melanchthon, as the most powerful of all states. It is even more absurd that they think they hold the empire of the Romans, which of course would seem laughable to all who have well in mind the map of the world. The empire of the Romans was most flourishing under Trajan. Never before had it been so great, and afterwards it constantly diminished, as may be seen in the pages of Appian and Sextus Rufus, who wrote in the time of Trajan. . . .

The Germans, however, hold no part of the Roman Empire except Noricum and Vindelicia. Germany is bounded by the Rhine, the Danube, the Vistula, the Carpathian Mountains, and the ocean, but all authority ends at the foothills of the Alps in the south; by the Rhine and a few cities this side of the Rhine in the west; by Silesia, in turn, in the east; by the Baltic regions in the north. How much truer it is of the king of the Turks, who took Byzantium, the capital of the empire, from the Christians, the region of Babylon, which is discussed in the book of Daniel, from the Persians, and joined a great part of his dominion beyond the Danube, up to the mouths of the Dnieper, to the old Roman provinces? Now, if we identify monarchy with force of arms, or with great wealth, or with fertility of areas, or with the number of victories, or with size of population, or with etymology of the name, or with the fatherland of Daniel, or with the seat of the Babylonian empire, or with the amplitude of sway, it will be more appropriate, certainly, to interpret the prophecy of Daniel as applied to the sultan of the Turks. . . .

Chapter 8. A System of Universal Time

Those who think they can understand histories without chronology are as much in error as those who wish to escape the windings of a labyrinth without a guide. The latter wander hither and thither and cannot find any end to the maze, while the former are carried among the many intricacies of the narrative with equal uncertainty and do not understand where to commence or where to turn back. But the principle of time, the guide for all histories, like another Ariadne tracing the hidden steps with a thread, not only prevents us from wandering, but also often makes it possible for us to lead back erring historians to the right path. So we see all very good writers have so much regard for time as to include not only the years, but even the separate parts of the year. Others do not omit even the very months and days, or the moments of the day, in which a thing happened, because they understand that without a system of time hardly any advantage is culled from history.

Then, since the most important part of the subject depends upon the chronological principle, we have thought that a system of universal time is needed for this method of which we treat. Both on account of its great usefulness and also on account of the discrepancy which appears among historians concerning the antiquity and the succession of events, I should like to shed some light on this topic also. . . .

Sequence of times   Now our system of chronology from the Creation must be taken out of historical documents; this cannot be obtained from the arid sources of the Greeks. They had nothing older than the Trojan history, which Thucydides said was fabulous for the most part, and since Homer himself, the most ancient writer after Orpheus and Linus, flourished two hundred years after the Trojan War, it is natural that they reported common errors and fables instead of true history. However that may be, Plutarch, beginning the lives of the princes with Theseus, affirmed that the earlier events were mixed with fables. Theseus is said to have flourished about five hundred years before Romulus, in the time when Abimelech was the leader of the Hebrews. The year is 2740 from the Creation. For that reason let us inquire about the antiquity of time from [sources] other than the Greeks. From all writers of other races I see no one older than Moses. . . .

Chapter 9. Criteria by Which
to Test the Origins of Peoples

No question has exercised the writers of histories more than the origin of peoples; they record the decline of states or the course of civil wars for no reason more frequently than to attest the fame and splendor of their race. Some people, having achieved noble rank through riches, or crime, or the valor of their ancestors, prefer to separate themselves from the others and repudiate their affinity with them. The extreme type of arrogance is seen in those who, forgetful of their human nature, boast that they are descended from gods. This happened not only in the case of foolish and stupid men but also of men who achieved the highest reputation for wisdom and virtue. Caius Caesar was not ashamed to boast in the assembly of the Roman people that in the maternal line he was descended from kings, but in the paternal from the gods. Aristotle also traced his family back to Aesculapius and Apollo. The haughty pride of powerful men is reflected even in the humblest, who, because they did not know their own racial origin, or because they concealed it on account of dislike for foreigners, called themselves sprung from the parent land, that is, autochthonous and earth-born. Aristides, in the Panathenaea, claimed for the Athenians the boon of highest nobility, because they traced their descent from no other source than from this very earth, mother of the gods.

This error is common not only to the older writers but to the younger ones also, since Polydore Virgil, otherwise a reliable author, affirmed that the Britons lived in the interior, were indigenous there, and had not come from any other place—following Caesar, I suppose. Althamer, imitating Tacitus, also wrote that the Germans were born in Germany itself and were not descended from any other race; he did not hesitate to credit this story relying on the authority of Tacitus, Sabellicuse, and Sipontinus. What more stupid, shall I say, or more impious can be imagined than this? . . .

There are three proofs in the light of which origins can be known and evaluated when reported by historians: first, in the proved reliability of the writer; second, in traces of language; third, in the situation and character of the region. We have spoken earlier about the choice of historians and how much credit can be given to a writer who deals with his own fellow citizens or with an enemy. Conrad Peutinger, Irenicus, Hermann Neuernar, Lupold of Bamberg, Jacob Wimpheling, Andreas Althamer, Wolfgang Lazius, Paul Jovius, Antonius Sabellicus, and among us Robert Ceneau wrote so vaingloriously about their own fellow countrymen, that they made no concessions to others and thought that the gods themselves were not their equals. More truthful were Beatus Rhenanus and Abbot Trithemius. Others in praise of their own names wrote many things, which, though they may be true, still could be written in more moderate vein without scorn for others. Let us grant that the Franks originated among the Germans. What can be more excellent for the fame of our name, or better for forming alliances and friendships, or more useful for the vigor of both states than to trace the origin of the Franks to the valiant and noble race of the Germans? However, for questions of this sort let us use the tests which I have mentioned to obtain definite and well-authenticated origins of all peoples. . . .

Then the word "indigenous" must be abandoned, and the origin of all peoples must be sought in the Chaldeans; since in their country, or certainly near it, came to rest that ship which served as nursery of the human race. From there men scattered hither and thither and propagated their kind in the way in which Moses and the teachers of the Jews have most truthfully and fully described. But I omit what each reader may obviously find in the same books.

92. PIERRE DROIT DE GAILLARD (fl. late sixteenth century) wrote various historical chronologies and, in the wake of Bodin's work, published his own *Method for the Reading of History* in 1574, celebrating the self-knowledge and understanding of human culture which the study of histories of all sorts provides.

Preface containing the explication of the oracle "Know Thyself," and that self-knowledge which consists mainly in the principle of the immortality of the soul, and of its excellent function.

Among the apothegms and proverbs proposed by the ancients, even those apparently enlightened only by the light of nature, I think there is none more remarkable than that of the Lacedaemonium Chilon, one of the seven sages—a statement which for its excellence and divinity was attributed to the wisest of gods, Apollo, and which contains two words: GNOTHI SEAUTON: Know thyself. For this includes all that a man can learn to guide his actions well and to conduct his life happily, prudently warning of his purpose: the question so obscurely and diversely treated by philosophers, of which Varro (as we learn from Saint Augustine) repeats two or three hundred opinions.

This sentence warns man to understand first how many miseries and calamities his life is subject to in order to remove himself from pride and arrogance. The great God has created an infinite number of things, of which man is perhaps the least, as Pliny well observed, following the divine Plato and many other Greek, Latin, and barbarian philosophers. . . .

But such speculations fail badly if they contemplate only the misery of man and not his dignity and excellence, which is the other part of his knowledge and all the weightier because of his reasonable soul and intellect, which alone belong wholly to man. If then we consider man in the state in which God first created him, he was his masterpiece in the creation of the universe, and everything was created for man (as the Stoics learnedly taught), so that he would be glorified as the most noble of all creatures. But if we consider man in the state of general corruption passed on to all the posterity of Adam, we will see his soul, monstrous, hideous, deformed, subject to many irregularities, deprived of blessedness, impotent, variable, hypocritical, in short, the slave of sin, in

Pierre Droit de Gaillard, *Methode qu'on doit tenir en la lecture de l'histoire*. Paris: Chez Pierre Cauellat, 1579. Pp. 1, 46, and 548–556. My translation.

which he is born and conceived. . . . This is what, at least in part, the Oracle recommends: Know thyself, which cannot be done without first knowing God to honor and to serve him, in whom is the end, happiness, and sovereign good of man.

Now this knowledge depends on history, sacred as well as profane (in which we include natural history), universal as well as particular, of which I have made a little collection in the form of an "institution," containing what is most memorable in the best authors, Hebrew, Greek, Latin, and others, and leading as by the hand the lovers of antiquity in the reading of these. . . .

Definition and division of history, with a discourse on the words "witness of times," which contains the order and continuation of all historiographers.

Following the path of the most learned and observing the precepts left by those three excellent preceptors, Plato, Aristotle, and Cicero, we propose first the definition of history, which alone shows us ("with finger and eye") its dignity, utility, and all the fruits which we can gather from it. History thus is as Cicero defines it truly and gravely.

Let us see the meaning of the first phrase or part of the definition, "witness of times." Certainly, as the great God has created this great and beautiful theater of the world, the sky, sun, moon, stars, elements, planets, animals, and all other things to be contemplated and considered by us (which consideration is called "natural history"), that by this contemplation we may see some vestiges of his divine bounty and wisdom, so he wants us to remark the order and continuation of the times, the great and admirable things which he has accomplished in the deeds of men, especially in the church, from the beginning of the world. . . . And all this we know through the gift of history, especially sacred history. For these admirable facts are for the most part unknown to the other [profane history], whose principal purpose is to describe the beginning, progress, and ruin of kingdoms and republics of the world, the causes, counsels, and deliberations of great and illustrious personages in peace as well as in war, with an account of various political and moral virtues. . . . Is not the principal point of difference between us and the brute beasts that, by memory of past things, their causes, occasions, progress, and consequences, by comparison of past and present, we may foresee the future?

. . . As for the other parts of the definition ("light of truth, life of memory, messenger of antiquity"), all this seems to signify the same thing. . . . Who is so ignorant or lacking in spirit as to deny the title, "messenger of antiquity"? Without the benefit of history, how could we know the deeds of the ancients by which we might be incited to virtue and deflected from vice?

. . . Let us discuss a little the phrase by which [history] assumes the quality of "mistress of life." Certainly, this phrase is the greatest which one can make, and we should attribute it to God and to the law [Decalogue] containing his will. . . .

Comparison of history with other disciplines.

And in this [demonstration of virtues and vices] history infinitely surpasses moral philosophy. . . . As for jurisprudence, it has emerged from history, as is sufficiently witnessed by the jurists Gaius and Pomponius, speaking of its origin. For it consists in ancient laws, decrees of the people, sentences and decisions of the senate, ordinances of the prince, edicts of the pretor, and responses of the wise men and jurisconsults. And what is the source of all this if not history? . . . And to put it in a word, all disciplines take their source and the origin of their principles, which we have from nature, as from an overflowing fountain.

> 93. THOMAS BLUNDEVILLE (fl. late sixteenth century) was a popularizer of European ideas; in this *True Order and Method of Writing and Reading Histories,* he summarizes the art of history as viewed in the Italianate *Artes historicae,* especially that of Francesco Patrizi.

A history ought to declare the things in such order as they were done. And because everything has its beginning, augmentation, state, declination, and end; the writer ought therefore to tell the things so as thereby a man may perceive and discern that which appertains to every degree, and that not only as touching the country or city but also as touching the rule or dominion thereof. For the beginning, augmentation, state, declynation, and end of a country or city, and of the empire thereof, be not all one but diverse things.

Four things would be dispersed throughout the history: that is to say, the trade of life, the public revenues, the force, and the manner of government. By knowing the trade of life, the country and city in every time and season has used, we learn how to have like in like times. Again,

Thomas Blundeville, *The True Order and Method of Writing and Reading Histories.* London: William Seres, 1574. No pagination.

by knowing the revenues and what things have been done therewith, we come to know what the country or city is able to do. The force consists in soldiers, in the manner of the military discipline, in the navies, in munition, and instruments of war. And the writer must not forget to show whither the soldiers be hired foreigners or home soldiers, for lack whereof Polybius has given great cause of wonder unto this age, because all Italy at this present [time] is not able to levy the tenth part of the number of soldiers which the Romans levied in his time, enjoying all that time neither Liguria, Lombardy, Romania, nor Marcapiana. And yet as the foresaid Polybius writes, they were able to set forth four score thousand footmen and three score thousand horsemen. And in their first wars against Carthage, being only lords of Italy, they did send a navy to the sea of three hundred and thirty great galleys, called *Quinqueremi*, and now the Turk for all his greatness is scant able to fend to the sea so many small galleys.

The writer also must show what kind of government the country or city had in its beginning, augmentation, state, declination, and end. And whither there were any change[s] of government, for what cause, and how the same was done, and what good or evil ensued thereof.

Histories be made of deeds done by a public weal, or against a public weal, and such deeds be either deeds of war, of peace, or else of sedition and conspiracy. Again, every deed, be it private or public must needs be done by some person for some occasion in some time and place with means and order and with instruments, all which circumstances are not to be forgotten of the writer, and specially those that have accompanied and brought the deed to effect. Every deed that man does springs either of some outward cause, as of force or fortune (which properly ought not to be referred to man), or else of some inward cause belonging to man, of which causes there are two: that is, reason and appetite. Of reason springs counsel and election, in affairs of the life, which not being letted do cause deeds to ensue. Of appetite does spring passions of the mind, which also does cause men to attempt enterprises. . . . Again, if there be a principal doer there is also a principal cause, ruling all other inferior causes, and also a principal time, place, mean, and instrument. And as deeds have outwardly belonging unto them all the aforesaid circumstances, so inwardly they do comprehend three special things which do run throughout all the circumstances from the beginning to the ending. And they be these: possibility, occasion, and success, Which things the writer must declare, even as they were.

. . . Now as touching the time, the writer ought to show the very moment as well of the beginning as of the ending of the deed, to the intent that the reader may know the continuance of the principal deed, and also of the inferior deeds. . . .

The place may be either general, special, or particular, as England, Norfolk, and Norwich. The means be diverse, for everything is done either secretly or openly, orderly or without order. And hereto appertains all means and ways that be used in governing states, in making laws, in creating magistrates, in deliberating, in judging, in appointing places, in providing victuals, in gathering up the public revenues, and a thousand such like things, of all which things it behooves that the writer have consideration, and when need is, that he declare the same at large. . . .

What profit histories do yield. Every city and country stands upon three principal points, unto one of which all public actions do appertain: that is, peace, sedition, and war; and the first is the end of the two last, in the which end, the happiness . . . [through]out life consists and [also] the accomplishment of three desires which we naturally have: first, to live; secondly, to live contentedly or blessedly; and thirdly, to live always in that happiness so far is as possible to man's nature, which three things the Latins do briefly utter in this sort: *esse, bene esse,* and *semper esse.* . . .

Of the duty and office of historiographers and what order and disposition in writing histories they ought to use. Of those that make anything, some do make much of nothing, as God did when creating the world [out] of naught, and as poets in some respect also do while they fein fables and make thereof their poesies and poetical histories; some again of more do make less, as carvers and gravers of images, and other such like artificers, some of little do make much and of much little, as the orators why left sometime they extol small things and sometime abase great things. And some do make of so much as much, as true philosophers and historiographers, whose office is to tell things as they were done without either augmenting or diminishing them or swerving one iota from the truth. Whereby it appears that the historiographers ought not to fein any orations nor any other thing but truely to report every such speach and deed, even as it was spoken or done.

What order and method is to be observed in reading histories. Who is so desirous to know how histories are to be read had need first to know the ends and purposes for which they are written. Whereof though there be diverse [ends and purposes] as some to win fame to the writer and some to delight the reader's ears that read only to pass away the time and such like; yet in my opinion there are but three chief and principal [ones]. First, that we may learn thereby to acknowledge the providence of God, whereby all things are governed and directed. Secondly, that by the examples of the wise we may learn wisdom wisely to behave our selves in all our actions, as well private and public, both in time of peace and war.

Thirdly, that we may be stirred by example of the good to follow the good and by example of the evil to flee the evil.

> 94. FRANCIS BACON (1561–1626), elaborating on his own distinctive conception of method, regarded history as the experiential data from which reason drew general conclusions as well as a literary genre. He also included history in the famous scheme of learning formulated in his *New Organon,* distinguishing, like Bodin, between civil, sacred, and natural history and discussing its uses.

History is Natural, Civil, Ecclesiastical, and Literary; whereof the three the first I allow as extant, the fourth I note as deficient. For no man hath propounded to himself the general state of learning to be described and represented from age to age, as many have done the works of nature and the state civil and ecclesiastical; without which the history of the world seemeth to me to be as the statue of Polyphemus with his eye out; that part being wanting which doth most shew the spirit and life of the person. And yet I am not ignorant that in divers particular sciences, as of the jurisconsults, the mathematicians, the rhetoricians, the philosophers, there are set down some small memorials of the schools, authors, and books; and so likewise some barren relations touching the invention of arts or usages. But a just story of learning, containing the antiquities and originals of knowledges, and their sects; their inventions, their traditions; their diverse administrations and managings; their flourishings, their oppositions, decays, depressions, oblivions, removes; with the causes and occasions of them; and all other events concerning learning, throughout the ages of the world; I may truly affirm to be wanting. The use and end of which work I do not so much design for curiosity, or satisfaction of those that are the lovers of learning; but chiefly for a more serious and grave purpose, which is this in few words, that it will make learned men wise in the use and administration of learning. For it is not St. Augustine's or St. Ambrose's works that will make so wise a divine,

Francis Bacon, *On the Advancement of Learning.* In *The Philosophical Works of Francis Bacon,* ed. John M. Robertson. London: George Routledge and Sons, 1905. Pp. 79 and 80.

as ecclesiastical history thoroughly read and observed; and the same reason is of learning.

¶ The Division of Civil History into Ecclesiastical, Literary, and Civil (which retains the name of the Genus) and that the History of Literature is wanting. Precepts for the Construction of it.

Civil History may rightly be divided into three species. First, Sacred or Ecclesiastical; next, that which we call Civil History (using the generic name specially); lastly, the History of Learning and the Arts. I will begin with the kind last-mentioned; for the two former are extant, while the latter—the History of Learning—(without which the history of the world seems to me as the statue of Polyphemus without the eye; that very feature being left out which most marks the spirit and life of the person), I set down as wanting. Not but I know that in the particular sciences of the jurisconsults, mathematicians, rhetoricians, philosophers, we have some slight mention or some barren narrations about the sects, schools, books, authors, and successions belonging to them; also that there exist some meagre and unprofitable memoirs of the inventors of arts and usages; but I say that a complete and universal History of Learning is yet wanting. Of this therefore I will now proceed to set forth the argument, the method of construction, and the use.

The argument is no other than to inquire and collect out of the records of all time what particular kinds of learning and arts have flourished in what ages and regions of the world; their antiquities, their progresses, their migrations (for sciences migrate like nations) over the different parts of the globe; and again their decays, disappearances, and revivals. The occasion and origin of the invention of each art should likewise be observed; the manner and system of transmission, and the plan and order of study and practice. To these should be added a history of the sects, and the principal controversies in which learned men have been engaged, the calumnies to which they have been exposed, the praises and honours by which they have been rewarded; an account of the principal authors, books, schools, successions, academies, societies, colleges, order,—in a word, everything which relates to the state of learning. Above all things (for this is the ornament and life of Civil History) I wish events to be

Francis Bacon, *De augmentis scientiarum*. In *The Philosophical Works of Francis Bacon*, ed. John M. Robertson. London: George Routledge and Sons, 1905. Pp. 431–439.

coupled with their causes. I mean, that an account should be given of the characters of the several regions and peoples; their natural disposition, whether apt and suited for the study of learning, or unfitted and indifferent to it; the accidents of the times, whether adverse or propitious to science; the emulations and infusions of different religions; the enmity or partiality of laws; the eminent virtues and services of individual persons in the promotion of learning, and the like. Now all this I would have handled in a historical way, not wasting time, after the manner of critics, in praise and blame, but simply narrating the fact historically, with but slight intermixture of private judgment.

For the manner of compiling such a history I particularly advise that the matter and provision of it be not drawn from histories and commentaries alone; but that the principal books written in each century, or perhaps in shorter periods, proceeding in regular order from the earliest ages, be themselves taken into consultation; that so (I do not say by a complete perusal, for that would be an endless labour, but) by tasting them here and there, and observing their argument, style, and method, the Literary Spirit of each age may be charmed as it were from the dead.

With regard to the use of the work, it is not so much to swell the honour and pomp of learning with a profusion of images; nor because out of my exceeding love for learning I wish the inquiry, knowledge, and preservation of everything that relates thereto to be pursued even to curiosity; but chiefly for a purpose more serious and important; which, in a word, is this: I consider that such a history as I have described would very greatly assist the wisdom and skill of learned men in the use and administration of learning; that it would exhibit the movements and perturbations, the virtues and vices, which take place no less in intellectual than in civil matters; and that from the observation of these the best system of government might be derived and established. For the works of St. Ambrose or St. Augustine will not make so wise a bishop or divine as a diligent examination and study of Ecclesiastical History; and the History of Learning would be of like service to learned men. For everything is subject to chance and error which is not supported by examples and experience. And so much for the History of Learning.

On the Dignity and Difficulty of Civil History.

I come next to Civil History, properly so called, whereof the dignity and authority are pre-eminent among human writings. For to its fidelity are entrusted the examples of our ancestors, the vicissitudes of things, the foundations of civil policy, and the name and reputation of men. But the difficulties no less than the dignity. For to carry the mind in writing back into the past, and bring it into sympathy with antiquity; diligently to examine, freely and faithfully to report, and by the light of words to place as it were before the eyes, the revolutions of times, the characters of persons, the fluctuations of counsels, the courses and currents of actions, the bottoms of pretences, and the secrets of governments; is a task of great labour and judgment—the rather because in ancient transactions the truth is difficult to ascertain, and in modern it is dangerous to tell. Hence Civil History is beset on all sides with faults; some (and these are the greater part) write only barren and commonplace narratives, a very reproach to relations and trifling memoirs; others merely run over the heads of events: others, on the contrary, go into all the minutest particularities, and such as have no relation to the main action; some indulge their imaginations in bold inventions; while others impress on their works the image not so much of their minds as of their passions, ever thinking of their party, but no good witness as to facts; some are always inculcating their favourite political doctrines, and idly interrupting the narrative by going out of the way to display them; others are injudiciously prolix in reporting orations and harangues, and even in relating the actions themselves; so that, among all the writings of men, there is nothing rarer than a true and perfect Civil History. But my present purpose in this division of learning is to mark omissions, and not to censure faults. I will now pursue the divisions of Civil History, and those of the different kinds; for the species will be exhibited more clearly under several heads than under one head curiously traced through all its members.

The First Division of Civil History into Memorials, Antiquities, and Perfect History.

Civil History is of three kinds, not unfitly to be compared with the three kinds of pictures or images. For of pictures and images we see some are unfinished, and wanting the last touch; some are perfect; and some are mutilated and defaced by age. So Civil History (which is a kind of image of events and times) may be divided into three kinds, corresponding to these,—Memorials, Perfect History, and Antiquities. For Memorials are history unfinished, or the first rough drafts of history; and Antiquities are history defaced, or remnants of history which have casually escaped the shipwreck of time.

Memorials, or Preparatory History, are two sorts, whereof the one may be termed Commentaries, the other Registers. Commentaries set down a bare continuance and tissue of actions and events without the causes and pretexts, the commencements and occasions, the counsels and orations, and other passages of action. For this is the true nature of a commentary to the best history extant. But Registers have a twofold character; for they either contain titles of things and persons in order of time, such as are called Annals and Chronologies; or collections of public acts, such as edicts of princes, decrees of councils, judicial proceedings, public speeches, letters of state, and the like, without a perfect continuance or contexture of the thread of the narration.

Antiquities, or remnants of histories, are (as was said) like the spars of a shipwreck; when, though the memory of things be decayed and almost lost, yet acute and industrious persons, by a certain perseverance and scrupulous diligence, contrive out of genealogies, annals, titles, monuments, coins, proper names and styles, etymologies of words, proverbs, traditions, archives and instruments as well public as private, fragments of histories scattered about in books not historical,—contrive, I say, from all these things or some of them, to recover somewhat from the deluge of time; a work laborious indeed, but agreeable to men, and joined with a kind of reverence; and well worthy to supersede the fabulous accounts of the origins of nations, and to be substituted for fictions of that kind; entitled however to the less authority, because in things which few people concern themselves about, the few have it their own way.

In these kinds of Imperfect History I think no deficiency is to be assigned; for they are things, as it were, imperfectly compounded, and therefore any deficiency in them is but their nature. As for epitomes (which are certainly the corruptions and moths of histories) I would have them banished, whereto likewise most men of sound judgment agree, as being things that have fretted and corroded the bodies of many most excellent histories, and wrought them into base and unprofitable dregs.

The Division of Perfect History into Chronicles, Lives, and Relations; and the Explanation thereof.

But Perfect History is of three kinds, according to the object which it propounds for representation. For it either represents a portion of time, or a person worthy of mention, or an action or exploit of the nobler sort. The first we call Chronicles or Annals; the second, Lives; the third, Narrations or Relations. Of these the first excels in estimation and glory; the second in profit and examples; and the third in verity and sincerity. For History of Times represents the magnitude of public actions, and the public faces and deportments of persons, but omits and covers up in silence the smaller passages and motions of men and matters. But such being the workmanship of God, that he hangs the greatest weights upon the smallest wires, it comes commonly to pass that such a history, pursuing the greater things alone, rather sets forth the pomp and solemnity of business than the true and inward springs and resorts thereof. Moreover, when it does add and insert the counsels and motives, yet from its love of grandeur it introduces into human actions more gravity and prudence than they really have; so that a truer picture of human life may be found in a satire than in some histories of this kind. Whereas Lives, if they be well and carefully written (for I do not speak of elegies and barren commemorations of that sort), propounding to themselves a single person as their subject, in whom actions both trifling and important, great and small, public and private, must needs be united and mingled, certainly contain a more lively and faithful representation of things, and one which you may more safely and happily take for example in another case. But special Narrations and Relations of actions (as the Peloponnesian War, the Expedition of Cyrus, the Conspiracy of Catiline, and the like) cannot but be more purely and exactly true than the Perfect Histories of times; because they may choose a manageable and definite argument, whereof a perfect knowledge and certainty and full information may be had; whereas the story of a time (especially if it be of a period much before the age of the writer) is sure to meet with many gaps in the records, and to contain empty spaces which must be filled up and supplied at pleasure by wit and conjecture. But this which I say touching the sincerity of Relations, must be taken with reservation; for (seeing that everything human is subject to imperfection, and good is almost always associated with evil) it must certainly be confessed that relations of this kind, especially if published near the time of the actions themselves (being commonly written either in favour or in spite), are of all other histories the most to be suspected. But then again the evil carries this remedy along with it; that as these very relations are commonly put forth not by one side only, but by both, according to their several factions and parties, a way may be found to truth between the extremes on either hand; and after party heat has cooled down, a good and prudent historian will obtain from them no bad materials and provision for a more perfect history.

With regard to the deficiencies of these three kinds of history, it is certain that there are many particular histories (I speak of such as may be of some moderate worth and dignity) which have been hitherto neglected, with the greatest detriment to the honour and name of the kings and states to which they belong; though to mention them would take too much time. But leaving the care of foreign stories to foreign states (for I will not be a meddler in other nations' matters), I cannot fail to represent to your Majesty the unworthiness of the history of England as we now have it, in the main continuance thereof, and the partiality and obliquity of that of Scotland, in the latest and largest author that I have seen; supposing that it would be honour for your Majesty, and a work very acceptable to future ages, if this island of Great Britain, as it is now joined in one monarchy for the ages to come, so were joined in one history for the ages past; after the manner of the Sacred History, which draws down the story of the ten tribes and of the two tribes as twins together. And if it shall seem that the greatness of this work (and great and difficult it is) may prevent it from being exactly and worthily performed, there is a memorable period of a much smaller compass of time, as to the history of England; that is to say, from the Union of the Roses to the Union of the Kingdoms; a portion of time wherein to my understanding there has been a greater variety of strange events than in like number of successions of any hereditary monarchy has ever been known. For it begins with the mixed obtaining of a crown, partly by arms, partly by title; an entry by battle, an establishment by marriage; and therefore times corresponding to these beginnings, like waters after a tempest, full of working and swelling, though without extremity of storm; but well passed through by the wisdom of the pilot, who was the most conspicuous for policy of all the kings who preceded him. Then follows the reign of a king whose actions, though conducted more by impulse than policy, exercised no slight influence over the affairs of Europe; balancing and inclining them variably. In whose reign also begun that great alteration in the State Ecclesiastical, an action which seldom comes upon the stage. Then the reign of a minor. Then an attempt at a usurpation, though it was but as a diary ague. Then the reign of a queen matched with a foreigner; then of a queen that lived solitary and unmarried. And now, last, this most happy and glorious event, that this island of Britain, divided from all the world, should be united in itself, and that old oracle given to Aeneas (Antiquam exquirite matrem), which fore-showed the rest in store for him, should now be performed and fulfilled upon the most renowned nations of England and Scotland; being now reunited in the ancient mother name of Britain, as a pledge and token of the end and period of all instability and peregrinations; so that as it comes to pass in massive bodies, that they have certain trepidations and waverings before they fix and settle; so it seems to have been ordained by the providence of God that this monarchy, before it settled and was confirmed in your Majesty and your royal generations (in which I hope it is now established for ever), should undergo these prelusive changes and varieties.

For Lives, I find it strange, when I think of it, that these our times have so little esteemed their own virtues, as that the commemoration and writings of the lives of those who have adorned our age should be no more frequent. For although there be but few sovereign kings or abso-lute commanders, and not many princes in free states (so many free states being now turned into monarchies), yet are there many worthy person-ages (even living under kings) that deserve better than dispersed report or dry and barren eulogy. For herein the invention of one of the later poets, by which he has enriched the ancient fiction, is not inelegant. He feigns that at the end of the thread or web of every man's life there hangs a little medal or collar, on which his name is stamped; and that Time waits upon the shears of Atropos, and as soon as the thread is cut, snatches the medals, carries them off, and presently throws them into the river Lethe; and about the river there are many birds flying up and down, who catch the medals, and after carrying them round and round in their beak a little while, let them fall into the river; only there are a few swans, which if they get a medal with a name immediately carry it off to a temple consecrated to immortality. Now this kind of swan is for the most part wanting in our age. And although there are many men, more mortal in their cares and desires than in their bodies, who regard the desire of name memory but as a vanity and ventosity,

Animi nil magnae laudis egentes;

whose philosophy and severity springs no doubt from that root "Non prius laudes contempsimus, quam laudanda facere desivimus"—yet that will not alter Solomon's judgment, "The memory of the just is praised, but the name of the wicked shall rot." The one flourishes for ever; the other either consumes to present oblivion, or turns to an ill odour. And therefore in that style or form of words which is well appropriated to the dean—(of happy memory, of pious memory, of blessed memory),—we seem to acknowledge that which Cicero says (having borrowed it from Demosthenes), "That good fame is the only possession a dead man has"; which possession I cannot but note that in our times it lies in most part waste and neglected.

For Narrations and Relations, a greater diligence therein is also much to be wished; for there is hardly any great action which is not attended by some good pen that can describe it. And because it is an ability not common to write a perfect history as it ought to be written (as may well appear from the small number even of moderate historians), yet if particular actions were but tolerably reported as they pass, it might be expected that a writer would some time or other arise who by such help and assistance might compile a complete History of Times. For the collection of such Relations would be as a nursery, whereby to plant a fair and stately garden when time should serve.

The Division of the History of Times into History Universal and Particular—their Advantages and Disadvantages.

History of Times is either Universal or Particular; whereof the latter contains the deed of some kingdom, commonwealth, or people; the former those of the whole world. For there have been those who have affected to write the history of the world from its very beginning; exhibiting by way of history a medley of things and abridgments of narratives. Others have attempted to comprise, as in a perfect history, the memorable events of their own age all over the world; with noble enterprise, and no small result. For the affairs of men are not so far separated by the divisions of empires or countries, but they have a connexion in many things; and therefore it is certainly of use to have the fates, acts, and destinies of one age described and contained as it were on one tablet. It is true also that many writings of no contemptible character (such as are those Relations of which I previously spoke), which would otherwise perish and not be reprinted,—that these, or at all events the principal matters in them, find a place in a general history of this kind, and in this way are fixed and preserved. But if due attention be paid to the subject, it will be found that the laws of regular history are so strict, that they can scarce be observed in such a wide field of matter; so that the dignity of history is rather diminished than increased by the greatness of the mass of it. For the writer who has such a variety of things on all sides to attend to, will become gradually less scrupulous on the point of information; his diligence, grasping at so many subjects, will slacken in each; he will take up with rumours and popular reports, and thus construct his history from relations which are not authentic, or other frivolous materials of the kind. He will be obliged moreover (lest the work increase beyond measure) purposely to omit a number of things worthy of record, and often to sink into abridgments. He is liable likewise to another danger, not small, and diametrically opposed to the very utility which belongs to Universal History; for as Universal History preserves some narrations which would perhaps otherwise perish, so on the other hand it destroys many that are profitable enough in themselves and would otherwise live, for the sake of that compendious brevity of which men are so fond.

Another Division of the History of Times into Annals and Journals.

The History of Times is also rightly divided into Annals and Journals; which division, though it take its name from periods of time, yet has also reference to the choice of subjects. For it is well observed by Cornelius Tacitus, after touching upon the magnificence of certain buildings, "That it was found suitable to the dignity of the Roman people to commit to Annals only matters of note, but such things as these to the Journals of the City"; thus referring matters concerning the state to Annals, but the less important kind of actions or accidents to Journals. Certainly, in my judgment, there ought to be a kind of heraldry in arranging the precedence of books, no less than of persons. For as nothing derogates from the dignity of a state more than confusion of ranks and degrees, so it not a little embases the authority of a history to intermingle matters of lighter moment, such as triumphs, ceremonies, spectacles, and the like, with matters of state. And surely it were to be wished that this distinction came into fashion. But in our times journals are only used in sea-voyages and expeditions of war; whereas in ancient times it was a matter of honour with princes to keep journals of what passed day by day in their courts; as we see in the case of Ahasuerus, King of Persia, who, when he could not take rest, called for the Chronicles, where he read over again the account of the conspiracy of the Eunuchs. But the journals of Alexander's house expressed every small particularity, so that even if he happened to sleep at table it was registered. Not that, as none but grave matters were included in the Annals, so none but trifling ones were admitted into Journals; but everything, whether of greater or less concern, was promiscuously entered in the Journals as it passed.

The Second Division of Civil History into Pure and Mixed.

The last division of Civil History is into Pure and Mixed. Of the Mixed there are two principal kinds; the one taken from Civil Science, the other principally from natural. For some men have introduced a form of writing consisting of certain narratives not woven into a continuous history, but separate and selected according to the pleasure of the author; which he afterwards reviews, and as it were ruminates over, and takes occasion from them to make public discourse and observation. Now this kind of Ruminated History I greatly approve, provided that the writer keep to it and profess it. But for a man who is professedly writing a Perfect History to be everywhere introducing political reflexions, and thereby interrupting the narrative, is unseasonable and wearisome. For though every wise history is pregnant (as it were) with political precepts and warnings, yet the writer himself should not play the midwife.

Another kind of Mixed History is the History of Cosmography; which is indeed mixed of many things; of Natural History, in respects of the regions themselves, their sites and products; of History Civil, in respect of the habitations, governments, and manners of the people; and of Mathematics, in respect of the climate, and configurations of the heavens; beneath which the regions of the world lie. In which kind of history or science we may congratulate our own age. For this great building of the world has in our age been wonderfully opened and thorough-lighted; and though the ancients had knowledge of the zone and the antipodes, yet that might be by demonstration rather than by travel. But for a little vessel to emulate the heaven itself, and to circle the whole earth with a course even more oblique and winding than that of the heavenly bodies, is the privilege of our age; so that these times may justly bear in their motto not only plus ultra—further yet—in precedence of the ancient non ultra—no further; and "imitable Thunder" in precedence of the ancient "Inimitable Thunder,"

(Demens qui nimbos, et not imitable fulmen, etc.),

but likewise, that which exceeds all admiration, "Imitable Heaven," in respect of our sea-voyages, by which the whole globe of earth has, after the manner of the heavenly bodies, been many times compassed and circumnavigated.

And this proficience in navigation and discovery may plant also great expectation of the further proficience and augmentation of the sciences; especially as it may seem that these two are ordained by God to be coevals, that is, to meet in one age. For so the Prophet Daniel, in speaking of the latter time, foretells "That many shall go to and fro on the earth, and knowledge shall be increased," as if the opening and thorough passage of the world, and the increase of knowledge, were appointed to be in the same age; as we see it is already performed in great part; the learning of these our times, not much giving place to the two former periods or returns of learning (the one of the Grecians, the other of the Romans), but in some respects far exceeding them.

The Division of Ecclesiastical History into Ecclesiastical History Special, History of Prophecy, and History of Providence.

History Ecclesiastical receives nearly the same divisions as History Civil, for there are Ecclesiastical Chronicles, there are Lives of the Fathers, there are relations of Synods and other things pertaining to the Church. But in itself it is properly divided into History Ecclesiastical (using the general name in a special sense), History of Prophecy, and History of Divine Judgments or Providence. The first describes the times of the Church Militant, and its different states; whether fluctuant, as the ark of Noah; or moveable, as the ark in the wilderness; or at rest, as the ark in the Temple; that is, the state of the Church in persecution, in remove, and in peace. In this part I find no deficiency, but rather superfluities; only I would that the virtue and sincerity of the relations were in accordance with the mass and quantity of the matter.

The second, which is History of Prophecy, consists of two relatives, the Prophecy and the Accomplishment; and therefore the plan of such a work ought to be, that every prophecy of Scripture be sorted with the event fulfilling the same, throughout all ages of the world; both for the better confirmation of faith, and for better instruction and skill in the interpretation of those parts of prophecies which are yet unfulfilled; allowing nevertheless that latitude which is agreeable and familiar to divine prophecies, that the fulfillments of them are taking place continually and not at the particular time only. For they are of the nature of their Author, "to whom a thousand years are but as one day, and one day as a thousand years"; and though the height or fulness of them is commonly referred to some one age or particular period, yet they have at the same time certain gradations and processes of accomplishment through divers ages of the world. This is a work which I find deficient, but it is one that is to be done with great wisdom, sobriety, and reverence, or not at all.

The third part, which is History of Providence, has indeed been handled by the pens of some pious writers, but not without partiality. Its business is to observe that divine correspondence which sometimes exists between God's revealed and secret will. For though the judgments and counsels of God are so obscure that to the natural man they are altogether inscrutable, yea, and many times hidden from the eyes of those that behold them from the tabernacle, yet at some time it pleases the Divine Wisdom, for the better establishment of His people, and the confusion of those who are as without God in the world, to write it and report it to view in such capital letters that (as the Prophet saith) "He that runneth by may read it"; that is, that mere sensual persons and voluptuaries, who hasten by God's judgments, and never bend or fix their thoughts upon them, are nevertheless, though running fast and busy about other things, forced to discern them. Such are late and unlooked for judgments; deliverances suddenly and unexpectedly vouchsafed; divine counsels, through tortuous labyrinths and by vast circuits, at length manifestly accomplishing themselves; and the like; all which things serve not only to console the minds of the faithful, but to strike and convince the consciences of the wicked.

Of the Appendices to History; which deal with the Words of Men (as History itself deals with their Actions). The Division thereof into Orations, Letters, and Apophthegms.

But not only man's actions, but his words also should be recorded. And these are no doubt sometimes inserted in history itself, so far as they contribute to the perspicuity and weight of the narrative. But the saying or words of men are properly preserved in books of Speeches, Letters, and Apophthegms. Certainly the Speeches of wise men on business and matters of grave and deep importance conduce greatly as well to the knowledge of the things themselves as to eloquence. But for instruction in civil prudence, still greater help is derived from Letters written by great men on weighty subjects. For of all the words of man nothing is more solid and excellent than letters of this kind; for they are more natural than orations, and more advised than conferences on the sudden. And when there is a continued series of them in order of times (as we find in the letters of ambassadors, governors of provinces, and other ministers of state, to kings, senates, and other superior officers; or, again, in the letters of rulers to their agents), they are of all others the most valuable materials for history. Neither are Apophthegms themselves only for pleasure and ornament, but also for use and action. For they are (as was said) "words which are as goads," words with an edge or point, that cut and penetrate the knots of business and affairs. Now occasions are continually returning, and what served once will serve again; whether produced as a man's own or cited as an old saying. Nor can there be any question of the utility in civil matters of that which Caesar himself thought worthy of his labour; whose book of Apophthegms I wish were extant; for all the collections which we have of this kind appear to me to have been compiled without much judgment.

And so much concerning History; which is that part of learning which answers to one of the cells, domiciles, or offices of the mind of man, which is that of the Memory.

> 95. JEAN MABILLON (1623–1707) was a member of the Maurist community and a student of ecclesiastical antiquities, especially those of his own Benedictine order. Through his studies of saints' lives, his edition of the works of Saint Bernard, and his familiarity with documentary sources, and in response to the hypercritical and flawed work of the Jesuit scholar Papebrouk, Mabillon assembled his great work *On Diplomatics* (1681), which codified the humanist methods of historical criticism and manuscript study since the time of Valla.

Those who attempt to diminish the authority and trustworthiness of ancient documents and records do harm to the study of literature and, in my opinion, attack and undermine constitutional law, not to mention

Jean Mabillon, *On Diplomatics*. In *Historians at Work*, ed. Peter Gay and Victor G. Wexler and trans. Richard Wertis. New York: Harper and Row, 1972. 2:164–168 and 170–171.

legal privilege. For, in fact, from these sources each individual obtains his rights and without them there is no security in civil matters. Consider history: the knowledge we have of the Middle Ages and following periods will be uncertain and incomplete if it is not supported and supplemented by these documents. For, I ask, what will become of the Gallia Christiana, the Italia Sacra, the Sicilia Sacra, and other similar histories; what will become of the Annales Historici Francorum, not to mention the Annales Baroniani, if anyone should disparage and undermine these records? All these historical works will be not more than a badly confused catalogue of names and various events resembling a skeleton. . . .

. . . One cannot help seeing how important the treatment of this subject is, for it concerns not only literature and antiquities, but also churches, monasteries, and noblemen as well; in short, the status of one and all is at stake. Consequently, those who strive to diminish either in whole or in large part the trustworthiness and authority of ancient documents of that kind on very slight grounds or because of minor difficulties do great harm and damage to the entire commonwealth.

But, you say, most manuscripts of this kind are spurious or, at least, interpolated; and they make the authenticity of all the others suspect. First of all, I utterly deny that there are as many false or interpolated documents in churches or monasteries as critics charge. On the contrary, Peter Francis Chissleti of the Society of Jesus, the Bollandist, states that he very rarely found interpolated documents when he investigated the archives of a large number of churches. I do not deny that in fact some documents are false and others are interpolated, but all of them should not be dismissed for that reason. Rather, it is necessary to devise and hand down rules for distinguishing genuine manuscripts from those that are false and interpolated. This, to be sure, was my purpose or, at least, in what measure I succeeded. If I may estimate from the favorable judgment I have received from most scholars thus far, it seems that they not only approved of my work but were enthusiastic about it. Moreover, and this I can state without boasting, I spared no effort in investigating this difficult and little-discussed subject. For I did not undertake this task with only my own intelligence and judgment to guide me, nor did I rely upon the random inspection of a few documents or a hasty and cursory examination of them, nor did I spend only a few days reading them. Rather, I undertook this task after long familiarity and daily experience with these documents. For almost twenty years I had devoted my studies

and energies to reading and examining ancient manuscripts and archives, and the published collections of ancient documents. Finally, I
have carefully examined the ancient books, records, and authentic documents not of just one church, monastery, or province but of many
churches and regions; and I compared and weighed them with one another that I might be able to compile a body of knowledge which was not
merely scanty and meager, but as accurate and as well-tested as possible
in a field which had not been previously investigated.

Furthermore, since the archive of the royal monastery of St. Denis,
which I think is more famous and has more documents than any other
archive, at least in France, was more accessible to me, I did not rely upon
the evidence of my own eyes or upon my own judgment. Rather, I asked
the most learned men in Paris to examine diligently and carefully the
authentic documents of that sacred place and in particular the manuscripts which I wanted to use in this work, and to tell me frankly and
openly their opinion about them. Their unanimous opinion was that
they should be considered genuine and authentic documents, and that I
could use them as such to examine and judge others. . . .

At this point perhaps someone may object and say that there is no
certain method, no sure arguments by which genuine documents can be
distinguished from spurious ones; and, therefore, that these documents
cannot be used in historical matters with certainty and freedom from
error. And although we cannot use them, the loss is not serious since it
can be made up for more than satisfactorily from other records, namely
from the works of ancient authors. And, you will say, what certain and
proved marks of authenticity can be used for distinguishing these documents? No argument can be based upon the material on which the document is written, whether it be papyrus or paper or vellum, or upon the
type of script, or the style, or the dates, or the subscriptions, seals, or
any other characteristics, because any one of these could be duplicated by
a skilled forger and imposter.

But, granted that each and any one of these characteristics can be
duplicated, the genuineness and trustworthiness of ancient documents
depends not upon these things considered separately, but upon the total
interconnection of all of them. And all these characteristics cannot be
duplicated by any forger, no matter how skilled, without there being
some indication of spuriousness which can be detected by an experienced
and accomplished antiquarian. Real and genuine ancient documents
have a kind of appearance of genuineness stamped upon them which

those who are experienced often distinguish true gold from the false by touch alone; painters distinguish originals from copies at a glance; and those who know coins always distinguish the genuine from the false simply at sight. But if any of these things has been so skillfully forged that they very closely resemble the genuine, a skilled man will in the end detect the forgery by a careful examination. He does this not so much by arguments and methods as by experience. This experience is, as it were, the touchstone by which goldsmiths detect real gold, and anyone who does not have it will easily fall into error.

The same method of judgment should be applied to the art of distinguishing genuine documents from spurious or interpolated ones and of determining their dates. All who are experienced in this matter agree that this art cannot be learned except through constant comparison of manuscripts which give a certain indication of their date with others that do not. It is agreed that manuscripts written in capital letters are ancient. What is the reason? Even the great Sirmond, who especially liked that script, would give no other reason than that he knows this from experience.

The state of preservation of ancient works on any subject is no better. In fact, there is no class of author in which false and spurious works are not found mixed with true and genuine ones. Neither historical works, nor the writings of the Fathers, nor decretal letters, nor the records of Councils, nor the lives of the Saints—out of reverence I will not mention Scripture—were immune from this type of corruption. In what way will you distinguish the spurious from the genuine? Only by the testimony of the ancient authors, by the comparison of suspect works with genuine ones; and, finally, by a certain taste which is acquired by constantly reading the genuine works of each author. For in this way the genuine works of the Fathers are separated from the suppositions; genuine epistolary decrees are distinguished from spurious ones; and the genuine acts of the martyrs and other Saints are separated from the forgeries. . . .

. . . To put it briefly, for deciding a question of this kind one should not require a metaphysical reason or demonstration, but rather a moral one of the kind which can be applied in these matters, and which is no less certain in its own right than a metaphysical demonstration. For in these matters, just as in moral matters, we deal with falsehood and error as well as truth. Beyond a doubt moral certitude cannot be acquired without long and constant observation of all the coincidences and circumstances which can lead to attaining the truth. In exactly this way the authenticity or spuriousness of ancient documents can be demonstrated.

It is specified by law, and all intelligent judges of these documents agree that a document which cannot be proved spurious by any certain and invincible arguments must be considered authentic and genuine. Many fines have been imposed upon those who for no good reason accused an ancient document of spuriousness. Let those who capriciously deny the authenticity of all ancient documents see what others receive as their punishment. No one ever attempted to do this unless he was a complete novice who had no experience at all in antiquities, and who did not understand how useful and necessary such documents are not only to the study of literature but also to the commonwealth.

Therefore, those who wish to learn the art of criticizing ancient documents must consider themselves experts only after careful and thorough preparation. For if it is difficult for someone without experience in this field to give an authoritative judgment about one single document, how much more arduous and dangerous will it be for him to judge all kinds of documents if he does not have as his guide that experience which cannot be acquired without long familiarity with documents of this kind? The liberal arts, the study of finished oratory, and the constant reading of the classical authors are not enough to produce this ability to judge documents; rather, these studies are a great obstacle if the same elegance or purity or diction is expected in those ancient documents. For in rejecting and disputing those documents the student would be guided by his own fancy because he is so familiar with those polished authors. The stylistic niceties of these authors must in some way be unlearned so that the mind may become more accustomed to the vulger Latin of these documents. And yet often those who are so familiar with the classical authors arrogantly claim expertise in judging ancient documents, and they ridicule those who disagree with their judgments. Therefore, the same must be required of those who wish to call themselves experts in diplomatics as Quintilian demanded of children's tutors: "Either they should be completely educated or they should realize their deficiencies."

❡ UNIVERSAL HISTORY

96. WALTER RALEIGH (1552?–1618), gentleman and soldier of fortune, composed his *History of the World* while imprisoned in the Tower of London. The work was a rather uncritical but compre-

Walter Raleigh, *The History of the World*. Ed. C. A. Patrides. Philadelphia: Temple University Press, 1971. Pp. 45, 48–49, 50, 71, 72, and 78–81.

hensive (and unfinished) survey of world history from Creation down to the fall of Macedonia in 160 B.C., including essays on many learned subjects and, in this famous preface, a classic appreciation of history.

How unfits, and how unworthy a choice I haue made of my self, to undertake a worke of this mixture; mine owne reason, though exceeding weake, hath sufficiently resolued me. For had it beene begotten then with my first dawne of day, when the light of common knowledge began to open it selfe to younger yeares: and before any wound receiued, either from Fortune or Time: I might yet well haue doubted, that the darknesse of Age and Death would haue couered ouer both It and Mee, long before the performance. For, beginning with the Creation: I haue proceeded with the History of the World; and lastly purposed (some few sallies excepted) to confine my discourse, within this our renowned Iland of Great Brittaine. I confesse that it had better sorted with my dissability, the better part of whose times are runne out in other trauailes; to haue set together (as I could) the unoiynted and scattered frame of our English affaires, than of the universall: in whome had there beene no other defect, (who am all defect) then the time of the day, it were enough; the day of a tempestuous life, drawne on to the very evening ere I began. But those inmost, and soulepeircing wounds, which are ever aking while uncured: with the desire to satisfie those few friends, which I have tried by the fire of adversitie; the former enforcing, the latter perswading; have caused mee to make my thoughts legible, and my selfe the Subiect of every opinion wise or weake. . . .

To me it belongs in the first part of this praeface, following the common and approved custome of those who have left the memories of time past to after ages; to give, as neare as I can, the same right to History which they have done. Yet seeing therein I should but borrow other mens wordes; I will not trouble the Reader with the repetition. True it is, that among many other benefits, for which it hath beene honored; in this one it triumpheth over all humane knowledge, That it hath given us life in our understanding, since the world it selfe had life and beginning, even to this day; yea it hath triumphed over time, which besides it, nothing but eternity hath triumphed over: for it hath carried our knowledge over the vast and devouring space of so many thousands of yeares, and given so faire and peircing eies to our minde; that we plainely behould living now, as if we had lived then, that great World, *Magni Dei* sapiens opus, the wise worke (saith Hermes) of a great GOD, as it was then, when but new to it selfe. By it I say it is, that we live in the very time when it was created: we behold how it was governed: how it was covered with waters, and againe repeopled: How Kings and kingdomes have florished and fallen; and for what vertue and piety GOD made prosperous; and for what vice and deformity he made wretched, both the one and the other. And it is not the least debt which we owe unto History, that it hath made us acquainted with our dead Ancestors; and, out of the depth and darkenesse of the earth, delivered us their memory and fame. In a word, wee may gather out of History a policy no lesse wise than eternall; by the comparison and application of other mens fore-passed miseries, with our owne like errours and illdeservings.

But it is neither of Examples the most lively instructions, nor the words of the wisest men, nor the terror of future torments, that hath yet so wrought in our blind and stupified mindes; as to make us remember, That the infinite eye and wisdome of GOD doth peirce through all our pretences; as to make us remember, That the iustice of GOD doth require none other accuser, than our owne consciences: which neither the false beauty of our apparent actions, nor all the formallitie, which (to pacifie the opinions of men) we put on; can in any, or the least kind, cover from his knowledge. And so much did that Heathen wisdome confesse, no way as yet qualified by the knowledge of a true GOD. If any (saith Eurypides) having in his life committed wickednesse, thinke he can hide it from everlasting gods, he thinkes not well. . . .

For seeing the first bookes of the following story, I have undertaken the discourse of the first Kings and Kingdomes: and that it is impossible for the short life of a Preface, to travaile after and over-take farr-off Antiquity, and to iudge of it; I will, for the present, examine what profit hath beene gathered by our owne Kings, and their Neighbor Princes: who having beheld, both in divine and humane letters, the successe of infidelitie, iniustice, and crueltie; have (notwithstanding) planted after the same patterne. . . .

But it is now time to sound a retrait; and to desire to be excused of this long pursuit: and withall, that the good intent, which hath moved me to draw the picture of time past (which we call Historie) in so large a table, may also be accepted in place of a better reason.

The examples of divine providence, every where found (the first divine Histories being nothing else but a continuation of such examples) have perswaded me to fetch my beginning from the beginning of all things;

to wit, Creation. For though these two glorious actions of the Almightie be so neare, and (as it were) linked together, that the one necessarily implyeth the other: Creation, inferring Providence; (for what Father forsaketh the child that he hath begotten?) and Providence presupposing Creation: Yet many of those that have seemed to excell in worldly wise-dome, have gone about to disioyne this coherence; the Epicure denying both Creation & Providence, but granting that the world had a begin-ning; the Aristotelian granting Providence, but denying both the Crea-tion and the Beginning. . . .

But for my selfe, I shall never been perswaded, that GOD hath shut up all light of Learning within the lanthorne of Aristotles braines: or that it was ever said unto him, as unto Esdras, Accendam in Corde tuo Lucer-nam intellectus: that GOD hath given invention but to the Heathen; and that they onely have invaded Nature, and found the strength and bot-tome thereof; the same nature having consumed all her store, and left nothing of price to after-ages. . . .

Generally concerning the order of the worke, I have onely taken con-saile from the Argument. For of the Assyrians, which after the downefall of Babel take up the first part, and were the first great kings of the World, there came little to the view of posterity: some few enterprises, greater in fame than faith, of Ninus and Semiramis excepted.

It was the story of the Hebrewes, of all before the Olympiads, that over came the consuming disease of time; and preserved it selfe, from the very cradle and beginning to this day: and yet not so entire, but that the large discourses thereof (to which in many Scriptures wee are referred) are no where found. The Fragments of other Stories, with the actions of those Kings and Princes which shot up here and there in the same time, I am driven to relate by way of digression: of which we may say with Virgil.

> Apparent rari nantes in gurgite vasto;
> They appeare here and there floting in the great gulfe of time.

To the same first Ages do belong the report of many Inventions therein found, and from them derived to us; though most of the Authors Names, have perished in so long a Navigation: For those Ages had their Lawes; they had diversity of Government; they had Kingly rule; No-bilitie, Pollicie in warre; Navigation; and all, or the most of needfull Trades. To speake therefore of these (seeing in a generall Historie we should have left a great deale of Nakednesse, by their omission) it cannot properly bee called a digression. True it is that I have also made many others: which if they shall be layd to my charge, I must cast the fault into the great heape of humane error. For seeing wee digresse in all the wayes of our lives: yea seeing the life of man is nothing else but digression; I may the better bee excused, in writing their lives and actions. I am not altogether ignorant in the Lawes of Historie, and of the Kindes.

The same hath beene taught by many; but by no man better, and with greater brevity, than by that excellent learned Gentleman, Sir Francis Bacon. Christian Lawes are also taught us by the Prophets and Apostles; and every day preacht unto us. But wee still make large digressions: yea the teachers themselves do not (in all) keepe the path which they poynt out to others.

For the rest after such time as the Persians had wrested the Empire from the Chaldaeans, and had raised a great Monarchie, producing actions of more importance than were else-where to be found: it was agreeable to the Order of Story, to attend this Empire; whilest it so florished, that the affaires of the nations adjoyning had reference thereunto. The like observance was to bee used towards the fortunes of Greece, when they againe began to get around upon the Persians, as also towards the affaires of Rome, when the Romans grew more mighty than the Greekes.

As for the Medes, the Macedonians, the Sicilians, the Carthaginians, and other Nations, who resisted the beginnings of the former Empires, and afterwards became but parts of their composition and enlargement: it seemed best to remember what was knowne of them from ther severall beginnings, in such times and places, as they in their flourishing estates opposed those Monarchies; which in the end swallowed them up. And herein I have followed the best Geographers: who seldome give names to those small brookes, whereof many, joined together, make great Rivers; till such time as they become united, and runne in a maine streame to the Ocean Sea. If the Phrase be weake, and the Stile not every-where lit it else: the first, shewes their legitimation and true Parent; the second, will excuse it selfe upon the Variety of matter. For Virgill, who wrote his Eclogues, gracili auena, used stronger pipes when he sounded the warres of Aeneas. It may also bee layd to my charge that I use divers Hebrew words in my first booke, and else where: in which language others may thinke, and I my-selfe acknowledge it, that I am altogether ignorant: but it is true, that some of them I finde in Montanus; others in lattaine Caracter in S. Senensis, and of the rest I have borrowed the interpretation of some of my learned friends. But say I had been beholding to neither, yet were it not bee wondred at having had an eleven years leasure, to attaine the knowledge of that, or of any other tongue; How-so-ever, I know that it will bee said by many, That I might have beene more pleasing to the Reader, if I had written the Story of mine owne times; having been permitted to draw water as neare the Well-head as another. To this I answere, that who-so-ever in writing a moderne Historie, shall follow truth too neare the heeles, it may happily strike out his teeth. There is no mistresse or Guide, that hath led her followers and servants into greater miseries. He that goes after her too farre off, looseth her sight, and looseth him-selfe: and hee that walkes after her at a middle distance; I know not whether I should call that kind of course Temper or Basenesse. It is true, that I never travailed after men's opinions, when I might have made the best use of them: and I have now too few daies remayning, to imitate those, that either out of extreme ambition, or extreme cowardise, or both, doe yet, (when death hath them on his shoulders) flatter the world, betweene the bed and the grave. It is enough for me (being in that state I am) to write of the eldest times: wherein also why may it not be said, that in speaking of the past, I point at the present, and taxe the vices of those that are yet lyving, in their persons that are long since dead; and have it laid to my charge. But this I cannot helpe, though innocent. And certainly if there be any, that finding themselves spotted like the Tigers of old time, shall finde fault with me for painting them over a new; they shall therein accuse themselves justly, and me falsly.

For I protest before the Majesty of God, That I malice no man under the Sunne. Impossible I know it is to please all: seeing few or none are so pleased with themselves, or so assured of themselves, by reason of their subjection to their private passions; but that they seeme diverse persons in one and the same day. Seneca hath said it, and so doe I: Vnus mihi pro populo erat: and to the same effect Epicurus, Hoc ego non multis sed tibi; or (as it hath since lamentably fallen out) I may borrow the resolution of an ancient Philosopher, Satis est nullus. For it was for the service of that inestimable Prince Henry, the successive hope, and one of the greatest of the Christian World, that I undertooke this Worke. It pleased him to peruse some part thereof, and to pardon what was amisse. It is now left to the world without a Maister: from which all that is presented, hath received both blows & thanks. Eadem probamus, eadem reprehendimus: hic exitus est omnis iudicij, in quo lis secundum plures datur. But these discourses are idle. I know that as the charitable will judge charitably: so against those, qui gloriantur in malitia, my present adversitie hath disarmed mee. I am on the ground already; and therefore have not farre to fall: and for rysing againe, as in the Naturall privation their is no recession to habit; so is it seldome seene in the privation politique. I doe therefore for-beare to stile my Readers Gentle, Courteous, and Friendly, thereby to beg their good opinions, or to promise a second and third volume (which I also intend) if the first receive grace and good acceptance. For that which is already done, may be thought enough; and too much: and it is certaine, let us claw the Reader with never so many courteous phrases; yet shall we ever-more be thought fooles, that write foolishly. For conclusion; all the hope I have lies in this, That I have already found more ungentle and uncurteous Readers of my Love towards them, and well-deserving of them, than ever I shall doe againe. For had it beene otherwise, I should hardly have had this leisure, to have made myselfe a foole in print.

> 97. JAMES USSHER (1646–1716), archbishop and scriptural scholar, continued to improve on the work on comparative chronology begun by Scaliger and others; his results have been accepted, especially in Protestant biblical circles, down to the present century.

Censorinus, in his little book, written to Q. Cerellius of one's birthday, having in hand the Explications of Times Intervals, thought good thus to preface it: . . . If the origin of the world had been known unto man, I would thence have taken my beginning. And a little after, speaking of this time, . . . says he, . . . whether time had a beginning, or whether it always was, the certain number of years cannot be comprehended. Therefore Ptolemaeus, from astronomical supputations, thus renounces this epoch of the world as a thing most remote from the knowledge of man.

. . . Nor, truely is it strange that heathens, altogether of holy writ, should thus despair of ever attaining the knowledge of the world's rise; when as even among Christians, that most renowned chronographer Dionysius Petavius, being about to declare his opinion concerning the creation of the world and the number of years from thence down to us,

James Ussher, *The Annals of the World*. London: E. Tyler, 1658. No pagination.

first made . . . this resolution before his discourse: . . . that the number of years from the beginning of the world to these our days can by no reasons be certainly concluded nor any way found out without devine revelation. From whose opinion Philastrius Brixiensis did very much dissent, denoting it heresay . . . to affirm the number of years from the beginning of the world uncertain and that men knew not the spaces of time. And Lactantius Firmianus, whose assertion in his Divine Institutions, is somewhat more bold: . . . We whom the holy scriptures do train up to the knowledge of truth know both the beginning and the end of the world. For whatsoever may be done of things past, we are taught that the . . . Father hath reserved the knowledge of things future in his own power. Nor is there any mortal to whom the whole continuance of time is known, whither that [expression] of the Son of Sirac is thought to tend: . . . The sands of the sea, the drops of rain, and the days of the world, who can number? Which Lyranus thinking to have been spoken of time past (when as others interpret it here and in Chapter XVIII.ii of the days of eternity) draws thence this erroneous conclusion: that the days from the beginning of the world were never by any man cast up certainly and precisely.

The first Christian writer (that I have had a view of) who attempted from holy writings to deduce the age of the world was Theophilus, Bishop of Antioch, who, . . . concerning this whole account, thus generally declares: . . . All times and years are made known to them who are willing to obey the truth. But concerning the exactness of this calculation he thus afterwards proceeds: . . . And haply we may not be able to give an exact account of every year, because in the Holy Scriptures there is no mention of the months and days current.

. . . But if any one, well seen in the knowledge not only of sacred and exotic history but of astronomical calculation and the old Hebrew calendar, shall apply himself to these studies, I judge it indeed difficult but not impossible for such a one to attain not only the number of years but even of days from the creation of the world. . . . But in regard, in diverse ages and nations, diverse epochs of time were used and [also] several forms of years. Here it's necessary that some common and known account should be observed, to which the diversity of the rest may most appositely be reduced. And to us there is no measure of time more known and more accommodatious to the common collation of times than the form of the Julian years and months, deduced from the middle of the night beginning the Calends of January, of the first year of the common account from Christ; with those three cycles by which being joined every year is distinguished from all other years whatsoever.

. . . We find moreover that the year of our forefathers and the years of the ancient Egyptians and the Hebrews were of the same quantity with the Julian, consisting of twelve equal months, every [one] of them containing thirty days (for it cannot be proved that the Hebrews did use lunary months before the Babylonian Captivity) adjoining to the end of the twelfth month the addition of five days and every forth year six.

. . . The difficulties of chronologers, perplexed by that [philoueikia], or love of contention, so termed by Basil, being at last over-passed I encline to this opinion, that from the evening ushering in the first day of the world, to that midnight which began the first day of the Christian era, there was 4003 years, seventy days, and six temporary hours; and that the true nativity of our Savior was full four years before the beginning of the vulgar Christian era, as is demonstrable by the time of Herod's death.

. . . And whereas amongst a multitude of Historians, which were before Julius Caesar's time, the malice of time left only four remaining: Herodotus, Thucididies, Xenophon, and Polibius (and him also lame and imperfect in the general part of him), these, notwithstanding, I esteemed the most authentic for their antiquity.

> 98. JACQUES-BENIGNE BOSSUET (1627–1704), bishop of Meaux and champion of Gallicanism, wrote his *Discourse on Universal History* (1681) for the French dauphin, rehearsing the old providential plan of human history, especially the vicissitudes of empire and the progress of the church, down to the time of Charlemagne.

Even if history were useless to other men, princes should be made to read it. For there is no better way to show them what is wrought by passions and interest, time and circumstance, good and bad advice. Histories deal only with the deeds that concern princes, and everything in them seems to be made for their use. If they need experience to acquire the prudence of a good ruler, nothing is more useful for their instruction than to add the examples of past centuries to the experiences they have every day. While ordinarily they learn to evaluate the dangers they en-

Jacques-Bénigne Bossuet, *Discourse on Universal History* (Classic European Historians). Trans. Elborg Forster and ed. Orest Ranum. Chicago: University of Chicago Press, 1976. Pp. 3–6, 9–10, 339–340, 341, 370, and 372–374.

counter only at the expense of their subjects and their own glory, history will help them form their judgment on the events of the past without any risk. Seeing even the most hidden vices of princes exposed to everyone's sight, despite the spurious praise they receive during their life, they will be ashamed of the vain pleasure they take in flattery and will understand that true glory comes only with merit.

Furthermore, it would be shameful not only for a prince but for any gentleman in general to be ignorant of the human race and of the memorable changes the passage of time has wrought in the world. He who has not learned from history to distinguish different ages will represent men under the law of Nature or under written law as they are under the law of the Gospel; he will speak of the vanquished Persians under Alexander as he speaks of the victorious Persians under Cyrus; he will make the Greeks as free at the time of Philip as at the time of Themistocles or Miltiades, the Roman people as proud under Diocletian as under Constantine, and France during the upheavals of the civil wars under Charles IX and Henry III as powerful as at the time of Louis XIV, when, united under that great king, France alone triumphs over all of Europe.

It was in order to avoid these pitfalls, Monseigneur, that you have read so much ancient and modern history. Above all, it was necessary to make you read in the Scriptures the history of God's people, the foundation of religion. Nor were you left ignorant of Greek and Roman history; and, even more important for you, you were carefully taught the history of this great kingdom which you are obliged to make happy. But lest these histories, and those you will still have to learn, become confused in your mind, it is of the first importance to put before you distinctly, but in a condensed form, the entire course of the centuries.

This kind of universal history is to the history of every country and of every people what a world map is to particular maps. In a particular map you see all the details of a kingdom or a province as such. But a general map teaches you to place these parts of the world in their context; you see what Paris or the Ile-de-France is in the kingdom, what the kingdom is in Europe, and what Europe is in the world.

In the same manner, particular histories show the sequences of events that have occurred in a nation in all their detail. But in order to understand everything, we must know what connection that history might have with others; and that can be done by a condensation in which we can perceive, as in one place, the entire sequence of time.

Such a condensation, Monseigneur, will afford you a grand view. You will see all preceding centuries developing, as it were, before your very eyes in a few hours; you will see how empires succeeded one another and how religion, in its different states, maintains its stability from the beginning of the world to our own time.

It is the progression of these two things, I mean religion and empires, that you must impress upon your memory. And since religion and political government are the two points around which human affairs revolve, to see what is said about them in a condensation and thus to discover their order and sequence is to understand in one's mind all that is great in mankind and, as it were, to hold a guiding line to all the affairs of the world.

Just as, looking at a world map, you leave your native country and the place that holds you to travel all over the habitable world, seeing it in your mind with all its oceans and its lands; so also, looking at a chronological condensation, you leave the narrow confines of your age and extend yourself through all the centuries.

But just as, to help our memory in the knowledge of places, we must retain certain principal towns around which to place the others according to their distance, so also, in the succession of centuries, we must have certain times marked by some great event to which we can relate all the rest.

That is what we call an epoch, from a Greek word meaning to stop, because we stop there in order to consider, as from a resting place, all that has happened before or after, thus avoiding anachronisms, that is, the kind of error that confuses ages.

We must begin by firmly establishing a small number of epochs, such as they are found in the time of ancient history:

Adam, or the Creation
Noah, or the Flood
The Calling of Abraham, or the Beginning of the Covenant
    between God and Man
Moses, or the Written Law
The Fall of Troy
Solomon, or the Foundation of the Temple
Romulus, or the Building of Rome
Cyrus, or the Deliverance of the Chosen People from the
    Babylonian Captivity
Scipio, or the Fall of Carthage
The Birth of Jesus Christ
Constantine, or the Peace of the Church
Charlemagne, or the Establishment of the New Empire

I offer you the establishment of the new empire under Charlemagne as the end of ancient history, because it is here that you will see the conclusive end of the ancient Roman Empire. That is why I shall make you pause at such an important point of universal history. The sequence will be given you in a second part, which will bring you up to the century we see illuminated by the immortal actions of the king, your father, and in which your ardor in following his great example gives rise to hopes of further luster.

Having explained the plan of this work in general, I must do three things to make it as useful as I would hope it to be.

First, I must take you through the epochs I mentioned, and, briefly explaining the principal events belonging to each of them, I must accustom your mind to putting these events in their place without paying attention to anything but the sequence of time. But since my principal aim is to show you, in this progression of time, the course of religion and of great empires, I shall first treat the facts concerning these two things in chronological order and then treat separately, with appropriate reflections, first those facts that show us the perpetual duration of religion and finally those that show us the causes of the great changes in empires.

After that, whatever part of ancient history you may read, everything will be useful to you. You will see no fact without perceiving its consequences. You will admire the continuous direction of God in matters of religion; you will also see how human affairs are bound together. Hence, you will know with how much care and foresight they have to be conducted. . . .

First Epoch

Adam, or the Creation. First Age of the World   The first epoch begins with a grand spectacle: God creating heaven and earth through his word and making man in his image (1 A.M. [*anno mundi*], 4004 B.C.). This is where Moses, the first historian, the most sublime philosopher, and the wisest of legislators, begins.

On this foundation he builds his history as well as his teaching and his laws. Then he shows us all men within one man, even his wife fashioned from him; harmony in marriage and human society built on that foundation; the perfection and power of man so long as he bears the image of God in its entirety; his domination over the animals; his innocence and also his happiness in Paradise, whose memory is preserved in the Golden

Age of the poets; the divine precept given to our first parents; the malice of the tempting spirit and his appearance in the form of the serpent; the fall of Adam and Eve, so fateful to all their posterity; the first man justly punished in all his children and God's curse on the human race; the first promise of redemption and the future victory over the demon that was his downfall.

The earth begins to be populated, and crime increases (129 A.M., 3875 B.C.). Cain, the first child of Adam and Eve, shows the nascent world the first tragic action, and already virtue is beginning to be persecuted by vice. The contrasting ways of life of the two brothers appear: the innocence of Abel, his pastoral life, and his pleasing sacrifices; and those of Cain rejected, his rapacity, his impiety, his parricide, and his envy, the mother of murder; the punishment of that crime and the constant terror in the criminal's conscience; the building of the first town by that evildoer, who was seeking asylum from the hatred and horror of mankind. We see the invention of a few skills by his children; the tyranny of the passions and the prodigious depravity of the human heart, which is always ready to do evil. We also see the posterity of Seth, faithful to God despite that depravity; the pious Enoch (987 A.M., 3017 B.C.), miraculously taken from a world unworthy of him; the distinction between the children of man and those of God, meaning those that live according to the flesh and those that live according to the spirit; their mingling and the universal corruption of the world; the destruction of man decided by a just judgment of God (1536 A.M., 2468 B.C.); the announcement of his wrath to the sinners by his servant Noah; their hardhearted impenitence that was finally chastised in the Flood (1656 A.M., 2348 B.C.); Noah and his family, who were saved for the preservation of mankind.

This much happened in 1,656 years. Such is the beginning of all history, and here we discover the omnipotence, wisdom, and kindness of God; the happy innocence under his protection, his justice in punishing crime but also his patience in waiting for the conversion of sinners; the greatness and dignity of man in his first state; the nature of mankind since its corruption; man's natural bent toward envy and the secret causes of violence and war—in a word we discover all the cornerstones of religion and ethics.

Along with mankind, Noah preserved the arts—those that were basic to human existence, having been known from the beginning, as well as those that had been invented later. The arts that men learned first, apparently from their Creator, are agriculture, animal husbandry, and the art of making clothing and perhaps also that of finding shelter. That is why we seek the beginning of these arts in the East, the region whence mankind spread out.

The tradition of the great deluge is found everywhere on earth. The ark in which the last of mankind took refuge has always been famous in the East, especially around the place where it came to rest after the Flood. Several other circumstances relating to this famous event can be found in the annals and traditions of ancient peoples; their chronology tallies, and everything fits together as well as can be expected for a past so remote. . . .

There is no need to give you a detailed account of the causes for the fall of the kingdoms fashioned from the ruins of Alexander's empire, namely, Syria, Macedonia, and Egypt. All of them fell because they had to yield to a stronger power, the power of Rome. But if we were to consider the situation of these monarchies toward their end, we could easily recognize the immediate causes for their fall. Among other things, we would see that the most powerful among them, Syria, seriously weakened already by the effeminacy and luxury of the nation, was dealt the final blow by the division among its princes. . . .

Finally, we have come to the great empire which has engulfed all of the world's empires and has given rise to the greatest kingdoms of our world—the empire whose laws we still respect and which we consequently should know better than any other. You are aware, of course, that I am speaking of the Roman Empire. You have studied the entire course of its long and memorable history. But in order to gain a full understanding of the reasons for the rise of Rome and the great changes it underwent, you should carefully study not only the ways of the Romans but also the ages which gave rise to all the vicissitudes of that vast empire.

The world has never seen a prouder and bolder, but also a more steadfast and tradition-bound, as well as more astute, industrious, and patient people than those of Rome.

These traits created the best militia and the most farsighted, firm, and consistent policy that ever existed.

The very essence of a Roman, so to speak, was his attachment to his liberty and to his country. These feelings reinforced each other; for because he loved his liberty, he also loved his country as a mother who constantly fostered his generosity and his liberty.

To the Romans, as to the Greeks, the word liberty meant a state in which no one was subject to anything but the law and where the law was more powerful than men.

I might add that, although Rome was born under a royal government, the liberty it enjoyed even under its kings is not suitable to a monarchy as we know it. For not only was the king elected, and elected by all the people; it also fell to the assembled people to confirm the laws and to make decisions concerning war and peace. In certain cases, kings deferred even ultimate judgments to the people, as on the occasion when Tullus Hostilius, not daring either to condemn or to absolve Horatius—who was both honored for defeating the Curiatii and despised for killing his sister—had him judged by the people. Thus, properly speaking, the kings were responsible only for the command of the armies, and their authority was restricted to convoking lawful assemblies, where they proposed the measures to be taken, and to maintaining the laws and executing the public decrees. . . .

Liberty, then, was a treasure to them, and they preferred it to all the riches of the world. And you have seen how, early in their history and for a long time thereafter, they did not consider poverty an evil. On the contrary, they saw it as a means of preserving their most complete liberty; for who is freer or more independent than a man who is able to make do with very little and who, not expecting anything from anyone's protection or liberality, counts only on his own industry and his own work for his livelihood?

That is what the Romans did. They raised livestock, worked the land, denied themselves as much as they could, and lived by thrift and hard work. That was their life; and that is how they supported their families, whom they brought up to similar occupations.

Livy was correct when he said that there never was a people to hold frugality, thrift, and poverty in esteem for so long a time. . . .

Now you can easily perceive the causes of the rise and fall of the Roman Empire.

You can see that this state—founded as it was on war and therefore naturally inclined to encroach upon its neighbors—subjugated the world because it had brought political and military science to the highest point of perfection.

You see that the divisions within the republic and its eventual fall were caused by the jealousy of its citizens and by a love of liberty that was carried to an excessive and intolerable degree of sensitivity.

It is no longer difficult for you to recognize all the ages of Rome, whether you wish to consider it in itself or in relation to other nations; and you see what changes were bound to follow from the configuration of issues in each age.

Examining Rome in itself, you see it first in a monarchical state, which was based on its original laws; then in its liberty; and finally subject again to a monarchical rule, but this time by force and violence.

It is easy to understand how the popular state developed from the rudiments that had existed even at the time of the monarchy; and it is equally evident that the basis of the new monarchy was gradually forming during the time of liberty. . . .

These are the noteworthy ages which mark the changes in the Roman state considered in itself. Those which show us its situation in relation to others are equally easy to discern.

There was the age of its struggle against equals, during which Rome was in danger. This lasted for a little over 500 years and ended with the annihilation of the Gauls in Italy and of the Carthaginian Empire.

There was the age of struggle from a position of superior strength, which presented no danger to Rome, however great the wars undertaken. It lasted for 200 years and continued until the establishment of the Caesars.

There was the age in which Rome preserved its empire and its majesty. This lasted for 400 years and ended with the reign of Theodorus I, the Great.

There was the age, finally, when the empire, losing ground on all its sides, gradually declined. This stage, which also lasted for 400 years, began with the children of Theodosius and came to a definitive end with Charlemagne.

I am fully aware, Monseigneur, that many specific incidents could be added to the causes for the fall of Rome. The rigorous treatment of debtors by their creditors, for example, frequently stirred up great upheavals. The prodigious number of gladiators and slaves, of whom there were entirely too many in Rome and Italy, caused dreadful violence and even savage wars. Exhausted by a long period of civil and foreign wars, Rome created so many new citizens—who were admitted either by conniving or for good reasons—that it could hardly recognize itself in the throng of naturalized foreigners. The senate became filled with barbarians; Roman blood lost its purity; love of the fatherland, which had enabled Rome to rise above all the world's nations, did not come naturally to citizens of foreign origin; and the others were tainted by this admixture. More and more factions resulted from the great number of new citizens; and unruly elements used them as a new means for creating disturbances and for their own advancement.

Meanwhile, the number of poor was growing endlessly, because luxury, debauchery, and sloth had crept into Rome. Those who found themselves ruined found redress only in sedition; in any case, it was of little concern to them that their actions might lead to the collapse of the entire society. It is well known that this attitude prompted the Catalinian conspiracy. Men of great ambition, together with the wretched poor, who have nothing to lose, always favor change. These two kinds of citizens were the most numerous in Rome; and since the middle class, the only one which can create an equilibrium in a popular state, was weak, the republic was bound to fall.

To this we might also add the character and special aptitudes of those who brought about the great changes; I mean the Gracchi, Marius, Sulla, Pompey, Julius Caesar, Anthony, and Augustus. I have gone into this to a certain extent, but I have mainly focused your attention on the universal causes and the true root of the evil, namely, the jealousy between the two estates, since it is important that you see this with all its consequences.

Conclusion of the Entire Preceding Discourse, in Which It Is Shown That Everything Must Be Ascribed to a Providence

You should recall, however, Monseigneur, that this long concatenation of particular causes which make and unmake empires depends on the secret decrees of Divine Providence. From the highest heavens God holds the reigns of every kingdom and holds every heart in his hands. At times he bridles man's passions, at others he gives them free rein; and that is how he moves all of mankind. Should he wish to see a conqueror, he will spread terror before him and will inspire him and his armies with invincible boldness. Should he wish to see legislators, he will send them his spirit of wisdom and foresight; he will cause them to forestall the evils that can befall a state and to lay the foundation for public tranquility. Knowing that human wisdom always falls short in some way, he will enlighten it and give it scope—but then he will also leave it to its own ignorance, blind it, hasten it, and throw it into confusion. Then it will become perplexed by its own subtlety, and its very precautions will become so many snares. In this manner God renders his redoubtable judgments, according to the rules of his never-failing justice. It is he who plants the seeds of future events in their most remote causes and who strikes the great blows whose reverberations reach so far. When he wishes to unleash the final blow and to overthrow an empire, human conduct becomes fitful and weak. Egypt, once so wise, marched on like a nation drunken, staggering, and reeling because the Lord had struck its conduct with bewilderment—Egypt no longer knew what it did and lost its way. But let no man deceive himself: God will set aright the bewildered senses whenever it pleases him, and he who mocks the blindness of others will fall into even profounder darkness himself; and it may be that nothing more than this prolonged good fortune is needed to lead him astray.

Thus God reigns over every nation. Let us no longer speak of coincidence or fortune; or let us use these words to cover only our ignorance. What is coincidence to our uncertain foresight is concerted design to a higher foresight, that is, to the eternal foresight which encompasses all causes and effects in a single plan. Thus all things concur to the same end; and it is only because we fail to understand the whole design that we see coincidence or strangeness in particular events.

> 99. GOTTFRIED WILHELM LEIBNIZ (1646–1716), mathematician, scientist, jurist, and universal philosopher, was also an archival scholar who studied, and published the sources of, the history of the house of Braunschweig-Hanover. In the following letter to Duke Ernst Augustus in 1692, Leibniz suggests his theory of the structure and development of history and how it might be accommodated to his metaphysics.

To judge history distinctly, one may compare it to the body of an animal, where the bones support everything, the nerves form the connection, the spirit which moves the machine, the humors which consist of nourishing juices, and finally the flesh which gives completion to the whole mass. The parts of history correspond thus: chronology to bones, genealogy to nerves, hidden motives to invisible spirits, useful examples to juices, and the detail of circumstances to the whole mass of flesh. I

Gottfried Wilhelm Leibniz, *Preface*. In *A History of Historical Writing*, ed. and trans. James Westfall Thompson with Bernard J. Holm. Gloucester, Mass.: Peter Smith, 1967. 2:100.

consider, accordingly, chronology or the knowledge of time as the basis or skeleton of the whole body, which forms the foundation and support of all the rest. The genealogy of illustrious persons corresponds, in my opinion, to the nerves and tendons of history, for since history records what has passed among men, it is necessary that it pay attention to the natural connections among men, which consist of cosanguinity. And since succession has always given power and authority, . . . it follows that histories of nations, of kingdoms and of principalities depend much on connections, changes and families, whence came wars, unions of many countries to form a great monarchy, and the pretensions of one prince on another. . . .

Since history without truth is a body without life, it is necessary that one try to assert nothing without a basis of fact, and that gradually one purge history of fables, which have crept into it. . . . It is also necessary to admit that not all parts of history are equally susceptible to exactitude, for who could assure us of hidden motives reported in ancient history?

> 100. SAMUEL PUFENDORF (1632–1694), professor of law at the University of Lund and a founder of modern natural law, became royal historiographer to Charles IX. In his lectures (1682–1685) on the states of Europe, Pufendorf celebrated, in conventional terms, the value of universal history in the political education of the high-born offspring produced by the ruling elite of European society.

That history is the most pleasant and useful study for persons of quality, and more particularly for those who design for employments in the State, is well known to all Men of Learning.

It is therefore requisite, that young Gentlemen should be exhorted to apply themselves betimes to this Study, not only because their Memory is then vigorous, and more capable to retain what they learn, but likewise in regard it may be concluded, that he who has no relief for history, is very unlikely to make any great progress in the way of knowledge. It is a common custom, indeed, both in public and private schools, to read to their scholars some ancient historians; and there are a great many who employ several years in reading Cornelius Nepos, Curtius, Justin, and Livy, but never so much as take into their confidence the history of later

Samuel Pufendorf, *An Introduction to the History of the Principal Kingdoms and States of Europe*. London, 1806. No pagination. Orthography modernized.

times. 'Tis true, and it cannot be denied, but that we ought to begin with the ancient historians, they being equally useful and pleasant; but to neglect the history of later times is a notorious piece of indiscretion, and want of understanding in those to whom the education of youth is committed; for I lay down as a principle, that we are to study those things in our youth, which may prove useful to us hereafter, when we come to riper Years, and apply ourselves to business. Now I cannot, for my life, apprehend what great benefit we can expect to receive from Cornelius Nepos, Curtius, and the first decade of Livy, as to our modern affairs, though we had learned them by heart, and had, besides this, made a perfect index of all the phrases and sentences that are to be found in them: Or if we were so well versed in them, as to be able to give a most exact account, how many cows and sheep the Romans led in triumph when they had conquered the Aequi, the Vilsci, and the Hernici. But what a considerable advantage it is to understand the modern history as well as of our native country, as of its neighboring nations, is sufficiently known to such as are employed in state affairs. But after all it is not so easy a matter to acquire this knowledge, partly because those histories are comprehended in large and various volumes; partly because they are generally published in the native language of each country; so that he who intends to apply himself to this study, must be well versed in foreign languages. To remove in some measure this difficulty, I did some years, for the benefit of some young gentlemen in Sweden, compile a compendium of the history of such states as seemed to have any reference to that kingdom; with intent only to give them the first taste of those histories fitted for their private improvement. But after this rough draft had fallen into other hands, I had some reason to fear, that some progging bookseller or other would publish it imperfect, as I know it has happened to others, whose discourses undigested, have been published against their will and knowledge. So I found my self obliged, notwithstanding, I had but little leisure, to revise the said work, and after I had rendered it somewhat more perfect, rather to publish it, such as it is, than to suffer a surreptitious copy to appear. Upon this consideration, I hope the discreet reader will look favorably upon this work, as a piece not designed for men of advanced learning, but adapted to the apprehensions and capacities of young men, whom I was willing to show the way, and, as it were, to give them a taste, whereby they might be encouraged to make a further search into this study. I must here also advertise the reader, that as I have taken the history of each kingdom from its own historians, so a great difference is to be found in those several relations, which concern the transactions of some nations that were at enmity; it being a common observation, that the respective historians have magnified those actions which proved favourable to their native country, as they have lessened those that proved unfortunate. To reconcile and decide these differences, was not my business. But to give a clearer insight into the history of each country, I have added such observations as are generally made concerning the good and bad qualifications of each nation, without offering either to flatter or undervalue any; as also, what concerns the Nature, strength, and weakness of each country, and its form of government: all which I thought might be an inducement to young gentlemen when they travel or converse with men of greater experience in the affairs of the world, to be more inquisitive into those matters. What I have related concerning the interest of each state, is to be considered as relating chiefly to that time when I composed this work. And though I must confess that this is a matter more suitable to the capacity of men of understanding than of young people, yet I could not pass it by in silence, since this is to be esteemed the principle, from whence must be concluded, whether state-affairs are either well or ill managed. I must withal mention one thing more, which may serve as an instruction to young men; viz. that the interest of nations may be divided into the imaginary and the real interest. The first I understand to take place, when a prince judges the welfare of his state to consist in such things as cannot be performed without disquieting and being injurious to a great many other states, and which these are obliged to oppose with all their power: as for example, the monarchy of Europe, or an universal monarchy; such things being the fuel with which the whole world may be put into a flame. . . . If you would be the only masters of the world, does it thence follow, that all others should tamely lay their necks under your yoke? The real interest may be subdivided into perpetual and temporary. The former depends chiefly on the situation and constitution of the country, and the natural inclinations of the people; the latter, on the condition, strength, and weakness of the neighboring nations; for as those vary, the interest must also vary. Whence it often happens, that whereas we are, for our own security, sometimes obliged to assist a neighboring nation, which is likely to be oppressed by a more potent enemy; at another time we are forced to oppose the designs of those we before assisted; when we find they have recovered themselves to that degree, as that they may prove formidable and troublesome to us. But seeing this interest is so manifest to those who are versed in state-affairs, that they can't be ignorant of it; one might ask, how it oftentimes happens, that great errors are committed in this kind against the interest of the state. To this may be answered, that those who have the supreme administration of affairs, are oftentimes not sufficiently acquainted with the interest both of their own state, and of their neighbors; and yet being fond of their own sentiments, will not follow the advice of understanding and faithful ministers. Sometimes they are misguided by their passions, or by Time-serving ministers and favorites. But where the administration of the government is committed to the care of ministers of state, it may happen, that these are not capable of discerning it, or else are led away by private interest, which is opposite to that of the state; or else, being divided into factions, they are more concerned to ruin their rivals, than to follow the dictates of reason. And for this reason, some of the most exquisite parts of modern history consist in knowing the just character of the person who is the sovereign, or of the ministers, which rule a state; their capacity, inclinations, caprices, private interests, manner of proceedings, and the like; since upon this depends, in a great measure, the good and ill management of a state. For it frequently happens, that a state, which in itself considered is but weak, is made to become very considerable by the good conduct and vigilance of its directors; whereas a powerful state, by the ill management of those that sit at the helm, oftentimes declines apace. But as the knowledge of these matters appertains properly to those who are employed in the management of foreign affairs, so it is mutable, considering how often the scene is changed at court. Wherefore it is better learned from experience and the conversations of men well versed in these matters, than from any books whatsoever. And this is what I thought myself obliged to premise in a few words, before I entered upon the body of the work.

9

ℰ The Enlightenment

The practice and theory of history as conceived by Renaissance humanists was overshadowed by the Scientific Revolution of the seventeenth century and indeed was in many ways shaped and redirected by it. Though overshadowed by mathematics and natural philosophy, history benefitted from the empirical method of Bacon, from the elevated aspirations toward certainty promoted by Galilean science, and especially from the skepticism of Pierre Bayle, which contributed to historical criticism and to a sense of history that was by no means absent in the age of the philosophes. In the eighteenth century, the disparate traditions of erudite antiquities (with the auxiliary science of chronology, diplomatics, and the rest) and literary narrative (with its focus on pleasure and utility) again converged, most notably in the work of Edward Gibbon and the Scottish and German schools of historiography. The study of history again came to accommodate both learning and utility, with problems of certainty and authenticity as well as moral enhancement and political application. In the Enlightenment, history was, to resolve the ancient (and modern) debate, both science and art.

Once again, history acquired associations with philosophy. On the most elementary level, this meant the pursuit of reasoned history (*histoire raisonnée*) and Voltaire's "philosophy of history" in the sense of enlightened and critical narrative—history, in the famous formula of Dionysius of Halicarnassus repeated by Bolingbroke, as "philosophy teaching by example." For such philosophers as David Hume, the study of history represented one of the most direct paths to the understanding of the varieties of human nature, and for Voltaire the new history required emphasis especially on the encyclopedic achievements of humanity in the arts of civilization. But this conjunction can be seen in more comprehensive efforts to construct a philosophy of history, as in the work of Johann Gottfried von Herder and most especially in Giambattista Vico's "new science," which envisioned the reconstruction of human experience and thought from antiquity down to the present.

In many ways, history was a part of the enlightened program of the philosophes, not only as a prominent part of the post-Baconian structure of knowledge but also as an organizing principle for all the arts and sciences, a perspective on the story of the "advancement of learning" and the control over nature which social improvement required. This was worked out in more detail in Jean d'Alembert's *Preliminary Discourse* to Denis Diderot's *Encyclopédie,* which was built on an extended version of Bacon's scheme of learning, and especially in M. J. A. de Condorcet's epic celebration and prophetic vision of the *Progress of the Human Mind.* Here history paralleled the process of education and the progress of humanity as viewed by John Locke, E. B. Condillac, and others, so that history became, in G. E. Lessing's phrase, "the education of the human race." In these enlightened and "reasoned" views of the historical process, the conventional periodization (ancient-medieval-modern) was joined to the modern idea of human progress, which, based on a presumption about what Condorcet called "the perfectibility of man," encompassed both material accumulation and moral improvement—a thesis which came to dominate the nineteenth-century conception of history.

❡ THE USES OF HISTORY

101. EPHRAIM CHAMBERS (ca. 1680–1740), in his famous and seminal *Cyclopaedia* (1728), English forerunner of the French *Encyclopédie,* offers this standard definition of history and its various divisions.

History, a recital or description of things as they are, or have been; in a continued, orderly narration of the principal facts, and circumstances thereof. See *Annals.*

The word is Greek, . . . *historia,* and literally denotes a search of curious things, or a desire of knowing, or even a rehearsal of things we have seen; being formed of the verb [*historein*], which properly signifies

Ephraim Chambers, *Cyclopaedia; or an Universal Dictionary of Arts and Sciences.* London: J. and J. Knapton, 1728. 1:252.

to know a thing by having seen it. Though the idea appropriated to the term *history,* is now very much more extensive; and we apply it to a narration of divers memorable things, even though the relation only takes them from a report of others. . . .

History is divided, with regard to its subject, into the *history of nature,* and the *history of actions. History* with regard to actions, is a continual relation of a series of memorable events, in the affairs, either of a single person, a nation, or several persons and nations; and whether included in a great, or little space of time.

Sacred *history,* is that which lays before us the mysteries and cere-monies of religion, visions or appearances of the Deity, etc. miracles, and other supernatural things, whereof God alone is the author.

Civil *history,* is that of peoples, states, republics, communities, cities, etc.—Such as those of Thucydides, Halicarnassus, Livy, Polybius, Meze-ray, F. Daniel, Buchanan, etc. (also Personal History, Singular History, Simple History, Figurate History, Mixed History, romance. . . .)

Figurate *History* is that which is farther enriched with ornaments, by the art, ingenuity, and address of the historian—Such are the political, and moral *histories* of the Greeks, Romans, and most of the moderns. The latter is a kind of rational *history;* which is without stopping at the shell or outside, the appearance of things, discovers the springs and move-ments of the several events; enters into the thoughts, the breasts of the persons concerned therein; discovers their inventions and views; and by the result of enterprises, and undertakings, discovers the prudence or weakness, wherewith they were laid, conducted, etc.

These are much the more useful, and entertaining *histories.*—To this class, may peculiarly be referred the *histories* and annals of Tacitus, Thuanus, and bishop Burnet, among the moderns.

102. CLAUDE FRANÇOIS MENESTRIER (1631–1705) wrote *Les Divers Caracteres des ouvrages historiques* (1694), which is cited by Chambers's *Cyclopaedia* for its further subdivision of the field of history.

Reasoned history is not only political and moral; it is one which reasons about all the natural things which it describes, which discusses causes and effects and properties and which teaches the uses [of historical

Claude François Menestrier, "Introduction a la lecture de l'histoire." In *Les Divers Caracteres des ouvrages historiques.* Lyon: Chez J. Bapt. and Nicolas de Ville, 1694. No pagination. My translation.

knowledge, such as] the history of tea, coffee, chocolate . . . , many illnesses, earthquakes [etc.].

Critical history is what proposes to justify some particular action or the conduct of certain persons by reporting the facts and circumstances . . . and by undeceiving the public about the suspicions they may have about such persons. Those who are engaged in great negotiations are often obliged to write apologetic relations.

Authorized history is that which, besides the ornaments of "figured history," has proofs taken from "simple history" and which offers without art to support what is described with artistry and display. This sort of writing is especially evident in this century, which loving truth no less than new invention, has found the means of joining to "reasoned" and "figured" narrative the titles, charters, and extracts from chronicles and memoirs which serve to support it. Many things have contributed to this sort of history, the edition of old chronicles and ancient histories, with notes and other illustrations.

> 103. VOLTAIRE (François-Marie Arouet, 1694–1778) wrote a number of popular historical works, including his *Age of Louis XIV,* his *History of Charles XII,* and especially his *Essay on the Manners, Customs, and Spirit of the Nations.* This last work treated the whole range of cultural history—artistic, scientific, and social as well as political and military matters—in the spirit of the great enterprise of the philosophes, Diderot's *Encyclopédie ou dictionnaire raisonné des arts, des sciences et des métiers,* to which Voltaire submitted the following article summarizing his own view of history and its sources, certitude, and utility.

History, n.f., is the account of things represented as true, as contrasted with fable, which is the account of things represented as false.

There is a *history* of opinions, which is only the collection of human errors; a *history* of the arts, perhaps the most useful of all, when it joins the knowledge of the invention and progress of arts to a description of their working; and natural *history,* improperly called *history* and actually an essential part of physical science.

The *history* of events is divided into sacred and profane. Sacred *history* is an account of divine and miraculous operations by which God was formerly pleased to guide the Jewish nation and today guides our faith. I shall not pursue this respectable matter.

Voltaire, "Histoire." In [Denis Diderot], *Encyclopédie* (1751–1765). 3rd ed. Geneva: J. L. Pellet, 1778–1779. My translation.

The first foundations of all *history* are the accounts handed down from father to son and then transmitted from one generation to another; these are only probable in their original form and lose a degree of probability with each generation. With time the fabulous grows, and the true diminishes, whence it happens that the origins of all peoples are absurd. Thus the Egyptians were governed by the gods for many centuries; these were followed by demigods; later, the kings for 11,340 years, and during that time the sun changed four times from east to west.

The Phoenicians claimed to be established in their country for thirty thousand years; and these thirty thousand years were filled with as many prodigies as the Egyptian chronology. The marvelous absurdity ruling in the *history* of the Greeks is well known. The Romans, altogether serious as they were, also enveloped the *history* of their first ages in fables. . . . The first annals of all our modern nations are no less fabulous: prodigious and improbable things ought to be reported but only as proofs of human credulity; they are part of the *history* of opinions.

There is only one way to know with certainty something of ancient history, and this is to see if any incontestable monuments remain. We have only three in written form: the first is the collection of astronomical observations made during the nineteen hundred years of existence of Babylonia, sent by Alexander the Great and used in Ptolemy's *Almagest.* . . .

The second monument is the eclipse of the sun, calculated in China 2155 years before our [Christian] era and recognized as correct by our astronomers.

The third monument, much inferior to the two others, consists in the Arundel marbles; the chronicle here was engraved 263 years before our era; but it goes back only to Cecrops, 1319 years before the time it was carved. This is the only incontestable knowledge we have for the *history* of all antiquity.

It is not surprising that we have no ancient *history* going back as much as three thousand years: the cause is revolutions of the earth, the long and universal ignorance of that art which transmits facts through writing. There are many peoples lacking that ability. The art is common only in very small numbers of civilized nations and even then only in the hands of a few. Before the thirteenth and fourteenth centuries, nothing was more uncommon among the French and Germans than an interest in writing. In France only in 1454 did Charles VII have customs put down in writing. The art of writing was even less common among the Spanish, whence the fact that their history is so bare and uncertain. . . .

Herodotus is well informed and truthful in his *History* to the degree that he approaches his own time. We must conclude that for us *history* begins only with the enterprises undertaken by the Persians against the Greeks. Before these great events, only vague descriptions enveloped in puerile stories can be found. Herodotus becomes the model historian when he describes the prodigious preparations of Xerxes to subjugate Greece and then Europe.

Herodotus had the same merits as Homer; he was the first historian as Homer was the first poet, and both seized upon the beauty of an art unknown before then. . . .

Thucydides, the successor of Herodotus, limited himself to detailing the *history* of the war of the Peloponnesus, a country not larger than a province of France or Germany but which produced men of all sorts worthy of immortal reputation. . . .

The *history* of the Roman Empire is what most merits our attention, for the Romans have been our masters and our legislators. Their laws are still in force in most of our provinces, their language is still spoken, and long after their disappearance it is the only language in which are recorded the public acts of Italy, Germany, Spain, France, England, and Poland.

With the dismemberment of the Roman Empire in the West there began a new order of things, and this is called the *history of the Middle Ages,* barbaric *history* of barbarous people who became Christian but not the better for it.

It was at the end of the fifteenth century that the New World was discovered, and soon after the political form of Europe and the arts took a new shape. The art of printing and the restoration of the sciences finally produced fairly faithful *histories* instead of the ridiculous chronicles assembled in cloisters from the time of Gregory of Tours. Every nation in Europe soon had its historians. Former poverty was transformed into prosperity. There was no city that did not want its own particular *history.* We are overwhelmed with minutiae. A man who wants to be informed is obliged to follow the events and to notice all the facts which he comes across. He seizes on the multitude of revolutions, the spirit of the times and the manners of the peoples. He must attend above all to the *history* of his country, study it, possess it, reserve it for detailed study, and cast a more general glance at other nations. Their *history* is interesting only for the relations they have with us or for the great things they have accomplished. The first ages since the fall of the Roman Empire are only, as formerly remarked, barbarian events under the name of barbarians, except for the time of Charlemagne. The north was savage until the sixteenth century. Germany was for a long time in a state of anarchy. The quarrels of emperors and popes desolated Italy for six hundred years. [In Spain] all was confusion until the reign of Isabella and Ferdinand.

On the utility of history. This benefit consists in the comparison which a statesman or citizen can make between foreign laws and manners and those of his own country. This is what impels modern nations to draw near each other in arts of commerce and agriculture. The great errors of the past can also be used in this way. One cannot too often recall the crimes and misfortunes caused by absurd quarrels. It is certain that by reviewing the memory of these quarrels we can prevent them from being revived. . . .

Finally, the great utility of modern *history* over ancient is learning about all the rulers who, from the fifteenth century, have united against a too preponderant power. This system of equilibrium was unknown to the ancients, and that is the reason for the success of Rome. . . .

On the certitude of history. All certitude which is not from mathematical demonstrations is only extreme probability. There is no historical certitude.

Incertitude of history. Time is divided into fabulous and historical. But historical times should themselves be divided into true and false. I do not speak of fables recognized today as such—it is not a question, for example, of the prologues with which Livy adorned, or defaced, his history—but of the basis for the most commonly accepted facts. Consider that the Roman Republic was for five hundred years without a historian, that Livy himself deplored the lack of annals of the pontiffs and other monuments, almost all of which perished in the burning of Rome, and the fact that in the three previous centuries the art of writing was very rare. We may be permitted, then, to doubt all the things which are outside the ordinary course of human events.

Are monuments, annual ceremonies, and even medals historical proofs? One is naturally disposed to believe that a monument erected by a nation to celebrate an event testifies to its certitude. Yet if these monuments were not raised by contemporaries, can they prove anything except the desire to endorse popular opinion?

Of Cicero's maxim about history, that the historian should never tell anything false, nor hide the truth. The first part of the precept is incontestable, but we must examine the other. If a truth can be of some use to your state, your silence is condemnable. But supposing that you write the *history* of a prince who has given you a secret, should you reveal it? Should you tell posterity what you would be wrong to tell one man? Does the duty of the historian outweigh a larger duty?

On satirical history. If Plutarch charged Herodotus with not having sufficiently celebrated the glory of certain Greek cities, how much more reprehensible today are those who (without Herodotus's merits) impute without proof various actions to princes and nations. . . .

On the method and manner of writing history. So much has been said on this subject that here very little needs to be said. One knows well that the method and style of Livy, his gravity and eloquence, were appropriate to the majesty of the Roman Republic, that Tacitus was made for portraying tyranny, Polybius for giving lessons of war, and Dionysius of Halicarnassus for describing antiquities.

But in modeling oneself today on these great masters, one has a heavier burden than they carried. One requires of modern historians more details, better founded facts, more precise dates, better authorities, and more attention to usages, laws, manners, commerce, finances, agriculture, and population. It is the same with *history* as with mathematics and physics; its purpose is vastly increased. As it is easy to make a collection of periodicals, so it is difficult to write *history*. One expects that the history of a foreign country should not be cast in the same mold as that of your own fatherland.

> 104. The *ENCYCLOPEDIE* of Denis Diderot (1713–1784) contained other articles on the modern study of history, its achievements, and its problems, including the following discussions of antiquity (and associated words), chronology (in the wake of the pioneering studies of Scaliger, Ussher, and others), and erudition (critical scholarship as contrasted with the writing of historical narrative). The articles here on *ancien* and *chronologie* are by Diderot, that on *erudition* by Jean d'Alembert (see also no. 111).

Ancient, old, antique [*ancien, vieux, antique*]. These terms supplement each other. A fashion is old, when it ceases to be in use; it is ancient when it has not been in use for a long time; it is antique when it has not been

---

Encyclopédie (1751–1765), "Ancien," "Erudition" (Denis Diderot) and "Chronologie" (Jean d'Alembert). 3rd ed. Geneva: J. L. Pellet, 1778–1779. My translation.

ancient for a long time. "Recent" is opposed to old, "new" [*nouvel*] to ancient, "modern" to antique. Old age [*la vieillesse*] pertains to man, ancient [*l'ancienneté*] to a family, antiquity to monuments. . . .

Erudition. Considered in relation to the present stage of literature, *erudition* has three main branches, the knowledge of history, that of languages, and that of books.

The knowledge of history is subdivided into several branches: ancient and modern history, sacred, profane, and ecclesiastical history; the history of our own country and that of foreign countries; the history of science and arts; chronology; geography; antiquities and medals; and others. . . .

One who possesses perfectly each of these three branches is a true man of erudition [*erudit*] in all its forms; but this goal is too large for a single man to reach. . . .

From the knowledge of history, languages, and books arises that important part of *erudition* which is called *criticism* [*la critique*] and which consists either in establishing the meaning of an ancient author or of restoring his text or else (the principal part) of determining the degree of authority which can be given him for the facts which he reports. . . .

And here are the main rules. 1. One should count as proofs only the testimonies of original authors, that is, those who wrote in, or nearly in, the times of which they write. . . . 2. When, however, a sober and truthful author cites ancient writings which we no longer have, one should, or may, believe him; but if such ancient authors exist, it is necessary to compare them with the one who cites them, especially when the latter is modern. 3. Authors, even contemporary authors, should never be followed without examination: one should first know if the writings are indeed by this author, for it is well known that there have been many questionable attributions [*supposes*]; see *Decretals*. If the author is certain, it is still necessary to examine the degree of believability and to determine whether he is judicious, impartial, free from credulity and superstition, clear enough to distinguish the true and sincere enough not to substitute conjectures for the truth and suspicions which might attract him.

In criticism there are two kinds of excess to avoid, one of indulgence and another of severity. One can be a good Christian without giving credence to the great number of false acts of martyrs and lives of saints, to false gospels and apocryphal letters, to the golden legend of Jacques de Voraigne, to the fable of the Donation of Constantine and that of Pope Joan, to many miracles reported by Gregory of Tours and other credulous authors; but one cannot be a good Christian and reject the prodigies, revelations, and other extraordinary facts reported by Saint Irenaeus, Saint Cyprian, Saint Augustine, and other respectable authors who may not be regarded as visionaries.

Erudition is a kind of knowledge in which modern scholars are distinguished in two ways: the more the world grows, [*vieillet*], the more the material of *erudition* increases, and consequently the more erudite men are needed. Formerly, ancient Greece attended only to its history and language, and the Romans were only orators and politicians; and so *erudition* properly speaking was not cultivated by the ancients. At the end of the Republic, however, and then in the time of the emperors, there were a few erudite men, such as Varro, Pliny the naturalist, and some others.

The translation of the Empire to Constantinople and then the destruction of the Empire of the West soon ended all sorts of learning in that part of the world, which was barbarous until the end of the fifteenth century. See *Libraries. . . .*

It is usually believed that the destruction of the Eastern [Roman] Empire was the cause of the renewing of letters in Europe, that the scholars of Greece, driven from Constantinople by the Turks and invited by the Medicis, brought enlightenment [*la lumiere*] to the West. This is true to a certain extent, but the arrival of the scholars of Greece had been preceded by the invention of printing, followed a few years later by the works of Dante, Petrarch, and Boccaccio, who had brought to Italy the dawn of good taste, and finally a small number of scholars who began to study and even to cultivate Latin literature, such as Poggio [Bracciolini], Lorenzo Valla, Francesco Filelfo, and some others. But the main advantage produced by the study of languages was criticism, of which we spoke earlier: the ancient texts were purged of errors introduced by the ignorance or inattention of copyists; works disfigured by the effects of time were restored; obscure places were explained by learned commentaries; and rules were set down for distinguishing true from supposed works, rules based on the knowledge of history, chronology, the style of authors, of taste, and of the character of different centuries. These rules were mainly useful when such scholars, after having exhausted Latin and Greek literature, turned to the barbarous and shadowy time which is called *the Middle Ages.* It is well known how distinguished our nation is in this sort of study, by which the names of Pithou, Saint-Marthe, Du Cange, Valois, Mabillon, and others have been immortalized.

Thanks to the work of these scholars, antiquity and later times have become not only uncovered but almost wholly understood, or at least understood as well as possible, given the monuments that remain to us.

Chronology. In general *chronology* is, properly speaking, the *history of times.*

According to the Vulgate:	Ussher	4004 years
	Scaliger	3950
	Petau	3984
	Riccioli	4184
According to the Septuagint:	Eusebius	5200
	Alphonsine Tables . . .	6934
	Riccioli	5634

Let us finish this discussion which we have devoted to the interests of truth and to the honor of these famous chronologies. Most of those who complain of the differences in results do not seem to realize the moral impossibility of the precision they require. If they considered the prodigious multitude of facts to combine, the various characters of the peoples involved with these facts, the inexactitude of date, inevitable in times when facts were transmitted only by tradition, the mania for [claims of] antiquity which has infected almost all nations, the lies and involuntary errors of historians, the similarity of names, which often diminishes the number of persons, the differences which have often multiplied them, fables presented as truths, truths metamorphosed as fables, the diversity of languages and measures of times, and an infinity of other circumstances which conspire to increase the obscurity—if one considers all these things, one will be surprised not that there are so many differences in *chronological* systems which have been devised but that they have been devised at all.

> 105. Henry St. John, first Viscount BOLINGBROKE (1678–1751), politician and literary artist, retired in the 1730s to France, where he gained the acquaintance of Voltaire, Montesquieu, and others, and wrote a series of letters expressing the Enlightenment (and, more remotely, the humanist) conception of history, emphasizing its moral, educational, political, and philosophical value in contrast to narrow scholarship of the antiquarian tradition.

Bolingbroke, *Letters on the Study and Use of History.* In *Historical Writings,* ed. Isaac Kramnick. Chicago: University of Chicago Press, 1972. Pp. 7–9, 10–11, 17, 18–19, 29, 34–36, 42, 51–52, 53, 58, 59, 60, 68–69, and 77.

Concerning the True Use and Advantages of the Study of History

Letter 2   Let me say something of history, in general, before I descend into the consideration of particular parts of it, or of the various methods of study, or of the different views of those that apply themselves to it, as I had begun to do in my former letter.

The love of history seems inseparable from human nature, because it seems inseparable from self-love. The same principle in this instance carries us forward and backward, to future and to past ages. We imagine that the things, which affect us, must affect posterity: this sentiment runs through mankind, from Caesar down to the parish-clerk in Pope's Miscellany. We are fond of preserving, as far as it is in our frail power, the memory of our own adventures, of those of our own time, and of those that preceded it. Rude heaps of stones have been raised, and ruder hymns have been composed, for this purpose, by nations who had not yet the use of arts and letters. To go no farther back, the triumphs of Odin were celebrated in runic songs, and the feats of our British ancestors were recorded in those of their bards. The savages of America have the same custom at this day: and long historical ballads of their huntings and their wars are sung at all their festivals. There is no need of saying how this passion grows, among civilized nations, in proportion to the means of gratifying it: but let us observe that the same principle of nature directs us as strongly, and more generally as well as more early, to indulge our own curiosity, instead of preparing to gratify that of others. The child hearkens with delight to the tales of his nurse: he learns to read, and he devours with eagerness of fabulous legends and novels: in riper years he applies himself to history, or to that which he takes for history, to authorised romance: and, even in age, the desire of knowing what has happened to other men, yields to the desire alone of relating what has happened to ourselves. Thus history, true or false, speaks to our passions always. What pity is it, my lord, that even the best should speak to our understandings so seldom? That it does so, we have none to blame but ourselves. Nature has done her part. She has opened this study to every man who can read and think: and what she had made the most agreeable, reason can make the most useful, application of our minds. But if we consult our reason, we shall be far from following the examples of our fellow-creatures, in this as in most other cases, who are so proud of being rational. We shall neither read to soothe our indolence, nor to gratify our vanity: as little shall we content ourselves to drudge like grammarians and critics, that others may be able to study with greater ease and profit, like philosophers and statesmen; as little shall we affect the slender merit of becoming great scholars at the expense of groping all our lives in the dark mazes of antiquity. All these mistake the true drift of study, and the true use of history. Nature gave us curiosity to excite the industry of our minds; but she never intended it should be made the principal, much less the sole object of their application. The true and proper object of this application is a constant improvement in private and in public virtue. An application to any study that tends neither directly nor indirectly to make us better men and better citizens, is at best but a specious and ingenious sort of idleness, to use an expression of Tillotson: and the knowledge we acquire by it is a creditable kind of ignorance, nothing more. This creditable kind of ignorance is, in my opinion, the whole benefit which the generality of men, even of the most learned, reap from the study of history: and yet the study of history seems to me, of all other, the most proper to train us up to private and public virtue.

Your lordship may very well be ready by this time, and after so much bold censure on my part, to ask me, what then is the true use of history? In what respects may it serve to make us better and wiser? and what method is to be pursued in the study of it, for attaining these great ends? I will answer you by quoting what I have read some where or other, in Dionysiou Halicarn[assus], I think, that history is philosophy teaching by example. We need but to cast our eyes on the world, and we shall see the daily force of example: we need but to turn them inward, and we shall soon discover why example has this force. "Pauci prudentia," says Tacitus, "honesta ab deterioribus, utilia ab noxiis discernunt: lures aliorum eventis docentur." Such is the imperfection of human understanding, such is the frail temper of our minds, that abstract or general propositions, though ever so true, appear obscure or doubtful to us very often, till they are explained by examples; and that the wisest lessons in favor of virtue go but a little way to convince the judgment, and determine the will, unless they are enforced by the same means; and we are obliged to apply to ourselves what we see happen to other men. . . .

. . . The school of example, my lord, is the world: and the masters of this school are history and experience. I am far from contending that the former is preferable to the latter. I think upon the whole otherwise; but this I say, that the former is absolutely necessary to prepare us for the latter, and to accompany us whilst we are under the discipline of the latter, that is, through the whole course of our lives. No doubt some few men may be quoted, to whom nature gave what art and industry can give to no man. But such examples will prove nothing against me because I admit that the study of history, without experience, is insufficient, but assert, that experience itself is so without genius. Genius is preferable to the other two; but I would wish to find the three together: for how great soever a genius may be, and how much soever he may acquire new light and heat, as he proceeds in his rapid course, certain it is that he will never shine with the full lustre, nor shed the full influence he is capable of, unless to his own experience he adds the experience of other men and other ages. . . .

There is another advantage, worthy of our observation, that belongs to the study of history . . . that the examples which history presents to us, both of men and of events, are generally complete: the whole example is before us, and consequently the whole lesson, or sometimes the various lessons, which philosophy proposes to teach us by this example. For first, as to men; we see them at their whole length in history, and we see them generally there through a medium less partial at least than that of experience. . . .

Thus again, as to events that stand recorded in history; we see them all, we see them as they followed one another, or as they produced one another, causes or effects, immediate or remote. We are cast back, as it were, into former ages: we live with the men who lived before us, and we inhabit countries that we never saw. Place is enlarged, and time prolonged, in this manner; so that the man who applies himself early to the study of history, may acquire in a few years, and before he sets his foot abroad in the world, not only a more extended knowledge of mankind, but the experience of more centuries than any of the patriarchs saw. . . .

Letter 3 Mr. Locke, I think, recommends the study of geometry even to those who have no design of being geometricians: and he gives a reason for it, that may be applied to the present case. Such persons may forget every problem that has been proposed, and every solution that they or others have given; but the habit of pursuing long trains of ideas will remain with them, and they will pierce through the mazes of sophism, and discover a latent truth, where persons who have not this habit will never find it.

In this manner the study of history will prepare us for action and observation. History is the ancient author: experience is the modern language. We form our taste on the first, we translate the sense and reason, we transfuse the spirit and force; but we imitate only the particular graces of the original; we imitate them according to the idiom of our own tongue, that is, we substitute often equivalents in the lieu of them, and are far from affecting to copy them servilely. To conclude, as experience is conversant about the present, and the present enables us to guess at the future; so history is conversant about the past, and by knowing the things that have been, we become better able to judge of the things that are. . . .

. . . You see, my lord, not only how late profane history began to be written by the Greeks, but how much later it began to be written with any regard to truth; and consequently what wretched materials the learned men, who arose after the age of Alexander had to employ, when they attempted to form systems of ancient history and chronology. We have some remains of that laborious compiler Diodorus Siculus, but do we find in him any thread of ancient history, I mean, that which passed for ancient in his time? What complaints, on the contrary, does he not make of former historians? how frankly does he confess the little and uncertain light he had to follow in his researches? Yet Diodorus, as well as Plutarch, and others, had not only the older Greek historians, but the more modern antiquaries, who pretended to have searched into the records and registers of nations, even at the time renowned for their antiquity. . . .

Of Sacred History. What memorials therefore remain to give us light into the originals of ancient nations, and the history of those ages, we commonly call the first ages? The Bible, it will be said; that is, the historical part of it in the Old Testament. But, my lord, even these divine books must be reputed insufficient to the purpose, by every candid and impartial man who considers either their authority as histories, or the matter they contain. For what are they? and how come they to us? At the time when Alexander carried his arms into Asia, a people of Syria, till then unknown, became known to the Greeks: this people had been slaves to the Egyptians, Assyrians, Medes, and Persians, as the several empires prevailed: ten parts in twelve of them had been transplanted by ancient conquerors, and melted down and lost in the east, several ages before the establishment of the empire that Alexander destroyed: the other two parts had been carried captive to Babylon a little before the same era. This captivity was not indeed perpetual, like the other; but it lasted so long, and such circumstances, whatever they were, accompanied it, that the captives forgot their country, and even their language, the Hebrew dialect at least and character. . . .

In attributing the whole credibility of the Old Testament to the authority of the Jews, and in limiting the authenticity of the Jewish Scriptures to those parts alone that concern law, doctrine, and prophecy, by which their chronology and the far greatest part of their history are excluded, I will venture to assure your lordship that I do not assume so much, as is assumed in every hypothesis that affixes the divine seal of inspiration to the whole canon; that rests the whole proof on Jewish veracity; and that pretends to account particularly and positively for the descent of these ancient writings in their present state. . . .

Letter 4   I agree, then, that history has been purposely and systematically falsified in all ages, and that partiality and prejudice have occasioned both voluntary and involuntary errors, even in the best. Let me say without offence, my lord, since I may say it with truth and am able to prove it, that ecclesiastical authority has led the way to this corruption in all ages, and all religions. How monstrous were the absurdities that the priesthood imposed on the ignorance and superstition of mankind in the Pagan world, concerning the originals of religions and governments, their institutions and rites, their laws and customs? What opportunities had they for such impositions, whilst the keeping the records and collecting the traditions was in so many nations the peculiar office of this order of men? A custom highly extolled by Josephus, but plainly liable to the grossest frauds, and even a temptation to them. If the foundations of Judaism and Christianity have been laid in truth, yet what numberless fables have been invented to raise, to embellish, and to support these structures, according to the interest and taste of the several architects? That the Jews have been guilty of this will be allowed: and, to the shame of Christians, if not of Christianity, the fathers of one church have no right to throw the first stone at the fathers of the other. Deliberate, systematical lying has been practised and encouraged from age to age; and among all the pious frauds that have been employed to maintain a reverence and zeal for their religion in the minds of men, this abuse of history has been one of the principal and most successful: an evident, an experimental proof, by the way, of what I have insisted upon so much, the aptitude and natural tendency of history to form our opinions, and to settle our habits. . . .

This lying spirit has gone forth from ecclesiastical to other historians: and I might fill many pages with instances of extravagant fables that have been invented in several nations to celebrate their antiquity, to ennoble their originals, and to make them appear illustrious in the arts of peace and the triumphs of war. When the brain is well heated, and devotion or vanity, the semblance of virtue or real vice, and, above all, disputes and contests, have inspired that complication of passions we term zeal, the effects are much the same, and history becomes very often a lying panagyric or a lying satire; for different nations or different parties in the same nation, belie one another without any respect for truth, as they murder one another without any regard to right or sense of humanity. Religious zeal may boast this horrid advantage over civil zeal, that the effects of it have been more sanguinary, and the malice more unrelenting. In another respect they are more alike, and keep a nearer proportion: different religions have not been quite so barbarous to one another as sects of the same religion; and, in like manner, nation has had better quarter from nation, than party from party. But in all these controversies, men have pushed their rage beyond their own and their adversaries' lives: they have endeavored to interest posterity in their quarrels, and by rendering history subservient to this wicked purpose, they have done their utmost to perpetuate scandal, and to immortalise their animosity. . . .

What has been said concerning the multiplicity of histories, and of historical memorials, wherewith our libraries abound since the resurrection of letters happened, and the art of printing began, puts me in mind of another general rule, that ought to be observed by every man who intends to make a real improvement, and to become wise as well as better, by the study of history. I hinted at this rule in a former letter, where I said that we should neither grope in the dark, nor wander in the light. History must have a certain degree of probability and authenticity, or the examples we find in it would not carry a force sufficient to make due impressions on our minds, nor to illustrate nor to strengthen the precepts of philosophy and the rules of good policy. But besides, when histories have this necessary authenticity and probability, there is much discernment to be employed in the choice and the use we make of them. Some are to be read, some are to be studied; and some may be neglected entirely, not only without detriment, but with advantage. . . .

He who reads with discernment and choice, will acquire less learning, but as more knowledge is collected with design, and cultivated with art and method, it will be at all times of immediate and ready use to himself and others. . . .

He who reads without this discernment and choice, and, like Bodin's pupil, resolves to read, will not have time, no, nor capacity neither, to do any thing else. He will not be able to think, without which it is impertinent to read; nor to act, without which it is impertinent to read; nor to act, without which it is impertinent to think. . . .

Whatever political speculations, instead of preparing us to be useful to society, and to promote the happiness of mankind, are only systems for gratifying private ambition, and promoting private interests at the public expense; all such, I say, deserve to be burnt, and the authors of them to starve, like Machiavel, in a jail.

Letter 5   The age in which Livy flourished abounded with such materials as these: they were fresh, they were authentic; it was easy to procure them, it was safe to employ them. How he did employ them in executing the second part of his design, we may judge by his execution of the first: and, I own to your lordship, I should be glad to exchange, if it were possible, what we have of this history for what we have not. Would you not be glad, my lord, to see, in one stupendous draught, the whole progress of that government from liberty to servitude? the whole series of causes and effects, apparent and real, public and private? those which all men saw, and all good men lamented and opposed at the time; and those which were so disguised to the prejudices, to the partialities of a divided people, and even to the corruption of mankind, that many did not, and that many could pretend they did not, discern them, till it was too late to resist them? I am sorry to say it, this part of the Roman story would be not only more curious and more authentic than the former, but of more immediate and more important application to the present state of Britain. But it is lost: the loss is irreparable, and your lordship will not blame me for deploring it. . . .

There have been lawyers that were orators, philosophers, historians: there have been Bacons and Clarendons, my lord. There will be none such any more, till, in some better age, true ambition or the love of fame prevails over avarice; and till men find leisure and encouragement to prepare themselves for the exercise of this profession, by climbing up to the "vantage ground," so my Lord Bacon calls it, of science; instead of grovelling all their lives below, in a mean but gainful application to all the little arts of chicane. Till this happen, the profession of the law will scarce deserve to be ranked among the learned professions: and whenever it happens, one of the vantage grounds, to which men must climb, is metaphysical, and the other historical knowledge. They must pry into the secret recesses of the human heart, and become well acquainted with the whole moral world, that they may discover the abstract reason of all laws: and they must trace the laws of particular states, especially of their own, from the first rough sketches to the more perfect draughts; from the first causes or occasions that produced them, through all the effects, good and bad, that they produced.

❡ PHILOSOPHICAL HISTORY

106. DAVID HUME (1711–1776), who represented the culmination of English empirical philosophy, was led by his skepticism from philosophical criticism to moral philosophy and later to his practical-minded and opinionated survey of English history from the Roman invasion to the Revolution of 1688. In this letter to a woman friend, Hume offers his views of the study of history, ancient and modern, not only as knowledge but as the means of access to other kinds of knowledge, especially of human nature.

There is nothing which I would recommend more earnestly to my female readers than the study of history, as an occupation, of all others, the best suited both to their sex and education, much more instructive than their ordinary books of amusement, and more entertaining than those serious compositions, which are usually to be found in their closets. Among other important truths, which they may learn from history, they may be informed of two particulars, the knowledge of which may contribute very much to their quiet and repose; That our sex, as well as theirs, are far from being such perfect creatures as they are apt to imagine, and, That Love is not the only passion, which governs the

David Hume, *Of the Study of History.* In *Essays: Moral, Political, and Literary,* ed. T. H. Green and T. H. Grose. New York: Longmans, Green, 1808. Pp. 388–391.

male-world, but is often overcome by avarice, ambition, vanity, and a thousand other passions. Whether they be the false representations of mankind of those two particulars, which endear romances and novels so much to the fair sex, I know not; but must confess that I am sorry to see them have such an aversion to matter of fact, and such an appetite for falsehood. I remember I was once desired by a young beauty, for whom I had some passion, to send her some novels and romances for her amusement in the country; but was not so ungenerous as to take the advantage which such a course of reading might have given me, being resolved not to make use of poisoned arms against her. I therefore sent her Plutarch's Lives, assuring her, at the same time, that there was not a word of truth in them from beginning to end. She perused them very attentively, 'till she came to the lives of Alexander and Caesar, whose names she had heard of by accident; and then returned me the book, with many reproaches for deceiving her.

I may indeed be told that the fair sex have no such aversion to history, as I have represented, provided it be secret history, and contain some memorable transaction proper to excite their curiosity. But as I do not find that truth, which is the basis of history, is at all regarded in those anecdotes, I cannot admit of this as a proof of their passion for that study. However this may be, I see not why the same curiosity might not receive a more proper direction, and lead them to desire accounts of those who lived in past ages, as well as of their contemporaries. What is it to Cleora, whether Fulvia entertains a secret commerce of Love with Philander or not? Has she not equal reason to be pleased, when she is informed (what is whispered about among historians) that Cato's sister had an intrigue with Caesar, and palmed her son, Marcus Brutus, upon her husband for his own, tho' in reality he was her gallant's? And are not the loves of Messaline or Julia as proper subjects of discourse as any intrigue that this city has produced of late years?

But I know not whence it comes, that I have been thus seduced into a kind of raillery against the ladies: Unless, perhaps, it proceed from the same cause, which makes the person, who is the favourite of the company, be often the object of their good-natured jests and pleasantries. We are pleased to address ourselves after any manner, to one who is agreeable to us; and, at the same time, presume that nothing will be taken amiss by a person, who is secure of the good opinion and affections of every one present. I shall now proceed to handle my subject more seriously, and shall point out the many advantages which flow from the study of history, and show how suited it is to every one, but particularly to those who are debarred the severer studies, by the tenderness of their complexion, and the weakness of their education. The advantages found in history seem to be of three kinds, as it amuses the fancy, as it improves the understanding, and as it strengthens virtue.

In reality, what more agreeable entertainment to the mind, than to be transported into the remotest ages of the world, and to observe human society, in its infancy, making the first faint essays towards the arts and sciences: To see the policy of government, and the civility of conversation refining by degrees, and every thing which is ornamental to human life advancing towards its perfection. To remark the rise, progress, declension, and final extinction of the most flourishing empires: The virtues, which contributed to their greatness, and the vices, which drew on their ruin. In short, to see all human race, from the beginning of time, pass, as it were, in review before us; appearing in their true colours, without any of those disguises, which during their life-time, so much perplexed the judgment of the beholders. What spectacle can be imagined, so magnificent, so various, so interesting? What amusement, either of the senses or imagination, can be compared with it? Shall those trifling pastimes, which engross so much of our time, be preferred as more satisfactory, and more fit to engage our attention? How perverse must that taste be, which is capable of so wrong a choice of pleasures?

But history is a most improving part of knowledge, as well as an agreeable amusement; and a great part of what we commonly call Erudition, and value so highly, is nothing but an acquaintance with historical facts. An extensive knowledge of this kind belongs to men of letters; but I must think it an unpardonable ignorance in persons of whatever sex or condition, not to be acquainted with the history of their own country, together with the histories of ancient GREECE and ROME. A woman may behave herself with good manners, and have even some vivacity in her turn of wit; but where her mind is so unfurnished, 'tis impossible her conversation can afford any entertainment to men of sense and reflection.

I must add, that history is not only a valuable part of knowledge, but opens the door to many other parts, and affords materials to most of the science. And indeed, if we consider the shortness of human life, and our limited knowledge, even of what passes in our own time, we must be sensible that we should be for ever children in understanding, were it not for this invention, which extends our experience to all past ages, and to the most distant nations; making them contribute as much to our improvement in wisdom, as if they had actually lain under our observation. A man acquainted with history may, in some respect, be said to have been making continual additions to his stock of knowledge in every century.

There is also an advantage in that experience which is acquired by history, above what is learned by the practice of the world, that it brings us acquainted with human affairs, without diminishing in the least from the most delicate sentiments of virtue. And, to tell the truth, I know not any study or occupation so unexceptional as history in this particular. Poets can paint virtue in the most charming colours; but, as they address themselves entirely to the passions, they often become advocates for vice. Even philosophers are apt to bewilder themselves in the subtility of their speculations; and we have seen some go as far as to deny the reality of all moral distinctions. But I think it a remark worthy the attention of the speculative, that the historians have been, almost without exception, the true friends of virtue, and have always represented it in its proper colours, however they may have erred in their judgments of particular persons. Machiavel himself discovers a true sentiment of virtue in his history of Florence. When he talks as a Politician, in his general reasonings, he considers poisoning, assassination and perjury, as lawful arts of power; but when he speaks as an Historian, in his particular narrations, he shows so keen an indignation against vice, and so warm an approbation of virtue, in many passages, that I could not forbear applying to him that remark of Horace, That if you chace away nature, tho' with ever so great indignity, she will always return upon you. Nor is this combination of historians in favour of virtue at all difficult to be accounted for. When a man of business enters into life and action, he is more apt to consider the characters of men, as they have relation to his interest, than as they stand in themselves; and has his judgment warped on every occasion by the violence of his passion. When a philosopher contemplates characters and manners in his closet, the general abstract view of the objects leaves the mind so cold and unmoved, that the sentiments of nature have no room to play, and he scarce feels the difference between vice and virtue. History keeps in a just medium betwixt these extremes, and places the objects in their true point of view. The writers of history, as well as the readers, are sufficiently interested in the characters and events, to have a lively sentiment of blame or praise; and, at the same time, have no particular interest or concern to pervert their judgment.

107. EDWARD GIBBON (1737–1794), greatest of English historians, combined the virtues of antiquarian and narrative historian and, in his *Decline and Fall of the Roman Empire,* surveyed, with massive erudition, philosophical insight, and literary artistry, the dramatic trajectory of Rome and its posthumous fortunes from the Augustan Age to the Renaissance. Here he offers another Enlightenment view of the contemporary value of historical studies, praising the work of the "monkish historians" (Mabillon and his colleagues) as well as of chroniclers and national historiographers as a basis for modern interpretations.

That History is a liberal and useful study, and that the history of our own country is best deserving of our attention, are propositions too clear for argument, and too simple for illustration. Nature has implanted in our breasts a lively impulse to extend the narrow span of our existence, by the knowledge of the events that have happened on the soil which we inhabit, of the characters and actions of those men from whom our descent, as individuals or as a people, is probably derived. The same laudable emulation will prompt us to review, and to enrich our common treasure of national glory: and those who are the best entitled to the esteem of posterity, are the most inclined to celebrate the merits of their ancestors. The origin and changes of our religion and government, of our arts and manners, afford an entertaining, and often an instructive subject of speculation; and the scene is repeated and varied by the entrance of the victorious strangers, the Roman and the Saxon, the Dane and the Norman, who have successively reigned in our stormy Isle. We contemplate the gradual progress of society, from the lowest ebb of primitive barbarism, to the full tide of modern civilization. We contrast the naked Briton who might have mistaken the sphere of Archimedes for a rational creature, and the contemporary of Newton, in whose school Archimedes himself would have been an humble disciple. And we compare the boats of osier and hides that floated along our coasts, with the formidable navies which visit and command the remotest shores of the ocean. Without indulging the fond prejudices of patriotic vanity, we may assume a conspicuous place among the inhabitants of the earth. The English will be ranked among the few nations who have cultivated with equal success the arts of war, of learning, and of commerce; and Britain

Edward Gibbon, *An Address.* In *Miscellaneous Works,* ed. Lord John Sheffield. London: A. Straham and T. Cadell, 1796. 2:707–717.

perhaps is the only powerful and wealthy state which has ever possessed the inestimable secret of uniting the benefits of order with blessings of freedom. It is a maxim of our law, and the constant practice of our courts of justice, never to accept any evidence, unless it is the very best which, under the circumstances of the case, can possibly be obtained. If this wise principle be transferred from jurisprudence to criticism, the inquisitive reader of English History will soon ascend to the first witnesses of every period, from whose testimonies the moderns, however sagacious and eloquent, must derive their whole confidence and credit. In the prosecution of his inquiries, he will lament that the transactions of the Middle Ages have been imperfectly recorded, and that these records have been more imperfectly preserved: that the successive conquerors of Britain have despised or destroyed the monuments of their predecessors; and that by their violence or neglect much of our national antiquities has irretrievably perished. For the losses of history are indeed irretrievable: when the productions of fancy or science have been swept away, new poets may invent, and new philosophers may reason; but if the inscription of a single fact be once obliterated, it can never be restored by the united efforts of genius and industry. The consideration of our past losses should incite the present age to cherish and perpetuate the valuable relics which have escaped, instead of condemning the MONKISH HISTORIANS (as they are contemptuously styled) silently to moulder in the dust of our libraries; our candour, and even our justice, should learn to estimate their value, and to excuse their imperfections. Their minds were infected with the passions and errors of their times, but those times would have been involved in darkness, had not the art of writing, and the memory of events, been preserved in the peace and solitude of the cloister. Their Latin style is far removed from the eloquence and purity of Sallust and Livy; and connected the series of our ancient chronicles, from the age of Bede to that of Walsingham. In the eyes of a philosophic observer, these monkish historians are even endowed with a singular, though accidental merit; the unconscious simplicity with which they represent the manners and opinions of their contemporaries: a natural picture, which the most exquisite art is unable to imitate.

Books, before the invention of printing, were separately, and slowly copied by the pen; and the transcripts of our old historians must have been rare; since the number would be proportioned to the number of readers capable of understanding a Latin work, and curious of the history and antiquities of England. The gross mass of the laity, from the baron to

the mechanic, were more addicted to the exercises of the body than to
those of the mind: the middle ranks of society were illiterate and poor,
and the nobles and gentlemen, as often as they breathed from war, maintained their strength and activity in the chase or the tournament. Few
among them could read, still fewer could write; none were acquainted
with the Latin tongue; and if they sometimes listened to a tale of past
times, their puerile love of the marvellous would prefer the romance of
Sir Launcelot or Sir Tristram, to the authentic narratives most honourable to their country and their ancestors. Till the period of the reformation, the ignorance and sensuality of the clergy were continually increasing: the ambitious prelate aspired to pomp and power; the jolly monk
was satisfied with idleness and pleasure; and the few students of the
ecclesiastical order, perplexed rather than enlightened their understandings with occult science and scholastic divinity. In the monastery in
which a chronicle had been composed, the original was deposited, and
perhaps a copy; and some neighboring churches might be induced, by a
local or professional interest, to seek the communication of these historical memorials. Such manuscripts were not liable to suffer from the injury
of use; but the casualty of a fire, or the slow progression of damp and
worms, would often endanger their limited and precarious existence.
The sanctuaries of religion were sometimes profaned by aristocratic op-
pression, popular tumult, or military licence; and although the cellar
was more exposed than the library, the envy of ignorance will riot in the
spoil of those creatures which it cannot enjoy.

After the discovery of printing, which has bestowed immortality
on the works of man, it might be presumed that the new art would
be applied without delay, to save and to multiply the remains of our
national chronicles. It might be expected that the English, now wak-
ing from a long slumber, should blush at finding themselves strangers
in their native country; and that our princes, after the example of
Charlemagne and Maximilian I would esteem it their duty and glory to
illustrate the history of the people over whom they reigned. But these
rational hopes have not been justified by the event. It was in the year
1474 that our first press was established in Westminster Abbey, by
William Caxton: but in the choice of his authors, that liberal and industrious artist was reduced to comply with the vicious taste of his readers;
to gratify the nobles with treatises on heraldry, hawking, and the game
of chess, and to amuse the popular credulity with romances of fabulous
knights, and legends of more fabulous saints. The father of printing

expresses a laudable desire to elucidate the history of his country; but instead of publishing the Latin chronicle of Redulphus Higden, he could only venture on the English version by John de Trevisa; and his complaint of the difficulty of finding materials for his own continuation of that work, sufficiently attests that even the writers, which we now possess of the fourteenth and fifteenth centuries, had not yet emerged from the darkness of the cloister. His successors, with less skill and ability, were content to tread in the footsteps of Caxton; almost a century elapsed without producing one original edition of any old English historian; and the only exception which I recollect is the publication of Gildas (London 1526) by Polydore Virgil, an ingenious foreigner. The presses of Italy, Germany, and even France, might plead in their defence, that the minds of their scholars, and the hands of their workmen, were abundantly exercised in unlocking the treasures of Greek and Roman antiquity; but the world is not indebted to England for one first edition of a classic author. This delay of a century is the more to be lamented, as it is too probable that many authentic and valuable monuments of our history were lost in the dissolution of religious houses by Henry the Eighth. The protestant and the patriot must applaud our deliverance; but the critic may deplore the rude havoc that was made in the libraries of churches and monasteries, by the zeal, the avarice, and the neglect, of unworthy reformers.

Far different from such reformers was the learned and pious Matthew Parker, the first protestant Archbishop of Canterbury, in the reign of Queen Elizabeth. His apostolical virtues were not incompatible with the love of learning, and while he exercised the arduous office, not of governing, but of founding the Church of England, he strenuously applied himself to revive the study of the Saxon tongue, and of English antiquities. By the care of this respectable prelate, four of our ancient historians were successively published: the Flores of Matthew of Westminster (1570); the Historia Major of Matthew Paris (1572); the Vita Elfridi Regis, by Afferius; and the Historia Brevis, and the Upodigma Neustriae, by Thomas Walsingham. After Parker's death, this national duty was for some years abandoned to the diligence of foreigners. The ecclesiastical history of Bede had been printed and reprinted on the continent as the common property of the Latin church; and it was again inserted in a collection of British writers (Heidelberg 1587), selected with such critical skill, that the romance of Jeffrey of Monmouth, and a Latin abridgment of Froissard, are placed on the same level of historical evidence. An edition of Florence of Worcester, by Howard (1592) may be slightly noticed; but we should gratefully commemorate the labours of Sir Henry Saville, a man distinguished among the scholars of the age by his profound knowledge of the Greek language and mathematical sciences. A just indignation against the base and plebeian authors of our general and legitimate history: but his modest industry declining the character of an architect, was content to prepare materials for a future edifice. Some of the most valuable writers of the twelfth and thirteenth centuries were rescued by his hands from dirt, and dust, and rottenness (e situ squalore et pulvere), and his collection, under the common title of Scriptores post Bedam, was twice printed; first in London (1596), and afterwards at Frankfort (1601). During the whole of the seventeenth, and the beginning of the eighteenth centuries, the same studies were prosecuted with vigour and success: a miscellaneous volume of the Anglica Normanica, &c. (Frankfort 1603), and the Historia Nova of Eadmer (London 1623), were produced by Camden and Selden, to whom literature is indebted for more important services. The names of Wheele and Gibson, of Watts and Warton, of Dugdale and Wilkins, should not be defrauded by their due praise: but our attention is fixed by the elaborate collections of Twysden and Gale: and their titles of Decem and Quindecim Scriptores announce that their readers possess a series of twenty-five of our old English historians. The last who has dug deep into the mine was Thomas Hearne, a clerk of Oxford, poor in fortune, and indeed poor in understanding. His minute and obscure diligence, his voracious and undistinguished appetite, and the coarse vulgarity of his taste and style, have exposed him to the ridicule of idle wits. Yet it cannot be denied that Thomas Hearne has gathered many gleanings of the harvest; and if his own prefaces are filled with crude and extraneous matter, his editions will be always recommended by their accuracy and use.

I am not called upon to enquire into the merits of foreign nations in the study of their respective histories, except as far as they may suggest a useful lesson, or a laudable emulation to ourselves. The patient Germans have addicted themselves to every species of literary labour; and the division of their vast empire into many independent states would multiply the public events of each country, and the pens, however rude, by which they have been saved from oblivion. Besides innumerable editions of particular historians, I have seen (if my memory does not fail me) a list of more than twenty of the voluminous collections of the Scriptores

Rerum Germanicarum; some of these are of a vague and miscellaneous nature; others are relative to a certain period of time; and others again are circumscribed by the local limits of a principality or a province. Among the last I shall only distinguish the Scriptores Rerum Brunswicensium, compiled at Hanover in the beginning of this century by the celebrated Leibnitz. We should sympathize with a kind of domestic interest in the fortunes of a people to whom we are united by our obedience to a common sovereign; and we must explore with respect and gratitude the origin of an illustrious family, which has been the guardian near four-score years of our liberty and happiness. The antiquarian, who blushes at his alliance with Thomas Hearne, will feel his profession ennobled by the name of Leibnitz. That extraordinary genius embraced and improved the whole circle of human science; and after wrestling with Newton and Clark in the sublime regions of geometry and metaphysics, he could descend upon earth to examine the uncouth characters and barbarous Latin of a chronicle or charter. In this, as in almost every other active pursuit, Spain has been outstripped by the industry of her neighbours. The best collection of her national historians was published in Germany: the recent attempts of her royal academy have been languid and irregular, and if some memorials of the fourteenth and fifteenth centuries are lately printed at Madrid, her five oldest chronicles after the invasion of the Moors still sleep in the obscurity of provincial editions (Pamplona, 1615, 1634; Barcelona, 1663). Italy has been productive in every age of revolutions and writers; and a complete series of these original writers, from the year five hundred to the year fifteen hundred, are most accurately digested in the Scriptores Rerum Italicarum of Muratori. This stupendous work, which fills twenty-eight folios, and overflows into the six volumes of the Antiquitas Italiae Medii Aevi, was achieved in   years by one man; and candour must excuse some defects in the plan and execution, which the discernment, and perhaps the envy of criticism has too rigorously exposed. The antiquities of France have been elucidated by a learned and ingenious people: the original historians, which Duchesne had undertaken to publish, were left imperfect by his death, yet had reached the end of the thirteenth century; and his additional volume (the sixth) comes home to ourselves, since it celebrates the exploits of the Norman Conquerors and Kings of England. About   years ago the design of publishing Les Historiens des Gaules et de la France, was resumed on a larger scale, and in a more splendid form; and although the name of Dom Bouquet stands foremost, the merit must be shared among the veteran Benedictines of the Abbey of St. Germain des Prez at Paris. This noble collection may be proposed as a model of such national works: the original texts are corrected from the best manuscripts; and the curious reader is enlightened, without being oppressed, by the perspicuous brevity of the prefaces and notes. But a multitude of obstacles and delays seems to have impeded the progress of the undertaking; and the Historians of France had only attained to the twelfth century, and the thirteenth volume, when a general deluge overwhelmed the country, and its ancient inhabitants. I might here conclude this enumeration of foreign studies, if the Scriptores Rerum Danicarum of Langebeck and his successors, which have lately appeared at Copenhagen, did not remind me of the taste and munificence of a court and country, whose scanty revenues might have apologized for their neglect.

It is long, very long indeed, since the success of our neighbours, and the knowledge of our resources, have disposed me to wish, that our Latin memorials of the Middle Age, the Scriptores Rerum Anglicarum, might be published in England, in a manner worthy of the subject and of the country. At a time when the Decline and Fall of the Roman Empire has intimately connected me with the first historians of France, I acknowledged (in a note) the value of the Benedictine Collection, and expressed my hope that such a national work would provoke our own emulation. My hope has failed, the provocation was not felt, the emulation was not kindled; and I have now seen, without an attempt or a design, near thirteen years, which might have sufficed for the execution. During the greatest part of that time I have been absent from England: yet I have sometimes found opportunities of introducing this favourite topic in conversation with our literary men, and our eminent booksellers. As long as I expatiated on the merits of an undertaking, so beneficial to history, and so honourable to the nation, I was heard with attention; a general wish seemed to prevail for its success, and of reducing a pleasing theory into a real action, then we were stopped, at the first step, by an insuperable difficulty—the choice of an editor. Among the authors already known to the public, none, after a fair review, could be found, at once possessed of ability and inclination. Unknown, or at least untried abilities could not inspire much reasonable confidence: some were too poor, others too rich; some too busy, others too idle: and we knew not where to seek our English Muratori; in the tumult of the metropolis, or in the shade of the university. The age of Herculean diligence, which could devour and digest whole libraries, is passed away; and I sat down in hopeless despondency, till I should be able to find a person endowed with proper qualifications, and ready to employ several years of his life in assiduous labor, without any splendid prospect of emolument or fame.

The man is at length found, and I now renew the proposal in a higher tone of confidence. The name of this editor is Mr. John Pinkerton; but as that name may provoke some resentments, and revive some prejudices, it is incumbent on me, for his reputation, to explain my sentiments without reserve; and I have the satisfaction of knowing that he will not be displeased with the freedom and sincerity of a friend. The impulse of a vigorous mind urged him, at an early age, to write and to print, before his taste and judgment had attained to their maturity. His ignorance of the world, the love of paradox, and the warmth of his temper, betrayed him into some improprieties, and those juvenile follies, which candour will excuse, he himself is the first to condemn, and will perhaps be the last to forget. Repentance has long since propitiated the mild divinity of Virgil, against which the rash youth, under a fictitious name, had darted the javelin of criticism. He smiles at his reformation of our English tongue, and is ready to confess, that in all popular institutions, the laws of custom must be obeyed by reason herself. The Goths still continue to be his chosen people, but he retains no antipathy to a Celtic savage; and without renouncing his opinions and arguments, he sincerely laments that those literary arguments have ever been embittered, and perhaps enfeebled, by an indiscreet mixture of anger and contempt. By some explosions of this kind, the volatile and fiery particles of his nature have been discharged, and there remains a pure and solid substance, endowed with many active and useful energies. His recent publications, a Treatise on Medals, and the edition of the early Scotch Poets, discover a mind replete with a variety of knowledge, and inclined to every liberal pursuit; but his decided propensity, such a propensity as made Bentley a critic, and Rennel a geographer, attracts him to the study of the History and Antiques of Great Britain; and he is well qualified for this study, by a spirit of criticism, acute, discerning, and suspicious. His edition of the original Lives of the Scottish Saints has scattered some rays of light over the darkest age of a dark country: since there are so many circumstances in which the most daring legendary will not attempt to remove the well-known landmarks of truth. His Dissertation on the Origin of the Goths, with the Antiquities of Scotland, are, in my judgment, elaborate and satisfactory works; and were this a convenient place, I would gladly enumerate the important questions in which he has rectified my old opinions concerning the migrations of the Scythic or German nation from the neighbourhood of the Caspian and the Euxine to Scandinavia, the eastern coasts of Britain, and the shores of the Atlantic ocean. He has since undertaken to illustrate a more interesting period of the History of Scotland; his materials are chiefly drawn from papers in the British Museum, and a skillful judge has assured me, after a perusal of the manuscript, that it contains more new and authentic information than could be fairly expected from a writer of the eighteenth century. A Scotchman by birth, Mr. Pinkerton is equally disposed, and even anxious, to illustrate the History of England: he had long without my knowledge, entertained a project similar to my own; his twelve letters, under a fictitious signature, in the Gentleman's Magazine (1788), display the zeal of a patriot, and the learning of an antiquarian. As soon as he was informed, by Mr. Nicol the bookseller, of my wishes and my choice, he advanced to meet me with the generous ardour of a volunteer, conscious of his strength, desirous of exercise, and careless of reward; we have discussed, in several conversations, every material point that relates to the general plan and arrangement of the work; and I can only complain of his excessive docility to the opinions of a man much less skilled in the subject than himself. Should it be objected, that such a work will surpass the powers of a single man, and that industry is best promoted by the division of labour, I must answer, that Mr. Pinkerton seems one of the children of those heroes, whose race is almost extinct; that hard assiduous study is the sole amusement of his independent leisure; that his warm inclination will be quickened by the sense of duty resting solely on himself; and that he is now in the vigour of age and health; and that the most voluminous of our historical collections was the most speedily finished by the diligence of Muratori alone. I must add, that I know not where to seek an associate; that the operations of a society are often perplexed by the division of sentiments and characters, and often retarded by the degrees of talent and application; and that the editor will be always ready to receive the advice of judicious counsellors, and to employ the hand of subordinate workmen.

Two questions will immediately arise, concerning the title of our historical collection, and the period of time in which it may be circumscribed. The first of these questions, whether it should be styled the Scriptores Rerum Britannicarum, or the Scriptores Rerum Anglicarum, will be productive of more than a verbal difference: the former imposes the duty of publishing all original documents that relate to the history and antiquitie of the British islands; the latter is satisfied with the spacious, though less ample, field of England. The ambition of a conqueror might prompt him to grasp the whole British world, and to think, with Caesar, that nothing was done while any thing remained undone.

Nil actum reputans dum quid superesset agendum.

But prudence soon discerns the inconveniences of increasing a labour already sufficiently arduous, and of multiplying the volumes of a work, which must unavoidably swell to a very respectable size. The extraneous appendages of Scotland, Ireland, and even Wales, would impede our progress, violate the unity of design, and introduce into a Latin text a strange mixture of savage and unknown idiom. For the sake of the Saxon Chronicle, the editor of the Scriptores Rerum Anglicarum will probably improve his knowledge of our mother tongue; nor will he be at a loss in the recent and occasional use of some French and English memorials. But if he attempts to hunt the old Britons among the islands of Scotland, in the bogs of Ireland, and over the mountains of Wales, he must devote himself to the study of the Celtic dialects, without being assured that his time and toil will be compensated by any adequate reward. It seems to be almost confessed, that the Highland Scots do not possess any writing of a remote date; and the claims of the Welsh are faint and uncertain. The Irish alone boast of whole libraries, which they sometimes hide in the fastnesses of their country, and sometimes transport to their colleges abroad: but the vain and credulous obstinacy with which, amidst the light of science, they cherish the Milesian fables of their infancy, may teach us to suspect the existence, the age, and the value of these manuscripts, till they shall be fairly exposed to the eye of profane criticism. This exclusion, however, of the countries which have since been united to the crown of England must be understood with some latitude: the Chronicle of Melross is common to the borderers of both kingdoms: the Expugnatio Hibernie of Giraldus Cambrensis contains the interesting story of our settlement in the western isle; and it may be judged proper to insert the Latin Chronicle of Caradoc, (which is yet unpublished,) and the code of native laws which were abolished by the conqueror of Wales. Even the English transactions in peace and war with our independent neighbors, especially those of Scotland, will be best illustrated by a fair comparison of the hostile narratives. The second question, of the period of time which this Collection should embrace, admits of an earlier decision; nor can we act more prudently, than by adopting the plan of Muratori, and the French Benedictine, who confine themselves within the limits of ten centuries, from the year five hundred to the year fifteen hundred of the Christian era. The former of these dates coincides with the most ancient of our national writers; the latter approaches within nine years of the accession of Henry VIII., which Mr. Hume considers as the true and perfect era of modern history. From that time we are enriched, and even oppressed, with such treasures of contemporary and authentic documents in our own language, that the historian of the present or a future age will be only perplexed by the choice of facts, and the difficulties of arrangement. Exoriatur aliquis—a man of genius, at once eloquent and philosophic, who should accomplish, in the maturity of age, the immortal work which he had conceived in the ardour of youth.

> 108. WILLIAM ROBERTSON (1721–1793) followed Hume in the Scottish school of historiography and published a series of classic and colorful narrative works on modern European and American history, based on archival sources but, like Hume's and Gibbon's, concerned with the didactic and philosophical uses of history, showing especially the underlying pattern of material and moral progress. In this introduction to his *History of the Reign of the Emperor Charles V,* Robertson sets down his pioneering views concerning the interpretation of modern European history.

No period in the history of one's own country can be considered as altogether uninteresting. Such transactions as tend to illustrate the progress of its constitution, laws, or manners, merit the utmost attention. Even remote and minute events are objects of a curiosity, which, being natural to the human mind, the gratification of it is attended with pleasure.

But with respect to the history of foreign states, we must set other bounds to our desire of information. The universal progress of science during the last two centuries, the art of printing, and other obvious causes, have filled Europe with such a multiplicity of histories, and with such vast collections of historical materials, that the term of human life is too short for the study of even the perusal of them. It is necessary, then, not only for those who are called to conduct the affairs of nations, but for such as inquire and reason concerning them, to remain satisfied

William Robertson, *The History of the Reign of Charles V.* In *The Progress of Society in Europe* (Classic European Historians), ed. Felix Gilbert. Chicago: University of Chicago Press, 1972. Pp. 3–6.

with a general knowledge of distant events, and to confine their study of history in detail chiefly to that period, in which the several States of Europe having become intimately connected, the operations of one power so felt by all, as to influence their councils, and to regulate their measures.

Some boundary, then, ought to be fixed in order to separate these periods. An aera should be pointed out, prior to which, each country, little connected with those around it, may trace its own history apart; after which, the transactions of every considerable nation in Europe become interesting and instructive to all. With this intention I undertook to write the history of the Emperor Charles V. It was during his administration that the powers of Europe were formed into one great political system, in which each took a station, wherein it has since remained with less variation than could have been expected after the shocks occasioned by so many internal revolutions, and so many foreign wars. The great events which happened then have not hitherto spent their force. The political principles and maxims, then established, still continue to operate. The ideas concerning the balance of power, then introduced or rendered general, still influence the councils of nations.

The age of Charles V may therefore be considered as the period at which the political state of Europe began to assume a new form. I have endeavored to render my account of it, an introduction to the history of Europe subsequent to his reign. While his numerous Biographers describe his personal qualities and actions; while the historians of different countries relate occurrences the consequences of which were local or transient, it hath been my purpose to record only those great transactions in his reign, the effects of which were universal, or continue to be permanent.

As my readers could derive little instruction from such a history of the reign of Charles V without some information concerning the state of Europe previous to the sixteenth century, my desire of supplying this had produced a preliminary volume, in which I have attempted to point out and explain the great causes and events, to whose operation all the improvements in the political state of Europe, from the subversion of the Roman Empire to the beginning of the sixteenth century, must be ascribed. I have exhibited a view of the progress of society in Europe, not only with respect to interior government, laws and manners, but with respect to the command of the national force requisite in foreign operations; and I have described the political constitution of the principal states in Europe at the time when Charles V began his reign.

In this part of my work I have been led into several critical disquisitions, which belong more properly to the province of the lawyer or antiquary, than to that of the historian. These I have placed at the end of the first volume, under the title of Proofs and Illustrations. Many of my readers will, probably, give little attention to such researches. To some they may, perhaps appear the most curious and interesting part of the work. I have carefully pointed out the sources from which I have derived information, and have cited the writers on whose authority I rely with a minute exactness, which might appear to border upon ostentation, if it were possible to be vain of having read books, many of which nothing but the duty of examining with accuracy whatever I laid before the publick, could have induced me to open. As my inquiries conducted me often into paths which were obscure or little frequented, such constant recourse to the authors who have been my guides, was not only necessary for authenticating the facts which are the foundations of my reasonings, but may be useful in pointing out the way to such as shall hereafter hold the same course, and in enabling them to carry on their researches with greater facility and success.

Every intelligent reader will observe one omission in my work, the reason of which it is necessary to explain. I have given no account of the conquests of Mexico and Peru, or of the establishment of the Spanish colonies in the continent and islands of America. The history of these events I originally intended to have related at considerable length. But upon a nearer and more attentive consideration of this part of my plan, I found that the discovery of the new world; the state of society among its ancient inhabitants; their character, manners, and arts; the genius of the European settlements in its various provinces, together with the influence of these upon the systems of policy or commerce in Europe, were subjects so splendid and important, that a superficial view of them could afford little satisfaction; to treat of them as extensively as they merited, must produce an episode, disproportionate to the principal work. I have therefore reserved these for a separate history; which, if the performance now offered to the publick shall receive is approbation, I propose to undertake.

Though, by omitting such considerable but detached articles in the reign of Charles V I have circumscribed my narration within more narrow limits, I am yet persuaded, from this view of the intention and nature of the work which I thought it necessary to lay before my readers, that the plan must still appear to them too extensive, and the undertaking too arduous. I have often felt them to be so. But my conviction of the utility of such a history prompted me to persevere. With what success I have executed it, the publick must now judge. I wait, in sollicitude, for its decision; to which I shall submit with a respectful silence.

❡ THE IDEA OF PROGRESS

109. GIAMBATTISTA VICO (1668–1744), working out of the tradition of Renaissance humanism, Roman law, and post-Cartesian philosophy, constructed a cryptic, extraordinarily eclectic, yet original philosophy of history, which he called "the new science." In his autobiography, Vico suggests some of the major features, methods, and goals of his linguistic and mythological interpretations and his reconstruction of the universal history of nations.

Vico, by the reading of Bacon of Verulam's treatise *On the Wisdom of the Ancients,* more ingenious and learned than true, was incited to look for its principles farther back than in the fables of the poets. He was moved to do this by the example of Plato who in the Cratylus had sought to track them down within the origins of the Greek language. An added incentive was the feeling he had begun to entertain, that the etymologies of the grammarians were unsatisfactory. He applied himself therefore to search out these principles in the origins of Latin words; for certainly the wisdom of the Italic sect had in the school of Pythagoras a much earlier flowering and a greater depth than that which began later in Greece itself. . . .

In his *New Science* of 1725, Vico finally discovers in its full extent that principle which in his previous works he had as yet understood only in a confused and indistinct way. For he now recognizes as indispensable and even human necessity to seek the first origins of this science in the beginnings of sacred history. . . .

By the light of this new critical method the origins of almost all the disciplines, whether sciences or arts, which are necessary if we are to discuss with clarity of ideas and propriety of language the natural law of nations, are discovered to be quite different from those that have previously been imagined.

Hence he divides these principles into two parts: one of ideas, the other of languages. In the part devoted to ideas he discovers new historical principles of geography and chronology, the two eyes of history, and thence the principles of universal history hitherto lacking. He discovers new historical principles of philosophy, and first of all a metaphysics of the human race. That is to say, a natural theology of all nations by which each people naturally created by itself its own gods through a certain natural instinct that man has for divinity. Fear of these gods led the first founders of nations to unite themselves with certain women in a lifelong companionship. This was the first human form of marriage. Thus he discovers the identity of the grand principle of gentile theology with that of the poetry of the theological poets, who were the world's first poets as well as the first poets of all gentile humanity. From this metaphysics he derives a morality and thence a politics common to all the nations, and on this he bases a jurisprudence of the human race, varying with certain sects of the times, as the nations unfold the ideas of their nature, with consequent developmental changes in their governments. The final form of the latter he shows to be monarchy, in which the nations by nature come at last to rest. In this way he fills up the great void left in the principles of universal history, which begins with Ninus and the monarchy of the Assyrians.

In the part devoted to languages he discovers new principles of poetry, both of song and of verse, and shows that both it and they sprang up by the same natural necessity in all the first nations. By following up these principles, he discovers new origins of heroic insignia, which were the dumb language of all the first nations at a time when they were incapable of articulate speech. Thence he discovers new principles of the science of heraldry, which he shows to be the same as those of numismatics. Here he observes the heroic origins of the two houses of France and Austria with their four thousand years of continuous sovereignty. Among other results of the discovery of the origins of language, he finds certain principles common to all, and by a specimen essay reveals the true causes of the Latin language. By this example he opens the way for scholars to do the same for all other tongues. He gives an idea of an etymologicon common to all original languages, and then an idea of another etymologicon for words of foreign origin, in order finally to develop an idea of a universal etymologicon for the science of language which is necessary if we are to be able to discuss with propriety the natural law of the peoples.

By means of these principles of ideas and tongues, that is by means of this philosophy and philology of the human race, he develops an ideal eternal history based on the idea of the providence by which, as he shows throughout the work, the natural law of the peoples was ordained. This eternal history is traversed in time by all the particular histories of the nations, each with its rise, development, acme, decline and fall. Thus from the Egyptians, who twitted the Greeks for being always children and knowing nothing of antiquity, he takes and puts to use two great fragments of antiquity. One of these is their division of all preceding time into three ages: the age of gods, the age of heroes, and the age of men. The other is their reduction of the languages spoken before their time to three types, coeval respectively with the three ages. First, the divine, a dumb language of hieroglyphics or sacred characters. Second, the symbolic, consisting of metaphors as the heroic language did. Third, the epistolographic [demotic], consisting of expressions agreed upon for the everyday uses of life.

He shows that the first age and the first language coincide with the time of the families, which certainly preceded the cities among all nations, and out of which it is agreed the cities arose. . . .

Then he shows that the second age and the second or symbolic language coincide with the period of the first civil governments. These he shows were those of certain heroic kingdoms or ruling order of nobles, whom the ancient Greeks called "herculean races" and held to be of divine origin. The first plebeians, their subjects, on the other hand, were held to be of bestial origin. . . .

Finally he shows that the third age, that of common men and vernacular languages, coincides with the times of the ideas of a human nature completely developed and hence recognized as identical in all men. This developed human nature brought with it forms of human government, which he shows to be the popular and the monarchical. To this period belonged the Roman jurisconsults under the emperors. Thus he shows that monarchies are the final governments in which nations come to rest. On the fanciful hypothesis that the first kings were monarchs such as those of the present are, the commonwealths could not have begun. Nor could the nations have begun by fraud and force, as had been imagined hitherto.

Equipped with these and other less important discoveries, of which he makes a great number, he proceeds to discuss the natural law of the peoples, and shows at what certain times and in what determinate ways the customs were born that constitute the entire economy of this law. These are religions, languages, property rights, conveyances, classes, sovereign powers, laws, arms, trials, penalties, wars, peaces and alliances. And from the times and ways in which they were born he unfolds the eternal properties which show that the nature of each, that is the time and way of its origin, is such and not otherwise.

> 110. JOHANN GOTTFRIED von HERDER (1744–1803), philosopher, philologist, poet, and social theorist, developed a genetic and organicist theory of human history which presented national culture, including language, literature, and art, as the product of a natural, evolutionary process. He formulated his views in various works, including his *Outlines of a Philosophy of the History of Man* (1784–1791), which traced human history from cosmic origins through poetical, prosaic, and philosophical stages and projected it into a cosmopolitan future.

When I published ten years ago the little tract, entitled "Another Philosophy of History for the Improvement of Mankind," this title was by no means intended to proclaim, "anch'io son pittore," "I too am a painter." It was meant rather as a Supplement to many Supplements of the present Century, and the subjoined motto, as an expression of humility; implying, that the author far from exhibiting it as a complete philosophy of the history of our species, merely pointed out, amid the numerous beaten roads, that men are perpetually treading, one little foot-path, which had been neglected, and yet was probably worth exploring. The works quoted occasionally in the book were sufficient, to show the wellworn paths, from which the author wished to turn his steps; and thus his essay was intended for nothing more than a loose leaf, a supplement to supplements, as it's form likewise evinced.

The whole of the impression was soon sold, and I was encouraged to

Johann Gottfried von Herder, *Outlines of a Philosophy of the History of Man.* Trans. T. Churchill. London: Printed for J. Johnson, 1800. Pp. v–x and 239–244.

prepare a new edition; but it was impossible, that this should appear before the public in it's former state. I had observed, that some of the ideas contained in my tract had been introduced into other works, and applied in an extent of which I had never thought. It had never entered into my mind, by employing the few figurative expressions, the child-hood, infancy, manhood, and old age of our species, the chain of which was applied, as it was applicable, only to a few nations, to point out a highway, on which the history of cultivation, to say nothing of the phi-losophy of history at large, could be traced with certainty. Is there a people upon earth totally uncultivated? and how contracted must the scheme of Providence be, if every individual of the human species were to be formed to what we call cultivation, for which refined weakness would often be a more appropriate term? Nothing can be more vague, than the term itself; nothing more apt to lead us astray, than the applica-tion of it to whole nations and ages. Among a cultivated people, what is the number of those who deserve this name? in what is their preemi-nence to be placed? and how far does it contribute to their happiness? I speak of the happiness of individuals; for that the abstract being, the state, can be happy, when all the members that compose it suffer, is a contradiction, or rather a verbal illusion, evident to the slightest view.

If the book, therefore, would in any degree answer it's title, it must begin much deeper, and embrace a much wider compass of ideas. What is human happiness? how far does it exist in this world? considering the great difference of all the beings upon the earth, and especially of man, how far is it to be found in every form of government, in every climate, in every change of circumstances, of age, and of the times? Is there any standard of these various states? and has Providence reckoned on the well-being of her creatures, in all these situations, as upon her ultimate and grand object? All these questions must be investigated, they must be unravelled through the wild whirl of ages and governments, before a general result for mankind at large can be produced. Thus we have here a wide field to traverse, and profound depths to explore. I had read almost every thing, that was written upon the subject; and from my youth every new book that appeared, relative to the history of man, and in which I hoped to find materials for my grand work, was to me a treasure discov-ered. I congratulated myself, that this philosophy became more in vogue of late years, and neglected to collateral assistance, that fortune threw into my way.

An author, who produces a book, be it good or bad, in some measure exhibits his own heart to the world, provided this book contain thoughts, which, if he have not invented, and in our days there is little that is new left for invention, he has at least found, and made his own, nay which he has enjoyed for years as the property of his own heart and mind. He not only reveals the subjects, that have employed his thoughts at certain periods, the doubts, that have occurred to perplex him in his journey through life, and the solutions, with which he has removed them; but he reckons upon some minds in unison with his own, be they ever so few, to which these or familiar ideas will prove of importance in the labyrinth of life; for what else could excite him to turn author, and disclose what occurs within his own breast to the eyes of a rude multitude? With those he converses unseen, and to those he imparts his sentiments; expecting from them in return their more valuable thoughts and instructions, when they have advanced beyond him. This invisible commerce of hearts and minds is the one great benefit of printing, without which it would be of as much injury as advantage to a literary nation. The author considered himself as in a circle of those, who actually felt themselves interested in the subject on which he wrote, and on which he was desirous of calling forth and participating their better thoughts. This is the most estimable merit of authorship; and a man of a good heart will feel much less pleasure from what he says, than from what he excites. He who reflects, how opportunely this or that book, or merely this or that hint in a book, has sometimes fallen in his way; what pleasure it has afforded him, to perceive a distant mind, yet actively near to him, in his own, or in a better track; and how such a hint has often occupied him for years, and led him on still farther; will consider an author, who converses with him, and imparts to him his inmost thoughts, not as one who labours for hire, but as a friend, who confidentially discloses his yet imperfect ideas, that the more experienced reader may think in concert with him, and carry his crudities nearer to perfection.

On a subject like mine, the history of mankind, the philosophy of their history, such a disposition in the reader appears to me a prime and pleasing duty. He, who wrote it, was a man; and thou, who readest it, art a man also. He was liable to errour, and has probably erred: thou hast acquired knowledge, which he did not and could not possess; use, therefore, what thou canst, accept his good will, and throw it not aside with reproach, but improve it, and carry it higher. With feeble hands he has laid a few foundation stones of a building, which will require ages to finish: happy, if, when these stones may be covered with earth, and he who laid them forgotten, the more beautiful edifice be but erected over them, or on some other spot!

But I have imperceptibly wandered too far from the design, with which I set out, and which was, to give an account of the manner of my falling upon this subject, and returning to it again among other occupations and duties of a very different nature. At an early age, when the dawn of science appeared to my sight in all that beauty, which is greatly diminished at the noon of life, the thought frequently occurred to me, whether, as every thing in the world has it's philosophy and science, there must not also be a philosophy and science of what concerns us most nearly, of the history of mankind at large. Every thing enforced this upon my mind; metaphysics and morals, physics and natural history, and lastly religion above all the rest. Shall he, who has ordered every thing in nature, said I to myself, by number, weight, and measure; who has so regulated according to these the essence of things, their forms and relations, their course and subsistence, that only one wisdom, goodness, and power prevail from the system of the universe to the grain of sand, from the power that supports worlds and suns to the texture of a spider's web; who has so wonderfully and divinely weighed every thing in our body, and in the faculties of our mind, that, when we attempt to reflect on the only-wife ever so remotely, we lose ourselves in an abyss of his purposes; shall that God depart from his wisdom and goodness in the general destination and disposition of our species, and act in these without a plan? Or can he have intended to keep us in ignorance of this, while he has displayed to us so much of his eternal purpose in the inferior part of the creation, in which we are much less concerned? What are the human race upon the whole but a flock without a shepherd? In the words of the complaining prophet, are they not left to their own ways, as the fishes of the sea, as the creeping things that have no ruler over them? Or is it unnecessary to them, to know this plan? This I am inclined to believe: for where is the man, who discerns only the little purpose of his own life? though he sees as far as he is to see, and knows sufficiently how to direct to his own steps.

In the mean time perhaps this very ignorance serves as a pretext for great abuses. How many are there, who, because they perceive no plan, peremptorily deny the existence of one; or at least think of it with trembling dread, and doubting believe, believing doubt! They constrain themselves not to consider the human race as a nest of emmets, where the foot of a stranger, himself but a large emmet, crushes thousands, annihilates thousands in the midst of their little great undertakings, where lastly the two grand tyrants of the Earth, Time and Chance, sweep away the whole nest, destroying every trace of it's existence, and leaving the empty space for some other industrious community, to be obliterated hereafter in it's turn. Proud man refuses to contemplate his species as such vermin of the Earth, as a prey of all-destroying corruption: yet do not history and experience force this image upon his mind? What whole upon Earth is completed? What is a whole upon it? Is not Time ordained as well as Space? Are they not the twin offspring of one ruling power? That is full of wisdom; this, of apparent disorder: yet man is evidently formed to seek after order, to look beyond a point of time, and to build upon the past; for to this end is he furnished with memory and reflection. And does not his building of one age upon another render the whole of our species a deformed gigantic edifice, where one pulls down what another builds up, where what never should have been erected is left standing, and where in the course of time all becomes one heap of ruins, under which timid mortals dwell with a confidence proportionate to its fragility?

I will pursue no farther this chain of doubts, and the contradictions of man with himself, with his fellows, and with all the rest of the creation; suffice it, that I have fought for a philosophy of history wherever I could seek it.

Whether I have found it, let this work, but not it's first volume, decide. This contains only the basis, partly in a general view of the place of our abode, partly in an examination of the different organized beings, that enjoy with us the light of our sun. No one, I hope, will think this course too long, or beginning at too remote a distance: for, as there can be no other, to read the fate of man in the book of the creation, it cannot be too carefully or too extensively considered. He, who requires mere metaphysical speculations, may have them in a shorter way: but these, unconnected with experience and the analogy of nature, appear to me aerial flights, that seldom lead to any end. The ways of God in nature, the intentions which the eternal has actually displayed to us in the chain of his works, form the sacred book, the letters of which I have endeavored to spell, and shall still continue to do so, with skill inferior to that of a child it is true, but at least with honesty and zeal. Were I so happy as to impart only to one of my readers somewhat of that sweet impression of the eternal wisdom and goodness of the inscrutable creator in his operations, which I have felt with a confidence, for which I know not a name, this feeling of assurance would be a safe clue, with which in the subsequent part of the work we might venture into the labyrinth of human history. Every where the great analogies of nature have led me to religious truths, which, though I find it difficult, follow step by step that light, which every where beams upon me from the hidden presence of the creator in his works. It will be so much the greater satisfaction both to my reader and to myself, if, as we proceed on our way, this obscurely dawning light rise upon us at length with the splendour of an unclouded sun.

Let no one be misled, therefore, by my occasionally employing the term nature, personified. Nature is no real entity; but God is all in his works: this sacred name, however, which no creature, that comes under the cognizance of our senses, ought to pronounce without the profoundest reverence, I was desirous at least not to abuse by employing it too frequently, since I could not introduce it with sufficient solemnity on all occasions. Let him, to whose mind the term nature has been degraded, and rendered unmeaning, by many writers of the present day, conceive instead of it that almighty power, goodness, and wisdom, and mentally name that invisible being, for whom no language upon Earth can find an expression.

It is the same when I speak of the organic powers of the creation: I do not imagine, that they will be considered as occult qualities, since their operations are apparent to us, and I know not how to give them a more precise and determinate name. At some future period I intend, to enter more fully into these and other subjects, at which I must here give no more than a cursory glance.

In the mean time I rejoice, that this infantile attempt has been made in an age, when the hands of masters have collected materials, and laboured in so many particular sciences and branches of knowledge, to which it was necessary for me to have recourse. These, I am assured, will not despise the exoteric attempts of one uninitiated in their arts, but improve them; for I have constantly observed, that, the more real and firmly grounded a science is, so much the less empty altercation occurs among them, who are attached to it and cultivate it. Verbal disputes are left to those, who are learned only in words. Most parts of my book show, that a philosophy of the history of man cannot yet be written, thought it will probably before the end of this chiliad, if not in the present century.

Thus, great being, invisible supreme disposer of our race, I lay at thy feet the most imperfect work, that mortal ever wrote, in which he has ventured to trace and follow thy steps. It's leaves may decay, and it's characters vanish; forms after forms, too, in which I have discerned traces of thee, and endeavored to exhibit them to my brethren, may moulder into dust; but thy purpose will remain, and thou wilt gradually unfold them to thy creatures, and exhibit them in nobler forms. Happy, if then these leaves shall be swallowed up in the stream of oblivion, and in their stead clearer ideas rise in the mind of man. . . .

All the Arts and Sciences of Mankind have been invented through Imitation, Reason, and Language.

As soon as man, by whatever good and genius led, was brought to appropriate to himself a thing as a sign, and to substitute an arbitrary character for the sign he had found, in other words, as soon as the language of reason commenced with the slightest beginnings, he was in the road to every art and science. For what does human reason more, in the invention of all these, than remark and designate? Thus with language, the most difficult of arts, a prototype of all the rest was in a certain degree given.

The man, for example, who conceived a mark of designation from an animal, in so doing laid the foundation of domesticating tameable animals, benefitting himself by such as were useful, and rendering himself the general lord of every thing in nature; for in every one of his appropriations he does nothing in reality but mark the characters of a tameable, useful being, to be employed for his own convenience, and designate it by language or pattern. In the gentle sheep, for instance, he remarked the milk sucked by the lamb, and the wool that warmed his hand, and endeavored to appropriate each to his own use. In the tree, to the fruit of which he was guided by hunger, he remarked leaves, with which he might gird himself, wood, that would afford him heat. Thus he leaped on the back of the steed, that he might carry him; and kept him, that he might carry him again. He observed Nature, how she brought up her children, and protected them from danger: he observed the beasts, how they nourished and defended themselves. Thus he got into the road to every art, through nothing but the internal generation of a distinct mark, and the retention of it in a fact, or some other note; in short through language. Through it, and it alone, were observation, recognition, remembrance, possession, and a chain of thought, possible; and thus in time were born the arts and sciences, daughters of designating Reason, and Imitation for some purpose.

Bacon has already wished for an art of invention: but as its theory would be difficult, and perhaps useless, a history of inventions would probably be the most instructive work, that the divinities and geniuses of the human species could frame for an everlasting model to their successors. In this it would every where appear, how accident and fate had presented a new mark to the eye of one inventor, introduced a new character as an instrument into the mind of another and for the most part by a slight approximation of two long known thoughts given birth to an art, that operated on future ages. Such have often been invented and again forgotten; their theory existed, but they were not yet carried into practice, till some one more fortunate brought the hidden gold into circulation, or from a new station moved worlds with a trifling lever. Perhaps there is no species of history, that so evidently shows a superior destiny ruling over human affairs, as that of the invention and improvement of arts, of which we are apt to be most vain. The character, and the material of its designation, had long existed; but it was now for the first time remarked, now first designated. The production of an art, as of a human being, was an instant of pleasure, an union between idea and character, between body and spirit.

It is with reverence I trace the inventions of the human mind to this simple principle of its observing and describing understanding. For this is what is truly divine in man, this is his characteristic excellence. All, who use a learned language, wander, as if their reason were in a dream; they think with the reason of others, and are but imitatively wise: for is he, who employs the art of another, himself an artist? But he, in whose mind native thoughts arise, and form a body for themselves; he, who sees not with the eye alone, but with the understanding, and describes not with the tongue, but with the mind; he, who is so happy as to observe Nature in her creative laboratory, espy new marks of her operations, and turn them to some human purpose by implements of art; he is properly a man, and as such seldom appear, he is a god among men. He speaks, and thousands lisp his words: he creates, and others play with what he has produced: he was a man, and children perhaps come after him again for centuries. A view of the World, and the history of nations, give us numerous proofs, how rarely inventors appear among mankind, and how indolently men adhere to what they possess, without troubling themselves for what is still wanting; nay the history of civilization sufficiently demonstrates the same.

Thus with the arts and sciences a new tradition pervades the human species; and while it is given but to the happy few, to add new links to the chain, the rest cling to it like industrious slaves, and mechanically drag it along. As this sugared water passed through many hands ere it came to me, and I have no other merit than that of swallowing it; so are our reason and way of life, our learning and acquired arts, our military and political science, a combination of the thoughts and inventions of others, which have been derived to us from all parts of the World without any merit of our own, and in which we have sunk or swum from our earliest youth. Vain therefore is the boast of so many Europeans, when they set themselves above the people of all the other quarters of the Globe, in what they call arts, sciences, and cultivation, and, as the madman by the ships in the port of Piraeus, deem all the inventions of Europe their own, for no other reason, but because they were born and the confluence of these inventions and traditions. Poor creature! hast thou invented any of these arts? have thy own thoughts any thing to do in all the traditions thou hast sucked in? thy having learned to use them is the work of a machine: thy having imbibed the waters of science is the merit of a sponge, that has grown on the humid soil. Steer thy frigate to Otaheite, bid thy cannon roar along the shores of the New Hebrides, still thou art not superiour in skill or ability to the inhabitant of the South Sea islands, who guides with art the boat, which he has constructed with his own hand. Even the savages themselves have had an obscure perception of this, as soon as they became more intimately acquainted with Europeans. In the preparation of their implements they appeared to them unknown superiour beings, before whom they bowed themselves, and whom they saluted with reverence: but when the savage perceived, that they were vulnerable, mortal, liable to disease, and more feeble in bodily exercises than himself, he dreaded the art, but slew the man, whose art was not part of himself. This is applicable to all European cultivation. If the language of a people, even in books, be delicate and modest, every one who reads these books, and speaks this language, is not therefore to be concluded modest and delicate. How he reads, and how he speaks, are the question: and even then he thinks and speaks only after others, whose thoughts and expressions he follows. The savage,

who in his narrower circle thinks for himself, and expresses himself in it
with more truth, precision, and form: he, who in the sphere of his activity knows how to employ his mental and corporal faculties, his practical understanding, and few implements, with arts, and with presence
of mind; is palpably, man for man, more cultivated than the politic or
learned machine, that fits like a child on a lofty stage, erected, alas! by
the hands of others, nay perhaps by the labour of all preceding ages. The
man of nature, on the contrary, more limited indeed, but a sounder,
abler, man, stands firmly on the ground. No one will deny Europe to be
the repository of art, and of the inventive understanding of man: the
destiny of ages has deposited its treasures there: they are augmented and
employed in it. But every one, who makes use of them, has not therefore
the understanding of the inventors: nay, this very use tends to render the
understanding inactive; for while I have the instrument of another for
my purpose, I shall scarcely take the trouble, to invent one for myself.

It is a far more difficult point to determine, what the arts and sciences
have contributed to the happiness of mankind, or how far they have
increased it and I do not think the question is to be answered with a
simple affirmative or negative, since here, as in every thing else, all
depends on the use made of what has been invented. That there are finer
and more artificial implements in the World, so that more is done with
less exertion, and consequently much human labour is spared where it
can be dispensed with, admits not of question. It is equally contestable,
that every art and science knits a new bond of society, of that mutual
want, without which men of art cannot live. But, on the other hand,
whether this increase of wants extend the narrow circle of human happiness; whether art be capable of actually adding any thing to nature, or
whether nature be not rather debilitated and dispensed with in many by
means of art; whether all talents of art or science have not excited propensities in the human breast, which render the attainment of man's highest
blessing, content, much more rare and difficult, as the internal rest-
lessness occasioned by these propensities must be incessantly at war with
contentment; nay, finally, whether the concourse of men, and the augmentation of their sociability, have not converted many towns and countries into poor houses and artificial hospitals, in the close atmosphere of
which pallid human nature withers; and whether, while men are supported by so many unearned alms of science, art, and policy, they have
not for the most part assumed the nature of beggars, applying themselves to all the arts of begging, and consequently incurring the effects of

beggary: these, and many others, are questions, that luminous History, the daughter of Time, alone can solve.

Messengers of Fate, men of genius and invention, on what beneficial yet dangerous heights have you exercised your divine calling. You invented, but not for yourselves; it was not in your power to determine how the world, how posterity, should employ your inventions, what they should annex to them, what of new or opposite to them they would discover from analogy. The jewel often lay buried for centuries, and cocks scratched up the ground over it; till at length perhaps it was found by some unworthy mortal, and transferred to the crown of a monarch, not always to shine with beneficent splendour. You, however, performed your work, and gave posterity a treasure, dug up by your restless minds, or thrown into your lap by disposing Fate. Thus also you left to disposing Fate the effects and uses of your discoveries, who has done with them what seemed to her good. In periodical revolutions she has either perfected thoughts, or permitted them to perish, always contriving to mix and correct the poison with its antidote, the injurious with the beneficial. The inventor of gunpowder little thought, what destruction both of the political and physical powers of man would ensue from the explosion of his black dust; still less could he see, what we are scarcely able to conjecture, how the beneficent seeds of a different constitution of posterity will germinate from this barrel of powder, the fearful throne of many a despot. Does not thunder clear the air? When the giants of the Earth are destroyed, must not Hercules himself turn his hand to gentler works? The man, who first noticed the polarity of the magnet, saw neither the happiness nor misery, that this magic gift, aided by a thousand other arts, would confer on every quarter of the Globe; till here too, perhaps, some new catastrophe will compensate old evils, or engender new. So it is with the discoveries of glass, gold, iron, clothing, writing, printing, astronomy, and all the sciences. The wonderful connexion, that appears to prevail in the development and periodical improvement of these inventions; the singular manner, in which one limits and mitigates the effect of others; all belong to the sovereign economy of God with regard to our species, the true philosophy of our history.

111. JEAN D'ALEMBERT (1717–1783), mathematician, philosophe, and friend of Diderot, provided the best introduction to

Jean d'Alembert, *Discours préliminaire de "l'encyclopédie."* Paris: Libraire Armand Colin, 1919. Pp. 63–67. My translation.

Enlightenment thought in his "Preliminary Discourse" to the *Encyclopédie,* outlining both the extended Baconian structure of knowledge and, in the form of a "philosophical history of the mind" since the Renaissance, the basis for future intellectual, cultural, technological, and social progress.

From the beginning these three faculties form the three general divisions of our system and the three general objects of human understanding: History, which is related to memory; Philosophy, which is the fruit of reason; and the Fine Arts, which are born of imagination. Placing reason before imagination produces an order which seems well-founded and in agreement with the natural progress of the operations of the human mind, because imagination is a creative faculty, and the mind, before it thinks of creating, begins by reasoning about what it sees and knows. Another motive which should require placing reason before imagination is that in imagination the other two are to some extent brought together, so that reason is joined to memory. The mind creates and imagines objects only insofar as they are similar to those that it has known by direct ideas and by sensations: the more remote it is from these objects, the more bizarre and unpleasant are the beings that it forms. Thus, in the imitation of Nature, invention itself is subject to certain rules that are the principal basis of the philosophical part of the Fine Arts, which part is until now still rather imperfect because it can be the work only of genius, and genius would rather create than discuss.

Finally, if we examine the progress of reason in its successive operations, we will be persuaded that it should precede imagination in the ordering of our faculties, because in a way reason leads to imagination by the last operations which it makes on objects; for these operations consist entirely in, as it were, creating general beings which are no longer within the province of our senses, being separated from their subject by abstraction. Thus Metaphysics and Geometry are, of all the sciences that pertain to reason, those in which imagination plays the greatest part. I ask pardon of those fine spirits who are detractors of geometry; no doubt they do not regard themselves as close to it, although perhaps all that separates them from it is metaphysics. Imagination acts no less in a geometer who creates than in a poet who invents. It is true that the two operate differently on their object. The first strips imagination down and analyzes it, the second puts it together and embellishes it. It is true also that these different ways of operating belong to different sorts of minds, and for this reason the talents of a great geometer and those of a great poet will perhaps never be found together; but whether or not they are mutually exclusive, they have no right to scorn one another. Of all the great men of antiquity, Archimedes is perhaps the only one who deserves to be placed beside Homer. I hope that this digression by a geometer who loves his art will be pardoned and that he will not be accused of being an extravagant admirer, and I return to my subject.

The general distribution of beings into *spiritual* and *material* provides a subdivision of the three general branches. History and Philosophy are each occupied with these two kinds of beings, while the imagination deals only with purely material beings—a new reason for placing it last in the ordering of our faculties. At the head of the spiritual beings is God, who must hold the first rank because of His nature and of our need to know Him; below this supreme being are the *created spiritual beings* whose existance is taught us by Revelation; then comes *man,* who, composed of two principles, belongs because of his soul to the spiritual beings and because of his body to the material world; and finally comes this vast *universe* which we call the *corporeal world,* or *nature.* We do not know why the celebrated author [Bacon] who serves as our guide to this arrangement has placed nature before man in his system. On the contrary, it seems that everything requires us to put man in the passage that separates God and spiritual beings from bodies.

History, insofar as it is related to God, includes either *revelation* or *tradition,* and from these two points of view it is divided into *sacred history* and *ecclesiastical history.* The history of man has for its object either his *actions* or his *understanding,* and consequently it is either *civil* or *literary;* that is, it is divided between the great nations and the great geniuses, between the kings and the men of letters, between the conquerors and the philosophers. Finally, the history of Nature is the history of the innumerable productions that we observe in it, and it forms a quantity of branches almost equal in number to those diverse productions. Among these different branches, a distinct place should be given to the *history of the arts,* which is nothing else than the history of the use which men have for the productions of Nature to satisfy their needs or their curiosity.

Such are the principal objects of memory. Let us now turn to the faculty that reflects and reasons. Since the beings, both spiritual as well as material, on which that faculty acts have some general properties, such as existence, possibility, and duration; the examination of these properties constitutes from the beginning this branch of philosophy from which all others in part borrow their principles. This is called *ontology,* or the *science of being,* or *general metaphysics.* We descend from there to the different particular beings, and the divisions which make possible the knowledge of these different beings are formed on the same plan as the knowledge of history.

> 112. Marie-Jean-Antoine-Nicolas de CONDORCET (1743–1794), mathematician, philosophe, revolutionary, and victim of the Terror, composed, during his last months in prison, a *Sketch for a Historical Picture of the Progress of the Human Mind,* which summed up the Enlightenment conception of Western cultural and intellectual history, with its ten periods of human advancement through reason (and according to detectable laws) from a primitive age through the revival of learning and the arts down to an age of philosophy, civilization, and human "perfectibility," and culminating in a revolutionary vision of future scientific and moral progress on "positive" principles.

Man is born with the ability to receive sensations; to perceive them and to distinguish between the various simple sensations of which they are composed; to remember, recognize and combine them; to compare these combinations; to apprehend what they have in common and the ways in which they differ; to attach signs to them all in order to recognize them more easily and to allow for the ready production of new combinations.

This faculty is developed in him through the action of external objects, that is to say, by the occurrence of certain composite sensations whose constancy or coherence in change are independent of him; through communication with other beings like himself; and finally through various artificial methods which these first developments have led him to invent.

Sensations are attended by pleasure or pain; and man for his part has the capacity to transform such momentary impressions into permanent feelings of an agreeable or disagreeable character, and then to experience these feelings when he either observes or recollects the pleasures and pains of other sentient beings.

Condorcet, *Progress of the Human Mind.* In *Sketch for a Historical Picture of the Progress of the Human Mind,* trans. June Barraclough. New York: Noonday, 1955. Pp. 3–13. Reprinted by permission of George Weidenfeld and Nicholson Ltd.

Finally, as a consequence of this capacity and of his ability to form and combine ideas, there arise between him and his fellow-creatures ties of interest and duty, to which nature herself has wished to attach the most precious portion of our happiness and the most painful of our ills.

If one confines oneself to the study and observation of the general facts and laws about the development of these faculties, considering only what is common to all human beings, this science is called metaphysics. But if one studies this development as it manifests itself in the inhabitants of a certain area at a certain period of time and then traces it on from generation to generation, one has the picture of the progress of the human mind. This progress is subject to the same general laws that can be observed in the development of the faculties of the individual, and it is indeed no more than the sum of that development realized in a large number of individuals joined together in society. What happens at any particular moment is the result of what has happened at all previous moments, and itself has an influence on what will happen in the future.

So such a picture is historical, since it is a record of change and is based on the observation of human societies throughout the different stages of their development. It ought to reveal the order of this change and the influence that each moment exerts upon the subsequent moment, and so ought also to show, in the modifications that the human species has undergone, ceaselessly renewing itself through the immensity of the centuries, the path that it has followed, the steps that it has made towards truth or happiness.

Such observations upon what man has been and what he is today, will instruct us about the means we should employ to make certain and rapid the further progress that his nature allows him still to hope for.

Such is the aim of the work that I have undertaken, and its result will be to show by appeal to reason and fact that nature has set no term to the perfection of human faculties; that the perfectibility of man is truly indefinite; and that the progress of this perfectibility, from now onwards independent of any power that might wish to halt it, has no other limit than the duration of the globe upon which nature has cast us. This progress will doubtless vary in speed, but it will never be reversed as long as the earth occupies its present place in the system of the universe, and as long as the general laws of this system produce neither a general cataclysm nor such changes as will deprive the human race of its present faculties and its present resources.

The first stage of civilization observed amongst human beings is that of a small society whose members live by hunting and fishing, and know only how to make rather crude weapons and household utensils and to build or dig for themselves a place in which to live, but are already in possession of a language with which to communicate their needs, and a small number of moral ideas which serve as common laws of conduct; living in families, conforming to general customs which take the place of laws, and even possessing a crude system of government.

The uncertainty of life, the difficulty man experiences in providing for his needs, and the necessary cycle of extreme activity and total idleness do not allow him the leisure in which he can indulge in thought and enrich his understanding with new combinations of ideas. The means of satisfying his needs are too dependent on chance and the seasons to encourage any occupation whose progress might be handed down to later generations, and so each man confines himself to perfecting his own individual skill and talent.

Thus the progress of the human species was necessarily very slow; it could move forward only from time to time when it was favoured by exceptional circumstances. However, we see hunting, fishing and the natural fruits of the earth replaced as a source of subsistence by food obtained from animals that man domesticates and that he learns to keep and to breed. Later, a primitive form of agriculture developed; man was no longer satisfied with the fruits or plants that he came across by chance, but learnt to store them, to collect them around his dwelling, to sow or plant them, and to provide them with favourable conditions under which they could spread.

Property, which at first was limited to the animals that a man killed, his weapons, his nets and his cooking utensils, later came to include his cattle and eventually was extended to the earth that he won from its virgin state and cultivated. On the death of the owner this property naturally passed into the hands of his family, and in consequence some people came to possess a surplus that they could keep. If this surplus was absolute, it gave rise to new needs; but if it existed only in one commodity and at the same time there was a scarcity of another, this state of affairs naturally suggested the idea of exchange, and from then onwards, moral relations grew in number and increased in complexity. A life that was less hazardous and more leisured gave opportunities for meditation or, at least, for sustained observation. Some people adopted the practice of exchanging part of their surplus for labour from which they would then be absolved. In consequence there arose a class of men whose time was not wholly taken up in manual labour and whose desires extended beyond their elementary needs. Industry was born; the arts that were already known, were spread and perfected; as men became more experienced and attentive, quite casual information suggested to them new arts; the population grew as the means of subsistence became less dangerous and precarious; agriculture, which could support a greater number of people on the same amount of land, replaced the other means of subsistence; it encouraged the growth of the population and this, in its turn, favoured progress; acquired ideas were communicated more quickly and were perpetuated more surely in a society that had become more sedentary, more accessible and more intimate. Already, the dawn of science had begun to break; man revealed himself to be distinct from the other species of animals and seemed no longer confined like them to a purely individual perfection.

As human relations increased in number, scope and complexity, it became necessary to have a method of communicating with those who were absent, of perpetuating the memory of an event with greater precision than that afforded by oral tradition, of fixing the terms of an agreement with greater certainty than that assured by the testimony of witnesses, and of registering in a more enduring manner those respected customs according to which the members of a single society had agreed to regulate their conduct. So the need for writing was felt, and writing was invented. It seems to have been at first a genuine system of representation, but this gave way to a more conventional sign to every idea, to every word, and so by extension, to every modification of ideas and words.

And so mankind had both a written and spoken language, both of which had to be learnt and between which an equivalence had to be established.

Certain men of genius, humanity's eternal benefactors, whose names and country are for ever buried in oblivion, observed that all the words of a language were nothing but the combinations of a very limited number of primary sounds, but that their number, though very limited, was enough to form an almost limitless number of different combinations. They devised the notion of using visible signs to designate not the ideas or the words that corresponded to ideas, but the simple elements of which words are composed. And here we have the origin of the alphabet; a small number of signs sufficed to write everything, just as a small number of sounds sufficed to say everything. The written language was the same as the spoken language; all that was necessary was to know how to recognize and reproduce these few signs, and this final step assured the progress of the human race for ever. . . .

All peoples whose history is recorded fall somewhere between our present degree of civilization and that which we still see amongst savage tribes; if we survey in a single sweep the universal history of peoples we see them sometimes making fresh progress, sometimes plunging back into ignorance, sometimes surviving somewhere between these extremes or halted at a certain point, sometimes disappearing from the earth under the conqueror's heel, mixing with the victors or living on in slavery, or sometimes receiving knowledge from some more enlightened people in order to transmit it in their turn to other nations, and so welding an uninterrupted chain between the beginning of historical time and the century in which we live, between the first peoples known to us and the present nations of Europe.

So the picture that I have undertaken to sketch falls into three distinct parts.

In the first our information is based on the tales that travellers bring back to us about the state of the human race among the less civilized peoples, and we have to conjecture the stages by which man living in isolation or restricted to the kind of association necessary for survival, was able to make the first steps on a path whose destination is the use of a developed language. This is the most important distinction and indeed, apart from a few more extensive ideas of morality and the feeble beginnings of social order, the only one separating man from the animals who like him live in a regular and continuous society. We are therefore in this matter forced to rely upon theoretical observations about the development of our intellectual and moral faculties.

In order to carry the history of man up to the point where he practises certain arts, where knowledge of the sciences has already begun to enlighten him, where trade unites the nations and where, finally, alphabetical writing is invented, we can add to this first guide the history of the different societies which have been observed in all their intermediary stages, although none can be traced back far enough to enable us to bridge the gulf which separates these two great eras of the human race.

Here the picture begins to depend in large part on a succession of facts transmitted to us in history, but it is necessary to select them from the history of different peoples, to compare them and combine them in order to extract the hypothetical history of a single people and to compose the picture of its progress.

The history of man from the time when alphabetical writing was known in Greece to the condition of the human race at the present day in the most enlightened countries of Europe is linked by an uninterrupted chain of facts and observations; and so at this point the picture of the march and progress of the human mind becomes truly historical. Philosophy has nothing more to guess, no more hypothetical surmises to make; it is enough to assemble and order the facts and to show the useful truths that can be derived from their connections and from their totality.

When we have shown all this, there will remain one last picture for us to sketch: that of our hopes, and of the progress reserved for future generations, which the constancy of the laws of nature seems to assure them. It will be necessary to indicate by what stages what must appear to us today a fantastic hope ought in time to be come possible, and even likely; to show why, in spite of the transitory successes of prejudice and the support that it receives from the corruption of governments or peoples, truth alone will obtain a lasting victory; we shall demonstrate how nature has joined together indissolubly the progress of knowledge and that of liberty, virtue and respect for the natural rights of man; and how these, the only real goods that we possess, though so often separated that they have even been held to be incompatible, must on the contrary become inseparable from the moment when enlightenment has attained a certain level in a number of nations, and has penetrated throughout the whole mass of a great people whose language is universally known and whose commercial relations embrace the whole area of the globe. Once such a close accord had been established between all enlightened men, from then onwards all will be the friends of humanity, all will work together for its perfection and its happiness.

We shall reveal the origin and trace the history of those widespread errors which have somewhat retarded or suspended the progress of reason and which have, as often as forces of a political character, even caused man to fall back into ignorance.

The operations of the understanding that lead us into error or hold us there, from the subtle paralogism which can deceive even the most enlightened of men, to the dreams of a madman, belong no less than the methods of right reasoning or of discourse to the theory of the development of our individual faculties; on the same principle, the way in which general errors are insinuated amongst peoples and are propagated, transmitted and perpetuated is all part of the historical picture of the progress of the human mind. Like the truths that perfect and illuminate it, they are the necessary consequences of its activity and of the disproportion that for ever holds between what it knows, what it wished to know and what it believes it needs to know.

It can even be observed that, according to the general laws of the development of our faculties, certain prejudices have necessarily come into being at each stage of our progress, but they have extended their seductions or their empire long beyond their due season, because men retain the prejudices of their childhood, their country and their age, long after they have discovered all the truths necessary to destroy them.

Finally, in all countries at all times there are different prejudices varying with the standard of education of the different classes of men and their professions. The prejudices of philosophers harm the progress of truth; those of the less enlightened classes retard the propagation of truths already known; those of certain eminent or powerful professions place obstacles in truth's way: here we see three enemies whom reason is obliged to combat without respite and whom she vanquishes often only after a long and painful struggle. The history of these struggles, of the birth, triumph and fall of prejudices will occupy a great part of this work and will be neither the least important nor the least useful section of it.

10

❡ Conclusion: Looking Forward

*This riddling tale, to what does it belong? / Is't history? vision? or
an idle song?*

> —Samuel Taylor Coleridge, ca. 1830

History has continued, as it began, as a sort of inquiry and
judgment requiring written form. Coming into literary maturity in the
eighteenth century and methodological independence in the nineteenth
century, the study of history nevertheless preserved many of its old habits, concerns, patterns, and aspirations. There have been innumerable
carryovers from the earlier, often seminal, stages of historiography. By
nature history concentrates on, and is informed by, change; in the past
two centuries this discipline has itself been transformed as well as profes-
sionalized through contact with new fields and methods. Yet the more
enduring features have persisted in one form or another, and it is this
legacy, these factors of *longue durée,* that I wish to recall. Not that I deny
the value of the "new histories" of our own age; but it is obvious that
such novelty itself has a long tradition, though self-inflation and general
unfamiliarity with the history of history too often allow us to forget this
humbling fact.[1]

Among the ingredients of historical study, truthfulness and memo-
rability have perhaps been the most essential, and these qualities are still
the subject of concern and criticism. Problems of objectivity and truth
value have become even more worrisome in the wake of the "crisis of
historicism" of this century, when notions of objective truth were vic-

1. Gertrude Himmelfarb, *The New History and the Old* (Cambridge, Mass.,
1987).

timized by various forms of subjectivism and relativism.[2] "What is truth?" Pilate asked (and, Bacon added, "would not stay for an answer"), and many twentieth-century historians adopt a similarly skeptical attitude toward the possibility of attaining truth by means of evidence collected and evaluated within the limitations of the human condition. Yet truth and even objectivity remain the goal of most practicing historians. This is precisely where memory comes into play, for this mental faculty is a direct measure of the limits of truth. "History is not what you thought," is the facetious formulation of that small classic, *1066 and All That,* "it is what you can remember."[3] History, limited to what the evidence permits, must always be written down in a present; in this sense, at least, we may agree with Croce's famous dictum that "all history is contemporary history."

The problem of gaining access to a largely forgotten past may be overcome to some extent by limiting historical inquiry to contemporary events, or at least to matters for which there is fairly direct evidence. Thucydides' principle that history is best written by those who have participated in or witnessed the events in question was extended by modern scholars to criteria for selecting the best second-hand testimony—primary sources—but his skepticism about investigating the more remote past has persisted as an assumption for many historians. Because some scholars doubt the possibility of penetrating to levels of history innocent of written records, they have often questioned the reliability of antiquarian research in general, since it depends on interpretations or intuitions based on language, myth, oral tradition, and other nonliterate forms of collective memory. In modern times the Thucydidean prejudice has been extended by historians to many earlier periods of historical experience—not only ancient and medieval history but also prescientific, preindustrial, pretechnological ages being consigned in effect to the dustbin of antiquarian research. The persisting polarity of contemporary and antiquarian history is illustrated by Geoffrey Barraclough's belated, almost emotional, conversion from the first to the second form of historical writing and the light it may cast on the future.[4]

History, although the term has Homeric and preliterate roots, has

2. Franco Bianco, ed., *Il Dibatto sullo storicismo* (Bologna, 1978).

3. By Walter Carruthers Sellar and Robert Julian Yeatman (London, 1930), vii.

4. Barraclough, *History in a Changing World* (New York, 1955).

been a captive of scribal (and later of typographical) culture for some twenty-five centuries, and it has taken shape and generical form in the context of writing and publicity. The conventional distinction between annals, chronicles, and historical narrative has been accepted almost from the beginning. So has the distinction between poetry and history, in terms not only of form (prosaic versus poetic) but also of goals (truth versus fiction) and of its philosophical value (specificity versus the more general character of poetry). Yet the ancients recognized a historical connection between historical narrative and the poetic creations of primitive society—a connection analogous both to Vico's conception of poetic wisdom as the root of civilized discourse and to what a modern historian has called "the open boundaries of history and fiction."[5] Indeed, the historical study of myth, barbarism, and oral culture, including not only the works of Vico and his Romantic disciples but also those of B. G. Niebuhr and his more "scientific" following among classicists and mythologists, has been a permanent feature of the study of history.[6]

The modern "idea of history," despite the conceptual perspective established by R. G. Collingwood, was elaborated in the context not so much of philosophy (as Aristotle's famous distinction suggests—see above, no. 9) but rather of rhetoric and, in a longer view, of literary theory. With rhetoric, according to the ancients, history shared many fundamental elements, especially connected, narrative form; explanatory, persuasive force; and private or public (moral, social, or political) value. History told an amusing, horrifying, or convincing story, memorialized or defended a particular person or group, resolved a particular problem concerning the past, or constructed a larger interpretation about the historical process. The rhetorical nature of history has been conspicuous at several points in its history: in ancient Rome, Renaissance Europe, and more recently in the work of such neorhetoricians as Michel de Certeau and Hayden White, who have also assimilated history to literature in certain respects.[7]

5. Suzanne Gearhart, *The Open Boundaries of History and Fiction: A Critical Approach to the French Enlightenment* (Princeton, 1984).

6. Fritz Stern, ed., *The Varieties of History* (New York, 1956), 46ff.; see also Herbert Butterfield, *Man on His Past* (Cambridge, 1955), and Maurice Mandelbaum, *History, Man, and Reason: A Study in Nineteenth-Century Thought* (Baltimore, 1971).

7. Certeau, *The Writing of History,* trans. Tom Conley (Ithaca, 1988), and White, *Metahistory: The Historical Imagination in Nineteenth-Century Europe*

The literary dimension of history suggests one of the most persistent of all questions concerning the nature of history: is it an art or a science? In one way or another the topic has been debated since antiquity, notably in the Renaissance, in the Enlightenment, and more recently by J. B. Bury and G. M. Trevelyan.[8] One form of the debate, derived from antiquity and revived in the Renaissance, was between erudition and narrative history, or between the art and the method of history, and in the eighteenth century Voltaire, who wrote popular histories, still sneered at the monkish slaves of *érudition*—although Gibbon succeeded, peerlessly, in combining both traditions. Professional historians periodically call for their colleagues to reach out to a wider popular audience, or for a broader social role for the study and writing of history. Allan Nevins, for example, in his presidential address before the American Historical Association, celebrated history as a literary form and lauded more recent efforts to resurrect narrative history.[9]

Another perennial topic of debate has been the question of the proper subject matter for historical inquiry and writing. This issue, too, goes back to the ancient opposition established by Herodotus and Thucydides—or at least their followers and readers. The respective poles were the omnivorous curiosity of the first and the sharply political and analytical focus of the second: Herodotus was interested in a vast range of alien cultures and social customs, whereas Thucydides concentrated on questions of power, the causes—remote and immediate—of conflict, and the course of events in the wake of political and military crises.[10] Herodotus portrayed the cultural legacy of Hellas and the drama of confrontation with the "barbarians" over a long period, while Thucydides limited himself to the small horizons and swirling events of his own lifetime and national tradition. Later historians sometimes attempted to reconcile these divergent approaches, but the tensions between long-term cultural interests and short-term political analysis has persisted and perhaps intensified over the centuries.

(Baltimore, 1973); cf. Frank Ankersmit, *Narrative Logic* (The Hague, 1983), and Savoie Lottinville, *The Rhetoric of History* (Norman, Okla., 1976).

8. See above, chapter 1, at note 20; also Stern, *Varieties,* 209–245.

9. "Not Capulets, Not Montagues," *American Historical Review,* 65 (1960): 253–270; see also Herman Ausubel, *Historians and Their Craft* (New York, 1950), 120ff., 189ff.

10. See Randolph Starn, "Historians and Crisis," *Past & Present,* no. 52 (1971), 3–22.

The tradition of political narrative has been continuous from Thucydides and Tacitus down to Gibbon and Ronald Syme; that of cultural
history from Herodotus and Dionysius of Halicarnassus down to the
"new history" of Voltaire, the *Encyclopédie,* and works from the early part
of this century, in France and Germany as well as in the United States.
"New" histories have traditionally eschewed political analysis for
broader cultural vistas, from Pierre Droit de Gaillard and La Popelinière
in the sixteenth century down to John Richard Green (who shifted emphasis from "drums and trumpets" to the life of the English people as a
whole), James Harvey Robinson and his followers, and the "total history" of Henri Berr.[11] That the modern fields of cultural and intellectual history draw on this old impulse to extend, enrich, and humanize
historical research and writing has been most recently illustrated by the
so-called "new cultural history" and the "new historicism" of the past
decade.

Other topics have endured over the long career of Western historiography. The value of geography (though shifting from its original
medico-astrological to a more scientific base) has been unquestioned
from the time of Polybius and Strabo. Bodin, Montesquieu, Lucien
Febvre, and Fernand Braudel, in particular, stressed its importance.[12]
The inclusion of religious life, an integral part of Western conceptions of
history since the time of Eusebius, has not only opened up previously
neglected areas of social history but has also produced a special field of
historical scholarship which parallels and rivals other subfields, such as
economic, diplomatic, and military history—not to speak of the history
of particular disciplines, such as science (and the particular sciences),
philosophy, political thought, literature, and history itself. In a sense,
all of these genres may be traced back at least to the Renaissance vision of
the cultural past, which combined an "encyclopedic" view of culture
with an employment of history as an organizing principle.[13]

11. J. R. Green, *A Short History of the English People* (New York, 1884),
preface; James Harvey Robinson, *The New History* (New York, 1912); and
Stern, *Varieties,* 63–70, 256–266; cf. Georg Iggers, *New Directions in European
Historiography* (rev. ed., Middletown, Conn., 1984), and Stephen Vaughn, ed.,
The Vital Past (Athens, Ga., 1985).

12. Febvre, *A Geographical Introduction to History,* trans. E. Mountford and
J. H. Paxton (London, 1924); Braudel, *The Mediterranean and the Mediterranean
World in the Age of Philip II,* trans. Siân Reynolds (New York, 1972), Vol. 1.

13. D. R. Kelley, "Humanism and History," in *Renaissance Humanism,* ed.
A. Rabil (Philadelphia, 1988), 3:236–270 with further references.

Another old theme, an important subplot in the story of history, has been the emergence of the auxiliary sciences and especially the art of historical criticism. The development of such criticism is complex, many sided, and not at all to be represented by a simple trajectory of intellectual progress or as a byproduct of modern skepticism. It grew out of a mix of common sense, erudition, philology, a growing sense of anachronism, and the heuristic ingenuity of particular authors; but it was fundamentally shaped by religious, political, and cultural prejudices and partisanship. Lorenzo Valla scorned the Donation of Constantine and the tradition of which it was a part, and yet he idealized the history of ancient Rome beyond recognition. Historians have always been quick to point out the myths and misconceptions of aliens or enemies while at the same time being extraordinarily creative in producing their own often self-serving interpretations, fabrications, and legitimations. The old topos *anasceua,* a rhetorical device of critical rejection, has accompanied traditions of philological analysis in the development of historical methods.[14]

The subject of historical method in general has also been a part of the legacy of historical thought since ancient times. The Renaissance art of history followed and gave systematic form to the reflections of Lucian, Cicero, and others concerning the writing of history and the qualities of a good historiographer, while the discussions of the science and method of history, which superseded these *artes historicae,* employed the critical reading of histories and their exploitation for practical, whether moral, political, or philosophical, purposes. These treatises on the best way to study history explored the grounds, the limits, and the potential of historical knowledge; they inaugurated the formal history of historiography and produced a new genre that in later times was transformed into the handbooks of methodology—pedagogical as well as scientific—which furnish critical introductions to the professional study of history in modern times.[15]

"What is history?" Bodin asked over four centuries ago, "And how many categories does it have?" These questions are still asked, and the

14. Frank Borchardt, *German Antiquity in Renaissance Myth* (Baltimore, 1971).

15. D. R. Kelley, "The Theory of History," in *Cambridge History of Renaissance Philosophy,* ed. C. B. Schmitt and Q. Skinner (Cambridge, 1988), 746–761.

answers are often familiar. History today remains both a form of inquiry and also a source of endless speculation about meaning—not only about the way things "actually happened" (in the phrase of Lucian made famous by Ranke) but about the larger patterns which might resolve questions of value and purpose if not satisfy aspirations for prediction and prophecy.[16] The study of history continues to be shaped by a wide range of conventional myths: Greece and its "liberty"; Rome and its fate; Germany and its virtues; the New World and its Frontier (as envisioned by Frederick Jackson Turner);[17] the invidious distinction between civilization and barbarism; the intervention of a middle age between antiquity and modernity; persisting stereotypes of national character; the course of universal empire; the possibility of measurable progress; the advance of liberty and ideals of what has come to be known as civic humanism; notions of a golden age, whether secular or sacred; what Marc Bloch called "the idol of origins"; and finally, as Hans Blumenberg has argued, that greatest and last of all myths, the "end of myth."[18]

It is the quest for meaning that has drawn history and philosophy (or theology) together and that has created the field which, from the Enlightenment down to the twentieth century, has been referred to as "the philosophy of history."[19] The goal continues to be the search for larger patterns, a perceptible trajectory, or even the shape of the future. From Hesiod and Polybius to Eusebius, Augustine, and Otto of Freising, from Machiavelli, Bodin, and Vico to Spengler, Toynbee, Voegelin, and devotees of the Whig view of history, these efforts have continued, and a variety of metahistorical designs—regular or teleological, tragic or optimistic—has been imposed on the historical process and projected into the future, whether in terms of mythology, national or human destiny, religious conviction, or some other form of the historical imagination. In many ways historiography, if not history, has tended to repeat itself, or at least pass through cycles of intellectual fashion, over many centuries and across many cultural and disciplinary boundaries.

Most fundamental of all, perhaps, has been the question of the nature

16. Stern, *Varieties*, 57.

17. *The Frontier in American History* (New York, 1948).

18. Bloch, *The Historian's Craft*, trans. P. Putnam (New York, 1953), 29, and Blumenberg, *Work on Myth*, ed. R. Wallace (Cambridge, Mass., 1985).

19. See, for example, Patrick Gardiner, ed., *Theories of History* (Glencoe, Ill., 1959).

of historical understanding: does it reveal the Self or the Other? Is it a way (in the famous formula of Dilthey) of "finding the I in the Thou"? Or is the past truly a "foreign country," where "people do things differently"? If history teaches anything, it is that satisfactory resolutions to these problems will not be readily forthcoming. History remains, for us as it was for Herodotus, a way of asking, but not always of answering, the large questions provoked by the human condition.

Do we do this better than our forebears? There have undeniably been certain kinds of intellectual progress, and yet, despite technological advance, we are inevitably epigones in many human ways. That any high-school student of physics knows more than Newton did reflects an insight long familiar to historians. As Voltaire remarked (to himself), "[Dr. Hans] Boerhave is more useful than Hippocrates, Newton than all of antiquity, and Tasso than Homer. *Sed gloria primis.*" [20] Voltaire probably felt the same about the relationship between his historical work and that of Herodotus and Thucydides, but in many ways he respected their pioneering efforts and intellectual priority. And so may we—with him and on similar grounds—acknowledge a certain "glory to the first."

20. *Notebooks,* ed. Theodore Besterman (2nd ed., Toronto, 1968), 2:565.

❡ Select Bibliography

1. GENERAL

Breisach, Ernst. *Historiography: Ancient, Medieval, and Modern.* Chicago, 1983.
Collingwood, R. G. *The Idea of History.* Oxford, 1946.
Gay, Peter, et al., eds. *Historians at Work.* 4 vols. New York, 1972–1975.
Hay, Denys. *Annalists and Historians: Western Historiography from the Eighth to the Eighteenth Centuries.* London, 1977.
Lowenthal, David. *The Past Is a Foreign Country.* Cambridge, 1985.
Momigliano, Arnaldo. *Essays in Ancient and Modern Historiography.* Oxford, 1977.
Thompson, James Westfall. *A History of Historical Writing.* 2 vols. New York, 1942.

2. GREECE

Bury, J. B. *The Ancient Greek Historians.* New York, 1909.
Butterfield, Herbert. *The Origin of History.* New York, 1981.
Cochrane, Charles Norris. *Thucydides and the Science of History.* Oxford, 1929.
Cornford, F. M. *Thucydides Mythhistoricus.* London, 1907.
Edelstein, Ludwig. *The Idea of Progress in Classical Antiquity.* Baltimore, 1967.
Finley, John W., Jr. *Thucydides.* Cambridge, Mass., 1942.
Grant, Michael. *The Ancient Historians.* New York, 1970.
Hartog, François. *The Mirror of Herodotus: The Representation of the Other in the Writing of History.* Trans. Janet Lloyd. Berkeley, 1988.
Myres, J. L. *Herodotus, Father of History.* Oxford, 1953.
Starr, Chester G. *The Awakening of the Greek Historical Spirit.* New York, 1968.
Toynbee, Arnold J., ed. *Greek Historical Thought.* London, 1950.

3. ROME

Dorey, T. A., ed. *Latin Historians*. New York, 1966.
————. *Livy*. Toronto, 1971.
————. *Tacitus*. New York, 1969.
Laistner, M. L. W. *The Greater Roman Historians*. Berkeley, 1947.
Syme, Ronald. *Sallust*. Darmstadt, 1970.
————. *Tacitus*. 2 vols. Oxford, 1958.
Walsh, P. G. *Livy*. Cambridge, 1961.

4. THE JUDEO-CHRISTIAN TRADITION

Grant, Robert. *Eusebius as Church Historian*. Oxford, 1980.
Ladner, Gerhart B. *The Idea of Reform: Its Impact on Christian Thought and Action in the Age of the Fathers*. Cambridge, Mass., 1959.
Milburn, R. L. P. *Early Christian Interpretations of History*. New York, 1954.
Patrides, C. A. *The Grand Design of God: The Literary Form of the Christian View of History*. Toronto, 1972.
Wallace-Hadrill, D. S. *Eusebius of Caesarea*. London, 1960.

5. THE MIDDLE AGES

Archambault, Paul J. *Seven French Chroniclers: Witnesses to History*. Syracuse, N.Y., 1974.
Brandt, William J. *The Shape of Medieval History*. New Haven, Conn., 1966.
Gransden, Antonia. *Historical Writing in England*. 2 vols. Ithaca, N.Y., 1974–82.
Hanning, R. W. *The Vision of History in Early Britain: From Gildas to Geoffrey of Monmouth*. New York and London, 1966.
Poole, Reginald Lane. *Chronicles and Annals*. Oxford, 1926.
Reeves, Marjory. *The Influence of Prophecy in the Later Middle Ages*. Oxford, 1969.
Smalley, Beryl. *Historians in the Middle Ages*. London, 1974.
Southern, R. W. *Saint Anselm and His Biographer*. Cambridge, 1963.
Thompson, A. H., ed. *Bede, His Life, Times, and Writings*. London and Oxford, 1935.

6. THE RENAISSANCE

Baker, Herschel. *The Race of Time: Three Lectures on Renaissance Historiography*. Toronto, 1967.
Borchardt, Frank. *German Antiquity in Renaissance Myth*. Baltimore, 1971.
Burke, Peter. *The Renaissance Sense of the Past*. New York, 1969.

Cochrane, Eric W. *Historians and Historiography in the Italian Renaissance*. Chicago, 1981.

Ferguson, Wallace K. *The Renaissance in Historical Thought: Five Centuries of Interpretation*. Boston, 1948.

Gilbert, Felix. *Machiavelli and Guicciardini: Politics and History in Sixteenth-Century Florence*. Princeton, N.J., 1965.

Green, Louis. *Chronicle into History: An Essay on the Interpretation of History in Florentine Fourteenth-Century Chronicles*. Cambridge, 1972.

Hay, Denys. *Flavio Biondo and the Middle Ages*. London, 1959.

————. *Polydor Vergil: Renaissance Historian and Man of Letters*. Oxford, 1952.

Huppert, George. *The Idea of Perfect History*. Urbana, Ill., 1970.

Kelley, Donald R. *Foundations of Modern Historical Scholarship: Language, Law, and History in the French Renaissance*. New York, 1970.

Levine, Joseph. *Humanism and History: Origins of Modern English Historiography*. Ithaca, N.Y., 1987.

Phillips, Mark. *Francesco Guicciardini: The Historian's Craft*. Toronto, 1977.

Struever, Nancy S. *The Language of History in the Renaissance*. Princeton, 1970.

Weiss, Roberto. *The Renaissance Discovery of Classical Antiquity*. Oxford, 1969.

Wilcox, Donald. *The Development of Florentine Humanist Historiography in the Fifteenth Century*. Cambridge, Mass., 1969.

7. THE REFORMATION

Dickens, A. G., and Tonkin, John M. *The Reformation in Historical Thought*. Cambridge, Mass., 1985.

Fairfield, L. P. *John Bale: Mythmaker for the English Reformation*. West Lafayette, Ind., 1976.

Ferguson, Arthur B. *Clio Unbound: Perception of the Social and Cultural Past in Renaissance England*. Durham, N.C., 1979.

Fussner, F. S. *The Historical Revolution: English Historical Thought and Writing, 1580–1640*. London, 1962.

Hale, John R., ed. *The Evolution of British Historiography: From Bacon to Namier*. New York, 1964.

Haller, William. *Foxe's Book of Martyrs and the Elect Nation*. London, 1963.

Headley, John M. *Luther's View of Church History*. New Haven, Conn., 1963.

Levy, F. J. *Tudor Historical Thought*. San Marino, Calif., 1967.

Parry, G. J. R. *A Protestant Vision: William Harrison and the Reformation of Elizabethan England*. Cambridge, 1987.

Ranum, Orest A. *Artisans of Glory: Writers and Historical Thought in Seventeenth-Century France*. Chapel Hill, N.C., 1980.

Strauss, Gerald. *Historian in an Age of Crisis: Aventinus*. Cambridge, Mass., 1963.

Vogelstein, Ingeborg. *Johann Sleidan's Commentaries*. Lanham, Mass., 1986.

8. THE SCIENCE OF HISTORY

D'Amico, John. *Theory and Practice in Renaissance Textual Criticism: Beatus Rhenanus*. Berkeley, 1988.

Douglas, David. *English Scholars 1660–1730*. London, 1939.

Franklin, Julian H. *Jean Bodin and the Sixteenth-Century Revolution in the Methodology of Law and History*. New York, 1963.

Grafton, Anthony. *Joseph Scaliger: A Study in the History of the Classical Tradition*. Vol. 1. Oxford, 1983.

Kendrick, T. D. *British Antiquity*. London, 1950.

Knowles, David. *Great Historical Enterprises*. London, 1963.

Levine, Joseph. *The Ancients and the Moderns*. Ithaca, N.Y., 1990.

McCuaig, William. *Carlo Sigonio: The Changing World of the Late Renaissance*. Princeton, N.J., 1989.

Manuel, Frank. *Isaac Newton, Historian*. Cambridge, Mass., 1963.

Mendyk, Stan A. E. *"Speculum Britanniae": Regional Study, Antiquarianism, and Science in Britain to 1700*. Toronto, 1989.

Pocock, J. G. A. *The Ancient Constitution and the Feudal Law*. 2d ed. Cambridge, 1987.

9. THE ENLIGHTENMENT

Anderson, M. S. *Historians of Eighteenth-Century Europe, 1715–1789*. Oxford, 1979.

Barnard, F. M. *Johann Gottfried von Herder on Social and Political Culture*. Cambridge, 1969.

Berlin, Isaiah. *Vico and Herder: Two Studies in the History of Ideas*. New York, 1976.

Black, J. B. *The Art of History: A Study of Four Great Historians of the Eighteenth Century*. New York, 1926.

Brumfitt, J. H. *Voltaire, Historian*. New York, 1968.

Grimsley, Ronald. *Jean d'Alembert*. Oxford, 1963.

Kelley, Donald R. "Giovanni Battista Vico." In *European Writers*, ed. George Stade. Vol. 4. New York, 1984.

Mooney, Michael. *Vico in the Tradition of Rhetoric*. Princeton, N.J., 1985.

Porter, Roy. *Gibbon: Making History*. New York, 1988.

Reill, Peter. *The German Enlightenment and the Rise of Historicism*. Berkeley, 1975.

Schargo, Nellie. *History in the "Encyclopédie"*. New York, 1947.

Stern, Fritz, ed. *The Varieties of History*. New York, 1956.

❡ Index

Page numbers in italics refer to selected readings.